NAVIGATING THE SOCIAL WORLD

What Infants, Children, and Other Species Can Teach Us

EDITED BY

MAHZARIN R. BANAJI

SUSAN A. GELMAN

OXFORD
UNIVERSITY PRESS

OXFORD

UNIVERSITY PRESS

Oxford University Press is a department of the University of Oxford.
It furthers the University's objective of excellence in research, scholarship,
and education by publishing worldwide.

Oxford   New York
Auckland   Cape Town   Dar es Salaam   Hong Kong   Karachi
Kuala Lumpur   Madrid   Melbourne   Mexico City   Nairobi
New Delhi   Shanghai   Taipei   Toronto

With offices in
Argentina   Austria   Brazil   Chile   Czech Republic   France   Greece
Guatemala   Hungary   Italy   Japan   Poland   Portugal   Singapore
South Korea   Switzerland   Thailand   Turkey   Ukraine   Vietnam

Oxford is a registered trade mark of Oxford University Press
in the UK and certain other countries.

Published in the United States of America by
Oxford University Press
198 Madison Avenue, New York, NY 10016

© Oxford University Press 2013

First issued as an Oxford University Press paperback, 2014.

Library of Congress Cataloging-in-Publication Data
Navigating the social world : what infants, children, and other species can teach us /
edited by Mahzarin R. Banaji, Susan A. Gelman.
    pages cm.—(Oxford series in social cognition and social neuroscience)
  Includes bibliographical references and index.
  ISBN 978-0-19-936106-9
1. Social perception. 2. Social perception in children. 3. Social psychology.
I. Banaji, Mahzarin R., editor. II. Gelman, Susan A., editor.
  BF323.S63N385 2014
  302—dc23
  2013028085

9 8 7 6 5 4 3 2

Printed in the United States of America
on acid-free paper

For

Eleanor and Eleanor

CONTENTS

FOREWORD

In this inspiring book, *Navigating the Social World: What Infants, Children, and Other Species Can Teach Us,* the editors, Mahzarin R. Banaji and Susan A. Gelman, have done far more than put together a first-rate collection of chapters on social development. They have created a panoramic vision of social development that is vast in scope, theoretically rich, and empirically rigorous and ingenious.

In each of these excellent short chapters, the authors lay out a brief historical perspective of the issues they address, bring us up to date on more current contributions including their own cutting-edge research, and then point to outstanding questions or puzzles that remain to be solved. All of the authors deserve great credit for accomplishing this in a few short pages. The superb quality and enormous range of this volume make it indispensable for experts in the field, while the brevity and clarity of the essays also provide a comprehensible introduction for students.

Among the breathtakingly many research topics covered in this volume are questions about the origins and development of stereotypes, bias, and prejudice; of prosocial behavior, including helping, cooperation, honesty, and altruism; of folk theories of society; of Theory of Mind, including false belief, intention, and agency; of status seeking, ownership, conventionality, and conformity; and of learning from others, imitation, and evaluating others' expertise, reliability, and reputation. To address these questions, the contributors have conducted comparative studies with primates; they have studied infants, young children, individuals with autism and Williams Syndrome, and those experiencing social deprivation. Other disciplines that have informed this work include evolutionary biology, genetics, neuroscience, and philosophy.

Taken together, this collection forms a multifaceted jewel of a book. It defies traditional disciplinary boundaries to boldly redefine the field of social development.

Ellen M. Markman
Stanford University
Palo Alto, CA

EDITORS' PREFACE

From birth to adulthood, children grow and develop in ways that amaze all, especially their caregivers. Infants and children develop the cognitive abilities to understand the world of objects, navigate in physical space, represent abstract concepts, acquire language, develop memories, perform computations, and reason about complex ideas. Additionally, infants and children develop the repertoire of social abilities to understand the minds of others, their intentions and goals; to come to know who is self and other, us and them; to form attachments; to learn and teach; and even to engage with the hard moral questions of what is good and bad.

How do these two dimensions, mental and social, develop? Both, it is clear, are fundamental to defining us as a species and us as individuals. Both are present in "prepared" forms ready for action in the earliest moments of life. Both unfold to become immensely more sophisticated than their primitive forms through experience in particular cultural contexts. Importantly, our mental and social capacities are interdependent. Cognitive abilities develop in a world filled with other social beings, who as individuals and collectives facilitate (or thwart) their unfolding; on the other hand, social abilities are acquired and honed only as cognitive capacities and processes themselves come online, allowing social relations to emerge and flourish in species-specific and culturally nuanced ways.

Over the past two decades it has been our great pleasure to observe new and vigorous research on these two dimensions of cognitive and social development, not as they typically have been studied—as orthogonal processes—but rather as necessarily linked in the study of the intertwined process of social cognition.

In this volume we bring together a wide range of work on a core set of questions that concern the development of social cognition. Our primary focus is human development in infancy and early childhood, the years during which some of the greatest changes in both cognitive and social development occur. While understanding infants and young children forms the backbone of this volume, we also include some research on early adolescence as well as work on nonhuman primates. Together, these approaches provide a new and fuller picture of the antecedents and trajectories of social cognition across a broad spectrum of the various activities minds perform, from face perception to deception, from choosing food to learning words, from liking and disliking others based on their groups to overt exclusion, from imitating to engaging with imaginary companions.

As with many scientific advances, there was no grand, overarching plan behind this research. It was, as the best science often is, a grassroots effort. Individual investigators and collaborators trained in experimental social psychology found themselves asking questions about the origins of particular concepts they had studied for decades in adults (impression formation, attitudes, stereotypes, altruism) and recognized that no ready answers were available about the developmental origins of their favorite phenomena. In addition, in the laboratories of cognitive developmentalists, new generations of students sought to understand social cognition alongside the more bread-and-butter processes of traditional interest such as perception, categorization, causality, memory, reasoning, problem solving, and cognitive control. Then, of course, there were those prescient few who had been studying social cognition for decades and are no doubt delighted to see the broader community recognize the importance of that which they have long pursued passionately.

To all of us doing this work, whatever our own history, it is clear that an understanding of the development of social cognition is important to appreciating the evolutionary origins as well as the experiential development of mind and social behavior. Each of our own labs has witnessed these research developments and we enthusiastically bring forth this volume containing a wide-ranging set of theoretical position pieces and a wealth of empirical evidence.

It was clear to us from the outset that a traditional book containing a small number of lengthy chapters would not do justice to the remarkable range of work on this topic. Instead, we sought to gather a compendium of short, broadly accessible papers, each of which would communicate a critical theoretical opinion or a set of discoveries.

We asked authors to write for a relatively general audience, likening their responsibility to that of the author of an "op-ed" on their choice of topic. We invited about 70 authors to contribute and nearly every single one obliged promptly and with enthusiasm. Not only was the response enthusiastic, but with hardly any work on our part the products we received were dazzling. The unusual format seemed to release our authors to situate their ideas within the context of the Big Questions that motivate them, that have been central to their thinking over a long period of time.

The papers in this volume are, as such, a set of pithy "points of view" on core issues about the developing mind in social context as well as reports of evidence that enhance our knowledge of the development of social cognition. In many cases, the work surprises us by contradicting received wisdom. As with basic cognitive processes, social cognition is present in surprisingly sophisticated forms early in infancy and childhood, and young humans are, more than anything else, social and moral animals.

Section 1 (Framing the Issues) provides general commentaries on the topic of social cognitive development, beginning with a brief historical review. The papers that follow present seemingly oppositional ideas such as the importance of both universals and individual differences, on temperamental difference that accounts for distinct social orientations toward others (approach/avoidance), and on sophisticated social cognition even in infancy as well as continued brain development late into adolescence. When core capacities are present in young children in much the

same form they take in adults, the suggestion that they are psychologically fundamental presents itself. The automatic nature of social learning and social judgment provides one intriguing prospect. Others raise the possibility of placing social cognition broadly on the list of core capacities, with some arguing for it through the importance of relational orientations such as communality and hierarchy, others zeroing in on the importance of the concept of "group," and still others noting the obsessive interest children have in their surrounding social world as evidenced through the imperative of gossip.

Section 2 (Mentalizing) delves into the mystery of how we come to understand the minds of others. The act of understanding what another knows or thinks—mentalizing—can be seen in the behavior of infants who as early as 6 months of age begin to see biological movement as intentional rather than as simply movement in space. Research on mentalizing has been dominated by well-documented "false-belief" tasks, for example, in which a young child is asked to guess where somebody is likely to look for an object—the location where that other had seen the object last or the location to which the object has been moved in their absence. In Section 2 we cover both classic and exciting new perspectives on Theory of Mind (ToM). These include elegant experimental methods that reveal surprisingly early ToM (or ToM-like behaviors) in infants, how linguistic structures may promote ToM, how ToM is reflected in children's imagination, and how a "theory of society" rather than a "theory of mind" may be the way to conceptualize mentalizing. Finally, research on children with Williams syndrome suggests that super sociality in the form of approach and trust need not reveal appropriate development of social cognition.

Learning From and About Others (Section 3) contains papers on the central question of how cognition is situated within social contexts. We look at how human and primate infants imitate, model, share, and communicate in both species-general and species-specific ways. A diverse set of papers tackles the rich variety in domains of social learning—including language, interpersonal skills, causality, statistical evidence, food, and friendship.

In Section 4 (Trust and Skepticism) we begin with papers that show how deeply we care about the appraisal of others, from gaze to status and reputation. The first several papers in this section show that children are cognitively and socially attuned to deriving others' respect, caring about their reputation and seeking status alongside other social agents. Other papers in this section explore related questions of how children are born to believe, how they learn to trust and mistrust others, how they distinguish between reliable and unreliable sources of information quite early in life, as well as their vulnerability to misinformation, their emerging skepticism, and how they learn to defer to the authority of others in response to cultural demands.

At the heart of social cognition is the question of how we represent the collectives of which we are members and especially those of which we are not. In Section 5, Us and Them, we examine how children understand collectives, coalitions, and tribal affiliations. Children grapple with how social categories provide information about causality, and the role of essentialism in cementing categories. Next, we present papers that focus on specific aspects of social groups, such as how infants detect group differences via faces and how experiences modulate their social cognitive abilities. In this section, several commentaries focus on particular social groups based on gender, race/ethnicity, and language/accent, including more general analyses of the power of naïve theories and the desire to belong. A final set of papers in Section 5 takes up the question of attitude change as it pertains to the topic of prejudice reduction, both the possible ways to achieve this and the surprising resistance to it.

Section 6 (Good and Evil) tackles the thorny problem of moral cognition. To begin, the section first addresses comparative (primate-human) approaches to behavioral choice and the roots of morality more generally. This work addresses such questions as the general tendency of children to evaluate profligately, the active engagement of children in questions of morality, the limits to natural morality, the cross-cultural variations in morality, and the developmental shifts from deontological to utilitarian modes of moral thinking. A second subsection of Section 6 consists of papers that jointly demonstrate that the roots of prosociality are visible in infants favoring helpers over hinderers, and in children's own behavior of helping, altruism, and cooperation.

We placed Section 1 first because of its distinct focus on some of the broadest issues of how social cognition develops. The sections that follow represent the many and equally sturdy pillars that raise this topic to be the exciting one it is. You can sample these sections in any order of your choosing; there is no inherent progression to them. Each paper is strong in the empirical evidence it reviews, and each tells an engaging story about our development as social beings.

In the dedication to Eleanor and Eleanor, we of course refer to Eleanor Maccoby and Eleanor Gibson, two remarkable scientists we were moved to recognize. We do so in the hope that the influence of their studies of both social and cognitive development will continue to inspire new generations through the work of their descendants presented in this volume.

Mahzarin R. Banaji
Cambridge, MA
Susan A. Gelman
Ann Arbor, MI

ACKNOWLEDGMENTS

We are grateful to Ran Hassin for recognizing the need for such a book. We thank Joan Bossert at Oxford University Press for investing in it. We also acknowledge with gratitude the generous support of The Edmond J. Safra Center for the Study of Ethics, the Santa Fe Institute, and Harvard University (to MRB) and the Economic and Social Research Council (ESRC), the National Institute for Child Health and Human Development (R01 HD36043), the National Science Foundation (BCS-0817128), and the University of Michigan (to SAG) while we worked on this book. Most directly and deeply we thank Steven Lehr for his assistance in communicating with the many scientists who contributed and for doing far more by advising and supporting us intellectually in bringing the project of editing this volume to completion.

CONTRIBUTORS

Frances E. Aboud
McGill University
Montreal, Quebec, Canada

Naomi R. Aguiar
University of Oregon
Eugene, OR

Gizelle Anzures
Birkbeck, University of London
London, UK

Dare Baldwin
University of Oregon
Eugene, OR

Renée Baillargeon
University of Illinois
Champaign, IL

John A. Bargh
Yale University
New Haven, CT

Simon Baron-Cohen
Cambridge University
Cambridge, UK

Emily P. Bernier
Harvard University
Cambridge, MA

Rebecca S. Bigler
University of Texas
Austin TX

Susan Birch
Department of Psychology
University of British Columbia
Vancouver, Canada

Paul Bloom
Yale University
New Haven, CT

Sarah F. Brosnan
Georgia State University
Atlanta, GA
Keeling Center for Comparative
    Medicine and Research
University of Texas MD Anderson Cancer Center
Bastrop, TX

Patricia Brosseau-Liard
Department of Psychology
Concordia University
Montreal, Canada

Celia A. Brownell
University of Pittsburgh
Pittsburgh, PA

Daphna Buchsbaum
University of California at Berkeley
Berkeley, CA

Susan Carey
Harvard University
Cambridge, MA

Dorothy L. Cheney
University of Pennsylvania
Philadelphia, PA

Maciej Chudek
Department of Psychology
University of British Columbia
Vancouver, Canada

Andrei Cimpian
University of Illinois at
    Urbana-Champaign
Champaign, IL

Kathleen H. Corriveau
Harvard University
Cambridge, MA

Gergely Csibra
Central European University
Budapest, Hungary

Judith H. Danovitch
Michigan State University
East Lansing, MI

Jill de Villiers
Smith College
Northampton, MA

Juliane Degner
University of Amsterdam
Amsterdam, The Netherlands

Gil Diesendruck
Bar-Ilan University
Ramat Gan, Israel

Sabine Doebel
The University of Minnesota
Minneapolis, MN

Kristen A. Dunfield
Ohio State University
Columbus, OH

Yarrow Dunham
Princeton University,
Princeton, NK

Carol S. Dweck
Stanford University
Stanford, CA

Louisa C. Egan Brad
Bryn Mawr College
Bryn Mawr, PA

Angela Evans
Brock University
St. Catharines ON, Canada

Richard A. Fabes
Arizona State University
Tempe, AZ

Pier F. Ferrari
Universita di Parma
Parma, Italy

Ori Friedman
University of Waterloo
Waterloo, ON, Canada

Nathan A. Fox
University of Maryland
College Park, MD

György Gergely
Central European University
Budapest, Hungary

Alison Gopnik
University of California at Berkeley
Berkeley, CA

Laura D. Hanish
Arizona State University
Tempe, AZ

Brian Hare
Duke University
Durham, NC

Paul L. Harris
Harvard University
Cambridge, MA

Zijing He
University of Illinois
Champaign, IL

Sarah M. Helfinstein
Department of Neurobiology
The University of Texas at Austin
Austin, TX

Annette M. E. Henderson
University of Auckland
Grafton, New Zealand

Joseph Henrich
University of British Columbia
Vancouver, BC Canada

Gail D. Heyman
University of California, San Diego
San Diego, CA

Lawrence A. Hirschfeld
New School for Social Research
New York, NY

Aline Hitti
University of Maryland
College Park, MD

Lydia M. Hopper
Georgia State University
Atlanta, GA

Vikram K. Jaswal
University of Virginia
Charlottesville, VA

Mark H. Johnson
Birkbeck, University of London
London, UK

Susan C. Johnson
Ohio State University
Columbus, OH

Charles W. Kalish
University of Wisconsin—Madison
Madison, WI

Dina M. Karafantis
New York Institute of Technology
New York, NY

Frank C. Keil
Yale University
New Haven, CT

Melanie Killen
University of Maryland
College Park, MD

Katherine D. Kinzler
University of Chicago
Chicago, IL

Melissa A. Koenig
The University of Minnesota
Minneapolis, MN

Valerie Kuhlmeier
Queen's University
Kingston, ON, Canada

Tamar Kushnir
Cornell University
Ithaca, NY

Kang Lee
University of Toronto
Toronto, ON, Canada

Jukka M. Leppänen
University of Tampere
Tampere, Finland

Sheri R. Levy
Stony Brook University
Stony Brook, NY

Vivian Li
Yale University
New Haven, CT

David Liu
University of California, San Diego
San Diego, CA

Julie Lumeng
Department of Pediatrics
University of Michigan
Ann Arbor, MI

Derek E. Lyons
Yale University
New Haven, CT

Carol Lynn Martin
Arizona State University
Tempe, AZ

Andrew N. Meltzoff
University of Washington
Seattle, WA

Cindy Faith Miller
Arizona State University
Tempe, AZ

Henrike Moll
University of Southern California
Los Angeles, CA

Kelly Lynn Mulvey
University of Maryland
College Park, MD

Karen R. Neary
University of Waterloo
Waterloo, ON, Canada

Charles A. Nelson III
Children's Hospital Boston
Harvard Medical School
Cambridge, MA

Drew Nesdale
Griffith University
South Brisbane, Australia

Sara R. Nichols
University of Pittsburgh
Pittsburgh, PA

Kristina R. Olson
Yale University
New Haven, CT

Olivier Pascalis
Université Pierre Mendes
Grenoble, France

Annika Paukner
National Institute of Child Health
  and Human Development
NIH Animal Center
Poolesville, MD

David Pietraszewski
Yale University
New Haven, CT

Daniela Plesa Skwerer
Boston University
Boston, MA

Seth D. Pollak
University of Wisconsin
Madison, WI

Paul C. Quinn
University of Delaware
Newark, DE

Luisa Ramírez
Universidad del Rosario
Bogotá, Colombia

Marjorie Rhodes
New York University
New York, NY

Philippe Rochat
Emory University
Atlanta, GA

Lisa Rosenthal
Yale University
New Haven, CT

Diane N. Ruble
New York University
New York, NY

Adam Rutland
University of Kent
Canterbury, UK

Mark A. Sabbagh
Queen's University
Kingston, ON, Canada

Laurie R. Santos
Yale University
New Haven, CT

Rebecca Saxe
Massachusetts Institute of Technology
Cambridge, MA

Rose M. Scott
University of Illinois
Champaign, IL

Andrew Scott Baron
University of British Columbia
Vancouver, BC, Canada

Elizabeth Seiver
University of California at Berkeley
Berkeley, CA

Peipei Setoh
University of Illinois
Champaign, IL

Robert M. Seyfarth
University of Pennsylvania
Philadelphia, PA

Alex W. Shaw
Yale University
New Haven, CT

Kristin Shutts
University of Wisconsin—Madison
Madison, WI

Joan B. Silk
University of California, Los Angeles
Los Angeles, CA

Amy E. Skerry
Harvard University
Cambridge, MA

Alan Slater
University of Exeter
Exeter, UK

Stephanie Sloane
University of Illinois
Champaign, IL

Judith G. Smetana
University of Rochester
Rochester, NY

Elizabeth S. Spelke
Harvard University
Cambridge, MA

Stephen J. Suomi
National Institute of Child Health
    and Human Development
NIH Animal Center
Poolesville, MD

Margarita Svetlova
University of Pittsburgh
Pittsburgh, PA

Helen Tager-Flusberg
Boston University
Boston, MA

Catherine Tamis-LeMonda
New York University
New York, NY

James W. Tanaka
University of Victoria
Victoria, BC, Canada

Marjorie Taylor
University of Oregon
Eugene, OR

Lotte Thomsen
Harvard University
University of Copenhagen
Copenhagen, Denmark

Michael Tomasello
Max Planck Institute for Evolutionary
    Anthropology
Leipzig, Germany

Nim Tottenham
University of California, Los Angeles
Los Angeles, CA

Kimberly E. Vanderbilt
University of California, San Diego
San Diego, CA

Felix Warneken
Harvard University
Cambridge, MA

Sandra Waxman
Northwestern University
Evanston, IL

Henry M. Wellman
University of Michigan
Ann Arbor, MI

Andrew Whiten
University of St Andrews
St Andrews, UK

Victoria Wobber
Harvard University
Cambridge, MA

Amanda Woodward
University of Chicago
Chicago, IL

Karen Wynn
Yale University
New Haven, CT

Daniel Y.-J. Yang
University of Illinois
Champaign, IL

Kristina M. Zosuls
Arizona State University
Tempe, AZ

SECTION I

Framing the Issues

1.1

Social-Cognitive Development

A Renaissance

CAROL S. DWECK

In the beginning, social development and cognitive development were deeply intertwined. Founders of developmental psychology recognized that there was a natural alliance between the two. Lev Vygotsky (1896–1934), one of the early titans of developmental psychology, built his influential theory around the idea that social communication provides the input for the child's developing mental functions (Vygotsky, 1978). Piaget, the giant in the field of cognitive development, knew that cognitive and social development were inextricably bound, that they developed hand in hand, and that similar developmental processes were often at play in both (1945/1995; see DeVries, 1997). Indeed, Piaget asserted that the child's progress in social development and cognitive development "constitute[s] two indissociable aspects of a single reality" (1945/1995, p. 145) and even that "social life is a necessary condition for the development of logic" (Piaget, 1928/1995, p. 210).

Many followers of Piaget felt the same way (e.g., Hunt, 1961; Kohlberg, 1966). These scholars understood the deep connection between social and cognitive development. Children's minds develop in a social context, the concepts they develop are about both the social and the nonsocial world, and their developing concepts and conceptual abilities affect social attitudes and behavior.

In the 1970s and 1980s, however, social development and cognitive development went their separate ways. It is curious that they parted ways at that time, for that was precisely when the cognitive revolution was bringing other fields, such as cognitive and social psychology, closer together. In fact, social cognition overtook social psychology and led to such major works as Nisbett and Ross's (1980) book *Human Inference: Strategies and Shortcomings of Social Judgment* and several

era-defining books on attribution theory that showed how people's construals and explanations profoundly affect their social behavior (e.g., Jones et al., 1972). However, despite some major programs of research bringing social cognition into social development (e.g., Dodge, 1980; Dweck & Goetz, 1978; see Olson & Dweck, 2008), this approach did not penetrate to the heart of the field to become a dominant viewpoint.

Why not? Computers came into widespread use in the 1970s and made it possible to analyze unprecedented amounts of data about children, their families, and their environments. Social development researchers suddenly felt like kids in a candy store. Before then, all data were analyzed by hand on glorified adding machines. But now dozens of variables could be measured in thousands of participants over long periods of time and analyzed with ever-new and more wondrous data analysis programs. Fine-grained, moment-to-moment analyses of psychological processes became increasingly rare in social development. And experiments gave way to correlational methods.

Social development, at its core, has typically cared deeply about important childhood outcomes, such as children's social adjustment and well-being. And it has cared deeply about the environmental/social circumstances that affect these outcomes. Most researchers in this field did not see a way to use the concepts and methods of the cognitive revolution to illuminate the phenomena they cared about. For this reason, social development became more and more distant from cognitive development and from experimentally oriented psychology as a whole.

At the same time, the study of cognitive development became more purely a look at what's inside the child's mind—and became less relevant to children's functioning and well-being in the real world. Although many cognitive development researchers of the 1970s and the 1980s studied children's emerging "metacognitive" abilities (such as their ability to use strategies to enhance their cognitive performance), this fell out of fashion. In short, many researchers stopped making contact with "real" phenomena that directly affected children's lives, and instead focused on the processes that unfolded inside children's minds as children tried to understand what objects are, how space is organized, or how numbers work.

In both fields, many fascinating things were learned, but when the fields were separate, many fascinating questions were not and could not be asked. For example, experiments in cognitive development showed that young infants knew incredible things about the physical world and could perform astonishing feats of inference in that realm. Could they do the same things about the social world—the world they depended on for survival? Almost no one asked. And that's what makes today's research so exciting. Everyone is asking.

In the last few years, a reunion between social and cognitive development has taken place and a renaissance is afoot. This book heralds that reunion and exuberantly celebrates the renaissance, showing us, for example, how the concepts and methods of cognitive development researchers are now making contact with the deep concerns of social development researchers to create new questions, new methods, and new answers.

How did this come about? First, it was researchers who, like the founders of developmental psychology, no longer believed in a sharp distinction between the social and the cognitive. Indeed, many of the basic theories of cognitive development now place children squarely in their social environment (Gelman, 2009; Gergely & Csibra, 2005; Meltzoff, 2007; Tomasello, 1999), showing how much they already know as infants about other people's goals and intentions (Johnson, 2000; Woodward, 1998) and showing how prepared they are to learn from others (Csibra & Gergely, 2009).

Next, it happened because researchers brought the experimental methods of cognitive development to bear on social developmental phenomena, and thanks to them we now know how remarkably early it is that children can form in-group preferences (Kinzler, Dupoux, & Spelke, 2007), recognize good guys and bad guys (Hamlin, Wynn, & Bloom, 2007), know what other people believe (Onishi & Baillargeon, 2005), and have expectations for how people will behave (Johnson, Dweck, & Chen, 2007; Thomsen, Frankenhuis,

Ingold-Smith, & Carey, 2011). Without the methods that allow us to ask questions of preverbal infants (and have them answer us), we could never have learned these things about young children.

It came about because of the social psychologists, who wanted to understand the roots of important phenomena—like prejudice—in childhood (e.g., Dunham, Baron, & Banaji, 2008). It also happened because of the people who believed in this approach all along, who never gave up, and who at last have many, many colleagues. Finally, it is because of the people like the editors of this volume, who with their passion and vision are infusing the field with tremendous momentum.

Although the field of social-cognitive development has deep roots, it seems new. One can feel its growing energy and sense its unlimited horizons. As you dig into this volume, get ready to be amazed at what we have learned in a few short years about the roots of the human (social) mind in infants and children.

REFERENCES

Csibra, G., &, Gergely, G. (2005). Social learning and social cognition: The case for pedagogy. In M. H. Johnson & Y. Munakata (Eds.), *Processes of change in brain and cognitive development: Attention and performance, XXI*. Oxford, England: Oxford University Press.

Csibra, G., & Gergely, G. (2009). Natural pedagogy. *Trends in Cognitive Science, 13*, 148–153.

DeVries, R. (1997). Piaget's social theory. *Educational Researcher, 26*, 4–17.

Dodge, K. A. (1980), Social cognition and children's aggressive behavior. *Child Development, 51*, 162–170.

Dunham, Y., Baron, A. S., & Banaji, M. (2008). The development of implicit intergroup cognition. *Trends in Cognitive Science, 12*, 248–253.

Dweck, C. S., & Goetz, T. E. (1978). Attributions and learned helplessness. In J. Harvey, W. Ickes, & R. Kidd (Eds.), *New directions in attribution research* (Vol. 2,). Hillsdale, NJ: Erlbaum.

Gelman, S. A. (2009). Learning from others: Children's construction of concepts. *Annual Review of Psychology, 60*, 115–140.

Gergely, G., & Csibra, G. (2005). The social construction of the cultural mind. *Interaction Studies, 6*, 463–481.

Hamlin, J. K., Wynn, K., & Bloom, P. (2007). Social evaluation by preverbal infants. *Nature, 450*, 557–559

Hunt, J. McV. (1961). Intelligence and experience. New York: Ronald Press.

Johnson, S., Dweck, C. S., & Chen, F. (2007). Evidence for infants' internal working models of attachment. *Psychological Science, 18*, 501–502.

Johnson, S. C. (2000). The recognition of mentalistic agents in infancy. *Trends in Cognitive Science, 4,* 22–28.

Jones, E. E., Kanouse, D. E., Kelley, H. H., Nisbett, R. E., Valins, S., & Weiner, B. (Eds.) (1972). *Attribution: Perceiving the causes of behavior.* Morristown, NJ: General Learning Press.

Kinzler, K., Dupoux, E., & Spelke, E. S. (2007). The native language of social cognition. *Proceedings of the National Academy of Science, 104,* 12577–12580.

Kohlberg, L. (1966). A cognitive-developmental analysis of children's sex-role concepts and attitudes. In E. E. Maccoby (Ed.), *The development of sex differences.* Stanford, CA: Stanford University Press.

Meltzoff, A. N. (2007). "Like me": A foundation for social cognition. *Developmental Science, 10,* 126–134.

Nisbett, R. E., & Ross, L. (1980). *Human inference: Strategies and shortcomings of social judgment.* Englewood Cliffs, NJ: Prentice-Hall.

Olson, K. R., & Dweck, C. S. (2008). A blueprint for social cognitive development. *Perspectives on Psychological Science, 3,* 193–202.

Onishi, K. H., & Baillargeon, R. (2005) Do 15-month-old infants understand false beliefs? *Science, 308,* 255–258.

Piaget, J. (1995). *Logical operations and social life.* New York: Routledge. [Original work published in 1945].

Piaget, J. (1995). *Sociological studies.* New York: Routledge. [Original work published in 1928].

Thomsen, L., Frankenhuis, W. E., Ingold-Smith, M., and Carey, S. (2011). Big and mighty: Preverbal infants mentally represent social dominance. *Science, 331,* 477–480.

Tomasello, M. (1999). *The cultural origins of human cognition.* Cambridge, MA: Harvard University Press.

Vygotsky, L. (1978). *Mind in society: The development of higher psychological processes.* M. Cole, V. John-Steiner, S. Scribner, & E. Souberman (Eds.). Cambridge, MA: Harvard University Press.

Woodward, A. (1998). Infants selectively encode the goal object of an actor's reach *Cognition, 69,* 1–34.

1.2

The Paradox of the Emerging Social Brain

MARK H. JOHNSON

In recent years we have seen an explosion of interest in applying cognitive neuroscience methods to the emergence of human social perceptual and cognitive abilities. Dedicated conferences, books, and journal issues have all reflected this dramatic increase in research effort and data in this interdisciplinary branch of science. There is real excitement in the idea that by studying the brain, and its development, we can shed light on age-old issues concerning how individual infants and children become enculturated as active social members of our species. However, an overview of this new body of work reveals that two apparently opposing views are emerging. On the one hand, neuroimaging studies from my lab and others are providing clear neural evidence for apparently quite sophisticated aspects of social cognition in infants of only a few months old, and certainly at ages younger than most behavioral indicators reveal. On the other hand, work from various labs (including my own) also shows evidence for surprisingly late changes, even for some seemingly quite simple aspects of social brain function such as the perception of faces. How are we to make sense of these apparently diverging sets of results?

Evidence for apparently precocial specification of brain processing of social stimuli has been used to support the view that the human infant is born equipped to be ready for the social world in general, and for interacting with other individuals of our species in particular (Csibra & Gergely, 2011). By contrast, evidence for the late emergence of specialized neural circuitry for processing information about other humans has been used to support the view that the human brain only gradually acquires expertise with social stimuli (e.g., Gauthier & Nelson, 2001). In this contribution, I briefly outline a selection of the evidence for these views, before turning to ways in which neuroscience and brain imaging data might further inform our picture of emerging social abilities in infants and children.

Evidence that, to many, is surprising in that it shows precocial functioning of different regions of the cortical "social brain network" previously described in adults comes from studies using a new functional imaging technique suitable for use with babies: near infrared spectroscopy (NIRS). In an initial exploration of social brain function with this method, we (Lloyd-Fox et al., 2009) used NIRS to measure hemodynamic responses in the temporal lobes of the cortex in response to a complex social stimulus (a video of an actress playing nursery hand games) in 5-month-old infants. Our infants showed increased bilateral temporal lobe activation in response to this complex biological motion stimulus as compared to either static control images or complex nonbiological motion stimuli (video clips of machine cogs and pistons and moving mechanical toys). More specifically, we observed this selective activation around the posterior superior temporal cortex, a component of the adult social brain already known to be activated during dynamic social events in adults (see Beauchamp, Lee, Haxby, & Martin, 2002). In a more recent study with infants, we have decomposed this complex visual stimulus into some of its component features with videos of an actress making hand, eye, or mouth movements (Lloyd-Fox et al., 2011). To our surprise, we found evidence for preferential activation for eye, hand, or mouth movements in different portions of the infant temporal lobe in a pattern that was consistent with previously reported results from adults (Pelphrey, Morris, Michelich, Allison, & McCarthy, 2005). Thus, even at 5 months babies are activating some cortical regions in response to viewing social stimuli in a surprisingly "adult-like" way.

In another example of such precocial specificity within the social brain network, 4-month-old infants watched two kinds of dynamic scenarios in which a dynamic animated face either established mutual gaze (eye contact) with the viewing infant or had a matched eye movement away from the infant (averted gaze) (Grossmann et al., 2008). Once again, hemodynamic responses were measured by NIRS, permitting spatial localization of brain activation. The results revealed that processing mutual gaze interactions activates areas in the infant right superior temporal and prefrontal cortex that correspond to the brain regions implicated in these processes in adults (Kampe, Frith, & Frith, 2003; Pelphrey, Morris, & McCarthy, 2004). This pattern of data suggests the early specialization of brain processes involved in mutual gaze detection. These studies are merely illustrative of emerging findings showing a striking degree of adult-like specificity within the infant social brain network (for review, see Grossmann & Johnson, 2007).

In contrast to this evidence for early cortical specialization for biological motion in young infants, a flurry of recent functional magnetic resonance imaging (fMRI) papers have traced a much more gradual and delayed pattern of cortical specialization or "tuning" for the processing of social stimuli extending into the teenage years (Johnson, Grossman, & Cohen Kadosh, 2009). For example, we (Cohen-Kadosh & Johnson, 2007; Johnson et al., 2009) reviewed the currently available developmental fMRI literature on faces with regard to two questions: (1) Does cortical activation in response to viewing faces become more focal and localized during childhood? (2) Does the degree of functional specialization (as measured by the degree of tuning to faces) increase in specificity during development? Encouragingly, we found some consistency across the developmental fMRI studies conducted to that point. Collectively, these studies show that while faces activate specific areas of cortex in children, these areas may occupy more extensive, or slightly different, regions from those seen in adults. Furthermore, three of the most recent studies show evidence of increasing tuning of face-sensitive areas of cortex during mid-childhood (Golarai et al., 2007; Passarotti et al., 2003; Scherf, Behrmann, Humphreys, & Luna, 2007) accompanied in some cases by more focal patterns of activation in older children. More specifically, children over around 10 years selectively activate face areas of cortex in a similar way to adults. In contrast, however, in younger children these same areas are activated equally well by other complex objects, demonstrating that they are less finely tuned to process social stimuli. These differences in the

degree of selective activation relate to success in behavioral tests of face recognition ability (Furl, Garrido, Dolan, Driver, & Duchaine, 2011). Most recently, we (Cohen-Kadosh, Cohen-Kados, Dick, & Johnson, 2010) showed that even when regions on the core face network are tuned up to faces, the functional connectivity between these regions, and the modulation of this connectivity by task demands, continues to develop during the teenage years. In general, these dynamic developmental changes in cortical activation were consistent with an extended and gradual process of increased tuning or specialization of cortical circuitry for processing faces during development (Johnson, 2011).

These findings on the gradual tuning up of cortical processing of faces during mid and late childhood are consistent with other studies showing marked neural changes during social cognitive decision making in adolescents (for review, see Blakemore, 2010). In at least one developmental fMRI study we have conducted, we observed that while the processing of nonanimate object (tools) was adult-like from the earliest age we could scan (6 years), the processing of potentially social stimuli (animals) showed considerable development between 6 and 10 years (Dekker, Mareschal, Sereno, & Johnson, 2010), indicating that aspects of social brain function may be delayed in their development relative to equivalent processing for inanimate stimuli. This proposal will require further research.

RESOLVING THE PARADOX

How are we to reconcile the evidence reviewed earlier that is supportive both of precocial activity the social brain network, and of the progressive and gradual development of at least some component parts? This pattern of results challenges both the simple view that, due to its importance in evolution, the social brain network is innate (Kanwisher, 2010), and the opposing stance that social skills, and their neural substrates, are primarily acquired through the passive experience gained by being reared in a social environment (Gauthier & Nelson, 2001). With this in mind, I now consider three potential resolutions to this apparently conflicting neuroscience data that may, individually or in combination, advance our fundamental understanding of the emerging social brain.

The first type of explanation is centered on the idea that there are specific social cognitive functions that are critical for infants to possess in order to enable further social learning. These specific functions are precocial (or "innate") and serve to guide or elicit the necessary learning for constructing the rest of the social brain network. One prominent version of this kind of account has been advanced by Csibra and colleagues, and argues that infants are predisposed, probably from birth, to respond in a selective way to situations of face-to-face individual communication with another human being (e.g., Csibra & Gergely, 2011). This specific adaptation for infants to seek out communicative cues from other humans and then engage them in communication is argued to promote their learning about, and from, other human beings. These cues can also be provided in nonvisual sensory modalities such as infant-directed speech (Grossmann, Parise, & Friederici, 2010). In other words, babies' brains are adapted to tap into the richest source of new information in their early environment: other human beings. From this attention toward, and interaction with, other humans, they learn more about conspecifics and about the complex niche that we all inhabit. In terms of the neuroscience data, this view predicts that regions and circuits involved in detecting ostensive cues, and invitations to interact, from other humans should develop in advance of other social skills such as predicting the outcome of actions or inferring intentions. Some of the studies mentioned earlier are consistent with this prediction, for example, the early and specific sensitivity to viewing faces that engage the viewer with direct gaze (Grossmann et al., 2008). Furthermore, many of the behavioral studies with newborns can be interpreted as their preferentially orienting toward faces that are likely to engage them in communication, such as faces that contain positive affect (a smile) in addition to direct eye gaze (Farroni, Csibra, Simion, & Johnson, 2002; Johnson, 2005).

A second, and closely related, type of explanation is the drive that parents and caregivers have to communicate with babies and young children. Leaving aside traditional questions of parent–infant bonding, we can say that new brains are recruited into the world of social interaction by adult brains that have already operated in that environment for years. This active recruitment process has not yet been well studied with the methods of cognitive neuroscience. This active role of caregivers in recruiting the brains of infants into the world of social interaction could also be a feature of a related type of explanation that may also resolve the apparently opposing sets of data

discussed earlier. A neural manifestation of this recruitment of the infant brain into the social world may be observed in resting state or "default mode" network activity. This state (rather like the idling of a car engine) in adults often reflects a state of readiness of the mature social brain network (Bressler & Menon, 2010), and the degree of activity in this network can predict later performance in active social tasks, such as face recognition (Zhang, Tian, Liu, Li, & Lee, 2009). Since it is thought that brain resting states partly reflect the overall patterns of experience of the developing child, it is possible that frequent social interaction initiated by adults biases these idle states of the brain to be prepared for future social interaction. This biasing of resting states may, in turn, also help sculpt the emerging anatomical connections appropriate for the social brain network (Johnson, 2011), thus solidifying the recruitment of the child brain into the social world.

A third perspective on the apparently conflicting sets of findings on imaging the emerging social brain comes from the interactive specialization theory of human functional brain development mentioned earlier. Johnson et al. (2009) reviewed some of the literature mentioned earlier and a wide range of other studies showing dynamic changes in the patterns of brain activation that underlie emerging social cognitive abilities during later childhood and adolescence. According to this account, there will be different schedules of specialization (or "tuning up") for different regions of the social brain network. In particular, parts of the prefrontal cortex (PFC) may be critical for orchestrating the networks of specialized regions whose coordinated activity supports social perception and cognition. Specifically, knowledge-based cascade correlation (KBCC; Shultz, Rivest, Egri, Thivierge, & Dandurand, 2007) involves an algorithm and architecture that recruits previously learned functional networks when required during learning. Put simply, this kind of network can learn many tasks faster, or learn tasks that other networks cannot, because it can recruit the "knowledge" and computational ability of other self-contained networks as and when required. In a sense, it selects from a library of available computational regions to orchestrate the best combination for the learning problem at hand. While this class of model is not specifically intended to be a detailed model of brain circuits (Shultz & Rivest, 2001; Shultz et al., 2007), it has been used to characterize frontal systems (Thivierge, Titone, & Schultz, 2005) and may capture important elements of the emerging interactions between PFC and other parts of the cortical social brain at an abstract level. Under this scenario of the emerging social brain network, medial PFC may be activated from early on by social stimuli (Grossmann et al., 2008) but at that point may play little role in selectively activating other regions due to their own lack of functional specialization, and possibly also a lack of myelination of the relevant long-range connections. Once more posterior cortical regions (such as superior temporal sulcus and the fusiform face area) become more finely tuned to their different functions, the role of medial PFC, or other frontal areas, becomes even more important in orchestrating the combinations of regions activated for a given social cognition task. These prefrontal areas will be required more when learning a task, or acquiring a new skill, than once it is acquired (with the appropriate combination of other posterior regions already selected). This may explain the observation that there is a general migration of activity during childhood from greater activity in medial PFC than in more posterior cortical regions (superior temporal sulcus and fusiform face area) to the reverse pattern in later development. Once PFC has learned the appropriate pattern of posterior regional activation to succeed in a specific task context, cortical activity will tend to migrate to these posterior regions.

In conclusion, developmental cognitive neuroscience data are revealing that simple views of the development of the social brain as either being generated solely by learning processes, or by innate mechanisms, are unlikely to be adequate. Rather, more sophisticated and nuanced accounts are required that can potentially account for why some aspects of social brain function are evident shortly after birth, while others show a very prolonged and gradual sequence of development extending into the teenage years. Neurally inspired ideas and models such as those briefly outlined in this chapter may help resolve the initially puzzling and apparently contradictory patterns of results emerging from current studies in developmental social neuroscience. It may be that these reconceptualizations suggest new theories of the emergence of social perception and cognition in terms of cognitive and affective concepts.

REFERENCES

Beauchamp, M. S., Lee, K. E., Haxby, J. V., & Martin, A. (2002). Parallel visual motion processing streams for manipulable objects and human movements. *Neuron, 34*(1), 149–159.

Blakemore, S. (2010). The developing social brain: Implications for education. *Neuron, 65*(6), 744–747. doi:10.1016/j.neuron.2010.03.004

Bressler, S. L., & Menon, V. (2010). Large-scale brain networks in cognition: Emerging methods and principles. *Trends in Cognitive Sciences, 14*(6), 277–290. doi:10.1016/j.tics.2010.04.004

Cohen-Kadosh, K., Cohen-Kadosh, R., Dick, F., & Johnson, M. H. (2010) Developmental changes in effective connectivity in the emerging core face network. *Cerebral Cortex*, doi:10.1093/cercor/bhq215

Cohen Kadosh, K., & Johnson, M. H. (2007). Developing a cortex specialized for face perception. *Trends in Cognitive Sciences, 11*(9), 367–369. doi:10.1016/j.tics.2007.06.007

Csibra, G. & Gergely, G. (2011). Natural pedagogy as evolutionary adaptation. *Philosophical Transactions of the Royal Society B, Biological Sciences, 366*(1567), 1149–1157.

Dekker, T., Mareschal, D., Sereno, M. I., & Johnson, M. H. (2010). Dorsal and ventral stream activation and object recognition performance in school-age children. *NeuroImage.* doi:10.1016/j.neuroimage.2010.11.005

Farroni, T., Csibra, G., Simion, F., & Johnson, M. H. (2002). Eye contact detection in humans from birth. *Proceedings of the National Academy of Sciences USA, 99*(14), 9602–9605. doi:10.1073/pnas.152159999

Furl, N., Garrido, L., Dolan, R. J., Driver, J., & Duchaine, B. (2011). Fusiform gyrus face selectivity relates to individual differences in facial recognition ability. *Journal of Cognitive Neuroscience, 23*(7), 1723–1740.

Gauthier, I., & Nelson, C. A. (2001). The development of face expertise. *Current Opinion in Neurobiology, 11*(2), 219–224.

Golarai, G., Ghahremani, D. G., Whitfield-Gabrieli, S., Reiss, A., Eberhardt, J. L., Gabrieli, J. D. E., & Grill-Spector, K. (2007). Differential development of high-level visual cortex correlates with category-specific recognition memory. *Nature Neuroscience, 10*(4), 512–522. doi:10.1038/nn1865

Grossmann, T., & Johnson, M. H. (2007). The development of the social brain in human infancy. *European Journal of Neuroscience, 25*(4), 909–919. doi:10.1111/j.1460-9568.2007.05379.x

Grossmann, T., Johnson, M. H., Lloyd-Fox, S., Blasi, A., Deligianni, F., Elwell, C., & Csibra, G. (2008). Early cortical specialization for face-to-face communication in human infants. *Proceedings of the Royal Society B: Biological Sciences, 275*(1653), 2803–2811. doi:10.1098/rspb.2008.0986

Grossmann, T., Parise, E., & Friederici, A. D. (2010). The detection of communicative signals directed at the self in infant prefrontal cortex. *Frontiers in Human Neuroscience, 4,* 201. doi:10.3389/fnhum.2010.00201

Johnson, M. H. (2005). Subcortical face processing. *Nature Reviews Neuroscience, 6*(10), 766–774. doi:10.1038/nrn1766

Johnson, M. H. (2011). Interactive specialization: A domain-general framework for human functional brain development? *Developmental Cognitive Neuroscience, 1*(1), 7–21. doi:10.1016/j.dcn.2010.07.003

Johnson, M. H., Grossmann, T., & Cohen Kadosh, K. (2009). Mapping functional brain development: Building a social brain through interactive specialization. *Developmental Psychology, 45*(1), 151–159. doi:10.1037/a0014548

Kampe, K. K. W., Frith, C. D., & Frith, U. (2003). "Hey John": Signals conveying communicative intention toward the self activate brain regions associated with "mentalizing," regardless of modality. *Journal of Neuroscience, 23*(12), 5258–5263.

Kanwisher, N. (2010). Functional specificity in the human brain: A window into the functional architecture of the mind. *Proceedings of the National Academy of Sciences USA, 107*(25), 11163–11170. doi:10.1073/pnas.1005062107

Lloyd-Fox, S., Blasi, A., Everdell, N., Elwell, C. E., & Johnson, M. H. (2011). Selective cortical mapping of biological motion processing in young infants. *Journal of Cognitive Neuroscience, 23*(9), 2521–2532. doi:10.1162/jocn.2010.21598

Lloyd-Fox, S., Blasi, A., Volein, A., Everdell, N., Elwell, C. E., & Johnson, M. H. (2009). Social perception in infancy: A near infrared spectroscopy study. *Child Development, 80*(4), 986–999. doi:10.1111/j.1467-8624.2009.01312.x

Passarotti, A. M., Paul, B. M., Bussiere, J. R., Buxton, R. B., Wong, E. C., & Stiles, J. (2003). The development of face and location processing: An fMRI study. *Developmental Science, 6*(1), 100–117.

Pelphrey, K. A., Morris, J. P., & McCarthy, G. (2004). Grasping the intentions of others: The perceived intentionality of an action influences activity in the superior temporal sulcus during social perception. *Journal of Cognitive Neuroscience, 16*(10), 1706–1716. doi:10.1162/0898929042947900

Pelphrey, K. A., Morris, J. P., Michelich, C. R., Allison, T., & McCarthy, G. (2005). Functional anatomy of biological motion perception in posterior temporal cortex: An FMRI study of eye, mouth and hand movements. *Cerebral Cortex, 15*(12), 1866–1876. doi:10.1093/cercor/bhi064

Scherf, K. S., Behrmann, M., Humphreys, K., & Luna, B. (2007). Visual category-selectivity for faces, places and objects emerges along different developmental trajectories. *Developmental Science, 10*(4), F15–F30. doi:10.1111/j.1467-7687.2007.00595.x

Shultz, T. R, & Rivest, F. (2001). *Knowledge-based cascade-correlation: using knowledge to speed learning.* Retrieved November 4, 2010, from http://birkbeck.library.ingentaconnect.com/content/tandf/ccos/2001/00000013/00000001/art00002

Shultz, T. R., Rivest, F., Egri, L., Thivierge, J., & Dandurand, F. (2007). Could knowledge-based neural learning be useful in developmental robotics? The case of KBCC. *International Journal of Humanoid Robotics, 4*(2), 245. doi:10.1142/S0219843607001035

Thivierge, J. P., Titone, D., & Shultz, T. R. (2005). Simulating frontotemporal pathways involved in lexical ambiguity resolution. In *Proceedings of the Twenty-seventh Annual Conference of the Cognitive Science Society* (pp. 2178–2183). Mahwah, NJ: Erlbaum.

Zhang, H., Tian, J., Liu, J., Li, J., & Lee, K. (2009). Intrinsically organized network for face perception during the resting state. *Neuroscience Letters, 454*(1), 1–5. doi:10.1016/j.neulet.2009.02.054

1.3

Core Social Cognition

ELIZABETH S. SPELKE, EMILY P. BERNIER, AND AMY E. SKERRY

As a species, humans are distinguished by extraordinary capacities to learn and to socialize. A number of investigators of human cognitive development have proposed that these abilities are related: Our cognitive accomplishments are rooted in capacities and propensities for engaging with other people, learning from them, and navigating the social world (Csibra & Gergely, 2011; Meltzoff, Kuhl, Movellan, & Sejnowski, 2009; Tomasello, Carpenter, Call, Behne, & Moll, 2005). These proposals align with recent research testifying to the surprising social acumen of human infants, much of which is described in this volume. Here, we ask about the cognitive architecture underlying these abilities: Are infants endowed with an integrated, fundamental system of social reasoning, and if so, is this system responsible for any of the unique accomplishments of our species? Although researchers have not yet answered these questions, we suggest that the field can begin to do so by probing the signature limits of infants' social capacities and mounting an interdisciplinary research effort to characterize those capacities.

This suggestion is inspired by the success of the last several decades of research on the development of perception and cognition. Research on human infants and young children has characterized infants' abilities to perceive and reason about objects (e.g., Baillargeon, 2004), actions (e.g., Woodward, 1998), number (e.g., Feigenson, Dehaene, & Spelke, 2004), and geometry (e.g., Spelke, Lee, & Izard, 2010). One of us has argued that this research provides evidence for five *systems* of *core knowledge*: knowledge of objects and their motions, of agents and their goal-directed actions, of number and the operations of arithmetic, of places in the navigable layout and their distances and directions from one another, and of geometrical forms and their length and angular relations. Herein, we unpack this core knowledge hypothesis by considering each of its three claims: that infants' knowledge is guided by *systems*, that the systems are at the *core* of mature reasoning in these domains, and that these systems' computations give rise to *knowledge*. We then review how investigating boundary conditions and signature limits allowed the discovery and exploration of these systems across ages, species, and cultures. We suggest that understanding the nature of infants' social reasoning abilities will require a similar effort, and we discuss how such an approach could help to clarify current theories of human social cognitive development.

The core systems hypothesis states that infants represent and reason about the world in a way that accords with five specific, distinctive, and unitary bodies of principles. The principles are specific to a single domain (e.g., solid, bounded objects), because infants apply them to entities within the domain across wide variations in context and perceptual modality (for example, object principles are applied to tangible and hidden objects as well as to visible ones) and fail to apply them to perceptible entities outside the domain (Spelke, 1998). The five domains are distinct from one another, because the principles governing reasoning in each domain are different, producing systematic sets of double dissociations in infants' performance. Indeed, evidence for such dissociations has informed our understanding of mature cognition by suggesting that certain apparently unitary knowledge systems may in fact be founded on two distinct systems, as in the case of numerical and geometrical knowledge (Carey, 2009; Feigenson et al., 2004; Spelke et al., 2010). Finally, each set of principles forms a *system*, because when an entity is shown to behave in a manner that violates one principle, infants suspend the other principles (Huntley-Fenner, Carey, & Solimando, 2002; Van de Walle, Rubenstein, & Spelke, 1998).

The hypothesis that these are *core* systems is supported by research making systematic comparisons across species, across rearing conditions, and across human children and adults from different cultures or with differing access to the products of their culture. Diverse species represent objects, agents, number, places, and forms in the same ways human infants do, providing evidence for homologies in these cognitive capacities. In controlled-rearing experiments, animals have exhibited evidence of these representations on their very first encounters with entities in each of these domains (e.g., Chiandetti & Vallortigara, 2011). These systems do not disappear over later human development but rather continue to exist in children (e.g., Cantlon, Safford, & Brannon, 2011), appear in diverse cultures independently of formal education (e.g., Pica, Lemer, Izard, & Dehaene, 2004), and are relatively preserved in children and adults with limited access to language and other symbol systems (for reviews, see Carey, 2009; Spelke, 2011).

Finally, the hypothesis that these are core systems of *knowledge* is supported by evidence that the systems support knowledge acquisition in children and the use of that knowledge in adults. Core notions of objects support intuitive reasoning about the physical world (Carey & Spelke, 1994), core notions of agents allow us to infer goals from actions (Baker, Saxe, & Tenenbaum, 2009), and core notions of number and geometry undergird both the learning and the performance of formal mathematics (Dehaene, 2009; Spelke, 2011). The behavioral signatures of each system can then support the tracing of these representational systems into the human brain, where the same cortical systems are engaged for nonsymbolic tasks tapping core knowledge systems and for symbolic tasks tapping abilities that are unique to educated humans (for examples in the domain of number, see Dehaene, 2009; Piazza, 2010).

Critically, these conclusions are supported not by the mere demonstration of infant cognitive abilities but by research probing the generality and limits of those abilities. The discovery of signature limits in infants' representations of objects, number, and geometry allowed for experiments that revealed the scope and boundaries of core knowledge in different domains and that tested whether the signature limits found in human infants were shared by nonhuman animals. The discovery of those common signatures, in turn, allowed for experiments on animals that tested systematically for effects of experience on the development of these systems (e.g., Chiandetti & Vallortigara, 2011). The discovery of brain systems that show the same signatures allowed for experiments probing the neural mechanisms that support reasoning

in these domains (e.g., Dehaene, 2009). And finally, the discovery of adult cognitive systems that show the same signatures allowed for experiments testing for the persistence of core systems over later development, their universality across cultures, and the roles played by those systems in mature reasoning (e.g., Scholl, 2002).

In this context, we can return to our first question: Do humans also possess *a system of core social knowledge*? Is infants' early engagement with the social world underpinned by a coherent and distinct set of principles that continues to guide their social reasoning throughout life? If there is a core system for social reasoning, we must identify the entities and events that constitute its domain and the inferences that it supports. What sort of information can and cannot be taken as input to this system, and what computations does it perform?

Here we consider evidence for three different answers to this question: Gergely and Csibra's hypothesis of an innate system for learning in pedagogical contexts (Csibra & Gergely, 2011), Meltzoff's hypothesis of an innate system for matching one's own actions to the actions of others (Meltzoff, 2007), and Tomasello's hypothesis of an innate motivation to share attention and goals (Tomasello et al., 2005). We focus on these three theories for several reasons. First, each posits a system of social engagement that is unique to humans, and that promises to account for the development of our species' unique cognitive achievements. Second, each has generated an extensive body of research. Third, each is testable, we believe, through further research that follows the path of previous research on core cognition in other domains: research that defines the contours of the earliest developing social knowledge and then uses those contours in an interdisciplinary effort to probe the nature and development of this knowledge and its role in mature reasoning.

NATURAL PEDAGOGY

Following proposals by Premack and Premack (1996) and by Sperber and Wilson (1986), Gergely and Csibra suggest that our unique cultural heritage is a consequence of a species-specific adaptation for learning generalizable knowledge from communicative acts (Csibra & Gergely, 2011). Under this theory, humans are predisposed to identify self-directed communicative acts from innately specified cues. These intentional communications are then interpreted via pedagogy-specific assumptions, which support inferences about generic properties of the objects and events that the communications highlight.

Vivid signatures of pedagogy, sometimes in the form of departures from optimal learning, come from studies of older children. For example, nonhuman apes learn useful ways to manipulate novel objects from skilled performers, ignoring irrelevant actions, but 3- and 4-year-old children tested in the same tasks copy manifestly irrelevant actions (Horner & Whiten, 2005), as if trusting that the performer would not demonstrate actions unless they were causally relevant (Lyons, Young, & Keil, 2007). Symmetrically, when an apparently knowledgeable adult deliberately demonstrates only a single action on a novel object, children are less likely to explore other properties of the object than they are when no demonstration occurred at all, when the demonstrator expresses ignorance of the object's functions, or when the pedagogical demonstration is interrupted. In conditions of full pedagogy, children evidently assume that a knowledgeable adult would have demonstrated other object functions if they existed (Bonawitz et al., 2011).

Recent work has begun to test for similar pedagogical assumptions in infancy, with tantalizing results. When a socially engaging adult looks at and speaks to an infant about some object or event, the infant learns different things about the world than when the same person simply acts on the object or event with no prior social engagement (Topal, Gergely, Miklosi, Erdohegyi, & Csibra, 2008; Yoon, Johnson, & Csibra, 2008). Nevertheless, it is unclear whether these effects reflect a pedagogical stance: Does social communication merely heighten or redirect infants' attention, or does it lead infants to make specific inferences about the evidence provided (Skerry, Lambert, Powell & McAulliffe, in press)? This question could be addressed by testing for the effects of pedagogical learning found in older children. For example, will infants constrain their exploration of and learning about a new object based on an adult's completed pedagogical demonstration, and will this effect disappear if the communication is interrupted? Such experiments are necessary to distinguish pedagogy-specific inferences from lower level mechanisms for orienting attention to communicative adults. Only by linking learning in infants to learning in older children can we identify signatures by which to probe, through comparative research across ages and species, the nature, development, and evolution of this propensity to learn from communicative partners.

NATURAL SIMILARITY

Meltzoff (2007) has proposed that the crucial starting point for human social cognition is a propensity to learn from and affiliate with others who are represented as being like the self. Infants imitate the actions of others from birth (Meltzoff & Moore, 1977), and by 14 months, prefer others who imitate them in turn (Meltzoff, 2007). These actions propel infants' learning both about and from their social partners, fostering the acquisition of language, cognitive skills, and social knowledge.

If a propensity for imitation is at the root of our species-specific social cognitive abilities, then aspects of this propensity should be unique to humans. Given that some imitative tendencies and preferences have been documented in nonhuman primates, both in neonates (Ferrari et al., 2006) and beyond (Horner & Whiten, 2005), what are the specific features of human imitation that could support the rich social learning found in humans but not other species? One possibility, we suggest, is that a propensity to divide the social world into groups with common norms may serve to guide not only infants' own social interactions but also their understanding of the larger social landscape.

Human adults and older children not only behave like others with whom they wish to affiliate, and evaluate positively those who mirror their own behavior, but also conform to larger social groups and use evidence for conformity to reason about social relationships. Intriguing new work by Lindsey Powell suggests that by 8 months of age, human infants have a similar ability (Powell & Spelke, 2011). Infants were shown animated displays depicting two social groups whose members engaged in two different characteristic actions, one per group. After observing the two actions performed by a subset of group members, infants viewed new group members performing the action of either their own or the other group. Infants looked longer at the inconsistent event in which a group member did not behave like others in its group. These findings suggest that conforming actions may have social meaning for 8-month-old infants, outside the context of their own social actions. However, further research is necessary to test this suggestion: What features of third-party interactions influence infants' expectations of behavioral similarity, and to what class of entities are these expectations applied? Once the origins and limits of these expectations are better defined, psychologists can turn to the broader questions of whether these early-developing capacities are seeds of our propensities for understanding and evaluating social conformity as adults, and whether they are unique to humans or shared by other animals.

NATURAL COOPERATION

Finally, Tomasello (2009) has proposed that the crucial differences between humans and other species stem from our unique biological predisposition to share psychological states with others. Evidence for this claim comes from a variety of studies examining the communicative and cooperative behaviors of toddlers. Within the second year of life children are predisposed to share attention and information (Liszkowski, Carpenter, Striano, & Tomasello, 2006) and to engage in helpful actions toward others, even in the absence of any explicit request or reward (Warneken & Tomasello, 2006). These observations raise the possibility that a core propensity to share mental states traces back to the beginning of human life.

Although active helping has not been reported systematically in the first year of life, a series of experiments on infants suggest that prosocial motivations may extend far back in development. Like Powell's studies, moreover, these experiments suggest that this propensity guides not only infants' own social interactions but also their understanding of the social interactions of others whom they observe as third parties. Building on research by Premack and Premack (1997), Hamlin and her collaborators presented infants with puppet shows in which two agents respectively help and hinder a third agent in achieving its goal. Six-month-old infants preferentially reached toward the agent who facilitated the goal over the agent who hindered it; 3-month-old infants showed a similar pattern of preferential looking at the helpful agent over the harmful one (Hamlin, Wynn, & Bloom, 2010). These findings, and related findings with older infants, have been taken as evidence that infants appropriately valence the helper's and hinderer's behaviors, providing a foundation for social or moral evaluation (Hamlin, Wynn, & Bloom, 2007).

These findings raise many questions concerning the conditions under which infants exhibit such preferences. One set of questions concerns the domain of these phenomena: Are they specific to completed and thwarted goal-directed actions, or might infants show preferences based on other social primitives such as harm or battery? A second set of questions concerns the inferences guiding infants' evaluations: Do infants infer the intentions, that is, the second-order goals, of helpers and hinderers? Do they impute emotional experiences to those who are in need of help, or to those who are wronged? As these questions are answered, investigators will gain tools for probing the role of these capacities in the development and practice of moral reasoning at later ages, and for reconstructing the evolution of these capacities through systematic comparisons across animal species.

These three examples illustrate a few of the more intriguing findings from the rich and growing body of research on social cognition in infancy. They begin to test general claims about the human mind while also providing ways to probe for the nature and development of human social knowledge. Nevertheless, none of these studies yet reveals whether a system of core social knowledge exists in infants. Moreover, this research does not reveal whether any of the social abilities and propensities found in young infants are unique to our species. Because all of the evidence for distinctively human patterns of pedagogy, conformity, and cooperation come from studies of older children, it is possible that these patterns develop from core social cognitive systems that humans share with other animals. Our uniquely human social propensities may result from the ways in which we build on these shared systems of core knowledge. To distinguish these possibilities, we must deepen our experiments and widen our view.

If a core system of social knowledge exists, it will be discovered by experiments that probe its contours, characterizing the input conditions that elicit specifically social reasoning and the principles that guide it (e.g., see Kinzler, Dupoux, & Spelke, 2007). If it is unique to humans, then systematic differences should emerge when the same experiments are conducted on other species. If it is a guide to social reasoning throughout human life, then the same principles and limits should be found in humans in all cultures and at all ages. All of these findings will depend on the discovery of signature properties or profiles that can be used to identify common processes operating over development and across species, cultures, and levels of analysis.

If the system is an evolutionary adaptation to life in a social world, then evolutionary analyses focusing on the selection pressures shaping human evolution may provide insights into its limits and idiosyncrasies (e.g., Kurzban, Cosmides, & Tooby, 2001). If the system lies at the center of our social reasoning as adults, then theories of mature human social reasoning, from social psychology, evolutionary and cultural anthropology (e.g., Henrich & Broesch, 2011), and computational cognitive science (e.g., Shafto & Goodman, 2008) may guide research into its foundations (e.g., Bonawitz et al., 2011). And if social cognitive development resembles development in other cognitive domains, then insights also will flow in the opposite direction: The search for the origins of social knowledge will shed light on the nature of mature social knowledge. As this volume attests, the study of social cognitive development is at an extremely exciting juncture, where all of the big questions are open, and where rich empirical and theoretical tools are available to address them.

REFERENCES

Baillargeon, R. (2004). Infants' physical world. *Current Directions in Psychological Science*, *13*, 89–94.

Baker, C. L., Saxe, R., & Tenenbaum, J. B. (2009). Action understanding as inverse planning. *Cognition*, *113*, 329–349.

Bonawitz, E., Shafto, P., Gweon, H., Goodman, N. D., Spelke, E., & Schulz, L. (2011). The double-edged sword of pedagogy: Instruction limits spontaneous exploration and discovery. *Cognition*, *120*, 322–330.

Cantlon, J. F., Safford, K. E., & Brannon, E. M. (2010). Spontaneous analog number representations in three-year-old children. *Developmental Science*, *13*, 289–297.

Carey, S. (2009). *The origin of concepts*. New York: Oxford University Press.

Carey, S., & Spelke, E. (1994). Domain-specific knowledge and conceptual change. In L. A. Hirshfeld & S. A. Gelman (Eds.), *Mapping the mind* (pp. 169–200). Cambridge, UK: Cambridge University Press.

Chiandetti, C., & Vallortigara, G. (2011). Intuitive physical reasoning about occluded objects by inexperienced chicks. *Proceedings of the Royal Society B: Biological Sciences*, *278*(1718), 2621–2627

Csibra, G., & Gergely, G. (2011). Natural pedagogy as evolutionary adaptation. *Philosophical Transactions of the Royal Society B*, *366*, 1149–1157.

Dehaene, S. (2009). Origins of mathematical intuitions: The case of arithmetic. *Annals of the New York Academy of Sciences*, *1156*, 232–259.

Feigenson, L., Dehaene, S., & Spelke, E. S. (2004). Core systems of number. *Trends in Cognitive Sciences*, *8*, 307–314.

Ferrari, P.F., Visalberghi, E., Paukner, A., Fogassi, L., Ruggiero, A., & Suomi, S. J. (2006). Neonatal imitation in rhesus macaques. *PLoS Biology*, *4*(9), e302.

Hamlin, J., Wynn, K., & Bloom, P. (2007). Social evaluation by preverbal infants. *Nature*, *450*, 557–559.

Hamlin, J. K., Wynn, K., & Bloom, P. (2010). 3-month-olds show a negativity bias in social evaluation. *Developmental Science*, *13*, 923–939.

Henrich, J., & Broesch, J. (2011). On the nature of cultural transmission networks: Evidence from Fijian villages for adaptive learning biases. *Philosophical Transactions of the Royal Society*, *366*, 1139–1148.

Horner, V., & Whiten, A. (2005). Causal knowledge and imitation/emulation switching in chimpanzees (Pan troglodytes) and children (Homo sapiens). *Animal Cognition*, *8*, 164–181.

Huntley-Fenner, G., Carey, S., & Solimando, A. (2002). Objects are individuals but stuff doesn't count: Perceived rigidity and cohesiveness influence infants' representations of small numbers of discrete entities. *Cognition*, *85*, 203–221.

Kinzler, K. D., Dupoux, E., & Spelke, E. S. (2007). The native language of social cognition. *Proceedings of the National Academy of Sciences USA*, *104*, 12577–12580.

Kurzban, R., Tooby, J. & Cosmides, L. (2001). Can race be erased? Coalitional computation and social categorization. *Proceedings of the National Academy of Sciences USA*, *98*, 15387–15392.

Liszkowski, U., Carpenter, M., Striano, T., & Tomasello, M. (2006). Twelve- and 18-month- olds point to provide information for others. *Journal of Cognition and Development*, *7*, 173–187.

Lyons, D., Young, A., & Keil, F. (2007). The hidden structure of overimitation. *Proceedings of the National Academy of Sciences USA*, *104*, 19751–19756.

Meltzoff, A. N. (2007). "Like me": A foundation for social cognition. *Developmental Science*, *10*, 126–134.

Meltzoff, A. N., Kuhl, P. K., Movellan, J., & Sejnowski, T. J. (2009). Foundations for a new science of learning. *Science*, *325*, 284–288.

Meltzoff, A. N., & Moore, M. K. (1977). Imitation of facial and manual gestures by human neonates. *Science*, *198*, 75–78.

Piazza, M. (2010). Neurocognitive start-up tools for symbolic number representation. *Trends in Cognitive Science*, *922*, 1–10.

Pica, P., Lemer, C., Izard, W., & Dehaene, S. (2004). Exact and approximate arithmetic in an Amazonian indigene group. *Science*, *306*, 499–503.

Powell, L., & Spelke, E. (2011, March 31-April 2). *Eight-month-olds expect conformity from social but not nonsocial entities*. Poster presented at the annual meeting of the Society for Research in Child Development, Montreal, Quebec.

Premack, D., & Premack, A. J. (1996). Why animals lack pedagogy and some cultures have more of it than others. In D. R. Olson (Ed.), *The handbook of education and human development: New models of learning, teaching and schooling* (pp. 302–323.). Malden, MA: Blackwell.

Premack, D., & Premack, A. J. (1997). Infants attribute value to the goal directed actions of self-propelled objects. *Journal of Cognitive Neuroscience, 9,* 848–856.

Scholl, B. J. (Ed.). (2002). *Objects and attention.* Cambridge, MA: MIT Press.

Shafto, P., & Goodman, N. (2008). Teaching games: Statistical sampling assumptions for pedagogical situations. In B. C. Love, K. McRae, & V. M. Sloutsky (Eds.), *Proceedings of the 30th Annual Conference of the Cognitive Science Society* (pp. 1632–1636). Austin, TX: Cognitive Science Society.

Skerry, A. E., Lambert, E., Powell, L. J. and McAulliffe, K. (in press). The origins of pedagogy: developmental and evolutionary perspectives. *Evolutionary Psychology.*

Spelke, E. S. (1998). Where perceiving ends and thinking begins: The apprehension of objects in infancy. In A. Yonas (Ed.), *Perceptual development in infancy. Minnesota Symposium on Child Psychology* (Vol. 20, pp. 197–233). Hillsdale, NJ: Erlbaum.

Spelke, E. S. (2011). Natural number and natural geometry. In E. Brannon & S. Dehaene (Eds.), *Space, time, and number in the brain: Searching for the foundations of mathematical thought. Attention & Performance XXIV* (pp. 287–313). Amsterdam: Elsevier..

Spelke, E. S., Lee, S. A., & Izard, V. (2010). Beyond core knowledge: Natural geometry. *Cognitive Science, 34*(5), 863–884.

Sperber, D., & Wilson, D. (1986). *Relevance: Communication and cognition.* Oxford, England: Blackwell.

Tomasello, M. (2009). *Why we cooperate.* Cambridge, MA: MIT Press.

Tomasello, M., Carpenter, M., Call, J., Behne, T., & Moll, H. (2005). Understanding and sharing intentions: The ontogeny and phylogeny of cultural cognition. *Behavioral and Brain Sciences, 28,* 675–735.

Topal, J., Gergely, G., Miklosi, A., Erdohegyi, A., & Csibra, G. (2008). Infants' perseverative search errors are induced by pragmatic misinterpretation. *Science, 321*(5897), 1831–1834.

Van de Walle, G., Rubenstein, J., & Spelke, E. S. (1998). Infant sensitivity to shadow motions. *Cognitive Development, 13,* 387–419.

Warneken, F., & Tomasello, M. (2006). Altruistic helping in human infants and young chimpanzees. *Science, 311,* 1301–1303.

Woodward, A. L. (1998). Infants selectively encode the goal object of an actor's reach. *Cognition, 69,* 1–34.

Yoon, J. M. D., Johnson, M. H., & Csibra, G. (2008). Communication-induced memory biases in preverbal infants. *Proceedings of the National Academy of Sciences USA, 105,* 13690–13695.

1.4

Core Cognition of Social Relations

LOTTE THOMSEN AND SUSAN CAREY

Humans are an ultrasocial species. All children must discover the social structure of their world: who is friend or foe, who should lead and who should follow, who is a peer. Such social learning has cognitive, affective, and motivational components. Cognitively, the child must acquire representations of categories of social relations and specific instantiations of each category. Affectively and motivationally, the child must acquire the emotional reactions and behavioral responses to ensure that he or she acts appropriately in different kinds of social situations. Here we concentrate on the conceptual representations that underlie our interpretations of the social world.

Parents may spend a good deal of energy teaching their children how to behave in different kinds of situations. But how do children figure out which new social contexts are alike—that is, when to share (or not), when to obey (or not), and so on? We rarely instruct or explicitly discuss the relational rules of social situations, and our social experiences vary greatly. Yet we share enough relational expectations to be able to coordinate our social life, even in new encounters. We readily perceive the kind of social relationship that is in play and adapt our actions in myriad ways. In present-day Denmark, for instance, it is obvious to us that food in the fridge generally belongs to everybody within a family and anyone who is hungry is allowed to eat it regardless of who bought it at the supermarket. But it goes without saying that this is not the case when it is the refrigerator at the office that is in question. The question of how it is that humans can understand and coordinate infinitely varying and novel instances of meaningful social interactions is roughly parallel to the classical *learnability question* in theoretical linguistics—how it is that all children within a language community converge in learning the same grammar of their mother tongue, although the verbal stimuli they meet are impoverished, noisy, and highly variable (Chomsky, 1967/2006).

Ultimately, it amounts to asking how human social life is understandable, and hence possible. The problem does not reduce to understanding that individuals are agents who act intentionally to fulfill their goals. Although by definition a social relationship takes place between intentional agents, knowing that several intentional agents are present does not specify what kind of social relationship they will have with one another.

ONE POSSIBLE SOLUTION: INNATE PRIMITIVES

Pursuing the analogy with language acquisition, it is possible that there is something analogous to universal grammar in the domain of social relations—a universal set of abstract kinds of social relations, and innate skeletal knowledge of these that guides learning, inference, and indeed experience in the social domain. Alternatively, some constructive learning process may create representations of the social world building on representations with no social content per se. Several sorts of data bear on adjudicating between these two broad possibilities. These include evidence for cross-cultural universality in the *types* of social relations and the features that indicate when each applies, as well as evidence from young infants suggesting knowledge of those relational types and indicators. Data from very young children will also bear on specific proposals for how knowledge of social relations might be learned because the proposed learning mechanisms must use evidence available to children before the age at which they understand social relationships (e.g., if preverbal infants understand social relations, they cannot have learned about them through explicit, verbal instruction).

The anthropologist Alan Fiske (e.g., 2004) has amassed evidence for cross-culturally universal types of social relations, such as communal sharing (e.g., members of a family), authority/dominance (e.g., different ranks in the military), and equality (e.g., peers at the same rank within the military). Each of these is realized in many specific social relations, differing both within and across cultures. The anthropological record indicates that *communal sharing* is prototypically implemented among close kin and marked by touch and spatial closeness, by sharing food and bodily substances (breast milk, semen, saliva, and blood), by moving in synchrony, and by marking the bodies to look alike. For instance, many communal rituals include eating or drinking out of a common pot, as in the sacrament of the Catholic Church. This is why many people find it disgusting if people they do not know take a sip from their glass, but not if their partner or child does. Fiske (2004) argues that these practices all create the impression of one social body with a shared essence that is the foundation for communal sharing. Hierarchical relations of leadership and authority are prototypically marked in time and space so that superiors are perceived to be, and placed so as to be, bigger, above, and coming before others and being more forceful than others. For instance, superiors ceremonially wear headdresses or sit on thrones that make them appear taller than others. Egalitarian relations are prototypically constituted through operational procedures such as turn-taking, tit-for-tat matching, and making outcomes *even*; these operations define what it means to be equal. Evolutionary precursors for communal sharing and social hierarchy, and some of their markers, are widely observed throughout the animal social world. Most basically, kinship co-occurs with the sharing of semen across species, breast-feeding among mammals, and with territoriality, huddling/affiliate touch, and altruistic sacrifice (e.g., feeding one's kin) at the very least among birds and mammals but also among some insects. Similarly, relative body size is associated with dominance rank across the animal kingdom, and so are dominance displays that make the body appear larger and taller versus submissive displays of prostration and constriction of the body. These spatial features and displays also play a role in our modern social life. Imagine, for instance, how odd a court trial would be if the person on trial was seated at a higher level than the judge, looking down on him or her. Actual body height is correlated with socioeconomic status, actual power, and perceived dominance of males—and even predicts the presidential candidates' likelihood of getting elected. Most people also intuitively respond to someone with a dominant, open posture (that makes the body look larger) by adopting a complementary submissive, constricted one, and those who do not are liked less than those who do (for review, see Schubert, Waldzus, & Seibt, 2008). Furthermore, being induced by some cover story to simply adopt an open posture rather than a constricted one for a few minutes affects how powerful participants feel, the risks they are willing to take to get what they want, and even the neuroendocrine signature of dominance (increased testosterone, decreased cortisol; Carney, Cuddy, & Yap, 2010). In other words, the meaning of dominance postures seems wired into our bodies in the sense that they solicit the appropriate chemical responses and behaviors to the dominance rank that an open versus constricted posture indicates.

In sum, Fiske's analysis provides a candidate set of conceptually primitive representations of social relations. If the hypothesis that representations of relational models have been shaped by evolution to guide social interactions and sociocultural learning is correct, then these core cognitive systems should be active as soon as the cultural learning process begins—perhaps even in infancy. If natural selection yielded an innate representational vocabulary, including concepts of communal sharing, social hierarchy, and equality, it will have also created sensitivity to some perceptually available indicators that identify instances of these relations in the infants' social world. Having a concept of dominance would be of no use if the infant had no way of recognizing when one agent is dominant over another. Cues infants are sensitive to concerning social relations among agents should affect infants' own actions toward others as well as their predictions about the relational interactions of third parties. And indeed, recent studies have shown this to be so, both for social dominance relations and communal sharing relations.

REPRESENTATIONS OF SOCIAL DOMINANCE IN CHILDHOOD

A body of ethological and ecological studies going back to the 1920s converges on the point that dominance plays an important role early in human life. Evidence from the win-lose patterns of dyadic contests shows that groups of toddlers and preschoolers form social dominance hierarchies not unlike those of chimpanzees. The more dominant children will assertively or aggressively take contested resources (e.g., toys) away from others, but these children are also the most watched, imitated, and preferred play partners by the other children (this changes by early elementary school).

Some studies also suggest that toddlers size up the social scene and the "resource holding power" of their opponents and use aggression strategically, only claiming resources from children who are smaller than themselves, do not have a reputation for winning fights, or have fewer allies around (for reviews, see Hawley, 1999; Pellegrini, 2008). Of course, it is entirely possible that toddlers and preschoolers simply learn about social dominance through their own experiences, struggling for contested resources within their group. Might preverbal infants, who are too young to have experience participating in such conflicts, nonetheless understand them and also understand that size predicts dominance, even among people they do not know? If there is innate core cognition of relational models, they might.

Since preverbal and just-linguistic infants cannot be interviewed, their knowledge must be assessed by their behavior—either with respect to their emotional reactions in social situations or with respect to their expectations as to how observed social interactions will play out. A much used way of assessing infants' mental representations is the violation-of-expectancy looking time method. Basically, infants tend to look longer when something surprises them. So we can test hypotheses about what they expect by measuring

how long they look at animated or play-acted scenarios that either violate or confirm their expectations. We used this methodology to demonstrate that preverbal infants from 10 months of age use relative size—a cue that varies with social dominance across culture and the animal kingdom—to predict which of two novel agents will prevail in a schematized conflict of goals (Thomsen, Frankenhuis, Ingold-Smith, & Carey, 2011). When a large and small agent repeatedly moved across a stage in opposite directions before they met in the middle, blocking each other's way, infants from 10 to 17 months of age looked much longer, and hence presumably were surprised, when the large agent bowed and scooted away, yielding the way so the smaller agent could pass it and make it to the end of stage, rather than vice versa (all infants watched both scenarios; see Fig. 1.4.1 or http://news.sciencemag.org/sciencenow/ 2011/01/ babies-size-up-the-social-scene.html for the actual stimuli shown to babies).

Several controls in Thomsen et al. (2011) and a subsequent follow-up study demonstrated that this effect depended crucially upon a context of conflicting goals and that the infants' greater interest to the smaller agent's prevailing in the conflicting goals scenario was not driven by differences of perceptual saliency across the test outcomes nor by

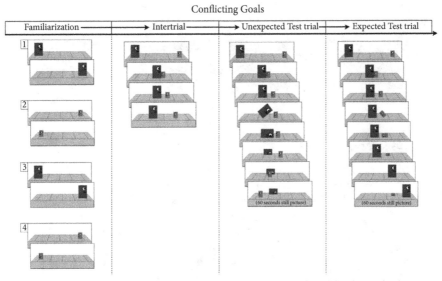

(presentation order of events, color, side and order of entry of the agents were fully counter-balanced across subjects)

FIGURE 1.4.1: Schematic of the animations used by Thomsen et al. (2011) to test whether preverbal infants understand social dominance and use relative size to predict who will yield or prevail when the goals of novel agents conflict.

knowledge that small agents are more likely to fall over than large ones. This experiment is the first to explore preverbal infants' representations of social dominance, and so it raises many more questions than it answers. Most important, it does not establish whether infants take the dominance relation between two agents to be stable over time nor does it address infants' evaluation of the participants in a dominance interaction: Are they more interested in the dominant agent? Do they prefer it? Do they selectively learn from it and imitate it? Doing so might benefit infants insofar as dominance rank reflects success in one's social context.

REPRESENTATIONS OF COMMUNAL SHARING IN INFANCY

There is also evidence that infants are motivated to participate in communal relations and that they automatically respond meaningfully to cues that signal communal sharing. First of all, toddlers (and under some conditions chimps) spontaneously help others (e.g., Warneken & Tomasello, 2006; see Chapter 6.11 in this volume), handing them what they cannot reach, removing barriers to achieving some goal, and so forth. Young infants also prefer those who help, rather than hinder, others in achieving their goals (Hamlin, Wynn, & Bloom, 2007). Thus, there seems to be

a fundamental motivation for humans (and perhaps other primates) to cooperate in helping others achieve their goals. These results do not bear on whether infants distinguish communal sharing relations, in which cooperation is expected, from other social relations in which it is less expected. To this end, Over and Carpenter (2009) demonstrated that spontaneous helping varies with exposure to a universal marker of communal sharing: affiliate touch. In this study, one experimenter showed 18-month-old toddlers photos of eight household objects (e.g., a teapot), drawing attention to it, and commenting on it. Each photo had one or two little figures in the background, to which no attention was drawn. Across the conditions, the background figures differed (see Fig. 1.4.2 for examples of the teapot photo from each of the four conditions). Children were subsequently more likely to spontaneously help another experimenter pick up a bunch of pencils she dropped later on in the study if the background figures were two dolls facing each other and touching (i.e., hugging; Fig. 1.4.2a) than if the background figure consisted of only one doll (Fig. 1.4.2b), the figures were not dolls (Fig. 1.4.2c), or the dolls were back to back (Fig. 1.4.2d). This is, to our knowledge, the first study to show priming of infants' social motivation by a cue for a specific kind of social relationship.

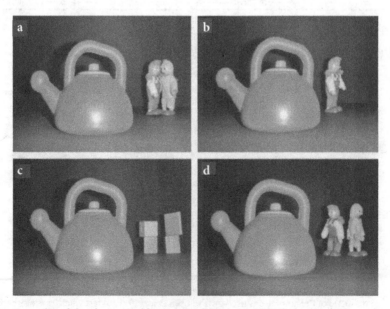

FIGURE 1.4.2: Examples of the photos used by Over and Carpenter (2009) to test whether exposure to affiliate touch affects altruistic behavior among just-linguistic infants.

MIGHT RELATIONAL MODELS BE LEARNED?

Taken together, the data reviewed show that pre-verbal infants have representations of abstract types of social relations, including those of communal sharing and dominance/hierarchy, as well as ways of recognizing instances of them in their social world. Young children appear to see closeness and touch as a cue to communal relationships and respond accordingly with altruistic and affiliative behavior, and at least in a context of conflicting goals they expect relative size and vertical posture to predict priority of right-of-way. Although these data are consistent with there being innate, core cognition of social relations, they obviously do not establish the truth of this hypothesis because the infants who demonstrated this knowledge were 10 months of age or older. The alternative is that concepts of social relations are constructed out of leaner primitives, and the indicators of distinct types of social relations are learned.

The cross-culturally universal metaphors for talking about social relations have been taken by some to reflect a construction process of representations of social relations in which these representations are built from more concrete, spatial and bodily primitives. These embodiment and conceptual metaphor theories of conceptual learning assume that "sensorimotor experiences in early life form a scaffold for the development of conceptual knowledge" (Ackerman, Nocera, & Bargh, 2010, p. 1713; see also Lakoff & Johnson, 1980/2003). For instance, infants' universal experiences of being held closely in their parents' arms might make them think of intimacy as closeness and love as warmth. Evidence in favor of this possibility is the fact that this conceptual metaphor is used across many languages (Lakoff & Johnson, 1980/2003). Furthermore, its reflex in nonlinguistic thought is revealed in the Over and Carpenter study reviewed earlier, as well as in many social psychological experiments. For instance, Williams and Bargh (2008) showed that holding a warm, rather than iced, cup of coffee made participants perceive the experimenter as a kinder person.

According to the conceptual metaphor account of the origin of abstract concepts, and the embodiment account of conceptual content, the meaning of social life is grounded in bodily sensations and spatial relations experienced in the course of each person's experience. According to these accounts, we each come to think in the same conceptual metaphors because we all have the same human body and hence roughly the same embodied learning experiences. But of course the phenomena brought to bear in support of these views also are consistent with core cognition accounts of the origin of social concepts. To put it simply, whereas the conceptual metaphor account argues that universal experiences lead to universal primary metaphors (i.e., closeness is intimacy, warmth is love), a core cognition approach would argue that universal, foundational core concepts lead to universal experiences.

There are several reasons we favor the latter alternative, namely that abstract representations of relational models are part of our innate conceptual repertoire. It is hard to see how one can learn that closeness goes with love without having some notion of love in the first place, unless the argument is the purely empiricist one that love is nothing whatsoever but embodied closeness. The conceptual metaphor approach also leaves open why our "embodied understanding" shifts from some image-schematic aspects in one context (e.g., being held *closely* by the mother, rather than picked *up* by her), to other aspects in a different context (being *on top* rather than being *close* in a physical fight for power). But children (and other cultural novices) cannot learn who has what kind of social relationships with whom unless they somehow know *what* are basic kinds of social relationships to look for between people, as well as *how* to recognize them in the world. In other words, something must constrain the child's attention to the relevant cues among the myriad aspects inherent in any social scenario. Ten-month-olds have experienced few dominance conflicts with peers, and surely the big creatures in their experience are deeply associated with love, comfort, feeding, and family—communal sharing, that is. Why then, does size not become metaphorically linked to love and nurturing? Children must somehow know that it matters who loves whom, and that you find out by looking for people holding hands or kissing like mom and dad, not by looking for people with the same size difference as mom and dad.

We do not deny, of course, that a vast amount of learning is required for children to come to understand their social worlds. On the picture of social learning argued for here, some of that learning will consist of identifying the particular social relationships that exemplify the abstract relational models the child knows innately. But additionally, associative learning could certainly enrich the cues that are useful for identifying specific types of social relations in a given social context (universal or not). That is, it certainly is possible that warmth is not an innate cue for communal sharing but comes to stand for it through embodied experiences (Lakoff & Johnson, 1980/2003). The difference between the view put forward here and conceptual metaphor theory is that we argue that infants must be able to conceptualize love, or communal sharing, or collaborative cooperation in the first place, and have *some* ways of recognizing it in the world, in order to learn to associate other cues, say, warmth with it. However, the empirical question as to which exact cues even very young infants use to identify elementary social relationships is still wide open.

CONCLUSIONS

We suggest that humans have evolved an innate, finite set of conceptual primitives that specify relational models for communal sharing, social hierarchy, and equality and are coupled with innate input analyzers that automatically identify some instances of each in the social world. Such a universal vocabulary of basic kinds of relational models would make it possible for young children to *learn* the relational makeup of their particular culture by specifying the kinds of social relationships they should be looking for and at least some initial ways of recognizing them.

REFERENCES

Ackerman, J. M., Nocera, C. C., & Bargh, J. A. (2010). Incidental haptic sensations influence social judgments and decisions. *Science, 328*, 1712–1715.

Carney, D. R., Cuddy, A. J. C., & Yap, A. J. (2010). Power posing: Brief nonverbal displays affect neuroendocrine levels and risk tolerance. *Psychological Science, 21*, 1363–1368.

Chomsky. N. (1967/2006). *Language and mind* (3rd ed.). Cambridge, England: Cambridge University Press.

Fiske, A. P. (2004). Four modes of constituting relationships: Consubstantial assimilation; space, magnitude, time, and force; Concrete procedures: Abstract symbolism. In N. Haslam (Ed.), *Relational Models Theory. A contemporary overview* (pp. 61–146). Mahwah, NJ: Erlbaum.

Hamlin, J. K., Wynn, K., & Bloom, P. (2007). Social evaluation by preverbal infants. *Nature, 450*, 557–559.

Hawley, P. (1999). The ontogenesis of social dominance: A strategy-based evolutionary perspective. *Developmental Review, 19*, 97–132.

Lakoff, G., & Johnson, M. (1980/2003). *Metaphors we live by*. Chicago, IL: University of Chicago Press.

Over, H., & Carpenter, M. (2009). Eighteen-month-old infants show increased helping following priming with affiliation. *Psychological Science, 20*, 1189–1193.

Pellegrini, A. D. (2008). The roles of aggressive and affiliative behaviors in resource control: A behavioral ecological perspectives. *Developmental Review, 28*, 461–487.

Schubert, T. W., Waldzus, S., & Seibt. B. (2008). The embodiment of power and communalism in space and bodily contact. In G. R. Semin & Smith, E. R. (Eds.), *Embodied grounding: Social, cognitive, affective, and neuroscientific approaches* (pp. 160–183). Cambridge, England: Cambridge University Press.

Thomsen, L. Frankenhuis, W. E., Ingold-Smith, M., & Carey, S. (2011). Big and mighty: Preverbal infants mentally represent social dominance. *Science, 331*, 477–480.

Warneken, F., & Tomasello, M. (2006). Altruistic helping in human infants and young chimpanzees. *Science, 311*, 1301–1303.

Williams, L. E., & Bargh. J. A. (2008). Experiencing physical warmth promotes interpersonal warmth. *Science, 322*, 606–607.

1.5

Infant Cartographers

Mapping the Social Terrain

KAREN WYNN

Some aspects of adult social psychology appear intriguingly similar to certain aspects of infant social psychology. Specifically, some of the kinds of social information that are particularly salient, important, and meaningful, as suggested by the extent to which they occur in adult conversation—that is, *gossip*—appear also to be salient, important, and meaningful aspects of very young humans' social-world representations, as indicated by scientific findings in the study of infant cognition.

As a highly social species, we humans are critically attuned to the goings-on in our social worlds and to the relationships of the individuals within these worlds. We monitor many features of our complex social network, including the following:

(a) Which individuals are fast friends and which are firm enemies

(b) Which individuals are allies with respect to a given cause and which are in conflict with each other (for example, who's in agreement with whom on controversial and important issues within our community—and which individuals share our *own* attitudes and viewpoints)

(c) Who is a dependable "team player" and who is "looking out for number one"

(d) Whether someone reciprocates support or a favor appropriately or inappropriately

(e) Where different individuals fall, with respect to ourselves and to each other, on the social status hierarchy (i.e., "keeping up with the Joneses" entails, among other things, knowing *where* the Joneses are in the race overall as well as relative to oneself)

Because social relationships are not fixed but are in constant flux and evolution, our mapping of our "social terrain" is never complete but constantly in need of confirmation and updating. Accordingly, over two thirds of all human conversation consists of "gossip"—that is, social information, discussions of the goings-on of others, and obtaining and passing on updates of their interactions and frictions with each other (e.g., Dunbar, Marriott, & Duncan, 1997). Gossip may be an evolutionarily rooted pastime of our species. It serves many adaptive functions—facilitating social comparisons (Wert & Salovey, 2004), tracking and influencing social reputations (such as who is a "cooperator" and who is a social "cheater" or defector; Sommerfeld, Krambeck, Semmann, & Milinski, 2007), and facilitating the monitoring of changes that occur within the social network (e.g., Dunbar, 2004). Put simply, we, as a species, are deeply interested in and focused upon mapping our local social terrain—accurately placing the new individuals we encounter within that landscape, as well as continually updating the changing topography of the relationships between individuals.

Interestingly, this mapping of the social landscape is not the sole province of adults. I will come back to the topic of gossip among mature humans, but will first highlight some aspects of the social world that young humans are busily mapping, even before their first birthday.

INFANTS ATTEND TO SOCIAL RELATIONSHIPS

Even preverbal infants attend to the socially relevant behaviors and attributes of others, and they represent several distinct types of relationships between individuals. For just a few examples: (1) Infants are sensitive to whether one individual aids or interferes with the efforts of another—that is, *whether two individuals are cooperating toward a common end or are in conflict*—and they expect an individual to be positively disposed toward one who has helped him or her in the past but to find aversive one who has previously opposed his or her efforts (Hamlin, Wynn, & Bloom, 2007; Kuhlmeier, Wynn, & Bloom, 2003; see Wynn, 2008). (2) Infants are able to make astute assumptions about the likely *dominance relationship between two individuals* of differing physical size (Mascaro & Csibra, 2012; Thomsen, Frankenhuis, Ingold-Smith, & Carey, 2011). For example, they expect a smaller individual to yield and give way to a larger one, rather than the reverse, if the two are on a collision course. And (3) infants are sensitive to *dependent/caregiver relationships*. In several experimental studies, their expectations of how an interaction between an animated schematic "child" and "parent" would unfold reflected their own individual attachment styles (e.g., Johnson et al., 2010).

INFANTS HAVE SOCIAL PREFERENCES

Infants not only note the nature of social relationships between others, they also determine the relevance of other individuals to *themselves*, generating social preferences for some individuals over others in meaningful and predictable ways. As early as the first 3 to 6 months of life (the youngest ages tested), infants prefer strangers who more closely resemble highly familiar individuals (such as their own primary caregivers), both in looks (e.g., race: Bar-Haim, Ziv, Lamy, & Hodes, 2006; gender: Quinn, Yahr, Kuhn, Slater, & Pascalis, 2002) and in behavior (language spoken: Kinzler, DuPoux, & Spelke, 2007).

My colleagues and I have found that infants themselves prefer an individual seen to have acted prosocially over one seen acting in an antisocial manner. Across a number of studies, we have found that infants preferentially attend to, approach, and reward individuals previously observed helping or engaging in a reciprocal interaction with another. In contrast, infants avoid, and even actively punish, individuals observed hindering another's efforts or acting in their own self-interest at another's expense (e.g., Hamlin, Wynn, & Bloom, 2007, 2010; Hamlin, Wynn, Bloom, & Mahajan, 2011; Hamlin & Wynn, 2011). To give a specific example from one of our studies: Infants saw a puppet playing with a ball, who rolled the ball in turn to each of two distinct individuals (also puppets). One of the recipients picked up the ball, then rolled it back to the first individual (a prosocial, reciprocal interaction); but the other recipient took the ball and ran away with it (a self-interested, nonreciprocal behavior). When given a choice between which of the two recipient puppets to reach for

(5-month-old infants) or look at (3-month-olds, who are too young to reach for objects), almost 90% of infants preferred the prosocial puppet (Hamlin & Wynn, 2011).

Infants also prefer others who are psychologically similar to them over those who are different: They prefer someone who has expressed the same tastes (in food, toys, or clothing) as the infant him- or herself, over someone who has expressed different tastes (Mahajan & Wynn, 2012; see, e.g., Billig & Tajfel, 1973, for parallel results in adults, and Fawcett & Markson, 2010, for parallel results in preschool-aged children).

The social information infants encode about others has wide-ranging psychological effects, influencing not only babies' early preferences but also their subsequent behaviors and even their future tastes. For example, when provided the opportunity to give a treat to a prosocial character or an antisocial actor, infants will selectively reward the do-gooder; but if the situation instead requires they *take* a treat from one of the actors, they will take it from the bad character (Hamlin, Wynn, Bloom, & Mahajan, 2011). Infants also want to be like, and model themselves after, characters they prefer; they selectively emulate the food choices of prosocial actors, but not of antisocial ones (Hamlin & Wynn, 2012).

INFANTS USE INFORMATION ABOUT OTHERS TO "FILL IN" ADDITIONAL ELEMENTS ON THE SOCIAL MAP

These early social preferences actively enable the generation of attitudes toward *new* individuals introduced into the social landscape. For example, infants not only reward prosocial characters and punish antisocial ones themselves but also prefer *others* who do the same, by 8 months of age (Hamlin, Wynn, Bloom, & Mahajan, 2011).

Using existing information to inform additional aspects of the social map can be quite useful. For example, if an infant observes that person A is closely allied with person B, even if the two are unknown to the infant and are not related to any known individuals, representing their relationship may later be helpful. The infant may later learn that (say) his or her own mother is friends with A; in this eventuality, the prior knowledge of A's and B's positive relationship enables the infant to assign (even if tentatively) a positive value to B ("the friend of my friend is my friend," or in this case, "The friend of my mother's friend is [absent other information] a friend"). Similarly, if the infant observes that stranger A is dominant over stranger B, and later learns that known individual C outranks A, he or she has the potential to infer that C outranks B. In this way, knowledge of various relational elements of the social network can aid the process of filling in other elements, even informing links that connect directly to the baby him- or herself.

HOW MIGHT GOSSIP INFORM THE STUDY OF DEVELOPMENTAL SOCIAL COGNITION?

But what does all of this have to do with gossip among adults? It has been argued that the kinds of information adults are most interested in discussing are precisely those kinds which are most adaptively useful to us (such as information relevant to mapping the social network of alliances and conflicts, reputation monitoring and management, monitoring changes in the social network, social comparison, identifying in-group and out-group members, and so on). Complex social information—that is, the relational interactions of third-party agents—is of enduring salience and interest in adult conversations, more so than socially less complex information about, for example, the nonsocial behaviors of others (Mesoudi, Whiten, & Dunbar, 2006). We appear to be especially interested in negative information about our rivals, our enemies, and those of higher social status than ourselves; in positive information about those allied with us (i.e., friends and relatives); in information of all kinds about our peers (those similar to us, especially in age and in gender); and in information about those who violate the social norms of a group and those whose actions most admirably benefit the group (e.g., Kniffin & Wilson, 2005; McAndrew, Bell, & Garcia, 2007).

As research on infants' attention to the social world continues to unfold, we may find that it is largely these same kinds of information that infants are most interested in tracking, and most attentive to. For example, will babies represent negative information about foes more strongly (e.g., have better memory for it) than positive information? Will they attend more closely to information about those who outrank their parents in social status than about those whom their parents outrank, and to individuals who violate social norms? I suspect we will find considerable developmental continuity, given the fundamental importance of such information for successful social navigation and social learning.

Of course, there will be important exceptions. Types of social information that are selectively relevant to specific developmental ages or life milestones will not be of equal interest to all ages. (I would not, for example, expect infants to be focused on information primarily relevant to someone's potential quality as a mate.) Also, there are unique selection pressures that apply during infancy and childhood (evolutionarily, a developmental period of high mortality; Volk & Atkinson, 2008), and thus, certain social concerns that may be specific to infants (see, e.g., Wynn, 2009). Interest in information about peers may differ between younger and older humans: Children (of all ages) may be selectively more attentive to the interests, alliances, and proclivities of those slightly *older* than themselves, as these individuals will tend to dominate them in physical size for many years, while they in turn will tend to dominate those younger than themselves—at least until the equalizing forces of puberty have come into play. Finally, while we should observe high rates of interest at all ages in those who are engaged in conflict with kin, infants and young children might be far more highly sensitized than adults in detecting enemies of their parents, given their exceptional vulnerability and utter dependence upon them.

I have suggested here that the kinds of social information that most matter to adults (at least, as represented in their conversations) may help inform our investigations of infants' representations of the social world. The reverse may be equally true—the social information infants track may help shed light on the origins and nature of adult social cognition. Those aspects of the social world that are sufficiently important that we represent them from the earliest moments of our entrée into social life may be (some of) the ones that are most fundamental to successfully navigating the social terrain, at any age.

REFERENCES

Bar-Haim, Y., Ziv, T., Lamy, D., & Hodes, R.M. (2006). Nature and nurture in own-race face processing. *Psychological Science, 17*, 159–163.

Billig, M., & Tajfel, H. (1973). Social categorization and similarity in intergroup behavior. *European Journal of Social Psychology, 3*, 27–52.

Dunbar, R. I. M. (2004). Gossip in evolutionary perspective. *Review of General Psychology, 8*, 100–110.

Dunbar, R. I. M., Marriott, A., & Duncan, N. D. C. (1997). Human conversational behavior. *Human Nature, 8*, 231–246.

Fawcett, C. A., & Markson, L. (2010). Similarity predicts liking in 3-year-old children. *Journal of Experimental Child Psychology, 105*, 345–358.

Hamlin, J. K., & Wynn, K. (2011). Young infants prefer prosocial to antisocial others. *Cognitive Development, 26*, 30–39.

Hamlin, J.K., & Wynn, K. (2012). Who knows what's good to eat? Infants fail to match the food preferences of antisocial others. *Cognitive Development, 27*, 227–239.

Hamlin, J. K., Wynn, K., & Bloom, P. (2007). Social evaluation by preverbal infants. *Nature, 450*, 557–559.

Hamlin, J. K., Wynn, K., & Bloom, P. (2010). Three-month-old infants show a negativity bias in social evaluation. *Developmental Science, 13*, 923–929.

Hamlin, J. K., Wynn, K., Bloom, P., & Mahajan, N. (2011). How infants and toddlers react to antisocial others. *Proceedings of the National Academy of Sciences, 108*, 19931–19936.

Johnson, S. C., Dweck, C. S., Chen, F. S., Stern, H. L., Ok, S-J., & Barth, M. (2010). At the intersection of social and cognitive development: Internal working models of attachment in infancy. *Cognitive Science, 34*, 807–825.

Kinzler, K. D., Dupoux, E., & Spelke, E. (2007). The native language of social cognition. *Proceedings of the National Academy of Sciences USA, 104*(30), 12577–12580.

Kniffin, K. M., & Wilson, D. S. (2005). Utilities of gossip across organizational levels. *Human Nature, 16*, 278–292.

Kuhlmeier, V., Wynn, K., & Bloom, P. (2003). Attribution of dispositional states by 12-month-old infants. *Psychological Science, 14*, 402–408.

Mahajan, N. & Wynn, K. (2012). Origins of "us" versus "them": Prelinguistic infants prefer similar others. *Cognition, 124*, 227–233.

Mascaro, O., & Csibra, G. (2012). Representation of stable social dominance relations by human infants. *Proceedings of the National Academy of Sciences, 109*, 6862–6867.

McAndrew, F. T., Bell, E. K., & Garcia, C. M. (2007). Who do we tell and whom do we tell on? Gossip as a strategy for status enhancement. *Journal of Applied Social Psychology, 37*, 1562–1577.

Mesoudi, A., Whiten, A., & Dunbar, R. (2006). A bias for social information in human cultural transmission. *British Journal of Psychology, 97*, 405–423.

Quinn, P., Yahr, J., Kuhn, A., Slater, A., & Pascalis, O. (2002). Representation of the gender of human faces by infants: A preference for females. *Perception, 31*, 1109–1121.

Sommerfeld, R., Krambeck, H-J., Semmann, D., & Milinski, M. (2007). Gossip as an alternative for direct observation in games of indirect reciprocity. *Proceedings of the National Academy of Sciences USA, 104*, 17435–17440.

Thomsen, L., Frankenhuis, W., Ingold-Smith, M., & Carey, S. (2011). Big and mighty: Preverbal infants represent social dominance. *Science, 331*, 477–480.

Volk, T., & Atkinson, J (2008). Is child death the crucible of human evolution? *Journal of Social, Evolutionary, and Cultural Psychology, 2*, 247–260.

Wert, S., & Salovey, P. (2004). A social comparison account of gossip. *Review of General Psychology, 8*, 122–137.

Wynn, K. (2008). Some innate foundations of social and moral cognition. In P. Carruthers, S. Laurence, & S. Stich (Eds.), *The innate mind: Foundations and the future* (pp. 330–347). Oxford, England: Oxford University Press.

Wynn, K. (2009). Constraints on natural altruism. *British Journal of Psychology, 100*, 481–485.

1.6

The Evolution of Concepts About Agents

ROBERT M. SEYFARTH AND DOROTHY L. CHENEY

We now know that the mind of a human infant is neither a blank slate nor, in William James's words, "one great blooming, buzzing confusion" (1890, p. 462). Instead, infants are born with what Carey (2009) has called "a set of innate, representational primitives" that "get learning off the ground" and "guide an infant's expectations of which objects go together and how they are likely to behave." Armed with these concepts, infants begin life with several "core" systems of knowledge, each specialized for representing and reasoning about entities of different kinds (Carey & Spelke, 1996). Three core systems have been widely discussed: one that deals with the causal and spatial relations among objects, another that concerns number, and a third that deals with agents, including their goals, attentional states, and the causal mechanisms that underlie their behavior.

How did conceptual thinking evolve? What advantages did it bring? Here we consider the evolution of conceptual knowledge about agents. We argue that the origin of human concepts of agents can be found in the predisposition of monkeys, apes, and perhaps many other animals to recognize members of their own species as individuals and group them into categories based on their behavior. In primates, conceptual thinking about agents has evolved because it helps individuals form stable, adaptive social relationships.

Social knowledge in animals is of particular interest because, unlike the recognition of quantities and objects (now the most widely cited examples of conceptual thinking in animals), it involves the recognition and classification of animate creatures according to behavior. It therefore includes implicit theories about motivation and action.

INDIVIDUAL RECOGNITION

Individual recognition is widespread in animals (Tibbetts & Dale, 2007). Many species have specialized brain cells that respond particularly strongly to faces (Leopold & Rhodes, 2010),

voices (Petkov et al., 2008), and familiar speakers (Belin & Zattore, 2003). Although individual recognition has most often been documented in the auditory mode through playback experiments (e.g., Rendall, Rodman, & Emond, 1996), subjects in these experiments often seem to be engaged in more complex cross-modal or even multimodal processing. A baboon who looks toward the source of the sound when she hears her offspring's call (Cheney & Seyfarth, 2007) acts as if the sound has created an expectation of what she will see if she looks in that direction. Dogs (Adachi, Kuwahata, & Fujita, 2007) and squirrel monkeys (Adachi & Fujita, 2007) associate the faces and voices of their caretakers, rhesus macaques integrate the faces and voices of conspecifics (Sliwa, Duhamel, Pascalis, & Wirth, 2011), and horses associate the whinny of a specific herd member with the sight of that individual (Proops, McComb, & Reby, 2008). Such cross-modal integration is not surprising, given the extensive connections between auditory and visual areas in mammalian brains (Cappe & Barone, 2005). Humans, of course, routinely integrate the perception of faces and voices to form the rich, multimodal concept of a person (Campanella & Belin, 2007).

How do animals learn to recognize individuals? Obviously, recognition cannot be entirely innate: Animals require experience to recognize the members of their group and any new animals who join it. Such learning almost certainly begins with the formation of classical, Pavlovian associations. Neural structures specialized for the recognition of faces, voices, and their cross-modal integration, however, suggest that many animals have an innate predisposition to organize what they have learned into concepts: in this case, the concept of a specific individual. These concepts cannot be reduced to or defined by any single sensory attribute but involve, instead, the integration of many different attributes into a single percept, such that the sound of a specific individual's voice creates an expectation of what one will see and the sight of that individual creates an expectation of what one will hear. Such concepts are implicit and, needless to say, formed without language: Animals do not, as far as we know, give names to each other. But they are concepts, nonetheless, and they are widespread in the animal kingdom. Perhaps the earliest concept was a social one—what in our species we call the concept of a person.

OTHER SOCIAL CLASSIFICATIONS

Many animals not only recognize individuals but also classify them into groups, organizing them according to close social bonds, linear dominance ranks, and transient sexual relations. Like the recognition of individuals, these classifications appear to involve the formation of concepts. Baboons provide some good examples.

Baboons live throughout Africa in groups of 50 to 150 individuals. Males and females have very different life histories. When they reach adult size, at 6 to 9 years of age, males leave the group where they were born and emigrate to other groups. Females, in contrast, remain in their natal group throughout their lives, maintaining close bonds with their matrilineal kin through frequent grooming, mutual support in coalitions, tolerance at feeding sites, and interactions with each other's infants (Cheney & Seyfarth, 2007; Silk et al., 2010a). Adult females can also be ranked in a stable, linear dominance hierarchy that determines priority of access to resources. From birth, daughters acquire ranks immediately below those of their mothers. As a result, the stable core of a baboon group consists of a hierarchy of matrilines, in which all members of, say, matriline B outrank or are outranked by all members of matrilines C and A, respectively. Rank relations are generally stable over time, with few reversals occurring either within or between families. When reversals do occur, however, their consequences differ significantly depending on who is involved. If the third-ranking female in matriline B (B3) rises in rank above her second-ranking sister (B2), the reversal affects only these individuals; the B family's rank relative to other families remains unchanged. However, a rank reversal between females from different matrilines (for example, C1 rising in rank above B3) usually causes all members of matriline C to rise above all members of matriline B (Cheney & Seyfarth, 1990, 2007). The ranked, matrilineal society of baboons is typical of many Old World monkeys.

Baboons, then, are born into a social world that is filled with statistical regularities: Animals interact in highly predictable ways. A young baboon quickly learns to recognize these patterns. By the time she is an adult, she recognizes both the close bonds among matrilineal kin and the linear rank relations within and between families (Cheney & Seyfarth, 2007). She also appears to recognize other animals' motives and the causal relations that govern their interactions; she knows, for example, when another individual is vocalizing to her (Engh, Hoffmeier, Cheney, & Seyfarth, 2006), and when an animal's grunt signals reconciliation after a fight (Cheney & Seyfarth, 1997; Wittig, Crockford, Wikberg, Seyfarth, & Cheney, 2007a). Does her knowledge of kin and rank relations involve the formation of concepts? Does her knowledge of motives and causality constitute a rudimentary theory of social life?

ALTERNATIVE HYPOTHESES

One hypothesis argues that memory and classical conditioning are entirely sufficient to explain primates' social knowledge. As they mature, baboons recognize patterns of behavior that link individuals in predictable ways. Their knowledge cannot be described as conceptual because there is no direct evidence for the existence of such concepts, and social knowledge can just as easily be explained by simpler hypotheses based on learned associations and prodigious memory (e.g., Schusterman & Kastak, 1998).

Explanations based on memory and associative learning are powerful and appealing under simplified laboratory conditions, but they strain credulity when applied to behavior in nature, where animals confront more complex sets of stimuli. A young baboon, for example, must learn thousands of dyadic (and tens of thousands of triadic) relations in order to predict other animals' behavior. The magnitude of the problem makes one wonder whether simple associations, even coupled with prodigious memory, are equal to the task. Faced with the problem of memorizing a huge, ever-changing dataset, humans are predisposed to search for a higher order rule that makes the task easier (Macuda & Roberts, 1995). Why should baboons be any different?

In fact, several observations suggest that baboons' social knowledge is organized into units of thought that resemble our concepts. To begin, consider the speed of their reactions to events. When baboons hear a sequence of vocalizations that violates the dominance hierarchy, they respond within seconds (Cheney & Seyfarth, 2007). When a male macaque, involved in a fight, tries to recruit an ally, he seems instantly to know which individuals would be the most effective partners (Silk, 1999). The speed of these reactions suggests that animals are not searching through a massive, unstructured database of associations but have instead—as a kind of cognitive shortcut—organized their knowledge into concepts: what we call dominance hierarchies and matrilineal (family) groups.

Social categories qualify as concepts because they cannot be reduced to any one, or even a few, sensory attributes. Family members do not look alike, sound alike, or share any other physical features that make them easy to tell apart. Infants are black whereas juveniles are olive brown, males are larger than females, and many individuals have idiosyncratic wounds or postures, yet none of this variation affects other animals' classifications: A three-legged member of family X is still a member of family X.

Nor is the classification of individuals into family groups based on behavior. The members of high-ranking families are not necessarily more aggressive than others, do not range in separate areas or groom or play together more often. In fact, because mothers generally groom daughters more than sons, grooming within families can be highly variable—yet this has no effect on other animals' perception of who belongs in which family.

Social categories, moreover, persist despite changes in their composition. Among females and juveniles, the recognition of families is unaffected by births and deaths; among adult males, the recognition of a linear, transitive hierarchy persists despite frequent changes in the individuals who occupy each rank. In the mind of a baboon, social categories exist independent of their members.

The classification of individuals into families seems to occur not because outsiders treat family members as identical, but because outsiders regard the family as an assemblage of different individuals who share a common attribute. While the individuals within a family can sometimes be substituted for one another—one member of the A matriline, for example, can reconcile "on behalf of" another (Wittig et al., 2007a)—they nonetheless retain their distinct identities. In this respect, baboons appear to be "psychological essentialists" (Medin, 1989): They act as if each animal, though a distinct individual, has an "essence or underlying nature" (Gelman, 2003) that makes her a member of family X. The same essentialist thinking applies to each family.

Finally, the classification of individuals into families and their arrangement into a dominance hierarchy are cognitive operations that affect behavior. When listeners hear vocalizations from two individuals interacting elsewhere, their response depends not just upon the animals' identities but also upon their ranks and family membership (Bergman, Beehner, Seyfarth, & Cheney, 2003). Social categories are units of thought that determine how individuals behave.

Bound up in the baboons' concepts are expectations: If a member of the A family threatens the member of another matriline, listeners expect that other family members will come to the threatener's aid (Wittig et al., 2007b). Baboons' concepts thus concern not only which entities "go together" but also how category membership affects behavior. Indeed, the baboons' concepts and their expectations about behavior are intimately entwined: They use their observations of behavior to create concepts and, having done so, use their concepts to predict behavior. For baboons, it is difficult if not impossible to separate concepts from the theory-like relations that underlie them.

Long-term data show that female baboons with the strongest social bonds experience less stress, have higher infant survival, and live longer than others (Silk et al., 2009, 2010b; Wittig et al., 2008). We propose that the ability to form concepts helps an individual both to monitor other animals' relations and to form relationships of her own. For these reasons natural selection has favored the evolution of conceptual thinking about individuals, their motives, and their relationships.

ACKNOWLEDGMENTS

We thank Daniel Swingley, Lila Gleitman, and Susan Gelman for comments.

REFERENCES

Adachi, I., & Fujita, K. (2007). Cross-modal representation of human caretakers in squirrel monkeys. *Behavioral Processes, 74*, 27–32.

Adachi, I., Kuwahata, H., & Fujita, K. (2007). Dogs recall their owner's face upon hearing the owner's voice. *Animal Cognition, 10*, 17–21.

Belin, P., & Zattore, R. (2003). Adaptation to speaker's voice in right anterior temporal lobe. *NeuroReport, 14*, 2105–2109.

Bergman, T., Beehner, J., Seyfarth, R. M., & Cheney, D. L. (2003). Hierarchical classification by rank and kinship in female baboons. *Science, 302,* 1234–1236.

Campanella, S., & Belin, P. (2007). Integrating face and voice in person perception. *Trends in Cognitive Science, 11,* 535–543.

Cappe, C., & Barone, P. (2005). Heteromodal connections supporting multisensory integration at low levels of cortical processing in the monkey. *European Journal of Neuroscience, 22,* 2886–2902.

Carey, S. (2009). *The origin of concepts.* Oxford, England: Oxford University Press.

Carey, S., & Spelke, E. (1996). Science and core knowledge. *Philosophy of Science, 63,* 515–533.

Cheney, D. L., & Seyfarth, R. M. (1990). *How monkeys see the world.* Chicago, IL: University of Chicago Press.

Cheney, D. L., & Seyfarth, R. M. (2007). *Baboon metaphysics.* Chicago, IL: University of Chicago Press.

Engh, A. L., Hoffmeier, R., Cheney, D. L., & Seyfarth, R. M. (2006). Who, me? Can baboons infer the target of vocalizations? *Animal Behavior, 71,* 381–387.

Gelman, S. (2003). *The essential child: Origins of essentialism in everyday thought.* New York: Oxford University Press.

James, W. (1890). *Principles of psychology.* New York: H. Holt & Co.

Leopold, D. A., & Rhodes, G. (2010). A comparative view of face perception. *Journal of Comparative Psychology, 124,* 233–251.

Macuda, T., & Roberts, W. A. (1995). Further evidence for hierarchical chunking in rat spatial memory. *Journal of Experimental Biology: Animal Behavior Processes, 21,* 20–32.

Medin, D. (1989). Concepts and conceptual structure. *American Psychology, 44,* 1469–1481.

Petkov, C. I., Kayser, C., Steudel, T., Whittingstall, K., Augath, M., & Logothetis, N. (2008). A voice region in the monkey brain. *Nature Neuroscience, 11,* 367–374.

Proops, L., McComb, K., & Reby, D. (2008) Cross-modal individual recognition in domestic horses. *Proceedings of the National Academy of Sciences USA, 106,* 947–951.

Rendall, D., Rodman, P., & Emond, R. (1996). Vocal recognition of individuals and kin in free-ranging rhesus monkeys. *Animal Behavior, 51,* 1007–1015.

Schusterman, R. J., & Kastak, D. (1998) Functional equivalence in a California sea lion: Relevance to animal social and communicative interactions. *Animal Behavior. 55,* 1087–1095.

Silk, J. B. (1999). Male bonnet macaques use information about third party rank relationships to recruit allies. *Animal Behavior, 58,* 45–51.

Silk, J. B., Beehner, J., Bergman, T., Crockford, C., Engh, A. L., Moscovice, L., ... Cheney, D. L. (2009). The benefits of social capital: Close social bonds among female baboons enhance offspring survival. *Proceedings of the Royal Society B: Biological Sciences, 276,* 3099–3014.

Silk, J. B, Beehner, J. C., Bergman, T. J., Crockford, C., Engh, A. L., Moscovice, L. R., ... Cheney, D. L. (2010a). Female chacma baboons form strong, equitable, and enduring social bonds. *Behavioral Ecology and Sociobiology, 64,* 1733–1747.

Silk, J. B., Beehner, J., Bergman, T., Crockford, C., Engh, A. L., Moscovice, L., ... Cheney, D. L. (2010b). Strong and consistent social bonds enhance the longevity of female baboons. *Current Biology, 20,* 1359–1361.

Sliwa, J., Duhamel, J-R., Pascalis, O., & Wirth, S. (2011). Spontaneous voice-face identity matching by rhesus monkeys for familiar conspecifics and humans. *Proceedings of the National Academy of Sciences USA, 108,* 1735–1740.

Tibbetts, E., & Dale, J. (2007). Individual recognition: It is good to be different. *Trends in Ecology and Evolution, 22,* 529–537.

Wittig, R., Crockford, C., Lehmann, J., Whitten, P., Seyfarth, R. M., & Cheney, D. L. (2008). Focused grooming networks and stress alleviation in wild female baboons. *Hormones and Behavior, 54,* 170–177.

Wittig, R., Crockford, C., Wikberg, E., Seyfarth, R. M., & Cheney, D. L. (2007a). Kin-mediated reconciliation substitutes for direct reconciliation in female baboons. *Proceedings of the Royal Society B: Biological Sciences, 274,* 1109–1115.

Wittig, R. M., Crockford, C., Seyfarth, R. M., & Cheney, D. L. (2007b). Vocal alliances in chacma baboons, *Papio hamadryas ursinus. Behavioral Ecology and Sociobiology, 61,* 899–909.

1.7

The Evolution of Human Sociocognitive Development

VICTORIA WOBBER AND BRIAN HARE

For nearly a century, the field of developmental psychology has provided insight into the nature of social cognition by elucidating the patterns in which cognitive skills emerge over the course of ontogeny. Meanwhile, comparative psychology has revealed the unique elements of human cognition through comparisons with our closest evolutionary relatives, nonhuman primates, or species more distant such as rats and dogs. However, the majority of these comparative studies have contrasted the performance of adult animals with that of human infants or children (e.g., Herrmann, Call, Hernandez-Lloreda, Hare, & Tomasello, 2007). Building on previous work, we argue that the next frontier in developmental psychology will be to investigate comparative cognitive development (Gomez, 2005; Matsuzawa, 2007) with a particular focus on humans' closest living relatives, chimpanzees (*Pan troglodytes*) and bonobos (*Pan paniscus*). Pioneering comparative developmental studies have focused intensively on the development of a few chimpanzee individuals and for the first time have begun to map social cognitive development across multiple tasks in these individuals (Matsuzawa, Tomonaga, & Tanaka, 2006; Tomasello & Carpenter, 2005). The next step will be to extend this research by examining a wide range of physical and social cognitive skills in a larger sample. A broader comparative developmental approach will be particularly useful in identifying the cognitive components that are "missing" in other species' sociocognitive development that lead them to possess differing adult abilities from our own. This can in turn clarify the elements of the human developmental process that allow our species' rich social psychology as adults. Finally, comparative developmental psychology can be integrated with the growing field of evolutionary developmental biology (or "evo-devo"), where increasing evidence suggests that differences between species in a number of traits stem from shifts in developmental processes (Carroll, 2008; Wobber, Wrangham, & Hare, 2010a).

WHY CHIMPANZEES AND BONOBOS?

We propose that large-scale comparative developmental studies of both chimpanzees and bonobos are essential to best understand the human mind. While these two species are equally related to humans genetically, they represent significantly different models of the behavior and psychology of their last common ancestor with humans (Hare, 2009, 2011; Won & Hey, 2005; Wrangham & Pilbeam, 2001). For example, chimpanzee males engage in more severe forms of aggression than bonobo males, including lethal "warfare" that in many ways parallels that of our own species (Furuichi & Ihobe, 1994; Kano, 1992; Mitani, Watts, & Amsler, 2010; Muller, 2002; Wrangham, 1999). Meanwhile, bonobos show striking parallels with humans in sharing food more readily, even with strangers, than do chimpanzees, and exhibiting greater nonconceptive sexual behavior (Hare, Melis, Woods, Hastings, & Wrangham, 2007; Hare & Kwetuenda, 2010; Wobber, Wrangham, & Hare, 2010b; Woods & Hare, 2011 Tan & Hare, in press). The two species differ markedly in their preferences, with bonobos more risk averse in their decision making and less patient in a temporal discounting task (Heilbronner, Rosati, Stevens, Hare, & Hauser, 2008; Rosati, Stevens, Hare, & Hauser, 2007). They also differ in their temperaments, as bonobos are shyer when presented with novel objects (Herrmann et al., in press). Finally, they differ in their cognitive abilities, with bonobos more sensitive to human social cues and less skillful in tool use tasks relative to chimpanzees (Herrmann, Hare, Call, & Tomasello, 2010).

Again these distinctions provide mixed evidence in regard to the species' relative similarity to humans, with bonobos more similar to humans in their levels of patience while chimpanzees are more comparable to humans in their competency in using tools (Herrmann et al., 2007; Rosati et al., 2007). Thus, studies of chimpanzees and bonobos can each provide insight into differing facets of human psychology.

The majority of comparative cognitive development research up to this point has been performed with chimpanzees, rather than bonobos (e.g., Povinelli, Rulf, Landau, & Bierschwale, 1993; Reaux, Theall, & Povinelli, 1999; Tomasello, Hare, & Fogleman, 2001). This is due to bonobos being largely unavailable for study until recently (living only in the war-torn Democratic Republic of Congo), and correspondingly less familiar to both the public and the scientific community (Hare, 2009). However, research in African ape sanctuaries provides the opportunity to work with large populations of both bonobos and chimpanzees. These facilities house orphans of the bushmeat trade, apes whose mothers were hunted and who themselves have been sold as pets. Local governments have been more effective in recent years in making the sale of these young apes illegal and in confiscating any animals found in markets or private homes. Sanctuaries provide care for these confiscated individuals until they can (potentially) be returned to the wild, and as such there are growing populations of infant test participants at these facilities (Woods & Hare, 2010). Our research suggests that despite these apes' potential early life stress, the rich social and physical environments at the sanctuaries allow them to exhibit species-typical behavior, physiology, and psychology (Wobber & Hare, 2011). Work at these sites thus allows researchers to study comparative developmental psychology in both of our closest living relatives.

COMPARATIVE COGNITIVE DEVELOPMENT IN HUMANS, CHIMPANZEES, AND BONOBOS

A great deal of research has compared the cognitive abilities of human children and adult chimpanzees, searching for what makes human psychology unique (e.g., Barth & Call, 2006; Hermann et al., 2007; Herrmann, Call, Hernandez-Lloreda, Hare, & Tomasello, 2010; Warneken, Hare, Melis, Hanus, & Tomasello, 2007). However, one question that remains is whether our process of cognitive development in and of itself is unique as well. If humans and chimpanzees acquire cognitive skills in a similar pattern, this would suggest that cognitive abilities must emerge in a certain sequence in order to produce fully functional adults, with this sequence fairly inflexible across species. Alternatively, it is possible that there are significant differences in the patterns of cognitive development between humans, chimpanzees, and bonobos, with these patterns reflecting a species' needs in its particular environment.

One study of human children and chimpanzee adults provides evidence to discriminate between these two hypotheses (Hermann et al., 2007). In this study, 2.5-year-old children and adult apes were presented with a battery of 16 social and physical cognition tasks. In one of the social cognition tasks, assessing social learning, subjects were presented with an easy but not obvious problem to solve (for example, a balloon or banana lodged in a clear plastic tube). Before being allowed to attempt to solve the problem, each subject watched an experimenter demonstrate one potential solution (in this case, hitting the tube on the ground until the reward fell out). The dependent measure for this task was whether the subject used the demonstrated means to solve the problem and obtain the reward, thus copying the experimenter's means, or whether the subject used his or her own means to solve the problem (though potentially the subject could also fail to solve the problem altogether) (Call, Carpenter, & Tomasello, 2005; Whiten, Custance, Gomez, Teixidor, & Bard, 1996). In one of the physical cognition tasks used in this task battery, subjects were asked to discriminate between relative quantities of a reward (small toys or peanuts). The experimenter presented each subject with two reward arrays, allowing him or her to look at both for several seconds, and then let the subject choose between the two. If the subject knew that one quantity was greater than the other, he or she should choose the greater reward, while if the subject was not able to perceive the difference between the two quantities, he or she should choose randomly. Varying pairs of quantity discriminations were presented (e.g., 1 versus 4, 3 versus 6) for a total of 13 trials (Boysen & Berntson, 1995; Hanus & Call, 2007). Tasks in the battery were chosen to assess a wide range of abilities based on a theoretical analysis of human and nonhuman primate cognition (Herrmann et al., 2007; Tomasello & Call, 1997).

Comparing performance across the social and physical cognition domains in children and apes, this study revealed that while human 2.5-year-olds and chimpanzee adults perform similarly on physical cognition tasks, humans at this age far outperform adult chimpanzees (and orangutans) in social cognition tasks. The authors of this study thus proposed that social cognition abilities emerge earlier on in human development than in chimpanzee development to enable human children to participate in culture, termed the Cultural Intelligence Hypothesis (Herrmann et al., 2007). Children's performance across the broad battery of tasks also exhibited a different factor structure from that of chimpanzee adults, with a distinct social cognition factor present in humans but not chimpanzees, supporting the notion that different cognitive mechanisms—and potentially, developmental trajectories—underlie performance on these tasks in the two species (Herrmann, Call, et al., 2010). We have further tested the Cultural Intelligence Hypothesis through direct comparisons of human and nonhuman ape juveniles (discussed later).

Beyond the differences in the patterns of cognitive development, the rate of cognitive development may differ between humans and other apes as well. Humans live longer than any other primate species, so it is conceivable that we acquire our cognitive skills more slowly, having more time to do so. Our postnatal physical growth is much slower than that of a chimpanzee, with chimpanzees achieving adult body size around the age of 10 years and humans doing so anywhere from 14 to 18 years (Walker et al., 2006). We are also born considerably more altricial, or underdeveloped, than other ape species (DeSilva & Lesnik, 2006), so it may take longer for human neural development to "catch up" with the development accomplished prenatally in nonhuman apes.

Early comparative cognitive development research supported the hypothesis that the rate of cognitive development scales with a species' life span and growth rate (Antinucci, 1990; Langer, 2000, 2001). This work indicated that humans acquire cognitive skills (measured by Piaget's sensorimotor stages) more slowly (in absolute time) than a chimpanzee, and a chimpanzee acquires these skills more slowly than a rhesus macaque (in line with its relatively longer life span and slower somatic growth rate) (see Figure 1 of Hawkes, O'Connell, Blurton Jones, Alvarez, & Charnov, 1998; Langer, 2000). Yet this work largely did not explore sociocognitive abilities, leaving it open to debate whether these abilities are subject to differing evolutionary pressures. Alternative to the hypothesis that human cognitive development is slow relative to other species, the Cultural Intelligence Hypothesis proposes that humans instead have accelerated cognitive development. According to this hypothesis, our early emergence of social cognition facilitates greater social learning skills that allow us to acquire a broad range of cognitive skills more quickly (Herrmann et al., 2007). These alternative hypotheses provide a compelling case to compare the patterns and rate of cognitive development in juvenile chimpanzees, bonobos, and humans.

One comparative developmental study supports the hypothesis that patterns of cognitive development differ between chimpanzees and humans (Tomasello & Carpenter, 2005). This study built on the research of Carpenter and colleagues investigating patterns of sociocognitive development longitudinally in typically developing children and cross-sectionally in children with an autism spectrum disorder (Carpenter, Nagell, & Tomasello, 1998; Carpenter, Pennington, & Rogers, 2002). Utilizing a battery of social cognition tasks, Carpenter et al. (1998) found that for typically developing infants, social cognitive skills emerge in a predictable sequence. Infants tend to acquire skills of joint engagement early on in ontogeny, looking to others' faces as a source of information to share in a given activity. Subsequently, they begin to follow others' attention to specific targets and then to direct others' attention by producing communicative gestures. Finally, after understanding and directing attention, they begin to comprehend and direct others' behavior as well (Carpenter et al., 1998). In contrast, for children in the autism spectrum, these same sociocognitive abilities were found to emerge in a different sequence. Autism spectrum children followed and directed others' behavior before they were able to follow and share attention with others (Carpenter et al., 2002). Furthermore, skills of joint engagement were less prevalent and later to emerge in autism spectrum children, in line with previous work (e.g., Charman et al., 1997).

To compare the patterns found in human cognitive development to those of chimpanzees, Tomasello and Carpenter (2005) presented three human-reared chimpanzee infants with the same battery of tasks (longitudinally). These chimpanzees showed a pattern of performance on the social cognition tasks similar to that of autism spectrum children, with their abilities to follow and direct others' behavior preceding their abilities to follow and direct others' attention (Tomasello & Carpenter, 2005). The chimpanzee infants never engaged in joint attention with humans despite their being reared by human caregivers. This suggests that skills of joint engagement are fundamental to the sociocognitive differences between humans and chimpanzees, as has been argued elsewhere (Tomasello, Carpenter, Call, Behne, & Moll, 2005). In addition, these findings indicate that a reorganization of sociocognitive development—both between species and between individuals of the same species—may be central to sociocognitive differences among adults. Further research can investigate the developmental trajectories of specific sociocognitive abilities in chimpanzees and bonobos (e.g., those pertaining to theory of mind) to clarify how shifts in cognitive development manifest themselves in adult psychology.

Our recent work has built upon these previous findings with the larger sample size available in African ape sanctuaries. We have found that there are developmental differences between humans and nonhuman apes, and also between chimpanzees and bonobos themselves. For example, we found that the differences between adult chimpanzees and bonobos in food sharing (described earlier) derive from shifts in the patterns of development between the two species. Chimpanzees develop increased intolerance of sharing food with age, while bonobos maintain juvenile (high) levels of sharing tolerance into adulthood. Bonobos also exhibit developmental delays relative to chimpanzees in their performance on several social inhibition tasks pertaining to feeding competition, leading them to be less skillful in these paradigms as adults in comparison to adult chimpanzees (Wobber et al., 2010a, 2010b). These results suggest that shifts in cognitive and behavioral development can lead to species differences in the behavior and cognition of adults.

We further investigated these differences by presenting a large sample of bonobos ($n = 50$) and chimpanzees ($n = 138$) of all ages with a battery of 10 cognitive tasks designed to assess a wide variety of social and physical cognition skills, based on previous comparative work (Herrmann et al., 2007). We found that chimpanzees and bonobos performed similarly on physical cognition tasks as infants, but chimpanzees significantly improved in their performance on the physical cognition tasks from infancy to adulthood while bonobos did not. This enabled chimpanzee adults to significantly outperform bonobo adults in the physical cognition domain. Meanwhile, there were no differences between the two species in the social cognition domain on the whole (though they did differ in social tasks pertaining to feeding competition) (Wobber et al., unpublished data).

These results support the hypothesis that physical and social cognition abilities are distinct from one another, since chimpanzees and bonobos performed comparably on social cognition tasks but showed differences in their physical cognition abilities. Furthermore, these findings suggest that cognitive mechanisms related to foraging (quantified as skills such as object permanence or tool use) have changed between these two ape species via shifts in the rate of cognitive development during evolution. For example, while chimpanzees become more proficient in fashioning and using tools with age, bonobos—despite showing comparable performance to chimpanzees in this domain as infants—do not significantly improve in their use of tools as they mature. This suggests that across species, differences in patterns of cognitive development should underlie differences in adult cognition (though the degree to which this is canalized within each species is open to question). While this conclusion would not surprise most developmental psychologists, such findings provide a compelling case to integrate research in psychology with that of biology. Recent research in anatomy and physiology has demonstrated that species differences frequently occur through evolution acting on developmental parameters (by shortening or lengthening the period of development, or altering the rate of development through shifting patterns of gene expression) (Abzhanov et al., 2006; Francis, Diorio, Liu, & Meaney, 1999). In the case of bonobos and chimpanzees in particular, certain skeletal differences have been found to result from delays in bonobo cranial development relative to chimpanzees (Lieberman, Carlo, Ponce de Leon, & Zollikofer, 2007; Wrangham & Pilbeam, 2001). Thus, our finding of delays in the development of bonobos' physical cognition abilities promotes continued interdisciplinary inquiry into the relationship between physiological maturation and psychological development.

To assess whether these shifts in cognitive development within nonhuman apes also extend to humans, we compared human children ranging from 2 to 4 years of age ($n = 48$) to chimpanzee and bonobo juveniles ($n = 42$) in the same age range (Wobber et al., unpublished data). We presented these individuals with a battery of 14 cognitive and 3 motivational control tasks similar to that described earlier (Herrmann et al., 2007), incorporating tasks from the previous investigation of sociocognitive development in three infant chimpanzees (Tomasello & Carpenter, 2005). We found that, relative to chimpanzee and bonobos (genus *Pan*) infants, humans develop at an accelerated rate in this period in both social and physical cognition. In addition, human infants significantly outperform *Pan* infants in their sociocognitive abilities at 2 years, in tasks assessing skills such as social learning and gaze following. However, human infants at 2 years perform comparably to same-age *Pan* infants in their physical cognition abilities, in tasks ranging from discriminating relative quantities to using tools. After 2 years, humans then proceed to outperform *Pan* in both the social and physical domains, doing so at 3 years and increasingly at 4 years. This suggests that there is an acceleration in cognitive development in our own species relative to other apes. As proposed by the Cultural Intelligence Hypothesis discussed earlier (Herrmann et al., 2007; Hermann, Call, et al., 2010), the early emergence of sociocognitive skills in human infants may enable our species to acquire cognitive abilities more quickly by learning from others in a way that is not possible for other animals. It is in fact remarkable to think of the number of social cognitive abilities that humans have early on in development. Children can follow others' gaze, discriminate nice from mean individuals, imitate rationally, and help an individual in need before they are able to overcome a gravity bias or to use a novel tool (Brooks & Meltzoff, 2002; Brown, 1990; Gergely, Bekkering, & Kiraly, 2002; Hamlin, Wynn, & Bloom, 2007; Hood, 1995; Warneken & Tomasello, 2006). Our results further support the notion that physical and social cognition represent distinct domains, since in this case their developmental trajectories changed discretely. Detailed comparisons of the relationship between physical and social cognition across ontogeny in apes can illuminate the degree to which these skills rely on shared processes versus independent mechanisms.

In sum, targeted comparisons of cognitive development between humans and other apes provide an exciting direction for future research. We contend that the inclusion of the bonobo is essential to fully understand human psychology. The comparative developmental framework will challenge traditional theories of cognitive development by elucidating whether the structure of cognition is achieved through similar developmental processes across species. Such inquiry will further our knowledge of human social psychology and provide the opportunity for interdisciplinary collaboration integrating psychology and biology.

REFERENCES

Abzhanov, A., Kuo, W., Hartmann, C., Grant, B., Grant, P., & Tabin, C. (2006). The calmodulin pathway and evolution of elongated beak morphology in Darwin's finches. *Nature*, *442*, 563–567.

Antinucci, F. (1990). The comparative study of cognitive ontogeny in four primate species. In S. Parker & K. Gibson (Eds.), *"Language" and intelligence in monkeys and apes* (pp. 157–171). Cambridge, England: Cambridge University Press.

Barth, J., & Call, J. (2006). Tracking the displacement of objects: A series of tasks with great apes (*Pan troglodytes, Pan paniscus, Gorilla gorilla, and Pongo pygmaeus*) and young children (*Homo sapiens*). *Journal of Experimental Psychology: Animal Behavior Processes*, *32*(3), 239–252.

Boysen, S. T., & Berntson, G. G. (1995). Responses to quantity—perceptual versus cognitive mechanisms in chimpanzees (Pan troglodytes). *Journal of Experimental Psychology-Animal Behavior Processes*, *21*(1), 82–86.

Brooks, R., & Meltzoff, A. N. (2002). The importance of eyes: How infants interpret adult looking behavior. *Developmental Psychology*, *38*(6), 958–966.

Brown, A. (1990). Domain-specific principles affect learning and transfer in children. *Cognitive Science*, *14*(1), 107–133.

Call, J., Carpenter, M., & Tomasello, M. (2005). Copying results and copying actions in the process of social learning: Chimpanzees (Pan troglodytes) and human children (Homo sapiens). *Animal Cognition*, *8*(3), 151–163.

Carpenter, M., Nagell, K., & Tomasello, M. (1998). Social cognition, joint attention, and communicative competence from 9 to 15 months of age. *Monographs of the Society for Research in Child Development*, *63*(4), 1–143.

Carpenter, M., Pennington, B. F., & Rogers, S. J. (2002). Interrelations among social-cognitive skills in young children with autism. *Journal of Autism and Developmental Disorders*, *32*(2), 91–106.

Carroll, S. B. (2008). Evo-devo and an expanding evolutionary synthesis: A genetic theory of morphological evolution. *Cell*, *134*(1), 25–36.

Charman, T., Swettenham, J., Baron-Cohen, S., Cox, A., Baird, G., & Drew, A. (1997). Infants with autism: An investigation of empathy, pretend play, joint attention, and imitation. *Developmental Psychology*, *33*(5), 781–789.

DeSilva, J., & Lesnik, J. (2006). Chimpanzee neonatal brain size: Implications for brain growth in Homo erectus. *Journal of Human Evolution*, *51*(2), 207–212.

Francis, D., Diorio, J., Liu, D., & Meaney, M. (1999). Nongenomic transmission across generations of maternal behavior and stress responses in the rat. *Science, 286,* 1155.

Furuichi, T., & Ihobe, H. (1994). Variation in male relationships in bonobos and chimpanzees. *Behaviour, 130,* 211–228.

Gergely, G., Bekkering, H., & Kiraly, I. (2002). Rational imitation in preverbal infants. *Nature, 415,* 755.

Gomez, J. C. (2005). Species comparative studies and cognitive development. *Trends in Cognitive Sciences, 9*(3), 118–125.

Hamlin, K., Wynn, K., & Bloom, P. (2007). Social evaluation by preverbal infants. *Nature, 450*(7169), 557–559.

Hanus, D., & Call, J. (2007). Discrete quantity judgments in the great apes (Pan paniscus, Pan troglodytes, Gorilla gorilla, Pongo pygmaeus): The effect of presenting whole sets versus item-by-item. *Journal of Comparative Psychology, 121*(3), 241–249.

Hare, B. (2009). What is the effect of affect on bonobo and chimpanzee problem solving? In A. Berthoz & Y. Christen (Eds.), *The Neurobiology of the Umwelt: How living beings perceive the world* (pp. 89–102). New York: Springer Press.

Hare, B. (2011). From hominoid to hominid mind: what changed and why? *Annual Review of Anthropology, 40,* 293–309.

Hare, B., & Kwetuenda, S. (2010). Bonobos voluntarily share their own food with others. *Current Biology, 20*(5), R230-R231.

Hare, B., Melis, A. P., Woods, V., Hastings, S., & Wrangham, R. (2007). Tolerance allows bonobos to outperform chimpanzees on a cooperative task. *Current Biology, 17*(7), 619–623.

Hawkes, K., O'Connell, J., Blurton Jones, N., Alvarez, H., & Charnov, E. (1998). Grandmothering, menopause, and the evolution of human life histories. *Proceedings of the National Academy of Sciences USA, 95,* 1336–1339.

Heilbronner, S., Rosati, A., Stevens, J., Hare, B., & Hauser, M. (2008). A fruit in the hand or two in the bush? Divergent risk preferences in chimpanzees and bonobos. *Biology Letters, 4*(3), 246–249.

Herrmann, E., Call, J., Hernandez-Lloreda, M., Hare, B., & Tomasello, M. (2007). Humans have evolved specialized skills of social cognition: The cultural intelligence hypothesis. *Science, 317,* 1360–1366.

Herrmann, E., Hare, B., Call, J., & Tomasello, M. (2010). Differences in the cognitive skills of bonobos and chimpanzees. *PLOS One, 5*(8), e12438.

Herrmann, E., Call, J., Hernandez-Lloreda, M., Hare, B., & Tomasello, M. (2010). The structure of individual differences in the cognitive abilities of children and chimpanzees. *Psychological Science, 21*(1), 102–110.

Herrmann, E., Hare, B., Cissewski, J., & Tomasello, M. (in press). The origins of human temperament: Children avoid novelty more than other apes. *Developmental Science.*

Hood, B. (1995). Gravity rules for 2- to 4-year olds? *Cognitive Development, 10*(4), 577–598.

Kano, T. (1992). *The last ape: Pygmy chimpanzee behavior and ecology.* Stanford, CA: Stanford University Press.

Langer, J. (2000). The descent of cognitive development. *Developmental Science, 3*(4), 361–388.

Langer, J. (2001). The heterochronic evolution of primate cognitive development. In S. Parker, J. Langer, & M. McKinney (Eds.), *Biology, brains, and behavior: The evolution of human development* (pp. 215–235). Santa Fe, NM: School of American Research Press.

Lieberman, D. E., Carlo, J., Ponce de Leon, M., & Zollikofer, C. (2007). A geometric morphometric analysis of heterochrony in the cranium of chimpanzees and bonobos. *Journal of Human Evolution, 52,* 647–662.

Matsuzawa, T. (2007). Comparative cognitive development. *Developmental Science, 10*(1), 97–103.

Matsuzawa, T., Tomonaga, M., & Tanaka, M. (2006). *Cognitive development in chimpanzees.* Tokyo: Springer-Verlag.

Mitani, J., Watts, D., Amsler, S. (2010). Lethal intergroup aggression leads to territorial expansion in wild chimpanzees. *Current Biology, 20,* R507–R508.

Muller, M. (2002). Agonistic relations among Kanyawara chimpanzees. In C. Boesch, G. Hohmann, & L. Marchant (Eds.), *Behavioural diversity in chimpanzees and bonobos* (pp. 112–123). Cambridge, England: Cambridge University Press.

Povinelli, D., Rulf, A., Landau, K., & Bierschwale, D. (1993). Self-recognition in chimpanzees (Pan troglodytes): Distribution, ontogeny, and patterns of emergence. *Journal of Comparative Psychology, 107,* 347–372.

Reaux, J., Theall, L., & Povinelli, D. (1999). A longitudinal investigation of chimpanzees' understanding of visual perception. *Child Development, 70,* 275–290.

Rosati, A., Stevens, J., Hare, B., & Hauser, M. (2007). The evolutionary origins of human patience: Temporal preferences in chimpanzees, bonobos, and human adults. *Current Biology, 17*(19), 1663–1668.

Tomasello, M., & Call, J. (1997). *Primate cognition.* New York: Oxford University Press.

Tomasello, M., & Carpenter, M. (2005). The emergence of social cognition in three young chimpanzees. *Monographs of the Society for Research in Child Development, 70*(1), 1–155.

Tomasello, M., Carpenter, M., Call, J., Behne, T., & Moll, H. (2005). Understanding and sharing intentions: The origins of cultural cognition. *Behavioral and Brain Sciences, 28,* 675–735.

Tomasello, M., Hare, B., & Fogleman, T. (2001). The ontogeny of gaze following in chimpanzees, *Pan troglodytes,* and rhesus macaques, *Macaca mulatta. Animal Behaviour, 61,* 335–343.

Walker, R., Gurven, M., Hill, K., Migliano, H., Chagnon, N., De Souza, R., . . . Yamauchi, T. (2006). Growth rates and life histories in twenty-two small-scale societies. *American Journal of Human Biology, 18*(3), 295–311.

Warneken, F., & Tomasello, M. (2006). Altruistic helping in human infants and young chimpanzees. *Science, 311,* 1301–1303.

Warneken, F., Hare, B., Melis, A., Hanus, D., & Tomasello, M. (2007). Spontaneous altruism by chimpanzees and young children. *PLOS Biology, 5*(7), 1414–1420.

Whiten, A., Custance, D., Gomez, J., Teixidor, P., & Bard, K. (1996). Imitative learning of artificial fruit processing in children (*Homo sapiens*) and chimpanzees (*Pan troglodytes*). *Journal of Comparative Psychology, 110*(1), 3–14.

Wobber, V., Wrangham, R., & Hare, B. (2010a). Application of the heterochrony framework to the study of behavior and cognition. *Communicative and Integrative Biology, 3*(4), 1–2.

Wobber, V., Wrangham, R., & Hare, B. (2010b). Bonobos exhibit delayed development of social behavior and cognition relative to chimpanzees. *Current Biology, 20*(3), 226–230.

Wobber, V., & Hare, B. (2011). Psychological health in orphan bonobos and chimpanzees in African sanctuaries. *PLOS One, 6*(6), e17147.

Won, Y., & Hey, J. (2005). Divergence population genetics of chimpanzees. *Molecular Biology and Evolution, 22*(2), 297–307.

Woods, V., & Hare, B. (2010). Think outside the lab: African sanctuaries as a new resource for 'non-invasive research on great apes. In D. Mills (Ed.), *Encyclopedia of applied animal behavior and welfare.* CABI.

Woods, V., & Hare, B. (2011). Bonobo but not chimpanzee infants use socio-sexual contact with peers. *Primates, 52*(2), 111–116.

Wrangham, R. (1999). Evolution of coalitionary killing. *Yearbook of Physical Anthropology, 42,* 1–30.

Wrangham, R., & Pilbeam, D. (2001). African apes as time machines. In B. Galdikas, N. Briggs, L. Sheeran, G. Shapiro, & J. Goodall (Eds.), *All apes great and small* (Vol. 1, pp. 5–18). New York: Kluwer Academic/Plenum Publishers.

1.8

Teleological Understanding of Actions

GERGELY CSIBRA AND GYÖRGY GERGELY

All organisms pursue goals that promote their survival and reproduction. For many species, the small repertoire of basic drive-related goals and behavioral means to achieve them are genetically specified and are triggered by appropriate releasing stimuli. Other species, most notably, but not exclusively, mammals and birds, have much more flexible ways to accomplish their goals, tailoring their behavior to the local environment and adjusting it according to their past experience with similar situations. Humans also display adaptability and learning capacities in their goal-directed actions, but they are flexible in another way as well: They regularly pursue goals that hold only a remote connection to their survival and reproductive potential (Csibra & Gergely, 2006; Gergely, 2010). These include social goals (e.g., increasing one's reputation), culturally defined desires (e.g., enjoying heavy metal music), and idiosyncratic aspirations (e.g., climbing Mount Everest); and in many cultures even the most basic survival needs, like consumption of food, are fulfilled by chains of goal-directed sequences composed of actions (e.g., sowing seeds, calling a restaurant to reserve a table) that are far detached from their biologically useful outcome.

Beyond pursuing goals, animals may also benefit from observing other individuals' behaviors because they may provide information (1) about what the observed agents would do next and (2) about the environment. Interpreting behaviors as goal-directed actions is especially valuable as it carries direct information about likely future events (the expected outcome) and its context (e.g., potential food source). What kinds of information are available in a goal-directed action that would help observers to interpret it as a means directed at a certain end (Csibra & Gergely, 2007)? First, as in many domains, statistical information about the co-occurrence of observed behaviors and their outcomes could assist the formation

of bidirectional action-effect associations. Such information may contribute to gradual learning about goal-directed actions, but it does not help when an observer is confronted with novel instrumental behaviors. The second source of information for interpreting actions as goal directed comes from the observer's own motor (or more generally, instrumental) competence. One can rely on the internal mechanisms of motor planning, which chain actions to bring about desired outcomes, to simulate observed actions and to link them to their likely goals. While such simulatory mechanisms play important roles in action prediction (Csibra, 2007), their use is restricted to actions that are within the observer's own motor competence, and they are unavailable for interpretation of the behavior of unfamiliar agents or novel actions of familiar actors.

We have proposed that a third source of information that, beyond temporal association and motor mediation, may link actions to goal states is the efficiency of the observed action to the observed or inferred goal in the given environment (Gergely & Csibra, 2003). Briefly, an observed behavior is interpreted as an action directed to a particular end state if it is judged to be the most efficient means available to the agent for achieving this goal in the given environment. When such an interpretation is established, it creates a teleological representation of the action, which is held together by the principle of efficiency. The paradigmatic situation in which the functioning of teleological interpretation can be tested is when one observes a behavior (e.g., an agent jumps into the air while moving in a certain direction) leading to an end state (e.g., the agent stops next to another object). If, and only if, the behavior (jumping) is justified by environmental factors (by the presence of a barrier over which the jumping occurs) will this behavior be interpreted as a means action to achieve the end state

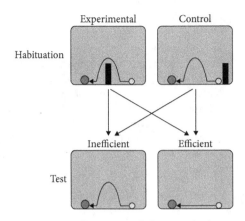

FIGURE 1.8.1: Illustration of the stimuli that were used to demonstrate the link between goal attribution and efficiency evaluation in infants (after Gergely et al., 1995). Infants were habituated to an event in which an agent (the small circle) approached another one (the larger circle) by a jumping action, which was either justified (Experimental condition, top left) or not (Control condition, top right) by the presence of an obstacle in between the agents. Their interpretation of these events was probed in the test trials (bottom row), in which the black box was removed from the screen. The looking times to these test events suggested that infants in the Experimental condition expected the agent to take the shortest pathway (Efficient approach, bottom right) instead of repeating the jumping action (Inefficient approach, bottom left) in the absence of the obstacle. In contrast, infants in the Control condition did not develop any specific expectation for the agent's action in the new situation.

as the goal of the action (to get in contact with the other object) (Fig. 1.8.1). We and others have published extensive evidence that infants from at least 6 months of age form this kind of teleological representations of actions (e.g., Gergely, Nádasdy, Csibra, & Bíró, 1995; Csibra, 2008).

Instead of listing evidence and arguments that support the proposal that such a representational system operates early in human development, we attempt to clarify commonly raised issues about this theory in a question-and-answer format.

Would it not be a simpler interpretation of these findings that infants expect agents to always follow the "shortest pathway"?

It would, but it would be misleading for two reasons. First, such an interpretation hides, rather than reveals, that infants represent the observed actions as goal directed. Whether a certain trajectory is

"the shortest pathway" can only be judged by reference to its end point ("shortest pathway" requires a "to" argument). Thus, if infants form this expectation, it implies that infants interpret the observed movement as goal directed. Second, "shortest pathway" is not the only factor that infants can apply to judge the efficiency of actions. They think, for example, that action sequences that contain fewer steps are more efficient than those with more steps (Southgate, Johnson, & Csibra, 2008), and that the shorter pathway is not necessarily better than a longer detour if it requires the agent to effortfully squeeze through a narrow aperture (Csibra & Gergely, 1998b; Gergely, 2003).

What is the advantage of forming such abstract representations of actions?

Teleological action interpretation enables at least three kinds of inferences to be made. First, it allows action predictions in situations in which the environment changes but the goal does not. In this case, one can predict that the agent would adjust its action to the modified environment, choosing the more efficient action alternative to the goal. In fact, this is exactly how goal attribution is tested in infant paradigms (e.g., Csibra, Bíró, Koós, & Gergely, 2003; Csibra, Gergely, Bíró, Koós, & Brockbank, 1999; Gergely et al., 1995). Second, teleological action representations support the prediction and attribution of goals to ongoing actions even before such outcomes have been realized. Answering the question, "Toward what end state is the observed behavior an efficient action in this environment?" enables the observer to infer the goal of unfinished, partly hidden, or even failed actions. Infants can definitely make such inferences at 10 to 12 months of age (Brandone & Wellman, 2009; Csibra et al., 2003), even on the basis of the observation of a single action (Southgate & Csibra, 2009). Third, the assumption of efficiency can provide a basis for inferring situational constraints of an observed goal-directed action. For example, 1-year-old infants infer the presence of an occluded barrier when an agent approaches its goal by a jumping action (Csibra et al., 2003). Thus, teleological action interpretation can be a productive process, which is especially important when a child observes novel instrumental actions.

To what kinds of agents do infants attribute goals via teleological interpretation?

Common sense dictates that the interpretation of goal directedness should be reserved to behaviors of agents, like animals, who do pursue goals.

However, feature-based identification of agency does not seem to constrain the application of teleological interpretation in infants. They readily attribute goals to people (Kamewari, Kato, Kanda, Ishiguro, & Hiraki, 2005; Sodian, Schoeppner, & Metz, 2004), hands (Biro, Verschoor, & Coenen, 2011; Brandone & Wellman, 2009; Phillips & Wellman, 2005; Southgate et al., 2008; Woodward & Sommerville, 2000), puppets (Sodian et al., 2004), robots (Kamewari et al., 2005), boxes (Csibra, 2008), balls (Southgate & Csibra, 2009), and computer-animated two-dimensional shapes (Biro, Csibra, & Gergely, 2007; Csibra et al., 1999, 2003; Gergely et al., 1995; Wagner & Carey, 2005). It may be true that teleological action interpretation is easier to elicit for familiar than for unfamiliar agents (Kamewari et al., 2005), but it is not denied of inanimate boxes even among the youngest age groups (Csibra, 2008). Another proposal suggested that goal attribution might be triggered only by actions of self-propelled agents (Leslie, 1994; Premack, 1990). We were unable to confirm this hypothesis in a study in which we found that infants interpreted the actions of an agent as goal directed even if they had no evidence of how it started to move and neither were there other disambiguating cues available (such as biomechanical movement) to indicate animacy (Csibra et al., 1999). Indeed, the only agency cue that seems to be reliably linked to goal attribution is some kind of evidence of "freedom" or "choice" in terms of variability of the agent's behavior (Csibra, 2008; see also Biro & Leslie, 2007; Luo, 2011).

Is teleological goal attribution a kind of mental attribution?

It does not have to be. An important insight of this proposal is that the computations that are necessary to set up teleological representations of actions are performed not on mental states but on real (present) and hypothetical (future) states of affairs. These states of affairs correspond to the contents of mental states (beliefs, desires, and intentions) that are involved in mentalistic action explanations (Csibra & Gergely, 1998a; Gergely & Csibra, 2003). We think that even adults do not normally appeal to mental states when they explain and predict others' actions, only when they have good reason to assume that the content of those states differs from real states of affairs (e.g., when the agent acts on false beliefs). When we take the "intentional stance" (Dennett, 1987) and interpret an action by attributing causally efficacious mental states to the agent, the

assumption of efficiency is not sufficient; we have to assume that the agent acts rationally, that is, efficiently in the world described by her beliefs. Thus, the principle of rational action applies calculations of efficiency either on real states of affairs or on contents of mental states (that represent real, hypothetical, or counterfactual state of affairs). However, when we find evidence of teleological action understanding in infants, it does not tell us whether it is based on mental attribution.

So, does the teleological nature of early action understanding suggest that infants are unable to attribute representational mental states?

No. In fact, evidence suggests that even 7-month-old infants attribute representational mental states based on observed perceptual access (Kovács, Téglás, & Endress, 2010), and that they use this ability for the interpretation of goal-directed actions in the second year of life (Onishi & Baillargeon, 2005; Surian, Caldi, & Sperber, 2007; Southgate, Senju, & Csibra, 2007). Although infants under 1 year of age can attribute belief states and evaluate the efficiency of goal-directed actions, it is not yet clear whether they can utilize the former ability in the service of the latter (but see Luo & Baillargeon, 2010). In fact, one way in which experience with goal-directed actions can contribute to the development of action understanding is by providing opportunities to learn to recognize the conditions under which taking into considerations representational mental states of the actor is necessary for correct action understanding. Note also that teleological action interpretation is not the only mechanism of action understanding: Communicative-referential actions invite different types of inferences and representations (Csibra, 2003; Gergely, 2010).

Do infants have sufficient knowledge of agents to assess the efficiency of their actions?

To evaluate efficiency, observers will have to estimate and compare the effort (the cost) that an agent does or would invest in action alternatives. Such calculations require detailed knowledge of biomechanical factors that determine the motion capabilities and energy expenditure of agents. However, in the absence of such knowledge, one can appeal to heuristics that approximate the results of these calculations on the basis of knowledge in other domains that is certainly available to young infants. For example, the length of pathways can be assessed by geometrical calculations, taking also into account some physical factors (like the impenetrability of solid objects). Similarly, the fewer steps an action sequence takes, the less effort it might require, and so infants' numerical competence can also contribute to efficiency evaluation. As infants learn the biomechanical constraints of familiar agents, like humans, by observation and by experiencing their own movement capabilities, they gradually take into account this knowledge in interpreting observed actions. Until this knowledge base is well established, however, they may make the mistake of expecting human agents to perform an impossible action if it seems the most efficient by some heuristics borrowed from other domains (Southgate et al., 2008).

Is teleological interpretation the only mechanism of goal attribution available to infants?

No. As we mentioned in the beginning of this chapter, there are also other ways to link actions to goals. We hypothesize that infants always attempt to find teleological explanations (i.e., explanations in terms of goal states) for observed actions (a phenomenon that we termed "teleological obsession"; see Csibra & Gergely, 2007). If no reliable information of means adjustment is present in the action, they can use alternative information, like the agent's apparent choice between two objects (Woodward, 1998). Recent studies have found that a goal that is attributed to an agent on the basis of efficiency of the means action is used by infants to predict which of two objects the agent would choose in a new situation (Biro et al., 2011; Hernik & Southgate, 2012). This transfer of goal attribution suggests that whatever information infants use to infer the goal of the action, it feeds into a unitary goal concept (Biro et al., in press). However, when efficiency information is pitted against goal selection, infants tend to rely more on the former than on the latter (Verschoor & Biro, 2012).

Is teleological action understanding human-specific?

Since nonhuman animals, for example primates, attribute goals, we find it unlikely that they would not use such a simple mechanisms of action evaluation, and evidence supports that they do so (Rochat, Serra, Fadiga, & Gallese, 2008). However, we think that teleological action understanding is not as productive in other animals as in humans; not because their teleological action representation would not support such productive inferences, but because they lack the "teleological obsession" with which humans, including human infants, approach actions. Thus, when no other cue indicates a potentially valuable goal (e.g.,

food) for an observed action, nonhuman animals do not necessarily start to engage in reasoning about what goal the action is directed to, while we suggest that human infants do so. The reason for this difference is that human infants also make use of teleological understanding of actions for social learning of instrumental actions and artifact functions (Csibra & Gergely, 2007).

Is teleological reasoning applied outside the domain of action perception?

Yes, it is. Humans tend to look for teleological explanations in many domains, most notably to interpret artifacts, social institutions, biological mechanisms, and even nonbiological phenomena (Kelemen, 1999, 2004). In all these cases the underlying intuition is that the explanation must satisfy some kind of optimality criterion: A tool should be better to achieve its desired effect than the available alternatives, biological mechanisms should be adaptive, and so on. Whether these explanations draw on the same underlying cognitive mechanisms is not known. However, it is plausible to assume that action interpretation and artifact understanding are closely linked in development (Csibra & Gergely, 2007). Infants seek to find functions for artifacts just like they search for action goals (Futó, Téglás, Csibra, & Gergely, 2010; Träuble & Pauen, 2007), and in many cases the answers to these queries coincide: The function of a tool is the goal which can efficiently be accomplished by its use.

Teleological understanding provides a powerful mechanism of learning because it specifies formal criteria of organization of information into a specific representational system. As such, it allows the learning of completely novel action-goal relations from the simplest level of single motor acts to complex actions linking spatially and temporally distant events. It also forms one of the basic representational systems from which our intuitive mentalistic psychology is built, without which human social cognition would be quite different.

ACKNOWLEDGMENTS

This work was supported by an Advanced Intestigator Grant (OSTREFCOM) from the European Research Council.

REFERENCES

Biro, S., Csibra, G., & Gergely, G. (2007). The role of behavioral cues in understanding goal-directed actions in infancy. *Progress in Brain Research, 164,* 303–322.

Biro, S. & Leslie, A. M. (2007). Infants' perception of goal-directed actions: Development through cue-based bootstrapping. *Developmental Science*, 10, 379–398.

Biro, S., Verschoor, S. A., & Coenen, L. (2011). Evidence for a unitary goal concept in 12–month-old infants. *Developmental Science*, 14(6), 1255–1260.

Brandone, A. C., & Wellman, H. M. (2009). You can't always get what you want: Infants understand failed goal-directed actions. *Psychological Science*, 20, 85–91.

Csibra, G. (2003). Teleological and referential understanding of action in infancy. *Philosophical Transactions of the Royal Society, London B*, 358, 447–458.

Csibra, G. (2007). Action mirroring and action interpretation: An alternative account. In P. Haggard, Y. Rosetti, & M. Kawato (Eds.), *Sensorimotor foundations of higher cognition. Attention and performance XXII* (pp. 435–459). Oxford, England: Oxford University Press.

Csibra, G. (2008). Goal attribution to inanimate agents by 6.5-month-old infants. *Cognition*, 107, 705–717.

Csibra, G., Bíró, S., Koós, S., & Gergely, G. (2003). One-year-old infants use teleological representations of actions productively. *Cognitive Science*, 27, 111–133.

Csibra, G., & Gergely, G. (1998a). The teleological origins of mentalistic action explanations: A developmental hypothesis. *Developmental Science*, 1, 255–259.

Csibra, G., & Gergely, G. (1998b, September). Beyond least effort: The principle of rationality in teleological interpretation of action in 1-year-olds. Poster presented at the Swansong Conference of the Medical Research Council Cognitive Development Unit, London.

Csibra, G., & Gergely, G. (2006). Social learning and social cognition: The case for pedagogy. In Y. Munakata & M. H. Johnson (Eds.), *Processes of change in brain and cognitive development. Attention and performance XXI* (pp. 249–274). Oxford, England: Oxford University Press.

Csibra, G., & Gergely, G. (2007). "Obsessed with goals": Functions and mechanisms of teleological interpretation of actions in humans. *Acta Psychologica*, 124, 60–78.

Csibra, G., Gergely, G., Bíró, S., Koós, O., & Brockbank, M. (1999). Goal attribution without agency cues: The perception of "pure reason" in infancy. *Cognition*, 72, 237–267.

Dennett, D. (1987). *The intentional stance.* Cambridge, MA: MIT Press.

Futó, J., Téglás, E., Csibra, G., & Gergely, G. (2010). Communicative function demonstration induces kind-based artifact representation in preverbal infants. *Cognition*, 117, 1–8.

Gergely, G. (2003). What should a robot learn from an infant? Mechanisms of action interpretation and observational learning in infancy. *Connection Science*, 13, 191–209.

Gergely, G. (2010). Kinds of agents: The origins of understanding instrumental and communicative agency. In U. Goshwami (Ed.), *Blackwell handbook of childhood cognitive development* (2nd ed., pp. 76–105). Oxford, England: Blackwell.

Gergely, G., & Csibra, G. (2003). Teleological reasoning in infancy: The one-year-old's naïve theory of rational action. *Trends in Cognitive Sciences*, 7, 287–292.

Gergely, G., Nádasdy, Z., Csibra, G., & Bíró, S. (1995). Taking the intentional stance at 12 months of age. *Cognition*, 56, 165–193.

Hernik, M., & Southgate, V. (2012). Nine-month-old infants do not need to know what the agent prefers in order to reason about its goals: on the role of preference and persistence in infants' goal-attribution. *Developmental Science*, 15, 714–722.

Kamewari, K., Kato, M., Kanda, T., Ishiguro, H., & Hiraki, K. (2005). Six-and-a-half-month-old children positively attribute goals to human action and to humanoid-robot motion. *Cognitive Development*, 20, 303–320.

Kelemen, D. (1999). Functions, goals and intentions: Children's teleological reasoning about objects. *Trends in Cognitive Sciences*, 12, 461–468.

Kelemen, D. (2004). Are children "intuitive theists"? Reasoning about purpose and design in nature. *Psychological Science*, 15, 295–301.

Kovács, Á. M., Téglás, E., & Endress, A. D. (2010). The social sense: Susceptibility to others' beliefs in human infants and adults. *Science*, 330, 1830–1834.

Leslie, A. M. (1994). ToMM, ToBy, and agency: Core architecture and domain specificity, In L. A. Hirschfeld & S. A. Gelman (Eds.), *Mapping the mind: Domain specificity in cognition and culture* (pp. 119–148). Cambridge, England: Cambridge University Press.

Luo, Y. (2011). Three-month-old infants attribute goals to a non-human agent. *Developmental Science*, 14, 453–460.

Luo, Y., & Baillargeon, R. (2010). Toward a mentalistic account of early psychological reasoning. *Current Directions in Psychological Science*, 19, 301–307.

Onishi, K. H., & Baillargeon, R. (2005). Do 15-month-old infants understand false beliefs? *Science*, 308, 255–258.

Phillips. A. T., & Wellman, H. M. (2005). Infants' understanding of object-directed actions. *Cognition*, 98, 137–155.

Premack, D. (1990). The infant's theory of self-propelled objects. *Cognition, 36,* 1–16.

Rochat, M. J., Serra, E., Fadiga, L., & Gallese, V. (2008). The evolution of social cognition: Goal familiarity shapes monkeys' action understanding, *Current Biology, 18,* 227–232.

Sodian, B., Schoeppner, B., & Metz, U. (2004). Do infants apply the principle of rational action to human agents? *Infant Behavior and Development, 27,* 31–41.

Southgate, V., & Csibra, G. (2009). Inferring the outcome of an ongoing novel action at 13 months. *Developmental Psychology, 45,* 1794–1798.

Southgate, V., Johnson, M. H., & Csibra, G. (2008). Infants attribute goals to even biologically impossible actions. *Cognition, 107,* 1059–1069.

Southgate, V., Senju, A., & Csibra, G. (2007). Action anticipation through attribution of false belief by two-year-olds. *Psychological Science, 18,* 587–592.

Surian, L., Caldi, S., & Sperber, D. (2007). Attribution of beliefs by 13-month-old infants. *Psychological Science, 18,* 580–586.

Träuble, B., & Pauen, S. (2007). The role of functional information for infant categorization. *Cognition, 105,* 362–379.

Verschoor, S. A., & Biro, S. (2012). The primacy of means selection information over outcome selection information in infants' goal attribution. *Cognitive Science, 36(4),* 714–725.

Wagner, L., & Carey, S. (2005). 12-month-old infants represent probable endings of motion events. *Infancy, 7,* 73–83.

Woodward, A. L. (1998). Infants selectively encode the goal object of an actor's reach. *Cognition, 69,* 1–34.

Woodward, A. L., & Sommerville, J. (2000). Twelve-month-old infants interpret action in context. *Psychological Science, 11,* 73–77.

1.9

How Universals and Individual Differences Can Inform Each Other

The Case of Social Expectations in Infancy

SUSAN C. JOHNSON, CAROL S. DWECK, AND KRISTEN A. DUNFIELD

Infant social cognition is an exciting research area to be in these days. It seems that new results are announced every week and a new perspective on infants' social reasoning is clearly emerging. As we have seen in other domains, it now appears that infants understand far more about the ways of the social world than we had imagined. Yet not all of the new findings fit together easily, revealing points of tension in our emerging framework.

This essay explores one key point of tension. In the emerging literature on infants' expectations about social interactions, about good and bad, about prosocial and antisocial behavior, the evidence for universals in social cognition appears at first glance to be at odds with evidence for individual differences. Does this tension reflect the familiar conflict between nativist and empiricist claims or is something deeper and more subtle at play? As we embark on a resolution to these issues, we hope to offer the possibility of a richer theoretical perspective than currently exists.

EVIDENCE FOR UNIVERSAL SOCIAL EXPECTATIONS IN INFANCY: HELPING AND HINDERING

One area in which researchers have observed universal expectations is within the domain of positive and negative social interactions. Several studies, using the visual habituation method, have examined infants' reasoning about an agent's positive and negative actions, such as helping versus hindering another. These studies have found that infants distinguish between these positive and negative interactions, attribute dispositions based on them, and prefer positive versus negative actors (Hamlin, Wynn, & Bloom, 2007, 2010;

Kuhlmeier, Wynn, & Bloom, 2003; Kuhlmeier, Dunfield, Stewart, Wynn, & Bloom, unpublished data; Premack & Premack, 1997). For example, Premack and Premack (1997) repeatedly showed infants displays of two animated balls interacting in either a positive manner (soft, "caressing" contact or one ball assisting the other in getting over a wall) or a negative manner (hard, "hitting" contact or one preventing the other from getting over a wall). They showed the infants these displays until they became bored with them. Then all infants were shown a new display with a brand new negative event. Infants who had originally viewed the positive interactions showed renewed interest in this novel event. But infants who had seen the negative displays, even though this was a new one, seemed to think "Ho-hum, just another negative interaction." Interestingly, this means they had the concept of a "negative interaction" that transcended any particular interaction.

In a related series of studies, Kuhlmeier, Wynn, and Bloom (2003; Kuhlmeier et al., unpublished data) found that infants' expectations of an agent's behavior was influenced by the agent's previous interactions. In these studies infants repeatedly watched a short animated video in which a geometric shape (a small red ball) interacted with two other shapes on a hillside. The small red ball attempted to climb a steep hill, but halfway up the hill the ball got "stuck." On alternating trials a yellow square helped the ball up the hill, or a green triangle hindered the ball, pushing it down the hill. Later, in a novel context, infants expected the ball to approach the helper and avoid the hinderer, suggesting that the infants understood how the ball's positive or negative interactions affected its subsequent behavior.

Finally, Hamlin, Wynn, and Bloom (2007, 2010) have extended this line of research using puppets. Replicating the original helping and hindering interactions, they have demonstrated that infants themselves possess robust social preferences for agents that engage in positive helping interactions as opposed to negative hindering. Specifically, when infants watched two puppets engage in either positive or negative interactions, they not only looked longer at the positive puppet but also reached out and took the positive puppet when offered a choice between the two. Importantly, in Hamlin and colleagues' studies, when individual responses were reported, the overwhelming majority of the infants (more than 80%) shared this social preference. Taken together, these elegant studies provide a strong case for universality in infants' interpretation and evaluation of others' positive versus negative interactions.

EVIDENCE FOR INDIVIDUAL DIFFERENCES IN SOCIAL EXPECTATIONS IN INFANCY: ATTACHMENT

Contrary to the results we have just described, researchers in the social developmental tradition have long claimed that infants' expectations of others, or at least of their caregivers' behavior, differs as a function of their experiences. And indeed, as we will see, the research shows that whereas some infants expect positive (responsive or helpful) behavior from a caretaker toward a child in need, others appear to expect less positive behavior from a caretaker. Perhaps even more at odds with the research described earlier, some infants even expect children to *prefer* the more negative (unhelpful) caretaker.

The view that such individual differences exist in what infants seek and expect from caretakers is most clearly developed in the context of attachment research (Ainsworth, Blehar, Waters, & Wall, 1978; Bowlby, 1969/1982). An infant's attachment style refers to his or her willingness and ability to seek and accept comfort from a caregiver and is thought to reflect an *internal working model* of how the infant expects social interactions to work (Bowlby, 1969/1982). It is commonly assessed using Ainsworth's Strange Situation (Ainsworth et al., 1978). In this procedure, infants are briefly separated twice from their caregiver. Over the course of the separations, infants universally become distressed; however, stable, robust individual differences are observed in infants' behavior upon reunion. These behaviors can be classified into two classes of strategies. The most common strategy, termed *secure,* is shown by infants who readily approach their caregivers and willingly accept comfort, as though confident in the expectation that caregivers will be accepting of their distress and comforting in their behavior. The remainder of infants typically employ *insecure* strategies such as avoidance or resistance, reflecting, it is thought, a lack of confidence in their caregiver's response, believing it to be unpredictable or rejecting.

Recently, we tested whether infants' behavior in the Strange Situation corresponded to their expectations of social interactions using more direct cognitive measures. To test infants' expectations of social interactions in this context, we used the same visual habituation method employed by Premack, Wynn, and others that we described earlier. Like those studies, the present study used abstract geometric shapes interacting in short animated events to test infants' expectations. Unlike these other studies, however, we found no universal patterns of response. Instead, we found unique patterns of social expectations, corresponding to attachment styles.

In our first study, infants repeatedly saw a display of two animated circles enacting a separation event. Each scene began with the larger, "mother" circle and the smaller, "child" circle together at the bottom of a steep incline. With the infant watching from below, the mother proceeded halfway up the incline to a small plateau, and as the mother came to rest at this midway position, the child left behind began to cry. The animation then paused and the infant was allowed to look at this final scene as long as she liked. The animation sequence was repeated until the infant was no longer interested in it. Once this happened, each infant was shown two test events, one depicting a positive response by the mother and the other depicting a negative response.

Each test event opened with the mother still positioned halfway up the incline as the child continued to cry. In the positive test event, the mother came back down the incline to the child. In the negative test event, the mother continued away from the child to the top of the slope. Infants' reactions to the test events showed clear individual differences. Infants who were securely attached to their own caregivers were surprised to see the mother ignore the crying baby and continue on her way. Infants who were insecurely attached showed the opposite pattern. They were surprised when the mother came back (Johnson, Dweck, & Chen, 2007; Johnson, Dweck, Chen, Stern, Ok, & Barth, 2010).

A second study tested which of two adult actors an infant would expect the child to seek out—one who had responded positively by returning when the child had cried for help or one who had responded negatively by ignoring the child's bids. In this case, securely attached infants seemed to expect the child to seek out the positive and responsive adult, while insecurely attached infants seemed to expect the child to seek out the negative adult, as though the unhelpful behavior of the rejecting caregiver represented normal, familiar behavior to them.

Thus, across these studies using a standard visual habituation method, unique patterns of social expectations emerged. Securely attached infants expected infants to gain comfort from caregivers and expected infants to seek that comfort. Insecurely attached infants not only expected caregivers to withhold comfort, they also expected infants to seek out the withholding caregiver over the more positive one. These data converge with the conclusions derived from more traditional methods in social development and with Bowlby's original claims—that infants form different expectations about how the social world works and what they then seek from it.

RECONCILING THE TWO SETS OF DATA

Let's review. On the one hand, we have a series of studies in which infants view a small abstract character (a circle) heading up a hill. Two other abstract characters (a triangle and a square) interact with the circle either positively (by helping it up the hill) or negatively (by blocking its progress and pushing it back down the hill). Later, the vast majority of the infants expect the circle to "prefer" or approach the supportive character, and the vast majority of infants themselves prefer to interact with the supportive character as well—suggestive of a universal pattern of expectations and preferences.

On the other hand, we have a series of studies employing a similar method, in which infants view a small abstract character (a circle) at the foot of a hill. Another, larger abstract character interacts with the circle in ways that are either positive (by attending and responding to the circle) or negative (by ignoring the circle). Yet, in contrast to the previous examples, no single, universal pattern emerges in infants' expectations; instead infants seem to expect interactions that are consistent with their own individual attachment styles.

Both sets of studies purport to test infants' expectations of positive and negative social interactions and positive and negative social actors. Yet they get considerably different kinds of results. What are the possible sources of these apparently contradictory results?

Perhaps, as is often the case in science, seemingly divergent results can be traced to significant differences in methodology or measurement. That does not seem to be the case here. Both sets of studies use a visual habituation method. Both sets of studies use similar abstract, animated displays. Just as important, both sets of data converge with other data based on different methodologies in their respective areas of research—the help/hinder looking time studies are consistent with infants' toy preferences and the caregiver responsiveness looking time studies with infant attachment behavior.

Another possibility is that we see only what we are looking for. Perhaps we would have found a universal pattern in the attachment data had we collapsed the data across attachment styles. Consider the distribution of individual attachment styles within a population. In a hypothetical sample with 75% securely attached infants and only 25% insecurely attached, the securely attached pattern could potentially dominate, yielding a group-level pattern. However, in our population, we typically had only 50%–60% securely attached infants. Collapsing the secure and insecure groups together never resulted in results at the group level that were distinguishable from chance. It was the individual difference variable that provided insight into the true nature of infants' responses to positive and negative events.

Conversely, perhaps meaningful subgroups could have been found in the help/hinder studies had the authors looked for them. However, the distribution of individual patterns within their samples does not support this possibility. Depending on the study, around 85% of the infants in the help/hinder studies showed the pattern reflected by the overall group. This distribution leaves only 15% of the population to represent any meaningful minority patterns. This is probably too small a proportion to account for the insecurely attached infants that were likely to have existed in all the samples that have been tested.

A THEORETICAL ADVANCEMENT

Once the methodological explanations are eliminated, we can concentrate on the interesting possibility that these two sets of studies, similar as they are on the surface, do in fact tap into two cognitively distinct mental processes. Pursuit along these lines might yield new insights into the structure of this area of social cognition. Indeed, recent proposals regarding the diverse nature of prosocial behavior may provide a theoretical framework within which to interpret these apparently divergent results. Specifically, it has been suggested that within the general domain of prosocial behavior there may be three unique subtypes of other-oriented action (helping, sharing, and comforting) which rely on the identification and response to three distinct types of needs (instrumental, material, and emotional; Dunfield & Kuhlmeier, in press; Dunfield, Kuhlmeier, O'Connell, & Kelley, in press).

If this is true, it stands to reason that the representations underpinning the different forms of prosocial behavior humans engage in might differ (e.g., Svetlova, Nichols, & Brownell, in press; Warneken & Tomasello, 2009), especially since the inputs for each form of prosocial behavior are slightly different (Dunfield & Kuhlmeier, in press). *Helping* is a response to someone's frustrated instrumental goals, for instance, his or her goal of climbing a hill. *Comforting*, on the other hand, is a response to someone's frustrated emotional goals, for instance, the goal of reunion with an attachment figure. To recognize the potentially positive role that the helper or the comforter could play, one must first recognize the frustrated goal, which in the case of instrumental versus emotional actions are quite distinct. Indeed, the cognitive processes that underpin reasoning about instrumental and emotional actions may have not only independent developmental trajectories (e.g., Dunfield & Kuhlmeier, in press), but one may be far more plastic and dependent on experience (comfort) than the other (helping), leading to more individual differences in the first than the second.

To test this hypothesis, Dunfield and Johnson (unpublished data) have designed a new series of abstract animated events in which the helping and comforting events have been pared back to show only the initial actor's need—either an instrumental need, for which helping would be in order, or a socioemotional need, for which comforting would be in order. Two 20-second animations were created in which a small and a large yellow circle appear against a green landscape that depicts a flat plane in front of a small hill. In the instrumental video, the small circle tries unsuccessfully to climb the hill, falling back down each

time, while the large circle looks on from the side. In the social video, the large circle leaves the small circle at the base of the hill, moving along the flat plane, such that the small circle could follow, but instead remains stationary while crying. Adult participants were asked to view each video and describe in their own words "what the video was about." Participants were also asked to fill out a short questionnaire that allowed us to classify them as having either secure or insecure attachment styles (ECR; Brennan, Clark, & Shaver, 1998). Coders scored participants' verbal descriptions specifically for their tendency to spontaneously report the small circle's goal—to get up the hill in the instrumental case or to get the mother's attention in the emotional case.

Preliminary results are striking. Sixty percent of adults with secure attachment styles and 62% of adults with insecure styles spontaneously reported the small circle's need in the instrumental video. By contrast, in response to the emotional video, 40% of the secure adults but none of the insecure adults volunteered a description of the small circle's emotional need. Whether the insecure adults' lack of response is due to an inability to recognize the small circle's goal or a reluctance to acknowledge it is unclear. Regardless, these results suggest universal similarity in the processing of instrumental goals, and individual differences in the processing of emotional goals. Moreover, these results provide an example of how attempts to understand and integrate *both* universal similarities, and individual differences, within a common theoretical framework can aid in understanding the course of social cognitive development.

The goal of this chapter was to examine two seemly divergent perspectives on social cognitive development—universal similarities versus individual differences. These two approaches are usually taken by different researchers: researchers who are interested in innate or early-emerging social-cognitive tendencies versus researchers who are interested in the role of experience in shaping social cognition. Most often, little attempt is made to integrate findings across the approaches. However, our proposed integration illustrates how identifying meaningful points of contact can result in a deeper understanding of important, even foundational, phenomena than would otherwise have been achieved.

REFERENCES

Ainsworth, M. D. S., Blehar, M. C., Waters, E., & Wall, S. (1978). *Patterns of attachment: A psychological* study of the strange situation. Hillsdale, NJ: Erlbaum.

Bowlby, J. (1982). Attachment and loss: Vol. 1. Attachment. Middlesex, England: Pelican Books. [Original work published 1969].

Brennan, K. A., Clark, C. L., & Shaver, P. R. (1998). Self-report measurement of adult romantic attachment: An integrative overview. In J. A. Simpson & W. S. Rholes (Eds.), Attachment theory and close relationships (pp. 46–76). New York: Guilford Press.

Dunfield, K. A., & Kuhlmeier, V. A. (in press). Classifying prosocial behavior: Helping, sharing, and comforting subtypes.

Dunfield, K. A., Kuhlmeier, V. A., O'Connell, L. J., & Kelley, E. A. (2011). Examining the diversity of prosocial behaviour: Helping, sharing, and comforting in infancy. Infancy, 16(3), 227–247.

Hamlin, J. K., Wynn, K., & Bloom, P. (2007). Social evaluation by preverbal infants. Nature, 450, 557–559.

Hamlin, J. K., Wynn, K., & Bloom, P. (2010). Three-month-olds show a negativity bias in their social evaluations. Developmental Science, 13, 923–929.

Johnson, S. C., Dweck, C., & Chen, F. S. (2007). Evidence for infants' internal working model of attachment. Psychological Science, 18, 501–502.

Johnson, S. C., Dweck, C., Chen, F. S., Ok., S. J., Stern, H. L., & Barth, M. E. (2010). At the intersection of social and cognitive development: Internal working models of attachment in infancy. Cognitive Science, 34, 807–825.

Kuhlmeier, V. A., Wynn, K., & Bloom, P. (2003). Attribution of dispositional states by 12-month-olds. Psychological Science, 14, 402–408.

Premack, D., & Premack, A. J. (1997). Infants attribute value +- to the goal-directed actions of self-propelled objects. Journal of Cognitive Neuroscience, 9, 848–856.

Svetlova, M., Nichols, S. R., & Brownell, C. A. (2010). Toddlers' prosocial behaviour: From instrumental to empathic to altruistic helping. Child Development, 81(6), 1814–1827.

Warneken, F., & Tomasello, M. (2009). Varieties of altruism in children and chimpanzees. Trends in Cognitive Sciences, 13, 397–402.

1.10

The Contribution of Temperament to the Study of Social Cognition

Learning Whether the Glass Is Half Empty or Half Full

NATHAN A. FOX AND SARAH M. HELFINSTEIN

Temperament refers to individual differences in the manner, intensity, and frequency of response to stimuli in the environment. Differences in responsivity can be identified early in life and can have a meaningful impact on a child's trajectory of social development. One temperament, behavioral inhibition, first identified some years ago by Jerome Kagan and his colleagues, describes a group of children who exhibit heightened vigilance and attention to their surroundings, are hesitant and wary of novel things, and are less likely to initiate social interaction with peers (Kagan & Snidman, 1991). Moreover, these children display an overarching pattern of withdrawal behavior: They avoid novelty and risky situations that hold potential for both positive and negative outcomes. As they get older, behaviorally inhibited youngsters are more likely to have difficulties with friendships and peer relationships, and they may find themselves neglected and excluded from peer groups. Of course, not all behaviorally inhibited children have these social problems. For some time now, we have studied the development of these children, with a particular focus on understanding the neural mechanisms underlying behavioral inhibition (Fox, Henderson, Marshall, Nichols, & Ghera, 2005) as well as the factors responsible for either continuity or discontinuity of this disposition over time. One question that has long guided our research is how basic neural circuitry present early in life could lead to the tendencies toward social withdrawal that are often seen in behaviorally inhibited children and adolescents. We now believe that temperament biases children's learning, filtering their experiences so that, over time, they develop tendencies to either approach or withdraw from particular situations: Learning about reward or punishment as a result

of initial temperamental dispositions determines whether children come to see the glass as half empty or half full. Imagine a young child who is temperamentally fearful and more sensitive and attentive to negative events. She finds herself in a social situation where she is rejected or ignored. While this might minimally influence another child's feelings about social interactions, the negative event will have a greater impact on the behaviorally inhibited child and significantly affect her perceptions of social interactions. That child may learn to expect or anticipate bad things the next time she finds herself in a similar context. Over time, with additional aversive interactions, such a child may learn to avoid risky social situations altogether.

There is evidence from social cognitive research with anxious children that seems to support this biased interpretation of the world. This is work in which anxious adults or children are presented with tasks in which they receive an ambiguous word or scenario, and they are asked either to generate a similar word, or how they would respond to a particular situation. For example, when subjects are presented with the word "growth," anxious subjects are more likely to favor the threat-related meaning (i.e., cancer), while nonanxious individuals are more likely to favor the nonthreat meaning (i.e., height/development) (Taghavi, Moradi, Neshat Doost, Yule, & Dalgleish, 2000). Glass half-empty versus glass half-full. Or when subjects are presented with a scenario in which they walk past a group of other children who stop and look at them as they walk past, the anxious child tends to endorse a threatening interpretation of the scenario (likely thinking the children are judging her or were talking about her), compared to the nonanxious child (Bogels & Zigterman, 2000;

Waters, Wharton, Zimmer-Gembeck, & Craske, 2008). Glass half-empty versus glass half-full. What, then, are the neural mechanisms that can bias a child to develop a glass half-empty perception of the world?

Our initial work described the behaviors and physiological responses of these children when they were confronted with mild stress and social novelty. We found that behaviorally inhibited children displayed heightened autonomic reactivity, heightened cortisol responses, and elevated startle responses (Schmidt et al., 1997). As the amygdala plays an important role in the regulation of each of these processes, it was suggested that the temperament of behavioral inhibition may be, in part, a result of an overactive amygdala (Kagan, Reznick, & Snidman, 1987). Consistent with this theory, Kagan and colleagues found that young adults who were characterized in childhood as behaviorally inhibited displayed heightened amygdala activation to novel faces relative to their noninhibited, same-age peers (Schwartz, Wright, Shin, Kagan, & Rauch, 2003). We replicated and extended this finding with our own neuroimaging study of adolescents who were characterized in childhood with behavioral inhibition. These subjects displayed heightened amygdala activation in response to fear and threat faces (Pérez-Edgar et al., 2007) compared to noninhibited controls.

In recent research, we have attempted to examine the neural bases of reward and punishment within a group of adolescents who were characterized as behaviorally inhibited since early childhood using functional imaging studies. The teens completed a task called the Monetary Incentive Delay task that is known to elicit activation in the striatum (Knutson, Westdorp, Kaiser, & Hommer, 2000). This task measures neural response to cues that indicate the potential for reward or punishment, and at first, we expected that it would elicit greater reward activation in noninhibited control subjects. However, unexpectedly, the behaviorally inhibited subjects—and not typical controls—showed greater striatal activation to cues that indicated potential reward or punishment on the Monetary Incentive Delay task. Indeed, the more money that was at stake on a given trial, the greater the increase of activation in the inhibited teens relative to the noninhibited (Guyer et al., 2006).

We were puzzled. Why would behaviorally inhibited children show greater activity in brain structures that are described as reward-processing centers? To gain a better understanding of what was going on, we conducted a second study with a different group of behaviorally inhibited teens, again designed to elicit activation in the striatum. This study used a reward contingency task where subjects saw two types of cues. One cue indicated that the subject had to make a simple motor response to receive money; the other indicated that subjects had to guess which of two options was correct, and if they guessed correctly, they would receive money. In this task, behaviorally inhibited subjects showed greater striatal activation than their peers only to the cues that indicated that subjects had to make a choice. Behaviorally inhibited and noninhibited subjects responded equally to the cues that indicated a certain monetary gain (Bar-Haim et al., 2009).

To better understand these findings, we decided to learn more about the striatum and how it functions. What we learned surprised us; it made us realize that the striatum is positioned to play a key role in approach and avoidance behavior and may drive the enhanced avoidance seen in behaviorally inhibited individuals. The neural connections of the striatum allow it to function as a limbic-motor interface: It is positioned to integrate information about salient stimuli in the environment and use this information to shape behavior. It sends output along a pathway that terminates both in motor cortex, and in the prefrontal cortex, which is critical for goal-setting and goal-directed behavior. In turn, it receives input from "limbic" regions such as the amygdala, the hippocampus, and the ventromedial prefrontal cortex. Additionally, it is densely innervated by dopaminergic neurons from two small nuclei: the substantia nigra and the ventral tegmental area, usually referred to as the VTA (Mogenson, 1980).

The dopaminergic input from the VTA plays a particularly important role in encoding salient environmental stimuli. These neurons show short, phasic bursting responses to salient cues. The earliest research describing these neurons demonstrated their sensitivity to reward (Romo & Schultz, 1990; Schultz, 1986), earning the tegmento-striatal pathway its description as "reward circuitry." However, subsequent research has shown that these neurons fire to many types of salient cues, including stimuli that are aversive (Sorg & Kalivas, 1991; Young, Joseph, & Gray, 1993) or novel (Horvitz, 2000; Ljungberg, Apicella, & Schultz, 1992). Moreover, these neurons are tuned in to *change* in the goodness or badness of the environment: an unexpected cue that indicates a reward is forthcoming will elicit a burst, but the reward itself, which was fully predicted by the cue, will not (Ljungberg, Apicella, & Schultz, 1992; Mirenowicz & Schultz, 1994). A cue that indicates a higher probability of a reward will elicit a larger burst than one that indicates a lower probability of a reward (Hollerman & Schultz, 1998), and a cue that indicates a larger reward will elicit a larger burst than one that indicates a smaller reward. Wolfram Schultz and colleagues (Schultz, Dayan, & Montague, 1997) noted that the firing pattern of these dopaminergic neurons mimicked the prediction error signal that is a critical part of the temporal difference model of Pavlovian conditioning (Rescorla & Wagner, 1972), which describes reinforcement learning in animals. Schultz and colleagues theorized that the purpose of these signals was to allow for shifts in goal-directed behavior when environmental contingencies changed: If a rewarding cue suddenly appeared in the environment, these signals would allow an individual to shift from pursuing the current goal to approaching a rewarding cue. Presumably, the same would be true for an aversive cue: A dopaminergic burst to an aversive cue would lead to a shift from pursuing the current goal to escaping an impending threat. If the pathway that translated unexpected aversive cues into avoidance behavior were somehow more sensitized than the pathway that translated unexpected appetitive cues into approach behavior, could this lead to the heightened tendency toward avoidance seen in behavioral inhibition?

There is already some evidence that provides support for this idea, both in humans and animals. Reynolds and Berridge (2001, 2002, 2008) have conducted a number of elegant studies demonstrating that stimulating the front portion of the shell of the nucleus accumbens—a region of the striatum—causes rats to engage in approach behavior, while stimulating the back portion of the shell leads them to engage in defensive behaviors. They have demonstrated that this effect is dopamine dependent (Faure, Reynolds, Richard, & Berridge, 2008), and perhaps most interestingly, they have shown that the relative likelihood of approach and avoidance behaviors can be manipulated. When rats are placed in dark, quiet, comfortable environments, stimulation of most of the shell elicits approach behavior and only the back tip elicits avoidance; when they are instead placed in a bright, loud, unfamiliar environment, stimulation of most of the shell produces avoidance behavior, and only the very front elicits approach (Reynolds & Berridge, 2008). At least transiently, then, it is possible for the environment to shape

approach and avoidance tendencies via striatal pathways.

In humans, there is neuroimaging research that suggests a relation between striatal activation to reward cues and approach behavior. Numerous studies have shown that in functional magnetic resonance imaging studies, striatal BOLD response follows a prediction error pattern both to reward (Abler, Walter, Erk, Kammerer, & Spitzer, 2006; Cohen et al., 2010; Seymour, Daw, Dayan, Singer, & Dolan, 2007) and to punishment (Seymour et al., 2004, 2007). One study measuring prediction error response to reward cues showed that the amount of prediction error response in the striatum was related to subjects' self-reported levels of exploratory excitability and thrill and adventure seeking. Another study that examined prediction error response to novelty (Wittmann, Daw, Seymour, & Dolan, 2008) found that it was related to self-reported novelty seeking. Thus, it seems that enhanced sensitivity to particular types of salient stimuli in the striatal pathway is related to certain personality traits. Perhaps this could also be true for enhanced sensitivity to aversive stimuli? Indeed, perhaps the individual differences we found in our initial imaging study using the Monetary Incentive Delay task were specifically the result of an enhanced sensitivity to punishment.

Because the cues in our studies were ambiguous—they indicated an opportunity to perform correctly but also an opportunity to perform incorrectly—we could not infer from our findings whether inhibited individuals were showing greater striatal sensitivity to positive events, negative events, or both. To home in on this question, we examined striatal response to feedback on contingent trials in the second imaging study we had conducted, the reward contingency task (Bar-Haim et al., 2009). Because subjects were guessing on these trials, half the time they would receive positive feedback and half the time they would receive negative feedback. In this way, we could determine whether subjects showed heightened activation specifically to positive events, negative events, or both. Consistent with our hypothesis, we found (Helfinstein et al., 2011) that behaviorally inhibited subjects showed heightened striatal activation only to negative feedback; they actually showed reduced activation to positive feedback relative to their peers.

At present we are extending these findings in two directions. First, we are using an imaging paradigm with both rewarding and punishing cues

that vary in the level of prediction error they elicit. If behaviorally inhibited subjects display enhanced prediction errors to punishment, this should be seen in a prediction error paradigm, not just to a single negative and single positive stimulus, as we have already seen. Second, we are measuring approach and avoidance learning in the same subjects so that we can examine the relations between their striatal prediction error response and the ability to learn to approach and avoid. This is critical. We are trying to do more than simply describe neural correlates of behavioral inhibition; we wish to determine the underlying behavioral and neural mechanisms that are associated with a specific characteristic of the behaviorally inhibited phenotype: increased avoidance behavior.

The study of human infant and child temperament has much to contribute to understanding the mechanisms by which individual differences in social cognition emerge. From early childhood, some individuals are more disposed to withdraw rather than approach. We believe that this may be the result of a greater neural attentiveness to novelty (amygdala activation) and sensitivity to negative events (striatal activation) that makes it easier to learn to approach than avoid. These dispositions and learning mechanisms contribute to children's cognitions about the social world. While this model still needs to be carefully tested, for us the glass is definitely half-full as we move ahead with this program of research.

REFERENCES

Abler, B., Walter, H., Erk, S., Kammerer, H., & Spitzer, M. (2006). Prediction error as a linear function of reward probability is coded in human nucleus accumbens. *NeuroImage, 31*, 790–795.

Bar-Haim, Y., Fox, N., Benson, B., Guyer, A., Williams, A., Nelson, E.,...Ernst, M. (2009). Neural correlates of reward processing in adolescents with a history of inhibited temperament. *Psychological Science, 20*, 1009–1018.

Bogels, S. M., & Zigterman, D. (2000). Dysfunctional cognitions in children with social phobia, separation anxiety disorder, and generalized anxiety disorder. *Journal of Abnormal Child Psychology, 28*(2), 205–211.

Cohen, J., Asarnow, R., Sabb, F., Bilder, R., Bookheimer, S., Knowlton, B., & Poldrack, R. (2010). A unique adolescent response to reward prediction errors. *Nature Neuroscience, 13*(6), 669–671.

Faure, A., Reynolds, S., Richard, J., & Berridge, K. (2008). Mesolimbic dopamine in desire and dread: Enabling motivation to be generated by localized glutamate disruptions in nucleus accumbens. *Journal of Neuroscience, 28*, 7184–7192.

Fox, N. A., Henderson, H. A., Marshall, P. J., Nichols, K. E., & Ghera, M. M. (2005). Behavioral inhibition: Linking biology and behavior within a developmental framework. *Annual Review of Psychology, 56*, 235–262

Guyer, A., Nelson, E., Perez-Edgar, K., Hardin, M., Roberson-Nay, R., Monk, C.,...Ernst, M. (2006). Striatal functional alteration in adolescents characterized by early childhood behavioral inhibition. *Journal of Neuroscience, 26*, 6399–6405.

Helfinstein, S., Benson, B., Perez-Edgar, K., Bar-Haim, Y., Detloff, A., Pine, D.,...Ernst, M. (2011). Striatal responses to negative monetary outcomes differ between behaviorally inhibited and non-inhibited adolescents. *Neuropsychologia, 49*, 479–485.

Hollerman, J., & Schultz, W. (1998). Dopamine neurons report an error in the temporal prediction of reward during learning. *Nature Neuroscience, 1*, 304–309.

Horvitz, J. (2000). Mesolimbocortical and nigrostriatal dopamine responses to salient non-reward events. *Neuroscience, 96*, 651–656.

Kagan, J., Reznick, J. S., & Snidman, N. (1987). The physiology and psychology of behavioral inhibition in children. *Child Development, 58*, 1459–1473.

Kagan, J. J., & Snidman, N. (1991). Temperamental factors in human development. *American Psychologist, 46*, 856–862.

Knutson, B., Westdorp, A., Kaiser, E., & Hommer, D. (2000). FMRI visualization of brain activity during a monetary incentive delay task. *NeuroImage, 12*, 20–27.

Ljungberg, T., Apicella, P., & Schultz, W. (1992). Responses of monkey dopamine neurons during learning of behavioral reactions. *Journal of Neurophysiology, 67*, 145–163.

Mirenowicz, J., & Schultz, W. (1994). Importance of unpredictability for reward responses in primate dopamine neurons. *Journal of Neurophysiology, 72*, 1024–1027.

Mogenson, G., Jones, D., & Yim, C. (1980). From motivation to action: Functional interface between the limbic system and the motor system. *Progress in Neurobiology, 14*, 69–97.

Pérez-Edgar, K., Roberson-Nay, R., Hardin, M. G., Poeth, K., Guyer, A. E., Nelson, E. E.,...Ernst, M. (2007). Attention alters neural responses to evocative faces in behaviorally inhibited adolescents. *NeuroImage, 35*, 1538–1546.

Rescorla, R., & Wagner, A. (1972). A theory of pavlovian conditioning: Variations in the effectiveness of reinforcement and nonreinforcement. In A.H.

Black, & W.F. Prokasy (Eds.), *Classical conditioning II: Current research and theory* (pp. 64–99). New York: Appleton-Century-Crofts.

Reynolds, S., & Berridge, K. (2001). Fear and feeding in the nucleus accumbens shell: Rostrocaudal segregation of GABA-elicited defensive behavior versus eating behavior. *Journal of Neuroscience, 21*, 3261–3270.

Reynolds, S., & Berridge, K. (2002). Positive and negative motivation in nucleus accumbens shell: Bivalent rostrocaudal gradients for GABA-elicited eating, taste "liking"/"disliking" reactions, place preference/avoidance, and fear. *Journal of Neuroscience, 22*, 7308–7320.

Reynolds, S., & Berridge, K. (2008). Emotional environments retune the valence of appetitive versus fearful functions in nucleus accumbens. *Nature Neuroscience, 11*, 423.

Romo, R., & Schultz, W. (1990). Dopamine neurons of the monkey midbrain: Contingencies of responses to active touch during self-initiated arm movements. *Journal of Neurophysiology, 63*, 592–606.

Schmidt, L. A., Fox, N. A., Rubin, K. H., Sternberg, E. M., Gold, P. W., Smith, C. C., & Schulkin, J. (1997). Behavioral and neuroendocrine responses in shy children. *Developmental Psychobiology, 30*, 127–140.

Schultz, W. (1986). Responses of midbrain dopamine neurons to behavioral trigger stimuli in the monkey. *Journal of Neurophysiology, 56*, 1439–1461.

Schultz, W., Dayan, P., & Montague, P. (1997). A neural substrate of prediction and reward. *Science, 275*, 1593–1599.

Schwartz, C. E., Wright, C. I., Shin, L. M., Kagan, J., & Rauch, S. L. (2003). Inhibited and uninhibited infants "grown up": Adult amygdalar response to novelty. *Science, 300*, 1952–1953.

Seymour, B., Daw, N., Dayan, P., Singer, T., & Dolan, R. (2007). Differential encoding of losses and gains in the human striatum. *Journal of Neuroscience, 27*, 4826–4831.

Seymour, B., O'Doherty, J., Dayan, P., Koltzenburg, M., Jones, A., Dolan, R., ... Frackowiak, R. S. (2004). Temporal difference models describe higher-order learning in humans. *Nature, 429*, 664.

Sorg, B., & Kalivas, P. (1991). Effects of cocaine and footshock stress on extracellular dopamine levels in the ventral striatum. *Brain Research, 559*, 29–36.

Taghavi, M. R., Moradi, A. R., Neshat Doost, H. T., Yule, W., & Dalgleish, T. (2000). Interpretation of ambiguous emotional information in clinically anxious children and adolescents. *Cognition and Emotion, 14*(6), 809–822.

Waters, A. M., Wharton, T. A., Zimmer-Gembeck, M. J., & Craske, M. G. (2008). Threat-based cognitive biases in anxious children: Comparison with non-anxious children before and after cognitive behavioural treatment. *Behavioral Research Therapy, 46*(3), 358–374.

Wittmann, B., Daw, N., Seymour, B., & Dolan, R. (2008). Striatal activity underlies novelty-based choice in humans. *Neuron, 58*, 967–973.

Young, A., Joseph, M., & Gray, J. (1993). Latent inhibition of conditioned dopamine release in rat nucleus accumbens. *Neuroscience, 54*, 5–9.

1.11

Emotion and Learning

New Approaches to the Old Nature-Nurture Debate

SETH D. POLLAK

Traditional approaches to understanding the origins of social behavior tend to be hybrids of two venerable perspectives. One, a nativist approach, is that humans are biologically prepared to develop and behave in certain ways; on this view, the basic building blocks of emotions are hardwired into the brain. The other approach is empiricist or constructivist and focuses more on the roles of observation and modeling in shaping the schemas through which social interactions are interpreted. But most theories of socioemotional development end up in a nature-nurture gridlock of "easy" answers that attempt to accommodate both views and ultimately explain very little about exactly how it is that change in behavior occurs across development. In this chapter, I suggest that current advances in the neurobiology of learning are a fruitful way to examine the mechanisms that underlie children's acquisition of social skills.

While the old nature-nurture conundrum is always fun for impassioned debate, an exciting current perspective in socioemotional development concerns questions about how our brains instantiate behavioral change. How is it that our social experiences subsequently shape our thoughts, feelings, and behaviors? My own research has begun to integrate the neurobiology of learning into these questions. The history of psychology is rich with examples of the immediacy and power of basic learning processes. For example, we need only become ill once to create a strong food aversion, and changes in the frequency of reward schedules can quickly change behavior. Contemporary aspects of learning theory have enriched and even dominated some fields, such as the understanding of drug addiction and sensory perception. But this research has not yet infused the study of socioemotional development. This may be because the learning theories so dominant

a half-century ago seem stale to psychologists interested in thoughts and feelings.

There is, however, compelling evidence that basic learning theories can uncover rich information about powerful sources of human motivation. My own interest in bridging the neurobiology of learning with the development of socioemotional behavior came from studies of parent–child bonding in rodents. As an example, experimental disruption of reward circuitry in the brain prevents mice pups from emitting vocalizations when removed from their mothers; interfering with brain reward systems also prevents mice from showing a preference for their own mothers (Moles, Kieffer, & D'Amato, 2004). This association also works in the opposite direction: When attachment to the parent is disrupted, other aspects of the animals' reward systems are also affected. For example, animals with disrupted attachments to their parents also have abnormal responses to novelty, altered appetitive conditioning, and unusually high sensitivity to dopamine antagonists and reactivity to other drug administrations (for review, see Matthews & Robbins, 2003). This type of data has led me to think of emotions like love and affection as operating on the brain in the same way—and perhaps through the same learning mechanisms—as drugs; after all, in different ways, both are rewarding.

LEARNING AND SOCIOEMOTIONAL DEVELOPMENT

My research has focused upon the emotional development of school-aged children who have had adverse early experiences as a way to better understand the processes of emotional development. We have learned a tremendous amount about the role of the social environment from studying children who have been maltreated by the adults who ought to have been providing protection and security for them. Children who have suffered physical abuse are exposed to inconsistent or poorly conveyed emotional signals in their environments. The adults responsible for their care tend to vacillate between extreme emotional states and social withdrawal (Shackman et al., 2010). Yet these social interactions are the primary basis upon which these children begin to learn about their social environment. We hypothesized that this social context might affect the brain regions associated with learning which features of the environment lead to reward or punishment.

We have found that 4- to 6-year old children who are neglected have difficulty differentiating facial expressions of emotion—for example, perceiving that a facial expression is sad rather than angry (Pollak, Cicchetti, Hornung, & Reed, 2000). Conversely, children who have been physically abused appear to become very adept at recognizing cues of anger and hostility (Pollak, Vardi, Putzer Bechner, & Curtin, 2005; Shackman, Shackman, & Pollak, 2007). These patterns reflect ways in which the environment, through learning, directs children's attention to salient and meaningful information. A recent study suggests that these processes influence children's social cognition. Five- and six-year-old abused children in our study believed that almost any kind of interpersonal situation could result in an adult becoming angry; in contrast, most other children saw anger as likely only in particular interpersonal circumstances (Perlman, Kalish, & Pollak, 2008).

The results from these experiments raise new questions about how probabilistic information about other people's behaviors becomes instantiated in children's thinking about their social interactions. Given that children have a limited processing capacity and that there are limitless aspects of the world that can be attended to at any given moment, it may be the case that abused children prioritize negative social cues at the expense of positive cues. Consistent with this view, on a probabilistic reward task, most children respond more quickly as their chances of winning a reward increases. In contrast, maltreated children were not sensitive to the likelihood of reward (Guyer et al., 2006). And primate models also report that maltreated monkeys display less interest in rewards relative to control monkeys (Pryce, Dettling, Spengler, Schnell, & Feldon, 2004).

A potentially important implication of this focus on sensitivity to reward concerns the high rates of depression experienced by maltreated individuals. Although depression is frequently considered to be a problem involving sadness, one of the core symptoms is anhedonia, or reduced experience of pleasure. Indeed, depressed adults experience less pleasure and less reward-related brain activity than nondepressed individuals (Knutson, Bhanji, Cooney, Atlas, & Gotlib, 2008). Impairments in reward learning may lead to reduced engagement with positive stimuli in the environment; such deficits have been linked to problems in social functioning (Fareri, Martin, & Delgado, 2008; Finger et al., 2011). My own work has also suggested that in addition to overattending to threat, 10-year-old abused children underattend to positive cues, which may undermine feelings of safety and pose risk for aggression or depression (Pollak & Tolley-Schell, 2003).

CANDIDATE NEURAL SYSTEMS

There are some clues about which brain mechanisms are ripe for exploration about learning and social cognition. These include the basal ganglia (BG) and orbitofrontal cortex (OFC), which seem to represent the outcomes of situations that the organism has experienced. The BG is a diverse network of subcortical structures that work in concert to orchestrate and execute planned, motivated behaviors that require integration of movement, thinking, and feeling (Haber, 2003). The OFC is a rapidly flexible associative-learning area that is crucial for signaling outcome expectancies such as reward/punishment and the regulation of flexible behavior (Kringelbach & Rolls, 2004). Current thinking is that the BG guides learning based on assessments of the probability of a positive outcome, while the OFC represents gain–loss information and, together, these systems provide a robust way for the organism to learn from and adapt to the environment (Frank & Claus, 2006). As expected, impairments in these systems are associated with poor learning from environmental cues.

With regard to social cognition, it is especially interesting that OFC neurons do not stop firing in response to the reward after learning, suggesting that these neurons support predictions on the basis of afferent input and anticipation prior to other emotion-processing regions such as the amygdala (Schoenbaum, Roesch, Stalnaker, & Takahashi, 2009). Consistent with this view, damage to the OFC causes deficits in reversal learning, reduces the speed of reward learning, and is activated in humans during processes such as regret and counterfactual reasoning (Honey, Kotter, Breakspear, & Sporns, 2007; Murray & Wise, 2010; Passingham, Stephan, & Kotter, 2002). Common to these examples is the need to signal, in real time, information about outcomes predicted by circumstances in the environment. Some emerging evidence suggests functional changes in the OFC and BG during reward processing in adolescents, further suggesting that these systems are a source of developmental changes in social behavior (Galvan et al., 2006).

There is also some evidence that functioning of these systems may account, in part, for how early-life stressors confer pervasive lifetime risks for children. Many kinds of early-life stressors (e.g., maternal separation, social defeat, chronic stress exposure, abuse) appear to alter neurotransmitters and receptors in the BG that are subsequently associated with impairments in learning (DeSteno & Schmauss, 2010). Child maltreatment has been associated with lower BG recruitment during a reward task (Mehta et al., 2010), and research from my own lab has found that children who experienced early-life stress have smaller brain volumes in the OFC (Hanson et al., 2010).

CONCLUSION
The concept of learning situates brain development within an environmental context. Integrating research and methods about the neurobiology of reward learning, in particular, may prove to be a powerful way to test novel hypotheses about children's developing abilities to understand social cues and regulate social behavior. Successful social adaptation reflects children's ability to learn from complex and varied interpersonal experiences. Children need to discern cues for approach versus withdrawal, which actions lead to punishments versus rewards, which behaviors lead to success in having their needs and desires met. These processes become increasingly intricate and fine-tuned as relevant neuroanatomical and neurobiological systems develop and as the range, complexity, and amount of social information increase for the developing child.

Although psychologists often like to see their subjects of study—emotion, language, social cognition, visual perception—as distinct from other domains of behavior, it may well be the case that general processes underlie many aspects of early learning. In this regard, there may be similarities in the neural processes that children use to track and encode features of their environments, parse and categorize these inputs into meaningful units,

and begin to experience these interactions with the sensory world as rewarding or punishing. For this reason, the infusion of new perspectives and experimental techniques, such as those from the neurobiology of learning, can advance the study of social cognition.

A focus on learning processes allows us to formulate questions about which neural mechanisms we use to process socioemotional information, how these mechanisms are themselves shaped by social context, why adverse social environments confer risks for children, and, perhaps, what sorts of neurally informed interventions might remediate deficits in social cognition.

ACKNOWLEDGMENTS
The writing of this chapter was supported by the National Institute of Mental Health through grant number R01-MH61285.

REFERENCES
Desteno, D., & Schmauss, C. (2009). A role for dopamine D2 receptors in reversal learning. *Neuroscience, 162*, 118–127.

Fareri, D., Martin, L., & Delgado, M. (2008). Reward-related processing in the human brain: Developmental considerations. *Development and Psychopathology, 20*, 1191–1211.

Finger, E., Marsh, A., Blair, K., Reid, M., Sims, C., & Ng, P. (2011). Disrupted reinforcement signaling in the orbitofrontal cortex and caudate in youths with conduct disorder or oppositional defiant disorder and a high level of psychopathic traits. *American Journal of Psychiatry, 168*(2), 152–162.

Frank, M., & Claus, E. (2006). Anatomy of a decision: Striato-orbitofrontal interactions in reinforcement learning, decision making, and reversal. *Psychological Review, 113*(2), 300–326.

Galvan, A., Hare, T. A., Parra, C. E., Penn, J., Voss, H., Glover, G., & Casey, B. J. (2006). Earlier development of the accumbens relative to orbitofrontal cortex might underlie risk-taking behavior in adolescents. *Journal of Neuroscience, 26*(25), 6885–6892.

Guyer, A., Kaufman, J., Hodgdon, H., Masten, C., Jazbec, S., Pine, D., & Ernst, M. (2006). Behavioral alterations in reward system function: The role of childhood maltreatment and psychopathology. *Journal of the American Academy of Child and Adolescent Psychiatry, 45*(9), 1059–1067.

Haber, S. (2003). The primate basal ganglia: Parallel and integrative networks. *Journal of Chemical Neuroanatomy, 26*(4), 317–330.

Hanson, J., Chung, M., Avants, B., Shirtcliff, E., Gee, J., Davidson, R., & Pollak, S. D. (2010). Early stress is associated with alterations in the orbitofrontal cortex: A tensor-based morphometry investigation of brain structure and behavioral risk. *Journal of Neuroscience, 30*(22), 7466–7472.

Honey, C. J., Kotter, R., Breakspear, M., & Sporns, O. (2007). Network structure of cerebral cortex shapes functional connectivity on multiple time scales. *Proceedings of the National Academy of Sciences USA, 104*(24), 10240–10245.

Knutson, B., Bhanji, J. P., Cooney, R. E., Atlas, L. Y., & Gotlib, I. H. (2008). Neural responses to monetary incentives in major depression. *Biological Psychiatry, 63*, 686–692.

Kringelbach, M., & Rolls, E. (2004). The functional neuroanatomy of the human orbitofrontal cortex: Evidence from neuroimaging and neuropsychology. *Progress in Neurobiology, 72*(5), 341–372.

Matthews, K., & Robbins, T. (2003). Early experience as a determinant of adult behavioural responses to reward: The effects of repeated maternal separation in the rat. *Neuroscience and Biobehavioral Reviews, 27*(1–2), 45–55.

Mehta, M., Gore-Langton, E., Golembo, N., Colvert, E., Williams, S., & Sonuga-Barke, E. (2010). Hyporesponsive reward anticipation in the basal ganglia following severe institutional deprivation early in life. *Journal of Cognitive Neuroscience, 22*(10), 2316–2325.

Moles, A., Kieffer, B., & D'Amato, F. (2004). Deficit in attachment behavior in mice lacking the mu-opioid receptor gene. *Science, 304*(5679), 1983–1986.

Murray, E. A., & Wise, S. P. (2010). Interactions between orbital prefrontal cortex and amygdala: advanced cognition, learned responses and instinctive behaviors. *Current Opinion in Neurobiology, 20*(2), 212.

Murray, E. A., Wise, S. P., & Rhodes, S. E. V. (2011). What can different brains do with reward? In J. A. Gottfried (Ed.), *The neurobiology of sensation and reward* (pp. 61–98). Boca Raton, FL: Taylor & Francis.

Passingham, R. E., Stephan, K. E., & Kotter, R. (2002). The anatomical basis of functional localization in the cortex. *Nature Reviews Neuroscience, 3*(8), 606–616.

Perlman, S., Kalish, C., & Pollak, S. D. (2008). The role of maltreatment experience in children's understanding of the antecedents of emotion. *Cognition and Emotion, 22*(4), 651–670.

Pollak, S. D., & Tolley-Schell, S. A. (2003). Selective attention to facial emotion in physically abused children. *Journal of Abnormal Psychology, 112*, 323–338.

Pollak, S. D., Cicchetti, D., Hornung, K., & Reed, A. (2000). Recognizing emotion in faces: Developmental effects of child abuse and neglect. *Developmental Psychology, 36*(5), 679–688.

Pollak, S. D., Vardi, S., Putzer Bechner, A., & Curtin, J. (2005). Physically abused children's regulation of attention in response to hostility. *Child Development, 76*(5), 968–977.

Pryce, C., Dettling, A., Spengler, M., Schnell, C., & Feldon, J. (2004). Deprivation of parenting disrupts development of homeostatic and reward systems in marmoset monkey offspring. *Biological Psychiatry, 56*(2), 72–79.

Schoenbaum, G., Roesch, M. R., Stalnaker, T. A., & Takahashi, Y. K. (2009). A new perspective on the role of the orbitofrontal cortex in adaptive behaviour. *Nature Reviews Neuroscience, 10*(12), 885–892.

Shackman, J., Fatani, S., Camras, L., Berkowitz, M., Bachorowski, J-A., & Pollak, S. D. (2010). Emotion expression among abusive mothers is associated with their children's emotion processing and problem behaviours. *Cognition and Emotion, 24*(8), 1421–1430.

Shackman, J., Shackman, A., & Pollak, S. (2007). Physical abuse amplifies attention to threat and increases anxiety in children. *Emotion, 7*(4), 838–852.

1.12

Early Childhood Is Where Many Adult Automatic Processes Are Born

JOHN A. BARGH

Research on the development of adult social cognitive processes has the potential to revolutionize the way we think about adult social cognition—especially those forms that operate implicitly, automatically, or unconsciously. Traditionally, the development of automatic processes has been understood in terms of *skill acquisition*, processes that start out as conscious and intentional, and only after considerable experience become capable of operating nonconsciously (e.g., Shiffrin & Schneider, 1977). By this dominant view, then, all processes start out as conscious and strategic, and only become unconscious after considerable use. However, this basic assumption has blinded us, historically speaking, to the possibility that unconsciously or implicitly operating influences could be present and operating at birth or soon thereafter, influences gleaned over the eons through the workings of natural selection or through the considerable early experiences of the child.

In other words, "not all automatic processes are habit forming" (Bargh, 2001). Evidence that this was the case started to emerge about 10 years ago, when Duckworth et al. (2002) published data indicating the "automatic attitude activation" effect held for novel as well as familiar attitude objects. Up until then, these automatic activation capabilities were believed to develop out of frequent and consistent expression of a given attitude, which increased that attitude's "strength" or accessibility to the point where its activation was automatic upon the mere perception of the attitude object. But if the effect held for entirely novel stimuli (e.g., nonrepresentational art, nonsense sounds), then clearly extensive experience with the attitude object was not needed for the automatic evaluation effect.

The Duckworth et al. (2002) findings suggested that automatic processes operating in adult social cognition were not all the result of

extensive experience or skill acquisition. Some instead appear to be natural and perhaps innate mechanisms that would be expected therefore to have clear survival value. An immediate default first-pass screening of one's current environment in terms of positive (beneficial) versus negative (dangerous) would seem to be of clear utility to the individual (e.g., LeDoux, 1996), especially if, as research has found, these automatic appraisals then produce immediate approach and avoidance behavioral tendencies (Chen & Bargh, 1999), even for the entirely novel stimuli in the Duckworth et al. (2002, Study 3) experiments. If the automatic evaluation mechanism is innate, we should be able to observe its operation in young childhood, prior to the individual having the extensive experience with the world of attitude objects. Indeed, recent research has demonstrated automatic social evaluation effects in preschool children (Dunham, Baron, & Banaji, 2008), with immediate implicit biases in favor of in-group over out-group members.

At about the same time there was an even more dramatic demonstration that automatic social cognition was not the exclusive domain of adults. Ambady et al. (2001) showed that even children as young as 5 years of age showed stereotype-priming effects on their behavior. Asian American girls primed with line drawings of two Asian American children together (in order to activate the Asian aspect of their social identities) were found to outperform the other children on an age-appropriate math test; but if the female aspect of their identities had been primed instead with drawings of two (non-Asian) girls together, this same group of girls performed significantly less well than the other groups. This startling finding revealed not only that cultural stereotypes were already so ingrained in the minds of preschool children that they could be activated implicitly or nonconsciously (shocking news in its own right), but that (even worse news) these stereotypes could operate automatically and unconsciously to influence the children's actual academic performance (i.e., stereotype threat effects).

However, from the vantage point of evolutionary biology, the discovery of adult-like automatic processes in young children makes much more sense. "Open-ended" genetic programs and influences (Mayr, 1976) operate in interaction with the infant's local environment as a second wave of fine-tuning, of learning what is safe and appropriate (socially safe) behavior and what is not. Recent developmental research such as the Ambady et al. (2001) study shows that children do indeed quickly and voraciously "soak up" these cultural norms and influences through natural imitation tendencies (e.g., Meltzoff & Moore, 1983), which shape their behavior and later their beliefs to be in line with those of their parents and peers and other cultural inputs (e.g., from television). As Pinker (1994) noted, you can take any newborn and transport him or her to any part of the world, and that child will quickly learn the local language and cultural norms and values as well as those children who were born there. Open-ended genetic programs such as those involved in language (and culture) acquisition enable very young children to adapt quickly to wherever in the world and at what point in history they happen to be born. To take another example of this "second-wave" cultural absorption process, newborn infants do not show any preference for same-race faces at birth (an innate or "first-wave" effect), but they do show this preference after only 3 months (Kelly et al., 2005).

Early childhood is the origin of many of the implicit effects that social cognition researchers demonstrate in adults. The early concepts formed during this period serve as the basis for later developing, abstract concepts and thus are also an important "bridge" to language acquisition (Mandler, 1992; Williams, Huang, & Bargh, 2009). In this way the implicit groundwork being laid by early life experiences continues to exert an influence through life, as the associative connections formed between the early and later concepts enable the former to prime the latter in an entirely unconscious, unseen manner. Illustrative of the importance of early childhood to the later operation of implicit effects is the finding that implicit measures of stereotyping and prejudice reveal no change in the size of implicit bias effects from early childhood through adolescence and adulthood, whereas measures of explicit bias and prejudice show a significant decrease over the same period (Dunham et al., 2008). And we will not have explicit knowledge or access to these influences, so they are able to operate to influence our feelings, judgments, and behavior outside of our conscious awareness.

Scholars in diverse fields (developmental psychology, philosophy of mind) have argued that many of the earliest concepts to develop in infancy and preverbal childhood are those having to do with the physical world, and with physical experiences (e.g., Clark, 1973; Lakoff & Johnson, 1980; Mandler, 1992). Most important, these early concepts should then be used as the basis for the later development of more abstract concepts, as argued by Mandler (1992) in her model of language acquisition. Lakoff and Johnson (1980) held that the use of these early physical concepts in the formation of more abstract concepts is the reason for our pervasive metaphorical use of these physical concepts to describe social and psychological phenomena (among others), as in a "close relationship," a "hard bargainer," and a "warm father."

Williams et al. (2009) hypothesized that the close associations formed in early childhood between basic physical concepts and more abstract psychological concepts built or "scaffolded" onto them (e.g., warm, distant, soft, high, backward) should enable one level to prime the other, and indeed many such physical or metaphoric priming effects are now being demonstrated. Briefly holding something warm causes a person to perceive another person as socially "warm" (friendly, generous) and also to behave oneself in a warm, generous manner (Williams & Bargh, 2008). And the priming effects are bidirectional, as (in the case of the physical temperature metaphor) experiencing social "coldness" (exclusion from a group) causes people to estimate the room temperature as being colder than otherwise (Zhong & Leonardelli, 2008). Similar physical-to-psychological effects have been demonstrated for physical distance manipulations (creating emotional and psychological distance effects; Williams & Bargh, 2008), manipulations of haptic (touch) physical sensations (e.g., sitting on hard chairs causes negotiators to take a "hard line" and compromise less than those sitting on soft chairs; Ackerman, Nocera, & Bargh, 2010), verticality (the "your highness" effect in which "up" is related to power; Schubert, 2005), among many others (see Landau, Meier, & Keefer, 2010).

If the physical experience primes or activates the corresponding psychological concept, then our daily life in the physical world provides many, perhaps even continuous priming experiences. But as we assume that the very early development of these associations makes them as opaque to explicit access as our memories of very early childhood experiences, these priming effects will operate only at an implicit level. Now, think of the boon these implicit connections would be for the self-regulation of emotion and other psychological states. The negative emotional impact of socially "cold" experiences such as being rejected or excluded by others could then be ameliorated at least to some extent by the self-application of physical warmth. Yet the implicit nature of the effect prevents us from consciously knowing about it and using it strategically. Therefore, if we were found to make use of these physical-to-social associations in response to threat or social need states (belonging, affiliation), it would have to be a case of *implicit self-regulation.* hmm

A recent study of the substitutability of physical warmth for missing social warmth (Bargh & Shalev, 2012) has documented such implicit use of the physical-psychological associations we assume develop in early childhood. Two correlational studies revealed a significant correlation between loneliness (social coldness) and extraction of warmth from bathing activity, which can be done either by taking warm baths or showers more often, using higher temperature water, or staying under the warm water longer each time. Further experimental tests showed that the social coldness produced by being excluded by a group, which usually triggers a compensatory need to affiliate with others, was eliminated by merely holding something physically warm. The physical warmth experience thus satisfied the need for social warmth produced by the rejection experience. However, our participants showed no explicit awareness of the effect of physical warmth on their emotional state or affiliative needs.

Thus, people tend to make use of implicit mechanisms to self-regulate their emotional state in the absence of explicit knowledge of the underlying mechanism or actual reason for their warmth-seeking behavior. The absence of explicit awareness of this effect is even more surprising given how pervasive the "warm" and "cold" metaphors are in everyday language use. Indeed, the metaphorical connection between physical and social coldness can be found in writings as long as 2,000 years ago. First, Dante in the *Inferno* (ca. 1308 AD) reserved the lowest circle of Hell for those who betrayed the trust of others (extreme social coldness) and assigned them the "poetic justice" of being frozen in ice for all eternity. (This

[margin note: Lady Macbeth washing hands]

punishment is even more remarkable in the midst of an otherwise fiery location.) But Dante himself was influenced by the Apocalypse of St. Peter, written in the first century AD, which referred to hell as "rivers of fire, and of ice for the cold-hearted" (see Bargh & Shalev, 2011).

The physical-to-psychological associations formed in early childhood thus bubble up in our language and poetic expression and even our self-regulatory behavior, but all at an implicit level. The substitutability of physical for social warmth in daily language and behavior thus serves as a prototypic example of how the associative connections formed in early childhood continue to affect our behavior and phenomenal experiences throughout the rest of life, but in the absence of any explicit access or conscious appreciation of this impact.

The same principles are argued to apply to motivations and goal pursuits (Williams et al., 2009), such that later acquired, more abstract motivations at the psychological and social level are hypothesized to scaffold onto more basic, innate physical motivational circuits, such as for survival and safety. In a classic recent example, cleansing one's hands (physical purity) is found to "wash away guilt" (abstract, moral purity) induced by remembering a time when one transgressed against others (the "MacBeth effect"; Zhong & Liljenquist, 2006). Relatedly, Huang et al. (in press) have shown that satisfying concrete physical self-protection needs also satisfies the social self-protection needs scaffolded onto them—that is, after receiving an inoculation against the flu virus (thus protecting them from physical "invasion" by viruses), people are significantly less prejudiced against out-group members than they were before the inoculation. (Note that the scaffolding principle applies equally to phylogenetic as well as ontogenetic concept development, so that potentially innate social motives such as for cooperation and helping [e.g., Tomasello, Carpenter, Call, Behne, & Moll, 2005] would also be expected to have close associational ties to the physical concept substrate.)

In conclusion, recent theoretical (especially embodiment and neural reuse) and empirical developments have cast strong doubt on the exclusively "habit formation" model of adult automatic or unconscious processes. The habit-formation assumption continues to blind much of the field of psychology (especially in the areas of self-regulation and social cognition) from the possibility that automatic and unconscious influences are operating in childhood as well as adulthood, and from taking seriously the principles of evolution and natural selection that strongly imply the presence of innate concepts and structures operating in early childhood as well as throughout the life span. The research described earlier illustrates the viability of this evolutionary approach and of taking seriously the role of early childhood experiences in the development of implicit or automatic social cognitive processes, including implicit self-regulatory strategies. For all of these reasons, I for one am "all in" for the continued and expanded study of developmental social cognition, a research area that will significantly advance our understanding not only of how adult social cognitive processes develop but of human nature itself.

REFERENCES

Ackerman, J. M., Nocera, C. C., & Bargh, J. A. (2010). Incidental haptic sensations influence social judgments. *Science, 328,* 1712–1715.

Ambady, N., Shih, M., Kim, A., & Pittinsky, T. L. (2001). Stereotype susceptibility in children: Effects of identity activation on quantitative performance. *Psychological Science, 12,* 385–390.

Bargh, J. A. (2001). Caution: Automatic social cognition may not be habit forming. *Polish Psychological Bulletin, 32,* 1–8.

Bargh, J. A., & Shalev, I. (2012). The substitutibility of physical and social warmth in everyday life. *Emotion, 12,* 154–162.

Chen, M., & Bargh, J. A. (1999). Consequences of automatic evaluation: Immediate behavioral predispositions to approach or avoid the stimulus. *Personality and Social Psychology Bulletin, 25,* 215–224.

Clark, H. H. (1973). Space, time, semantics, and the child. In T. E. Moore (Ed.), *Cognitive development and the acquisition of language* (pp. 27–63). New York: Academic Press.

Duckworth, K. L., Bargh, J. A., Garcia, M., & Chaiken, S. (2002). The automatic evaluation of novel stimuli. *Psychological Science, 13,* 513–519.

Dunham, Y., Baron, A. S., & Banaji, M. R. (2008). The development of implicit intergroup cognition. *Trends in Cognitive Sciences, 12,* 248–253.

Huang, J. Y., Ackerman, J. M., Sedlovskaya, A., & Bargh, J. A. (2011). Inoculation against physical disease removes bias against social outgroups. *Psychological Science, 22,* 1550–1556.

Kelly, D. J., Quinn, P. C., Slater, A. M., Lee, K., Gibson, A., Smith, M., … Pascalis, O. (2005). Three-month-olds, but not newborns, prefer own-race faces. *Developmental Science, 8,* F31–F36.

Lakoff, G., & Johnson, M. (1980). *Metaphors we live by.* Chicago, IL: University of Chicago Press.

Landau, M. J., Meier, B. P., & Keefer, L. A. (2010). A metaphor-enriched social cognition. *Psychological Bulletin, 136,* 1045–1067.

LeDoux, J. E. (1996). *The emotional brain.* New York: Simon & Schuster.

Mandler, J. M. (1992). How to build a baby: II. Conceptual primitives. *Psychological Review, 99,* 587–604.

Mayr, E. (1976). *Evolution and the diversity of life.* Cambridge, MA: Harvard University Press.

Meltzoff, A. N., & Moore, M. K. (1983). Newborn infants imitate adult facial gestures. *Child Development, 54,* 702–709.

Pinker, S. (1994). *The language instinct.* New York: William Morrow.

Schubert, T. W. (2005). Your Highness: Vertical positions as perceptual symbols of power. *Journal of Personality and Social Psychology, 89,* 1–21.

Shiffrin, R. M., & Schneider, W. (1977). Controlled and automatic human information processing: II. Perceptual learning, automatic attending, and a general theory. *Psychological Review, 84,* 127–190.

Tomasello, M., Carpenter, M., Call, J., Behne, T., & Moll, H. (2005). Understanding and sharing intentions: The origins of cultural cognition. *Behavioral and Brain Sciences, 28,* 675–691.

Williams, L. E., & Bargh, J. A. (2008). Experiencing physical warmth promotes interpersonal warmth. *Science, 322,* 606–607.

Williams, L. E., Huang, J. Y., & Bargh, J. A. (2009). The scaffolded mind: Higher mental processes are grounded in early experience of the physical world. *European Journal of Social Psychology, 39,* 1257–1267.

Zhong, C-B., & Leonardelli, G. J. (2008). Cold and lonely: Does social exclusion literally feel cold? *Psychological Science, 19,* 838–842.

Zhong, C-B., & Liljenquist, K. (2006). Washing away your sins: Threatened morality and physical cleansing. *Science, 313,* 1451–1452.

1.13

Social Evaluation

GAIL D. HEYMAN

In 2008, voters in California faced a ballot proposition to redefine marriage so as to exclude same-sex couples. Several children in my daughter's first-grade classroom demanded that each student declare a position on this proposition, and then refused to associate with those who reported a position that differed from their own. The fact that the children who were directing this informal polling effort were not able to answer even the most basic questions about the nature of the proposition did not seem to get in the way of the impassioned positions they had staked out. I will argue that the eagerness of young children to make these types of evaluative judgments plays a central role in their social-cognitive development, a role that is often overlooked or misunderstood.

The tendency to view the social world through an evaluative lens begins early. Children as young as 2 years apply terms such as "nice" and "naughty" to people (Bretherton & Beeghly, 1982) and seek to police violations of social rules (Rakoczy, Warneken, & Tomasello, 2008; Ross & Bak-Lammers, 1998). Even preverbal infants assess individuals with reference to the positive or negative behaviors that they direct toward others (Hamlin, Wynn, & Bloom, 2007).

To date, developmental psychologists have often treated children's tendency to make social evaluations as a potential artifact to be controlled for (e.g., when measuring reasoning ability; Alvarez, Ruble, & Bolger, 2001; Heyman, 2009; Liu, Gelman, & Wellman, 2007; Ruble & Dweck, 1995), and there is no question that it can make research findings more difficult to interpret. However, this possible source of methodological noise is worthy of careful examination in its own right.

INSIGHTS INTO CHILDREN'S COGNITIVE DEVELOPMENT

Limitations in Critical Thinking

By examining children's evaluative judgments we can gain insights into limitations in their critical thinking skills. Although children may be capable of making rational assessments when they evaluate others as sources of information (Gelman, 2009; Harris, 2007; Heyman, 2008), their judgments can be colored by the perceived desirability of potential outcomes. Woolley, Boerger, and Markman (2004) told young children about an imaginary being named "the Candy Witch" who visits children's homes to offer them new toys in exchange for candy. The participants in a 4- to 5-year-old group who preferred toys to candy, and presumably had more to gain by a visit from the Candy Witch, were more willing to accept that she is real than were other 4- and 5-year-olds.

Desirability-related effects have been seen even among children who have no personal stake in the outcome. Heyman, Fu, and Lee (in press) presented 7- and 10-year-olds from the United States and China with scenarios in which they were asked to assess the credibility of teachers' evaluations of unfamiliar peers. In one scenario, a teacher told a student that her essay was the best in the class, and in another a teacher told a student that her essay was the worst in the class. Children within each age group in each country showed a pattern of *selective skepticism*, in which they reported that they found the less desirable evaluations to be less credible. One child illustrated this pattern of reasoning by saying, "When a teacher compliments your work you should take pride in it, but if a teacher doesn't compliment your work, it's only one person, so it doesn't mean much."

Children younger than 8 years seem to have difficulty reasoning about the possibility that people are not always motivated to accurately communicate what they know. Heyman and Legare (2005) found that a group of 6- and 7-year-olds assumed that people can be trusted to accurately report on their own level of honesty. Participants frequently justified this assumption with reference to the moral imperative to tell the truth, as one child explained: "If you ask them to tell the truth, then they better tell the truth; otherwise it would be a lie."

Young children have difficulty rejecting the advice of individuals who have antisocial motives. Vanderbilt, Liu, and Heyman (2011) found that 4-year-olds followed the advice of an individual who had a history of lying, even after predicting that the lying would continue in the future. Heyman, Sritanyaratana, and Vanderbilt (in press) found evidence suggesting that children's failure to reject advice in this context is due to a difficulty with representing an individual as having a prosocial motive (i.e., the willingness to offer advice) and an antisocial motive (i.e., the intent to deceive) simultaneously (see also Mascaro & Sperber, 2009).

Children's Cognitive Capacities

The way children make evaluative judgments can offer insights into their reasoning abilities, including their capacity to take into account the psychological and interpersonal context in which behavior occurs. Children as young as 5 years are more critical of peers whose actions upset others if they are told that negative consequences had been anticipated (Heyman & Gelman, 1998). When evaluating the prosocial tendencies of others, children are sensitive to perceived fairness in the distribution of resources (Ng, Heyman, & Barner, 2011).

Young children also show context sensitivity in their interactions with individuals who exhibit positive and negative personal qualities. Cluver, Heyman, and Carver (in press) found that 32- to 36-month-olds who were faced with a problem-solving task tended to seek help from an individual who appeared competent and friendly, rather than one who appeared incompetent and unfriendly. However, all of their spontaneous offers of help were directed toward the individual who appeared incompetent and unfriendly, who presumably was in greater need of assistance. This finding suggests that young children do not always apply a simple heuristic of approaching individuals who behave in ways that are associated with positive traits and avoiding those who behave in ways that are associated with negative traits.

IMPLICATIONS FOR INTERPERSONAL PROCESSES

Once children reach an evaluative conclusion, they may need to decide whether to convey it to others. To make these decisions effectively, children must take a range of possible consequences into account. For example, a decision about whether to tell a teacher about a rule violation may involve anticipating the reactions of the teacher, the transgressor, and other classmates.

Each potential audience for the evaluation may carry a different set of dynamics, such as gratitude from classmates for an effort to enforce rules that prevent harm and promote fairness, or hostility and accusations of disloyalty. To address children's reasoning about this type of dilemma, Loke, Heyman, Forgie, MacCarthy, and Lee (2011) asked 6- to 11-year-olds to respond to scenarios in which a child observes a classmate committing a transgression and decides to inform the teacher about it or keep quiet. Both older and younger participants approved the reporting of serious violations, but there were strong age-related differences in judgments about minor transgressions. For example, although 6- to 7-year-olds and 10- to 11-year-olds agreed that a teacher should be informed if a classmate is seen stealing money, only the younger children approved of informing the teacher when a classmate brings large pieces of paper to school after having been told to bring small pieces. This age-related shift was interpreted in terms of a changing peer culture in which the social costs of reporting transgressions increase for older children, and a developmental increase in children's understanding of the ways in which telling the truth can come into conflict with other values.

The social implications of value-laden information are also important when children decide what information to disclose to others. For example, telling peers about one's failures can elicit support and encouragement, but it can also lead to perceptions of incompetence and the loss of social status; telling peers about one's successes can elicit admiration, but it can create perceptions of arrogance.

Even young children have some understanding that not all value-laden information about the self is equally worthy of disclosure, as is evident by the fact that 2-year-olds share their successes with others more frequently than they share their failures (Stipek, Recchia, McClintic, & Lewis, 1992). As children get older they develop more nuanced ideas about how to present themselves to others. Elementary school-age children understand that the acceptability of different types of communication about the self varies with the audience (Heyman, Fu, & Lee, 2008; Watling & Banerjee, 2007), and as children grow into adolescence they become increasingly aware of ways in which the same message can be perceived differently by different audiences. Juvonen and Murdock (1995) found that 14-year-olds, like younger children, reasoned that they could gain approval from teachers by portraying themselves as hardworking. However, unlike younger children, 14-year-olds reasoned that the same strategy would lead to disapproval if used with popular peers. This understanding can lead children to portray themselves in different ways for different audiences or scale back their academic goals to gain the approval of peers.

In a cross-cultural study on beliefs about self-disclosure, Heyman, Fu, and Lee (2008) examined how elementary school children coordinate the goal of presenting themselves as competent while avoiding the social disapproval associated with appearing immodest. Children in the United States generally disapproved of disclosing academic successes to poorly performing peers. One might expect that in China, where modesty is more highly valued than in the West (Lee, Cameron, Xu, Fu, & Board, 1997), children would be even more disapproving of this practice, but the Chinese participants were actually more accepting of it. Heyman, Fu, and Lee (2008) found that these results may reflect cross-cultural differences in default assumptions about the situation. The predominant interpretation among children from the United States was that the disclosure constituted showing off, whereas the predominant interpretation among children from China was that the successful performer was making an implicit offer of help to the unsuccessful performer. The salience of this interpretation among children from China suggests that they may be using disclosure of academic successes as a way to draw positive attention to themselves without appearing blatantly immodest. Taken together, the findings may reveal the presence of a universal process of seeking the esteem of one's peers while simultaneously avoiding a public image that is seen as unacceptable by one's culture.

CONCLUSION

Zajonc (1980, p. 153) described the pervasiveness of social evaluation, noting that "we evaluate each other constantly, we evaluate each others' behavior, and we evaluate the motives and consequences of their behavior." I argue that this tendency to view the social world through an evaluative lens is central to children's social cognition, and it is more nuanced and complex than the standard treatment of children's social cognition would suggest. Evaluative tendencies play an important role in children's development as they strive to meet central psychological needs, such as gaining the esteem of others. More broadly, the pervasiveness of social evaluations, and the ease with which even very young children apply them, may underlie the

in-group–out-group dynamics and social hierarchies that serve to structure human societies.

ACKNOWLEDGMENTS
This work was supported by NICHD grant R01 HD048962. Address correspondence to Gail D. Heyman, Department of Psychology, University of California, San Diego, 9500 Gilman Dr., La Jolla, CA 92093–0109; gheyman@ucsd.edu.

REFERENCES

Alvarez, J. M., Ruble, D. N., & Bolger, N. (2001). Trait understanding or evaluative reasoning? An analysis of children's behavioral predictions. *Child Development, 72*, 1409–1425.

Bretherton, I., & Beeghly, M. (1982). Talking about internal states: The acquisition of an explicit theory of mind. *Developmental Psychology, 18*, 906–921.

Cluver, A., Heyman, G.D., & Carver, L.J. (in press). Young children selectively seek help when solving problems. *Journal of Experimental Child Psychology*.

Gelman, S. A. (2009). Learning from others: Children's construction of concepts. *Annual Review of Psychology, 60*, 115–140.

Hamlin, J. K., Wynn, K., & Bloom, P. (2007). Social evaluation by preverbal infants. *Nature, 450*, 557–559.

Harris, P. L. (2007). Trust. *Developmental Science, 10*, 135–138.

Heyman, G. D. (2008). Children's critical thinking when learning from others. *Current Directions in Psychological Science, 17*, 344.

Heyman, G. D. (2009). Children's reasoning about traits. In P. J. Bauer (Ed.), *Advances in child development and behavior* (Vol. 37, pp. 105–143). New York: Academic Press.

Heyman, G. D., Fu, G., & Lee, K. (2008). Reasoning about the disclosure of success and failure to friends among children in the United States and China. *Developmental Psychology, 44*, 908–918.

Heyman, G. D., Fu, G., & Lee, K. (in press). Selective skepticism: American and Chinese children's reasoning about evaluative academic feedback. *Developmental Psychology*.

Heyman, G. D., & Gelman, S. A. (1998). Young children use motive information to make trait inferences. *Developmental Psychology, 34*, 310–321.

Heyman, G. D., & Legare, C. H. (2005). Children's evaluation of sources of information about traits. *Developmental Psychology, 41*, 636–647.

Heyman, G. D., Sritanyaratana, L., & Vanderbilt, K. E. (in press). Young children's trust in overtly misleading advice. *Cognitive Science*.

Juvonen, J., & Murdock, T. B. (1995). Grade-level differences in the social value of effort: Implications for self-presentation tactics of early adolescents. *Child Development, 66,* 1694–1705.

Lee, K., Cameron, C. A., Xu, F., Fu, G., & Board, J. (1997). Chinese and Canadian children's evaluations of lying and truth telling: Similarities and differences in the context of pro- and antisocial behaviors. *Child Development, 68,* 924–934.

Loke, I.C., Heyman, G.D., Forgie, J. MacCarthy A. & Lee, K. (2011). Children's moral evaluations of reporting the transgressions of peers: Age differences in evaluations of tattling. *Developmental Psychology, 47,* 1757–1762.

Liu, D., Gelman, S. A., & Wellman, H. M. (2007). Components of young children's trait understanding: Behavior-to-trait inferences and trait-to-behavior predictions. *Child Development, 78,* 1543–1558.

Mascaro, O., & Sperber, D. (2009). The moral, epistemic, and mindreading components of children's vigilance towards deception. *Cognition, 112,* 367–380.

Ng, R., Heyman, G.D., & Barner, D. (2011). Collaboration promotes proportional reasoning about resource distribution in young children. *Developmental Psychology, 47,* 1230–1238.

Rakoczy, H., Warneken, F., & Tomasello, M. (2008). The sources of normativity: Young children's awareness of the normative structure of games. *Developmental Psychology, 44,* 875–881.

Ross, H. S., & Bak-Lammers, I.M. (1998). Consistency and change in children's tattling on their siblings: Children's perspectives on the moral rules and procedures of family life. *Social Development, 7,* 275–300.

Ruble, D. N., & Dweck, C. S. (1995). Self-conceptions, person conceptions and their development. In N. Eisenberg (Ed.), *Review of personality and social psychology: Vol. 15. Social development* (pp. 109–139). Thousand Oaks, CA: Sage Publications.

Stipek, D., Recchia, S., McClintic, S., & Lewis, M. (1992). Self-evaluation in young children. *Monographs of the Society for Research in Child Development, 57,* 1–98.

Vanderbilt, K. E., Liu, D., & Heyman, G. D. (2011). The development of distrust. *Child Development, 82,* 1372–1380.

Watling, D., & Banerjee, R. (2007). Children's understanding of modesty in front of peer and adult audiences. *Infant and Child Development, 16,* 227–236.

Woolley, J. D., Boerger, E. A., & Markman, A. B. (2004). A visit from the candy witch: Factors influencing young children's belief in a novel fantastical being. *Developmental Science, 7,* 456–468.

Zajonc, R. B. (1980). Feeling and thinking: Preferences need no inferences. American Psychologist, *35,* 151–175.

SECTION II

Mentalizing

2.1

Universal Social Cognition

Childhood Theory of Mind

HENRY M. WELLMAN

Some sage once said: All people everywhere are different, *and* all people everywhere are the same. I agree. Our task is to properly understand how differences illuminate the universal human condition, and how commonalities frame the differences. An especially informative place in which to examine how all this plays out is childhood development of a theory of mind.

Theory of mind refers to our everyday construal of each other in terms of underlying mental states (desires, beliefs, emotions), including understanding how human action is shaped by such states. *People* magazine ran an article, in September 2010, "Hope and Survival," about the Chilean miners. Upon being discovered alive underground, here is the first message one man sent to his wife:

> We *thought* we were going to starve to death down here. You can't *imagine* how much my soul hurt *wanting* to tell you, but unable to let you *know* we were alive. What I *want* now is to *see* you as I emerge from the belly of the earth.

An everyday mentalistic construal of persons—in terms of hopes, thoughts, wants, imagining, knowing—radiates from this message and in the whole Chilean drama.

An everyday Western understanding of persons, our folk psychology, rests heavily on such a mentalistic construal. But folk psychologies vary greatly worldwide. For example, anthropologist Jane Fajans (1985) has claimed:

> The most challenging and interesting thing about the Baining [of Papua New Guinea], from the point of view of ethnopsychological studies, is that they appear not to have a folk psychology ....If [folk psychology] includes a

concern with affect and emotions, concepts of person and self, theories of deviance, interpretations of behavior, and ideas about cognition and personality, the Baining manifest very little interest in these areas.

This is one of many such ethnographic descriptions of other folk thinking about people in ways that seem strikingly foreign (Lillard, 1998). We do not need to aggregate (or believe) them all to validly conclude that various ways of thinking about people exist—various folk psychologies exist—that are quite different one from another and different from our own. But I claim we should also conclude that everyday theory of mind is universal. How can both these things be true—theory of mind is universal, but folk psychologies differ profoundly worldwide? The pieces of this puzzle assemble themselves around two clarifying themes. One concerns *levels of analysis*: We need to distinguish core, framework understandings from detailed, specific ones. The other theme concerns *development*: We need to appreciate how theory of mind is both early achieved and dynamic—it develops on the basis of experience.

EVERYDAY THEORY OF MIND

Psychologists and philosophers agree that everyday theory of mind is organized around three large categories of mind and behavior: beliefs, desires, actions. Basically, in our everyday thinking we construe people as engaging in acts they *think* will get them what they *want*. The miner assured his wife he was alive, because he believed she would think him dead and he wanted to ease her mind.

Theory of mind reasoning goes beyond this, of course; it is an organized system (a theory) of interconnected constructs and implications that includes perception, emotion, mistakes, ignorance, and so on overlapping with beliefs-desires-actions.

Thus, the miners could *see* they were running out of food (only milk and canned tuna were left, and very little of that) and had *heard* no contact from anyone since the cave-in 3 weeks earlier and that led them to *think* "we're going to starve to death down here"; and their actions and inactions, desires and beliefs led to *emotions* big and small ("my soul hurt ...unable to let you know").

The Chilean examples show that everyday theory of mind is always fleshed out in personal specifics. But beneath the flesh is the more skeletal belief-desire-action frame: Generically, agents do things they think will achieve their desires; generally, perception (of whatever specific sort) leads to beliefs (of some specific sort); generally, not getting what you want leads to negative emotions. At this crucial, generic level theory of mind is a framework. It leaves many, many specific things unspecified. What exactly are the miners' beliefs and desires? *People* magazine tells us; the framework does not. It just tells us that they will have beliefs and desires, and that they are important. Are cows or newborns belief-desire agents? The framework does not say.

Central to this everyday framework is a dualist slippage between mind and action, or mind and world. "You can't always get what you want." The miners thought they would starve but (fortunately) did not. The centrality of this slippage is why there has been so much research on children's understanding of false belief.

Figure 2.1.1 presents a classic false-belief task. Theory of mind encompasses many understandings beyond false belief, but false belief is a good initial focus because such tasks have been used worldwide, with many children in many cultural communities speaking many different languages. Thus, Figure 2.1.2 also presents a key initial finding with regard to universality. Young children everywhere develop an understanding of false belief. They come to understand that a person's actions are importantly controlled by what she *thinks*, not just reality itself. Really, the candy is in the cupboard, but Jill looks in the drawer. Indeed, there is a similar developmental trajectory in all countries from below-chance incorrect judgments to above-chance correct judgments in the years from 2 to 6 or 7. False-belief understanding is a developmental achievement.

Amid universality, Figure 2.1.2 shows there is some obvious variation in timetables, too, across countries and across individuals. Although almost all typically developing children eventually master false belief, some children in some places come to this understanding earlier and some later. This

variation helps researchers confirm the impact of achieving preschool theory-of-mind understanding. Children's performance on false-belief tasks is just one marker of these understandings, but differences in false-belief understanding alone predict how and how much preschool children talk about people in everyday conversation, their engagement in pretense, their social interactional skills, and consequently their interactions with and popularity with peers (e.g., Astington & Jenkins, 1995; Watson, Nixon, Wilson, & Capage, 1999). These findings importantly confirm the real-life relevance of theory of mind. They also demonstrate that important changes take place in children's theory of mind understandings in the preschool years. Recent research claims that infants—at 10 to 15 months—already have an awareness that actors act on the basis of their beliefs (e.g., Onishi & Baillargeon, 2005). It is not yet clear how best to interpret these emerging findings. But it is clear that initial infant recognitions cannot gainsay the progress made in the preschool years or its importance. And it is research on preschool theory of mind that most clearly addresses universality and variation.

False-belief data provide an intriguing initial look at universality in childhood social cognition. But actually the data—as standard as they are for research in cognitive development—are not very developmental. True, they show some sort of developmental progress with age. But the data really only encompass passing/failing one sort of understanding averaged across age. And, true, the data show some universality (and some variability). But what sorts? Newer data unpack universality and variability more clearly and do so by clarifying more extended developmental progressions.

Consider these related things a child could know (or not know) about persons and minds: (a) People can have different desires for the same thing (diverse desires [DD]); (b) people can have different beliefs about the same situation (diverse beliefs [DB]); (c) something can be true, but someone might not know that (knowledge-access [KA]); (d) something can be true, but someone might falsely believe something different (false belief [FB]); and (e) someone can feel one way but display a different emotion (hidden emotion [HE]). These notions capture aspects of mental subjectivity, albeit different aspects (including mind-mind, mind-world, and mind-action distinctions). Listing them in this manner suggests that one could devise a set of tasks all with similar formats and procedures—similar to that in

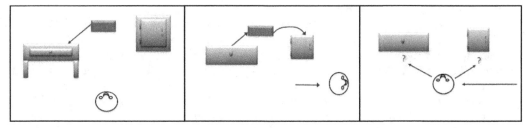

FIGURE 2.1.1: False-belief tasks ask children to reason about an agent whose actions should be controlled by a false belief. Such tasks have many forms, but here the child (not shown) sees the character, Jill, put her candy in one of two locations. Jill leaves and, while she cannot see, the candy gets moved. Jill returns, wants her candy, and the child is asked, "Where will Jill look for her candy?" or "Where does Jill think her candy is?" Older children answer correctly, like adults. Younger children answer incorrectly; they consistently say Jill will search in the cupboard (where it really is). A frequent alternative task uses deceptive contents (rather than change of location). For example, children see a crayon box, say they think it holds crayons, then upon opening see it holds candies. They are asked what someone else who has never looked inside will think the box holds—crayons or candies.

false-belief tasks, for example—and see how children do. Several studies have now done just that.

Studies using a battery of such tasks, encompassing more than 500 preschoolers in the United States, Canada, Australia, and Germany, evidence a clear and consistent order of difficulty. It is the order listed earlier, with diverse desires easiest and hidden emotions hardest. For shorthand we can call this sequence, DD>DB>KA>FB>HE. This sequence is highly replicable and significant—80% of these children show this pattern (Kristen, Thoermer,

Hofer, Aschersleben, & Sodian, 2006; Peterson, Wellman, & Liu, 2005; Wellman & Liu, 2004).

So these tasks—constituting a Theory of Mind Scale—reveal a robust sequence of understandings. What accounts for the consistency of sequence demonstrated so far? Clearly, a consistent sequence could result from innately programmed maturations. (Or similarly it could result from maturationally unfolding gains in basic cognitive processes, such as increases in executive function or in cognitive capacity.) But alternatively, a consistent sequence might result from processes of

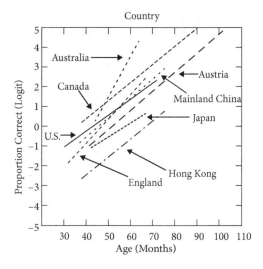

FIGURE 2.1.2: As shown in this graph (combining results from Liu, Wellman, Tardif, & Sabbagh, 2008; Wellman, Cross, & Watson, 2001), children in different cultural-linguistic communities can achieve false-belief understanding more quickly or more slowly. Yet in all locales they evidence the same trajectory—from below chance (0 = chance, in this scoring) to above-chance performance in early childhood. This is true even for children growing up in non-Western cultural communities speaking non-Indo-European languages, and it is true for children in traditional, nonliterate societies.

conceptual learning in which initial conceptions lead to later conceptions, shaped by relevant information and experiences. If they are more shaped by relevant information and experiences, however, then, in principle, sequences could be very different.

Additional cross-cultural research, for example in China, addresses these possibilities. Assume that theory-of-mind understandings *are* the products of social and conversational experiences that vary from one community to another. Western and Chinese childhood experiences could be crucially different. Various authors have described an Asian focus on persons as sharing group commonalities and interdependence and a contrasting Western focus on persons as distinctively individual and independent (e.g., Nisbett, 2003). These differences include differing emphases on common knowledge and perspectives versus diversity of individual beliefs and perspectives. Moreover, Western and Chinese adults seem to manifest very different everyday epistemologies. Everyday Western epistemology is focused on truth, subjectivity, and belief; Confucian-Chinese epistemology focuses more on pragmatic knowledge acquisition and the consensual knowledge that all right-minded persons should learn (Nisbett, 2003). Indeed, in conversation with young children, Chinese parents comment predominantly on "knowing," whereas US parents comment more on "thinking" (Tardif & Wellman, 2000).

In accord with such conversational-cultural preferences for emphasizing knowledge acquisition versus belief differences, Chinese preschoolers evidence a consistent but different theory of mind sequence in which KA and DB are reversed: DD>KA>DB>FB>HE (Wellman, Fang, Liu, Zhu, & Liu, 2006; Wellman, Fang, & Peterson, 2011). Both Western and Chinese children first understand basic aspects of desire (DD), but after that Western children first appreciate belief differences (DB), whereas Chinese children instead first appreciate knowledge acquisition (KA). This is not some singular peculiarity of Chinese mind and development; the same alternative sequence appears in Iranian preschool children. Despite profound differences in Iran's Muslim traditions and beliefs in contrast to Chinese Confucian/Buddhist/Communist ones, both China and Iran share collectivist family values emphasizing consensual learning, knowledge acquisition, and low tolerance for childhood assertions of disagreement and independent belief (Shahaeian, Peterson, Slaughter, & Wellman, 2011).

Of course, sequences are not the only issue—developmental timetables also matter. The false-belief data in Figure 2.1.2 already show that timetables can vary; some children are quicker, some slower to achieve false-belief understanding. But in the bigger picture this may not be all that much variation. Nearly everywhere children achieve a similar understanding of false belief in the preschool years. A similar suspicion might taint the sequence data as well: Sequence differences are intriguing, but children seem to proceed through more or less the same steps and at more or less the same time—in the preschool years. Tightly restricted—not identical, but restricted—timetables might well reflect development of theory-of-mind understandings as largely under maturational control. But if early progressive theory-of-mind understandings are built one upon the next, shaped by relevant information and experience, that process should be able to produce very different timetables.

Most people know that false-belief understanding *is* seriously (not modestly) delayed in children with autism. Most adolescents and adults with autism perform poorly on false-belief tasks. But, then, autism is replete with neurological impairments, general across-the-board cognitive impairment and delays. Autism could certainly have its own delayed maturational timetable. A more telling test case concerns deaf children. Deaf children do not suffer from the same central neurological impairments and retardation as individuals with autism; they have peripheral hearing loss instead.

Moreover, there are two main groups of deaf children to consider. Deaf children of deaf parents grow up with ordinary conversational, language experiences—albeit in sign language—and so grow up with others who communicate and interact with them profusely. But most deaf children—about 95%—are born to hearing parents. They grow up with very different early experiences. For example, despite valiant efforts to learn sign language, hearing parents rarely achieve real proficiency. Especially when their child is young, hearing parents mostly communicate with their deaf child using simple signs or gestures to refer to here-and-now objects. Also, usually only one person in the family—often the mother—is the "designated" primary communicator and interactor for the child. The deaf child in a hearing family begins with little discourse about persons' inner states, thoughts, and ideas; is likely to have restricted play with others; and generally has less access to the free-flowing, turn-taking, perspective-negotiating dance of social interactions.

Deaf children of hearing parents (but *not* deaf children of deaf parents) are substantially delayed in understanding false belief, often as delayed as high-functioning children with autism. Again, however, a focus on false belief alone is limiting. So, consider the performance of deaf children of hearing parents when they receive the Theory of Mind Scale. These deaf children evidence a consistent sequence of progression, like their hearing peers, but one that is delayed every step of the way. It takes deaf children 12 or more years to progressively achieve what hearing children (and deaf children of deaf parents) progressively achieve in 4 to 6 years (Wellman et al., 2011). The data for these deaf children also speak strongly against any maturational, critical-period analysis of theory of mind. Deaf children of hearing parents continue to progress in these "preschool" theory-of-mind understandings as adolescents and adults.

FRAMEWORK DEVELOPMENT

How do these findings clarify how theory of mind both constitutes universal social cognition yet allows vast differences in social cognition across cultures and societies? Here's how, I propose: Children worldwide share a framework theory of mind. Accordingly, children tend to assume that people have subjective experiences and internal mental states. Such assumptions, strongly evident at ages 2 or 3, are themselves the products of earlier developments in infancy.

Levels of analysis and development both importantly clarify this story. For levels, a general childhood expectation that people possess thoughts, wants, perceptions, and feelings provides only a very general framework, and children must engage in much specific instantiation of the framework, prominently including much culture-specific learning. The framework constrains the sorts of hypotheses that children make about people early on, but it does not specify a great many things: Are cows as well as people belief-desire agents? (Yes, in India.) Should I privilege individualized beliefs over consensual knowledge? (Yes, in the United States.)

As for development, an early theory-of-mind framework is dynamic, not static. In fact, it can revise and change to the extent of becoming in some parts and respects quite different from its initial form. As an example of the extensive change possible, think of the momentous preschool changes represented by achieving awareness of false beliefs and hidden emotions.

My shorthand for this scenario is *framework development*; notably, the framework itself develops *and* it frames further development. Framework development predicts constraints on cultural variability in folk psychologies—not maturational constraints but developmental-learning constraints. After all, any specific folk psychology must be learnable by children. Cultural communities cannot sustain a specially developed construal of *anything* that their members cannot learn.

Constrained variability should be especially notable in childhood—when learning and development are in their early stages. Adults' conceptions of people can be much more dissimilar worldwide than childhood ones. Why? Because the initial framework is enabling (as well as constraining) precisely in that it is a general framework and it works developmentally. Initially, the framework provides a helpful ground for a community's members to communicate with their children. But, in part through this communication, communities teach and socialize their children into their group's practices and beliefs. In terms of individual development, cultural communities have many years (at the least from infancy to adulthood) in which to enculturate their children into their beliefs and worldviews. In terms of historical development, those groups have centuries in which to develop unique understandings of persons, selves, psyches, and societies. Resulting adult folk psychologies could be quite different from one another worldwide, although grounded in the initial framework assumptions of young children. A long path, studded with progressive novelties, connects early theory of mind to the profusion of divergent folk psychologies.

Framework development is different from other scenarios that dominate discussion of universality and variation in our thinking about concepts. One dominant alternative is *nativist knowledge*, according to which there are early, evolved understandings that do not change. Nativist knowledge scenarios (most recently, core knowledge and mental module accounts) privilege and easily account for universality. The other dominant alternative is *empiricist knowledge*, which posits that young children begin ignorant and pick up—learn, match, and mirror—whatever their societies tell them. Empiricist knowledge scenarios (most recently, connectionist and dynamic systems proposals) privilege and easily account for variability in timetable and sequences. Framework development embraces, and accounts for, both universality and variability. It does so by emphasizing development and levels of analysis. If we insist there are several levels of analysis—framework versus specifics—and if we insist there is developmental change, then the full pattern of the data makes sense.

The full pattern of the data coupled with framework development underwrite my title and claim: Universal social cognition exists. If you want to see it, look at childhood theory of mind.

REFERENCES

Astington, J. W., & Jenkins, J. M. (1995). Theory of mind development and social understanding. *Cognitive Emotion, 9,* 151–165.

Fajans, J. (1985). The person in social context: The social character of Baining "psychology". In G. White & J. Kirkpatrick (Eds.), *Person, self, and experience: Exploring pacific ethnopsychologies* (pp. 367–397). Los Angeles: University of California Press.

Kristen, S., Thoermer, C., Hofer, T., Aschersleben, G., & Sodian, B. (2006). Skalierung von "theory of mind" aufgaben (Scaling of theory of mind tasks). *Zeitschrift fur Entwicklungspsychologic und Padagogische Psychologie, 38,* 186–195.

Lillard, A. (1998). Ethnopsychologies: Cultural variations in theories of mind. *Psychology Bulletin, 123,* 3–32.

Liu, D., Wellman, H. M., Tardif, T., & Sabbagh, M. A. (2008). Theory of mind development in Chinese children: A meta-analysis of false-belief understanding across cultures. *Developmental Psychology, 44,* 523–531.

Nisbett, R. E. (2003). *The geography of thought: How Asians and Westerners think differently—and why.* New York: Free Press.

Onishi, K. H., & Baillargeon, R. (2005). Do 15-month-old infants understand false beliefs? *Science, 308,* 255–258.

Peterson, C. C., Wellman, H. M., & Liu, D. (2005). Steps in theory of mind development for children with autism and deafness. *Child Development, 76,* 502–517.

Shahaeian, A., Peterson, C. C., Slaughter, V., & Wellman, H. M. (2011). Culture and the sequence of steps in theory of mind development. *Developmental Psychology, 47,* 1239–1247.

Tardif, T., & Wellman, H. M. (2000). Acquisition of mental state language in Mandarin- and Cantonese-speaking children. *Developmental Psychology, 36,* 25–43.

Watson, A. C., Nixon, C. L., Wilson, A., & Capage, L. (1999). Social interaction skills and theory of mind in young children. *Developmental Psychology, 35,* 386–391.

Wellman, H. M., Cross, D., & Watson, J (2001). Meta-analysis of theory of mind development: The truth about false belief. *Child Development, 72,* 655–684.

Wellman, H. M., Fang, F., Liu, D., Zhu, L., & Liu, G. (2006). Scaling of theory of mind understanding in Chinese children. *Psychological Science, 17,* 1075–1081.

Wellman, H. M., Fang, F., & Peterson, C. C. (2011). Sequential progressions in a theory of mind scale: Longitudinal perspectives. *Child Development, 82(3),* 780–792.

Wellman, H. M., & Liu, D. (2004). Scaling of theory of mind tasks. *Child Development, 75,* 523–541.

2.2

Infant Foundations of Intentional Understanding

AMANDA WOODWARD

People are built for a social world. An impressive number of our perceptual and cognitive resources are dedicated to perceiving, making sense of, and responding to our social partners, including processes that support identifying and categorizing individuals, perceiving biological motion, responding empathically, rendering moral judgments, learning from social partners, and engaging in theory of mind reasoning. Among these processes, and foundational to many of them, is the ability to see others' movements as structured by intentions. When we watch others act, we see more than bodies in motion; we see agents whose actions are structured by intentions. Imagine a woman making her way through a crowded plaza, basket in hand, in order to reach a fruit vendor. We automatically view her movements as structured by goals (avoiding obstacles in her path, searching for the vendor, buying supplies for dinner, etc.). In viewing her actions in this way, we engage a specifically social analysis. If we were to see a piece of newspaper blow across the plaza taking a similarly complex path, we would not view its movements as intentional.

This way of viewing human action has been described in terms of "intentional relations" (Barresi & Moore, 1996) because actions are represented as structured by the relation between the agent and the object at which his or her actions are directed. A reaching hand is seen not just as an appendage in motion, but rather as an action directed at a goal object. A gaze shift is seen not just as the movement of eyes and head, but rather as an act of attention directed at a referent in the environment. Intentional relations can be understood at many levels of analysis, from the concrete (reaching for a lemon) to the abstract (making a tart, feeding one's guests, or preparing a celebration). The apprehension of intentional relations is deeply embedded in mature social perception, and it is also foundational for much of early social and cognitive development. As examples, not long after their first birthdays, infants recruit their understanding of others' intentional actions to inform their word learning (Baldwin & Moses, 2001; Tomasello, 1999), their imitative learning (Meltzoff, 1995), and their learning from others' emotional messages (Moses Baldwin, Rosicky, & Tidball, 2001). It is not surprising, then, that sensitivity to intentional relations can be traced back to early in infancy.

INFANTS' UNDERSTANDING OF GOAL-DIRECTED ACTION

By 6 months of age, infants view others' actions not simply as movements through space, but rather as actions structured by intentional relations. The first evidence for this conclusion came from visual habituation experiments. When infants were habituated to repeated examples of an action directed at a particular goal, they subsequently showed longer looking (a response to novelty) to events that disrupted the original relation between the agent and her goal than to events which preserved this relation while varying the physical details of the agent's movements (Woodward, 1998; see Woodward, Sommerville, Gerson, Henderson, & Buresh, 2009 for a review). This pattern emerges early in the first year for simple instrumental actions, like reaching (Luo & Johnson, 2009; Sommerville, Woodward, & Needham, 2005; Woodward, 1998), and later in the first year for actions that relate agents to objects at a distance, like looking and pointing (Johnson, Ok, & Luo, 2007; Phillips, Wellman, & Spelke, 2002; Woodward, 2003), or reaching from afar (Brandone & Wellman, 2009), and for intentional relations that involve actions on intermediaries, such as tools (Hofer, Hauf, & Aschersleben, 2005; Sommerville et al., 2005; Sommerville, Hildebrand, & Crane, 2008).

Across these experiments, infants' encoding of intentional relations has been found to be selective for the well-formed actions of agents. When actions are ambiguous (Henderson & Woodward, 2011; Sommerville et al., 2005; Woodward, 1999) or agents are difficult to identify as animate (Biro & Leslie, 2007; Guajardo & Woodward, 2004; Hofer et al., 2005), infants do not respond selectively to the "goal" of the action. These ambiguous agents and actions direct infants' attention to the events in the same way that intentional actions do, but even so, infants do not respond to them as if they are goal directed (see Woodward, 1998, 2005 for discussions). Thus, it is not the low-level patterns of movement and contact that drive infants' responses to others' actions, but rather infants' analyses of these actions as goal directed.

Infants express their understanding of intentional relations with their hands as well as with their eyes. By 18 months, children show a robust propensity to selectively imitate the aspects of others' actions that are relevant to the actor's intentions (e.g., Meltzoff, 1995). The findings of visual habituation experiments with younger infants suggested that this tendency might be evident much earlier in life if the experimental procedures were made sensitive to the knowledge and abilities of younger infants. To investigate this question, Hamlin, Hallinan, and I (2008) showed 7-month-old infants events in which an experimenter reached toward one of two objects, and then gave infants the chance to choose between the two objects. We reasoned that if infants selectively reproduce the goal-relevant aspects of others' actions, they should systematically choose the experimenter's prior goal object, and this is what we found. Of course, infants might have selected the experimenter's goal for other reasons. In particular, the effects of the experimenter's reach in directing infants' attention to the toy might have led infants to choose that toy. To evaluate this possibility, we tested other groups of infants in the same procedure but showed them events in which the experimenter produced a novel or ambiguous action on the object (e.g., touching it with the back of her hand) or in which an inanimate object moved toward and contacted the toy (Gerson & Woodward, 2012; Hamlin et al., 2008; Mahajan & Woodward, 2009). These conditions entrained infants' attention in the same way that the reaching actions did, but infants responded to them differently: They chose randomly between the two toys. Thus, on parallel with their visual responses, infants' overt responses to others' goals are selective for the well-formed goal-directed actions of agents.

Infants' understanding of intentional relations goes beyond the perception of isolated events. To start, infants integrate information about a person's intentional actions over time. As examples, they generate rapid, on-line predictions about a person's reaching actions based on her prior goals (Cannon & Woodward, 2012), and they use a person's prior focus of attention to interpret her subsequent actions, for example, inferring that she is likely to reach for an object that she has previously attended to (Luo & Baillargeon, 2007; Phillips et al., 2002; Vaish & Woodward, 2010; see also Onishi & Baillargeon, 2005). In addition, infants use information about a person's actions in one context to interpret his actions in a new context. As examples, seeing an agent express a preference for an object influences infants' subsequent interpretation of his actions in a novel means-end sequence (Sommerville & Crane, 2009), seeing a person engage in a specific action with one object leads infants to expect she will seek out new objects on which that action can be performed (Song & Baillargeon, 2007), and seeing a person engage in a collaborative action informs infants' expectations about how she will later act on her own (Henderson & Woodward, 2011). Critically, infants understand that the individual person is the right unit of analysis for tracking intentional actions over time. By 9 months of age, infants know that an agent's actions provide information about her likely next actions, but not someone else's (Buresh & Woodward, 2007; Henderson & Woodward, 2012). Thus, although concepts of intention clearly continue to develop throughout early childhood, infants appreciate at least two critical aspects of intentions: They reside in the individual, and they serve to organize the individual's actions over time and across contexts.

ORIGINS

The research just reviewed shows that the infant mind, like the adult mind it will become, is built to make sense of the intentional structure of the social world. A pressing question for developmental psychologists is how the "building" takes place. Clearly, the ability to discern intentional structure in others' actions is essential for mature human social life, and, as discussed earlier, it is also critical for the acquisition of other foundational human abilities, including language and culture. When abilities that are critical for survival are found to emerge very early in life, it is often concluded that their emergence reflects evolutionary processes but not learning or experience during ontogeny. Along these lines, a number of recent proposals consider infants' understanding of intentional action to be an expression of an inborn representational module that is triggered by the presence of certain visual cues, such as self-propelled movement (e.g., Biro & Leslie, 2007; Gergely & Csibra, 2003; Luo & Baillargeon, 2005). According to these proposals, infants respond selectively to the intentional relations in human action because human actions reliably exhibit the cues to trigger this inborn representation.

However, it is not the case that all critical, naturally selected abilities emerge independent of experience. In fact, developmental processes often exploit reliable learning opportunities to ensure the emergence of critical abilities. As examples, social imprinting, navigation, and birdsong are all clearly shaped by natural selection and important for survival, yet in many species experience and learning play an essential role in their development (Gallistel, Brown, Carey, Gelman, & Keil, 1991; Gottlieb, 1991; Marler, 1991). Thus, another possible explanation for the early emergence of infants' sensitivity to others' intentions is that this ability depends on early and reliable aspects of infants' experience. Consistent with this viewpoint, several recent proposals posit that infants' sensitivity to intentional relations is shaped by two kinds of experience: (1) producing, and refining, one's own intentional actions and (2) acting in coordination with social partners (Barresi & Moore, 1996; Meltzoff, 2007; Woodward et al., 2009). Each of these experiences is ubiquitous in human infancy and each could, in principle, provide the infant with information about the intentional structure of action. As detailed later, there is now clear evidence that the first of these contributes to infants' intentional understanding, and there is initial evidence for a role of the second.

In the first postnatal year, infants experience dramatic changes in their abilities to direct actions toward goals and objects of attention. At around 6 months, after months of practice, infants become able to launch efficient goal-directed reaches. At 9 to 12 months, infants begin to be able to orchestrate means-end actions, and during this same time they begin to produce referential gestures, like pointing. As infants become increasingly skilled at coordinating these actions, they gain insight into the intentional structure of those same actions in others. Infants begin to respond systematically to others' reaching, means-end, and referential actions at around the ages that these actions emerge in their own repertoires (Woodward et al., 2009). Furthermore, infants' action production and action understanding are correlated during periods when both are emerging (Brune & Woodward, 2007; Cannon, Woodward, Gredebäck, von Hofsten, & Turek, 2012; Gredeback & Kochuhkova, 2010; Sommerville & Woodward, 2005; Woodward & Guajardo, 2002). For example, at 9 months, infants who themselves produce object-directed points also understand others' points in terms of the relation between the person and the object, whereas infants at this age who do not yet point do not (Brune & Woodward, 2007; Woodward & Guajardo, 2002; see also Liszkowski & Tomasello, 2011).

Critically, interventions that support infants' engagement in new goal-directed actions also support their ability to detect the intentional structure of those actions in others (Libertus & Needham, 2010; Sommerville & Woodward, 2005; Sommerville et al., 2008). For example, 3-month-old infants are too young to yet produce efficient goal-directed reaches, and they also fail to show sensitivity to others' reaching actions as goal directed. Training with Velcro-covered "sticky" mittens enables infants at this age to apprehend objects with their hands, and this training also leads infants to respond systematically to others' goal-directed actions in the habituation paradigm described earlier (Sommerville et al., 2005; see also Libertus & Needham, 2010). That is, learning to act causes changes in infants' understanding of others' actions.

Recent studies point to the potential neural correlates of the effects of acting on action understanding: Motor cortex activity occurs selectively when infants view other people producing actions that are within their own motor repertoire (Nystrom, 2008; Southgate, Johnson, El Karoui, & Csibra, 2010; van Elk, van Schie, Hunnius, Vesper, & Bekkering, 2008). To illustrate, when infants who can crawl view films of other infants crawling, there is selective responding of the motor system, as indicated by shifts in chronic electroencephalographic activity measured over motor cortex, and this neural response is correlated with the observing infant's own degree of crawling experience (van Elk et al., 2008). These findings, which parallel similar findings in adults (e.g., Calvo-Merino, Glaser, Grezes, Passingham, & Haggard, 2005), suggest that neurocognitive systems for action production play a role in action perception, and that as new modes of action are acquired, new neurocognitive resources become available for action perception. As yet, however, it is not known which aspects of action perception or action understanding are related to these patterns of neural activation in infants.

Learning from one's own actions is a useful first step, but it also has an important limitation. Social life requires understanding actions one has never performed. An infant viewing even the most mundane parental activities confronts many actions that are well beyond her own capacities. One way that infants could gain insight into novel actions is by analogy to actions they already understand. Analogical learning has been found to support children's, and infants', analysis of relational structure in a range of domains, including spatial relations (Christie & Gentner, 2010), causal relations in problem solving (Chen, Sanchez, & Campbell, 1997), and verb learning (Pruden, Shallcross, Hirsh-Pasek, & Golinkoff, 2008). It seems possible that this process could also support infants' detection of intentional relations in others' actions (see Barresi & Moore, 1996). By comparing a new action, for example, using tongs to pick up food, to a familiar one, for example, grasping objects, infants may detect the relational similarity between these two actions, and thus come to understand tong use as goal directed. The interactions that are common in infants' lives offer opportunities to engage in this kind of comparison. When infants coordinate actions with caretakers, their own actions are often aligned with those of the adult, for example, when the adult offers the infant an object or when the adult and infant jointly attend to an object. Under these conditions, comparison could support infants' understanding of the adult's actions.

Gerson and I (2012) tested this hypothesis by attempting to teach 7-month-old infants about a novel action, the use of a claw-shaped tool to grasp objects. Prior findings had shown that infants at this age do not spontaneously understand this action as goal directed. To assess infants' understanding of the tool action, we used the goal imitation procedure described earlier. In the critical condition, infants first engaged in joint actions involving the tool. The experimenter used the tool to hand the infant several toys, and this ensured that the infants' grasping actions co-occurred with the tool's action on the toys. This experience led infants to respond systematically in the imitation procedure, indicating that they now saw the tool action as goal directed. Infants in control conditions who interacted with the tool, or saw it move objects, but did not engage in joint action, responded randomly. Thus, the alignment of the infant's actions with the tool action seemed to be critical. By providing infants with the opportunity to compare the tool action with their own actions, joint action supported infants' understanding of this novel action. This laboratory demonstration highlights a process that could play a powerful role in enriching infants' understanding of others' actions because joint actions are common in infants' everyday lives.

CONCLUSIONS

Infants, like adults, experience a social world populated by intentional agents. Well before their first birthdays, infants see others' actions as structured by intentional relations. Moreover, infants view these intentional relations as organizers of people's actions over time and across situations. This foundational social worldview sets the stage for much of early social, cognitive, and linguistic development. When organized cognition is found to exist in young infants, this is often taken as evidence that learning is not needed to explain its emergence. However, as recent work has begun to highlight (Johnson, 2010; Woodward & Needham, 2009), this conclusion underestimates both the richness of the information present in infants' early experiences and the learning processes at infants' disposal. Recent findings highlight these factors in infants' developing ability to analyze others' intentions. The massive developments in infants' own actions during the first year yield action knowledge that seems to generalize readily to others' observed actions. Furthermore, in the context of everyday interactions, infants experience events in which their own actions are coordinated with those of adults, and this co-occurrence can support infants' detection of intentional relations in novel actions. Our findings, as well as other recent results (e.g., Pruden et al., 2008), suggest that the cognitive learning processes required to benefit from these learning opportunities operate during infancy. Taken together, these findings indicate that the human social worldview is structured, in no small part, by pervasive and early aspects of human experience.

ACKNOWLEDGMENTS

Grants from the NICHD (R01 HD035707 and P01 HD064653) and the NSF (DLS 0951489) provided support for the preparation of this chapter and for much of the research reviewed in it.

REFERENCES

Baldwin, D. A., & Moses, J. A. (2001). Links between social understanding and early word learning: Challenges to current accounts. *Social Development, 10*, 311–329.

Barresi, J., & Moore, C. (1996). Intentional relations and social understanding. *Behavioral and Brain Sciences, 19*, 107–154.

Biro, S., & Leslie, A. M. (2007). Infants' perception of goal-directed actions: Development through cue-based bootstrapping. *Developmental Science, 10*, 379–398.

Brandone, A. C., & Wellman, H. M. (2009). You can't always get what you want: Infants understand failed goal-directed actions. *Psychological Science, 20*, 85–91.

Brune, C. W., & Woodward, A. L. (2007). Social cognition and social responsiveness in 10-month-old infants. *Journal of Cognition and Development, 8*, 133–158.

Buresh, J. S., & Woodward, A. L. (2007). Infants track action goals within and across agents. *Cognition, 104*, 287–314.

Calvo-Merino, B., Glaser, D. E., Grezes, J., Passingham, R. E., & Haggard, P. (2005). Action observation and acquired motor skills: An fMRI study with expert dancers. *Cerebral Cortex, 15*, 1243–1249.

Cannon, E., & Woodward, A. L. (2012). Infants generate goal-based action predictions. *Developmental Science, 15(2)*, 292–298.

Cannon, E., Woodward, A., Gredebäck, G., von Hofsten, C., & Turek, C. (2012). Action production influences 12-month-old infants' attention to others' actions. *Developmental Science, 15(1), 35–42*.

Chen, Z., Sanchez, R. P., & Campbell, T. (1997). From beyond to within their grasp: The rudiments of analogical problem solving in 10- and 13-month-olds. *Developmental Psychology, 33*, 790–801.

Christie, S., & Gentner, D. (2010). Where hypotheses come from: Learning new relations by structural alignment. *Journal of Cognition and Development, 11*, 356–373.

Gallistel, C. R., Brown, A. L., Carey, S., Gelman, R., & Keil, F. C. (1991). Lessons from animal learning for the study of cognitive development. In S. Carey & R. Gelman (Eds.), *The epigenesis of mind: Essays on biology and cognition* (pp. 3–36). Hillsdale, NJ: Erlbaum.

Gergely, G., & Csibra, G. (2003). Teleological reasoning in infancy: The naive theory of rational action. *Trends in Cognitive Sciences, 7*, 287–292.

Gerson, S., & Woodward, A. (2012). A claw is like my hand: Comparison supports goal analysis in 7-month-old infants. *Cognition, 122(2)*, 181–192.

Gottlieb, G. (1991). Experiential canalization of behavioral development: Results. *Developmental Psychology, 27*, 35–39.

Gredebäck, G., & Kochukhova, O. (2010). Goal anticipation during action observation is influenced by synonymous action capabilities, a puzzling developmental study. *Experimental Brain Research, 202*, 493–497.

Guajardo, J. J., & Woodward, A. L. (2004). Is agency skin-deep? Surface features influence infants' sensitivity to goal-directed action. *Infancy, 6*, 361–384.

Hamlin, J. K., Hallinan, E. V., & Woodward, A. L. (2008). Do as I do: 8-month-old infants selectively reproduce others' goals. *Developmental Science, 11*, 487–494.

Henderson, A. M. E., & Woodward, A. L. (2011). Let's work together: What do infants understand about collaborative goals? *Cognition, 121(1), 12–21*.

Henderson, A. M. E., & Woodward, A. (2012). Nine-month-olds appreciate the shared nature of linguistic labels. *Developmental Science, 15(5)*, 641–652.

Hofer, T., Hauf, P., & Aschersleben, G. (2005). Infant's perception of goal-directed actions performed by a mechanical device. *Infant Behavior and Development, 28*, 466–480.

Johnson, S. C., Ok, S-J., & Luo, Y. (2007). The attribution of attention: Nine-month-olds' interpretation of gaze as goal-directed action. *Developmental Science, 10*, 530–537.

Johnson, S. P. (Ed.). (2010). *Neo-constructivism*. New York: Oxford University Press.

Libertus, K., & Needham, A. (2010). Teach to reach: The effects of active versus passive reaching experiences on action and perception. *Vision Research, 50*, 2750–2757.

Liszkowski, U., & Tomasello, M. (2011). Individual differences in social, cognitive, and morphological aspects of infant pointing. *Cognitive Development, 26*, 16–29.

Luo, Y., & Baillargeon, R. (2005). Can a self-propelled box have a goal? Psychological reasoning in 5-month-old infants. *Psychological Science, 16*, 601–608.

Luo, Y., & Baillargeon, R. (2007). Do 12.5-month-old infants consider what objects others can see when interpreting their actions? *Cognition, 105*, 489–512.

Luo, Y., & Johnson, S. C. (2009). Recognizing the role of perception in action at 6 months. *Developmental Science, 12*, 142–149.

Mahajan, N., & Woodward, A. L. (2009). Infants imitate human agents but not inanimate objects. *Infancy, 14*, 667–679.

Marler, P. (1991). The instinct to learn. In S. Carey & R. Gelman (Eds.), *The epigenesis of mind: Essays on biology and cognition* (pp. 37–66). Hillsdale, NJ: Erlbaum.

Meltzoff, A. N. (1995). Understanding the intentions of others: Re-enactments of intended acts by 18-month-old children. *Developmental Psychology, 31,* 838–850.

Meltzoff, A. N. (2007). The 'like me' framework for recognizing and becoming an intentional agent. *Acta Psychologica, 124,* 26–43.

Moses, L., Baldwin, D. A., Rosicky, J. G., & Tidball, G. (2001). Evidence for referential understanding in the emotions domain at 12 and 18 months. *Child Development, 72,* 718–735.

Nystrom, P. (2008). The infant mirror neuron system studied with high density EEG. *Social Neuroscience, 3,* 334–347.

Onishi, K. H., & Baillargeon, R. (2005). Do 15-month-old infants understand false belief? *Science, 308,* 255–258.

Phillips, A. T., Wellman, H. M., & Spelke, E. S. (2002). Infants' ability to connect gaze and emotional expression to intentional action. *Cognition, 85,* 53–78.

Pruden, S. M., Shallcross, W. L., Hirsh-Pasek, K., & Golinkoff, R. M. (2008). Foundations of verb learning: Comparison helps infants abstract event components. In H. Chan, H. Jacob, & E. Kapia (Eds.), *Proceedings of the 32nd Annual Boston University Conference on Language Development* (pp. 402–414). Somerville, MA: Cascadilla Press.

Sommerville, J. A., & Crane, C. C. (2009). Ten-month-old infants use prior information to identify an actor's goal. *Developmental Science, 12,* 314–325.

Sommerville, J. A., Hildebrand, E. A., & Crane, C. C. (2008). Experience matters: The impact of doing versus watching on infants' subsequent perception of tool use events. *Developmental Psychology, 44,* 1249–1256.

Sommerville, J. A., & Woodward, A. L. (2005). Pulling out the intentional structure of human action: The relation between action production and processing in infancy. *Cognition, 95,* 1–30.

Sommerville, J. A., Woodward, A. L., & Needham, A. (2005). Action experience alters 3-month-old infants' perception of others' actions. *Cognition, 96,* B1–B11.

Song, H., & Baillargeon, R. (2007) Can 9.5-month-old infants attribute to an agent a disposition to perform a particular action on objects? *Acta Psychologica, 124,* 79–105.

Southgate, V., Johnson, M. H., El Karoui, I., & Csibra, G. (2010). Motor system activation reveals infants' on-line prediction of others' goals. *Psychological Science, 21,* 355–359.

Tomasello, M. (1999). *The cultural origins of human cognition.* Cambridge, MA: Harvard University Press.

Vaish, A., & Woodward, A. (2010). Infants use attention but not emotions to predict others' actions. *Infant Behavior and Development, 33,* 79–87.

van Elk, M., van Schie, H. T., Hunnius, S., Vesper, C., & Bekkering, H. (2008). You'll never crawl alone: Neurophysiological evidence for experience-dependent motor resonance in infancy. *Neuroimage, 43,* 808–814.

Woodward, A. L. (1998). Infants selectively encode the goal object of an actor's reach. *Cognition, 69,* 1–34.

Woodward, A. L. (1999). Infants' ability to distinguish between purposeful and non-purposeful behaviors. *Infant Behavior and Development, 22,* 145–160.

Woodward, A. L. (2003). Infants' developing understanding of the link between looker and object. *Developmental Science, 6,* 297–311.

Woodward, A. L. (2005). Infants' understanding of the actions involved in joint attention. In N. Eilan, C. Hoerl, T. McCormack, & J. Roessler (Eds.), *Joint attention: Communication and other minds* (pp. 110–128). Oxford: Oxford University Press.

Woodward, A. L., & Guajardo, J. J. (2002). Infants' understanding of the point gesture as an object-directed action. *Cognitive Development, 17,* 1061–1084.

Woodward, A. L., & Needham, A. (Eds.). (2009). *Learning and the infant mind.* Oxford, England: Oxford University Press

Woodward, A. L., Sommerville, J. A., Gerson, S., Henderson, A. M. E., & Buresh, J. S. (2009). The emergence of intention attribution in infancy. In B. Ross (Ed.), *The psychology of learning and motivation* (Vol. 51, pp. 187–122). Burlington, VT: Academic Press.

2.3

Why Don't Apes Understand False Beliefs?

MICHAEL TOMASELLO AND HENRIKE MOLL

To give away our punch line at the beginning: We don't know why apes don't understand false beliefs. But it turns out that looking at precisely what they do and do not understand about the psychological states of others in general—what they understand about goals, intentions, perceptions, and epistemic states—helps us to be much more specific about what it takes to understand that someone has a false belief.

APES UNDERSTAND GOALS AND PERCEPTION

Great apes (most of the research is with chimpanzees) understand that others have goals and intentions (where intentions include not just a goal but a chosen behavioral means to that goal; Tomasello, Carpenter, Call, Behne, & Moll, 2005). The evidence is as follows:

- When a human passes food to a chimpanzee and then fails to do so, the ape reacts in a frustrated manner if the human is doing this for no good reason (i.e., is unwilling), whereas she waits patiently if the human is making good-faith attempts to give the object but failing or having accidents (i.e., is unable, Call, Hare, Carpenter, & Tomasello, 2004).
- When a human or conspecific needs help reaching an out-of-reach object or location, chimpanzees help them—which requires an understanding of their goal (Warneken & Tomasello, 2006; Warneken, Hare, Melis, Hanus, & Tomasello, 2007).
- When a human shows a human-raised chimpanzee an action on an object that is marked in various ways as a failed attempt toward a goal, the ape, in her turn, actually executes the intended action, not the actual action (Tomasello & Carpenter, 2005).
- When a human shows a human-raised chimpanzee a series of two actions on an object, one of which is marked in various ways as accidental, the ape, in her turn, usually executes only the intended action (Tomasello & Carpenter, 2005).
- When a human-raised chimpanzee sees a human perform an unusual action to produce an interesting result, she only reproduces it if the human did so freely, not if she was constrained to do so by the situation—she understands something of the circumstances under which the human pursued her goal (Buttelmann, Carpenter, Call, & Tomasello, 2007).

Great apes (most of the research is again with chimpanzees) also understand that others have perceptions and knowledge (where knowledge means just acquaintance with, e.g., someone saw an object at a location a few moments ago and so knows it is now there). Evidence is as follows:

- When a human peers behind a barrier, apes move over to get a better viewing angle to look behind it as well (Bräuer, Call, & Tomasello, 2006; Tomasello, Hare, & Agnetta, 1999).
- When a human gazes at a barrier and there is also an object further along the scan path, apes look only to the barrier and not to the object—unless the barrier has a window in it, in which case they look to the object (Okamoto-Barth et al., 2007).
- When apes beg a human for food, they take into account whether the human can see their gesture (Kaminski, Call, & Tomasello, 2004; Liebal, Call, Tomasello, & Pika, 2004).
- When chimpanzees compete with one another for food, they take into account whether their competitor can see the contested food (Hare, Call, Agnetta, & Tomasello, 2000), and they even attempt to conceal their approach from a competitor

(Hare, Call, & Tomasello, 2006; Melis, Call, & Tomasello, 2006).

- When chimpanzees compete with one another for food, they take into account whether their competitor knows the location of the contested food (because he witnessed the hiding process a few moments before; Hare, Call, & Tomasello, 2001; Kaminski, Call, & Tomasello, 2008).

Interestingly and importantly, the vast majority of these studies have counterparts in human children, with the typical age of success being around 1 to 2 years of age. The conclusion is thus that apes and young children both understand in the same basic way that individuals have goals (and intentions) in the form of an internal representation of some desired state of the world. They also understand in the same basic way as young children that individuals perceive (and know) things in the world and that this affects their goal-directed actions. In a review of all the extant literature, Call and Tomasello (2008) conclude that great apes, like human 1-year-olds, operate with a kind of perception-goal psychology about how others "work" as psychological beings.

BUT NOT FALSE BELIEFS

In contrast to all of these positive findings on the social cognition of great apes, in the past few years our laboratory has produced four solid negative results on the ability of great apes to understand others' false beliefs. What makes the negative results solid is that we have appropriate control conditions that rule out the possibility that subjects did not understand basic task requirements, were overwhelmed by task demands, and so forth. In addition, two of the studies were conducted with human 4- to 5-year-olds with positive results, and the other two are very similar to experimental paradigms in the literature in which 4- to 5-year-old children also show pro-

ficiency (the standard change-of-location and change-of-content tasks).

Table 2.3.1 lists some of the specifics of the four studies. For the sake of simplicity, let us simply describe two of them. In one of the studies of food competition cited earlier (Hare et al., 2001), we directly compared a knowledge-ignorance test and a false-belief test. The basic idea was this. In a competitive situation, a subordinate chimpanzee knew that a dominant would get the food if she could see it. In one study we manipulated whether the dominant saw the hiding process: Was she knowledgeable or ignorant about the hidden food's location? If the dominant was ignorant, then the subordinate should expect her to go to the two hiding locations randomly. In another study, the dominant saw the food being hidden in one location, but then while she was not looking it was moved to another location—and the subordinate saw all of this. In this case, the dominant was not just ignorant but had a false belief about where the food was located. If subordinates understood this, then they should have been able to predict that she would go to the "false" location, that is, the place where the food was no longer hidden. But they did not. In general, they behaved similarly in the ignorance condition and the misinformed (false belief) condition: In both cases they assumed she would be guessing where the food was located. Kaminski et al. (2008) used a very different experimental paradigm—but also with both a knowledge-ignorance and a false-belief test—and found exactly the same result.

In another one of these studies, Krachun et al. (2010) use a change of contents paradigm. Chimpanzee subjects first learned that a human experimenter always placed grapes in one bucket and banana pieces in a different bucket. Then the experimenter continued this training, but first placed the grape or the banana in a small box before putting the box inside the bucket. Now came the test. The experimenter placed, for example, a grape in the box and closed it in preparation

TABLE 2.3.1. SUMMARY CHARACTERISTICS OF FIVE STUDIES FINDING THAT CHIMPANZEES DO NOT UNDERSTAND FALSE BELIEFS

	Partner	Social Relation	Control	Training	Response
Call & Tomasello (1999)	Human	Cooperation	Various	Train	Object choice
Krachun et al. (2009)	Human	Cooperation	True belief	Little train	Object choice
Hare et al. (2001)	Chimp	Competition	Ignorance	No train	Food competition
Kaminski et al. (2008)	Chimp	Competition	Ignorance	Little train	Chimp chess
Krachun et al. (2010)	Human	Neutral	Ignorance	Train	Object choice

for putting it in the bucket. But then a research assistant switched the grape for a piece of banana and re-closed the box. In the false-belief condition this occurred while the experimenter had her back turned or was out of the room, whereas in a true-belief condition the experimenter watched the assistant making the switch. In such studies with young children, by about 4 to 5 years of age they understand that in the true-belief condition the experimenter knows about the switch and so will place the box in the bucket corresponding to its new content, whereas in the false-belief condition she does not know about the switch and so will place the box in the bucket corresponding to the old content (what she falsely believes to still be in there). In contrast, Krachun et al. (2010) found that chimpanzees made no difference between the two conditions. In an otherwise very different paradigm employing a change-of-location task with both false-belief and true-belief conditions, Krachun et al. (2009) found very similar results.

It is a truism in experimental psychology that negative results can have many different explanations. To conclude with any confidence that subjects do not have a certain competency, there must be control conditions, which share all of the task demands of the main conditions in which the subjects perform competently. Each of these four studies of chimpanzees' understanding of false beliefs—that is, their lack of understanding—had a very convincing control condition in which subjects performed well, two of them a true-belief control and two of them a knowledge-ignorance control. This means that the negative results cannot be attributed to subjects not following the procedures or otherwise being distracted by task demands. One can never say never in science—perhaps someone will come up with a more clever, more sensitive test next week—but our considered opinion at this point is that chimpanzees and other great apes simply do not comprehend false beliefs.

WHAT IS THE EXPLANATION?

So what is so different about knowledge and belief? Or about true belief and false belief? We think there are two answers to this question that are not mutually exclusive.

The first is that understanding a belief as false involves some kind of conflict, and indeed, in the tasks used, a conflict in which the most salient alternative, namely the agent's own knowledge of what is the case, must be suppressed or ignored. When a child is asked about another person's knowledge or true belief, the correct answer is

what she, the child, already believes to be true. No conflict. But, as is well known, questions about false belief require the child to suppress or ignore her own knowledge (overcome the pull of the real or the curse of knowledge) in order to identify what the other person falsely believes.

Evidence that this conflict between perspectives is a cause of children's difficulty with false-belief tasks is provided by studies correlating children's executive function skills with their false-belief skills (e.g., Carlson, Moses, & Breton, 2002; Sabbagh, Moses, & Shiverick, 2006). While working memory and some inhibitory skills such as planning and delay of gratification do not predict success on the false-belief task, inhibitory control tasks that involve some conflict (e.g., the bear-dragon test) do (Carlson et al., 2002). Because chimpanzees and other apes never pass the false-belief task, correlational studies of this type are not possible. It is widely believed that great apes have poor skills of inhibitory control and other executive functions, but in actuality the evidence is mixed depending on the task applied (Call, 2010; Vlamings, Hare, & Call, 2010). We are currently assessing a wide battery of tasks of self-regulation with chimpanzees, and it is already clear that they are not without some skills. Whether they have the kind of skills necessary to suppress their own belief to assess another's false belief is at the moment unknown.

Another explanation—which shares some features with the first but aims to particular more precisely why the difficulty arises in specific tasks—is that great apes lack some specific cognitive capacities that are needed in order to understand false beliefs. In the philosophical literature, beliefs occupy a special place. The reason is that beliefs are differentiated from knowledge-by-acquaintance because with beliefs the subject knows that she might be wrong. If I am familiar with something, I just am familiar with it. But if I believe something, that means that there is some possibility that I might be in error.

The best-known philosophical analysis is that of Davidson (1982). Davidson introduces the notion of "triangulation," which is very similar to the notion of "joint attention" from developmental psychology. The claim is that the notion of error can only arise in social situations in which another person and I simultaneously focus on the same object or event—but somehow differently. If I believe one thing, and then round the corner to find out that something else is the case, this does not require me to notice, let alone conceptualize, the discrepancy between reality and my former belief, because they are not two different perspectives on the same situation simultaneously—perhaps the world changed as I was rounding the corner. However, when two people are looking at the same thing at the same time, "space is created" (to use Davidson's metaphor) for the concept of error to enter the picture.

The issue was formulated in a developmental context by Moll and Tomasello (2007a) as follows. The notion of triangulation presupposes that we are both focused on the same object and that we share the knowledge that we do. Only if this shared knowledge (or joint attention or intersubjectivity) about this shared object structures our social interaction is the notion that we have different perspectives intelligible. If you look out of the window at the house across the street and I look out of the window as well but focus on a bicycle in front of the house, we do not have different perspectives, but simply different objects of perception: We just see different things. However, if we share attention to the bicycle but see it from different points of view, then it is appropriate to say that you have one perspective on it while I have another. Of course, once children understand that there are different ways of seeing the same thing, another person need not be present to complete the triangle in every case: The "generalized other" can now take the place of another individual. The child has come to realize that "one" (whether self or other) could be wrong about things or see things differently. But, initially in ontogeny, a joint attentional interaction with another person is required to elicit the clash of perspectives necessary in order to comprehend perspectival differences.

This analysis is relevant in the current context because it is arguably the case that great apes do not participate in joint attention or any other form of triangulation. From the empirical studies cited earlier, we know that chimpanzees can detect when someone cannot see something, even in situations where they themselves can see it. But they do not need the concept of perspective to do this. They are competing with the other, and they are computing his line of sight to see whether he has seen the food they are contesting. Either he does or he does not, but this does not involve the kind of confrontation of perspectives that false belief understanding entails, and the reason it does not is that the food is not a shared target of "our" attention—it is simply blocked from your vision. What creates the possibility of error and doubt is a common epistemic target but with a "space" between you and me that enables the possibility of different perspectives and error to arise.

At the moment there is no evidence that great apes engage in anything like joint attention (or shared knowledge or intersubjectivity) in the human manner. They do look back and forth from objects to social interactants (Carpenter Tomasello, & Savage-Rumbaugh, 1995), but they show none of the phenomena of child development that depend on joint attention. They do not comprehend human pointing gestures whose intended referent is recoverable only if they are in joint attention with the human pointer (see Tomasello, 2006, for a review); they do not attempt to establish joint attention with others by pointing themselves, even when given adequate opportunities; and they are not able to judge whether something is old or new to a person based on whether they have shared attention on that item with the person previously (Tomasello & Carpenter, 2005). With one another in the wild, whereas again there is mutual visual monitoring of conspecifics, there are no phenomena that would seem to be generated by any form of joint attention or mutual knowledge (e.g., such things as communicative conventions, social norms, social institutions, etc., which all depend in one way or another on shared "agreements" on how we do things).

And so the second answer is that because apes do not participate with others in any form of joint attention, they do not have any sense of different perspectives on the same entity, and therefore they do not comprehend that it is possible for someone to be in error or to have doubts about whether their own "take" on the situation is the right one.

WHAT ABOUT CHILDREN?

There is currently a very important debate in developmental psychology about when young children understand false beliefs, and perhaps the current analysis of apes is relevant to this debate. Classically, as everyone knows, young children were thought to understand false beliefs when they passed either the Sally Anne task (change of location) or the Smarties task (change of content), at about 4 to 5 years of age (Wellman, Cross, & Watson, 2001). But, as everyone also knows, several recent studies have been interpreted as demonstrating false-belief understanding (or at least sensitivity to false beliefs) in 1- to 2-year-olds (e.g., Buttelmann, Carpenter, & Tomasello, 2009; Onishi & Baillargeon, 2005; Senju, Csibra, & Southgate, 2007). These studies use different methods than the classic tasks, and so the debate represents clashes about methods and definitional criteria as well as substantive theories.

In the current analysis, we can argue that children should actually be expected to begin understanding false beliefs soon after their first birthdays because that is when they start sharing attention with others and begin to show an understanding that others may not know things they themselves know—where "knowing" in this context simply means to be familiar or acquainted with an object (e.g., Moll & Tomasello, 2007b; Tomasello & Haberl, 2003). However, something is still missing at this point. In the analysis of Moll and Meltzoff (in press), infants during the second year of life can *take* the perspective of others, but they struggle when different perspectives *confront* one another (see Perner, Stummer, Sprung, & Doherty, 2002). In the case of false beliefs and different visual perspectives the clash or confrontation may be obvious because the alternatives are mutually exclusive: believing an object to be in a certain location or seeing a visual array from a specific viewpoint makes it impossible to have a different construal or view of the situation at that time (I cannot at the same time believe the chocolate to be in the drawer and in the cupboard, or see the turtle right-side-up and upside-down). But a confrontation of perspectives can come about even when they are not incompatible or mutually exclusive in this sense. For example, a particular animal can be called both a "horse" and a "pony" (in the alternative naming task; Doherty & Perner, 1998) or a "deceptive object" can be a sponge that has an appearance of a rock (in the appearance-reality task; e.g., Flavell, 1993). However, children younger than 4 to 5 years nonetheless *treat them* as somehow mutually exclusive or as competing for the same "role" of naming the object's identity. They do not allow for, at least in their explicit judgments, other ways of "seeing" an object besides the one that is most obvious to them at the time. The ability to resolve confronting perspectives thus enables children at around 4 to 5 years of age to pass not just false-belief and visual perspective-taking tasks but also appearance-reality and alternative naming tests.

For this account to work, it would need to be the case that the infant studies showing an understanding of or sensitivity to false beliefs do not involve confronting perspectives. This is clearly true in a study using active behavioral measures. Buttelmann et al. (2009) had 18-month-olds watch while an adult placed her favorite toy into a box. He then left the room (in the false-belief condition) and the child and a research assistant moved the toy to a different box. The adult then returned and approached the box in which she had placed her toy and tried to open it. The research assistant told the child to "help him." The children did not try to help him open the box he was struggling with, but rather went and retrieved the toy from the other box. In a true-belief condition in which the adult stayed in the room and watched the transfer, children did not go fetch the toy but rather tried to help them open the box he was struggling with. The reason why there are no conflicting perspectives here is that the infant is not trying to determine the adult's belief but rather his goal. She is asking herself: "What is he trying to do?" and she is answering it differently depending on the knowledge state of the adult: But because the focus is not on the belief itself, it does not end up being confronted with the child's own knowledge of the situation. In Senju, Csibra, and Southgate's (2007) study, infants simply looked to the location in anticipation of where an agent would emerge based on his belief (i.e., one location if he believed the reward was there and another location if he believed the reward was there), but again, without having to make a reference to the other's belief directly, which would lead to a confrontation with the child's own knowledge. In Onishi and Baillargeon's (2005) study, since it simply involves looking times, infants only need to notice that something is not going as it normally does (people usually look for objects where they last saw them, but this adult is not doing that). The more general point is that there is no possibility of error in looking-time experiments, because the infant is just attending to what grabs her attention, not making a judgment.

In any case, the current proposal is that understanding false beliefs requires understanding that another person and I share attention to or knowledge of one and the same reality (which we know together), while at the same time having different perspectives on it. Although chimpanzees and other great apes understand goals and perception, they do not understand false beliefs because they do not fulfill the prerequisite of sharing attention with others (in the sense that they do not mutually know they are doing this), and so the notion of perspective does not arise at all. One-year-old human children share attention and develop a rudimentary and, at first, implicit understanding of perspectives inside such joint attentional frames. They thus perform well in tests that are set up in a way that other agents act in accordance with a false belief—as long as they need not explicitly reason about the false belief or predict the behavior that follows from it, because this is exactly what requires comparing or confronting of perspectives. Older children become much better at comparing different perspectives when they confront one another in various ways, and this enables them to pass false belief and many other tasks from the standard "theory of mind" battery that are more demanding than the infant studies in these ways (see Moll & Tomasello, in press).

The larger theoretical perspective—brought into especially clear relief in the great apes—is that understanding false beliefs is not like understanding goals, perception, and other "simple" mental states. Understanding false beliefs requires grasping the possibility of different views of the same thing, which relies on more basic skills of joint attention to establish the shared reality about which there may be differing beliefs.

REFERENCES

Bräuer, J., Call, J., & Tomasello, M. (2006). Are apes really inequity averse? *Proceedings of the Royal Society of London, 273,* 3123–3128.

Buttelmann, D., Carpenter, M., Call, J., & Tomasello, M. (2007). Enculturated chimpanzees imitate rationally. *Developmental Science, 10,* F31–F38.

Buttelmann, D., Carpenter, M., & Tomasello, M. (2009). Eighteen-month-old infants show false belief understanding in an active helping paradigm. *Cognition, 112,* 337–342.

Call, J. (2010). Do apes know that they can be wrong? *Animal Cognition, 13,* 689–700.

Call, J., Hare, B., Carpenter, M., & Tomasello, M. (2004). "Unwilling" versus "unable": Chimpanzees' understanding of human intentional action. *Developmental Science, 7,* 488–498.

Call, J., & Tomasello, M. (1999). A nonverbal false belief task: The performance of children and great apes. *Child Development, 70,* 381–395

Call, J., & Tomasello, M. (2008). Does the chimpanzee have a theory of mind? 30 years later. *Trends in Cognitive Sciences, 12,* 187–192.

Carlson, S., Moses, L., & Breton, C. (2002). How specific is the relation between executive function and theory of mind? Contributions of inhibitory control and working memory. *Infant and Child Development, 11,* 73–92.

Carpenter, M., Tomasello, M., & Savage-Rumbaugh, S. (1995). Joint attention and imitative learning in children, chimpanzees, and enculturated chimpanzees. *Social Development, 4,* 217–237.

Davidson, D. (1982). Rational animals. *Dialectica, 36,* 317–327.

Doherty, M., & Perner, J. (1998). Metalinguistic awareness and theory of mind: Just two words for the same thing? *Cognitive Development, 13,* 279–305.

Flavell, J. (1993). The development of children's understanding of false belief and the appearance-reality distinction. *International Journal of Psychology, 28,* 595–604.

Hare, B., Call, J., Agnetta, B., & Tomasello, M. (2000). Chimpanzees know what conspecifics do and do not see. *Animal Behaviour, 59,* 771–785.

Hare, B., Call, J., & Tomasello, M. (2001). Do chimpanzees know what conspecifics know? *Animal Behaviour, 61,* 139–151.

Hare, B., Call, J., & Tomasello, M. (2006). Chimpanzees deceive a human competitor by hiding. *Cognition, 101,* 495–514.

Kaminski, J., Call, J., & Tomasello, M. (2004). Body orientation and face orientation: Two factors controlling apes' begging behavior from humans. *Animal Cognition, 7,* 216–223.

Kaminski, J., Call, J., & Tomasello, M. (2008). Chimpanzees know what others know, but not what they believe. *Cognition, 109,* 224–234.

Krachun, C., Carpenter, M., Call, J., & Tomasello, M. (2009). A competitive, nonverbal false belief task for children and apes. *Developmental Science, 12,* 521–523

Krachun, C., Carpenter, M., Call, J., & Tomasello, M. (2010). A new change-of-contents false belief test: Children and chimpanzees compared. *International Journal of Comparative Psychology, 23,* 145–165.

Liebal, K., Call, J., Tomasello, M., & Pika, S. (2004). To move or not to move: How apes adjust to the attentional state of others. *Interaction Studies, 5,* 199–219.

Melis, A., Call, J., & Tomasello, M. (2006). Chimpanzees conceal visual and auditory information from others. *Journal of Comparative Psychology, 120,* 154–162.

Moll, H., & Tomasello, M. (2007a). Cooperation and human cognition: The Vygotskian intelligence hypothesis. *Philosophical Transactions of the Royal Society B, 362,* 639–648.

Moll, H., & Tomasello, M. (2007b). How 14- and 18-month-olds know what others have experienced. *Developmental Psychology, 43,* 309–317.

Moll, H., & Meltzoff, A. N. (2011). Perspective-taking and its foundation in joint attention. In N. Eilan, H. Lerman, & J. Roessler (Eds.), *Perception, causation, and objectivity. Issues in philosophy and psychology* (pp. 286–304). Oxford, England: Oxford University Press.

Moll, H., & Tomasello, M. (in press). Social cognition in the second year of life. In A. Leslie & T. German

(Eds.), *Handbook of theory of mind*. Mahwah, NJ: Erlbaum.

Okamoto-Barth, S., Call, J., & Tomasello, M. (2007). Great apes understanding of others' line of sight. *Psychological Science, 18*, 462–468.

Onishi, K., & Baillargeon, R. (2005). Do 15-month-old infants understand false beliefs? *Science, 308*, 255–258.

Perner, J., Stummer, S., Sprung, M., & Doherty, M. (2002). Theory of mind finds its Piagetian perspective: Why alternative naming comes with understanding belief. *Cognitive Development, 17*, 1451–1472.

Sabbagh, M., Moses, L., & Shiverick, S. (2006). Executive functioning and preschoolers' understanding of false beliefs, false photographs, and false signs. *Child Development, 77*, 1034–1049.

Southgate, V., Senju, A., & Csibra G. (2007). Action anticipation through attribution of false belief by two-year-olds. *Psychological Science, 18*, 587–592.

Tomasello, M. (2006). Why don't apes point? In N. J. Enfield & S. C. Levinson (Eds.), *Roots of human sociality: Culture, cognition and interaction* (pp. 506–524). Oxford, England & New York: Berg.

Tomasello, M., & Carpenter, M. (2005). The emergence of social cognition in three young chimpanzees. *Monographs of the Society for Research in Child Development, 70*, 133–152.

Tomasello, M., Carpenter, M., Call, J., Behne, T., & Moll, H. (2005). Understanding and sharing intentions: The origins of cultural cognition. *Behavioral and Brain Sciences, 28*, 675–735.

Tomasello, M., & Haberl, K. (2003). Understanding attention: 12- and 18-month-olds know what is new for other persons. *Developmental Psychology, 39*, 906–912.

Tomasello, M., Hare, B., & Agnetta, B. (1999). Chimpanzees, Pan troglodytes, follow gaze direction geometrically. *Animal Behaviour, 58*, 769–777.

Vlamings, P., Hare, B., & Call, J. (2010). Reaching around barriers: The performance of the great apes and 3- to 5-year-old children. *Animal Cognition, 13*, 273–285

Warneken, F., Hare, B., Melis, A. P., Hanus, D., & Tomasello, M. (2007). Spontaneous altruism by chimpanzees and young children. *PLoS Biology, 5*, e184.

Warneken, F., & Tomasello, M. (2006). Altruistic helping in human infants and young chimpanzees. *Science, 31*, 1301–1303.

Wellman, H., Cross, D., & Watson, J. (2001). Meta-analysis of theory-of-mind development: The truth about false belief. *Child Development, 72*, 655–684.

2.4

False-Belief Understanding and Why it Matters

The Social-Acting Hypothesis

RENÉE BAILLARGEON, ZIJING HE, PEIPEI SETOH, ROSE M. SCOTT,
STEPHANIE SLOANE, AND DANIEL Y.-J. YANG

From a very early age, infants attempt to make sense of the world around them. This causal reasoning appears to be carried out by a small number of special-purpose reasoning systems; each system operates without explicit awareness and is triggered whenever infants attend to events, or aspects of events, that fall within the purview of the system. Thus, the physical-reasoning system deals with the interactions of objects and other physical entities; the psychological-reasoning system deals with the intentional actions of agents; and the sociomoral-reasoning system deals with the interactions of individuals within and across social groups. Each reasoning system has at its core a distinct explanatory framework that enables infants to form specific expectations about events. Because each framework is at best skeletal, early expectations tend to be highly abstract and lacking in all mechanistic detail; nevertheless, they play a critical role in determining how infants respond to and learn about events. To a remarkable degree, all reasoning systems are able to operate jointly: Thus, when infants watch a complex event with salient physical, psychological, and social components, the relevant reasoning systems work together seamlessly to yield a causally coherent interpretation of the event.

In this chapter, we focus primarily on the psychological-reasoning system. We first briefly describe its two subsystems and then discuss the long-standing and controversial question of when the second subsystem—the one responsible for our uniquely human ability to understand that others may hold and act on false beliefs—becomes operational in development. Finally, we propose that, beyond false-belief understanding, this second subsystem (when recruited by the sociomoral-reasoning system) allows individuals to decouple what they think and feel from what they choose to communicate to others in everyday social interactions. We speculate that the primary function of social acting—in the form of white lies, tactful omissions, feigned interest, hidden disappointments, false cheer, and the like—is that of maintaining positivity within social groups, thereby supporting in-group loyalty (for related ideas, see, e.g., DePaulo & Bell, 1996; Lakoff, 1973; Lee & Ross, 1997; Sweetser, 1987).

THE PSYCHOLOGICAL-REASONING SYSTEM

When infants identify an entity—whether human or nonhuman—as an agent and attend to its actions, their psychological-reasoning system enables them to infer some of the likely mental states underlying the agent's actions. Two subsystems are assumed to be involved in the attribution of mental states, subsystem-1 (SS1) and subsystem-2 (SS2) (e.g., Leslie, 1995; Scott & Baillargeon, 2009).

When infants watch an agent act in a scene, SS1 enables them to attribute at least two kinds of mental states to the agent: motivational states, which specify the agent's motivation in the scene (e.g., goals, dispositions), and epistemic states, which specify what the agent knows and what the agent does not know about the scene. When an agent is ignorant about some aspect of a scene (e.g., the agent cannot see an object, or a portion of an object, that the infant sees), a masking mechanism blocks the information that is unavailable to the agent, enabling the infant to predict and interpret the agent's actions in terms of the remaining, shared information (e.g., Luo & Beck, 2010).

SS2 extends SS1 and enables infants to attribute counterfactual states to agents; these states include false and pretend beliefs. When an agent holds information about a scene that is incompatible with the information available to the infant (e.g., the agent believes a toy is in location-A, but the infant knows the toy has been moved to location-B; the agent pretends to be riding a horse, but the infant knows the horse is really a broom), SS2 allows the infant to represent these divergent beliefs. A decoupling mechanism enables the infant to create a separate representation of the scene that incorporates the agent's false or pretend beliefs but otherwise functions as expected, making it possible for the infant to predict and interpret the agent's actions (e.g., Leslie, 1994).

Why Two Subsystems?

There are at least four reasons for positing two separate subsystems in infants' psychological-reasoning system. First, the masking mechanism of SS1 seems intuitively very different from the decoupling mechanism of SS2; masking or blocking out the portion of reality that is unavailable to an agent seems computationally far simpler than creating a second, alternative version of reality that incorporates an agent's false or pretend beliefs (e.g., Scott & Baillargeon, 2009). Second, recent evidence from neuroscience suggests that the brain regions associated with SS1 and SS2 tasks do not fully overlap (e.g., Yang & Pelphrey, in press; Young & Saxe, 2009). Third, although there is extensive evidence that nonhuman primates possess psychological-reasoning abilities akin to those carried out by SS1, there is currently no robust evidence that they can either attribute false beliefs or comprehend pretense (e.g., Call & Tomasello, 2008). Finally, children and adults living with autism appear to have specific difficulties with false-belief and pretense tasks (e.g., Senju, Southgate, White, & Frith, 2009). Together, these results suggest that the decoupling mechanism of SS2 emerged late in evolution, is relatively fragile, and is somewhat impaired or deficient in individuals living with autism.

WHEN DOES SUBSYSTEM-2 BECOME OPERATIONAL?

SS1 is operational early in life: There is considerable evidence that young infants can attribute simple goals and dispositions to agents and that they hold different expectations for the actions of knowledgeable and ignorant agents (e.g., Luo & Baillargeon, 2010). The question of when SS2 becomes operational has been far more controversial.

Elicited-Response False-Belief Tasks

Beginning with the seminal work of Wimmer and Perner (1983), much of the research on early psychological reasoning has focused on the question of when children become able to attribute false beliefs to others. Initial investigations used elicited-response tasks in which children answer a direct question about the likely behavior of an agent who holds a false belief about a scene. In a classic task (Baron-Cohen, Leslie, & Frith, 1985), children listen to a story enacted with props: Sally hides a marble in a basket and then leaves; in her absence, Anne moves the marble to a nearby box; Sally then returns, and children are asked where she will look for her marble. Beginning at about age 4, children typically answer correctly and point to the basket (where Sally falsely believes the marble is); in contrast, most 3-year-olds point to the box (where the marble actually is), suggesting that they do not yet understand that Sally holds a false belief about the marble's location. This developmental pattern was subsequently confirmed with elicited-response tasks testing different false beliefs and with children from different countries (e.g., Liu, Wellman, Tardif, & Sabbagh, 2008).

Broadly speaking, two very different accounts were proposed for these findings. In the dominant (late-emergence) account, researchers suggested that false-belief understanding did not emerge until the preschool years, as a result of conceptual, executive-function, or linguistic advances (e.g., Carlson & Moses, 2001; Wimmer & Perner, 1983). The other (early-emergence) account argued that (1) SS2 had to be operational much earlier, since the same decoupling mechanism underlies pretense and false-belief reasoning and infants in the second year of life already engage in pretense, and therefore (2) preschoolers' failures at elicited-response false-belief tasks had to reflect performance limitations, such as inhibition difficulties (e.g., Leslie, 1994; Leslie & Polizzi, 1998). In line with the early-emergence account, 3-year-olds performed somewhat better at elicited-response false-belief tasks when inhibition demands were reduced through various means; however, children's performance was typically no better than chance, providing only weak support for the account (e.g., Kovács, 2009; Yazdi, German, Defeyter, & Siegal, 2006).

A critical new research direction began with the discovery that 3-year-olds gave evidence of

[handwritten marginal note: Why age 4? what's so special about 4?]

[handwritten marginalia: is the confounding issue the linguistic? decoupling thing? masking?]

false-belief understanding when the experimenter delivered the standard test question (e.g., "Where will Sally look for her marble?") as a self-addressed prompt, rather than as a direct question: Upon hearing the prompt, children spontaneously looked at the marble's original location, thus correctly anticipating where Sally's false belief would lead her to search (e.g., Clements & Perner, 1994). These positive results gave rise to the possibility that children younger than age 3 might also demonstrate false-belief understanding in tasks designed to measure their spontaneous—instead of their elicited—responses to test scenes.

Spontaneous-Response False-Belief Tasks

Beginning with the work of Onishi and Baillargeon (2005), several different spontaneous-response false-belief tasks have been developed for use with infants and toddlers. Positive results have now been obtained with children ages 7 months to 2.5 years, indicating that SS2 is already operational in the first year of life and as such supporting the early-emergence account (e.g., Baillargeon, Scott, & He, 2010; He, Bolz, & Baillargeon, 2011; Kovács, Téglés, & Endress, 2010; Scott, Baillargeon, Song, & Leslie, 2010). To illustrate false-belief reasoning in young infants, we next describe a recent violation-of-expectation experiment with 11-month-olds (He & Baillargeon, 2012); this experiment was based on prior physical-reasoning findings that, by about 7.5 months, infants realize that a tall object can be hidden in a tall but not a short container (e.g., Hespos & Baillargeon, 2006).

Infants were assigned to a false-belief, a knowledge, or an ignorance condition. In the false-belief condition, infants first received four familiarization trials (see Fig. 2.4.1). In each trial, a female agent sat at a window in the back wall of a puppet-stage apparatus, and a female experimenter knelt at

False-belief Condition

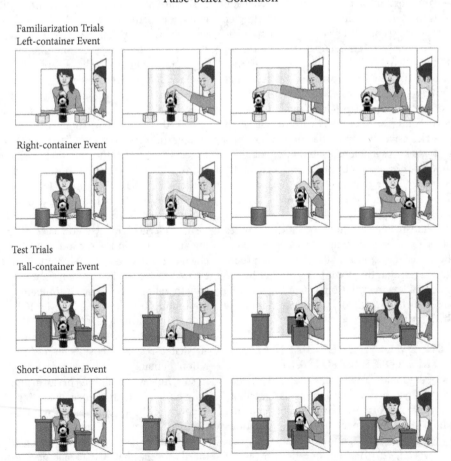

FIGURE 2.4.1: Familiarization and test events shown in the false-belief condition of He and Baillargeon (2012).

a window in the right wall; on the apparatus floor were two short open containers and a tall toy dog. The agent played with the dog briefly, returned it to the apparatus floor, and then hid herself by lifting a large cloth that filled her window. The experimenter placed the dog in one of the containers and then signaled the agent to return ("Ok!"). At that point, the agent lowered her cloth, grasped the dog's head, and paused until the trial ended. Across trials, different containers were used, and the dog was placed in the left or the right container (order was counterbalanced); the familiarization trials thus served to establish that the agent wanted the dog and reached for it wherever the experimenter happened to place it. Next, infants received two test trials involving a tall and a short container, each closed with a lid; the dog was taller than the short but not the tall container. As before,

the agent played with the dog and then hid behind her cloth. Next, the experimenter shortened the dog (its body was a rigid cylinder that could be collapsed by pressing firmly on its head) and placed it in the short container. When the agent returned, she grasped the lid of either the tall container (tall-container event) or the short container (short-container event), and then she paused until the trial ended. If infants reasoned that the agent (1) should falsely believe that the dog was still tall and hence (2) should falsely infer that it was hidden in the tall container (since tall objects cannot be hidden in short containers), then they should expect the agent to reach for the tall container and they should look reliably longer when she reached for the short container instead. Infants in the knowledge condition (see Fig. 2.4.2) saw similar test events except that the agent watched all of the

FIGURE 2.4.2: Test events shown in the knowledge and ignorance conditions of He and Baillargeon (2012). Infants in these conditions saw the same familiarization events as in the false-belief condition, with one exception: In the knowledge condition, the agent's cloth had a large hole that enabled her to watch the experimenter's actions.

[handwritten margin note: unable to put others perspectives first → selfishness↗]

experimenter's actions through a large hole in her cloth and hence knew where the dog was hidden. Infants in this condition should thus expect the agent to reach for the short container, and they should look reliably longer when she reached for the tall container instead. Finally, infants in the ignorance condition again saw test events similar to those in the false-belief condition except that, before the agent hid behind her cloth, she saw the experimenter shorten the dog. Because the shortened dog could be hidden in either container, infants should expect the agent to reach randomly for the tall or the short container, and they should thus look about equally at the two events.

As predicted, infants in the false-belief condition looked reliably longer at the short- than at the tall-container event, infants in the knowledge condition showed the reverse looking pattern, and infants in the ignorance condition looked about equally at the two events. Together, these results indicate that, by 11 months of age, infants can already attribute false beliefs to others.

Why Are Elicited-Response False-Belief Tasks Difficult for Young Children?

If children succeed at spontaneous-response false-belief tasks before they reach their first birthday, why do they fail at elicited-response false-belief tasks until about age 4? According to our processing-load account, elicited-response tasks not only require children to represent the agent's false belief but also involve at least two executive-function · processes (e.g., Scott, He, Baillargeon, & Cummins, 2012). One is an inhibition process: When children are asked the test question (and thus shift from merely observing the test scene to engaging in a verbal interaction about it), their own perspective on the scene naturally becomes prominent and must be inhibited to allow them to adopt the agent's perspective. The other process is a response-selection process: Children must select a response to the test question. The inhibition and response-selection processes are both important. In low-demand false-belief tasks where little inhibition is required (e.g., where Anne, instead of moving the marble to the box, takes it away to an undisclosed location), 2.5-year-olds typically perform at chance, because the simultaneous activation of the false-belief-representation and response-selection processes overwhelms their limited information-processing resources; children do succeed, however, if first given practice trials designed to reduce response-selection demands (Setoh, Scott, & Baillargeon, 2011). In

more typical high-demand false-belief tasks (e.g., where Anne moves the marble to the box), young children fail even if given response-selection practice trials because their inhibitory skills are too immature to enable them to inhibit their own prominent perspective on the scene.

According to the processing-load account, spontaneous-response false-belief tasks are thus easier because (1) children observe the false-belief scene as bystanders so that their own perspective is less salient, leaving them free to reason about the scene from the agent's perspective, and (2) children respond spontaneously, so that the response-selection process is not engaged.

WHY DOES SUBSYSTEM-2 MATTER?

We have reviewed evidence that SS2 is typically operational in the first year of life, is impaired in individuals living with autism, and is absent in nonhuman primates. Why does SS2 matter? As alluded to in the Introduction, we suspect that, beyond false-belief understanding, an intact SS2 enables individuals to engage in everyday social acting. Whether one is pretending to ride a horse or pretending to adore the latest inspirational window ornament offered by Great-Aunt Petunia, one is still pretending.

In-Group Support, Positivity, and Social Acting

One of the principles guiding sociomoral reasoning in adults and children is that of in-group support (Baillargeon et al., in press). Like adults, young children tend to prefer members of their own groups, to help in-group members in need of assistance, to display in-group favoritism when distributing resources, and so on (e.g., Brewer, 1999; Kinzler, Dupoux, & Spelke, 2007; Olson & Spelke, 2008; Over & Carpenter, 2009; Sloane, Baillargeon, & Premack, 2010; Warneken & Tomasello, 2006). Recent evidence from our laboratory suggests that infants also expect individuals from the same social group to maintain positivity; for example, mild negative actions (e.g., throwing someone's toy on the floor), when produced without provocation, are viewed as unexpected or impermissible if directed at in-group members, but not if directed at out-group members or at individuals whose group membership is unspecified (e.g., He & Baillargeon, 2011). From an evolutionary standpoint, it does not seem implausible that, during the millions of years our ancestors lived in small bands of hunter-gatherers, selective pressures supported the acquisition of various pro-group biases, including positivity; after all, positivity would facilitate cooperation within a group and as such would contribute to the group's long-term prosperity and survival.

Our findings concerning early positivity led us to the hypothesis—termed the social-acting hypothesis—that one ubiquitous advantage conferred by an intact SS2 is that it allows individuals to engage in social acting with in-group members for the specific purpose of maintaining positivity: preventing aggressive confrontations, avoiding hurt or embarrassed feelings, smoothing over awkward situations, bolstering feelings of trust, and so on.

The brilliant actor Marlon Brando insisted that acting is something all of us do every day. When interviewed on *The Dick Cavett Show* in 1973, Mr. Brando said: "We couldn't survive a second if we weren't able to act. Acting is a survival mechanism. It's a social unguent and it's a lubricant.... People lie constantly every day by not saying something that they think, or [by] saying something that they didn't think" (as reported by Susan Stamberg on Morning Edition, National Public Radio, November 9, 2010). Judith Martin, in her essential *Miss Manners' Guide to Excruciatingly Correct Behavior* (1983), lobbied for more acting. When asked the question "You wouldn't want me to pretend to something I don't really feel, would you?" Miss Manners answered, "Why, yes. Please." She went on to explain that she was forever "trying to persuade people to fake such feelings as delight upon receiving useless presents, curiosity about the welfare of the terminally boring, [and] pleasure in the success of competitors" (p. 243).

According to the social-acting hypothesis, SS2 is one of the critical structures that enable us to decouple what we privately think and feel from what we display outwardly in everyday interactions. As Mr. Brando and Ms. Martin aptly observed, we do not, and should not, speak our minds at every turn; instead, we convey more or less than we believe, we exaggerate some sentiments while suppressing others, we embellish, we equivocate, we feign interest and approval, all in a constant and semi-successful effort to limit aggression and to "lubricate" everyday encounters with members of our social groups (e.g., DePaulo & Bell, 1996; DePaulo & Kashy, 1998). Of course, SS2 also helps us understand that others, too, engage in social acting, allowing us to respond appropriately (Yang & Baillargeon, in press).

From a developmental perspective, the social-acting hypothesis views skillful, nuanced, and context-sensitive social acting as a staggering accomplishment, not fully achieved until late in development, and profoundly shaped by familial, social, and cultural practices (e.g., Broomfield, Robinson, & Robinson, 2002; Heyman & Sweet, 2009; Ma, Xu, Heyman, & Lee, 2011; Xu, Bao, Fu, Talwar, & Lee, 2010). By comparison, demonstrating an understanding of false belief, deception, or pretense in a laboratory experiment seems like an easy feat.

Testing the Social-Acting Hypothesis

The social-acting hypothesis makes several interesting predictions, which we are beginning to test. For example, in an ongoing violation-of-expectation experiment by Setoh, He, and Baillargeon, 2.5- to 3-year-old toddlers watch an individual pretend to eat and to enjoy a food she does not like; the experiment tests whether children view the individual's pretense and deception as expected when she is interacting with an in-group member (i.e., the individual is engaging in social acting), but as unexpected when she is interacting with an out-group member. The two social groups used in the experiment are novel, arbitrary groups identified by nonsense labels.

Children are assigned to an in-group or an out-group condition. In the in-group condition, children first receive two category-induction trials. In each trial, three female individuals sit on the three sides of a puppet-stage apparatus (the child sits at the front) and label themselves: the individual on the right (R) says, "I am a lumi!"; the individual at the back (B) says, "I am a lumi, too!"; and the individual on the left (L) says, "I am a tarfen!" R and B thus belong to the same social group, and L to a different group. In the next, familiarization trial, B is alone; R' and L's positions are closed with curtains. B finds a distinctive cracker, eats it, and expresses disgust ("Yucky!"). In the test trials, L is again absent, and B watches as R opens her window and brings in a box of the same crackers. R eats two crackers with obvious enjoyment, places a third cracker in front of B, and then leaves briefly. While R is gone, B looks at the cracker with distaste ("Eww!") and drops it on the room floor. When R returns, B pretends to be chewing and smiles at R as though enjoying the cracker ("Yummy!"); R and B then pause until the trial ends. Children in the out-group condition see identical events except that in the category-induction trials B states that she is a tarfen, making her a member of the same group as L rather than R. Test results indicate that children in the out-group condition look reliably longer than those in the in-group condition, suggesting that children can make sense of B's pretense and deception when she belongs to the same social group as R (i.e., B's actions serve to maintain in-group positivity), but not when she belongs to a different social group than R. Results from control conditions support this interpretation.

CONCLUDING REMARKS

Until recently, it was generally assumed that the achievement of false-belief understanding marked a critical milestone in the development of children's "Theory of Mind." In this article, we have argued that false-belief understanding can in fact be demonstrated in the first year of life, as long as one uses spontaneous-response tasks; that preschoolers' difficulties with traditional, elicited-response tasks stem primarily from immature executive-function processes; and that the psychological-reasoning system's decoupling subsystem (SS2), which enables infants to understand false beliefs, deception, and pretense, is also used by the sociomoral-reasoning system for the purpose of comprehending and performing social acting. According to the hypothesis proposed here, social acting serves the principle of in-group support: Maintaining a modicum of positivity within a group limits the number of aggressive or negative interactions and facilitates cooperation, thereby supporting the group's long-term prosperity and survival. In line with this hypothesis, we presented evidence that toddlers expect social acting between members of the same social group, but not between members of different social groups; future research will examine whether infants share the same expectation.

ACKNOWLEDGMENTS

The redaction of this article was supported by an NICHD grant to Renée Baillargeon (HD-021104). We thank Clark Barrett and Glenn Roisman for helpful suggestions.

REFERENCES

Baillargeon, R., Scott, R. M., & He, Z. (2010). False-belief understanding in infants. *Trends in Cognitive Sciences, 14*, 110–118.

Baillargeon, R., Scott, R. M., He, Z., Sloane, S., Setoh, P., Jin, K., & Bian, L. (in press). Psychological and sociomoral reasoning in infancy. In P. Shaver & M. Mikulincer (Eds.-in-chief) & E. Borgida & J. Bargh (Vol. Eds.), *APA Handbook of Personality and Social Psychology: Vol.1. Attitudes and Social Cognition*. Washington, D.C.: APA.

Baron-Cohen, S., Leslie, A. M., & Frith, U. (1985). Does the autistic child have a "theory of mind"? *Cognition, 21*, 37–46.

Brewer, M. B. (1999). The psychology of prejudice: Ingroup love or outgroup hate? *Journal of Social Issues, 55*, 429–444.

Broomfield, K. A., Robinson, E. J., & Robinson, W. P. (2002). Children's understanding about white lies. *British Journal of Developmental Psychology, 20*, 47–65.

Call, J., & Tomasello, M. (2008). Does the chimpanzee have a theory of mind? 30 years later. *Trends in Cognitive Sciences, 12*, 187–192.

Carlson, S. M., & Moses, L. J. (2001). Individual differences in inhibitory control and children's theory of mind. *Child Development, 72*, 1032–1053.

Clements, W. A., & Perner, J. (1994). Implicit understanding of belief. *Cognitive Development, 9*, 377–395.

DePaulo, B. M., & Bell, K. (1996). Truth and investment: Lies are told to those who care. *Journal of Personality and Social Psychology, 71*, 703–716.

DePaulo, B. M., & Kashy, D. A. (1998). Everyday lies in close and casual relationships. *Journal of Personality and Social Psychology, 74*, 63–79.

He, Z., & Baillargeon, R. (2011, March). *Infants expect individuals to retaliate more severely against outgroup members*. Paper presented at the Biennial Meeting of the Society for Research in Child Development, Montreal, Canada.

He, Z., & Baillargeon, R. (2012, June). *Young infants attribute to others knowledge based on memory and on inference*. Paper presented at the Biennial International Conference on Infant Studies, Minneapolis, MN.

He, Z., Bolz, M., & Baillargeon, R. (2011). False-belief understanding in 2.5-year-olds: Evidence from change-of-location and unexpected-contents violation-of-expectation tasks. *Developmental Science, 14*, 292–305.

Hespos, S. J., & Baillargeon, R. (2006). Décalage in infants' knowledge about occlusion and containment events: Converging evidence from action tasks. *Cognition, 99*, B31–B41.

Heyman, G. D., & Sweet, M. A. (2009). Children's reasoning about lie-telling and truth-telling in politeness contexts. *Social Development, 18*, 728–746.

Kinzler, K. D., Dupoux, E., & Spelke, E. S. (2007). The native language of social cognition. *Proceedings of the National Academy of Sciences USA, 104*, 12577–12580.

Kovács, Á. M. (2009). Early bilingualism enhances mechanisms of false-belief reasoning. *Developmental Science, 12*, 48–54.

Kovács, Á. M., Téglás, E., & Endress, A. D. (2010). The social sense: Susceptibility to others' beliefs in human infants and adults. *Science, 24*, 1830–1834.

Lakoff, R. (1973). The logic of politeness, or minding your P's and Q's. In C. Corum, T. C. Smith-Stark, & A.

Weiser (Eds.), *Papers from the Ninth Regional Meeting of the Chicago Linguistics Society* (pp. 292–305). Chicago, IL: Chicago Linguistics Society.

Lee, K., & Ross, H. J. (1997). The concept of lying in adolescents and young adults: Testing Sweetser's folkloristic model. *Merrill-Palmer Quarterly, 43,* 255–270.

Leslie, A. M. (1994). Pretending and believing: Issues in the theory of ToMM. *Cognition, 50,* 211–238.

Leslie, A. M. (1995). A theory of agency. In D. Sperber, D. Premack, & A. J. Premack (Eds.), *Causal cognition: A multidisciplinary debate* (pp. 121–141). Oxford, England: Clarendon Press.

Leslie, A. M., & Polizzi, P. (1998). Inhibitory processing in the false belief task: Two conjectures. *Developmental Science, 1,* 247–253.

Liu, D., Wellman, H. M., Tardif, T., & Sabbagh, M. A. (2008). Theory of mind development in Chinese children: A meta-analysis of false-belief understanding across cultures and languages. *Developmental Psychology, 44,* 523–531.

Luo, Y., & Baillargeon, R. (2010). Towards a mentalistic account of early psychological reasoning. *Current Directions in Psychological Science, 19,* 301–307.

Luo, Y., & Beck, W. (2010). Do you see what I see? Infants' reasoning about others' incomplete perceptions. *Developmental Science, 13,* 134–142.

Ma, F., Xu, F., Heyman, G. D., & Lee, K. (2011). Chinese children's evaluations of white lies: Weighing the consequences for recipients. *Journal of Experimental Child Psychology, 108,* 308–321.

Martin, J. (1983). *Miss Manners' guide to excruciatingly correct behavior.* New York: Warner Books.

Olson, K. R., & Spelke, E. S. (2008). Foundations of cooperation in young children. *Cognition, 108,* 222–231.

Onishi, K., & Baillargeon, R. (2005). Do 15-month-old infants understand false beliefs? *Science, 8,* 255–258.

Over, H., & Carpenter, M. (2009). Eighteen-month-old infants show increased helping following priming with affiliation. *Psychological Science, 20,* 1189–1193.

Scott, R. M., & Baillargeon, R. (2009). Which penguin is this? Attributing false beliefs about identity at 18 months. *Child Development, 80,* 1172–1196.

Scott, R. M., Baillargeon, R., Song, H., & Leslie, A. M. (2010). Attributing false beliefs about non-obvious properties at 18 months. *Cognitive Psychology, 61,* 366–395.

Scott, R. M., He, Z., Baillargeon, R., & Cummins, D. (2012). False-belief understanding in 2.5-year-olds: Evidence from two novel verbal spontaneous-response tasks. *Developmental Science, 15(2), 181–193.*

Senju, A., Southgate, V., White, S., & Frith, U. (2009). Mindblind eyes: An absence of spontaneous theory of mind in Asperger Syndrome. *Science, 325,* 883–885.

Setoh, P., Scott, R. M., & Baillargeon, R. (2011, March). *False-belief reasoning in 2.5-year-olds: Evidence from an elicited-response low-inhibition task.* Paper presented at the Biennial Meeting of the Society for Research in Child Development, Montreal, Canada.

Sloane, S., Baillargeon, R., & Premack, D. (2010, March). *Expectations of fairness are modified by group membership in 18-month-old infants.* Paper presented at the Biennial International Conference on Infant Studies, Baltimore, MD.

Stamberg, S. Retrieved November 2012, from the NPR Web site: http://www.npr.org/templates/story/story.php?storyId=131161215. Cavett's Conversations: 'When People Simply Talk'. Copyright National Public Radio.

Sweetser, E. E. (1987). The definition of lie: An examination of the folk models underlying a semantic prototype. In D. Holland (Ed.), *Cultural models in language and thought* (pp. 43–66). New York: Cambridge University Press.

Warneken, F., & Tomasello, T. (2006). Altruistic helping in human infants and young chimpanzees. *Science, 311,* 1301–1303.

Wimmer, H., & Perner, J. (1983). Beliefs about beliefs: Representation and constraining function of wrong beliefs in young children's understanding of deception. *Cognition, 13,* 103–128.

Xu, F., Bao, X., Fu, G., Talwar, V., & Lee, K. (2010). Lying and truth-telling in children: From concept to action. *Child Development, 81,* 581–596.

Yang, D. Y.-J., & Baillargeon, R. (in press). Difficulty in understanding social acting (but not false beliefs) mediates the link between autistic traits and ingroup relationships. *Journal of Autism and Developmental Disorders.*

Yang, D. Y.-J., & Pelphrey, K. A. (in press). Dissociable neural systems for mindreading and their disruption in autism. In S. Baron-Cohen, H. TagerFlusberg, & M. Lombardo (Eds.), *Understanding Other Minds* (3rd ed.). New York: Oxford University Press.

Yazdi, A. A., German, T. P., Defeyter, M. A., & Siegal, M. (2006). Competence and performance in belief-desire reasoning across two cultures: The truth, the whole truth, and nothing but the truth. *Cognition, 100,* 343–368.

Young, L., & Saxe, R. (2009). Innocent intentions: A correlation between forgiveness for accidental harm and neural activity. *Neuropsychologia, 47,* 2065–2072.

2.5

Language and Reasoning About Beliefs

JILL DE VILLIERS

I would never consider myself any kind of expert on social cognition. I have neither the training nor an affinity for the theories in that domain, but I have spent several years now working on the interface of language and Theory of Mind. Language hijacked me.

The empirical work began with a mundane idea, the exact reverse of the final story: Children would not be able to handle certain kinds of linguistic structures without having mastered Theory of Mind. If a child could not conceive of false beliefs, how could he handle a sentence such as:

The girl thinks she caught a fish. (but she did not, she caught something else).

At the time I was deep in research on wh-questions (de Villiers, 1996), and we were testing whether children could answer questions such as:

What did the girl think she caught?

We wanted to be sure that the child's answer included both verbs in the scope of the question, so we designed the scenarios so that the children were told a story in which what the girl caught was not what she *said* she caught. Young children failed; they answered only what the girl actually caught. So we began a year-long longitudinal study (ultimately de Villiers & Pyers, 2002) to determine whether children needed to pass false-belief reasoning before they could properly answer our syntactic questions. But the data were different than expected. It became very clear that, in fact, children answered the questions properly before they could pass the classic tests of false belief.

We endeavored to remove confounds from the syntactic test: We studied mental verbs (*think*, *believe*) but also communication verbs (*say*, *tell*) in the same structures, and we provided the children with the answers in the story, so that no special "mind reading" was needed. Had we just succeeded in making a really easy false-belief task? Or was the story a deeper one: Could the language that expresses propositional attitudes actually be required for explicit false-belief reasoning? Were children actually using these linguistic forms to think in a new way?

The way to answer that question seemed to be to find a group of children who had delayed language but were otherwise typically developing, social, tuned-in, and intelligent. The group we chose to study were deaf children born to hearing parents (as 95% of deaf children are), learning to speak English, but delayed by the problems of access to the primary linguistic data (de Villiers & de Villiers, 2000). If we had just found an easier false-belief task that was linguistic in form, it shouldn't be easier for these children than a *low-verbal* task of false beliefs, since they were delayed in syntactic development. On the other hand, if the syntax mastery was prerequisite for reasoning, then deaf children might also need to pass the test of syntax before they passed the low-verbal test of false beliefs. The answers were clear: Deaf children also needed to master the syntactic form before they could pass the false-belief reasoning, even when the linguistic demands of the latter were made minimal (Schick, de Villiers, de Villiers, & Hoffmeister, 2007).

It occurred to two different groups of researchers to put to real experimental test whether the linguistic mastery were requisite for false-belief reasoning. Hale and Tager-Flusberg (2003) and Lohmann and Tomasello (2003) tested whether children who initially failed both tasks were trained on the syntactic task using verbs of communication would improve on false-belief tasks. The results were positive after a very brief intervention: Training on the language of complements helped the false-belief reasoning.

A further experimental study (Newton & de Villiers, 2007) used a dual-task procedure with adults in a false-belief task. Adults who shadowed a linguistic message while watching an unseen displacement task failed to predict how the movie would end, that is, failed to consider the character's state of false belief, though they could choose the right ending in a true-belief case. A control task requiring the shadowing of rhythmic patterns, shown to be equivalently demanding on a non-belief task, had no effect on false-belief responses. The study suggested that even adults, or perhaps *especially* adults, need to have access to their language faculty while reasoning about others' minds, even when the task is a nonverbal choice task. Unfortunately, the experimental result is at variance with other results from aphasic adults who nevertheless retain some false-belief ability, so it is controversial (Apperly, Samson, & Davies, 2009), even though it is a highly replicable finding. I am continuing to pursue these studies with adults and test the variety of tasks—both false belief and the dual task—that show an interference effect.

The theory underlying these empirical findings has been gradually adapted as new results have emerged. In our early speculations, we seriously considered the possibility, and still do, that children use the language around them as a source of evidence about other minds; that is, in working out the meanings of words such as *think* and *know*, children become aware of social circumstances and truth conditions that would otherwise have been opaque to a creature just absorbed in behavior. In exploring the issue with deaf children, we were aware of work that suggested that deaf children's input was impoverished not only because of hearing loss but also because of a tendency to simplify discourse, engaged in by their caregivers and teachers (Peterson & Siegal, 1999). As a result, deaf children with a language delay might simply have less to work with to build the theory about beliefs. The same might be true of children with autism, but in that case added to an existing neglect of or inattention to social clues. But if language is just useful as an evidence source for the Theory of Mind, then once a child has the theory, the language faculty should no longer be necessary for the task of mind-reading. Newton and de Villiers's results suggested otherwise. And over a longer period of time, surely deaf children would eventually get the evidence, though by a more painstaking route? The evidence from Pyers and Senghas (2009) on adult users of the not-yet-fully-developed Nicaraguan Sign Language contradicts that assumption, in that they were still delayed as adults on false-belief tasks.

It was Helen Tager-Flusberg who first urged me to consider a more radical form of the thesis, namely that linguistic structures such as complementation might be the representational medium for entertaining thoughts of others' beliefs. In 1998, Gabriel Segal, a philosopher of language, published an interesting paper in which he argued that adults' judgments about beliefs were exactly as subtle as the natural language in which they are described. Fodor (1975) had previously made the claim that our thinking must be couched in a Language-of-Thought (LoT), a full propositional language, to capture all the intricacies of what we can think about (see also the updated defense in Fodor, 2008). But Fodor denied that this was natural language, denied that it was unique to humans, and denied that it was learned. Despite the implausibilities, I had always liked the logical arguments in Fodor and found an immediate affinity in Segal's claims that a natural language had the right format for belief representation. For example, only language can represent falsity or negation: An image cannot do this. Furthermore, language has recursion, allowing it to capture propositional attitudes, where a proposition is designated as belonging to an individual, and that process can be recursive:

Jason thinks Mary believes that Harry knows . . . . .

If so, why duplicate machinery in the mind for both a LoT *and* natural language?

In 2002, Carruthers made a similar argument about the potential role of natural language (in particular, Logical Form) in complex reasoning, based on Spelke's (2003) view of language as a possible "bridge" between otherwise informationally encapsulated modules of the mind. Though I was not convinced yet that there were two modules that needed bridging for Theory of Mind, the role of language in thinking was irresistible. In part this was because of Chomsky's (2010) increasingly strong assertions that the evolutionary advantage of human language (now that he was discussing it at all) was in the service of cognition, not communication, a proposition that infuriates almost everyone else (Pinker & Jackendoff, 2005).

Invited to a conference on "Whither Whorf?" in 2003 (de Villiers & de Villiers, 2003), we tried to distinguish our point of view on the role of language in thinking from the neo-Whorfians, who argue that the particular language one speaks plays a formative role in the kinds of thinking that come habitually to you. At the time, I was convinced that the theory applied universally, that all languages had sentential complements (several syntacticians at the time assured me of this), and that there was essentially no variance across linguistic populations in the age of achievement of complements or false-belief reasoning. Since then, the matter has become more controversial. Tardif, So, and Kaciroti (2007) demonstrated some slowing of Theory of Mind attainments in Cantonese, a language with very little surface marking of complements but a special verb to indicate "think falsely." Everett (2005) has famously proclaimed that the Brazilian Indian language, Pirahã, lacks embedding of any sort, though the linguistic evidence is highly disputed (Nevins, Pesetsky, & Rodrigues, 2009). I have actively explored the possibility in the last few years that evidential marking in some languages (e.g., Turkish, Bulgarian, Romani, Tibetan) might serve as a different linguistic route for promoting or establishing false-belief understanding. The evidence is not at all compelling for such an account (de Villiers, Garfield, Gernet-Girard, Roeper, & Speas, 2009).

A further development addressed the thorny question of whether syntax or semantics constitutes the basic linguistic development in the complements task (Perner, Sprung, Zauner, & Heider, 2003; de Villiers, 2005). Is it just the verb meaning, or something about the falsity of the embedded proposition, and can these be separated? The verbs in question have the unique property that the complement that they take can be a false proposition, one whose truth lies in the world in the mind of the sentence subject, not the speaker of the sentence. So the two are inextricably linked. Recently I have argued that the verb transfers the "point of view" of the sentence subject onto its complement as it subordinates it, and this point of view is evident not just in the "truth" of the clause but also in its noun phrases, which are designations from the point of view of the subject (de Villiers, 2005). It is not the lexical meaning of the terms in question, but their sentential role, that is key. These linguistic arguments are still being refined (de Villiers, 2010) in the light of new work in syntax.

There has been much recent work that threatens the viability of the linguistic determinism thesis. Most central to the critique is the burgeoning empirical work on "implicit" Theory of Mind in infants and toddlers. Earlier, many theorists had been relatively sympathetic to the idea that language might play *some* kind of role in at least enhancing false-belief understanding, though the particular version I espoused was never popular. However, with new studies coming out that suggested infants might have an understanding of others' minds as part of a core knowledge system, there was a growing suspicion that the fault

in the classic false-belief tasks was precisely that they made too many task demands: linguistic and executive function in particular. A resolution might be that even infants could reason about the false beliefs or states of ignorance of another person provided:

a) The lure of reality was removed.
b) No behavioral choice was required, merely a natural response such as anticipatory or prolonged eye gaze.

Fodor (1992), Leslie (2000), and Baillargeon, Scott, and He (2010) all reason that the infant does have the ability to attend to others' mental states, but that there is an additional factor that must be added before explicit false-belief reasoning is demonstrated with behavioral choices. The most likely candidate in their view is *executive function or inhibitory control* (but see Apperly and Butterfill, 2009, for a cogent critique). Despite good evidence that executive function skills are highly correlated with false-belief achievement in typically developing children, the correlation fails in language-delayed deaf children. The hearing-impaired children perform at age level on the popular executive function tasks, and the best predictor of their success on false-belief tasks is their syntactic skill at complements (de Villiers & de Villiers, 2012).

Yet another side of the current debate is as follows: Are infants just *apparently* engaging in mental state reasoning? Since the first result emerged (Onishi & Baillargeon, 2005) with prolonged eye gaze as an index of infant's surprise at an ignorant protagonists' choice in an unseen displacement task, the search has been on for an alternative explanation of what the infants are responding to, short of mental state reasoning. Perner and Ruffman (2005) responded by suggesting the result was due to a kind of low-level associative link between persons, places, and objects that was broken in the false-belief scenario. But subsequent work has made that less plausible (Baillargeon et al., 2010). In particular, work by Southgate, Senju, and Csibra (2007) on anticipatory looking to where someone's hand will emerge to retrieve an object belies an associative explanation of the simplest sort. Nevertheless, other explanations abound, such as an early understanding of intention rather than belief (Hutto, 2008), or a set of behavior rules that lack the flexibility of a full-fledged Theory of Mind (Perner, 2010). But Perner is now convinced that the infants are showing behavior that *takes mind into account*, albeit implicitly.

I really wish I had taken linguistics right now.

The most compelling recent synthesis by Apperly and Butterfill (2009) proposes that there may be two systems: an early developed, evolutionarily prior, automatic, and relatively inflexible system for anticipation of others' behavior, to which is added a more sophisticated, representational Theory of Mind that is successful at a wider range of circumstances and allows reflection, deliberation, and overt reasoning. Quite naturally, this latter is tied to language. They model their ideas on a proposal by Carey (2004) on number, in which infants possess a module for small numerosities that allows them to predict the addition and subtraction of objects up to number four but fails thereafter. Grafted onto this is a true number system that relies in part on insights transferred from the counting system within language.

The analogy is a tempting one, if one could carefully identify what the limits are to the early Theory of Mind. Apperly and Butterfill give a sketch of what would be required to complete the analogy: a signature of early belief reasoning, a clear limitation, that would make it dissociable from the later kind. At the moment, the successes of the early module are proliferating. Work on prosocial helping has squelched the suggestion that the early module cannot be recruited for an overt response (Buttelmann, Carpenter, & Tomasello, 2009), and tantalizing work by Scott and Baillargeon (2009) has at least threatened, if not contradicted, a favorite notion of my own, also entertained by Apperly and Butterfill (2009), that the early module might be able to track the *direction or orientation* of another's search (where) but not the *contents* (what) of another's beliefs. But hope springs eternal.

Finally, and I should stop with the trouble I am in already, I have begun to ask whether the role that syntax plays in (explicit) false-belief representation is unique, or whether syntax of the simplest sort opens up conceptual possibilities that are not available to prelinguistic infants or nonlinguistic creatures. Inspired by Hinzen (2007), a philosopher who has acted as an "interpreter" of contemporary work by Chomsky, I have begun asking whether even the notion of a transitive event: "X verbs Y," where X and Y are variables, is possible in the absence of a linguistic faculty. Fundamentally, and roughly, a sentence represents a proposition, something that can have a truth value in the world. The sentence "a woman is kissing a baby" is only truth-evaluable if one can recognize that the woman in question belongs to the class of women, that the baby in question is a part of the set of babies, that the act is one of kissing, that there is finiteness to the act, namely tense, and

the direction of action is from the woman to the baby, not vice versa. All of these components presumably exist in prelinguistic conceptual space, but are they evaluable together in the absence of syntax to bind them appropriately into roles? In particular, do different instances of the event, with different tokenings of women, babies, and kissing, plus direction, have any conceptual unity without language to unite them? We shall see. If syntax does bind them, this opens up a whole new array of tantalizing questions about how the social world is construed before and after language.

REFERENCES

Apperly, I., & Butterfill, S. A. (2009). Do humans have two systems to track beliefs and belief-like states? *Psychological Review, 116*(4), 953–970.

Apperly, I., Samson, D., & Humphreys, G. (2009). Studies of adults can inform accounts of theory of mind development. *Developmental Psychology, 45,* 190–201.

Baillargeon, R., Scott, R., & He, Z. (2010). False-belief understanding in infants. *Trends in Cognitive Science, 14,* 110–118.

Buttelmann, D., Carpenter, M., & Tomasello, M. (2009). Eighteen-month-old infants show false belief understanding in an active helping paradigm. *Cognition, 112,* 337–342.

Carey, S. (2004). Bootstrapping and the origin of concepts. *Daedalus, 133,* 59–68.

Carruthers, P. (2002). The cognitive functions of language. *Behavioral and Brain Sciences, 25,* 657–719.

Chomsky, N. (2010). Some simple evo-devo theses: How true might they be for language? In R. K. Larson, V. Deprez, & H. Yamakido (Eds.), *The evolution of human language* (pp. 45–62). Cambridge, England: Cambridge University Press.

de Villiers, J. G. (1996). Defining the open and closed program for acquisition: The case of wh-questions. In M. Rice (Ed.), *Toward a genetics of language* (pp. 145–184). Mahwah, NJ: Erlbaum.

de Villiers, J. G. (2005). Can language acquisition give children a point of view? In J. W. Astington & J. A. Baird (Eds.), *Why language matters for theory of mind* (pp. 186–219). Oxford, England: Oxford University Press.

de Villiers, J. G. (2010) On building up a sufficient representation for belief: Tense, point of view and wh-movement. In J. Costa, A. Castro, M. Lobo, & F. Pratas (Eds.), *Language acquisition and development: Proceedings of Gala 2009* (pp. 121–134). Newcastle, England: Cambridge Scholars Press.

de Villiers, J. G. & de Villiers, P. A. (2000). Linguistic determinism and false belief. In P. Mitchell & K. Riggs (Eds.), *Children's reasoning and the mind* (pp. 191–228). Hove, UK: Psychology Press.

de Villiers, J. G., & de Villiers, P. A. (2003). Language for thought: Coming to understand false beliefs. In D. Gentner & S. Goldin-Meadow (Eds.), *Language in mind: Advances in the study of language and thought* (pp. 335–384). Cambridge, MA: MIT Press.

de Villiers, J. G., Garfield, J., Gernet Girard, H., Roeper, T., & Speas, P. (2009). Evidentials in Tibetan: Acquisition, semantics, and cognitive development. In S. Fitneva & T. Matsui (Eds.), Evidentiality: A window into language and cognitive development [Special issue]. *New Directions for Adolescent and Child Development, 125,* 29–48.

de Villiers J. G., & Pyers, J. (2002). Complements to cognition: A longitudinal study of the relationship between complex syntax and false-belief understanding, *Cognitive Development, 17,* 1037–1060.

de Villiers, P. A., & de Villiers, J. G. (2012). Deception dissociates from false belief reasoning in deaf children: Implication for the implicit versus explicit theory of mind debate. *British Journal of Developmental Psychology, 30,* 188–209.

Everett, D. (2005). Cultural constraints on grammar and cognition in Pirahã. *Current Anthropology, 46,* 621–646.

Fodor, J. (1975). *The language of thought.* New York: Harvester Press.

Fodor, J. (1992). A theory of the child's theory of mind. *Cognition, 44,* 283–296.

Fodor, J. (2008). *LoT2: Language of thought revisited.* Oxford, England: Oxford University Press.

Hale, C. M., & Tager-Flusberg, H. (2003). The influence of language on theory of mind: A training study. *Developmental Science, 6,* 346–359.

Hinzen, W. (2007). *An essay on names and truth.* Oxford, England: Oxford University Press.

Hutto, D. (2008). *Folk psychological narratives.* Cambridge, MA: MIT Press.

Leslie, A. M. (2000). "Theory of mind" as a mechanism of selective attention. In M. Gazzaniga (Ed.), *The new cognitive neurosciences* (pp. 1235–1247). Cambridge, MA: MIT Press.

Lohmann, H., & Tomasello, M. (2003). The role of language in the development of false belief understanding: A training study. *Child Development, 74,* 1130–1144.

Nevins, A., Pesetsky, D., & Rodrigues, C. (2009). Pirahã exceptionality: A reassessment. *Language, 85,* 355–404.

Newton, A., & de Villiers, J.G. (2007). Thinking while talking: Adults fail non-verbal false belief reasoning. *Psychological Science, 18,* 574–579.

Onishi, K. H., & Baillargeon, R. (2005). Do 15-month-old infants understand false beliefs? *Science, 308,* 255–258.

Perner, J. (2010). Who took the cog out of cognitive science: Mentalism in an era of anti-cognitivism. In P. A. Frensch & R. Schwarzer (Eds.), *Cognition and neuropsychology: Proceedings of the 29th International Congress of Psychology* (Vol. 1, pp. 241–262). London: Psychology Press.

Perner, J., Sprung, M., Zauner, P., & Haider, H. (2003) Want that is understood well before say that, think that, and false belief: A test of de Villiers' linguistic determinism on German-speaking children, *Child Development, 74,* 179–188.

Perner, J., & Ruffman, T. (2005). Infants' insight into the mind: How deep? *Science, 308,* 214–216.

Peterson, C. C., & Siegal, M. (1999). Representing inner worlds: Theory of mind in autistic, deaf, and normal-hearing children. *Psychological Science, 10,* 126–129.

Pinker, S., & Jackendoff, R. (2005). The nature of the language faculty and its implications for evolution of language (Reply to Fitch, Hauser, and Chomsky). *Cognition, 97,* 211–225.

Pyers, J., & Senghas, A. (2009). Language promotes false-belief understanding: Evidence from learners of a new sign language. *Psychological Science, 20,* 805–812.

Schick, B., de Villiers, P. A., de Villiers, J. G., & Hoffmeister, R. (2007). Language and theory of mind: A study of deaf children. *Child Development, 78,* 376–396.

Scott, R. M., & Baillargeon, R. (2009). Which penguin is this? Attributing false beliefs about identity at 18 months. *Child Development, 80,* 1172–1196.

Segal, G. (1998). Representing representations. In P. Carruthers & J. Boucher (Eds.), *Language and thought* (pp. 146–161). Cambridge, England: Cambridge University Press.

Southgate, V., Senju, A., & Csibra, G. (2007). Action anticipation though attribution of false belief by 2-year-olds. *Psychological Science, 18,* 587–592.

Spelke, E. (2003). What makes us smart? Core knowledge and Natural language In D. Gentner & S. Goldin-Meadow (Eds.), *Advances in the investigation of language and thought* (pp. 277–311). Cambridge, MA: MIT Press.

Tardif, T., So, C., & Kaciroti, N. (2007). Language and false belief: Evidence for general, not specific, effects in Cantonese-speaking preschoolers. *Developmental Psychology, 43,* 318–340.

2.6

The Myth of Mentalizing and the Primacy of Folk Sociology

LAWRENCE A. HIRSCHFELD

Evolution may not select the best of all possible solutions, but it does select among the best of those available at any given moment. Over the past 30 years an extensive literature on Theory of Mind has emerged, much implicitly or explicitly presuming that mentalizing—imagining that others have thoughts and feelings and other mental states that motivate them to action—provides a better way of predicting and interpreting the behavior of others than more evolutionarily ancient social strategies. Here I argue against this position, proposing that mentalizing is not a particularly useful tool for predicting and interpreting the behavior of others. I suggest that this is true for three reasons. First, mentalizing often, perhaps typically, misattributes the mental states of others, either by inferring that an individual holds a particular mental state that he or she does not in fact hold or by ignoring other aspects of mentalizing, such as the influence that norms and statuses have on an individual's mental states. Second, in addition to mentalizing, humans and other social animals possess an early developing, both in ontogenesis and over evolutionary time, capacity for predicting and interpreting the behavior of others, a faculty that we might call a Theory of Society. This capacity allows, indeed compels, actors to parse the environment into groups and calibrate the importance of particular group membership in a given circumstance. Third, following the lead of the social sciences concerned with aggregations, I consider the possibility that a folk capacity for Theory of Society is generally a more "accurate" strategy for predicting and interpreting the actions of others because social position(ing) fundamentally shapes social behavior.

Theory of Mind, mentalizing, mind reading, Machiavellian intelligence, social intelligence, social brain hypothesis, folk psychology, naïve psychology. All these name a particular cognitive phenomenon: the capacity to attribute mental states to others and use these attributions as the basis for interpreting and predicting their actions. Human society, a broad consensus agrees, rests on a bedrock of mentalizing (Tomasello, 2006), in significant measure because more highly developed mentalizing skills allow an individual to manipulate and deceive cohabiting group mates (Humphrey, 1976). The mentalizing corollary of the prevailing assumption that the more accurate a creature's beliefs the more its survival is enhanced (McKay & Dennett, 2009) is that the more accurate an individual's beliefs about what others think and feel, the better is that individual's chances of survival.

To the contrary, in what follows I suggest that mentalizing, despite the attention it has received and the importance attributed to it, is ultimately of sharply limited utility in interpreting and predicting the behavior of others in both the contemporary world and the sociocultural environments in which mentalizing evolved. I will argue that humans are in fact quite poor at appraising what others and indeed what we ourselves are thinking and feeling. In contrast, humans excel at interpreting and predicting behavior in terms of unseen social and cultural (nonmental) qualities (ranging from "fixed" qualities such as gender or race, to "variable" ones such as age, rank, or occupation, and to "episodic" or transient ones such as coalition partner or teammate). In negotiating social interactions, mentalizing is less important than attention to the contingencies of context, normative constraints on action, epistemic affordances of the cultural environment, and the group dynamics of the social milieu. These capacities allow us to identify, interpret, and extrapolate from experience—and ultimately guide our actions. The mental states of others may be good to think about; still, knowing who actors are and where they find themselves (e.g., the social situations they are in, their goals, the social positions they and their interlocutors occupy, etc.) ultimately are more important to understanding why they behave as they do.

Assessing these alternative claims—the one about mentalizing, the other about folk sociology or group-based reasoning—involves posing a series of narrower queries. Regarding mentalizing, we ask two linked questions: (a) How accurately do people appraise the states of mind of others? and (b) Does an ability to accurately appraise mental states enhance our understanding of others' actions? Regarding group-based reasoning, we ask whether the ability to reliably identify who someone is (which in part requires reliably identifying the nature of the relevant context) is more useful as a strategy.

We know surprisingly little about either the accuracy with which mental states are attributed to others or the degree to which mentalizing enhances an individual's survival. In one relevant study, although adults were found to be *capable* of distinguishing their own, accurate beliefs from the false beliefs of others, routinely they did not do so, even on a task that appeared to require it (Keysar, Lin, & Barr, 2003). Indeed, enhancing survival may turn on inaccurate attributions regarding one's own mental states. Trivers (2010) has recently argued that our success at deceiving others (the supposed evolutionary payoff of a mentalizing capacity) is enhanced when we deceive ourselves (by reducing the social and cognitive costs of deception). In short, deceiving others works better if we do not know we are doing it.

Mentalizing is also surprisingly sensitive to context, including culturally specific context. Status differences affect how accurately one predicts another's mental states (Rutherford, 2004), the number of siblings a child has affects when more highly developed mentalizing is achieved (McAlister & Peterson, 2007), and the moral valence of an action affects judgments of intentionality (Knobe, 2003). To illustrate the contextual contingencies of mentalizing, consider moral valence and attribution of intentionality. A morally bad side effect of an action (say, damage to the environment as an unforeseen consequence of commercial exploitation)—but not a morally good one—is judged intentional (Knobe, 2003), a pattern of reasoning also found among preschoolers (Leslie, Knobe, & Cohen, 2006). The cultural specificity of such judgments is underscored by Uttich & Lombrozo's (2010) finding that this asymmetry turns on whether a *norm* is violated,

regardless of its moral status. Thus, mentalizing is shaped by *culturally varying* aspects of context (to which even infants evince sensitivity; Onishi, Baillargeon, & Leslie, 2007).

One interpretation of these results is that mentalizing encompasses not only beliefs/desire psychology but also "social influences on action and thought" (Wellman & Miller, 2008). On this view, mentalizing is the key process for interpreting social experience, but it is tweaked or enhanced with an understanding of social influences, to make it even more *informative* of the actions of others. Yet little direct evidence speaks to how accurately people attribute mental states to others (beyond measures of false belief) or whether such attributions enhance survival. This is not surprising if we consider the accuracy of conscious deliberation about our *own* thought processes. In a classic study, Nisbett and Wilson (1977) found that verbal reports "are so removed from the processes that investigators presume to have occurred as to give grounds for considerable doubt that there is direct access to these processes" (p. 238).

This is not to say that we do a poor job of interpreting and predicting the behaviors of others. For many—arguably most—encounters, we seem to do pretty well. We do not manage this, however, by mind reading. One class of lay interpretation and prediction involves inferring another's actions based on what we know about the situation or social context. The move is a corrective to a widespread (among lay and professional psychologists alike) overestimation of the influence of traits and dispositions (i.e., predilections to behave in similar ways despite contingencies and cultural affordances) in shaping our own behavior, and especially that of others (Ross & Nisbett, 1991). This overestimation of the importance of traits and dispositions can in part be traced to the parallel confidence that (conscious) mental states are the fundamental determiner of action, as traits and dispositions are interpreted as crystallized mental states (Wellman, 1990).

The situational turn in social psychology has vitally changed the field, but it has ironically also encouraged an impoverished notion of situation. Often the situation is treated as if it means little more than local contingency embedded in a particular setting—"the environmental attractions, repulsions, and constraints" that shape behavior (Mason & Morris, 2010). Little effort has been made to develop models of what a situation actually *is*. A hint emerges from another area of social psychology, intergroup relations. Much of our attention in interpreting and predicting behavior is focused on groups, particularly the *sorts of* people their members are rather than what they might think. Groups are *cultural entities*, defined and justified by norms and systems of moral belief, sustained by commitment to the web of common sense, and implicated in the organization and distribution of power and authority.

Recent work suggests that group-based social reasoning (what I have called elsewhere "folk sociology") is governed by a distinct, arguably core, cognitive knowledge structure (Hirschfeld, 1996; Spelke & Kinzler, 2007) that is orthogonal to mentalizing (Clément, Bernard, & Kaufmann, 2011). Relative to group-based reasoning, mentalizing may in fact be a later emerging, and more limited, tool in our arsenal for social thinking (Hirschfeld, Bartmess, White, & Frith, 2007). More speculatively, rather than being the foundation of human sociality, mentalizing may be a by-product of a by-product, a way to think about the causal potential of conscious mental states enabled by the emergence of self-awareness relatively recently in human evolutionary history. Indeed, its importance in the literature may be overestimated because of its importance to the particular cultural environment from which that literature emerges. As a set of papers in a recent issue of *Anthropology Quarterly* illustrate, in many cultural environments the predominant expectation is that it is difficult if not impossible to know what others think and feel; indeed, the emphasis on interpreting others in terms of (crystallized) mental states (rather than the social categories they occupy) is characteristic of a rather limited range of cultures in North America and Northern Europe, and for the most part the White males living in them (Robbins & Rumsey, 2008).

If knowing who and what people are is a fundamental strategy for interpreting and predicting their actions, then discovering who and what people are—in short, discovering the sorts of groups there are in society and who their members are—is a fundamental task for the child. Not surprisingly, as noted earlier, there is growing evidence of a special-purpose cognitive device, a component of core knowledge, dedicated to guiding the child's acquisition of this specific sort of knowledge. Like other special-purpose devices, this one is robust, requiring modest levels of environmental input, early emerging, and operates outside conscious awareness. Precursor saliencies are evident in infants' sensitivity to those social dimensions that ultimately become culturally articulated and play predominant roles in all known societies, including age (Brooks & Lewis, 1976), gender (Quinn,

Yahr, Kuhn, Slater, & Pascalis, 2002), language spoken (Mehler et al., 1988), and even race (Kelly et al., 2005).

A recent study demonstrates the independence of group-based reasoning and mentalizing (Hirschfeld et al., 2007), two of whose findings are particularly relevant to this discussion: first, adult-like competence in group-based reasoning emerges earlier than the corresponding adult-like competence in mentalizing; second, culturally specific, adult-like competence in group-based reasoning develops intact, even when there is significant impairment in social communication generally, and mental state reasoning in particular. *[handwritten margin note: deaf? autistic?]* Specifically, the study demonstrated that highly impaired 6-year-old autistic children (who failed a false-belief task) recruited culturally transmitted racial and gender stereotypes *as readily as unimpaired controls* when interpreting novel situations (e.g., when asked to select the helpful person, they chose a drawing of a White woman over a Black woman more than two thirds of the time). As the performance of unimpaired 3-year-olds (whose use of gender and racial stereotypes did not differ from those of older, autistic children and unimpaired controls) in the same study demonstrated, adult-like competence in group-based reasoning emerges before similarly advanced mentalizing skills (i.e., the ability to grasp false beliefs). Indeed, in some respects group-based reasoning trumps the nascent mentalizing skills mastered by younger preschoolers and impaired autistic children (viz., the ability to recognize that individuals have desires and habitual preferences, such as the recognition that a particular girl prefers to play with trucks rather than dolls). Both unimpaired 3-year-olds and highly impaired autistic 6-year-olds were more likely than unimpaired controls and less impaired autistic 6-year-olds to predict that the person would act in accord with a cultural stereotype than a personal desire/habitual preference, when the two conflicted (e.g., that despite knowing that a particular girl prefers to play with trucks over dolls, these subjects, when asked whether she would play with a truck or a doll, predicted that she would play with a doll).

What accounts for the priority of group-based reasoning? The divergent natural histories of the two competencies seems a reasonable explanation. Highly developed mentalizing skills appear to be unique to humans (Povinelli & Vonk, 2003); in contrast, humans are among many creatures that live in groups. Moreover, the complex social (group) lives of some primate species are strikingly evocative of extant human societies (i.e., presence of multiple and often strategic affiliations, opportunistic as well as enduring group commitments, transitive and inheritable statuses, and so on; Cheney & Seyfarth, 2007). Such cross-species parallels, although informative, may obscure crucial features of human group living. Although small-scale human societies with relatively low levels of socioeconomic integration are often (accurately) described as based on relations of kinship, the parallel with kin-based nonhuman primate group structures risks being overdrawn. First, human groups are seldom kin based *in a strict biological sense*, even when the language (both indigenous and scholarly) for describing them seems to be. Human systems of kin reckoning never accurately reflect degrees of biological relatedness; in fact, they almost always distort it (as biological relatedness is understood by the indigenous populations themselves). For example, in one well-studied class of kinship systems, individuals who are related biologically to the same degree are the most sought-after marriage partners if the relationship is reckoned through the mother's line, whereas if it is reckoned through the father's line, they are incestuously close relatives (Lévi-Strauss, 1969).

A more crucial difference between human and other primate societies is the nature of and extent to which human groups are linked in enduring confederations (using the term broadly), some of which define people of a single "kind," some of which define people of essentially other "kinds." Studies of neocortex across species have revealed a close association between relative neocortex size and number of individuals typically in a single group (Dunbar, 1992). The association seems to break down with humans; our neocortex seemingly supports groups much larger than the typical residential bands found among hunter-gathering populations. The reason is that unlike other primates, human groups have invariably embraced multiple residential bands, even when face-to-face contact between members was infrequent. Moreover, ethnographic and archaeological evidence shows that these bands are systematically linked in enduring exchange relationships. Not only did modern humans engage in continuing long-distance trade in goods (Tattersall & Schwartz, 2000) but also in the exchange of women between groups (Chapais, 2008; Lévi-Strauss, 1969). First contact reports suggest that people moved easily and regularly between cultural groups and across cultural "boundaries" (Fried, 1975). The human capacity to learn multiple languages as readily as acquiring a single language suggests that this

social openness may be supported by an evolved mechanism (Hirschfeld, 2008).

One way to imagine much group-based reasoning is as cultural affordances, predilections to act that are shaped not by interiorized and personal motivations but by commitment to cultural expectations. These affordances support the emergence of "communities of sentiment," which Appadurai (1990) illustrates with one strategy South Asian beggars use to extract gifts. Beggars, he argues, literally entrap their "audience" into a fleeting sense of debt by evoking the sentiments associated with the web of obligation and counterobligation that ordinarily links *kinds of people* rather than *individuals* per se. Neither the beggar nor the donor believes that the evoked web of obligation in fact actually reigns; only that the participants are compelled to act in the short run as if it does in virtue of expectations of mutual knowledge and commitments to a mutually acknowledged set of cultural entanglements.

This kind of engagement—and the powerful ways it shapes behaviors independent of variation in individual psychological motivation—is not limited to "tradition-bound" cultural environments rich in interpersonal obligations and counterobligations, and the political, economic, and religious structures supporting them. We can see this in the pull of patriotism and nationalist sentiments. Personally I believe that nationalist chauvinism is pernicious, yet every 2 years I find myself rooting for American athletes at the Olympics. How do I reconcile this discrepancy? On one interpretation—a version of a dual processing model—I consciously hold a set of beliefs consistent with a broader political position that favors, say, an internationalist perspective. "Hidden" behind these beliefs are a set of nonconscious or implicit beliefs and attitudes that, although inconsistent with this conscious perspective, are widely held among those with whom I live (Banaji & Greenwald, 1994). The force of the latter ultimately trumps the former, so that my conscious, internationalist perspective is less a competing ethos than a cognitive veneer over "truer" biases. An alternative explanation is that my beliefs are shaped by a range of cultural affordances, situations, and relations that render certain engagements more readily effected (as action) than readily accepted (as belief).

Claude Steele (1995) and his associates have documented a similarly involuntary but nontrivial instance of this process. When minority (or in another way stigmatized), but otherwise confident and competent, test takers were even briefly primed for representations disparaging their "kind," performance declined relative to performance in unprimed conditions. Like the South Asian beggar's audience, test takers need not endorse these representations for the manipulation to have effect; indeed, they may well actively reject them. Perhaps as distressing—and the reason that I prefer to conceptualize stereotypes as cultural affordances—nonminority test takers' performance is also sensitive to cultural representations disparaging some groups over others. But in this case the effect is inverse: When primed with the same cultural representations that negatively affect performance among members of minority groups, White test takers experience a *boost* in performance compared to scores in unprimed conditions (Walton, 2003)

In brief, behavior is often best understood in terms of how the dynamics of social positionings play out as they are mediated by group affiliation, independent of an individual's desires. Interpreting and predicting others' behaviors is less a function of identifying whether dyadic relations are marked by sincerity or deception than by situating actors in cultural environments—and the roles the environments afford—that define and preserve the possibilities for action. Mentalizing is of limited utility not because we lack interior landscapes that are singular or opaque but because how we act is so often despite rather than in virtue of them.

REFERENCES

Appadurai, A. (1990). Topographies of the self: Praise and emotion in Hindu India. In C. A. Lutz & L. Abu-Lughod (Eds.), *Language and the politics of emotion* (pp. 92–112). New York: Cambridge University Press & Editions de la Maison des Sciences de l'Homme.

Banaji, M., & Greenwald, A. G. (1994). Implicit stereotyping and prejudice, *The psychology of prejudice: The Ontario symposium* (Vol. 7, pp. 55–76). Hillsdale, NJ: Erlbaum.

Brooks, J., & Lewis, M. (1976). Infants' responses to strangers: Midget, adult, and child. *Child Development, 47*(2), 323–332.

Chapais, B. (2008). *Primeval kinship: How pair-bonding gave birth to human society.* Cambridge, MA: Harvard University Press.

Cheney, D. L., & Seyfarth, R. M. (2007). *Baboon metaphysics: The evolution of a social mind.* Chicago, IL: University of Chicago Press.

Clément, F., Bernard, S., & Kaufmann, L. (2011). Social cognition is not reducible to theory of mind: When children use deontic rules to predict the behaviour of others. *British Journal of Developmental Psychology, 29*(1), 1–19.

Dunbar, R. (1992). Neocortex size as a constraint on group size in primates. *Journal of Human Evolution, 22*(6), 469–493.

Fried, M. (1975). *The notion of the tribe.* Menlo Park, CA: Cummings.

Hirschfeld, L. A. (1996). *Race in the making: Cognition, culture, and the child's construction of human kinds.* Cambridge, MA: MIT Press.

Hirschfeld, L. A. (2008). The bi-lingual brain revisited. *Evolutionary Psychology, 6*(1), 182–185.

Hirschfeld, L. A., Bartmess, E., White, S., & Frith, U. (2007). Can autistic children predict behavior by social stereotypes? *Current Biology, 17*(12), R451–R452.

Humphrey, N. K. (1976). The social function of intellect. In P. P. Bates & R. A. Hinde (Eds.), *Growing points in ethology* (pp. 303–317). Oxford, England: Oxford University Press.

Kelly, D. J., Quinn, P. C., Slater, A. M., Lee, K., Gibson, A., Smith, M., ... Pascalis, O. (2005). Three-month-olds, but not newborns, prefer own-race faces. *Developmental Science, 8*(6), F31–F36.

Keysar, B., Lin, S., & Barr, D. J. (2003). Limits on theory of mind use in adults. *Cognition, 89*(1), 25–41.

Knobe, J. (2003). Intentional action in folk psychology: An experimental investigation. *Philosophical Psychology, 16*(2), 309–324.

Leslie, A. M., Knobe, J., & Cohen, A. (2006). Acting intentionally and the side-effect effect: Theory of mind and moral judgment. *Psychological Science, 17*(5), 421–427.

Lévi-Strauss, C. (1969). *The elementary structures of kinship.* Boston, MA: Beacon Press.

Mason, M. F., & Morris, M. W. (2010). Culture, attribution and automaticity: A social cognitive neuroscience view. *Social Cognitive and Affective Neuroscience, 5*(2–3), 292–306.

McAlister, A., & Peterson, C. (2007). A longitudinal study of child siblings and theory of mind development. *Cognitive Development, 22*(2), 258–270.

McKay, R. T., & Dennett, D. C. (2009). The evolution of misbelief. *Behavioral and Brain Sciences, 32*(6), 493–561.

Mehler, J., Jusczyk, P., Lambertz, G., Halsted, N., Bertoncini, J., & Amiel-Tison, C. (1988). A precursor of language acquisition in young infants. *Cognition, 29*, 143–178.

Nisbett, R. E., & Wilson, T. D. (1977). Telling more than we can know: Verbal reports on mental processes. *Psychological Review, 84*(3), 231–259.

Onishi, K. H., Baillargeon, R. E., & Leslie, A. M. (2007). 15-month-old infants detect violations in pretend scenarios. *Acta Psychologica, 124*(1), 106–128.

Povinelli, D. J., & Vonk, J. (2003). Chimpanzee minds: Suspiciously human? *Trends in Cognitive Sciences, 7*(4), 157–160.

Quinn, P. C., Yahr, J., Kuhn, A., Slater, A. M., & Pascalis, O. (2002). Representation of the gender of human faces by infants: A preference for female. *Perception, 31*(9), 1109–1121.

Robbins, J., & Rumsey, A. (2008). Cultural and linguistic anthropology and the opacity of other minds. *Anthropological Quarterly, 81*(2), 407–420.

Ross, L., & Nisbett, R. E. (1991). *The person and the situation: Perspectives of social psychology.* Philadelphia, PA: Temple University Press.

Rutherford, M. D. (2004). The effect of social role on theory of mind reasoning. *British Journal of Psychology, 95*(1), 91–103.

Spelke, E. S., & Kinzler, K. D. (2007). Core knowledge. *Developmental Science, 10*(1), 89–96.

Steele, C. M., & Aronson, J. (1995). Stereotype threat and the intellectual test performance of African Americans. *Journal of Personality and Social Psychology, 69*(5), 797–811.

Tattersal, I., & Schwartz, J. (2000). *Extinct humans.* New York: Westview Press.

Tomasello, M. (2006). Uniquely human cognition is a product of human culture. In S. C. Levinson & J. Pierre (Eds.), *Evolution and culture: A Fyssen Foundation symposium.* (pp. 203–217). Cambridge, MA: MIT Press.

Trivers, R. (2010). Deceit and self-deception. In P. Kappeler & J. Silk (Eds.), *Mind the gap: Tracing the origins of human universals* (pp. 373–393). Dordrecht, The Netherlands: Springer.

Uttich, K., & Lombrozo, T. (2010). Norms inform mental state ascriptions: A rational explanation for the side-effect effect. *Cognition, 116*(1), 87–100.

Walton, G. (2003). Stereotype lift. *Journal of Experimental Social Psychology, 39*(5), 456–467.

Wellman, H. M. (1990). *The child's theory of mind.* Cambridge, MA: MIT Press.

Wellman, H. M., & Miller, J. G. (2008). Including deontic reasoning as fundamental to theory of mind. *Human Development, 51*(2), 105–135.

2.7

The New Puzzle of Theory of Mind Development

REBECCA SAXE

Human children make a remarkable discovery: Other people have minds, similar to but disconnected from their own. Other people see a slightly different world; have different desires, preferences, and values; and have different knowledge or beliefs from their own. That is, other people's minds contain representations of the world that are often true and reasonable but may be perverse, incomplete, or even totally false. This discovery helps children to make sense of some otherwise mystifying behavior: why mom would eat broccoli even though there is chocolate cake available (e.g., Repacholi & Gopnik, 1997), for example, or why she is looking for the milk in the fridge even though dad just put it on the table (e.g., Wimmer & Perner, 1983). Beyond simple action understanding, though, inferences about what other people know, want, or believe (collectively called a "Theory of Mind"; Gopnik & Wellman, 1992) inform children's growing understanding of many aspects of human social life: empathy, morality, deception, metaphor, irony, and fiction (e.g., Baird & Astington, 2004; Capelli, Nakagawa, & Madden, 1990; Peterson, Wellman, & Liu, 2005; Winner & Leekam, 1991). Thinking about other minds becomes one of the most impressive, and distinctive, accomplishments of human abstract cognition.

How, and when, do children learn to think about other people's thoughts? In developmental psychology, most research has focused on one key transition in this developmental process: when children understand that people can have false beliefs. In the past three decades, thousands of children, in hundreds of studies around the world, have been shown a scenario involving a simple false belief: for example, mother thinks the milk is in the fridge, but really it is on the table. Children are asked: "Where will she look for the milk?" or "Why is she looking in the fridge?" If you've never tried asking a 3-year-old this kind of question, I strongly encourage it. It is astonishing to watch a bright, articulate, verbal child confidently predict that she will look for the milk on the table, and if she is looking in the fridge, she must not want the milk. Five-year-old children, by contrast, usually predict that she will look in the fridge, because that's where she thinks the milk is (Wellman, Cross, & Watson, 2001).

This profile of developmental change in children's Theory of Mind is so reliable, across methods and across cultures (e.g., Avis & Harris, 1991; Liu, Wellman, Tardif, & Sabbagh, 2008; Wellman, Cross, & Watson, 2001), that it has become diagnostic of typical human social development. Children with autism spectrum disorders, for example, are specifically delayed in understanding false beliefs (e.g., Baron-Cohen, Leslie, & Frith, 1985; Leslie & Thaiss, 1992; Peterson, Wellman, & Liu, 2005). And nonhuman animals, in spite of rich social cognition in other respects, never quite reach a full and flexible understanding of false beliefs (e.g., Kaminski, Call, & Tomasello, 2008; Santos, Flombaum, & Phillips, in press).

Something about the typically developing human brain seems to be specially designed to help children make this critical cognitive leap. The advent of neuroimaging allowed researchers to look directly into human brains to find it—in what may be the most spectacular novel contribution of functional neuroimaging to cognitive science. In human adults, a group of brain regions is specifically devoted to social cognition (e.g., Gallagher et al., 2000). At least one of these, located near the right temporo-parietal junction (and therefore frequently called "the RTPJ" for short), is active specifically when people are thinking about other people's thoughts (Saxe, in press).

This introduction takes us to the state of the art around 2005, when developmental psychology and cognitive neuroscience appeared to provide converging support for a strong theory of when and how children acquire a Theory of Mind. Building on simpler foundations (e.g., concepts of "agent," "action," "intention," and "perception,"; Csibra & Gergely, 2007; Woodward, 2009), children make a key leap in their understanding of other minds between ages 3 to 5 years. Adult Theory of Mind depends distinctively on a group of brain regions, predominantly including the RTPJ. So it seemed plausible that key maturational changes typically occurred in the RTPJ between ages 3 and 5 years, supporting the cognitive advances, and that this maturation was specifically and adversely impacted by the etiology of autism (e.g., Saxe, Carey, & Kanwisher, 2004). Indeed, this view still seems appealing to me.

Recently, though, aspects of this picture have begun to unravel, creating a new puzzle of Theory of Mind, a key challenge for our understanding of social development. The puzzle is as follows: Recent advances in developmental psychology suggest that children have some understanding of false beliefs much *earlier* than age 3 years, and initial neuroimaging studies of children's brains suggests that key maturational changes in the RTPJ occur much *later* than age 5 years. To accommodate these data, a new theoretical picture will be needed.

Most of the troublesome new developmental data come from studies of infants' gaze. Before infants can talk or follow instructions, their eye movements already reveal their expectations about the world around them. Infants look longer at an object or event that surprises them and will look anticipatorily at a place where they expect something interesting to happen. Capitalizing on these simple behaviors, researchers have designed experiments that ask infants what they expect to happen when a person has a false belief. If mom last saw the milk in the fridge, even if it is now at the table, will infants look anticipatorily toward the fridge, expecting her to open it? If she goes instead to the table, will infants treat that action as surprising, and look longer than if she had gone to the fridge? In essence, the recent experiments answer: yes (e.g., Onishi & Baillargeon, 2005). Young infants appear to expect people to act in accordance with their beliefs about objects, whether they are true or false.

How young are these infants? Slightly confusingly, it differs across experiments. Some find evidence for understanding of false beliefs in 24- but not 18-month-olds (Southgate, Senju, & Csibra, 2007), whereas others find it in 18-, 15-, or even

13-month-olds (Scott & Baillargeon, 2009; Song & Baillargeon, 2008; Surian, Caldi, & Sperber, 2007). In all of the studies, though, the children are much younger than 3 years old—the age of the classic, reliable, and quite dramatic failures on traditional measures of false-belief understanding.

So, how can infants successfully make the very inferences that elude 3-year-old children? It is tempting to answer that the old studies were wrong and underestimated the 3-year-olds. Perhaps the experiments were unnecessarily complicated, and/or the young children were confused, rushed, and intimidated, or trying to give the answer the experimenter wanted. If the experimenters would just proceed more slowly and clearly, and give the children more practice, 3-year-olds (and even 2-year-olds) would show their true competence. The problem with this answer is that it has been tested and proven wrong. Hundreds of attempts to make the experiment simpler and the question clearer (e.g., Where will mom look *first* for the milk?) made only a modest difference at best (Wellman, Cross, & Watson, 2001), and 3-year-olds still predict that mom will look in the fridge even after dozens of trials of practice over many weeks (Baker & Leslie, 2008).

Renee Baillargeon, who pioneered the study of false-belief understanding in infants, argues that predicting where mom will look requires children to make inferences about the invisible future; in this demanding context, children go for the salient easy answer (where the milk actually is) because they do not have the cognitive resources left over to inhibit the easy answer and retrieve the more complicated answer (where she thinks it is), which they also know (Baillargeon, Scott, & He, 2010). Again, though, experimental data disagree. In some experiments, 3-year-olds get to watch mom look in the fridge and are then asked why she did that; there is no future to predict, and the "easy" answer should now be the one right in front of their eyes. Still 3-year-olds do not just say what infants appear to know, that mom thinks the milk is there. Instead, they generate whole new explanations (Goodman et al., 2006; Moses & Flavell, 1990): Apparently she does not want milk, so maybe she is looking in the fridge because she wants orange juice.

Another way out of the bind is to claim there is something wrong with the way the infant studies are conducted, so that the infants' concepts are being overestimated. Perhaps something else is catching infants' attention in the scenarios they are watching, creating differences in gaze without any real understanding of false belief. But this is also too easy. Specific evidence for infants' understanding of false beliefs now comes from almost a dozen studies done in multiple labs, across multiple countries (Scott & Baillargeon, 2009; Song, Onishi, Baillargeon, & Fisher, 2008; Southgate, Senju, & Csibra 2007; Surian et al., 2007). More generally, in other domains of cognition, measurements of infants' conceptual development based on gaze behavior converge perfectly with more traditional measurements like reaching actions (e.g., Feigenson & Carey, 2005; Sommerville, Woodward, & Needham, 2005). It will not be easy to simply write off the gaze measurements as meaningless or irrelevant.

Instead, it seems that both sets of data are right: Infants do expect people to act in accordance with false beliefs, but 3-year-olds do not predict or explain actions in terms of false beliefs. In fact, individual children can show both patterns simultaneously, looking anticipatorily at the fridge, but predicting verbally (and betting very confidently) that mom will go to the table (Ruffman, Garnham, Import, & Connolly, 2001).

At this point, many developmental psychologists, myself included, are drawn to the idea that there must be two different *ways* of understanding false beliefs. Young infants have one way; it is simple, fast, and efficient, but it is limited in scope and precision. So infants can formulate accurate expectations about others' actions in some simple contexts, like reaching for the milk you saw a moment ago. This system might be called an "implicit" Theory of Mind; it supports action understanding in the moment, but not reflection, deliberation, or revision. This simple system cannot expand to handle the complexities of adult Theory of Mind, though, so young children have to develop a whole second system of concepts of beliefs, desires, and actions, which has much larger scope and greater precision, is more flexible and easier to expand: an "explicit" Theory of Mind.

The proposed distinction between implicit and explicit Theory of Mind gains plausibility because a similar pattern occurs in another area of cognitive development: infants' understanding of numbers (e.g., Apperly & Butterfill, 2009). Very young infants do understand something about number and quantity, but their understanding is limited in scope and precision. As they slowly acquire their culture's words and concepts for numbers, they can acquire massively expanded computational power and flexibility (e.g., Le Corre & Carey, 2007).

Unfortunately, there is no actual evidence supporting a distinction between implicit and explicit Theory of Mind. So far, no one has found limits in scope or precision of infants' Theory of Mind. Nor is it perfectly clear why eye movements should reveal infants' implicit understanding, while pointing or talking requires the later developing explicit theory, even when giving the same answer to the same question. By contrast, the limits on young infants' numerical concepts are evident both in eye movements and reaching actions (Feigenson & Carey, 2005).

One of my chief hopes is that measurements of brain activity will help resolve this puzzle. If infants and children both have the same Theory of Mind, but different abilities to use inhibition to answer difficult questions, we should see it in the pattern of their brain activity. In adult brains, thinking about thoughts engages one group of brain regions, while solving difficult problems with high inhibitory demands depends on a distinct group of brain regions. If Baillargeon's theory is right, older children should show different brain activity from younger children (correlated with false-belief predictions) in the "problem-solving" brain regions, but not in the Theory of Mind brain regions. By contrast, if infants and children understand false beliefs using two different mechanisms—one "implicit" and the other "explicit," for example—we predict a different neural pattern. Infants and 3-year-olds watching mom looking in the fridge should show activity in different brain regions from the classic Theory of Mind pattern, while 5-year-olds' brains should look like adults'.

It is just now becoming possible to test these questions, by using functional neuroimaging of young children's brains. For better and for worse, though, the few neuroimaging studies of Theory of Mind development only deepen the puzzle. The contrasting hypotheses derived from developmental psychology predict change in Theory of Mind brain regions around age 1 year versus 4 years; the neuroimaging data show changes in Theory of Mind brain regions around age 9 years (Gweon, Dodell-Feder, Bedny, & Saxe, 2012; Kobayashi, Gloverb, & Templec, 2007; Saxe, Whitfield-Gabrieli, Scholz, & Pelphrey, 2009).

The pattern of functional change we have observed is fascinating. In adults, the RTPJ is highly specialized for thinking about thoughts; you use your RTPJ to think about someone's beliefs and desires, but not to think about their appearance, social background, or personality traits (Saxe & Kanwisher, 2003; Saxe & Powell, 2006). In 5- to 8-year-old children, the RTPJ shows robust activity when thinking about *anything* about another person: their thoughts and plans but also their appearance, relationships, and social background. In late childhood, then, this brain region seems to change its function by becoming more specialized (Gweon et al., unpublished data; Saxe et al., 2009). Starting with a more general role in social cognition, the RTPJ gradually focuses on one specific cognitive challenge: thinking about thought. It would have been very gratifying and simple, if this pattern of functional maturation in the brain underlay children's growing ability to understand false beliefs around age 4 years. But it does not.

Of course, the neural measurements do not directly contradict either of the developmental hypotheses. There are only a handful of neuroimaging studies of children's Theory of Mind. The measurement tool most commonly used in adults, functional magnetic resonance imaging (fMRI), is challenging for young children, since it requires lying completely still in a small, loud tube for at least half an hour. To date, no fMRI studies of Theory of Mind have been conducted with children younger than 5 years old. Key functional changes may very well occur in younger children's brains, but they have not yet been observed. Indeed, using another more child-friendly neuroimaging technique, electroencephalograms (EEG), Mark Sabbagh has found evidence of biological maturation in RTPJ, specifically related to 4-year-olds' action predictions based on false beliefs (Sabbagh, Bowman, Evraire, & Ito, 2009).

Here is one possible resolution. Young infants' foundational understanding of other people is rich enough to support some basic understanding of false belief, but it is in other respects seriously limited in scope, precision, and flexibility, in ways we will discover. Perhaps infants can only attribute beliefs and desires about objects and events that are currently present in the environment, or only about simple features (like location and identity), or only with very simple logical structures (a simple proposition). Correctly designed tasks will reveal these limits, in both eye gaze and other behavioral measurements. Adults also use the same fast efficient system in certain contexts; and so the limits on this system will appear on appropriate tests of spontaneous Theory of Mind in adults. Moreover, infants' Theory of Mind is housed in a distinct neural system, not in the RTPJ; and this system is functionally mature early in development. This alternative neural system will be revealed by future neuroimaging studies of infants.

Then, beginning around age 2 years but continuing throughout childhood into adolescence, children slowly form a second system of concepts for understanding other minds. These explicit concepts are much more computationally powerful and flexible, allowing us to attribute beliefs and desires on any topic, and with much more complex logical structure. They are formulated as common explanations of multiple kinds of evidence: children's own experience of their own mind, their observations of human behavior, the intuitions derived from their foundational (culturally universal) concepts of actions and agent, and the (culturally specific) verbal descriptions of the mind provided by people around them. The later system is housed in the slowly developing RTPJ (among other brain regions), and it provides the basis for explaining one's own and others' behaviors in a wide range of contexts, for moral judgment, for strategic planning, for spreading gossip, and for writing fiction.

I am drawn to this picture. So far there is very little evidence to support or contradict it, but many of the predictions are testable with behavioral and neural measurements. I worry, though, that it is an evasion; whenever cognitive scientists encounter two sets of data that do not fit nicely into one of our existing theories, we simply posit two separate cognitive systems. It would be much more satisfying to construct a single theory, in which each of the observed patterns arises as a special case or in a defined context (e.g., Saxe, 2005; Tenenbaum & Griffiths, 2001). But I do not yet know what such a theory would be.

I do believe that the new puzzle of Theory of Mind is one of the key open challenges in the science of social development, and in cognitive science more broadly. Once again, we need a new theory of Theory of Mind.

REFERENCES

Apperly, I. A., & Butterfill, S. A. (2009). Do humans have two systems to track beliefs and belief-like states? *Psychology Review, 116*, 953–970.

Avis, J., & Harris, P. (1991). Belief-desire reasoning among Baka children: Evidence for a universal conception of mind. *Child Development, 62*, 460–467.

Baillargeon, R., Scott, R. M., & He, Z. (2010). False-belief understanding in infants. *Trends in Cognitive Science, 14*, 110–118.

Baird, J. A., & Astington, J. W. (2004). The role of mental state understanding in the development of moral cognition and moral action. *New Directions in Child and Adolescent Development, Spring, 103*, 37–49.

Baillargeon, R., Scott, R. M., & He, Z. (2010). False-belief understanding in infants. *Trends in cognitive sciences, 14*(3), 110.

Baker, S., & Leslie, A. M. (2008, April 2). *A new method for developmental research reveals profiles and sources of change in individual preschoolers' theory of mind.* Paper presented at the meeting of the Experimental Psychology Society, Cambridge, England.

Baron-Cohen, S., Leslie, A. M., & Frith, U. (1985). Does the autistic child have a "theory of mind"? *Cognition, 21*, 37–46.

Capelli, C. A., Nakagawa, N., & Madden, C. M. (1990). How children understand sarcasm: The role of context and intonation. *Child Development, 61*(6), 1824–1841.

Csibra, G., & Gergely, G. (2007). "Obsessed with goals": Functions and mechanisms of teleological interpretation of actions in humans. *Acta Psychologica (Amsterdam), 124*, 60–78.

Feigenson, L., & Carey, S. (2005). On the limits of infants' quantification of small object arrays. *Cognition, 97*, 295–313.

Gallagher, H. L., Happe, F., Brunswick, N., Fletcher, P. C., Frith, U., & Frith, C. D. (2000). Reading the mind in cartoons and stories: An fMRI study of "theory of mind" in verbal and nonverbal tasks. *Neuropsychologia, 38*, 11–21.

Goodman, N. D., Bonawitz, E. B., Baker, C. L., Mansinghka, V. K, Gopnik, A., Wellman, H., Schulz, L. and Tenenbaum, J. B. (2006). Intuitive theories of mind: A rational approach to false belief. *In Proceedings of the Twenty-Eighth Annual Conference of the Cognitive Science Society* (pp. 1382–1387). Cognitive Science Society.

Gopnik, A., & Wellman, H. M. (1992). Why the child's theory of mind really is a theory. *Mind and Language, 7*, 145–171.

Gweon, H., Dodell-Feder, D., Bedny, M., & Saxe, R. (2012). Theory of Mind Performance in Children Correlates With Functional Specialization of a Brain Region for Thinking About Thoughts. *Child Development.*

Kaminski, J., Call, J., & Tomasello, M. 2008. Chimpanzees know what others know, but not what they believe. *Cognition, 109*, 224–234.

Kobayashi, C., Gloverb, G. H., & Templec, E. (2007). Children's and adults' neural bases of verbal and nonverbal "theory of mind" *Neuropsychologia, 45*, 1522–1532.

Le Corre, M., & Carey, S. (2007). One, two, three, four, nothing more: An investigation of the conceptual sources of the verbal counting principles. *Cognition, 105*, 395–438.

Leslie, A. M., & Thaiss, L. (1992). Domain specificity in conceptual development: Neuropsychological evidence from autism. *Cognition, 43*, 225–251.

Liu, D., Wellman, H. M., Tardif, T., & Sabbagh, M. A. (2008). Theory of mind development in Chinese children: A meta-analysis of false-belief understanding across cultures and languages. *Developmental Psychology, 44*, 523–531.

Moses, L. J., & Flavell, J. H. (1990). Inferring false beliefs from actions and reactions. *Child Development, 61*, 929–945.

Onishi, K. H., & Baillargeon, R. (2005). Do 15-month-old infants understand false beliefs? *Science, 308*, 255–258.

Peterson, C. C., Wellman, H. M., & Liu, D. (2005). Steps in theory-of-mind development for children with deafness or autism. *Child Development, 76*, 502–517.

Repacholi, B. M., & Gopnik, A. (1997). Early reasoning about desires: Evidence from 14- and 18-month-olds. *Developmental Psychology, 33*, 12–21.

Ruffman, T., Garnham, W., Import, A., & Connolly, D. (2001). Does eye gaze indicate implicit knowledge of false belief? Charting transitions in knowledge. *Journal of Experimental Child Psychology, 80*, 201–224.

Sabbagh, M. A., Bowman, L. C., Evraire, L. E., & Ito, J. M. (2009). Neurodevelopmental correlates of theory of mind in preschool children. *Child Development, 80*, 1147–1162.

Santos, L. R., Flombaum, J. I., & Phillips, W. (2007). The evolution of human mindreading: How non-human primates can inform social cognitive neuroscience. *Evolutionary Cognitive Neuroscience*, 433–456.

Saxe, R. (2005). Hybrid vigour: Reply to Mitchell. *Trends in Cognitive Sciences, 9*, 364.

Saxe, R. (2010). The right temporo-parietal junction: A specific brain region for thinking about thoughts. In *Handbook of theory of mind Philadelphia, PA: Psychology Press.*

Saxe, R., Carey, S., & Kanwisher, N. (2004). Understanding other minds: linking developmental psychology and functional neuroimaging. *Annual Review of Psychology, 55*, 87–124.

Saxe, R., & Kanwisher, N. (2003). People thinking about thinking people. The role of the temporo-parietal junction in "theory of mind." *Neuroimage, 19*, 1835–1842.

Saxe, R., & Powell, L. J. (2006). It's the thought that counts: Specific brain regions for one component of theory of mind. *Psychology Science, 17*, 692–699.

Saxe, R. R., Whitfield-Gabrieli, S., Scholz, J., & Pelphrey, K. A. (2009). Brain regions for perceiving and reasoning about other people in school-aged children. *Child Development, 80*, 1197–1209.

Scott, R. M., & Baillargeon, R. (2009). Which penguin is this? Attributing false beliefs about object identity at 18 months. *Child Development, 80*, 1172–1196.

Sommerville, J. A., Woodward, A. L., & Needham, A. (2005). Action experience alters 3-month-old infants' perception of others' actions. *Cognition, 96*, B1–B11.

Song, H. J., & Baillargeon, R. (2008). Infants' reasoning about others' false perceptions. *Developmental Psychology, 44*(6), 1789.

Song, H. J., Onishi, K. H., Baillargeon, R., & Fisher, C. (2008). Can an agent's false belief be corrected by an appropriate communication? Psychological reasoning in 18-month-old infants. *Cognition, 109*, 295–315.

Southgate, V., Senju, A., & Csibra, G. (2007). Action anticipation through attribution of false belief by 2-year-olds. *Psychology Science, 18*, 587–592.

Surian, L., Caldi, S., & Sperber, D. (2007). Attribution of beliefs by 13-month-old infants. *Psychology Science, 18*, 580–586.

Tenenbaum, J. B., & Griffiths, T. L. (2001). Generalization, similarity, and Bayesian inference. *Behavior and Brain Science, 24*, 629–640.

Wellman, H. M., Cross, D., & Watson, J. (2003). Meta-analysis of theory of mind development: the truth about false belief. *Child development, 72*(3), 655–684.

Wimmer, H., & Perner, J. (1983). Beliefs about beliefs: Representation and constraining function of wrong beliefs in young children's understanding of deception. *Cognition, 13*, 103–128.

Winner, E., & Leekam, S. (1991). Distinguishing irony from deception: Understanding the speaker's second-order intention. *British Journal of Developmental Psychology*, 257–270.

Woodward, A. L. (2009). Infants' grasp of others' intentions. *Current Directions in Psychological Science, 18*, 53–57.

2.8

How Real Is the Imaginary?

The Capacity for High-Risk Children to Gain Comfort From Imaginary Relationships

MARJORIE TAYLOR AND NAOMI R. AGUIAR

He kind of looks like me... we like to play sword fighting... we pretend to play Lego Star Wars. He's super funny... nice, generous, crazy sometimes. He tells me jokes... shares his snacks with me... When I'm upset, he makes me talk sometimes; he makes me feel a little bit better. He's really good at doing things... helping me with my homework. He can run super fast. He's super nice... a good friend.

—9-year-old boy's description of his friend "Bob"

This description includes many of the features that signal high quality in a friendship—a combination of recreation, guidance, validation, and intimate exchange (Parker & Asher, 1993). The support and companionship of such friends are important to our happiness and psychological health throughout life and in childhood are widely believed to promote social competence and resilience. Thus, having a friend like Bob might seem to be obviously a good thing—except for a caveat. Does it matter that Bob is imaginary? That he eats bugs, can read a 150-page book in a minute, and likes to shape shift into animals or sometimes plants (e.g., a tree)?

Imaginary companions are invented characters that children interact with and/or talk about on a regular basis. (Sometimes they are invisible and sometimes they are based on special stuffed animals or dolls referred to as personified objects.) There is a history of ambivalence about the meaning and significance of such friends. On the one hand, Developmental Psychology has backed away from Piaget's view that they reflect "a lack of coherence... an immature mind that had not yet adapted to reality" (1962, p. 131), and recent studies have overturned the lay stereotype of the child with an imaginary friend as a shy, unusual, and withdrawn individual with emotional problems. The findings from our lab and elsewhere show that in Western cultures having an imaginary companion during the preschool years is relatively common

(Singer & Singer, 1990; Taylor, 1999) and tends to be associated with positive characteristics such as referential communication skills (Roby & Kidd, 2008) and narrative depth in storytelling (Trionfi & Reese, 2009). And contrary to the stereotype, imaginary companions do not seem to be associated with fewer friendships with real children (Gleason, 2004). Yet imaginary companions are quick to elicit adult concern and suspicion if they are not well behaved—even though many children describe their imaginary companions as unruly, bossy, or disobedient (Taylor, Carlson, & Shawber, 2007)—or if they appear after the preschool years—even though it is not particularly unusual for older children and adolescents to have them (Pearson et al., 2001; Seiffge-Krenke, 1997).

While not all friendships, be they real or imaginary, have the depth and stability to become significant in our lives, do at least some imaginary companions evolve into an important source of real-world support? This is what we mean when we ask how "real" is the imaginary. Note that we are not asking if children are confused and think their imaginary companions are real. For the record, the evidence clearly indicates that even preschool children are well aware that they are pretend (Taylor & Mottweiler, 2008; Taylor, Shawber, & Mannering, 2009). Children who participate in our research frequently make explicit and spontaneous references to the fantasy status of their imaginary companions (e.g., "I just made him up in my head," "he's not in real life," "I pretend they're real, but they're not," "her is a fake animal"). In fact, their pretend status is often convenient; imaginary companions can bear the brunt of a child's anger, be blamed for mishaps, and provide an especially private audience for secrets. But can self-generated imaginary friendships, like high-quality friendships with real children, provide the companionship and support that is associated with resilience in the face of adversity? To the extent that this is true, we think that these relationships can be considered "real."

THE IMAGINARY COMPANIONS OF LOW SOCIOECONOMIC STATUS, HIGH-RISK, MIDDLE-SCHOOL CHILDREN

As sometimes is the case, our evidence for resilience comes from a study of risk (Taylor, Hulette, & Dishion, 2010). In this work, we departed from our usual practice of interviewing preschool children and their parents from a normative community sample. Our goal was to investigate the forms and functions of imaginary companions created by older children to learn more about the developmental course of this type of pretending and to determine if having an imaginary companion might be the red flag for older children that some have claimed (Gupta & Desai, 2006). To increase the base rates of problem behaviors and negative outcomes, we recruited low socioeconomic status, 12-year-old children who were identified by their teachers as being at high risk for developing problems. The use of a high-risk sample limits the generalizability of our results but provides an increased prevalence of problem behaviors and therefore more power to examine the relation between early adolescent imaginary companions and adjustment. Of the 152 children in this sample, 13 children told us that they currently had imaginary companions (e.g., a brainiac who is cool, knows everything, and tries to keep the child out of trouble; a boy with dirty blonde hair and long lashes who always know what the child is going to say). The question was whether having an imaginary companion at age 12 in this sample was predictive of particularly negative outcomes down the road or, alternatively, if such friendships might contribute to resilience.

The initial wave of data collection when the children were in middle school presented a mixed picture. On one hand, the children with current imaginary companions scored higher than the other children on a measure of positive strategies for making themselves feel better when they were upset (e.g., go for a walk instead of hitting someone). But these children were rated by their parents as having more behavioral problems and they were not well accepted by their peers. However, this partly negative picture was not what we found 6 years later at the follow-up assessment. By the end of high school, the majority of the children who had had imaginary companions in middle school (72.7%) were doing reasonably well (i.e., they had no mental illness, were not using illegal drugs, had no history of arrest, and had graduated from high school). This result was in marked contrast to the other adolescents in the sample who did not report having imaginary companions at age 12; only 27.5% showed this positive pattern of outcomes at the end of high school.

It is tempting to conclude that the imaginary companions contributed directly to these adolescents' resilience by helping them work through difficulties. Or perhaps adolescents who have the capacity and inclination to supplement their social world with their imagination are less vulnerable to the attractions of involvement with deviant peers. However, the limitations of this study constrain its interpretation. The sample of middle school children with current imaginary companions was small and highly selective. Our 12-year-old participants were among the children considered by their teachers to show the highest levels of poor school adjustment, and by extension, the most likely to continue and escalate problem behavior in later adolescence. In addition, the results of this study might not generalize across cultures. Retrospective studies with adults include isolated reports of imaginary companions from many countries (e.g., United States, Canada, England, New Zealand, Italy, Israel, Hong Kong, Japan, Gabon, Australia, Mexico), but it is an open question whether imaginary companions are created to the same extent or serve the same psychological and social purposes for children and youths in other cultural contexts.

However, given the extensive data collection and the longitudinal design of our study, we can say with some confidence that there was at least no evidence that having an imaginary companion was a sign of impending behavioral or mental health problems for high-risk adolescents in our sample. To draw stronger conclusions about causality, one needs an experimental design in which children are randomly assigned to an imaginary companion condition or a control condition. We have not done that, but Sadeh, Hen-Gal, and Tikotzky (2008) have. In two experiments conducted after the 2006 Israeli-Lebanon war, they examined the extent that having a personified object might reduce the stress symptoms related to having lived in a war zone (e.g., difficulty falling asleep, nightmares, excessive crying, anxiety and fears, clinging, strong reactions to noise). Children (3 to 6 years old) were randomly assigned to a condition in which they were asked to take care of a stuffed animal who was described as sad, lonely, and in need of a friend. At a 2-month follow up, the 191 children who were given the stuffed animals showed significant improvement in stress-related symptoms compared to a control group of 101 children. The design of this study allows for the conclusion that the personified object was causally related to the children's improvement.

Taken together, these studies suggest that imaginary relationships might provide a powerful tool for coping with life stress. Although we cannot be sure of direct effects in adolescence, creating an imaginary companion is clearly not an early marker of pathology for high-risk youth. In fact, having an imaginary companion in middle school predicted a positive pattern of adjustment at the end of high school. For preschool children, an intervention that built on a natural strength of young children—their imaginations—was beneficial in helping them cope with the negative effects of being exposed to war and related trauma.

THE IMAGINARY COMPANIONS OF CHILDREN WHO HAVE BEEN IN FOSTER CARE

The Sadeh et al. research inspired us to begin an investigation of how imaginary companions might help children cope with other challenging situations. Here we describe the beginning step in research with children who have been in the US foster care system. The experience of foster care can be traumatizing for children who are already in a vulnerable state due to the situations that resulted in their entering the foster care system (e.g., a history of poverty, severe neglect, physical and/or sexual abuse). In particular, the stress associated with foster care (e.g., disruption of family relationships, changes in schools, ineffective foster parenting, frequent transitions in and out of multiple foster care homes) can have deleterious effects on friendships (Shook, Vaughn, Litschge, Kolivoski, & Schelbe, 2009).

This population is at very high risk for a range of negative outcomes (Fisher, Gunnar, et al., 2006), but not all foster children inevitably grow up to be troubled adolescents and adults. Some are able to overcome the adversity in their early lives to become healthy and highly functioning members of society. Not much is known about the variables that are associated with positive outcomes in these children, but maybe some children are able to use their imaginations as an effective tool for coping.

More specifically, perhaps the creation of imaginary companions—healthy and stable friendships that are not prone to disruption—contributes to resilience for children in foster care.

Our first goal was to learn more about the extent that children in foster care create imaginary companions spontaneously and to collect qualitative data about their characteristics. In collaboration with Candice Mottweiler and Phil Fisher, we have recently competed interviews with 60 children between the ages of 9 and 14 years old. Twenty-one of these children had been removed from their families of origin when they were 3 to 6 years old and were placed in foster care (48% had imaginary companions); 39 were in a control group from a low socioeconomic status community (41% had imaginary companions). Both groups of children described how their imaginary companions helped them by simply being there ("she was there when I needed her"; "was there for giving me ideas"; "followed through and helped me"). Children also reported practical, everyday ways in which their imaginary companions supported them, such as helping with math homework, teaching them new things (e.g., the colors of the rainbow), and participating in joint activities (e.g., playing board games). And some of the children who had lived in foster care provided detailed accounts of the ways in which their imaginary companions helped them with particularly difficult experiences. For example, a 13-year-old boy described how his stuffed gorilla helped him cope with his grandfather's death, "…when I would get upset about something that I didn't want to happen—like…when our grandpa died—he helped me with that." Another child reported, "whenever I got sad or mad or…I wanted to throw something and break it…it was…like what a mom would do, try to calm someone down." Overall, the imaginary companions created spontaneously by the children in our sample were consistently described as powerful allies who provided them with steadfast companionship and support. The children themselves clearly believed that their imaginary companions had helped them cope with the challenges in their lives.

CONCLUSION

Recent studies in our lab indicate that imaginary companions in children and at-risk adolescents are not markers of mental and behavioral problems. Instead, our findings combined with experimental work by Sadeh et al. suggest that real comfort and support can be gained from imaginary relationships. We see a connection between our developmental work and the research of others with adults showing how fantasy activities (e.g., reading fiction, imagining interpersonal interactions) enhance our capacity for real-world empathy, social inference, and effective coping (Honeycutt, 2010; Mar & Oatley, 2008). While there is a long history in clinical practice of using imagination to change real-world behavior (Leuner, 1969), there is now a growing appreciation across other areas of psychology for the role that imagination plays in everyday cognitive and emotional experiences (Harris, 2000; Pascual-Leone et al., 1995).

A wide range of recent studies, many with adult participants, suggest that imaginative processes are fundamental to everyday thought throughout life and are inextricably linked to our understanding of reality and our everyday behavior. Along with these studies, our research with children is consistent with the view that imagination can be "real." Like living and breathing friends, we believe that imaginary ones can provide love and support and serve as sounding boards; they can also be provocative, challenging, neglectful, or infuriating, but ultimately they enrich our lives.

REFERENCES

Fisher, P. A., Burraston, B., & Pears, K. (2005). The early intervention foster care program: Permanent placement outcomes from a randomized trial. *Child Maltreatment, 10*(1), 61–71.

Fisher, P. A., Gunnar, M. R., Dozier, M., Bruce, J., & Pears, K. C. (2006). Effects of therapeutic interventions for foster children on behavioral problems, caregiver attachment, and stress regulatory neural systems. *Annals of the New York Academy of Sciences, 1094*, 215–255.

Gleason, T. R. (2004). Imaginary companions and peer acceptance. *International Journal of Behavioral Development, 28*, 204–209.

Gupta, A., & Desai, N. G. (2006). Pathological fantasy friend phenomenon. *International Journal of Psychiatry in Clinical Practice, 10*, 149–151.

Harris, P. L. (2000). *The work of the imagination.* Oxford, England; Oxford University Press.

Honeycutt, J. M. (Ed.). (2010). *Imagine that: Studies in imagined interactions.* Cresskill, NJ: Hampton.

Leuner, H. (1969). Guided affective imagery: A method of intensive psychotherapy. *American Journal of Psychotherapy, 23*, 4–22.

Mar, R. A., & Oatley, K. (2008). The function of fiction is the abstraction and simulation of social experience. *Perspectives on Psychological Science, 3*, 173–192.

Parker, J. G. & Asher, S. R. (1993). Friendship and friendship quality in middle childhood: Links with peer group acceptance and feelings of loneliness and social dissatisfaction. *Developmental Psychology, 29*, 611–621.

Pascual-Leone, A., Dang, N., Cohen, L. G., Brasilneto, J. P., Cammarota, A., & Hallett, M. (1995). Modulation of muscle responses evoked by transcranial magnetic stimulation during the acquisition of new fine motor skills. *Journal of Neurophysiology, 74*(3), 1037–1045

Pearson, D., Rouse, H., Doswell, S., Ainsworth, C., Dawson, O., Simms, K.,... Falconbridge, J. (2001). Prevalence of imaginary companions in a normal child population. *Child: Care, Health and Development, 27*, 13–22.

Piaget, J. (1962). *Play, dreams and imitation.* New York: W.W. Norton.

Roby, A.C., & Kidd, E. (2008). The referential communication skills of children with imaginary companions. *Developmental Science, 11*, 531–540.

Sadeh, A., Hen-Gal, S., & Tikotzky, L. (2008). Young children's reactions to war-related stress: A survey and assessment of an innovative intervention. *Pediatrics, 121*, 46–53.

Seiffge-Krenke, I. (1997). Imaginary companions in adolescence: Sign of a deficient or positive development? *Journal of Adolescence, 20*, 137–154.

Shook, J. J., Vaughn, M. G., Litschge, C., Kolivoski, K., & Schelbe, L. (2009). The importance of friends among foster youth aging out of care: Cluster profiles of deviant peer associations. *Children and Youth Services Review, 31*, 284–291.

Singer, D. G., & Singer, J. L. (1990). *The house of make-believe: Children's play and developing imagination.* Cambridge, MA: Harvard University Press.

Taylor, M. (1999). *Imaginary companions and the children who create them.* New York: Oxford University Press.

Taylor, M., Carlson, S, M., & Shawber, A. B. (2007). Autonomy and control in children's interactions with imaginary companions. In I. Roth (Ed.), *Imaginative minds* (pp. 81–100). Oxford, England: British Academy and Oxford University Press.

Taylor, M., Hulette, A. C., & Dishion, T. J. (2010). Longitudinal outcomes of young high-risk adolescents with imaginary companions. *Developmental Psychology, 46*, 1632–16–36.

Taylor, M., & Mottweiler, C. M. (2008). Imaginary companions: Pretending they are real but knowing they are not. *American Journal of Play, 1*, 47–54.

Taylor, M., Shawber, A. B., & Mannering, A. M. (2009). Children's imaginary companions: What is it like to have an invisible friend? In K. Markman, W. Klein, & J. Suhr (Eds.), *The handbook of imagination and mental simulation* (pp. 211–224). New York: Psychology Press.

Trionfi, G., & Reese, E. (2009). A good story: Children with imaginary companions create richer narratives. *Child Development, 80*, 1301–1313.

2.9

Social Engagement Does Not Lead to Social Cognition

Evidence From Williams Syndrome

HELEN TAGER-FLUSBERG AND DANIELA PLESA SKWERER

For over two decades now, cognitive scientists have been captured by the promise that Williams syndrome (WS), a rare genetic disorder in which about 25 genes are missing from one copy of the long arm of chromosome 7, will highlight the core architecture of human cognition because of the apparent unique phenotype that characterizes individuals with this disorder. In the early days, attention focused on the putative dissociations between language and cognition, though as research progressed it seemed that the reality was far less interesting: Language abilities are essentially commensurate with mental age levels (for reviews, see Martens, Wilson, & Reutens, 2008; Mervis & Becerra, 2007). The significance of the social phenotype of WS has been more enduring; however, the precise nature of the mechanisms that underlie the essential features that distinguish children and adults with WS from others has been more elusive to pinpoint than was initially anticipated.

People with WS are strikingly social creatures. They are outgoing, gregarious, warm, and socially engaged with other people. Despite their mild to moderate levels of intellectual disability, children and adults with WS will approach new people they meet, strike up a conversation, and show intense interest in them. These characteristics are often documented in descriptive studies and highlight the positive aspects of their social phenotype, which researchers have pursued in the hopes of discovering the genetic bases of human social cognitive architecture (Bellugi et al., 2007; Tager-Flusberg & Plesa Skwerer, 2006). But these same descriptive studies also reveal a darker side to the social world of people with WS. First, the social engagement, especially in young children, can be so extreme that their fearlessness and willingness

to accompany complete strangers pose real potential danger. And second, by middle childhood they experience difficulties forming friendships, have limited conversational and other discourse skills, and are vulnerable to teasing and social rejection. This is the essential paradox of the social phenotype of WS that has captured the attention of researchers in the field of social cognition (Plesa Skwerer & Tager-Flusberg, 2006).

WHAT ARE THE MECHANISMS THAT UNDERLIE THE SOCIAL PHENOTYPE IN ADOLESCENTS AND ADULTS?

In the early days, researchers ignored the darker side of the phenotype and boldly proposed that WS exemplified a relatively preserved "social module" in the context of general cognitive impairment (Karmiloff-Smith, Klima, Bellugi, Grant, & Baron-Cohen, 1995). However, later carefully designed studies, in which the WS participants were compared to well-matched control groups on developmentally appropriate Theory of Mind tasks, including basic false-belief tasks as well as more advanced tasks such as distinguishing between lies and ironic jokes, using personality traits to make intentionality attributions, and moral attributions, demonstrated unambiguous impairments in social cognition in children and adolescents with WS, on a par with their general level of cognitive and language abilities (Porter, Coltheart, & Langdon, 2008; Tager-Flusberg & Sullivan, 2000). In retrospect, these findings were not surprising given the high linguistic and cognitive-inferential demands of the experimental paradigms that were used to probe Theory of Mind in WS.

The next round of studies that were carried out in the hopes of capturing the distinctive profile of social cognition hypothesized to characterize socially driven people with WS focused on tasks that tap mentalizing abilities related directly to social perception, such as tests of emotion or mental state recognition from nonverbal channels, including faces and voices. Repeating the history of research on Theory of Mind in WS, after one false start, which claimed to find relative sparing in a small sample of adolescents with WS on the "Reading the Mind in the Eyes" task (Tager-Flusberg, Boshart, & Baron-Cohen, 1998), a later study failed to replicate this initial finding when a more rigorous version of the task was employed with larger matched groups of adolescents (Plesa Skwerer, Verbalis, Schofield, Faja, & Tager-Flusberg, 2006). Moreover, several studies using various emotion recognition tasks revealed difficulties in the WS participants with labeling or matching emotional expressions from faces and voices, despite their relatively intact performance in face identity recognition (Gagliardi et al., 2003; Plesa Skwerer, Faja, Schofield, Verbalis, & Tager-Flusberg, 2006; Porter, Coltheart, & Langdon, 2007).

Several studies probed more complex social judgments in WS based on Ralph Adolphs's Approachability task (Adolphs, Tranel, & Damasio, 1998). Depending on the particular face stimuli used and the age of the participants, findings varied, with some studies reporting that adults with WS gave significantly more positive ratings overall, judging the unfamiliar faces as more approachable and more trustworthy than did the controls (Bellugi, Adolphs, Cassady, & Chiles, 1999; Martens, Wilson, Dudgeon, & Reutens, 2009), while other studies using emotionally expressive faces reported that the WS group rated only the *happy* faces as more approachable than the matched controls (Frigerio et al., 2006; Porter et al., 2007). Difficulties in distinguishing between negative facial expressions of emotion (e.g., fearful, sad, angry) and a bias toward rating happy faces as more trustworthy and approachable (Frigerio et al., 2006) demonstrate that individuals with WS are *not* adept at decoding perceptual cues to mental states from faces and voices; instead they rely on superficial strategies in making social judgments in the absence of spared social cognitive skills.

The conclusions from experimental studies on social cognition and social perception in WS fit well with the lack of social savvy, difficulties forming and maintaining meaningful social relationships over time, and generally poor social outcomes, including some degree of social isolation by adulthood that both parents and adults with WS report (e.g., Howlin & Udwin, 2006; Plesa

Skwerer, Sullivan, Joffre, & Tager-Flusberg, 2004). But these studies, which relied on explicit experimental tasks, do not provide insight into what might be distinctive about the WS social phenotype: Poor performance on experimental tasks and impaired social functioning are found not only in WS but also in others with intellectual disability and different genetic syndromes, and none of this research explains the more positive heightened social engagement and social approach behaviors that are uniquely characteristic of children and adults with this disorder.

A clearer picture about what might genuinely distinguish WS from other people and which may account for the most striking aspects of the social phenotype is beginning to emerge from studies that employ *implicit* measures of social information processing, such as spontaneous attention deployment, autonomic arousal, and functional neuroimaging with adolescents and young adults. This more recent line of research has revealed two distinctive aspects of processing social information compared to matched controls: (1) increased attention to the social content of visual stimuli, especially human faces (Ammerman et al., 2010; Riby & Hancock, 2008, 2009); and (2) decreased autonomic arousal to signals of social threat, as conveyed in negatively valenced images of human faces or social scenes (Plesa Skwerer et al., 2009).

Evidence for unusual attention deployment processes in WS has come from studies using eye-tracking methods and from experimental studies of attentional biases based on reaction time measures. Eye-tracking studies have found that people with WS look more at social aspects of complex scenes and faces compared to typical controls (Ammerman et al., 2010; Riby & Hancock, 2008, 2009). These biases toward looking more at faces appear to be modulated by emotional expression. For example, in one recent study using a dot-probe detection task with pairs of faces displaying happy, angry, or neutral expressions, the WS group exhibited a significantly greater attentional bias for happy faces than age- and mental-age-matched controls, but not for neutral or angry faces (Dodd & Porter, 2010). This bias was primarily driven by difficulties disengaging attention from the happy faces rather than attention capture, which is consistent with other findings from eye-tracking research (Riby & Hancock, 2009).

Several studies have examined autonomic responses to emotionally valenced social and nonsocial stimuli in WS, in an effort to explore whether there are differences in physiological reactivity related to processing of social information (Andre, Olufemi, Plesa Skwerer, & Tager-Flusberg, 2009; Doherty-Sneddon, Riby, Calderwood, & Ainsworth, 2009; Plesa Skwerer et al., 2009). Across different psychophysiological measures, skin conductance responses, heart rate changes, and pupil dilation, adolescents and adults with WS show overall lower levels of autonomic arousal under a variety of conditions, but especially when viewing images conveying, directly or indirectly, social threat. This lower level of arousal is experienced in social encounters with strangers and may partly explain the tendency of people with WS to maintain prolonged eye contact, beyond the point when others would find the unbroken gaze uncomfortable (Doherty-Sneddon et al., 2009).

Such distinctive responses in WS, reflected in attentional and physiological indices, suggest abnormalities in the neurocognitive systems involved in processing social and affective information, and in interpreting the salience of this information at implicit levels of processing. The hypothesis of amygdala dysfunction is consistent with the behavioral and physiological findings, and so the amygdala and its complex regulatory interactions with cortical areas has been the focus of several brain imaging studies conducted with adults with WS. Using fMRI with a group of adults with WS who had normal-range IQ scores, Meyer-Lindenberg and colleagues (2005) found hypoactivation of the amygdala in response to pictures of negative facial affect (fear, anger), but increased activation when viewing threatening nonsocial scenes, relative to controls. Furthermore, brain functional connectivity analyses revealed that the WS group did not activate the orbito-frontal cortex to the face stimuli but showed equivalent activation to the social and nonsocial stimuli in medial and dorso-lateral prefrontal regions, suggesting that abnormalities in the regulatory interactions between the prefrontal cortex and the amygdala may explain the pattern of decreased social fear (and perhaps increased nonsocial fear) in people with WS. In another study comparing neural responses to viewing happy, fearful, neutral, and scrambled faces, using both functional magnetic resonance imaging and event-related potential measures, Haas and his colleagues (2009) found that WS participants showed elevated amygdala activation to happy but not to fearful faces, in contrast to the activation pattern found in controls, and suggested that "abnormal amygdala reactivity in WS may possibly function to increase attention to and encoding of happy expressions and to decrease arousal to fearful expressions" (Haas et al., 2009, p. 1132). A follow-up investigation of a small subset of the adults from this study linked reduced amygdala activation to fearful faces to a greater propensity to approach strangers, as reported by their parents (Haas et al., 2010). Although the findings across these small-scale studies of adults are not entirely consistent, they do highlight the role of the amygdalae, particularly their connectivity with prefrontal cortical areas, as the neural structures responsible for the distinctive pattern of affective responses to social stimuli found in older individuals with WS.

The experimental research summarized earlier provides different strands of evidence—from subjective ratings of approachability, to attention biases, arousal measures, and neural responses—that converge on the idea that atypical processing of social signals of potential threat underpins the unusual social fearlessness and approach behavior seen in people with WS.

THE DEVELOPMENT OF SOCIAL ENGAGEMENT IN WILLIAMS SYNDROME

But when do these unique processing patterns begin, and how do they develop in early childhood? The origins and the trajectory of developmental changes in the social engagement phenotype of WS remain poorly understood, in part because no longitudinal studies of the social phenotype have been conducted. Still, there is a growing body of behavioral studies which suggest that the unique social phenotype of WS begins early in infancy. Careful behavioral observations of infants and young children with WS have highlighted that prolonged and intense looking at faces of both familiar and unfamiliar people is seen in WS starting at least by 8–12 months (Jones et al., 2000; Mervis et al., 2003). Reporting on the looking behavior of one toddler with WS observed in free play interaction with his mother and with unfamiliar partners, Mervis and her colleagues (2003) described the intensity of the toddler's gaze as "boring through." An intense attentional focus on faces is especially obvious during the second and third years of life (Mervis et al., 2003), but it appears to moderate with age, as attention disengagement mechanisms begin to mature. However, an eagerness to approach and engage strangers even at ages when children are normally shy has been consistently reported by parents and demonstrated in studies using laboratory-based measures of temperament (Jones et al., 2000).

We recently conducted a multiple-methods study of social-emotional development in 3- to 6-year-olds with WS. To investigate their emotional responses, the children were confronted with a variety of situations selected from the Laboratory Assessment of Temperament (Lab-TAB; Goldsmith et al., 1995), several of which were designed to elicit social and nonsocial fear. For instance, in the "Stranger Approach" episode the child encounters an unfamiliar person who enters the room where the child was left alone for a brief period of time, sits down in a chair, and asks the child several questions; in other episodes the child is asked to touch fear-eliciting objects (a jumping spider toy and a large gorilla mask). Child behaviors were coded on critical aspects of emotional responses (e.g., fearful facial affect, approach and avoidance behaviors, vocal distress, postural fear) and compared to groups of age-matched children with Down syndrome (DS), and typically developing controls (Lindeke, Plesa-Skwerer, Ciciolla, & Tager-Flusberg, 2008). As expected, in a variety of social contexts children with WS exhibited significantly less fear and were more likely to approach the stranger than the other children. However, somewhat surprisingly, the WS children were also less wary than controls in their responses to nonsocial stimuli, readily touching the jumping spider and gorilla mask, suggesting an underlying temperamental approach-propensity that is not restricted to the social domain in WS, at least in early childhood. To complement the behavioral observations, parents completed questionnaires assessing their children's temperament, emotional intensity, and assessments of family functioning. According to parent ratings, only the "social fear" scale yielded significant differences between the WS and the DS children, with the children with WS being rated significantly lower, whereas both the WS and DS groups scored lower on inhibitory control, interest, and attention compared to the typically developing controls. Parents rated their children with WS higher than both control groups in emotional intensity expression across contexts, suggesting a distinctive profile of high sociability, high emotionality, lack of fear, and high approach in young children with WS.

The overfriendliness toward strangers shown by many children with WS, even at ages when stranger wariness is expected to emerge, raises the question of whether dysfunction in the formation of attachment bonds with a primary caregiver might underlie their indiscriminate approach behavior. We examined this issue using both laboratory-based observational paradigms (the Strange Situation Procedure) and extensive interviews with the parents of the children who were part of this developmental investigation (Plesa Skwerer, Lindeke, Ogrodnik, & Tager-Flusberg, 2008). Coding of attachment-related behaviors showed that most of the children in all three groups were classified as securely attached. The parental interviews confirmed that children with WS show clear preferential affective bonds with primary caregivers, differentiate between familiar people in the family, and show a hierarchical arrangement of caregivers in terms of strength of preference. Nevertheless, almost all the parents of WS children interviewed (95%) readily declared that their child would willingly go off with a stranger, and admitted that this behavior worried them. These findings suggest that the indiscriminate friendliness and approach toward strangers shown by children with WS cannot be related to the absence of focused attachment bonds or to characteristics of the child's rearing environment.

Another highly distinctive characteristic also manifest from an early age in WS is their emotional responsivity toward others, especially their empathy for people in distress. In a simulated pain procedure, in which children witness an experimenter "accidentally" hurting herself and displaying facial and vocal signs of suffering, 3- to 7-year-olds with WS showed significantly more comforting behavior, expressions of sympathy and overall concern than matched control groups (e.g., Ciciolla, Plesa Skwerer, & Katz, 2007). In a different type of task, in which children witnessed an adult expressing likes or dislikes for certain food items through facial and vocal affective expressions, children with WS were more likely to mimic or imitate the adult's facial and vocal affect compared to a matched control group, but, just like the mental age-matched controls, they failed to give the adult more of the food that they liked based on their nonverbal communicative signals (Fidler, Hepburn, Most, Philofsky, & Rogers, 2007). At this early stage then, greater sensitivity and responsiveness to affective communication does not translate into appropriate social action. This conclusion from work with very young children with WS foreshadows the disconnection found between heightened social interest and poor social cognition that characterizes older children and adults with WS.

Taken together, these studies demonstrate that the distinctive aspects of emotional responsiveness seen in young children with WS may signal a developmental precursor to social disinhibition in WS (Fidler et al., 2007). Children with WS, while hypersocial and empathic, have difficulties linking their affective responsiveness to appropriate social behavior or competence.

SUMMARY AND CONCLUSIONS

Beginning very early in development, infants with WS show increased attention to social stimuli, especially faces, far greater social approach behaviors, and an affective connection to others as expressed in their empathy and nonverbal communicative displays. These components of social engagement are coupled with a more generalized disinhibited temperament and reduced fear of both social and nonsocial threat. Even at these early stages there is a clear disconnection between these unique aspects of the prosocial phenotype of WS and the development of social competence. In older children with WS, disinhibition and overly focused attention to social stimuli (or difficulty disengaging attention) are modulated, probably as a result of the development of general cognitive control processes, though they still show increased attention to social information. Reduced arousal to threat stimuli is also still evident in older individuals, perhaps only in social contexts (cf. Meyer-Lindenberg et al., 2005). Despite their interest and engagement with social stimuli, older children and adults with WS still have quite limited social cognitive competencies, which remain at a level predicted by their cognitive and linguistic levels, not their social motivation. The take-home message from research on WS is that early social interest and social-affective connectivity does not necessarily translate into later social cognitive skills.

There is still much that we do not know about the social phenotype of WS. Given that this is a genetic disorder of known origin, we have the opportunity to identify the genetic bases of the unique aspects of the social affiliative drive that distinguishes people with WS from other people, but so far the specific genes in the deleted region that might be implicated in this behavior have not been specified. New work on animal models of WS may soon provide some answers (Li et al., 2009). As children with WS get older, anxiety increases, often taking the form of phobias or generalized anxiety disorder (Leyfer, Woodruff-Borden, Klein-Tasman, Fricke, & Mervis, 2006). Is this anxiety related to aspects of the social phenotype? Paradoxically, anxiety disorders coexist with hypersocial fearless behavior and reduced autonomic arousal that characterizes people with WS. This intriguing dissociation between social and nonsocial anxiety in WS is another facet of the puzzle at the heart of the WS phenotype that needs to be unraveled in developmental and neuroimaging studies. Much has been learned from studying the complex, often contradictory, phenotype that is at the core of WS. The future of this line of research may eventually lead to finding the genetic origins of social engagement, which lies at the heart of our human nature.

ACKNOWLEDGMENTS

This chapter was written with support from the NICHD (RO1 HD 33740; RO3 HD 51943).

REFERENCES

Adolphs, R., Tranel, D., & Damasio, A. R. (1998). The human amygdala in social judgment. *Nature, 393*, 470–474.

Ammerman, E., Andre, M. C., Storer, A., Fine, A., Ciciolla, L., Lindeke, M., … Tager-Flusberg, H. (2010, May). *Differential appraisal of social and nonsocial affective images in Williams syndrome.*Presented at the 22nd Annual Convention of the Association for Psychological Science, Boston, MA.

Andre, M. C., Olufemi, O. L., Plesa Skwerer, D., & Tager-Flusberg, H. (2009, October). *Pupillary responses to images with social-affective content in Autism and Williams Syndrome.* Presented at the 2nd Tufts University Conference: The neuroscience of emotion: From reaction to regulation, Boston, MA.

Bellugi, U., Adolphs, R., Cassady, C., & Chiles M. (1999). Towards the neural basis for hypersociability in a genetic syndrome. *Neuroreport, 10*, 1653–1657.

Bellugi, U., Järvinen-Pasley, A., Doyle, T. F., Reilly, J., Reiss, A. L., & Korenberg, J. R. (2007). Affect, social ehavior, and the brain in Williams syndrome. *Current Directions in Psychological Science, 16*, 99–104.

Ciciolla, L., Plesa Skwerer, D., & Katz, R. (2007, March). *Exploring helping behaviors and empathy in young children with Williams syndrome.* Presented at the Biennial Meetings of the Society for Research in Child Development, Boston, MA.

Dodd, H. F., & Porter, M. A. (2010). I see happy people: Attention towards happy but not angry facial expressions in Williams syndrome. *Cognitive Neuropsychiatry, 15*, 549–567.

Doherty-Sneddon, G., Riby, D, Calderwood, L., & Ainsworth, L. (2009). Stuck on you: Face -to- face arousal and gaze aversion in Williams syndrome. *Cognitive Neuropsychiatry, 14*, 1–14.

Fidler, D. J., Hepburn, S. L., Most, D. E., Philofsky, A., & Rogers, S. J. (2007). Emotional responsivity in young children with Williams syndrome. *American Journal on Mental Retardation, 112*, 194–206.

Frigerio, E., Burt, D. M., Gagliardi,C., Cioffi, G., Martelli, S., Perrett, D. I., & Borgatti, R. (2006). Is everybody always my friend? Perception of approachability in Williams syndrome. *Neuropsychologia, 44,* 254–259.

Gagliardi, C., Frigerio, E., Burt, D. M., Cazzaniga, I., Perrett, D., & Borgatti, R. (2003). Facial expression recognition in Williams syndrome. *Neuropsychologia, 41,* 733–738.

Goldsmith, H. H., Reilly, J., Lemery, K. S., Longley, S., & Prescott, A. (1995). Laboratory Temperament Assessment Battery: Preschool version. Unpublished manuscript.

Haas, B., Mills, D., Yam, A., Hoeft, F., Bellugi, U., & Reiss, A. (2009). Genetic influences on sociability: Heightened amygdala reactivity and event-related responses to positive social stimuli in Williams syndrome. *Journal of Neuroscience, 29,* 1132–1139.

Haas, B., Hoeft, F., Searcy, Y., Mills, D., Bellugi, U., & Reiss, A. (2010). Individual differences in social behavior predict amygdale response to fearful facial expressions in Williams syndrome. *Neuropsychologia, 48,* 1283–1288.

Howlin, P., & Udwin, O. (2006). Outcome in adult life for people with Williams syndrome—results from a survey of 239 families. *Journal of Intellectual Disability Research, 50,* 151–160.

Jones, W., Bellugi, U., Lai, Z., Chiles, M., Reilly, J., Lincoln, A., & Ralphs, A. (2000). Hypersociability in Williams syndrome. *Journal of Cognitive Neuroscience, 12*(Suppl.), 30–46.

Karmiloff-Smith, A., Klima, E., Bellugi, U., Grant, J., & Baron-Cohen, S. (1995). Is there a social module? Language, face processing and theory of mind in individuals with Williams syndrome. *Journal of Cognitive Neuroscience, 7,* 196–208.

Leyfer,O.,Woodruff-Borden,J.,Klein-Tasman,B.,Fricke, J., & Mervis, C. G. B. (2006). Prevalence of psychiatric disorders in 4 to 16 year-olds with Williams syndrome. *American Journal of Medical Genetics, B Neuropsychiatric Genetics, 141B,* 615–622.

Lindeke, M., Plesa Skwerer, D., Ciciolla, L., & Tager-Flusberg, H. (2008, July). *Strangers and spiders: How young children with Williams syndrome respond to social and nonsocial fear-eliciting events.* Paper presented at the International Professional Conference on Williams Syndrome, Anaheim, CA.

Li, H., Roy, M., Kuscuiglu, U., Spencer, C., Halm, B., Harrison, K.,…Francke, U. (2009). Induced chromosome deletions cause hypersociability and other features of Williams-Beuren syndrome in mice. *Molecular Medicine, 1,* 50–65.

Martens, M. A., Wilson, S. J., & Reutens, D. C. (2008). Research review: Williams syndrome: A critical review of the cognitive, behavioral and neuroanatomical phenotype. *Journal of Child Psychology and Psychiatry, 49,* 576–608.

Martens, M. A., Wilson, S. J., Dudgeon, P., & Reutens, D. C. (2009). Approachability and the amygdala: Insights from Williams syndrome. *Neuropsychologia, 47,* 2446–2453.

Mervis, C. B., & Becerra, A. M. (2007). Language and communicative development in Williams syndrome. *Mental Retardation and Developmental Disabilities Research Reviews, 13,* 3–5.

Mervis, C., Morris, C. A., Klein-Tasman, B. P., Bertrand, J., Kwitny, S., Appelbaum, L. G., & Rice, C. E. (2003). Attentional characteristics of infants and toddlers with Williams syndrome during triadic interactions. *Developmental Neuropsychology, 23*(1&2), 243–268.

Meyer-Lindenberg, A., Hariri, A. R., Munoz, K. E., Mervis, C. B., Mattay, V. S., Morris, C. A., & Berman, K. F. (2005). Neural correlates of genetically abnormal social cognition in Williams syndrome. *Nature Neuroscience, 8,* 991–993.

Plesa Skwerer, D., Borum, L., Verbalis, A., Schofield, C., Crawford, N., Ciciolla, L., & Tager-Flusberg, H. (2009). Autonomic responses to dynamic displays of facial expressions in adolescents and adults with Williams syndrome. *Social Cognitive and Affective Neuroscience, 4,* 93–100.

Plesa Skwerer, D., Faja, S., Schofield, C., Verbalis, A., & Tager-Flusberg, H. (2006). Perceiving facial and vocal expression of emotion in Williams syndrome. *American Journal on Mental Retardation,111,* 15–26.

Plesa Skwerer, D., Lindeke, M., Ogrodnik, K., & Tager-Flusberg, H. (2008, July). *Observational assessments of attachment and temperament in young children with Williams syndrome: Toward a profile of early socio-emotional functioning.* Paper presented at the 11th International Professional Conference on Williams Syndrome, Anaheim, CA.

PlesaSkwerer,D.,Sullivan,K.,Joffre,K.,&Tager-Flusberg, H. (2004). Self-concept in people with Williams syndrome and Prader-Willi syndrome. *Research in Developmental Disabilities, 25,* 119–138.

Plesa Skwerer, D., & Tager-Flusberg, H. (2006). Social cognition in Williams-Beuren syndrome. In C. A. Morris, H. M. Lenhoff, & P. Wang (Eds.), *Williams-Beuren syndrome: Research and clinical perspectives* (pp. 237–253). Baltimore, MD: Johns Hopkins University Press.

Plesa Skwerer, D., Verbalis, A., Schofield, C., Faja, S., & Tager-Flusberg, H. (2006). Social-perceptual abilities in adolescents and adults with Williams syndrome. *Cognitive Neuropsychology 23,* 338–349.

Porter, M., Coltheart, M., & Langdon, R. (2007). The neuropsychological basis of hypersociability in Williams and Down syndrome. *Neuropsychologia, 45,* 2839–2849.

Porter, M. A., Coltheart, M., & Langdon, R. (2008). Theory of mind in Williams syndrome assessed using a nonverbal task. *Journal of Autism and Developmental Disorders, 38,* 806–814

Riby, D. M., & Hancock, P. J. (2008). Viewing it differently: Social scene perception in Williams syndrome and autism. *Neuropsychologia, 46,* 2855–2860

Riby, D. M., & Hancock, P. J. (2009). Do faces capture the attention of individuals with Williams syndrome or Autism? *Journal of Autism and Developmental Disorders, 39,* 421–431.

Tager-Flusberg, H., Boshart, J., & Baron-Cohen, S. (1998) Reading the windows to the soul: Evidence of domain-specific sparing in Williams syndrome. *Journal of Cognitive Neuroscience, 10,* 631–639.

Tager-Flusberg, H., & Plesa Skwerer, D. (2006). Social engagement in Williams syndrome. In P. J. Marshall & N. A. Fox (Eds.), *The development of social engagement: Neurobiological perspectives* (pp. 331–354). New York: Oxford University Press Series in Affective Science.

Tager-Flusberg, H., & Sullivan, K. (2000). A componential view of theory of mind: Evidence from Williams syndrome. *Cognition, 76,* 59–89.

SECTION III ———————————

Imitation, Modeling, and Learning From and About Others

3.1

Natural Pedagogy

GYÖRGY GERGELY AND GERGELY CSIBRA

While socially transmitted population-specific cultural skills exist both in human and nonhuman primate species (Whiten et al., 1999), the scope and kinds of cultural knowledge forms transmitted by humans suggest that our hominin ancestors may have evolved species-specific social cognitive adaptations specialized for cultural learning (Csibra & Gergely, 2006; Tomasello, 1999). There are a number of significant properties that differentiate the types of knowledge contents that are transmitted and maintained across generations in human cultures when compared to the much more restricted range of socially transmitted cultural skills that characterize nonhuman primate cultures.

First, human cultures are unique in that they involve the transmission of cognitively opaque cultural knowledge that is not (or not fully) comprehensible for the naïve observational learner in terms of their relevant causal and/or teleological properties. The variety of such cognitively opaque forms of cultural knowledge includes relevant information about novel means-end skills and practical know-how embedded in relatively complex forms of tool use and tool manufacturing procedures, behavioral traditions that "ought to" be performed in specific ways in particular types of social situations, normative conventions, shared knowledge about social rules and roles, or arbitrary referential symbols. Second, human cultures involve the transmission of generic (or semantic) knowledge of properties that specify and generalize to kinds. Third, human cultures involve conveying shared cultural knowledge that is presumed to be equally accessible to all members of one's cultural group.

These three unique properties of human cultural knowledge forms would represent a serious learnability problem for naïve juvenile learners if they relied on purely observational learning strategies to acquire them from others. This is so because standard mechanisms of individual observational learning lack the appropriate informational basis that would allow the novice to (1) differentiate the relevant aspects of the observed but cognitively opaque behavior (which should be selectively retained) from those that are incidental or nonrelevant (and should therefore be omitted), (2) infer whether or how to generalize it to other situations, and (3) identify whether it represents shared knowledge that can be assumed to be available to other members of the cultural community as well (Csibra & Gergely, 2009; Gergely, 2010).

We hypothesized that this learnability problem would have endangered the successful intergenerational transmission of highly useful and fitness-enhancing but cognitively opaque technological skills that emerged during hominin evolution (Gergely & Csibra, 2005). In our view, this challenge represented selective pressure for a new type of social communicative learning mechanism, technically termed "natural pedagogy," to become selected in humans (Csibra & Gergely, 2006, 2011; Gergely & Csibra, 2006). Relying on ostensive-referential demonstrations of the relevant aspects of the opaque skills, communicative knowledge transfer could alleviate the learnability problem by having the knowledgeable conspecific actively guide the novice through selectively manifesting "for" the learner the relevant information to be acquired and generalized. Thus, we propose that the mechanism of natural pedagogy is ostensive communication, which incorporates evolved interpretive biases that allow and foster the transmission of generic and culturally shared knowledge to others (Csibra & Gergely, 2006, 2009). Such communication is not necessarily linguistic but always referential.

There is extensive evidence that infants and children are especially sensitive to being communicatively addressed by adults and that even newborns attend to and show preference for ostensive signals, such as eye contact, infant-directed speech, or infant-induced contingent reactivity (Csibra, 2010). Such ostensive cues generate referential expectations in infants triggering a tendency to gaze-follow the other's subsequent orientation responses (such as gaze-shifts) to their referential target (Csibra & Volein, 2008; Deligianni, Senju, Gergely, & Csibra, 2011; Senju & Csibra, 2008; Senju, Csibra, & Johnson, 2008), which may contribute to learning about referential signals such as deictic gestures and words. We now know that human infants are prepared to be at the receptive side of verbal as well as preverbal communication from the beginning of their lives.

The most unique proposal of the theory of natural pedagogy is the hypothesis that the information extracted from the other's ostensive-referential communication is encoded and represented qualitatively differently from the interpretation of the same behavior when it is observed being performed in a noncommunicative context. In particular, infants have been shown to expect that (1) kind-relevant features of ostensively referred objects (such as their shape or texture) are more important to encode than their other properties that are not informative about and do not generalize to object kinds (such as their location, Yoon, Johnson, & Csibra, 2008; or numerosity, Chen, Volein, Gergely, & Csibra, 2011), (2) ostensively demonstrated functional properties of novel objects specify the artifact kinds they belong to (resulting in kind-based object individuation; Futó, Téglás, Csibra, & Gergely, 2010), (3) object properties revealed in ostensive communicative demonstrations are relevant to judging object categories (Kovács, Teglas, Gergely, & Csibra, 2011), (4) a novel means action should be learned despite its apparent cognitive opacity as long as it has been communicatively demonstrated for them (Gergely, Bekkering, & Kiraly, 2002; Király, 2009; Király, Csibra, & Gergely, in press), and (5) ostensive attitude expressions communicate shared cultural knowledge about referents (Egyed Király, & Gergely, in press; Gergely, Egyed, & Kiraly, 2007). These effects suggest that infants assume that ostensive communication licenses certain inductive inferences that pure observation does not allow them to make, and this assumption enables fast learning of culturally shared knowledge about object and action kinds.

Next we briefly address some of the most frequently asked questions about natural pedagogy in order to resolve some typical misunderstandings about what is and what is not claimed by our theory.

Is natural pedagogy restricted to communication to children?

No. We believe that the interpretative biases that characterize natural pedagogy are essential constituents of human communication and are perhaps derivable from general relevance-seeking mechanisms (Sperber & Wilson, 1995). In fact, recent evidence indicates that an ostensive communication automatically generates the same kind of genericity bias of referential interpretation in adults that has been demonstrated in infants (Marno, Davelaar, & Csibra, 2009). Nevertheless, it should be clear that novices, and especially infants and children, are the natural targets of relevance-guided teaching through natural pedagogy as they are most in need of acquiring a large amount of generic and shared cultural knowledge in a variety of epistemic domains, while they possess the least amount of background knowledge that could help them infer such cultural information from pure observation alone. Thus, we expect that cultural learning in young children would rely and depend on ostensively communicated information and relevance guidance by knowledgeable and benevolent adults to a significantly larger degree than does cultural learning among adults. In contrast to infants and young children, adult cultural learners have access to a much larger variety of epistemic sources and can more competently employ inductive statistical learning and inferential reasoning processes that do not (and often need not) involve ostensive communication.

Does any kind of teaching count as an example of natural pedagogy?

No. We believe that natural pedagogy is a special kind of teaching that should be distinguished from many other behavioral skills that function to support and facilitate learning in naïve conspecifics, and, as such, can be also considered to fulfill the function of teaching (Caro & Hauser, 1992). Examples are conditioning, in which the teacher distributes rewards and punishments to the learner, or scaffolding (Wood, Bruner, & Ross, 1976), where the teacher modifies the learner's environment to promote individual learning (cf. opportunity teaching; Caro & Hauser, 1992). Several forms of teaching in this wider sense can be found both in human and in nonhuman species alike (Hoppit et al., 2008). However, we reserve the term "natural pedagogy" to refer to instances of ostensive communication that promotes the learning of generic knowledge by the addressee.

Does the theory of natural pedagogy claim that adult communication to children primarily serves teaching functions?

No. Communication to children, just like communication between adults, serves various kinds of functions, which include supporting coordination of joint action and cooperation to achieve shared goals (Tomasello, 2008) as well as transferring relevant episodic information about individuals (Dunbar, 1998). However, infants and children seem prepared and, indeed, biased to acquire generic and culturally shared knowledge from ostensive communications of adults whenever the content of their communication enables such learning to occur. This propensity can, in fact, give rise to the potential of pragmatic misinterpretation of infant-directed communication especially at the early stages of development. For example, when adults attempt to play an episodic hide-and-search game with 10-month-olds (as in the classical Piagetian AnotB object search task; Piaget, 1954), the young infants who do not yet understand the nature of the game may mistake the adult's ostensive communications during object hiding actions as teaching events, and thus fail to encode the episodic information about current object location, which would be relevant for finding the object hidden but irrelevant for learning anything generalizable about it. That such a pragmatic misinterpretation may, indeed, be induced by the adult's ostensive communication is suggested by our finding that when the object search task is presented without accompanying ostensive communicative gestures by the adult, young infants perform significantly better on the task, showing a robust reduction of their characteristic perseverative search errors (Topál Gergely, Miklósi, Erdőhegyi, & Csibra, 2008). Thus, children will have to learn the communicative and contextual cues that inform them about the episodic nature of instances of ostensive communication, making it possible to inhibit their default tendency to interpret the content to be generalizable beyond the "here and now."

Does the theory of natural pedagogy claim that children acquire most of their generic knowledge through communication?

No. Inductive learning can be based on different kinds of information. For example, inductive generalization can be licensed by strong preexisting biases built in by evolution as innate priors (such as fear of snakes), by experience as acquired priors, or by statistical information accumulated over a longer period. Children are likely to learn the majority of their knowledge via individual learning, observational social learning, or overhearing. However, learning from communication becomes important for transmitting generic knowledge that has no preexisting content bias, provides no frequent opportunities for statistical learning, and/or its relevant aspects are cognitively too opaque to be properly identified and extracted through pure observational learning. In such cases, communicative support and ostensive referential relevance guidance may be necessary to ensure fast and efficient cultural learning.

Can infants really comprehend the communicative intention in the ostensive acts addressed to them?

This, indeed, seems to be a necessary requirement for the system of natural pedagogy to work at early ages. When perceiving an ostensive cue, infants minimally have to be able to interpret it as indicating a second-order intention referring to the presence of further signals that carry some communicative (and potentially, but not necessarily, pedagogical) content (Csibra, 2010). Such comprehension of ostensive acts does not guarantee that the infant will also be able to recover the content of the informative intent (cf. Sperber & Wilson, 1995, 2002) from the available signals, but it ensures that she will expect to find such relevant content. The assumptions that, according to the theory of natural pedagogy, infants adopt in searching for the content of the communication act as constraints on the hypothesis space for the inferential process that interpret infant-directed communication.

Is natural pedagogy human specific?

It probably is. Animal communication is restricted to transmit only episodic information about particular referents, whose relevance is tied to the specific situational context of the "here and now." Nonhuman animals do not convey messages that are generalizable to different objects, locations, or situations. Although some species of nonhuman animals teach their young (in the wider sense of teaching, see Hoppit et al., 2008), they do not achieve this through transferring knowledge by communication (Csibra & Gergely, 2011). We believe that the reason for the absence of natural pedagogy in nonhuman animals is related to the fact that their behavioral repertoire, even when it incorporates local and socially transmitted traditions, does not include cognitively opaque elements that characterize many human instrumental actions and social conventions. Therefore, the social transmission of the relatively small repertoire of such cognitively transparent cultural skills is sufficiently served by noncommunicative observational learning mechanisms such as emulation (Tomasello, 1996).

Does dogs' sensitivity to human communication demonstrate an adaptation to natural pedagogy?

No. Dogs preferentially attend to human ostensive cues and learn to interpret referential signals, such as gaze, pointing, and words (Kaminski, 2009). They may expect to receive commands by human communication and by obeying them they can learn new routines. However, there is no evidence that they would generalize the content of single communicative acts as being relevant beyond the constraints of the "here and now" to other objects or situations as human infants appear to do. For example, while they tend to make similar mistakes in the AnotB object search task as the perseverative search errors that is so characteristic of 10-month-old infants (Topál et al., 2008), the learning that underlies their errors is revealed to be closely tied to the local stimulus situation and even to the specific person demonstrating the hiding acts (Topál, Gergely, Erdohegyi, Csibra, & Miklosi, 2009). This suggests that, although dogs have been adapted to interpret human communication signals, they expect that these signals express episodic imperatives for them to act in a certain way in the here and now rather than as conveying generalizable information about referents.

Is natural pedagogy universal across human cultures?

We believe it is. However, it should be noted that the theory we propose is about evolved cognitive mechanisms that enable the efficient transmission of certain types of cultural contents, rather than being about universal aspects of human behavioral forms across cultures that may, or may not, capitalize on these mechanisms. Nevertheless, we have found no convincing example of a human society in which verbal and nonverbal communication would be used exclusively to convey episodic content (Csibra & Gergely, 2011). Undoubtedly, there are enormous cultural differences in how societies organize child rearing and how they ensure that children acquire the knowledge and skills they need. Considering the variability of relevant cultural and environmental factors, most important the extent of cognitive opacity of local traditions

and artifact use, one should expect a variable amount of reliance on communicative knowledge transmission across different cultural communities. This cross-cultural variability, however, should not conceal the fact that even the minimal amount of natural pedagogy that a child in a traditional society receives is much more than any nonhuman primate infant is subjected to (Csibra & Gergely, 2011).

Do children teach or just learn from teaching?

This is an empirical question. We have seen no convincing data on young (less than 4-year-old) children attempting to teach their generic knowledge to others by means of communicative demonstrations. We would not find it surprising if the application of natural pedagogy would be characterized by an asymmetry of developmental progression. If the function of such communication is the transmission of cultural knowledge, only children who have already acquired some of this knowledge would be expected to act in the role of a teacher. It is possible, however, that one could trigger productive communication of acquired knowledge even in younger children in certain situations.

We have argued that during hominin evolution a specialized social cognitive system for "natural pedagogy" has been selected to enable the intergenerational transfer of uniquely human forms of cognitively opaque, generic, and shared cultural knowledge whose transmission would have posed a learnability problem for purely observational learning mechanisms. Natural pedagogy recruits ostensive communication to support inferential learning of such cultural contents from infant-directed manifestations provided by knowledgeable conspecifics. Ostensive signals induce built-in cognitive biases of referential interpretation (such as the genericity bias) that support the transfer of generic knowledge about object and action kinds from communicative demonstrations through particular referents even in preverbal infants.

ACKNOWLEDGMENTS

This work was supported by an Advanced Intestigator Grant (OSTREFCOM) from the European Research Council.

REFERENCES

Caro, T. M., & Hauser, M. D. (1992). Is there teaching in nonhuman animals? *Quarterly Review of Biology, 67,* 151–174.

Chen, M., Volein, Á., Gergely, G., & Csibra, G. (2011, April). Differential effects of communicative presentation on the encoding of visual features vs. numerosity of sets of objects in infants. Paper presented at the Biennial Meeting of the Society of Research in Child Development, Montreal, Canada.

Csibra, G. (2010). Recognizing communicative intentions in infancy. *Mind and Language, 25,* 141–168.

Csibra, G., & Gergely, G. (2006). Social learning and social cognition: The case for pedagogy. In Y. Munakata & M. H. Johnson (Eds.), *Processes of change in brain and cognitive development. Attention and performance XXI* (pp. 249–274). Oxford, England: Oxford University Press.

Csibra, G., & Gergely, G. (2009). Natural pedagogy. *Trends in Cognitive Sciences, 13,* 148–153.

Csibra, G., & Gergely, G. (2011). Natural pedagogy as evolutionary adaptation. *Philosophical Transactions of the Royal Society B, 366,* 1149–1157.

Csibra, G., & Volein, A. (2008). Infants can infer the presence of hidden objects from referential gaze information. *British Journal of Developmental Psychology, 26,* 1–11.

Deligianni, F., Senju, A., Gergely, G., & Csibra, G. (2011). Automated gaze-contingent objects elicit orientation following in 8-months-old infants. *Developmental Psychology, 47(6), 1499–1503.*

Dunbar, R. (1998). *Grooming, gossip, and the evolution of language.* Cambridge, MA: Harvard University Press.

Egyed, K., Király, I., & Gergely, G. (in press). Communicating shared knowledge in infancy. *Psychological Science.*

Futó, J., Téglás, E., Csibra, G., & Gergely, G. (2010). Communicative function demonstration induces kind-based artifact representation in preverbal infants. *Cognition, 117,* 1–8

Gergely, G. (2010). Kinds of agents: The origins of understanding instrumental and communicative agency. In U. Goshwami (Ed.), *Blackwell handbook of childhood cognitive development* (2nd ed., pp. 76–105). Oxford, England: Blackwell Publishers.

Gergely, G., Bekkering, H., & Kiraly, I. (2002). Rational imitation in preverbal infants. *Nature, 415,* 755.

Gergely, G., & Csibra, G. (2005). The social construction of the cultural mind: Imitative learning as a mechanism of human pedagogy. *Interaction Studies, 6,* 463–481.

Gergely, G., & Csibra, G. (2006). Sylvia's recipe: The role of imitation and pedagogy in the transmission of human culture. In N. J. Enfield & S. C. Levinson (Eds.), *Roots of human sociality: Culture,* *cognition, and human interaction* (pp. 229–255). Oxford, England: Berg.

Gergely, G., Egyed, K., & Kiraly, I. (2007). On pedagogy. *Developmental Science, 10,* 139–146.

Hoppit, W. J. E., Brown, G. R., Kendal, R., Rendell, L., Thornton, A., Webster, M. M., & Laland, K. N. (2008). Lessons from animal teaching. *Trends in Ecology and Evolution, 23,* 486–493.

Kaminski, J. (2009). Dogs (Canis familiaris) are adapted to receve human communication. In A. Berthoz & Y. Christen (Eds.), *Neurobiology of "umwelt": How living beings perceive the world* (pp. 103–107). Berlin: Springer.

Király, I. (2009). The effect of the model's presence and of negative evidence on infants' selective imitation. *Journal of Experimental Child Psychology, 102,* 14–25.

Király, I., Csibra, G., & Gergely, G. (in press). Beyond rational imitation: Learning arbitrary means actions from communicative demonstrations. *Journal of Experimental Child Psychology.*

Kovacs, A. M., Teglas, E., Gergely, G., & Csibra, G. (2011, April). Ostensive communication modulates how 12-month-olds categorize ambiguous objects. Paper presented at the Biennial Meeting of teh Society of Research in Child Development, Montreal, Canada.

Marno, H., Davelaar, E., & Csibra, G. (2009, August). The effect of communicative context on the perception and memory of objects. Poster presented at the European Society for Philosophy and Psychology Conference, Budapest, Hungary.

Piaget, J. (1954). *The construction of reality in the child.* New York: Basic Books.

Senju, A., & Csibra, G. (2008). Gaze following in human infants depends on communicative signals. *Current Biology, 18,* 668–671.

Senju, A., Csibra, G., & Johnson, M. H. (2008). Understanding the referential nature of looking: Infants' preference for object-directed gaze. *Cognition, 108,* 303–319

Sperber, D., & Wilson, D. (1995) *Relevance: Communication and cognition* (2nd ed.). Oxford, England: Blackwell.

Sperber, D., & Wilson, D. (2002). Pragmatics, modularity and mind-reading. *Mind and Language, 17,* 3–23.

Tomasello, M. (1996). Do apes ape? In C. M. Heyes & B. G. Galef (Eds.), *Social learning in animals: The roots of culture* (pp. 319–346). New York: Academic Press.

Tomasello, M. (1999). *The cultural origins of human cognition.* Cambridge, MA: Harvard University Press.

Tomasello, M. (2008). *Origins of human communication.* Cambridge, MA: MIT Press.

Topál, J., Gergely, G., Erdohegyi, A., Csibra, G., & Miklosi, A. (2009). Differential sensitivity to human communication in dogs, wolves and human infants. *Science, 325*, 1269–1272.

Topál, J., Gergely, G., Miklósi, Á., Erdőhegyi, Á., & Csibra, G. (2008). Infant perseverative errors are induced by pragmatic misinterpretation. *Science, 321*, 1831–1834.

Whiten A., Goodall J., McGrew, W. C., Nishida, T., Reynolds, V., Sugiyama. Y., . . . Boesch, C. (1999). Cultures in chimpanzees. *Nature, 399*, 682–685.

Wood, D., Bruner, J. S., & Ross, G. (1976). The role of tutoring in problem solving. *Journal of Child Psychology and Psychiatry, 17*, 89–100.

Yoon, J. M. D., Johnson, M. H., & Csibra, G. (2008). Communication-induced memory biases in preverbal infants. *Proceedings of the National Academy of Sciences USA, 105*, 13690–13695.

3.2

A Comparison of Neonatal Imitation Abilities in Human and Macaque Infants

ANNIKA PAUKNER, PIER F. FERRARI, AND STEPHEN J. SUOMI

Human infants are capable of imitating facial gestures such as mouth opening and tongue protrusion within the first days if not hours of life. What started as a hypothesis and was hotly debated for several years is now supported by numerous research reports, and the pertinent questions have moved from "Does it exist?" to "Why is it done?" "How is it done?" and "Why should we care?" (Meltzoff & Moore, 1999). The discovery that neonatal imitation can also be observed in chimpanzees (Bard, 2007) and rhesus macaques (Ferrari et al., 2006) has added critically important information to these questions, suggesting that neonatal imitation may have evolved in a common ancestor of humans, apes and Old World monkeys. In the following, we will briefly summarize what is known about neonatal imitation abilities in human infants and compare these findings with our recent discoveries of neonatal imitation in rhesus macaque infants. We propose that despite differences in physiology, behavioral ecology, and cognitive abilities, neonatal imitation may represent a basic behavioral adaptation and may serve to shape the fundamental stepping stones toward adult social cognition in both species.

NEONATAL IMITATION IN HUMANS

Face-to-face interactions between mothers and infants during the infants' first year are common in humans, and reports of mutual imitation were known anecdotally since early in the 20th century (e.g., Valentine, 1930), if not before. More rigorous experimental work in the 1970s and beyond confirmed that under controlled laboratory conditions, human infants are able to match a variety of gestures, including mouth opening, tongue protrusion, lip pursing, and finger movements (Meltzoff & Moore, 1977). This seminal work changed the prevailing view at the time, which purported that

infants are not able to imitate until 9–10 months old (Piaget, 1962) and turned the focus on newborn infants' ability to imitate. Subsequent studies discovered, for example, that infants can imitate facial gestures as early as 42 minutes after birth (Meltzoff & Moore, 1983) and thereafter for the first 2 months of life, after which imitation starts to wane and largely disappears by ca. 3 months old (Kugiumutzakis, 1999). In addition, newborns were found to initiate ("provoke") facial gestures even when the (previously gesturing) model was displaying a still face (Nagy & Molnar, 2004) and to remember gestures for delays of up to 24 hours at ca. 6 weeks old (Meltzoff & Moore, 1994). Since this latter achievement is thought to be based on recall memory and mental representation (Meltzoff & Moore, 1994), most subsequent work has focused on these extraordinary cognitive achievements under strictly controlled laboratory settings.

At the same time, infant intersubjectivity, the idea that human infants have an innate receptiveness to others and actively engage in social exchanges, was studied under less restrictive conditions using video recordings of mother–infant face-to-face games (Stern, 1985; Trevarthen & Aitken, 2001; Tronick, 1989). Instead of solely focusing on the infant, intersubjectivity research uses the mother–infant pair as the unit of analysis and emphasizes reciprocal regulation of feelings and interests using rhythmic patterns and multimodal signals during interactions. Neonatal imitation is recognized as an element of these affective communications, and it is thought to motivate companionship and cooperative awareness as well as an opportunity for infants to learn about social conventions of communication (Trevarthen & Aitken, 2001; Tronick, 1989). Unfortunately, few systematic studies have looked at mother–infant interactions during the neonatal period, and most data describe mother–infant interactions when infants are 12 weeks old or older. At this older age, mothers are more likely to imitate the infant than infants are to imitate the mother (Moran, Kripka, Tutton, & Symons, 1987), but the mother's imitative behavior appears to hold the infant's attention and may facilitate interactive regulation of affect (Reck et al., 2004). There is some indication that neonatal imitation may be related to the quality of these later interactions. Heimann (1989) found that infants who imitated facial gestures at 2–3 days and 3 weeks old were less likely to avert their gaze during playful interactions with their mothers at 3 months of age. Thus, neonatal imitation may predict later social responsiveness and play an important role in infants' social and emotional development.

NEONATAL IMITATION IN RHESUS MACAQUES

As others have done when studying human infants, we have investigated macaque neonatal imitation under two paradigms: naturalistic observations and controlled laboratory studies. We found that rhesus macaque mothers start engaging in mutual gaze with their infants even on the day of birth, sometimes gently pulling the infant's head to face them, and initiating mouth-to-eye and mouth-to-mouth contacts (Ferrari et al., 2009a). We also observed that macaque mothers directed lip-smacking (a communicative gesture conveying affiliation) at their infants, which happened as early as 3 days after birth. Mothers were prone to place themselves directly in front of the infant, lower their heads to the level of the infant's eyes, and engage in intense and exaggerated lip-smacking bouts accompanied by head bobbing (Ferrari et al., 2009a). These interactions were initiated almost exclusively by mothers rather than other adult females within the social group, and infants were likely to respond with lip-smacking gestures to these solicitations. Interestingly, mothers' lip-smacking bouts at infants remained high throughout the first 2 months of life, even after infants had mostly ceased to respond with lip-smacking gestures at ca. 1 month old. Although mothers appeared more active in initiating these lip-smacking exchanges, infants were not entirely passive in the process. In fact, while infants were most likely to respond with lip-smacking gestures at age 3–11 days old, they were most likely to initiate lip-smacking behaviors at 12–23 days old (Ferrari et al., 2009a).

Rhesus macaque infants also show imitation of facial gestures under controlled laboratory conditions. We tested several cohorts of infant macaques, who were being reared in a neonatal primate nursery for unrelated experimental studies. These infants typically had been separated from their mothers on the day they were born and were raised with visual, auditory, and variable physical contact with same-age peers in the laboratory's neonatal nursery. Even though their experiences with adult monkeys and observing facial gestures were severely limited, they nevertheless imitated lip-smacking gestures of human experimenters during the first week of life, with a peak in performance at 3 days old (Ferrari et al., 2006, 2009b). Interestingly, infants also matched tongue protrusion gestures of a human experimenter, a noncommunicative gesture that is not performed by macaque mothers (although their tongues may protrude slightly when performing lip-smacking, tongue protrusions in the absence of lip-smacking gestures are not part of macaques' communicative repertoire). Unlike human infants, however, they did not match a hand gesture. These results suggest that similar to human infants, infant macaques may be predisposed to match facial gestures of interaction partners at birth (see Fig. 3.2.1).

However, neonatal imitation in macaques is not an innate reflex-like fixed action pattern that can be triggered universally. We observed wide interindividual variation of neonatal imitation, with some infants consistently imitating facial gestures and others consistently failing to respond. Even in humans, only ca. 50% of infants respond with neonatal imitation under laboratory conditions (Heimann, Nelson, & Schaller, 1989). Interestingly, we also found that macaque infants who were able to match lip-smacking gestures of a human experimenter also initiated lip-smacking gestures after a 1-minute delay (Paukner, Ferrari, & Suomi, 2011). This finding supports the idea that infants are able to voluntarily control their own matched responses, and that neonatal imitation is part of an early communicative exchange.

Conceptually, in order to imitate, infants must be able to match the visual input from others' facial gestures with the proprioceptive and kinesthetic sensations of their own facial movements. Meltzoff and Moore (1999) proposed a cognitive model in which a common supramodel matches the perceived and performed gestures by means of goal-directed, active intermodal mapping (AIM). Similarly, Trevarthen (1998) suggested a common entity in the infant's nervous system that simultaneously processes sensory input and shapes motor output. Recent advances in neuroscience have been able to find neural correlates of these cognitive models in the form of mirror neurons, neurons in

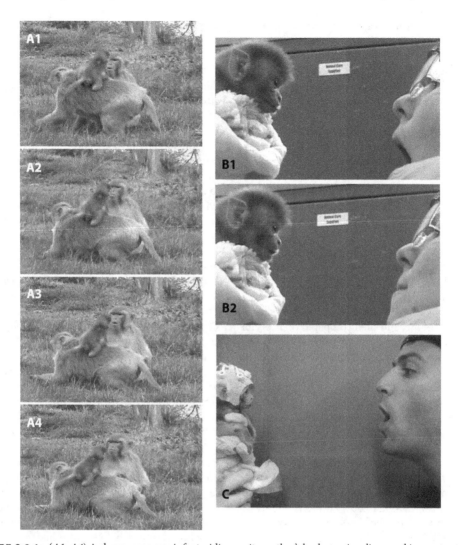

FIGURE 3.2.1: (*A1–A4*) A rhesus macaque infant, riding on its mother's back, receives lip-smacking gestures from another female. (Filmed at Poolesville, MD.) (*B1–B2*) A 3-day-old nursery-reared infant receives a lip-smacking gesture from a human experimenter (B1) and responds with lip-smacking (B2). (*C*) An infant watches lip-smacking gestures by a human experimenter during electroencephalographic recording.

the premotor cortex that fire both when a specific action is observed and when the same action is performed by an individual (Mukamel, Ekstrom, Kaplan, Iacoboni, & Fried, 2010; Rizzolatti, Fadiga, Gallese, & Fogassi, 1996). Several brain imaging studies in adult humans demonstrate an activation of the mirror neuron system both during the imitation of simple movements and facial gestures (Iacoboni et al., 1999) and during the imitation of novel action sequences that were not in the observer's motor repertoire (Buccino et al., 2004). By using electroencephalography (EEG) it has been shown that the observation and production

of action induces a suppression of alpha activity (8–13 Hz) recorded over the motor cortex (Pineda, 2005). This rhythm, known as the mu rhythm, is suggested to be a signature of the mirror neuron system, and it has also been found in children and infants within a 5 to 9 Hz frequency (Nyström, Ljunghammar, Rosander, & von Hofsten, 2011). While there is no evidence of a mirror neuron system being involved in neonatal imitation in human infants, we have recently been able to investigate this issue by means of EEG in infant rhesus macaques. We recorded brain activity during the observation and execution of facial gestures and found a significant desynchronization of the mu rhythm within the 5–6 Hz frequency band in the anterior electrodes approximately located above the motor cortex (Ferrari et al., 2012). Activation of these regions during action observation is consistent with those reported in the brain imaging literature (Iacoboni et al., 1999). These data are the first evidence that a mirror neuron system is operational at birth and that it might underpin neonatal imitative capacities.

If some rhesus macaque infants are able to imitate on the basis of a more responsive facial mirror neuron system, then other abilities that also rely on mirror neuron circuits may similarly differ between imitators and nonimitators. One such well-known mirror neuron circuit relates to intentional reaching and grasping actions. In another recent study, we classified macaque infants as either imitators or nonimitators based on the consistency of their imitative response during the first week of life, and then compared their performance on a standardized neurobehavioral assessment scale administered during the first month of life (Ferrari et al., 2009b). We found that there were no significant differences between imitators and nonimitators in body weight, visual attention, posture and general motor maturity, or emotionality. Two categories, however, indicated developmental divergence: Imitators scored significantly higher on a coordinated reach-and-grasp assessment, whereas nonimitators scored significantly higher on the expression of the palmar grasping reflex. Thus, there may be a connection between the ability to match facial gestures at birth and the ability to initiate intentional hand actions. In particular, areas of the brain that are known to contain mirror neurons are involved in the control of both intentional hand and mouth actions. Since sensory-motor coupling is necessary to control these intentional movements, it is likely that the cortical networks underpinning them are better developed in imitators than non-imitators. Together these results indicate that (1) imitators and nonimitators follow differential developmental pathways in a variety of domains, including social and motor development, and (2) imitation is not a reflexive-like phenomenon but rather an intentional form of exchange that might require complex cortical networks.

PROPOSED FUNCTIONS OF NEONATAL IMITATION IN HUMANS AND MACAQUES

Even though we have only just started to investigate neonatal imitation in rhesus macaques, we have already discovered surprising behavioral similarities between humans and macaques. For example, in both species the phenomenon is restricted to a few weeks after birth, and in both species the mother appears to initiate facial gestures more frequently than infants. We also see marked individual variation of imitation abilities in both species: Some human and macaque infants imitate; others do not. Finally, in both species we have indications that neonatal imitation may be predictive of later competencies. These commonalities appear to suggest a shared evolutionary root of neonatal imitation, indicating an important role of neonatal imitation in infant development, and leaving us to speculate about its possible functions.

In line with the two research areas of neonatal imitation outlined earlier, two conceivable functions of neonatal imitation have been proposed, which are not mutually exclusive (Heimann, 2002; Uzgiris, 1981). The cognitive explanation emphasizes that imitation serves to increase the infant's knowledge of the world. When presented with a new social situation, infants resolve the meaning of this situation through imitation, and feedback from the caregiver about their reproduced action ultimately leads to acquisition of new skills and knowledge (e.g., language skills, Legerstee, 1991; Nagy, 2006). The interpersonal explanation emphasizes the central role of infants' imitative behaviors in facilitating closeness to the mother, promoting intersubjective interactions and mutual regulations of affect (Trevarthen, 1998). The interconnection between the two proposed models is evident if one considers the role of communicative signals exchanged between mothers and infants during imitative interactions. Neonatal imitation might facilitate the appropriate use of existing communication signals, meaning that neonatal imitation may increase infants' ability to discern communicative and emotional signals from others (Heimann, 1989), and to respond with appropriate signals in various social situations. Correct use and understanding of communicative signals is central to the development of intersubjective exchange, which uses rhythmic patterns and multimodal signals to apprehend others' rudimentary intentions and emotions, which in turn leads to reciprocal regulation of affect. Studies in humans hint at this connection, e.g. mothers suffering from depression show less mimetic behaviors and positive affect, and infants of depressed mothers engage in more frequent self-comfort behavior in a presumed attempt to regulate themselves without the mother's interactive support (Reck et al., 2004). Thus, communicative signals, intersubjective exchanges, and emotional development are intricately linked and may form the basis of socio-cognitive functioning in later life.

What do studies of neonatal imitation in macaques contribute to this model? In terms of neural underpinnings, our recent EEG data show that the mirror neuron system may play a fundamental role in the development of these social skills, and they suggest that macaques and humans are likely to share basic elements that support early forms of social interactions. However, it has also been proposed that this system is shaped by social experience (Casile, Caggiano, & Ferrari, 2011), meaning that even though there is a common evolutionary root, this ability might have evolved further in humans to accommodate more complex, flexible, and lengthy exchanges between mother and infant. These include, for example, the extension of the facial motor repertoire and the inclusion of a vocalization-based form of communication. Although speculative, we propose that neonatal imitation may be a fundamental behavioral adaptation that serves to shape the basic building blocks of adult social cognition in both humans and macaques.

ACKNOWLEDGMENTS

This chapter is partly based on research supported by the Division of Intramural Research, NICHD.

REFERENCES

Bard, K. A. (2007). Neonatal imitation in chimpanzees (Pan troglodytes) tested with two paradigms. *Animal Cognition, 10*, 233–242.

Buccino, G., Vogt, S., Ritzl, A., Fink, G. R., Zilles, K., Freund, H. J., & Rizzolatti, G.. (2004). Neural circuits underlying imitation learning of hand actions: An event-related fMRI study. *Neuron, 42*, 323–334.

Casile, A., Caggiano, V., & Ferrari, P. F. (2011). The mirror neuron system: A fresh view. *Neuroscientist, 17*, 524–538.

Ferrari, P. F., Paukner, A., Ionica, C., & Suomi, S. J. (2009a). Reciprocal face-to-face communication between rhesus macaque mothers and their newborn infants. *Current Biology, 19*, 1768–1772.

Ferrari, P. F., Paukner, A., Ruggiero, A., Darcey, L., Unbehagen, S., & Suomi, S. J. (2009b). Interindividual differences in neonatal imitation and the development of action chains in rhesus macaques. *Child Development, 80*, 1057–1068.

Ferrari, P. F., Vanderwert, R., Paukner, A., Bower, S., Fox, N. J., & Suomi, S. J. (2012). Evidence for a mirror neuron system in newborn monkeys activates during the observation and imitation of facial gestures. *Journal of Cognitive Neuroscience, 24*, 1165–1172.

Ferrari, P. F., Visalberghi, E., Paukner, A., Fogassi, L., Ruggiero, A., & Suomi, S. J. (2006). Neonatal imitation in rhesus macaques. *PLoS Biology, 4*, e302.

Heimann, M. (1989). Neonatal imitation, gaze aversion, and mother-infant interaction. *Infant Behavior and Development, 12*, 495–505.

Heimann, M. (2002). Notes on individual differences and the assumed elusiveness of neonatal imitation. In A. N. Meltzoff & W. Prinz (Eds.), *The imitative mind: Development, evolution, and brain bases* (pp. 74–84). Cambridge, England: Cambridge University Press.

Heimann, M., Nelson, K. E., Schaller, J. (1989). Neonatal imitation of tongue protrusion and mouth opening: Methodological aspects and evidence of early individual differences. *Scandinavian Journal of Psychology, 30*, 90–101.

Iacoboni, M., Woods, R. P., Brass, M., Bekkering, H., Mazziotta, J. C., & Rizzolatti, G. (1999). Cortical mechanisms of human imitation. *Science, 286*, 2526–2528.

Kugiumutzakis, G. (1999). Genesis and development of early infant mimesis to facial and vocal models. In J. Nadel & G. Butterworth (Eds.), *Imitation in infancy* (pp. 36–59). Cambridge, England: Cambridge University Press.

Legerstee, M. (1991). The role of person and object in eliciting early imitation. *Journal of Experimental Child Psychology, 51*, 423–433.

Leslie, K. R., Johnson-Frey, S. H., & Grafton, S. T. (2004). Functional imaging of face and hand imitation: Towards a motor theory of empathy. *NeuroImage, 21*, 601–607.

Meltzoff, A. N., & Moore, M. K. (1977). Imitation of facial and manual gestures by human neonates. *Science, 178*, 75–78.

Meltzoff, A. N., & Moore, M. K. (1983). Newborn infants imitate adult facial gestures. *Child Development, 31*, 78–84.

Meltzoff, A. N., & Moore, K. M. (1994). Imitation, memory, and the representation of persons. *Infant Behavior and Development, 17*, 83–99.

Meltzoff, A. N., & Moore, M. K. (1999). Resolving the debate about early imitation. In A. Slater & D. Muir (Eds.), *The Blackwell reader in developmental psychology* (pp. 151–155). Oxford, England: Blackwell.

Moran, G., Kripka, A., Tutton, A., & Symons, D. (1987). Patterns of maternal and infant imitation during play. *Infant Behavior and Development, 10*, 477–491.

Mukamel, R., Ekstrom, A. D., Kaplan, I., Iacoboni, M., & Fried, I. (2010). Single-neuron responses in humans during execution and observation of actions. *Current Biology, 20*, 750–756.

Nagy, E. (2006). From imitation to conversation: The first dialogues with human neonates. *Infant and Child Development, 15*, 223–232.

Nagy, E., & Molnar, P. (2004). Homo imitans or homo provocans? Human imprinting model of neonatal imitation. *Infant Behavior and Development, 27*, 54–63.

Nyström, P., Ljunghammar, T., Rosander, K., & von Hofsten, C. (2011). Using mu-rhythm desynchronization to measure mirror neuron activity in infants. *Developmental Science, 14*, 327–335.

Paukner, A., Ferrari, P. F., & Suomi, S. J. (2011). Delayed imitation of lipsmacking by infant rhesus macaques (Macaca mulatta). *PLoS One, 6*, e28848.

Piaget, J. (1962). *Play, dreams, and imitation in childhood*. New York: Norton.

Pineda, J. A. (2005). The functional significance of mu rhythms: Translating "seeing" and "hearing" into "doing." *Brain Research Reviews, 50*, 57–68.

Reck, C., Hunt, A., Fuchs, T., Weiss, R., Noon, A., Moehler, E., Mundt, C. (2004). Interactive regulation of affect in postpartum mothers and their infants: An overview. *Psychopathology, 37*, 272–280.

Rizzolatti, G., Fadiga, L., Gallese, V., & Fogassi, L. (1996). Premotor cortex and the recognition of motor actions. *Cognitive Brain Research, 3*, 131–141.

Stern, D. N. (1985). *The interpersonal world of the infant: A view from psychoanalysis and developmental psychology*. New York: Basic Books.

Trevarthen, C. (1998). The concept and foundations of infant intersubjectivity. In S. Braten (Ed.), *Intersubjective communication and emotion in early ontogeny* (pp. 15–46). Cambridge, England: Cambridge University Press.

Trevarthen, C., & Aitken, K. J. (2001). Infant intersubjectivity: Research, theory, and clinical applications. *Journal of Child Psychology and Child Psychiatry, 42*, 3–48.

Tronick, E. Z. (1989). Emotions and emotional communication in infants. *American Psychologist, 44*, 112–126.

Uzgiris, I. C. (1981). Two functions of imitation during infancy. *International Journal of Behavioral Development, 4*, 1–12.

Valentine, C. W. (1930). The psychology of early imitation with special reference to early childhood. *British Journal of Psychology, 21*, 105–132.

3.3

Origins of Social Cognition

Bidirectional Self-Other Mapping and the "Like-Me" Hypothesis

ANDREW N. MELTZOFF

Human social cognition begins in the newborn period. When the human newborn opens its eyes and sees a human act for the first time, I have proposed that this engenders a feeling of interpersonal connectedness. To explain the idea, I offered the "Like-Me" developmental hypothesis. The key suggestion is that perceiving others as like me is a social primitive. The new empirical research shows that the core sense of similarity to others is not the culmination of social development, but the precondition for it. Without this initial felt connection to others, human social cognition would not take the distinctively human form that it does.

In the past, philosophers, social theorists, and psychologists have considered related ideas, but the foregoing departs from historical discussions in four ways. First, the relevant philosophers (e.g., Husserl, Merleau-Ponty, Ryle) did not imagine that this process begins at birth. These philosophers postulated that self-other mapping and first steps toward cracking the problem of Other Minds were late emerging and mediated by language and/or deliberate introspective reasoning.

Second, many sociologists and social psychologists working with adults gave priority to social learning from the outside in: An unformed self is given coherence by how others react to it (Cooley, Mead)—the "looking-glass self." Instead, as I will show, infants also use self-experience to give meaning to the observed behavior of others in ways these theorists missed.

Third, Piaget's work with infants led him to theorize that they start out as "solipsists" with no links between self and other. Piaget was unable to provide a satisfactory mechanism of change from initial solipsism to the rich social cognition of 5-year-olds, because he underestimated the initial state. Freud's and Baldwin's neonatal "adulism," merging, or lack of differentiation between self and other suffers from the same problem, and were precursors to Piaget's more sophisticated writing on the initial state.

Fourth, although contemporary work on social primitives has shown that infants have visual preferences for faces (Johnson and Morton), eyespots (Baron-Cohen), and self-mobile entities (Leslie), my proposal goes beyond cues that induce infant visual attention. Infants' supramodal representation of human action maps external events to the self. Crucially, this goes beyond heightened attention, preference, and visual expectations.

In this essay I will discuss empirical studies concerning two social learning mechanisms that build on the "like-me" primitive—imitation and gaze following. The studies illuminate three aspects of social cognition: (a) origins, (b) mechanisms of change, and (c) bidirectional learning between self and other. The studies support the view that "like me" is a social primitive that gives rise to a life-long ability to connect to other humans, which is vital to our survival as a species.

Humans have a long period of infantile immaturity compared to other animals. This immaturity has coevolved with powerful social learning mechanisms. Two of these social learning mechanisms—imitation and gaze following—are functional in human infancy, rare in the animal kingdom, and impoverished in autism. If one seeks to understand the birth, growth, and mechanisms of change in human social cognition, imitation and gaze following are promising domains to investigate.

Imitation supports rapid learning of behavioral skills, social customs, and causal relations by observation. Rather than relying purely on maturation (which is not responsive to cultural contingencies), independent invention (which is slow) or trial and error (which can be dangerous), humans excel in imitative learning from others in the environment. A key to human imitation is that it is not slavish or mindless duplication. Children and adults selectively regulate who, what, and when to imitate. Imitative learning is a chief avenue for social learning prior to language, but it also plays a role when adults are in novel social settings. Visiting a foreign country in which social greetings and eating implements differ from ours reminds us of the value of imitating experts rather than reliance on trial and error or invention.

Following the gaze of other people directs our attention to particular regions of space. Our attention is directed to locations, objects, and events that are particularly rich in information. These "information hot spots" do not stand out based on physical cues alone. They are not necessarily bigger, brighter, or more visually conspicuous. They gain psychological salience merely because a social other has looked at them. Perceptual alignment with others undergirds common ground for communication and supports pedagogy and collaborative learning.

IMITATION AS SOCIAL COGNITION

Bodily Imitation

In facial imitation, infants are duplicating a gesture they see with a gesture of their own that they cannot see themselves make. Developmentalists have known for more than 50 years that 1-year-olds imitate facial gestures, but it was a surprise to discover that newborns as young as 42 minutes old imitate such acts (Meltzoff & Moore, 1983).

Newborn facial imitation provides information about the initial state of social cognition. Newborns can see another person move but have never seen their own face. This apparent gulf between self and other is reminiscent of the Other Minds problem in philosophy (albeit at the level of actions and not intentional states). We know ourselves from the inside and others from the outside: How do we understand what it is like to be another person, to feel what the other person feels?

I have argued that imitation is based on active intermodal mapping, positing a primitive and foundational body scheme that allows infants to unify the seen acts of others and their own felt acts in a shared framework. Meltzoff and Moore (1997) postulated that human infants accomplish this via a "supramodal" representation of human acts. Links between perception and production do not have to be forged through associative learning but are available to the newborn. Imitation is a

congenital aspect of human social cognition, with much known at the behavioral-psychological level, and rapid progress being made illucidating infant neural mirroring mechanisms (e.g., Marshall & Meltzoff, 2011; Saby, Marshall, & Meltzoff, 2012).

Infants' self-experience may play a role in imitation. Even at birth infants have had experience with self-generated movements, which we call *body babbling* (Meltzoff & Moore, 1997). Films of prenatal behavior, for example, reveal that fetuses make repeated lip, tongue, and hand movements in utero. Body babbling provides infants with experience in how their own body moves. Body babbling is a mechanism for infants' learning about controlling their body, analogous to how vocal babbling provides experience in vocal maneuvers (Kuhl & Meltzoff, 1982). Tongues move differently from hinged joints such as fingers and elbows. Based on self-experience with the felt movements of one's own body, the kinetic signatures of a tongue protrusion/withdrawal (or mouth opening/closing, or finger flexing) could be recognized as crossmodally equivalent to those produced by others.

Personal Identity

Theories of developing social cognition must be concerned with personal identity. How does an infant distinguish one person from another and reidentify a person as the "same one" again despite changes in surface appearances? Infants' social worlds would be very different from ours if an interpersonal relationship were not maintained when the surface features of the other were altered. This is related to the topic of object individuation and numerical identity (Moore & Meltzoff, 2009; Spelke, Breinlinger, Macomber, & Jacobson, 1992; Xu & Carey, 1996), but considers the identity of people who disappear and reappear and change appearance.

We discovered that infant imitation contributes to infants' understanding of personal identity. Infants use both a person's spatial history (spatiotemporal parameters) and the prior experience of interacting with that person (functional parameters) to determine a person's identity. When infants are ambiguous about whether this is the same person they saw previously, infants show increased imitation of the person's past behavior, as if verifying "Are you the one who does x?" Body actions, mannerisms, and distinctive interactive games and routines played by particular people are akin to nonverbal shared memories that can be used as identity markers of people.

The value of using human acts as criteria for identity is that they allow infants to test as well as to observe. Instead of being limited to generalized reactions, such as smiling, cooing, and greeting of "humans in general," infants have a tool for intervening to actively probe whether they are re-encountering the same individual after a perceptual break or change in appearance. Social beliefs and attitudes are often about specific people, not categories. For infants who cannot yet use language to query a person, keeping track of individuals requires combining observation (spatiotemporal criteria) and action experience with that person (functional criteria) to make judgments about a person's identity.

The Imitation Game: Being Imitated Begets Social Bonding

One of the favorite activities of parents and children are reciprocal imitation games, and I argue that these games support social bonding and affiliation. Why are these mutual imitation games so alluring for infants? Temporal contingencies are part of the story, but it is often overlooked that people are special to infants because they can systematically match the form of their behavior in a generative fashion. This structural congruence is psychologically salient to infants (and adults).

In one study we gave infants a choice between two adults who were sitting side by side, one imitating what the infant did and the other acting contingently on the infant's actions but producing a mismatching action. The infants selectively looked longer and smiled more at the matching adult (Meltzoff, 1990). Infants' attention and positive emotions were directed at the one who acted "like me."

There are two key social-developmental sequelae. First, mutual imitation games deepen a sense of relationship. Mutual imitation indicates "communing" or "being with" someone else, even prior to the time that linguistic exchanges are possible. Adults develop positive feelings toward another person who is reflecting their behavior back to them, despite not being aware of the cause of these feelings in psychotherapeutic and everyday settings (Chartrand & Bargh, 1999; Ogden, 1982; van Baaren, Holland, Steenaert, & van Knippenberg, 2003). We see the seeds of this in the reciprocal imitation games in preverbal infants.

Second, caretakers' mirroring serves the functions as a physical mirror. Infants can use imitative interactions to learn what the self looks like. This provides a lever for developmental change, because early facial imitation is mediated by supramodal equivalence, and infants can accomplish it without modality-specific information

being preserved. Neonates can successfully imitate without yet knowing what their acts *look like* in a purely visual sense from the outside. Classical developmental and psychoanalytic theory (e.g., Lacan) implicated physical mirrors in the ontogenesis of a visual self, but this cannot be the only source. Mirrors are not culturally universal or historically ancient. Mutual imitation provides another mechanism. Through such social mirroring, infants gain a better sense of what their own felt acts look like.

Social neuroscience studies of mutual imitation in adults show that the right inferior parietal lobe is activated when people experience themselves being imitated (Decety, Chaminade, Grèzes, & Meltzoff, 2002). A speculation is that the right inferior parietal lobule is involved in differentiating self and other when they are both performing the same actions (a neural "who done it"). Related social neuroscience work is now emerging in infants (Saby, Marshall, & Meltzoff, 2012).

GAZE FOLLOWING

For adults, human attention implicates both external objects and the internal states of the viewer. When we see someone turn to look at an object, this is interpreted as more than a simple physical motion in space. It is recognized as an attempt to acquire information from afar despite the gap between the person and thing. Visual perception is a kind of psychological contact at a distance.

When do infants begin to ascribe visual perception to others' acts of looking, and how do they come to make this attribution? I believe that infants in part develop an understanding of the visual perception of others through their self-generated acts of turning in order to see and opening/shutting their eyes to cut off and reinstate visual experience. Self-experience changes their interpretation of the visual behaviors of others.

Self-Experience: Learning From the Inside Out

This idea that infants' own visual experiences contribute to their understanding of others' vision emerged from a puzzling finding. In a gaze-following study, an adult sat across from the infant and turned to face objects on a random schedule. Twelve-month-olds followed the adult significantly more when her eyes were open rather than closed (Brooks & Meltzoff, 2002). These infants seemed to understand that eye closure occludes vision, but this understanding was constrained—the same 12-month-olds turned when the adult wore a blindfold, which also occludes vision. Why?

Infants control their own vision by closing their eyes. We hypothesized that extensive self-experience turning off/on visual access through eye closing/opening provides a basis for understanding similar behaviors in others. This predicts that if infants are given experience that blindfolds block their view they should make new attributions to others, and they did. Meltzoff and Brooks (2008) gave 12-month-olds experience with blindfolds occluding their vision. After this experience, infants treated adults wearing blindfolds differently. Infants who received first-person experience with the blindfold treated the adult as though her view was blocked, suggesting that their first-person experiences changed their attributions to others. Self-experience provided a "like-me" framework for interpreting the other's experience.

We also discovered that self-experience can teach infants novel information that violates the notions of everyday visual opacity. It is well established that by 18 months infants know that opaque barriers such as walls, barriers, and blindfolds occlude the adult's line of regard. We provided 18-month-olds with biologically deviant self-experience. We designed a trick blindfold that looked opaque from the outside but was made of special material that could be seen through when held close to the eyes. Infants given an intense bout of this self-experience generalized from self to others and treated the blindfolded adult as if she too could see through it: They followed her gaze to distal objects (Meltzoff & Brooks, 2008). As infants gain first-person experience, they flexibly transform their understanding of others. Self-experience can induce a change in understanding the other.

Self-Experience Is Not the Sole Road to Social Cognition

Is self-experience the sole path for coming to understand the inner workings of other people? My research and theory, and those of others, strongly suggests not. Infants also come to understand others as bearers of psychological states by observing structured patterns of their behavior.

To test this, we modified the blindfold paradigm used with 18-month-olds. Infants were not given self-experience. They watched a blindfolded adult reach out and grab objects on the table in front of them. We thought that this "visually guided behavior" would be sufficient to support the inference that the adult is seeing. Infants in one control group saw the same adult wearing the

same blindfold and making fumbling reaches as if she could not see. Infants in another control saw the adult wearing the black cloth as a headband and successfully grabbing the objects.

Infants who saw the blindfolded adult make visually guided reaches were significantly more likely to follow the blindfolded adult's "line of regard" than the control infants. This suggests that infants draw inferences about whether the person can or cannot see based on observing a structured pattern of goal-directed behavior. The infants inferred sight because the blindfolded adult could systematically pick up distal objects in the gaze-following test. Thus, infants followed her gaze to the external object in the gaze-following test. This attribution to the adult is significant, because it contradicts the infants' own self-experience with opaque cloths. (For related work, see Williamson & Meltzoff, 2011.)

"SOCIAL ROBOTS"

Infants do not "gaze follow" in response to every movement in the visual field. If the wind blows the door opens, they are unlikely to follow where the doorknob is pointing. We investigated who or what infants would gaze follow. We showed 18-month-old infants a robot and experimentally varied how it interacted with others.

The effective manipulation was witnessing the robot having a social interaction: If the robot engaged in imitative exchanges with a person, the infants seemed to attribute sentience to the robot and to follow its gaze. When the robot simply moved its head (complete with eyespots) to the side, infants did not gaze follow. When the robot performed identical motions as in the social interaction group, but not as part of a reciprocal social exchange, gaze following did not occur (Meltzoff, Brooks, Shon, & Rao, 2010).

It is not solely the visual features or movements of an entity, but the *interactions* it engages in, that are cues of social cognition. Reciprocal imitation is interpreted as a marker of psychological agency. An entity that systematically imitates is one that perceives. Infants draw social-cognitive inferences from watching structured patterns of behavior—in this case social interaction—and do not require self-experience with the robot (in closely related studies such as Johnson, Slaughter, & Carey, 1998, there was contingent interaction between the infant and the nonhuman entity).

CONCLUSIONS

The primitive on which social cognition rests is the perceived "like me" equivalence between self and other. This provides infants, even newborns, with a feeling of kinship with fellow humans, and it supports bidirectional learning from and about people.

Going from the direction of inside out, infants' own self-experiences change their understanding of others. I have discussed instances of this projection from self to others. Infants who experience that a blindfold occludes their own vision make new attributions to others who wear it. Another example comes from infants' heightened attention and positive emotion at being imitated. Infants prefer those who act "like me" as manifest by prosocial acts such as smiling at the imitating adult. Later in development, children and adults exhibit positive attitudes toward those who share features of the self that go beyond action. "Like-me" preferences (initially based on shared actions) are building blocks for the in-group preferences that later develop based on gender and other characteristics (e.g., Cvencek, Greenwald, & Meltzoff, 2011; Dunham, Baron, & Carey, 2011). Adults prefer and feel empathy for those who are "like me" along abstract dimensions such as religion, nationality, and social class, but a sense of "us" versus "them" has its first instantiation in the felt kinship for those who *act* "like me."

Infants also acquire new information about themselves and the world simply by observing others—demonstrating outside-in learning. I discussed that observing a structured pattern of behavior supports infants' inferences about the psychology of others. At a more basic level, studies of infant imitation show that they do not require extensive prior experience with an action to imitate it. Infants readily imitate novel acts (Meltzoff, Kuhl, Movellan, & Sejnowski, 2009). They also learn novel causal relations based on observing the outcomes of others' goal-directed interventions (Meltzoff, Waismeyer, & Gopnik, 2012). The human capacity for the imitation of novel acts and observational causal learning are noteworthy—they free us from learning about people and things only via self-experience.

Developing social cognition, even in infancy, requires a bidirectional mapping between self and other, and children with autism have specific deficits in this bidirectional system. An initial "like-me" equivalence between self and other allows social cognition to get off the ground. Later bidirectional learning—from self to other and other to self—allows it to soar.

ACKNOWLEDGMENTS

Supported by the National Science Foundation (SMA-0835854), the National Institutes of Health (HD-22514), and the ONR (N00014-0910097). I thank P. Kuhl, R. Williamson, R. Brooks, D. Liu, and P. Marshall for helpful comments on an earlier draft, and K. Moore and A. Gopnik for useful discussions.

REFERENCES

Brooks, R., & Meltzoff, A. N. (2002). The importance of eyes: How infants interpret adult looking behavior. *Developmental Psychology, 38,* 958–966.

Chartrand, T. L., & Bargh, J. A. (1999). The chameleon effect: The perception-behavior link and social interaction. *Journal of Personality and Social Psychology, 76,* 893–910.

Cvencek, D., Greenwald, A. G., & Meltzoff, A. N. (2011). Measuring implicit attitudes of 4-year-olds: The Preschool Implicit Association Test. *Journal of Experimental Child Psychology, 109,* 187–200.

Decety, J., Chaminade, T., Grèzes, J., & Meltzoff, A. N. (2002). A PET exploration of the neural mechanisms involved in reciprocal imitation. *NeuroImage, 15,* 265–272.

Dunham, Y., Baron, A. S., & Carey, S. (2011). Consequences of 'minimal' group affiliations in children. *Child Development, 82,* 793–811.

Johnson, S. C., Slaughter, V., & Carey, S. (1998). Whose gaze will infants follow? The elicitation of gaze-following in 12-month-olds. *Developmental Science, 1,* 233–238.

Kuhl, P. K., & Meltzoff, A. N. (1982). The bimodal perception of speech in infancy. *Science, 218,* 1138–1141.

Marshall, P. J., & Meltzoff, A. N. (2011). Neural mirroring systems: Exploring the EEG mu rhythm in human infancy. *Developmental Cognitive Neuroscience, 1,* 110–123.

Meltzoff, A. N. (1990). Foundations for developing a concept of self: The role of imitation in relating self to other and the value of social mirroring, social modeling, and self-practice in infancy. In D. Cicchetti & M. Beeghly (Eds.), *The self in transition: Infancy to childhood* (pp. 139–164). Chicago, IL: University of Chicago Press.

Meltzoff, A. N., & Brooks, R. (2008). Self-experience as a mechanism for learning about others: A training study in social cognition. *Developmental Psychology, 44,* 1257–1265.

Meltzoff, A. N., Brooks, R., Shon, A. P, & Rao, R. P. N. (2010). "Social" robots are psychological agents for infants: A test of gaze following. *Neural Networks, 23,* 966–972.

Meltzoff, A. N., Kuhl, P. K., Movellan, J., & Sejnowski, T. J. (2009). Foundations for a new science of learning. *Science, 325,* 284–288.

Meltzoff, A. N., & Moore, M. K. (1983). Newborn infants imitate adult facial gestures. *Child Development, 54,* 702–709.

Meltzoff, A. N., & Moore, M. K. (1997). Explaining facial imitation: A theoretical model. *Early Development and Parenting, 6,* 179–192.

Meltzoff, A. N., Waismeyer, A., & Gopnik, A. (2012). Learning about causes from people: Observational causal learning in 24-month-old infants. *Developmental Psychology, 48,* 1215–1228.

Moore, M. K., & Meltzoff, A. N. (2009). Numerical identity and the development of object permanence. In S. Johnson (Ed.), *Neoconstructivism: The new science of cognitive development* (pp. 61–83). New York: Oxford University Press.

Ogden, T. H. (1982). *Projective identification and psychotherapeutic technique.* New York: Aronson.

Saby, J. N., Marshall, P. J., & Meltzoff, A. N. (2012). Neural correlates of being imitated: An EEG study in preverbal infants. *Social Neuroscience, 7,* 650–661.

Spelke, E. S., Breinlinger, K., Macomber, J., & Jacobson, K. (1992). Origins of knowledge. *Psychological Review, 99,* 605–632.

van Baaren, R. B., Holland, R. W., Steenaert, B., & van Knippenberg, A. (2003). Mimicry for money: Behavioral consequences of imitation. *Journal of Experimental Social Psychology, 39,* 393–398.

Williamson, R. A., & Meltzoff, A. N. (2011). Own and others' prior experiences influence children's imitation of causal acts. *Cognitive Development, 26,* 260–268.

Xu, F., & Carey, S. (1996). Infants' metaphysics: The case of numerical identity. *Cognitive Psychology, 30,* 111–153.

3.4

Overimitation and the Development of Causal Understanding

DEREK E. LYONS AND FRANK C. KEIL

Children are nature's master imitators, capable of extracting a wealth of knowledge from observing others. This precocity is usually coupled to an equally impressive degree of rational selectivity. Even prior to their second birthday, children will often ignore portions of observed action sequences that are not relevant to their goals (e.g., Meltzoff, 1995; Gergely, Bekkering, & Király, 2002; Schwier, Van Maanen, Carpenter, & Tomasello, 2006). However, this rational rule does have some puzzling exceptions.

Imagine a 4-year-old watching as an adult opens a novel but very simple clear plastic box to retrieve a toy. Some of the actions that the adult uses to reach the toy are necessary (for example, opening a door on the front of the object), while others are plainly irrelevant (e.g., removing a superfluous wooden rod attached to the top of the box). If the child later has an opportunity to retrieve the toy herself, how would we expect her to do it? In a notable comparative study, Horner and Whiten (2005) showed a version of this procedure to both preschool-aged children and chimpanzees. The chimpanzees were quite successful in avoiding the unnecessary actions modeled by the adult. The children, surprisingly, were not; they tended to copy everything the adult had done, including the actions with no causal bearing on the goal.

We refer to this phenomenon as *overimitation*: the tendency of young children to copy all of an adult model's actions, even components that are clearly irrelevant for the task at hand (Lyons, Young, & Keil, 2007). Once one is attuned to it, examples of overimitation can be found in literature dating back almost two decades (Nagell, Olguin, & Tomasello, 1993; see also Call, Carpenter, & Tomasello, 2005; Carpenter, Call, & Tomasello, 2002; Nielsen, 2006; Want & Harris, 2002; Whiten, Custance, Gomez, Teixidor, & Bard,

1996). What has always been unclear, however, is what overimitation means. What can account for situations in which children—usually so savvy in their imitative judgment—suddenly copy less rationally than chimpanzees?

PRIOR THEORIES OF OVERIMITATION

Prior theories have attempted to decipher overimitation by characterizing it as a deliberate response, one that children sometimes select in response to certain contextual or social cues. In Horner and Whiten's (2005) experiment, for example, children watched the adult demonstrate the same sequence of relevant and irrelevant actions three times in a row before being allowed to open the box themselves. Children may well have taken these repeated demonstrations as a strong implicit signal to open the box "like so," thus overimitating out of deference to perceived task demands. In a closely related vein, Kenward and colleagues (2011) have suggested that overimitation may reflect a kind of social norm learning. Observing the adult may cause children to "learn a prescriptive norm that the unnecessary action should be performed in the context of [the goal]," much as one might learn that it is proper (though not strictly necessary) to put the napkin in one's lap at the dinner table. Both of these views see overimitation as a voluntary response that children make when they believe that they are *supposed* to copy the adult precisely.

Alternatively, other theorists have argued that perhaps children overimitate because they *want* to. Noting the social importance of imitation in early childhood (cf. Uzgiris, 1981), Nielsen (2006) asserts that overimitation might simply reflect children's desire to "be like" the adult. Children may overimitate "to satisfy social motivations, to fulfill an interpersonal function of promoting shared experience with others" (Nielsen, 2006, p. 563). Taking a somewhat different tack, Whiten and colleagues (2009) have argued that children may overimitate because they have learned that (1) the cost of copying superfluous actions is generally low (i.e., there is plenty of time to fine-tune details later), and (2) deferring to adult expertise is usually a good bet.

THE AUTOMATIC CAUSAL ENCODING ALTERNATIVE

All of these theories are plausible, but as noted they share a common assumption: Each presumes that when children overimitate they understand that the irrelevant actions they copy are not actually necessary. Children are said to reproduce these actions not out of causal confusion, but rather because they assume that the actions are socially or normatively important. But is this always true? When we began our investigation of this topic in 2005 we wondered whether overimitation might have deeper roots. We were motivated by considering the causal learning challenges that our artifact-centric environment creates for young children.

Children grow up in a world dense with human-made objects. From tools to toys, these artifacts represent much of what makes our species unique; they also pose a significant developmental conundrum. How do children learn how the numerous artifacts in their environment "work"? That is, how do children learn enough about the causal structure of novel artifacts to interact with and use them effectively? A core difficulty is that the causal structure of human artifacts is often opaque to direct inspection: It cannot be determined simply by examining the physical object itself. This is readily apparent for modern devices such as televisions or cell phones, yet the problem extends much more broadly. As we and others have described (Csibra & Gergely, 2006; Gergely & Csibra, 2006; Lyons, 2008), this problem of *causal opacity* has arguably been with us since our ancestors' tool use first diverged from that of other primates.

Csibra and Gergely (2006; Gergely & Csibra, 2006) conceptualize the divergence of human tool use in terms of two primary innovations: (1) the ability to stably conceptualize tools qua tools—as objects that enable particular goals, even when those goals are not immediately present (inverse teleology), and (2) the ability to use tools as means for creating other tools (recursive teleology). Inverse and recursive teleology are significant because *they allow tool-mediated actions to be spatially and temporally separated from the goals*

they ultimately serve. Whereas chimpanzees create and use tools only in the presence of immediately perceptible goals (and discard them once the goal is fulfilled), human tool use can be directed at much more diverse and distal ends. This diversity has many advantages, but note how it complicates the task of observational learning. Because tool-mediated actions can be removed from their ultimate goals or embedded within chains of tool use, it is very difficult for an observer to draw firm conclusions about which features of a tool or which aspects of its employment are the important ones to attend to (see Lyons, 2008 for elaboration). This difficulty has nothing to do with the physical complexity of the tool itself; it is a property that arises from the mind of the tool's user. The consequence is that children, unlike other primates, cannot generally rely upon physical and environmental cues to disambiguate tools' causal structure; another form of support is needed.

Might overimitation reflect a unique human adaptation for coping with the problem of causal opacity? We hypothesized that when young children see an adult intentionally manipulating a novel object, they may automatically encode all of the adult's purposeful actions as causally necessary. They may, in effect, treat the adult's intentional actions as a guide to the novel object's causal structure, revising their beliefs about the object accordingly. This *automatic causal encoding* (ACE) process would often provide a reliable means of understanding even highly opaque artifacts. However, if a child were to see an adult purposefully performing *unnecessary* actions on a novel object, those irrelevant actions would be automatically encoded as causally meaningful. The resulting distortions in the child's causal beliefs about the object could then result in overimitation.

The ACE hypothesis represents a much different approach to overimitation than the prior theories we have described. Rather than casting overimitation as something that children *want* to do (for social reasons), or believe that they are *supposed* to do (due to task demands), ACE asserts that overimitation may be something that children sometimes *have* to do. Children may be locked into overimitation by a normally adaptive learning process that can be misdirected by observing purposeful but unnecessary actions.

PUTTING ACE TO THE TEST

The ACE hypothesis makes a crisp central prediction: If children are overimitating because of observationally induced distortions in their causal beliefs, then it should be very difficult to extinguish the effect. Children should continue to overimitate even when circumstances clearly disfavor the copying of unnecessary actions. To test this prediction, we designed a series of experiments in which preschool-aged participants watched an adult retrieve toys from inside simple but novel "puzzle objects." The adult's retrieval method was always markedly inefficient, incorporating obviously irrelevant actions alongside those that were actually necessary (note that because the puzzle objects were constructed mainly with transparent materials like Plexiglas, the causal significance for each action was always plainly visible). After watching the adult's actions, children were given the opportunity to open the puzzle objects themselves. Based on Horner and Whiten's results (2005), this procedure was expected to elicit high levels of overimitation. Critically though, we also manipulated implicit and explicit task demands to strongly *disfavor* the copying of irrelevant actions. Would overimitation persist despite this contrary pressure as our hypothesis predicted? Or would the effect disappear in a manner more consistent with prior voluntary accounts?

Overimitation and Contrary Task Demands

In our first experiment (Lyons et al., 2007, Exp. 1A) we used an extensive pretraining phase to discourage overimitation. Before observing the adult acting on the puzzle objects, each participant watched the experimenter use relevant and irrelevant actions to retrieve toys from a series of familiar household containers (clear plastic jars, zipper pouches, etc.). After each training object, children were asked to identify which things the experimenter "had to do" and which were "silly" and unnecessary; correctly identifying the experimenter's unnecessary actions was greeted with effusive praise and reinforcement. Immediately after this training, children moved into the test phase of the experiment, where they saw—to a first approximation—almost exactly the same thing. That is, they saw the same experimenter again using both relevant and irrelevant actions to retrieve toys, but this time from inside *novel* puzzle objects. We found that though the training phase made it clear that (1) performing irrelevant actions was undesirable, and (2) the experimenter was an especially unreliable model, children still showed a remarkably strong and consistent tendency to overimitate.

These results could not be explained by positing that the puzzle objects were too complex for children to understand; an age-matched baseline

group of participants almost never manipulated the irrelevant mechanisms when opening the objects independently (i.e., without first observing an adult). Nor was overimitation limited to children who found the training exercise difficult. In fact, there was no relationship between children's scores during training and their tendency to overimitate. Rather, the simple observation of the adult acting on the novel object caused even those children who had previously shown no difficulty with the relevant/irrelevant distinction to suddenly start reproducing obviously unnecessary actions.

Very similar results were obtained in follow-up studies (Lyons et al., 2007, Exps. 1B and 2A), where we steadily increased the strength and explicitness of the demands opposing overimitation. In one such study children were led to believe that the experiment had ended. The experimenter then "remembered" that another participant was scheduled to arrive at any moment and asked the child to help him prepare by verifying that an assistant had put toys back into the puzzle objects. Even in this putatively time-sensitive task, children continued to overimitate when opening the puzzle objects at the same rate observed in the original study. A third experiment demonstrated that even explicitly *telling* children not to overimitate was insufficient to dislodge the effect.

More recently, our work has documented that children will persist in overimitation even when doing so imposes a motivationally salient cost. For example, children in one study observed an adult opening one of a novel puzzle object's two identical ends using relevant and irrelevant actions. These children were then challenged to "race" with an orangutan puppet named Felix to see who could open an end of the object most quickly in order to claim a single toy turtle placed inside (Lyons, Damrosch, Lin, Macris, & Keil, 2011, Exp. 1). An opaque divider prevented children from watching Felix during the race itself, so participants had to rely on their own understanding of the object (gleaned from observing the adult) in order to open it as quickly as possible. Overimitation in this setting was clearly quite costly: Opening the box while performing the irrelevant actions required an average of 8 seconds, while only 2 seconds were needed if the irrelevant actions were skipped. Accordingly, participants who overimitated found that they always lost the race to Felix. Children were given up to three consecutive races to omit the irrelevant actions and thus beat Felix to the prize. We reasoned that if children had any doubt about the causal necessity of the irrelevant actions, this highly motivating setting would surely cause overimitation to crack. Surprisingly though, the majority of the 4- and 5-year-olds we tested remained "stuck" in overimitation even after three rounds of competition.

A second competitive study used a more real-world scenario to replicate and expand on these findings (Lyons et al., 2011, Exp. 2). Participants were again led to believe that the formal experiment had ended, and they watched as the experimenter used relevant and irrelevant actions to retrieve a prize for them from a novel prize container. The container's irrelevant mechanism had a bell attached, which jingled loudly when the unnecessary action was performed. Before the child could take the prize home, Felix returned to the room (ostensibly awakened by the bell) and unexpectedly stole the prize for himself. After Felix absconded with their reward, children were given the option of trying to retrieve a replacement from the prize container—now admonished to open the container as quietly as possible to avoid alerting Felix. Children took this competitive scenario quite seriously and made visible efforts to be "stealthy" (for example, muffling the noisy bell with their hands). Strikingly though, fully 70% of children continued to overimitate rather than simply avoiding the noisy irrelevant mechanism altogether.

Taken as a whole, this body of work constitutes a strong case for the ACE hypothesis. Children will continue to overimitate even when reproducing irrelevant actions is a costly and ill-advised strategy. Indeed, children overimitate as though they truly believe that they have no other choice.

THE LIMITS OF OVERIMITATION

Though the evidence presented thus far all favors the ACE proposal, the very consistency of the data actually poses an interesting paradoxical challenge. How do we reconcile the persistence of overimitation in these experiments with the fact that children's causal knowledge *usually* seems much more reliable? That is, if observing an adult acting on a novel object causes children to uncritically encode purposeful actions as causally necessary, why do we not see more overimitation errors outside of the psychology lab? For our theory to be tenable it must be the case that ACE is subject to constraints: boundary conditions that confine it to situations where it is likely to enhance children's causal understanding rather than undermining it.

What kind of constraints might we look for? In one of our original experiments (Lyons et al., 2007, Exp. 2B) we found that overimitation does

respect at least some fundamental physical constraints, as children will not overimitate irrelevant actions that appear to violate the contact principle (the rule that mechanical interactions cannot occur at a distance; Spelke, 1994). A more fundamental species of constraint, however, pertains to intentionality. Note that intentionality plays a critical role in the logic of the ACE hypothesis. That is, while encoding an adult's *intentional* actions as causally meaningful will often reveal something useful about a novel object, processing *unintentional* actions in the same way would clearly be a very poor strategy. Thus, a strong prediction of the ACE theory is that intentionality should regulate overimitation with a near binary precision.

In fact, one of our most recent studies (Lyons et al., 2011, Exp. 3) has demonstrated that this is exactly what occurs. As before, children in this experiment watched as an adult performed relevant and irrelevant actions while opening a novel puzzle object. The irrelevant actions in this case involved waving a small wand back and forth in space above the object, eventually knocking into and dislodging a wooden dowel mounted on top of it. Half of the children saw these irrelevant actions presented as though they were intentional. The other half, however, saw the very same actions presented in a context that suggested they were *unintentional*. In the unintentional case the experimenter received a call on his mobile phone in the middle of operating the puzzle object. Explaining that he had to take the call (it was his Mom phoning, after all), the experimenter engaged in a short conversation in which the waving actions were contextualized as gesturing. When the wand knocked into and dislodged the wooden dowel, therefore, it appeared to be an unintentional by-product of the conversation rather than a deliberate action. A control condition demonstrated that children had equally accurate memories for the experimenter's actions in both the intentional and unintentional cases. However, whereas 69% of children overimitated the intentional waving actions, only 7% reproduced them when they appeared unintentional. This striking difference clearly demonstrates the kind of strong "on/off" regulation that our theory predicts intentionality should provide. Though children will readily overimitate irrelevant actions that are deliberate, they will seamlessly ignore the very same actions when they appear unintentional.

CONCLUSION

As adults we often use social information to guide our causal learning, looking to the ways that others manipulate novel artifacts in order to infer causally important operations. Here we have argued that children engage in a very similar process, but that they do so in a way that is often surprisingly automatic. When children observe an adult performing intentional actions on a novel object, they have a strong tendency to encode those actions as causally meaningful—even when there is clear visible evidence to the contrary. This *automatic causal encoding* process gives children a powerful boost in understanding our species' artifact-rich cultural environment, but it can also lead to vivid errors. In particular, in the rare case of an adult intentionally performing *unnecessary* actions, children are extremely susceptible to encoding those actions as causally meaningful. We argue that the resulting distortions in children's causal beliefs are the true cause of overimitation. Though overimitation often appears illogical in the laboratory, in more naturalistic settings it would actually represent a profound learning advantage. Automatic causal encoding affords us a uniquely powerful mechanism for understanding and propagating our knowledge of artifacts, and it may be an important stepping stone in the development of more nuanced causal understanding.

REFERENCES

Call, J., Carpenter, M., & Tomasello, M. (2005). Copying results and copying actions in the process of social learning: chimpanzees (*Pan troglodytes*) and human children (*Homo sapiens*). *Animal Cognition, 8,* 151–163.

Carpenter, M., Call, J., & Tomasello, M. (2002). Understanding "prior intentions" enables two-year-olds to imitatively learn a complex task. *Child Development, 73,* 1431–1441.

Csibra, G., & Gergely, G. (2006). Social learning and social cognition: The case for pedagogy. In Y. Munakata & M. H. Johnson (Eds.), *Processes of change in brain and cognitive development. Attention and performance, XXI* (pp. 249–274). Oxford, England: Oxford University Press.

Gergely, G., Bekkering, H., & Király, I. (2002). Rational imitation in preverbal infants. *Nature, 415,* 755.

Gergely, G., & Csibra, G. (2006). Sylvia's recipe: The role of imitation and pedagogy in the transmission of cultural knowledge. In N. J. Enfield & S. C. Levenson (Eds.), *Roots of human sociality: Culture, cognition, and human interaction* (pp. 229–255). Oxford, England: Berg.

Horner, V., & Whiten, A. (2005). Causal knowledge and imitation/emulation switching in chimpanzees (*Pan troglodytes*) and children (*Homo sapiens*). *Animal Cognition, 8,* 164–181.

Kenward, B., Karlsson, M., & Persson, J. (2011). Over-imitation is better explained by norm learning than by distorted causal learning. *Philosophical Transactions of the Royal Society B, 278*(1709), 1239–1246.

Lyons, D. E. (2008). The rational continuum of human imitation. In J. A. Pineda (Ed.), *Mirror neuron systems* (pp. 77–103). New York: Humana Press.

Lyons, D. E., Damrosch, D., Lin, J. K., Macris, D. M., & Keil, F. C. (2011). The scope and limits of overimitation in the transmission of artifact culture. *Philosophical Transactions of the Royal Society B, 366*(1567), 1158–1167.

Lyons, D. E., Young, A. G., & Keil, F. C. (2007). The hidden structure of overimitation. *Proceedings of the National Academy of Sciences USA, 104*(50), 19751–19756.

Meltzoff, A. N. (1995). Understanding the intentions of others: Re-enactment of intended acts by 18-month-old children. *Developmental Psychology, 31*(5), 838–850.

Nagell, K., Olguin, K., & Tomasello, M. (1993). Processes of social learning in the tool use of chimpanzees (*Pan troglodytes*) and human children (*Homo sapiens*). *Journal of Comparative Psychology, 107,* 174–186.

Nielsen, M. (2006). Copying actions and copying outcomes: Social learning through the second year. *Developmental Psychology, 42,* 555–565.

Schwier, C., Van Maanen, C., Carpenter, M., & Tomasello, M. (2006). Rational imitation in 12-month-old infants. *Infancy, 10,* 303–311.

Spelke, E. (1994). Initial knowledge: Six suggestions. *Cognition, 50,* 431–445.

Uzgris, I. C. (1981). Two functions of imitation during infancy. *International Journal of Behavioral Development, 4.* 1–12.

Want, S. C., & Harris, P. L. (2002). How do children ape? Applying concepts from the study of non-human primates to the developmental study of "imitation" in children. *Developmental Science, 5,* 1–41.

Whiten, A., Custance, D. M., Gomez, J-C., Teixidor, P., & Bard, K. A. (1996). Imitative learning of artificial fruit processing in children (*Homo sapiens*) and chimpanzees (*Pan troglodytes*). *Journal of Comparative Psychology, 110,* 3–14.

Whiten, A., McGuigan, N., Marshall-Pescini, S., & Hopper, L. M. (2009). Emulation, imitation, over-imitation, and the scope of culture for child and chimpanzee. *Philosophical Transactions of the Royal Society B, 364,* 2417–2428.

3.5

Social Cognition

Making Us Smart, or Sometimes Making Us Dumb?
Overimitation, Conformity, Nonconformity, and
the Transmission of Culture in Ape and Child

ANDREW WHITEN

Human social cognition is uniquely sophisticated. This is amply illustrated in the social cognition that allows us to acquire and build our distinctively cumulative human cultures (Whiten, Hinde, Stringer, & Laland, 2011), the subject of this chapter. It is this cultural sophistication that has allowed our species to thrive and multiply in all manner of habitats around the globe, while our closest living relatives, chimpanzees, remain restricted to small islands of their preferred habitats in Africa. Not only are we smart in special ways that create and transmit our profoundly cultural nature, but we can also say that "culture makes us smart"—in the sense that the cumulative culture we each inherit allows us to achieve things vastly beyond the capabilities of any other species, as well as far beyond the repertoire of a human being lacking this cultural inheritance.

There is, however, another side to this coin, highlighted in my title: that the social cognition that underwrites culture, particularly the drive to copy the ways of others, can sometimes be so potent that instead of making us smart, it can appear to make us dumb. Such effects generally go by the name of conformity, which in the broadest sense can be defined as blindly copying others. This is not to say that all conformity is dumb: To the contrary, I will suggest that conformity is a vital and, in general, highly adaptive component of our deeply cultural nature. Perhaps, then, we can single out the more "dumb" consequences by referring to "overconformity," where an act is copied in the face of nontrivial evidence (such as from one's own experience) that it is maladaptive. Such personal evidence is overridden by the potency of certain processes of conformist social cognition. This appears to present us with an intriguing

paradox in our cultural makeup: What determines whether the outcomes of our cultural social cognition make us smart or instead sometimes lead us astray? In developmental psychology, this paradox has surfaced through surprising discoveries about an allied effect that has been dubbed "overimitation," which I visit in more detail later. I begin, however, with a broader evolutionary perspective on these phenomena, as analyzed in recent studies of nonhuman species.

THE EVOLUTION OF SOCIAL COGNITION: HAS CONFORMITY EVOLVED AMONG NONHUMAN ANIMALS?

One might expect conformity—particularly overconformity—to be a feature of only strongly cultural species—perhaps only one as deeply cultural as our own. The first sign that this might not be the case arose in our own studies as an unanticipated outcome of a social learning experiment. To test the capacity of chimpanzees to sustain cultural variations of the kinds we have described in the wild, we "seeded" two alternative tool-use techniques in two separate groups by training just one individual in each group how to use a stick-tool to extract food items from an artificial foraging device (Whiten, Horner, & de Waal, 2005). One individual learned a "poke" technique and the other, a quite different "lift" method. The study demonstrated that each of the seeded techniques spread, creating a lift tradition in one group and a poke tradition in the other. However, a few chimpanzees in each group discovered the technique customary in the other group, and some adopted it as their preferred approach. The unanticipated conformity effect came 2 months later when the two groups were retested. Now, there was a statistically significant tendency for individuals to "return to the fold," in that they were increasingly likely to use the technique most common in their group, an effect we interpreted as conformity and highlighted in the paper's title. More recently, we recorded an allied phenomenon among capuchin monkeys, with individuals in one group discovering the method customary for opening an "artificial fruit" in a second group, yet nevertheless persisting in maintaining their dominant group tradition (Dindo, de Waal, & Whiten, 2009).

Such effects illustrate one common sense of "conformity," which hinges on a tendency to adopt the response that is the most common in one's community. This is the sense made famous in the early human experiments of Solomon Asch and a host of social psychologists who followed in his footsteps. However, a different, but related sense of conformity sees it as a tendency to copy others (even just one individual), overriding countervailing personal evidence that would counsel against such copying. Interestingly, this was demonstrated in experiments performed by Galef and Whiskin (2008) with rats, in the wake of the primate studies outlined earlier. These experiments showed that rats that had learned through personal experience that certain foods were unpalatable or even toxic were prepared to reverse their choices to match those of other rats who ate these foods. In one experiment this effect occurred when just a single other rat made this choice, demonstrating an extraordinarily potent social effect. The bias in social cognition that counts as conformity may thus be much more widespread in the animal kingdom than hitherto expected (for example, shaping food choice in rats and extending to tool-use techniques in apes). Further evidence this may be the case is provided by a recent paper showing conformity in fish (sticklebacks: Pike & Laland, 2010), in respect of preferred foraging sites. However, the study of conformity in animals remains in its infancy, and the scope of such effects is still to be mapped out in any detail (Claidière & Whiten, 2012).

One curious additional, and I suggest related, effect was found in the course of an experiment that showed most chimpanzees in the study learning, by observation, how to join two sticks to make a longer tool and gain out-of-reach food (Price, Lambeth, Schapiro, & Whiten, 2009). However, a few chimps managed this by their own individual learning. The surprise came in tests with the food put closer, so that joining the sticks was unnecessary: In these conditions the individual learners stopped joining the sticks, but the social learners persisted, even though it was clearly awkward to use the resulting long tool. We accordingly described this as "a potent effect of social learning" and see it as allied to the conformity phenomena described earlier. Moreover, in this case we appear to see an effect of the kind hinted at the outset of this essay, where conformity led these chimps to relatively "dumb" approaches. This leads us directly into our next topic, overimitation.

THE DEVELOPMENT OF OVERIMITATION IN CHILDHOOD AND BEYOND

This story starts for our research group in a study that set out to test the prevailing view in the research literature that, while children are clearly great imitators, chimpanzees and other apes opt instead for "emulation," in which the focus is on the results of another's actions rather than on replicating the actions themselves. In one condition of the experiment, preschool children or young chimpanzees witnessed a familiar person use a stick tool to remove a bolt on top of an opaque box, revealing a hole into which they repeatedly rammed the stick, before shifting to a second door on the front of the box and inserting the tool to extract a desirable reward. In a second condition, other participants saw the same box except it was transparent, so they could see that the tool inserted in the top hole merely struck a partition and was an unnecessary element in gaining the reward. The young chimpanzees confirmed our prediction that they would tend to switch between a more emulative approach with the transparent box, omitting the irrelevant act and focusing on the final result, and a more complete imitative response with the opaque box, including doing the ramming actions in the top. But it was the child participants who surprised us, because they persisted in copying the whole routine even in the transparent box condition (Horner & Whiten, 2005).

Lyons et al. (2007; and see Chapter 3.4) replicated these results with young children and christened the effect "overimitation," an apt term insofar as the child is imitating more than is warranted by what she is witnessing, to her detriment (i.e., the child is wasting time and effort on the causally unnecessary action). This seems to be a case where conformity of this kind leads a young child to a surprisingly "dumb" response.

Lyons et al. considerably extended the scope of the phenomenon of interest, not only replicating the effect in other, analogous tasks, but more important, setting out to reduce the effect and discovering it to be much more robust than one would have imagined. Efforts to train children not to copy the irrelevant elements, and even urging them not to, were of no avail. Moreover, asking the child to check whether the reward were in place ready for the next participant while the experimenter busied himself with other tasks also failed to remove the overimitation effect, even though now the child was trying to act quickly and appeared free of any obvious social pressure to conform. Lyons et al. concluded that overimitation is an "automatic" process in these young children. We shall return to why this might be so later in the chapter.

Watching the videos of children in these various studies, one cannot help but be struck by their persistence in the face of stark evidence before them that what they are copying can have no causal relationship to the desired outcome. An obvious next question thus becomes, "When does children's cognitive development allow them to grow out of this nonselectivity?" The original Horner and Whiten study was of 3-year-olds, so McGuigan et al. (2007) replicated the study with 5-year-olds to explore this question. To our surprise, the effect was stronger. Moreover, consistent with this, we later found a weaker effect in children aged 2 to 2.5 years old (McGuigan & Whiten, 2009). Rather than growing out of the effect, it appears that over this age range children become increasingly prone to overimitate.

This is surprising for an additional reason, which is that there is considerable evidence that in some contexts young children do show selective imitation and this can be sophisticated (reviewed in Whiten, McGuigan, Marshall-Pescini, & Hopper, 2009). A particularly nice example is the demonstration by Gergely et al. (2002) that although preverbal infants would readily copy a bizarre act such as using one's head to switch on a light, they were much less likely to do so if the person's arms were wrapped in a blanket, such that their options were constrained to head use. The authors called this "rational imitation" and we can appreciate that term in two senses—the infant itself seems rational, in attributing a certain rationality to the model in what actions he chooses to make given contextual constraints, such as the blanket in the Gergely et al. experiment.

We thus appear to be faced with an almost perverse developmental trajectory, in which preverbal infants can show considerable imitative selectivity, while in later childhood there is a progressively stronger tendency toward unselective overimitation. However, that trend is supported and even extended by yet more recent studies. For example, Nielsen and Tomaselli (2010) showed not only that overimitation occurred in the very different cultural context of Kalahari Bushman children (thus concluding, perhaps a little prematurely given this one study, that "overimitation may be a universal human trait": p. 729), but that it occurred more strongly in a group as old as 6–13 years than in those aged 2–5 years.

We took this one step further by directly testing adults (mean age 42 years), as well as more 3- and 5-year-olds, using the same paradigm as in our earlier studies (McGuigan, Makinson, & Whiten, 2011). Again, to our surprise, adults not only did not show an amelioration of the effect but were significantly more overimitative than the children. In this experiment we also compared the effect of an adult versus a child model (the latter aged 5 years old), and for each of the three age groups, the adult model elicited more overimitation. Thus, although the basic overimitation effect appears remarkably nonselective, even into adulthood, it is coupled with significant selectivity in model choice. We suggested that despite the apparent "dumbness" of the basic effect, the coupling of this with other forms of selectivity, in this case concerning what we interpret as "confidence in the model" (see Harris and Corriveau, 2011, for more on this phenomenon), provides our species with a powerful cultural learning system, which I discuss further in the next section.

CONFORMITY IN THE CULTURAL GROUP CONTEXT

Although overimitation counts as conformity in the sense of social information being prioritized over personal information, it is conformity in the sense of copying the majority of one's social group that has been the dominant one in studies in social and comparative psychology. This phenomenon, however, appears only recently to have begun to be investigated in developmental studies (Corriveau & Harris, 2010).

We have started to address this in social "diffusion experiments" of the kind outlined earlier for nonhuman primates. In one of these we directly replicated the chimpanzee study described earlier, in which two different tool-use techniques to extract an otherwise unobtainable reward were seeded in separate groups, and the consequences tracked in detail (Flynn & Whiten, 2012; Whiten & Flynn, 2010). Given this was happening in preschool playgroups incorporating as many as 30 children, these consequences proved to be complex and here I merely pick out results bearing most directly on the question of conformity.

We found that most children could be classified as conformists insofar as they copied the technique they had seen most; but a significant minority, around 15%, were nonconformists against this criterion and adopted the technique they saw less of, to achieve their first successful extraction of a reward. These latter children, however, were still adopting a technique they had observed others use, and altogether we found 85% of children could be classed as "followers" in that they used one of the methods they had watched other children apply. Half of the remaining children modified a technique they had observed, to produced a recognizably different variant; the other half—thus only around one child in twelve—more radically generated a technique they had not seen and this minority of children could thus be seen as the real innovators. Together these analyses portray a children's "microculture" in which the great bulk of children are followers and conformists, complemented by a much smaller subset of nonconformists and innovators. Whether these classifications represent stable "personality types" remains an interesting subject for future research. In any case, I suggest it is a plausible hypothesis that these proportions represent adaptive strategies; for example, given a small number of innovators riskily exploring new ideas, it may pay for the majority to simply copy innovators' successful discoveries.

However, there is a more refined notion of conformity to address, which has been the subject of influential theoretical approaches to cultural transmission (see Richerson & Boyd, 2005 for an accessible overview). In this, conformists will perform a common behavioral variant they witness with a discriminably higher probability than its relative frequency in the community, a potentially potent cultural effect. Whiten and Flynn (see also Claidière & Whiten, 2012) distinguished this as "hyperconformity" and investigated whether preschool children's copying proclivities are consistent with such an effect. In fact, the data did not support this. In this study, children were predominantly conformist in the sense defined earlier, but not "hyperconformist."

WHAT DOES IT ALL MEAN?

The suite of findings briefly summarized here presents us with several intriguing puzzles and paradoxes. Why overimitate, why conform just to be like others, when this involves an apparently dumb repression of personal information suggesting that the action taken is far from a good one? The core of an answer offered by Whiten, Horner, and Marshall-Pescini (2005; see also Whiten et al., 2009)) is that overall, trustingly copying others is an adaptively functional disposition, even though occasionally it may lead one astray—an explanation somewhat parallel to those offered in social psychology for stereotypes (not always reliable but on balance providing an economic rule of thumb).

Lyons et al. (2007) offered an intriguing and more specific twist on this hypothesis, noting that a young child's world is full of objects whose inner workings are initially quite opaque; thus, it may be adaptive for children to "implicitly treat an adult's actions as highly reliable indicators of the object's 'inner workings' or causal structure, revising their causal beliefs about the object accordingly" (p. 19751). Nielsen and Tomaselli (2010) challenged this idea because in one of their experiments, children were allowed to discover the causal structure of the test object already before watching an adult model, yet they still went on to overimitate the unnecessary actions that the adult used. This does seem to conflict with the hypothesis of Lyons et al. as they expressed it, but could it be that instead, this experiment simply underlines the potency of overimitation in making a learner "revise their causal beliefs"? Whiten et al. (2009; see accompanying electronic supplementary information) and Kenward et al. (2010) debate these questions further.

Another paradox appears to lie in the contrasting findings in the literature of overimitation on the one hand, and of sophisticated, selective imitation on the other. One possible, if somewhat counterintuitive, explanation is that the selectivity that has largely been described in infants is superseded during development by a disposition to trustingly copy others, which is largely based on experience that this is a good rule of thumb. An alternative explanation is that the documented selectively typically concerns social causality (as in Gergely, Bekkering, & Kiraly, 2002, summarized earlier), as opposed to the physical causality at the core of demonstrations of overimitation, implying that social cognition enjoys a privileged trajectory in the course of development. This is perhaps an apt thought on which to end this contribution to a volume on the development of social cognition.

REFERENCES

Corriveau, K. H., & Harris, P. L. (2010). Prescoolers (sometimes) defer to the majority in making simple perceptual judgments. *Developmental Psychology, 46,* 437–445.

Claidière, N., & Whiten, A. (2012). Integrating the study of conformity and culture in humans and non-human animals. *Psychological Bulletin, 138*, 126–145.

Dindo, M., de Waal, F. B. M., & Whiten, A. (2009). In-group conformity sustains different foraging traditions in capuchin monkeys (*Cebus apella*). *PLoS One, 4*, e7858.

Flynn, E. G., & Whiten, A. (2012). Experimental "microcultures" in young children: Identifying biographic, cognitive and social predictors of information transmission. *Child Development, 83*, 911–925.

Galef, B. G., & Whiskin, E. E. (2008). "Conformity" in Norway rats? *Animal Behaviour, 75*, 2035–2039.

Gergely, G., Bekkering, H., & Kiraly, I. (2002). Rational imitation in pre-verbal infants. *Nature, 415*, 755.

Harris, P. L., & Corriveau, K. H. (2011). Young children's selective trust in informants. *Philosophical Transactions of the Royal Society B, 366*, 1179–1187.

Horner, V., & Whiten, A. (2005). Causal knowledge and imitation/emulation switching in chimpanzees (*Pan troglodytes*) and children (*Homo sapiens*). *Animal Cognition, 8*, 164–181.

Kenward, B., Karlsson, M., & Persson, J. (2010). Over-imitaiton is better explained by norm learning than by distorted causal learning. *Proceedings of the Royal Society B, 276*, 3377–3383.

Lyons, D., Young, A. G., & Keil, F. C. (2007). The hidden structure of overimitation. *Proceedings of the National Academy of Sciences USA, 104*, 19751–19756.

McGuigan, N., Makinson, J., & Whiten, A. (2011). From over-imitation to super-copying: Adults imitate causally irrelevant aspects of tool use with higher fidelity than young children. *British Journal of Psychology, 102*, 1–18.

McGuigan, N., & Whiten, A. (2009). Emulation and "over-emulation" in the social learning of causally opaque versus causally transparent tool use by 23-and 30-month-old children. *Journal of Experimental Child Psychology, 104*, 367–381.

McGuigan, N., Whiten, A., Flynn, E., & Horner, V. (2007). Imitation of causally-opaque versus causally-transparent tool use by 3- and 5-year-old children. *Cognitive Development, 22*, 353–364.

Nielsen, M., & Tomaselli, K. (2010). Overimitation in Kalahari Bushman children and the orgins of human cultural cognition. *Psychological Science, 21*, 729–736.

Pike, T. W., & Laland, K. N. (2010). Conformist learning in nine-spined sticklebacks' foraging decisions. *Biology Letters, 6*, 466–468.

Price, E. E., Lambeth, S. P., Schapiro, S. J., & Whiten, A. (2009). A potent effect of observational learning on chimpanzee tool construction. *Proceedings of the Royal Society B, 276*, 3377–3383.

Richerson, P. J., & Boyd, R. (2005). *Not by genes alone: How culture transformed human evolution.* Chicago, IL: Chicago University Press.

Whiten, A., & Flynn, E. G. (2010). The transmission and evolution of experimental "microcultures" in groups of young children. *Developmental Psychology, 46*, 1694–1709.

Whiten, A., Hinde, R. A., Stringer, C. B., & Laland, K. N. (2011). Culture evolves. *Philosophical Transactions of the Royal Society B, 366*, 938–948.

Whiten, A., Horner, V., & de Waal, F. B. M. (2005). Conformity to cultural norms of tool use in chimpanzees. *Nature, 437*, 737–740.

Whiten, A., Horner, V., & Marshall-Pescini, S. (2005). Selective imitation in child and chimpanzee: a window on the construal of others' actions. In S. Hurley & N. Chater (Eds.), *Perspectives on imitation: From mirror neurons to memes* (pp. 263–283). Cambridge, MA: MIT Press.

Whiten, A., McGuigan, N., Marshall-Pescini, S., & Hopper, L. M. (2009). Emulation, imitation, over-imitation and the scope of culture for child and chimpanzee. *Philosophical Transactions of the Royal Society B, 364*, 2417–2428.

3.6

Early Social Deprivation and the Neurobiology of Interpreting Facial Expressions

NIM TOTTENHAM

Successful social interaction depends upon on our ability to accurately process expressions from the faces of others, and persons with lower face processing skills have reported lowered social competence than those with higher skill (Nowicki & Mitchell, 1998). By adulthood, our ability to recognize social signals from the faces of others is a well-developed skill. Numerous studies have demonstrated that this skill results from a developmental process, and the current chapter presents an argument that this process relies on an early species-expected learning environment interacting with neurobiology involving the amygdala. It has been suggested that facial expressions are learned via principles of classical conditioning (Davis & Whalen, 2001; Tottenham, Hare, & Casey, 2009), and therefore, our understanding of the meaning of facial expressions in adulthood relies on associations that are formed throughout development. In this chapter, we consider the nature of these associations in the context of both species-expected and species-unexpected early social environments (e.g., caregiver deprivation). We argue that early social deprivation results in deviant facial expression processing because of two primary factors: deprived experience with human faces and atypical development of the neurobiology underlying facial expression processing, with particular emphasis on the amygdala. Children reared in deprived social environments are subject to both of these factors and should exhibit face expression processing behaviors that emerge in predictable, albeit atypical, ways.

The ability to understand facial expressions develops in a robust manner in most individuals, and this development most likely results from an expected early social environment including a parent who provides not only important caregiving functions but also informative facial expressions. The development of face expression processing undergoes a protracted time course that begins with perceptual discrimination in infancy (e.g. Amso, Fitzgerald, Davidow, Gilhooly, & Tottenham, 2010) and extends at least until adolescence to include interpretation of those expressions (e.g., Gao, Maurer, & Nishimura. 2010; Herba, Landau, Russell, Ecker, & Phillips, 2006). This extended time course allows for ample opportunities to learn from a highly regular social environment. This association between typical experience with faces and expression processing ability is supported by the primacy with which happy faces are correctly identified during development and the high frequency with which happy faces are typically perceived (Somerville & Whalen, 2006).

FACIAL EXPRESSION PROCESSING FOLLOWING EARLY DEPRIVATION

Highly deviant social environments have been shown to alter perceptual biases for emotional faces. For example, exposure to physically abusive caregivers results in expertise for threatening faces, such as angry faces (Pollak & Sinha, 2002). This behavioral effect is accompanied by differential brain electrical activity as measured by the P3b component in the event-related potential (ERP) measured at the scalp, suggesting an enhanced attentional bias when abused children view angry faces (Pollak, Klorman, Thatcher, & Cicchetti, 2001). This expertise seems rooted in their lowered threshold for identifying a face as angry. It has been argued that the high frequency with which physically abused children are exposed to hostility engenders expertise for angry faces (Pollak & Sinha, 2002). Whereas typical rearing results in expertise for happy faces (Gao & Maurer, 2010), abusive parenting increases expertise for angry faces. Parental neglect represents another deviation from typical early environments, and children who experience neglect exhibit extremely poor face expression processing skills in that they do not show expertise for any expressions, presumably because of the profound face deprivation they experience. Thus, for three different populations of children—typical, physically abused, and neglected—face expression processing skills mirror the experiences that children have with face stimuli.

Children raised in institutional care experience extreme neglect, including social, maternal, physical, and sensory (Gunnar, Bruce, & Grotevant, 2000). If face expression perception relies on species-typical experiences, then we should expect that children reared in institutional care, where the caregiver to child ratio is devastatingly low, will exhibit significant difficulties. However, as will be discussed, these impairments seem to be associated, not with an inability to discriminate facial expressions from each other, but rather with a difficulty assigning appropriate emotional meaning to expressions. Based on visual discrimination tests (visual paired comparisons task), looking performance did not differ between infants (13–30 months old) raised in an institutional setting and typically raised controls (Nelson, Parker, & Guthrie, 2006). That is, infants were able to demonstrate visual discriminations for emotions, including happy, sad, fear, and neutral. It is unlikely that group differences in discrimination are "masked" in infancy and emerge at a later age, since when this sample was assessed at a later age (42 months old), the same result was obtained (Jeon, Moulson, Fox, Zeanah, & Nelson, 2010).

While previously institutionalized children do not show evidence of poor discrimination, there is an emerging body of evidence showing atypical interpretation of facial expressions. For example, 4-year-olds who had spent the first 2 years of life in institutional care were significantly impaired in choosing appropriate emotional expressions for puppets in several emotional conditions (Vorria et al., 2006). Similarly, 4-year-olds demonstrated worse performance compared to typically raised children when asked to choose an appropriate facial expression to match emotional vignettes; these deficits could have been caused by difficulties understanding vignettes, but subjects also showed difficulty providing appropriate verbal labels for visually presented expressions (Camras, Perlman, Wismer Fries, & Pollak, 2004; Wismer Fries & Pollak, 2004). It was suggested that these behavioral differences reflected a delay, rather than a deviation, in the development of facial expression processing since the previously

institutionalized children had performed in a way characteristic of younger children (Wismer Fries & Pollak, 2004), that is, with highest accuracy for happy expressions and lowest for negatively valenced expressions. While as a group previously institutionalized children showed poor performance, accuracy was lower for children who had spent the longest periods in institutional care and improved the longer children lived with their postadoption families, providing a hint that the development of typical facial expression processing is contingent on amount of exposure to typical social environments. It may also be the case that this dose–response relationship reflects a sensitive period for facial expression learning, as has been the case for face identity processing (LeGrand, Mondloch, Maurer, & Brent, 2001). In a separate sample of previously institutionalized children, difficulty interpreting facial expressions continued to be observed into early adolescence. These group differences have been shown to persist in that 11-year-old, previously institutionalized children also showed lower expression recognition scores relative to same-aged peers (Colvert et al., 2008). When the children in all of these studies are adopted, they begin a life of relative enrichment, in which, by the time of testing, they have spent the majority of their lives. Therefore, the effects of early social deprivation on face expression processing seem long-lasting and resistant to recovery (at least without clinical intervention).

In addition to greater difficulty interpreting facial expressions, children with a history of early institutional care show evidence of a behavioral sensitivity to negatively valenced stimuli. During an emotional go/no-go task, where individuals are instructed to press a button in response to rapid presentations of certain expressions (e.g., neutral) and withhold pressing for other expressions (e.g., fear), group differences emerge in behavioral performance between children with a history of infant institutional care and a comparison group. The accuracy of previously institutionalized children was significantly impaired for negative facial expressions relative to the comparison group, and it was no different from the comparison group of children for positive expressions, such as happy (Tottenham et al., 2010). Additionally, there were effects of duration of institutionalization such that the older children were when they were adopted out of institutional care, the greater number of false alarm errors they made toward negatively (not positively) valenced stimuli. These results suggest that regulatory errors were more likely when children were presented with negatively valenced faces. There was also evidence of a negativity bias in that as a group, previously institutionalized children slowed down reaction times when responding to neutral faces, a behavioral hallmark characteristic of threatening faces (Hare, Tottenham, Davidson, Glover, & Casey, 2005). This interpretation is based on inference and thus should be taken with caution, but it might suggest that previously institutionalized children have a tendency to assign negative valence to facial expressions, even when such emotion is absent from the expression. All of the behavioral data taken together are consistent with the hypothesis that a history of early social deprivation is followed by poor facial expression processing ability (in terms of appropriate interpretation of emotional meaning) combined with greater reactivity to negatively valenced expressions. That previously institutionalized children continue to exhibit difficulties with the emotional meaning of faces years after removal from deprived environments suggests that early deprivation exerts a significant influence on the neurobiology that supports interpretation of facial expressions.

THE HUMAN AMYGDALA AND FACIAL EXPRESSIONS

The amygdala is one of the key neural structures that support learning about the emotional value of perceived stimuli. Much animal work has established the amygdala's role in emotional learning—in particular, fear learning (see Davis & Whalen, 2001 for review). The amygdala acts to determine the species-specific relevance of various stimuli, including faces. In humans, the amygdala responds best for faces that represent danger to the animal. The typical adult amygdala responds robustly to faces expressing highly arousing emotions, like fear, relative to faces with neutral expressions (Davis & Whalen, 2001), and this activity seems to reflect the fact that facial expressions are conditioned stimuli that hold informational value to the perceiver. An increase in amygdala activity while learning about the affective value of faces (Petrovic, Kalisch, Pessiglione, Singer, & Dolan, 2008) and facial expressions (Kim et al., 2004) provides support for the notion that our understanding and interpretations of facial expressions rely on amygdala-based emotional learning.

DEVELOPMENT OF AMYGDALA RESPONSE TO FACIAL EXPRESSIONS

Amygdala response to emotional facial expressions undergoes dramatic change during childhood and adolescence. Activity in response to facial expressions increases during the transition from childhood to adolescence, reaching an activity peak during adolescence (Guyer et al., 2008; Hare et al., 2008). Not only is there a change in overall response to facial expressions across development, but the typical child amygdala reacts to facial expressions in sometimes contrasting ways from the adult amygdala. Whereas with the adult, fearful faces result in greater amygdala activity than neutral, children's amygdala response to neutral faces exceeds the response to fear faces (Lobaugh, Gibson, & Taylor, 2006; Thomas et al., 2001; Tottenham et al., 2010). This pattern of responding may reflect learned associations with facial expressions that children have (which may differ from adults), the greater associative ambiguity (Whalen, 1998) of neutral faces for children, or relative immaturity of the amygdala response in general.

AMYGDALA DEVELOPMENT FOLLOWING EARLY-LIFE ADVERSITY

In contrast to the amygdala response of typically reared children, previously institutionalized children show an elevated amygdala response to fearful faces above neutral (Tottenham et al., 2011), much like the adult pattern. This result may be an indication that the amygdala, due to early-life adversity, has become prematurely activated by emotional stimuli (discussed in Tottenham, 2012). Numerous nonhuman animal studies have shown that early-life adversity prematurely activates and develops (e.g., myelination) the typically dormant juvenile amygdala via circulating stress hormones (e.g., glucocorticoids) that can pass the blood–brain barrier and bind to receptors within the amygdala (Moriceau, Roth, Okotoghaide, & Sullivan, 2004; Ono et al., 2008). That is, exposure to an atypically adverse postnatal environment promotes developmentally early engagement of the amygdala. As will be discussed, there is emerging structural and functional neuroimaging evidence to support the hypothesis that early-life adversity in humans is similarly followed by early and amplified amygdala development. Face expression processing in previously institutionalized children, therefore, likely occurs against the backdrop of early social deprivation and elevated amygdala activity.

The amygdala is a neural region involved in stress-regulatory processes that help the individual learn about the relative safety or danger in the environment. It is rich with stress hormone receptors (e.g., glucocorticoid and CRH receptors) particularly early in life (Avishai-Eliner, Yi, & Baram, 1996), and thus it is a neural target for early-life adversity. Effects of early adversity have been quantified in two separate samples of children using volumetric magnetic resonance imaging (MRI) techniques. Institutional care that occurred in the early postnatal period was associated with enlarged amygdala volumes relative to total brain size (Mehta et al., 2009; Tottenham et al., 2010), and the degree of enlargement was associated with behavioral indices of anxiety and internalizing difficulties (Tottenham et al., 2010). This pattern of amygdala development may amplify response to stimuli with negative value, and it may in part explain heightened behavioral reactivity to negative expressions observed in previously institutionalized children. Indeed, within this sample, there was a trend for a negative association between amygdala enlargement and accuracy for negative expressions during the emotional go/no-go task.

In addition to amygdala structural growth, a history of early social deprivation increases the risk of atypical amygdala activity. Functional neuroimaging has shown that children with a history of early institutional care exhibit significantly greater amygdala response to fearful faces relative to children who had experienced typical early care (that is, within a family) (Tottenham et al., 2011). However, this group difference was specific to fear (and not neutral expressions), suggesting a degree of specificity in amygdala response to negatively valenced expressions. Moreover, regions of the cortex (e.g., inferior frontal and fusiform gyrus) that receive input from the amygdala tend to exhibit relatively little activity in previously institutionalized children in response to face presentations, possibly suggesting certain downstream effects of atypical amygdala development. In support of this assertion are the findings of reduced white matter integrity between the amygdala and cortex (Govindan, Behen, Helder, Makki, & Chugani, 2010). Low cortical recruitment for faces has been shown using ERP in infants and preschoolers living in Romanian orphanages who exhibit decreased cortical electrical activity in response to facial expressions (Moulson, Fox, Zeanah, & Nelson, 2009; Parker & Nelson 2005) (e.g., smaller N170, midlatency negative central component, and positive slow wave component, P400). Importantly, these studies with Romanian infants were able to address issues of causality; random assignment into more typical caregiving environments (i.e., professional foster care) attenuated group differences in the ERP signal, providing more conclusive evidence that early caregiver deprivation disrupted neural development associated with facial expression processing.

Amygdala hyperactivation to facial emotion has been associated with the social behavior of previously institutionalized children. Those children who exhibited the greatest amygdala signal change to fearful faces were more likely to be rated by parents as having the lowest social competence (Tottenham et al., 2011). Additionally, measures of eye contact were taken using two different procedures—a high-precision eye-tracking procedure and an ecologically valid dyadic social interaction. As a group, the previously institutionalized children displayed decreased eye contact during both of these procedures. Moreover, there was a negative association between amygdala reactivity and eye contact. Several studies have suggested that avoiding eye contact is a means of decreasing some of the overarousal associated with face-to-face contact (Pilkonis, 1977; van Reekum et al., 2007), even though this strategy can interfere with successful interpersonal communication. Children who utilize this strategy may experience additional face deprivation in that they miss future opportunities to learn about facial expressions and their appropriate meaning.

In summary, the behavioral evidence suggests that children with an early history of social deprivation (that is, in the form of institutional care) are at risk for difficulties in facial expression processing. The difficulty seems to lie, not in an inability to discriminate based on perceptual features alone, but in a heightened reactivity to negative expressions and in a difficulty assigning appropriate meaning to expressions. The limited, but growing, data suggest that this behavioral profile results from heightened, and possibly premature, amygdala reactivity to arousing stimuli and from limited exposure to facial stimuli early in life. Appropriate assignment of emotional meaning to facial expression, particularly negative expressions which are slowest to be learned under all developmental circumstances, seems to rely heavily on exposure to those expressions and their emotional contexts. Difficulty interpreting faces may place children with histories of social deprivation at risk for future interpersonal challenges, including attachment relationships with parents and intimate relationships with peers.

REFERENCES

Amso, D., Fitzgerald, M., Davidow, J., Gilhooly, T., & Tottenham, N. (2010). Visual exploration strategies and the development of infants' facial emotion discrimination. *Frontiers in Developmental Psychology, 1*(180), 1–7.

Avishai-Eliner, S., Yi, S. J., & Baram, T. Z. (1996). Developmental profile of messenger RNA for the corticotropin-releasing hormone receptor in the rat limbic system. *Developmental Brain Research, 91*(2), 159–163.

Camras, L. A., Perlman, S. B., Wismer Fries, A. B., & Pollak, S. D. (2004). Post-institutionalized Chinese and Eastern European children: Heterogeneity in the development of emotion understanding. *International Journal of Behavioral Development, 30*(3), 193–199.

Colvert, E., Rutter, M., Beckett, C., Castle, J., Groothues, C., Hawkins, A.,…Sonuga-Barke, E. J. (2008). Emotional difficulties in early adolescence following severe early deprivation: Findings from the English and Romanian adoptees study. *Development and Psychopathology, 20*(2), 547–567.

Davis, M., & Whalen, P. J. (2001). The amygdala: Vigilance and emotion. *Molecular Psychiatry, 6*(1), 13–34.

Gao, X., & Maurer, D. (2010). A happy story: Developmental changes in children's sensitivity to facial expressions of varying intensities. *Journal of Experimental Child Psychology, 107*(2), 67–86.

Gao, X., Maurer, D., & Nishimura, M. (2010). Similarities and differences in the perceptual structure of facial expressions of children and adults. *Journal of Experimental Child Psychology, 105*(1–2), 98–115.

Govindan, R. M., Behen, M. E., Helder, E., Makki, M. I., & Chugani, H. T. (2010). Altered water diffusivity in cortical association tracts in children with early deprivation identified with tract-based spatial statistics (TBSS). *Cerebral Cortex, 20*(3), 561–569.

Gunnar, M. R., Bruce, J., & Grotevant, H. D. (2000). International adoption of institutionally reared children: Research and policy. *Development and Psychopathology, 12*(4), 677–693.

Guyer, A. E., Monk, C. S., McClure-Tone, E. B., Nelson, E. E., Roberson-Nay, R., Adler, A. D.,…Ernst, M. (2008). A developmental examination of amygdala response to facial expressions. *Journal of Cognitive Neuroscience, 20*(9), 1565–1582.

Hare, T. A., Tottenham, N., Davidson, M. C., Glover, G. H., & Casey, B. J. (2005). Contributions of amygdala and striatal activity in emotion regulation. *Biological Psychiatry, 57*(6), 624–632.

Hare, T. A., Tottenham, N., Galvan, A., Voss, H. U., Glover, G. H., & Casey, B. J. (2008). Biological substrates of emotional reactivity and regulation in adolescence during an emotional go-nogo task. *Biological Psychiatry, 63*(10), 927–934.

Herba, C. M., Landau, S., Russell, T., Ecker, C., & Phillips, M. L. (2006). The development of emotion-processing in children: effects of age, emotion, and intensity. *Journal of Child Psychology and Psychiatry, 47*(11), 1098–1106.

Jeon, H., Moulson, M. C., Fox, N. A., Zeanah, C. H., & Nelson, C. A. (2010). The effects of early institutionalization on the discrimination of facial expressions of emotion in young children. *Infancy, 15*(2), 209–221.

Kim, H., Somerville, L. H., Johnstone, T., Polis, S., Alexander, A. L., Shin, L. M., & Whalen, P. J. (2004). Contextual modulation of amygdala responsivity to surprised faces. *Journal of Cognitive Neuroscience, 16*(10), 1730–1745.

LeGrand, R., Mondloch, C. J., Maurer, D., & Brent, H. P. (2001). Neuroperception: Early visual experience and face processing. *Nature, 410*, 890.

Lobaugh, N. J., Gibson, E., & Taylor, M. J. (2006). Children recruit distinct neural systems for implicit emotional face processing. *Neuroreport, 17*(2), 215–219.

Mehta, M. A., Golembo, N. I., Nosarti, C., Colvert, E., Mota, A., Williams, S. C.,…Sonuga-Barke, E. J. (2009). Amygdala, hippocampal and corpus callosum size following severe early institutional deprivation: The English and Romanian adoptees study pilot. *Journal of Child Psychology and Psychiatry, 50*(8), 943–951.

Moriceau, S., Roth, T. L., Okotoghaide, T., & Sullivan, R. M. (2004). Corticosterone controls the developmental emergence of fear and amygdala function to predator odors in infant rat pups. *International Journal of Developmental Neuroscience, 22*(5–6), 415–422.

Moulson, M. C., Fox, N. A., Zeanah, C. H., & Nelson, C. A. (2009). Early adverse experiences and the neurobiology of facial emotion processing. *Developmental Psychology, 45*(1), 17–30.

Nelson, C. A., Parker, S. W., & Guthrie, D. (2006). The discrimination of facial expressions by typically developing infants and toddlers and those experiencing early institutional care. *Infant Behavior and Development, 29*(2), 210–219.

Nowicki, S. J., & Mitchell, J. (1998). Accuracy in identifying affect in child and adult faces and voices and social competence in preschool children. *Genetic, Social, and Genetic Psychology Monographs, 124*(1), 39–59.

Ono, M., Kikusui, T., Sasaki, N., Ichikawa, M., Mori, Y., & Murakami-Murofushi, K. (2008). Early weaning induces anxiety and precocious myelination in the anterior part of the basolateral amygdala of male Balb/c mice. *Neuroscience, 156*(4), 1103–1110.

Parker, S. W., & Nelson, C. A. (2005). The impact of early institutional rearing on the ability to discriminate facial expressions of emotion: An event-related potential study. *Child Development*, *76*(1), 54–72.

Petrovic, P., Kalisch, R., Pessiglione, M., Singer, T., & Dolan, R. J. (2008). Learning affective values for faces is expressed in amygdala and fusiform gyrus. *Social Cognitive and Affective Neuroscience*, *3*(2), 109–118.

Pilkonis, P. (1977). The behavioral consequences of shyness. *Journal of Personality*, *45*(4), 596–611.

Pollak, S. D., Klorman, R., Thatcher, J. E., & Cicchetti, D. (2001). P3b reflects maltreated children's reactions to facial displays of emotion. *Psychophysiology*, *38*(2), 267–274.

Pollak, S. D., & Sinha, P. (2002). Effects of early experience on children's recognition of facial displays of emotion. *Developmental Psychology*, *38*(5), 784–791.

Somerville, L. H., & Whalen, P. J. (2006). Prior experience as a stimulus category confound: An example using facial expressions of emotion. *Social Cognitive and Affective Neuroscience*, *1*(3), 271–274.

Thomas, K. M., Drevets, W. C., Whalen, P. J., Eccard, C. H., Dahl, R. E., Ryan, N. D., & Casey, B. J. (2001). Amygdala response to facial expressions in children and adults. *Biological Psychiatry*, *49*(4), 309–316.

Tottenham, N. (2012). Human amygdala development in the absence of species-expected caregiving. *Developmental Psychobiology*, *54*(6), 598–611.

Tottenham, N., Hare, T. A., & Casey, B. J. (2009). A developmental perspective on human amygdala function. In E. Phelps & P. Whalen (Eds.), *The human amygdala* (pp. 107–117). New York: Guilford Press.

Tottenham, N., Hare, T. A., Millner, A., Gilhooly, T., Zevin, J. D., & Casey, B. J. (2011). Elevated amygdala response to faces following early deprivation. *Developmental Science*, *14*(2), 190–204.

Tottenham, N., Hare, T. A., Quinn, B. T., McCarry, T., Nurse, M., Gilhooly, T., . . . Casey, B. J. (2010). Prolonged institutional rearing is associated with atypically large amygdala volume and emotion regulation difficulties. *Developmental Science*, *13*(1), 46–61.

van Reekum, C. M., Johnstone, T., Urry, H. L., Thurow, M. E., Schaefer, H. S., Alexander, A. L., & Davidson, R. J. (2007). Gaze fixations predict brain activation during the voluntary regulation of picture-induced negative affect. *Neuroimage*, *36*(3), 1041–1055.

Vorria, P., Papaligoura, Z., Sarafidou, J., Kopakaki, M., Dunn, J., Van Ijzendoorn, M. H., & Kontopoulou, A. (2006). The development of adopted children after institutional care: A follow-up study. *Journal of Child Psychology and Psychiatry*, *47*(12), 1246–1253.

Whalen, P. J. (1998). The ambiguous amygdala. *Current Directions in Psychological Science*, *7*(6), 177–188.

Wismer Fries, A. B., & Pollak, S. D. (2004). Emotion understanding in postinstitutionalized Eastern European children. *Developmental Psychopathology*, *16*(2), 355–369.

3.7

The Emergence of Perceptual Preferences for Social Signals of Emotion

JUKKA M. LEPPÄNEN AND CHARLES A. NELSON III

The capacity to recognize and share another individual's feelings and intentions is fundamental to human interpersonal interaction (e.g., Marsh, Kozak, & Ambady, 2007; Olsson & Phelps, 2007). Although a variety of cues are used to derive information about emotions and intentions (e.g., tone of voice, facial expressions, gestures, etc.), the majority of studies into this topic have focused on the recognition of facial expressions. In this chapter, we discuss a subset of these studies by focusing on those that have examined the early development of facial expression processing. We will pay particular attention to findings that show a clear developmental shift at the turn of the second half of the first year in perceptual processing of facial expressions. Studies by our groups and others have shown that it is at this age when infants begin to discriminate facial expressions of emotion and start to exhibit a robust perceptual preference for some emotional expressions (especially facial expressions of fear). We examine the mechanisms that might govern the appearance of this perceptual preference and discuss how future studies of the preference may shed light on the ontogenetic bases of typical and atypical social-cognitive development.

THE SEVEN-MONTH TRANSITION IN ATTENTION TO SOCIAL SIGNALS OF EMOTION

The ability to attend to and discriminate affect-relevant signals is a necessary first step for being able to process the emotional states and intentions of another individual. Human infants orient preferentially to faces at birth, but it is not before the age of 5 to 7 months when infants begin to reliably discriminate facial expressions (Bornstein & Arterberry, 2003; Flom & Bahrick, 2007; Kestenbaum & Nelson, 1990; Ludemann &

Nelson, 1988; Nelson, Morse, & Leavitt, 1979). At 7 months of age, infants also begin to exhibit an attentional bias toward affectively salient facial expressions, particularly facial expressions of fear. This well-documented bias is manifested in a slower rate of habituation to fearful versus happy expressions (Nelson et al., 1979), longer looking time for fearful than happy expressions in paired comparison tasks (Nelson & Dolgin, 1985), and less frequent or slower disengagement of attention from fearful than happy or neutral facial expressions (Leppänen et al., 2010; Peltola, Leppänen, Palokangas, & Hietanen, 2008). Studies recording event-related potentials (ERPs) have further shown that visual (e.g., N290, P400) and attention-sensitive (e.g., NC) components of the infant ERP are enhanced when infants view fearful as compared to happy facial expressions (Hoehl & Striano, 2010; Leppänen, Moulson, Vogel-Farley, & Nelson, 2007; Nelson & de Haan, 1996; Peltola, Leppänen, Mäki, & Hietanen, 2009).

There is no evidence that infants experience fear when they are viewing facial expressions of fear. Seven-month-old infants show a rapid heart rate deceleration (i.e., orientation response) but no sign of heart rate acceleration (indicative of sympathetic activation) when viewing fearful expressions (Leppänen et al., 2010). These findings suggest that 7-month-old infants find fearful facial expressions perceptually salient but do not associate them with specific emotional experiences, nor do they appear to experience a feeling of fearfulness.

There has been less research to examine whether the perceptual preference for fear generalizes to other negative facial expressions. However, a recently published study examined whether infants exhibit an attentional bias to other threat-related stimuli such as pictures of angry facial expressions (indicative of conspecific aggression) and pictures of snakes (LoBue & De Loache, 2010). Interestingly, 8- to 14-month-old infants in this study looked longer at fearful than happy expressions but did not look longer at angry relative to happy expressions or pictures of snakes versus flowers. The infants, however, oriented faster to both angry faces and pictures of snakes (i.e., moved their eyes from the fixation point to the location of the stimulus). These findings suggest that infants may adapt their responses to facial expressions depending on the specific nature of the signaled threat. Whalen (1998) has noted that fearful expressions signal the presence of threat in the environment and may hence engage prolonged processing (for example, to identify cues that provide information about the possible source of the threat), whereas angry faces (and snakes) pose a direct threat to the observer and may, thereby, elicit avoidance.

WHAT DRIVES INFANTS' PERCEPTUAL PREFERENCES?

It is tempting to interpret the perceptual preference for fear in infants as an evolved preparedness for preferential processing of danger-related cues. Specialized neural mechanisms may exist for prioritized processing of danger-related cues in the physical and social environment given the arguably central importance of such cues in adaptive behavior. Neuroimaging work in adults suggests that a network that involves limbic regions such as the amygdala and orbitofrontal cortex and their extensive connections to perceptual areas in the neocortex is important for prioritized processing of threat-related stimuli (Vuilleumier, 2005). The functional development of this network may be "time-locked" to the point in development at which the infant begins to locomote, spend increased time away from the caregiver, and actively explore the environment (i.e., when social signals of danger become behaviorally relevant, Leppänen & Nelson, 2009). It is further possible that the mechanisms for processing social signals of fear may be initially broadly tuned (i.e., respond to a range of cues) but become more specialized through experience for processing species-typical signals of emotion.

Interestingly, the concurrence of the emergence of exploratory behavior (or increased time away from the mother) and sensitivity to danger-related cues is also observed in rodents and macaque monkeys (see Bauman & Amaral, 2009; Sullivan & Holman, 2010). Detailed studies in rats have shown that endogenous increases in stress hormones and dopamine are important in initiating the functional onset of emotion-related neural circuits (i.e., amygdala) and the appearance of sensitivity to fear-related stimuli (Barr et al., 2009; Moriceau & Sullivan, 2004).

Kagan and Herschkowitz (2005) have suggested an alternative explanation for infants' perceptual preference for fearful facial expressions that emphasizes the physical characteristics of the fearful facial expression (e.g., open mouth and wide-open eyes) and their relative novelty in the infant's rearing environment instead of the emotional signal value. According to this view, the infant's representation (or schema) for faces allows him or her to recognize a fearful facial expression as a face because this expression shares the essential features of a face (such as the typical configuration of mouth, nose, and eyes), but the expression also receives increased attention because it contains features that are novel (such as the shape of the mouth and the eyes). Infants may attend for the longest period of time to a stimulus that can be recognized (shares essential features with the acquired representation) but also contains fewer essential features that are discrepant from the acquired representation. Kagan and Herschkowitz further argued that the transition in development at around 7 months reflects maturational changes in the prefrontal cortex and hippocampus, and associated improvements in working memory that allow the infant to retrieve schematic representation of the events encountered in the past and compare them with the present event.

A problem with the Kagan and Herschkowitz explanation is that a general preference for novel facial features would predict that infants prefer to attend to *any* facial expression that they have little experience of seeing during the first months of life. Contrary to this possibility, recent studies have shown that the perceptual preference is not observed for other negative expressions (e.g., expressions of anger, which are also likely to be novel for infants, see LoBue & de Loache, 2010) or novel, nonemotional facial expressions (Peltola et al., 2008).

DIRECTIONS FOR FUTURE RESEARCH

Clearly, further research is needed to test and directly contrast the alternative possible interpretations of the fear preference. It will be particularly important to determine whether infants are simply responding to the novel physical characteristic of fearful facial expressions (Kagan & Herschkowitz, 2005; see also Peltola et al., 2008) or whether they are also able to respond (at some level) to the emotional or social signal value of these expressions.

There is no straightforward test that would prove sensitivity to the emotional signal value of fearful expressions, but one criterion for such an ability is a functionally meaningful response to facial expressions (Nelson, 1987; Walker-Andrews, 1997). An example of such a response is provided by studies showing that 10- to 12-month-old infants avoid approaching an object if they see an adult expressing fear toward it (Carver & Vaccaro, 2007; Sorce, Emde, Campos, & Klinnert, 1985). It has been more challenging to examine whether younger infants show similar sensitivity to fearful expressions as "warning signals" because the paradigms are dependent on the infant's ability to move, but one promising line of recent research has started to address this question by investigating whether infants' attention to novel objects is affected by facial expressions (Hoehl, Palumbo, Heinisch, & Striano, 2008; Hoehl & Striano, 2010). These studies have shown that by 6 months of age, infants perceive the difference between fearful expressions that are directed toward a specific referent in the environment and expressions that have no referent (Hoehl & Striano, 2010). The studies have also shown that infants exhibit larger attention-sensitive ERPs to an object if they have seen an adult displaying a fearful expression toward the object as compared to a situation in which they have seen an adult displaying a neutral facial expression while looking at the object (Hoehl et al., 2008; Hoehl & Striano, 2010). More studies of this kind will be important for addressing the question of whether infants extract information about the signal value of fearful facial expressions.

If supported, the hypothesis that infants are sensitive to the emotional signal value of fearful expressions would have vast implications for understanding the ontogeny of emotion processing abilities. For example, such studies may offer insights into the typical developmental time course of fear processing during the first year of life. The evidence reviewed here suggests that, as is the case with rodents and monkeys (Bauman & Amaral, 2009; Sullivan & Holman, 2010), human infants may undergo a developmental shift from hyposensitivity to danger-related cues (i.e., period during which the infant shows no discrimination of safety- and threat-related cues) to differential processing of danger- and safety-related cues at a relatively well-defined developmental time point (at the onset of locomotion). If confirmed, such developmental periods may have wider implications for understanding the neurocognitive

bases and potential sensitive periods for the formation of attachment (formation of attachment may be facilitated during the hyposensitive period and become more difficult later in development; Sullivan & Holman, 2010) and also for understanding how sensitivity to environmental adversity is affected by the timing of the adverse experiences.

Electrophysiological and behavioral markers of fear processing would also open up new possibilities for examining early-emerging individual variability in processing danger-related cues. There is an increasing interest in investigating how genetic and experiential factors interact early in life to establish changes in emotion processing capacities (e.g., Ansorge, Zhou, Lira, Hen, & Gingrich, 2004; Gross et al., 2002; Hariri & Holmes, 2006). There is also evidence that heightened sensitivity to threat is causally associated with vulnerability to anxiety and negative mood (Bar-Haim, 2010; Mathews & MacLeod, 2005). The findings reviewed in this article suggest that developmental events during the first year of life are potentially important in the emergence of such biases in emotional information processing.

CONCLUSIONS

We have summarized and discussed studies examining the developmental foundations of the ability to perceive and adaptively respond to emotion-related information, focusing especially on infants' perceptual preference for fearful facial expressions. Our discussion highlights the important developmental events that take place during the second half of the first year and suggest ways in which future studies can shed light on the nature of this developmental change. This research may have vast implications for understanding the nature of infants' social cognitive capacities and how they relate to other aspects of development (e.g., attachment) and may also provide useful tools for studying individual variability in these capacities.

REFERENCES

Ansorge, M. S., Zhou, M., Lira, A., Hen, R., & Gingrich, J. A. (2004). Early-life blockade of the 5-HT transporter alters emotional behavior in adult mice. *Science, 306*, 879–881.

Bar-Haim, Y. (2010). Research review: Attention bias modification (ABM): A novel treatment for anxiety disorders. *Journal of Child Psychology and Psychiatry, 51*, 859–870.

Barr, G. A., Moriceau, S., Shionoya, K., Muzny, K., Gao, P., Wang, S., & Sullivan, R. M. (2009). Transitions in infant learning are modulated by dopamine in the amygdala. *Nature Neuroscience, 12,* 1367.

Bauman, M. D., & Amaral, D. G. (2009). Neurodevelopment of social cognition. In C. A. Nelson & M. Luciana (Eds.), *Handbook of developmental cognitive neuroscience* (2nd ed., pp. 161–185). Cambridge, MA: MIT Press.

Bornstein, M. H., & Arterberry, M. E. (2003). Recognition, discrimination and categorization of smiling by 5-month-old infants. *Developmental Science, 6,* 585–599.

Carver, L. J., & Vaccaro, B. G. (2007). 12-month-old infants allocate increased neural resources to stimuli associated with negative adult emotion. *Developmental Psychology, 43,* 54–69.

Flom, R., & Bahrick, L. E. (2007). The development of infant discrimination of affect in multimodal and unimodal stimulation: The role of intersensory redundancy. *Developmental Psychology, 43,* 238–252.

Gross, C., Zhuang, X., Stark, K., Ramboz, S., Oosting, R., Kirby, L., ... Hen, R. (2002). Serotonin1A receptor acts during development to establish normal anxiety-like behaviour in the adult. *Nature, 416,* 396–400.

Hariri, A. R., & Holmes, A. (2006). Genetics of emotional regulation: The role of the serotonin transporter in neural function. *Trends in Cognitive Sciences, 10,* 182–191.

Hoehl, S., Palumbo, L., Heinisch, C., & Striano, T. (2008). Infants' attention is biased by emotional expressions and eye gaze direction. *Neuroreport, 19,* 579–582.

Hoehl, S., & Striano, T. (2010). The development of emotional face and eye gaze processing. *Developmental Science, 13,* 813–825.

Kagan, J., & Herschkowitz, N. (2005). *A young mind in a growing brain.* Mahwah, NJ: Erlbaum.

Kestenbaum, R., & Nelson, C. A. (1990). The recognition and categorization of upright and inverted emotional expressions by 7-month-old infants. *Infant Behavior and Development, 13,* 497–511.

Leppänen, J. M., Moulson, M. C., Vogel-Farley, V. K., & Nelson, C. A. (2007). An ERP study of emotional face processing in the adult and infant brain. *Child Development, 78,* 232–245.

Leppänen, J. M., & Nelson, C. A. (2009). Tuning the developing brain to social signals of emotion. *Nature Reviews Neuroscience, 10,* 37–47.

Leppänen, J. M., Peltola, M. J., Mäntymaa, M., Koivuluoma, M., Salminen, M., & Puura, K. (2010). Cardiac and behavioral evidence for emotional influences on attention in 7-month-old infants. *International Journal of Behavioral Development, 34,* 547–553.

LoBue, V., & De Loache, J. S. (2010). Superior detection of threat-relevant stimuli in infancy. *Developmental Science, 13,* 221–228.

Ludemann, P. M., & Nelson, C. A. (1988). Categorical representation of facial expressions by 7-month-old infants. *Developmental Psychology, 24,* 492–501.

Marsh, A. A., Kozak, M. N., & Ambady, N. (2007). Accurate identification of fear facial expressions predicts prosocial behavior. *Emotion, 7,* 239–251.

Mathews, A., & MacLeod, C. (2005). Cognitive vulnerability to emotional disorders. *Annual Review of Clinical Psychology, 1,* 167–195.

Moriceau, S., & Sullivan, R. M. (2004). Maternal presence serves as a switch between learning fear and attraction in infancy. *Nature Neuroscience, 9,* 1004–1006.

Nelson, C. A. (1987). The recognition of facial expressions in the first two years of life: Mechanisms of development. *Child Development, 58,* 889–909.

Nelson, C. A., & de Haan, M. (1996). Neural correlates of infants' visual responsiveness to facial expressions of emotions. *Developmental Psychobiology, 29,* 577–595.

Nelson, C. A., & Dolgin, K. (1985). The generalized discrimination of facial expressions by 7-month-old infants. *Child Development, 56,* 58–61.

Nelson, C. A., Morse, P. A., & Leavitt, L. A. (1979). Recognition of facial expressions by 7-month-old infants. *Child Development, 50,* 1239–1242.

Olsson, A., & Phelps, E. A. (2007). Social learning of fear. *Nature Neuroscience, 10,* 1095–1102.

Peltola, M. J., Leppänen, J. M., Mäki, S., & Hietanen, J. K. (2009). The emergence of enhanced attention to fearful faces between 5 and 7 months of age. *Social Cognitive and Affective Neuroscience, 4,* 134–142.

Peltola, M. J., Leppänen, J. M., Palokangas, T., & Hietanen, J. K. (2008). Fearful faces modulate looking duration and attention disengagement in 7-month-old infants. *Developmental Science, 11,* 60–68.

Sorce, F. F., Emde, R. N., Campos, J. J., & Klinnert, M. D. (1985). Maternal emotional signaling: Its effect on the visual cliff behavior of 1-year-olds. *Developmental Psychology, 21,* 195–200.

Sullivan, R. M., & Holman, P. J. (2010). Transitions in sensitive period attachment learning in infancy: The role of corticosterone. *Neuroscience and Biobehavioral Reviews, 34,* 835–844.

Walker-Andrews, A. S. (1997). Infants' perception of expressive behaviors: Differentiation of multimodal information. *Psychological Bulletin, 121,* 437–456.

Whalen, P. J. (1998). Fear, vigilance, and ambiguity: Initial neuroimaging studies of the human amygdala. *Current Directions in Psychological Science, 7,* 177–188.

Vuilleumier, P. (2005). How brains beware: Neural mechanisms of emotional attention. *Trends in Cognitive Sciences, 9,* 585–594.

3.8

Some Thoughts on the Development and Neural Bases of Face Processing

CHARLES A. NELSON III

Among the numerous visual inputs that fall upon our retinas each moment, the human face is perhaps one of the most salient. The importance of the many signals it conveys (e.g., emotion, identity, gender, age, and so on), together with the alacrity and ease with which adults typically process this information, is a compelling reason to suppose that there may exist brain circuits specialized for processing faces. Neuropsychological studies provided the first evidence to support this view. For example, there are patients who show impaired face processing with relatively intact general vision and object processing, and others who show intact face processing but impaired object processing (e.g., Moscovitch, Winocur, & Behrmann, 1997). More recently, various neuroimaging tools have been used to identify the pathways involved in face processing in the intact brain. These studies have confirmed and extended findings from brain-injured patients, indicating that a distributed network of regions in the brain mediate face processing: Specifically, occipito-temporal regions are important for the early perceptual stages of face processing with more anterior regions, including areas of inferior temporal and orbitofrontal cortex and the amygdala, involved in processing aspects such as identity and emotional expression (Adolphs, 2002; Haxby, Hoffman, & Gobbini, 2002).

The Developing Brain

Developmental studies can provide important information to constrain and inform adult models of face processing. For example, by studying when and how face-specific brain responses emerge, developmental studies can provide some hints as to whether and how much experience might be needed for these responses to emerge. Behavioral studies suggest that face-processing pathways may be functional from very early in life: Newborns move their eyes, and sometimes their heads, longer to keep a moving face-like pattern in view than several other comparison patterns (Johnson, Dzuirwiec, Ellis, & Morton, 1991). Although there is a debate as to whether this reflects a specific response to face-like configurations or a lower level visual preference (e.g., for patterns with higher density of elements in the upper visual field; see Turati, Simion, Milani, & Umilta, 2002), the ultimate result is that face-like patterns are preferred to other arrangements from the first hours to days of life (reviewed in de Haan, Humphreys, & Johnson, 2002).

While this might seem evidence for the claim that face-specific cortical areas are already active from birth, the prevailing view is that this early preferential orienting to a face is likely mediated by subcortical mechanisms (e.g., superior colliculus; for a review of the evidence, see Johnson & Morton, 1991), and that cortical mechanisms do not begin to emerge until 2–3 months of age. At this early age, cortical areas are thought to be relatively unspecialized, as they await confirmation from visual input (Johnson & Morton, 1991; Nelson, 2001). One possible function of the earlier developing subcortical system is to provide a "face-biased" input to the slower developing occipito-temporal cortical system and to provide one mechanism whereby an initially more broadly tuned processing system becomes increasingly specialized to respond to faces during development (Johnson & Morton, 1991; Nelson, 2001).

Although the basic neural architecture of face processing is laid down in infancy, development continues well into adolescence. For example, behavioral studies have reported substantial improvement in sensitivity to subtle spacing differences among facial features between 8-year-olds and adults (Mondloch, Maurer, & Ahola, 2006) and studies using event-related potentials

(ERPs) suggest that there are gradual, quantitative improvements in face processing from 4 to 15 years of age rather than stage-like shifts (Taylor, McCarthy, Saliba, & Degiovanni, 1999). Finally, studies using functional magnetic resonance imaging reveal that 10- to 12-year-old children show a more distributed pattern of activation in brain networks involved in processing facial identity compared to adults (e.g., Passarotti et al., 2003).

Summary

Clearly the developmental course of face processing is protracted, with adult-like function not being obtained until perhaps adolescence. It is equally clear, however, that face processing advances rapidly during the infancy years, laying the groundwork for subsequent refinement, elaboration, and specialization. Indeed, the studies reviewed earlier suggest that the cortical systems involved in face processing become increasingly specialized for faces throughout the first decade of life.

The Role of Experience in Face Processing

Consistent with experience-dependent changes in brain function in general, experience seems to play a critical role in shaping the functional and anatomical networks involved in processing faces in the first years of life. Evidence comes both from studies of deprivation and/or abnormal or atypical experience, as well as from the so-called other face effect.

Studies of Altered Early Experience

In one series of studies, the face-processing abilities of patients with congenital cataracts who were deprived of patterned visual input for the first months of life were tested years after this period of deprivation. These patients show normal processing of featural information (e.g., subtle differences in the shape of the eyes and mouth) but show impairments in processing configural information (i.e., the spacing of features within the face; Geldart, Mondloch, Maurer, de Schonen, & Brent, 2002; Le Grand, Mondloch, Maurer, & Brent, 2001). This pattern was specific to faces in that both featural and configural aspects of geometric patterns were processed normally (Le Grand, Mondloch, Maurer, & Brent, 2001). These studies suggest that visual input during early infancy is necessary for the normal development of at least some aspects of face processing.

In a similar vein, maltreated children generally perform more poorly on emotion recognition tasks than do nonmaltreated children. For example, Pollak and colleagues have found that

compared to nonabused children, abused children show a response bias for anger (Pollak, Cicchetti, Hornung, & Reed, 2000), identify anger based on less perceptual input (Pollak & Sinha, 2002), and show altered category boundaries for anger (Pollak & Kistler, 2002). These results suggest that atypical frequency and content of emotional interactions with caregivers change the basic perception of emotional expressions in abused children. Finally, ERPs invoked to familiar and unfamiliar faces and to facial emotion among infants institutionalized since birth differ from those of never institutionalized infants (Moulson, Fox, Zeanah, & Nelson, 2009; Moulson, Westerlund, & Nelson, 2009; Parker & Nelson, 2005; Parker, Nelson, & the BEIP Core Group, 2005). As with Pollak's studies, in this work it was assumed that early deprivation includes limited access to facial emotion.

Studies of the "Other" Face Effect

Augmenting studies of altered early experience are studies focused on a set of phenomena often referred to as the "other" face effect, such as the other race effect, the other gender effect, the other species effect, and the other age effect. The essential observation here is that faces that are less familiar to the observer's tend to be less well identified/discriminated. For example, in the well-known "other race effect," adults find it easier to recognize faces from their own race (see Elfenbein & Ambady, 2002; O'Toole, Deffenbacher, Valentin, & Abdi, 1994), and increased exposure to members of another race improves discrimination of other-race faces (e.g., Chiroro & Valentine, 1995; Lavrakas, Buri, & Mayzner, 1976). Children show much less of the other race effect than do adults. Finally, there is also the "other species effect," in which both monkeys and human adults are better at recognizing faces from their own species (Pascalis & Wirth, 2012; Scott & Monesson, 2010). The interpretation of the other species effect is simply that we are best at recognizing faces similar to those we see most often (i.e., respectively, faces in an upright orientation and faces of individuals with whom we have most experience, be they the same race or the same species).

Collectively, experience clearly plays an important role in developing expertise in processing faces, which in turn leads to cortical specialization. How exactly might this occur?

Perceptual Narrowing of Face Processing

A number of models have been proposed to account for the development of face processing, all of which have in common (to varying degrees) the role of experience (Cohen Kadosh & Johnson, 2007; de Haan, 2008; Johnson, 2005; Nelson, 1993, 2001; Scott, Pascalis, & Nelson, 2007). The focus of the remainder of this chapter is a model put forth by the author, which focuses on the phenomenon of "perceptual narrowing" (Nelson, 1993, 2001). By "perceptual narrowing" I mean that prior to experience with certain faces (e.g., one's own species, one's own race), the perceptual window is tuned so broadly as to include virtually all faces. With specific experiences, however, this window narrows. This model suggests that infants mold their face-processing system based on the visual experiences they encounter. As is the case with speech perception, this model assumes a narrowing of the perceptual window through which faces are processed, which in turn results in an increase in cortical specialization. Thus, early in development humans possess the ability to discriminate among a wide range of faces and facial features, and based on experience with specific types of faces, this system becomes more specialized. Accordingly, the ability to discriminate between faces that one has not had exposure to (or has had less exposure to) is not as good as discrimination between faces with which one has had experience. This model of face processing differs to some degree from some of the previously discussed models by proposing (to use Greenough's term; see Greenough & Black, 1992) an experience-expectant mechanism that is activity dependent. Support for this model of perceptual narrowing comes from several adult and developmental investigations, three of which have been mentioned previously: the "other-race" and "other-species" effects, and research on the perceptual expertise effect (for recent discussion, see Slater et al., 2010).

In this model it is assumed that specific experiences with some stimuli lead to specialized expertise (hence, an active process of perceptual tuning), whereas stimuli that are never or rarely experienced fall out of the perceptual repertoire (a more passive process). Thus, those categories the perceiver becomes expert in recognizing lead to cortical specialization, whereas those stimuli that are infrequently experienced disappear from the behavioral repertoire. A corollary to the model is that if the organism has a particular experience during a sensitive period but the experience is not maintained, and if the perceptual/cognitive function requires such maintenance for its full expression, then in theory the circuitry that was initially committed to this function would be erased or damped down; the former would

predict that experience later in life would be of little use in regaining the function, and the latter implies that experience later in life might rekindle the function.

Why do some categories of stimuli lead to expertise (such as faces), whereas others do not? Presumably it is the lack of experience with one category of stimuli or another that is responsible, although it remains to be determined how broadly or narrowly tuned the categories are (e.g., for faces, would the category include faces from all species or all members of a species, or is the category more narrowly defined than that?).

The Future

Although there is strong support for the model of perceptual narrowing, much work remains to be done. First, we still know relatively little about the exact experiences that are required to facilitate the development of facial expertise, when these experiences must occur for development to proceed normally, and how much of these experiences are needed. For example, although some authors interpreted neonatal preferences for face-like stimuli as "innate" simply because they occur so early in life, perhaps the infant's face processing system benefits from the first minutes or hours of seeing a face after birth. Similarly, as Mondloch et al. (2006) have shown, development beyond age 8 years may be less driven by experience with faces than improvements in memory and other cognitive functions. Second, it is unclear whether the neural systems that subserve face processing are completely undifferentiated and thus entirely experience dependent, or in fact are at least partially assembled at birth. For example, monkeys completely deprived of viewing faces from birth are able to discriminate two monkey faces or two human faces immediately following the end of deprivation; however, from that point forward monkeys deprived of seeing only human faces lose the ability to discriminate such faces and similarly, monkeys deprived of seeing monkey faces lose the ability to discriminate monkey faces (Sugita, 2008). Thus, experience fully accounts for facial *expertise*, yet some degree of face processing appears experience independent or at least independent of *postnatal* experience (e.g., perhaps monkeys learned about faces prenatally by touching their own faces and through proprioception). Third, we know little about how much plasticity exists in face-processing circuits beyond the first months or years of life; for example, studies of deprivation (be it cataracts, neonatal brain damage, or early adversity) suggest there is remarkably little plasticity in such circuits.

Finally, we similarly know little about what happens to circuits that are no longer used (such as those used to process highly unfamiliar faces, such as faces from unfamiliar races or species); are these circuits fully erased, never to be used again, or do they go dormant, in which case reactivating them later in life might be possible?

CONCLUSIONS

Overall, the ability to process faces appears to be heavily experience dependent, and the window through which faces are viewed appears broadly tuned at birth and narrows with experience. The neural architecture that comes to be specialized for face processing does so over the first year of life, with perhaps a sensitive period occurring sometime in the second half of the first year (although experience may continue to exert its effects well into the second decade of life, essentially fine-tuning the system). The precise experiences that sculpt this system, as well as their timing and duration, remain to be established, as does the extent to which there might exist early in life some primitive architecture that has the potential to be dedicated to face processing.

ACKNOWLEDGMENTS

The author gratefully acknowledges support from the National Institutes of Health (MH078829) and the Richard David Scott endowment.

REFERENCES

Adolphs, R. (2002). Recognizing emotion from facial expressions: Psychological and neurological mechanisms. *Behavioral and Cognitive Neuroscience Reviews*, 1, 21–61.

Chiroro, P., & Valentine, T. (1995). An investigation of the contact hypothesis of the own-race bias in face recognition. *Quarterly Journal of Experimental Psychology: Human Experimental Psychology*, 48A, 879–894.

Cohen Kadosh, K., & Johnson, M. H. (2007). Developing a cortex specialized for face perception. *Trends Cognitive Science*, 11, 367–369.

de Haan, M. (2008). Neurocognitive mechanisms for the development of face processing. In C. A. Nelson & M. Luciana (Eds.), *Handbook of developmental cognitive neuroscience* (2nd ed., pp. 509–520). Cambridge, MA: MIT Press.

de Haan, M., Humphreys, K., & Johnson, M. H. (2002). Developing a brain specialized for face perception: A converging methods approach. *Developmental Psychobiology*, 40, 200–212.

Elfenbein, H. A., & Ambady, N. (2002). On the universality and cultural specificity of emotion recognition: A meta-analysis. *Psychological Bulletin*, 128, 203–235.

Geldart, S., Mondloch, C. J., Maurer, D., de Schonen, S., & Brent, H. P. (2002). The effect of early visual deprivation on the development of face processing. *Developmental Science*, 5(4), 490–501.

Greenough, W. T., & Black, J. E. (1992). Induction of brain structure by experience: Substrates for cognitive development. In M. R. Gunnar & C. A. Nelson (Eds.), *Developmental behavioral neuroscience. The Minnesota Symposia on Child Psychology* (Vol. 24, pp. 155–200). Hillsdale, NJ: Erlbaum.

Haxby, J. V., Hoffman, E. A., & Gobbini, M. I. (2002). Human neural systems for face recognition and social communication. *Biological Psychiatry*, 51, 59–67.

Johnson, M. H. (2005). Subcortical face processing. *Nature Reviews Neuroscience*, 6(10), 766–774.

Johnson, M. H., Dziurawiec, S., Ellis, H., & Morton, J. (1991). Newborns' preferential tracking of face-like stimuli and its subsequent decline. *Cognition*, 40, 1–19.

Johnson, M. H., & Morton, J. (1991). *Biology and cognitive development: The case of face recognition*. Oxford, England: Blackwell.

Lavrakas, P. J., Buri, J. R., & Mayzner, M. S. (1976). A perspective on the recognition of other-race faces. *Perception and Psychophysics*, 20, 475–481.

Le Grand, R., Mondloch, C., Maurer, D., & Brent, H. P. (2001). Early visual experience and face processing. *Nature*, 410, 890.

Mondloch, C. J., Maurer, D., & Ahola, S. (2006). Becoming a face expert. *Current Directions in Psychological Science*, 17, 930–934.

Moscovitch, M., Winocur, G., & Behrmann, M. (1997). What is special about face recognition? Nineteen experiments on a person with visual object agnosia but normal face recognition. *Journal of Cognitive Neuroscience*, 9, 555–604.

Moulson, M. C., Fox, N. A., Zeanah, C. H., & Nelson, C. A. (2009). Early adverse experiences and the neurobiology of facial emotion processing. *Developmental Psychology*, 45(1), 17–30.

Moulson, M. C., Westerlund, A., & Nelson, C. A. (2009). The effects of early experience on face recognition: An event-related potential study of institutionalized children in Romania. *Child Development*, 80(4), 1039–1056

Nelson, C. A. (1993). The recognition of facial expressions in infancy: Behavioral and electrophysiological correlates. In B. de Boysson-Bardies, S. de Schonen, P. Jusczyk, P. MacNeilage, & J. Morton (Eds.), *Developmental neurocognition: Speech and face processing in the first year of life* (pp. 187–193). Dordrecht, The Netherlands: Kluwer Academic Press.

Nelson, C. A. (2001).The development and neural bases of face recognition. *Infant and Child Development, 10*, 3–18.

O'Toole, A. J., Deffenbacher, K. A., Valentin, D., & Abdi, H. (1994). Structural aspects of face recognition and the other-race effect. *Memory and Cognition, 22*, 208–224.

Parker, S. W., & Nelson, C. A. (2005). The impact of early institutional rearing on the ability to discriminate facial expressions of emotion: An event-related potential study. *Child Development, 76*, 54–72.

Parker, S. W., Nelson, C. A., & the BEIP Core Group. (2005). An event-related potential study of the impact of institutional rearing on face recognition. *Development and Psychopathology, 17*, 621–639.

Passarotti, A. M., Paul, B. M., Bussiere, J. R., Buxton, R. B., Wong, E. C., & Stiles, J. (2003). The development of face and location processing: An fMRI study. *Developmental Science, 6*, 100–117.

Pascalis, O., & Wirth, S. (2012). Recognising the faces of other species: What can a limited skill tell us about face processing? In A. J. Calder, G. Rhodes, J. V. Haxby, & M. H. Johnson (Eds.), *The handbook of face perception* (pp. 719–730). Oxford, England: Oxford University Press.

Pollak, S. D., Cicchetti, D., Hornung, K., & Reed, A. (2000). Recognizing emotion in faces: Developmental effects of child abuse and neglect. *Developmental Psychology, 36*(5), 679–688.

Pollak, S. D., & Kistler, D. J. (2002). Early experience is associated with the development of categorical representations for facial expressions of emotion. *Proceedings of the National Academy of Sciences USA, 99*, 9072–9076.

Pollak, S. D., & Sinha, P. (2002). Effects of early experience on children's recognition and facial displays of emotion. *Developmental Psychology, 38*(5), 784–791.

Scott, L. S., & Monesson, A. (2010). Experience-dependent neural specialization during infancy. *Neuropsychologia, 48*(6), 1857–1861.

Scott, L. S., Pascalis, O., & Nelson, C. A. (2007). A domain-general theory of perceptual development. *Current Directions in Psychological Science, 16*, 197–201.

Slater, A., Quinn, P. C., Kelly, D. J., Lee, K., Longmore, C. A., McDonald, P. R., & Pascalis, O. (2010). The shaping of face space in early infancy: Becoming a native face processor. *Child Development Perspectives, 4*, 205–211.

Sugita, Y. (2008). Face perception in monkeys reared with no exposure to faces. *Proceedings of the National Academy of Sciences USA, 105*, 394–398.

Taylor, M. J., McCarthy, G., Saliba, E., & Degiovanni, E. (1999). ERP evidence of developmental changes in processing of faces. *Clinical Neurophysiology, 110*, 910–915.

Turati, C., Simion, F., Milani, I., & Umilta, C. (2002). Newborns' preferences for faces: What is crucial. *Developmental Psychology, 38*, 875–882.

3.9

Redescribing Action

DARE BALDWIN

Action is intentional behavior. Examples range from high-flown artistic enterprises (e.g., Michelangelo's sculpting of the Pietà) to the most mundane of everyday activities (e.g., eating breakfast). Making sense of action generally seems so effortless that we routinely take the skill involved for granted. Just imagine, however, what it would be like if this ability were suddenly snatched away. That is, suppose one could still see others' behavior but not penetrate to the meaning of that behavior. To illustrate, picture a family's school-day morning dash to get offspring breakfasted, cleansed, and in the car with all relevant gear in tow. What one actually experiences is a flurry of activity: bodies moving hither and thither, arms snaking in and out, a certain amount of clipped verbal exchange, and intermittent, rapidly changing contact between hands and a diverse range of objects and substances. The sheer volume of dynamic visual and auditory information contained in just a minute or two of such ordinary, everyday action is staggering. Given known constraints on working memory, any attempt to recall what happened in terms of simple surface information about sound or motion would surely be hopeless. In any case, such titanic efforts at recall would yield little benefit. Simply registering motion patterns (e.g., boy's arm arcing at Y angle with Z velocity in vicinity of kitchen counter) would not help much if the aim were to predict the actor's future behavior, to assist in getting things done, or to make sense of other forms of complex behavior also present, such as language or emotion. Clearly, our ability to go beyond surface registration of others' behavior to discern and interpret the motivations behind it lies at the heart of our social, cognitive, and linguistic functioning (Malle, Moses, & Baldwin, 2001; Tomasello, 1999).

A powerful perceptual/cognitive system is obviously at play here but much about this system is as yet mysterious. What are its components? How do they interact? How is this system acquired in normal human development, and what kinds of deficits arise when components are disrupted? What is unique about human action processing relative to that of other species? Among humans, what is universal about human action processing, and in what ways do experience and culture shape the action-processing system? Making progress toward answering these questions would represent a major leap forward on a topic central to cognitive science.

ACTION PROCESSING IN OUTLINE

Action processing seems to be a multimodal, massively parallel, and inferentially rich undertaking. That is, to make sense of others' action in terms of their goals, motivations, beliefs, desires, and the like, we engage in "broad-band observation"—integrating what we can glean from face, voice, action, gesture, and language to infer underlying states of mind to explain it all coherently. Such integration is likely possible only because somehow the underlying mechanisms that support processing across these multiple modalities and domains can deliver a common currency—the currency of social inference, meaning inference about another's intentions, goals, plans, beliefs, emotions, dispositions, attitudes, and the like.

Telltale signs of this inferential lingua franca are everywhere in human social interaction. For example, I might note that a new acquaintance is dictatorial. Likely I would leap to a similar conclusion regardless of whether the interaction was in person or in another format lacking one or another input source, such as a telephone call or an instant message. Clues to dispositional traits (and other social hypotheses) are littered in diverse ways across behavior, and we happily salvage whatever is available to tune them. Put in broader terms, we take many different threads of sensory input, process them in terms of considerable pre-established expertise, and weave a unified fabric of social inference. Recently, several researchers have suggested that a common set of underlying cognitive and perceptual mechanisms drive learning and inference across the diverse input sources (e.g., language, action, facial emotion) (e.g., Cassimatis, 2009). Such commonalities could help to support the formation of systems of knowledge across domains that are commensurable in terms of the social inferences that emerge. Along these lines, a small amount of recent evidence reveals fundamental processing commonalities across domains. For example, action is segmented in much the same way language is, and statistical learning subserves segmentation across these different domains (e.g., Baldwin, Andersson, Saffran, & Meyer, 2008). Additionally, action processing involves enhanced attention associated with closure of hierarchically higher order segments (Hard, Recchia, & Tversky, 2011), as does narrative processing (e.g., Haberlandt, Graesser, Schneider, & Kiely, 1986). And action processing shares with face processing telltale signs of being informed by two sources of information: featural and configural (Loucks & Baldwin, 2006, 2009).

One of the things that complicates inferences about the intentions underlying others' actions is that intention is not a monolithic beast: The intentions that motivate action can differ from one another in kind. One major taxonomic divide here (Baldwin, Loucks, & Sabbagh, 2008) is between action whose intended goal is communicative in nature (e.g., speech, signed language, and conventional gesture) versus action that is directed toward generating concrete effects in the world (e.g., tying one's shoelaces). Action of the first type—communicative action, such as language—has been the focus of intense interest to researchers since the advent of psychology as a field (e.g., James, 1890/1983). Oddly, action of the latter kind—what one might call object-oriented action—has received much less attention until quite recently.

Object-Oriented Action Under the Spotlight

Object-oriented action is directed toward achieving physical change in the world, rather than toward communicating a message to another. Processing object-oriented action, as an observer, involves discerning which physical change (or set of changes) in the world an actor intends to bring about. Phenomenologically, we typically experience this as a straightforward undertaking and often give the task little, if any, conscious effort. In fact, however, object-oriented action presents

major challenges to processing: Motion tends to be rapid, complex in its dynamic relations to other things in the world, and evanescent. As observers, we frequently have access only to fragments of the actual motion stream, and even those snippets are often degraded due to factors such as distance, darkness, or a poor viewing angle. For these reasons, we must rapidly register what is relevant in the motion stream and carry out extensive analysis (such as segmentation, categorization, integration, and inference) on the fly. In addition, this analytic process seems to be carried out on many levels simultaneously. At a fine-grained level, we need to be sensitive to small spatial and temporal details of motion in space. Such sensitivity enables us, for example, to differentiate between a slap and a caress, and we can recoil or bask accordingly. At the same time, at a more global level, we need to be sensitive to relations among lengthy sequences of action, often across extended periods of time. In this way, observation of an individual's tendencies across many contexts shapes the inferences one makes about new actions this individual undertakes. For example, one interprets a motion aimed straight at one's chin very differently depending on whether the actor has often exhibited hostile intent. Interestingly, if caresses are expected and it turns out to be a slap, one might nevertheless maintain the starting assumption that the actor's intent was benign despite the slap. For instance, one might cleverly infer the involvement of an unseen mosquito. Such examples illustrate that action processing not only yields inferences about others' goals and intentions but also interacts in complex ways with our general knowledge about the world. Action processing shapes our inferences about the nature of reality, and what we know about the world influences our inferences about intentions.

In broad outline, then, making sense of action seems to require parallel involvement of multiple perceptual/cognitive processes at numerous levels of analysis, and it both engages and enriches our massive fund of world knowledge. A common thread across all levels of analysis in action processing seems to be a joint requirement for detecting structure and redescribing that structure. A small body of research showcases this: Adults are skilled at capitalizing on structure inherent in action to organize processing and identify actions (Avrahami & Kareev, 1994; Baldwin, 2005; Baldwin et al., 2008; Johanssen, 1973; Newtson & Enquist, 1996; Troje, 2008; Zacks & Tversky, 2001; Zacks, Tversky, & Iyer, 2001), and display a powerful propensity to redescribe motion in intentional terms

(Hard, Tversky, & Lang, 2006; Scholl & Tremoulet, 2000). At this juncture, however, remarkably little is known about the kind of structure inherent in action, what aspects of such structure adults are sensitive to and track as action unfolds, or the precise nature of mechanisms subserving detection and redescription of such structure. Filling this knowledge vacuum is an important thrust for current and future research.

EPIGENESIS OF ACTION PROCESSING

Given the complexity of action, how do infants break into organized processing of the dynamic motion flow in the first place? When and how do they begin registering functional commonalities across diverse motions that ultimately give rise to inferences about others' intentions and goals? The structure detection/redescription framework described earlier provides a natural approach to tackling such questions. Inspired by the work of knowledge acquisition theorists such as Gentner, Holyoak, and Kokinov (2001) as well as causal learning theorists such as Cheng (1997) and Gopnik and colleagues (2004), this framework seeks to account for the epigenesis of action-processing skills in terms of domain-general learning mechanisms recruited by learners to detect patterns and infer causes that make sense of the barrage of motion information they encounter. What arises with development and experience is a specialized knowledge system responsive to structure inherent in action and the functional necessities of action. If this framework is on the right track, it should be possible to observe infants becoming increasingly tuned to structure in action with development, while redescription skills drive increasingly sophisticated levels of encoding that promote inferences about intentions, goals, causal efficacy, and related mental states.

Structure-Sensitive Segmentation

Infants as young as 10–12 months readily detect action segments within dynamic human action (Baldwin, Baird, Saylor, & Clark, 2001; Hespos, Grossman, & Saylor, 2010). Recently, we have gained evidence that structure-detection skills bootstrap infants' entry into such organized action processing. In one study, for example, we captured infants as young as 6–8 months in the act of discovering segmental structure inherent in an extended novel sequence of dynamic human action. In these studies, statistical regularities were the only available source of information to guide the discovery process. Other research has

documented infants' skill at segmenting dynamic action presented in a point-light format, which preserves structural information while minimizing contextual clues. This is a promising start: We now know infants are sensitive to structure in action and can capitalize on it to extract individual actions within the continuous motion stream. Our focus now is on identifying other sources of structure infants detect using looking-time and eye-tracking methodologies, and discovering the kinds of changes that occur in structure detection with development and experience. Along these lines, Loucks and Sommerville recently found that infants "tune" their processing of grasping actions to prioritize featural over configural aspects of motion between 6 and 10 months of age, and their ability to perform the actions at issue predicts their progress toward such tuning (Loucks & Sommerville, 2012a,b).

Action Redescribed

Motions that are dramatically different, on the surface, may nevertheless strike us as functionally the same. A push is a push, whether it is executed with a finger, toe, tool, or even a puff of air. We can detect the differences, but frequently we do not attend to them. Instead, we respond to the shared intentional content of these diverse physical methods of enactment. How and when do infants begin to engage in this very fundamental form of action redescription? Recent research hints that the period between 5 and 10 months may be a watershed in the epigenesis of action-redescription skills (Olofson, 2008; Olofson & Baldwin, 2011). For simple actions like *push* and *pull*, 10- to 11-month-olds systematically ignored surface motion differences that were functionally equivalent vis à vis future action, but they found equivalent motion differences noteworthy when functionally relevant. In contrast, 5- to 7-month-olds were unable to ignore surface changes even when they predicted the same functional outcome. Together, these findings document action redescription as early as 10–11 months of age but also suggest that infants in the second half of their first year may be in the midst of discovering functional commonalities across action scenarios that they soon will prioritize in processing. It will be interesting to discover whether the period between 5 and 10 months emerges as significant in infants' discovery of functional commonalities across a diverse range of actions, and whether infants' own motor repertoire predicts the set of actions to which they display a redescriptive pattern, as might be predicted by other recent findings

(Hauf, Aschersleben, & Prinz, 2007; Sommerville, Woodward, & Needham, 2005). More generally, an important goal is to discover what kinds of experiences and action input help to orient infants' processing away from surface characteristics toward redescription in terms of functional commonalities.

Motionese

Related to this, other research demonstrates that all action input is not equal: Some kinds seem to be more readily analyzable. In particular, we found that actions parents direct toward infants (relative to actions they direct toward adults) are riddled with a variety of modifications highlighting the structure inherent within the motion flow (Brand, Baldwin, & Ashburn, 2002). Without any conscious intention to do so, parents offer infants a form of action that is to the development of intentional understanding as "motherese" is to the development of language. Just as the melodic contours of child-directed speech exaggerate important aspects of the componential structure of language, infant-directed motion—we have coined the term "motionese"—highlights the componential structure of intentional action. Gaining a better understanding of motionese and how it benefits infants' structure detection and redescription will inform our general understanding of how action-processing skills develop, and it may also facilitate the design of new interventions for children with action-processing deficits.

DEFICITS IN ACTION PROCESSING

Autism seems to significantly undercut individuals' ability to discern others' internal states, which in turn undercuts knowledge acquisition and communicative skill (Baron-Cohen, Baldwin, & Crowson, 1997; Preissler & Carey, 2005; but see Gernsbacher, Stevenson, Khandakhar, & Goldsmith, 2009 and Sebanz, Knoblich, Stumpf, & Prinz, 2005 for an alternative perspective). These disruptions may arise, at least in part, from deficits in basic tendencies related to structure detection and/or redescription of complex, rapidly streaming visual information. Some existing evidence is generally consistent with this idea; for example, individuals with autism display differences in biological motion processing (Blake et al., 2003; Freitag et al., 2008; Klin et al., 2009) and in detecting motion coherence (Milne et al., 2002), both of which could arise from structure-detection difficulties.

As knowledge grows regarding the range of skills utilized in normal action processing, it may be possible to pinpoint some subset of these skills that is selectively impaired in autism. Additionally, with the infancy paradigms under development in tandem with adult research, it may be possible to use emerging methods to detect such impairments at a very early age. Such findings have the potential to guide the development of new interventions to assist early in development.

RELATION TO COGNITIVE NEUROSCIENCE RESEARCH

Recent cognitive neuroscience research has yielded a range of striking findings regarding the neurophysiological concomitants of action processing (Blakemore & Decety, 2001; Grossman, 2008), including discovery of a mirror-neuron system in monkeys and a functional homologue in humans that links actions one perceives with those one produces (e.g., Fogassi et al., 2005; Hamzei et al., 2003). Such evidence has generated a surge of interest in the topic of action processing. The mirror-neuron system responds even when key aspects of the observed action are invisible and must be inferred (Iacoboni et al., 2005), and expertise influences mirror-system responding (e.g., trained ballet dancers display stronger mirror-system activation than novices when viewing ballet; Calvo-Merino et al., 2005). Additionally, mirror-system activation to emotional facial expressions has been observed to differ in individuals with autism relative to normals (Dapretto et al., 2006), offering the possibility of identifying at least one specific neurophysiological marker of autism.

The mirror-neuron system research has produced impressive advances in understanding neurophysiological concomitants of action processing, but it is not without its problems. For example, actions of many different kinds are treated as functionally equivalent for purposes of drawing inferences about the mirror system (e.g., direct manipulative actions such as grasping, tool-based manipulation, facial expressions, actions embedded within sequences). This equivalence assumption is questionable. In some studies scant consideration is given to potentially significant artifacts such as superficial differences in motion trajectories, characteristics of targeted objects, and the like. These artifacts undercut clear interpretation of some of the findings. Additionally, mirror-system research has largely ignored questions of epigenesis, such as when and how the system is assembled developmentally and what kinds of plasticity constraints may impinge on it. These are important gaps in current knowledge begging for investigative attention.

In general, the contributions that neuroimaging techniques can make to understanding human action processing, while potentially groundbreaking, are at present conspicuously limited by a lack of basic starting knowledge about the domain of action processing. Progress is hampered by lack of information regarding the foundational issues under discussion here, such as what discriminations people actually make between actions, what information they focus on to make them, and what mechanisms guide discovery of the relevant information within the motion flow. Focus on these questions can sharpen neuroimaging research by illuminating phenomena and mechanisms for which a neurophysiological account is needed. As initial progress is made, neuroimaging methodologies can in turn benefit investigation of these issues.

BROADER IMPLICATIONS

The science of action processing has the potential to change the way we think about the human mind and the role of culture in shaping the mind. For example, there is strong reason to believe that some part of our skill set for action processing is uniquely human; the ability to infer intentions from action is at best limited even in closely related species such as chimpanzees (e.g., Povinelli & Vonk, 2003; Tomasello, Call, & Hare, 2003). At the same time, it is obvious that any social species must necessarily command a set of core skills for action processing in order to achieve organized social behavior. Sorting this out will provide a novel perspective on uniquely human cognitive mechanisms.

The propensity to adopt an "intentional stance" (Dennett, 1987)—a tendency to interpret others' actions in intentional terms—seems likely to be a universal aspect of human development. However, cultural diversity in human action processing is also likely. Across cultures, one and the same action can carry very different valence; to illustrate, an innocuous act of physical contact in one culture may be regarded as blatantly offensive in another. To be skilled in making sense of others' actions, children need to become attuned to clues providing high-fidelity information about intentions within their culture. Perhaps, as with language, early immersion in a culture's way of life is instrumental to establishing native levels of fluency in these subtleties. To illustrate, detecting a liar in action is known to be a challenging task of intentional inference under the best of circumstances, yet it may be considerably more difficult in a culture one does not encounter until adulthood.

Understanding the interplay of cultural universality and diversity in action processing, and the factors promoting fluency in intentional inference, will have a variety of implications ranging from a better understanding of the acquisition processes involved to new ideas for promoting cross-cultural understanding.

CONCLUSION

In *2001: A Space Odyssey*, Arthur C. Clarke (1968) foretold the advent of HAL, an artificial intelligence who could interpret our actions and, not liking their import, could even take steps to eliminate us. Yet in the year 2011, we still have much to learn about how any device—whether organic or inorganic—taking in dynamic, evanescent motion information over time can interpret that information in meaningful and heuristically valuable ways. We have developed machines that can "watch" us and "hear" us—such as video cameras—but they cannot yet understand us, at least not in anything like full humanistic terms. These devices cannot report on the goals, intentions, emotions, or other subjective experiences of the individuals they depict; only a live human observer can currently do that. Perhaps one day we will be able to flesh out, in detail, how that live human observer gains the ability to accomplish this interpretive feat. This enterprise can yield crucial knowledge about the nature of the human mind as well as information that enables us to promote the social and cognitive well-being of those for whom action processing does not come naturally.

ACKNOWLEDGMENTS

My gratitude to the colleagues who have helped to foster ideas and empirical progress on these topics, including Annika Andersson, Jodie Baird, Rebecca Brand, M. Angela Clark, Philip DeCamp, Jason Dooley, Bridgette Martin Hard, Jennifer LaBounty, Jeffery Loucks, Meredith Meyer, Lou Moses, Karen Myhr, Eric Olofson, Deb Roy, Mark Sabbagh, Jenny Saffran, Kara Sage, and Megan Saylor. I am also grateful to the University of Oregon and numerous funding agencies, most recently the Office of Naval Research, for their support of this research program.

REFERENCES

Avrahami, J., & Kareev, Y. (1994). The emergence of events. *Cognition*, 53, 239–261.

Baldwin, D. (2005). Discerning intentions: Characterizing the cognitive system at play. In B. Homer & C. Tamis-LeMonda (Eds.), *The *development of social cognition and communication* (pp. 117–144). Mahwah, NJ: Erlbaum.

Baldwin, D., Andersson, A., Saffran, J., & Meyer, M. (2008). Cognition. Segmenting dynamic human action via statistical structure. *Cognition, 106,* 1382–1407.

Baldwin, D. A., Baird, J. A., Saylor, M., & Clark, M. A. (2001). Infants parse dynamic human action. *Child Development, 72,* 708–717.

Baldwin, D., Loucks, J., & Sabbagh, M. A. (2008). Pragmatics of human action. In T. F. Shipley & J. M. Zacks (Eds.), *Understanding events: From perception to action* (pp. 96–129). New York: Oxford University Press.

Baron-Cohen, S., Baldwin, D. A., & Crowson, M., (1997). Do children with autism use the speaker's direction of gaze (SDG) strategy to crack the code of language? *Child Development, 68,* 48–57.

Blake, R., Turner, L. M., Smoski, M. J., Pozdol, S. L., & Stone, W. L. (2003). Visual recognition of biological motion is impaired in children with autism. *Psychological Science, 14,* 151–157.

Blakemore, S. J., & Decety, J. (2001). From the perception of action to the understanding of intention. *Nature Reviews Neuroscience, 2,* 561–567.

Brand, R., Baldwin, D. A., & Ashburn, L. (2002). Evidence for "motionese": Modifications in mothers' infant-directed action. *Developmental Science, 5,* 72–83.

Calvo-Merino, B., Glaser, D. E., Grezes, J., Passingham, R. E., & Haggard, P. (2005). Action observation and acquired motor skills: An fMRI study with expert dancers. *Cerebral Cortex, 8,* 1243–1249.

Cassimatis, N. L. (2009). Flexible inference with structured knowledge through reasoned unification. *IEEE Intelligent Systems, 24*(4), 59–67.

Cheng, P. W. (1997). From covariation to causation: A causal power theory. *Psychological Review, 104,* 367–405.

Clarke, A. C. (1968). *2001: A space odyssey.* New York: Signet.

Dapretto, M., Davies, M. S., Pfeifer, J. J., Scott, A. A., Sigman, M., Bookheimer, S. Y., & Iacoboni, M. (2006). Understanding emotions in others: mirror neuron dysfunction in children with autism spectrum disorders. *Nature Neuroscience, 9*(1), 28–30.

Dennett, D. C. (1987). *The intentional stance.* Cambridge, MA: MIT Press.

Fogassi, L., Ferrari, P. F., Gesierich, B., Rozzi, S., Chersi, F., & Rizzolati, G. (2005). Parietal lobe: From action organization to intention understanding. *Science, 308,* 662–667.

Freitag, C. M., Konrad, C., Haberlen, M., Kleser, C., von Gontard, A., Reith, W., Troje, N. F., & Krick, C. (2008). Perception of biological motion in autism spectrum disorders. *Neuropsychologia, 46,* 1480–1494.

Gentner, D., Holyoak, K. J., & Kokinov, B. N. (2001). *The analogical mind: Perspectives from cognitive science.* Cambridge, MA: MIT Press.

Gernsbacher, M. A., Stevenson, J. L., Khandakhar, S., & Goldsmith, H. H. (2009). Why is joint attention atypical in autism? *Child Development Perspectives.*

Gopnik, A., Glymour, C., Sobel, D., Schulz, L., Kushnir, T., & Danks, D. (2004). A theory of causal learning in children: Causal maps and Bayes nets. *Psychological Review, 111,* 1–31.

Grossman, E. D. (2008). Neurophysiology of action recognition. In T. F. Shipley & J. Zacks (Eds.), *Understanding events: How humans see, represent, and act on events* (pp. 335–362). New York: Oxford University Press.

Haberlandt, K., Graesser, A. C., Schneider, N. J., & Kiely, J. (1986). Effects of task and new arguments on word reading times. *Journal of Memory and Language, 25,* 314–322.

Hamzei, F., Rijntjes, M., Dettmers, C., Glauche, V., Weiller, C., & Büchel, C. (2003). The human action recognition system and its relationship to Broca's area: An fMRI study. *NeuroImage, 19,* 637–644.

Hard, B. M., Recchia, G., & Tversky, B. (2011). The shape of action. *Journal of Experimental Psychology: General, 140,* 586–604.

Hard, B. M., Tversky, B., & Lang, D. (2006). Making sense of abstract events: Building event schemas. *Memory and Cognition, 34,* 1221–1235.

Hauf, P., Aschersleben, G., & Prinz, W. (2007). Baby do—baby see: How action production influences action perception in infants. *Cognitive Development, 22*(1), 16–32.

Hespos, S., Grossman, S. R., & Saylor, M. M. (2010). Infants' ability to parse continuous actions: Further evidence. *Neural Networks, 23,* 1026–1032.

Iacoboni, M., Molnar-Szakacs, I., Gallese, V., Buccino, G., Mazziotta, J. C., & Rizzolatti, G. (2005). Grasping the intentions of others with one's own mirror neuron system. *PLoS Biology, 3,* 529–535.

James, W. (1983). *The principles of psychology.* Cambridge, MA: Harvard University Press. [Original work published in 1890].

Johanssen, G. (1973). Visual perception of biological motion and a model for its analysis. *Perception and Psychophysics, 14,* 201–211.

Klin, A., Lin, D. J., Gorrindo, P., Ramsay, G., & Jones, W. (2009). Two-year-olds with autism orient to nonsocial contingencies rather than biological motion. *Nature, 459*(7244), 257–261.

Loucks, J., & Baldwin, D. A. (2006). When is a grasp a grasp? Characterizing some basic components of human action processing. In K. Hirsh-Pasek & R. Golinkoff (Eds.), *Action meets words: How children learn verbs* (pp. 228–261). New York: Oxford University Press.

Loucks, J., & Baldwin, D. (2009). Sources of information for discriminating dynamic human actions. *Cognition, 111*(1), 84–97.

Loucks, J., & Sommerville, J. A. (2012a). The role of motor experience in understanding action function: The case of the precision grasp. *Child Development, 83*, 801–809.

Loucks, J., & Sommerville, J. A. (2012b). Developmental changes in the discrimination of dynamic human actions in infancy. *Developmental Science, 15*, 123–130

Malle, B. F., Moses, L. J. & Baldwin, D. A. (Eds.). (2001). *Intentions and intentionality: Foundations of social cognition* (pp. 193–206). Cambridge, MA: MIT Press.

Milne, E., Swettenham, J., Hansen, P., Campbell, R., Jeffries, H., & Plaisted, K. (2002). High motion coherence thresholds in children with autism. *Journal of Child Psychology and Psychiatry and Allied Disciplines, 43*, 255–263.

Newtson, D., & Enquist, G. (1976). The perceptual organization of ongoing behavior. *Journal of Experimental Social Psychology, 12*, 436–450.

Olofson, E. (2008). *Infants' processing of action for gist.* Unpublished Ph.D. dissertation, University of Oregon, Eugene.

Olofson, E., & Baldwin, D. (2011). Infants recognize similar goals across dissimilar actions involving object manipulation. *Cognition, 118*(2), 258–264.

Povinelli, D. J., & Vonk, J. (2003). Chimpanzee minds: suspiciously human? *Trends in Cognitive Sciences, 7*, 157–160.

Preissler, M. A., & Carey, S. (2005). The role of inferences about referential intent in word learning: Evidence from autism. *Cognition, 97*, B13–B23.

Scholl, B. J., & Tremoulet, P. D. (2000). Perceptual causality and animacy. *Trends in Cognitive Sciences. 4*, 299–309.

Sebanz, N., Knoblich, G., Stumpf, L., & Prinz, W. (2005). Far from action-blind: Representation of others' actions in individuals with autism. *Cognitive Neuropsychology, 22*, 433–454.

Sommerville, J. A., Woodward, A. L., & Needham, A. (2005). Action experience alters 3-month-old infants' perception of others' actions. *Cognition, 96*, B1–B11.

Tomasello, M. (1999). *The cultural origins of human cognition.* Cambridge, MA: Harvard University Press.

Tomasello, M., Call, J., & Hare, B. (2003). Chimpanzees understand psychological states—the question is which ones and to what extent. *Trends in Cognitive Sciences, 7*, 153–156.

Troje, N. (2008). Retrieving information from human movement patterns. In T. F. Shipley & J. Zacks (Eds.), *Understanding events: How humans see, represent, and act on events* (pp. 308–334) New York: Oxford University Press.

Zacks, J. M., & Tversky, B. (2001). Event structure in perception and cognition. *Psychological Bulletin, 127*, 3–21.

Zacks, J. M., Tversky, B., & Iyer, G. (2001). Perceiving, remembering, and communicating structure in events. *Journal of Experimental Psychology: General, 130*, 29–58.

3.10

Preschoolers Are Selective Word Learners

MARK A. SABBAGH AND ANNETTE M. E. HENDERSON

Children's capacity for rapid word learning is remarkable, particularly given the opacity of speakers' communicative intentions. When a speaker points to an object and uses a word in an ostensive frame, such as "This is a *blicket*," children make the usually correct guess that the word is a label for the whole object and that it will extend to other whole objects of similar shape or kind, even though there is no reason to make either inference based on the utterance itself (Markman, 1989). Children make these guesses even when the speaker is not obviously trying to teach a label, such as when labels are provided during the course of play (e.g., "Should we put on the baby's *shirt*?"), in indirect requests (e.g., "Could you hand me the *chromium* one?"), and even in talk that the child simply overhears (see Hall & Waxman, 2004 for a recent collection of papers). Adult humans are not even required to teach children words. Children learn words simply by sitting on their mother's lap while hearing a word from a stereo speaker co-occur with a line drawing presented on a computer screen (Werker, Cohen, Lloyd, Stager, & Cassosola, 1998).

Yet, recent work from our lab and others' shows that children are not simply remarkable word learners; they are remarkably *selective* word learners. In this chapter, we argue that preschool-aged children suspend their usual rapid semantic encoding processes when there is evidence that a word's meaning might not be shared by others within their linguistic communities.

THE IMPORTANCE OF BEING SELECTIVE

Most theories of cognitive and conceptual development admit a critical role for experience in shaping developmental timetables and trajectories. To some extent, these theories work from idealized models of experience whereby expert adults provide reliable (if subtle) information to children in settings that permit rapid and deep processing

of that information. Research has shown, however, that experience does not always conform to those ideals—even one-on-one parent–child conversation is complex, noisy, and occasionally unreliable. To illustrate, we recently explored the complexity of labeling in everyday settings by presenting parents and their preschool-aged children with groups of toys, some of which had labels that would be known by parents, others that would not (Henderson & Sabbagh, 2010). We reasoned that if parents were focused only on providing "reliable" labels for their children, they would avoid labeling objects when they were unsure of the label. However, parents used labels to refer to objects from a standpoint of ignorance regularly. Indeed, roughly 25% of their utterances directed to these objects of unknown labels were ostensive speech acts that are usually interpreted as having a goal of labeling (e.g., "That is some kind of car."). Thus, when parents come across objects with unknown labels, they frequently provide their word-learning children with data about word-referent associations that are only as reliable as their guesses. From the child's perspective, selectively avoiding learning in these circumstances would make word learning more efficient and less prone to frequent communicative failures.

ONE SPECIFIC STRATEGY: AVOID LEARNING FROM IGNORANT SPEAKERS

Such selective learning relies on two interrelated factors. The first is that children must have some principle that sensitizes them to the fact that they should not learn from ignorant speakers. This principle might be a specific one related directly to entailments of the concept of ignorance (i.e., ignorant speakers are "wrong"). Alternatively, there might be a more general principle, which is a possibility that we will discuss in the next section. The second factor is that there must be information present in the labeling context that can support inferences related to the principle. For instance, if children have a strategy of avoiding learning from ignorant speakers, there has to be some clue in the labeling context indicating that the speaker is ignorant.

In our naturalistic study, we found that when labeling things that they did not know the conventional labels for, parents typically provided an explicit statement of their ignorance or uncertainty (e.g., "I don't know…") or a paralinguistic marker of uncertainty (e.g., filled pause such as "uh…"). These signals were present in almost 90% of the cases in which parents labeled objects for their preschoolers from the standpoint of ignorance. Thus, children have plenty of information to work with to avoid learning from ignorant speakers. The question is whether they capitalize on this information.

There is a substantial body of research suggesting that children do not learn from speakers who explicitly signal their ignorance. In one study, Sabbagh and Baldwin (2001) presented 3- and 4-year-old children with a situation in which an experimenter wanted to help a friend ("Birdie") by sending her a "blicket" from a toy chest. For half the children the experimenter said he knew which of the three toys in the chest was the blicket, but for the other half, the experimenter said he did not know (i.e., "I'd like to help my friend Birdie, but I don't know what a blicket is."). Nonetheless, the experimenter in both conditions pointed to and labeled an object as a blicket, which was then sent to the friend along with the other objects. Immediately following the labeling, children were given an elicited production test and then later were given a multiple-choice comprehension test. Children who heard the label from the ignorant speaker showed no evidence of learning the label in either test, whereas children who heard the label from the knowledgeable speaker performed well.

A number of studies since have shown that children can also attend to even more subtle signs that a speaker may be ignorant, such as linguistic and paralinguistic expressions of uncertainty (Birch, Akmal, & Frampton, 2010; Jaswal & Malone, 2007; Sabbagh & Baldwin, 2001). These findings show that children are well equipped to capitalize on the kinds of information that parents naturally provide to avoid learning from ignorant speakers.

Another kind of information that children might be able to use to guide their word learning is the speaker's history of accuracy. A number of studies now have suggested that when confronted with a choice, children are more likely to learn a new word from a speaker who accurately named things in the past than from someone who was "inaccurate" in the past (i.e., called a shoe a "ball") (Koenig, Clement, & Harris, 2004). As some have noted, however, it is unclear that children necessarily take speakers' prior "inaccuracies" as evidence of ignorance (Lucas & Lewis, 2010). Nonetheless, the findings do provide some further evidence that children selectively learn from speakers who are "reliable" informants.

A MORE GENERAL STRATEGY: AVOID LEARNING INEFFECTIVE COMMUNICATIVE TOOLS

Words have meanings by social convention. There is nothing about an apple that demands that it be called as such, which is obvious when considering its different names across languages (e.g., *maçã*, *pomme*, *jabloko*). What makes a word "right" or "wrong" is the extent to which it is likely to be an effective communicative tool within a particular linguistic community. In the context of the present discussion, word meanings that issue from ignorant speakers are wrong because they are unlikely to be shared by others. There is some evidence that young children understand this social conventional nature of word meanings (Sabbagh & Henderson, 2007). This raises the intriguing hypothesis that children's selectivity in learning might stem from a more general principle of avoiding words that are unlikely to be effective communicative tools within their linguistic community.

We recently explored a strong prediction that comes out of this hypothesis (Henderson, Sabbagh, & Woodward, in press). We reasoned that if children are focused on learning words that are effective communicative tools within their own known group of speakers, they might not learn words for novel toys when they are told that those toys came from another community. After all, learning a word meaning that has no shared meaning within one's own community would have no immediate communicative utility to children. To test this possibility, an experimenter presented preschoolers with a group of three toys that belonged to a friend, one of which was an "uzma," though the experimenter was not sure which one. Half the children were told that the toys were purchased in a faraway country (Japan in one study, a novel country name in another study), and the other half were told that the toys were purchased close by ("downtown" in one study, "at the mall" in another). After the experimenter and child explored all three toys, the friend who owned the toys entered, established joint attention with the child and labeled one as an "uzma." After a brief delay, children were tested in a comprehension test. Results from three studies using this general setup showed that preschoolers were more likely to learn the names of the toys when they were told that the toys came from nearby than when they were told that the toys came from far away. Although there is still more work to do, these results are consistent with the view that children avoid learning words that are unlikely to be useful communicative tools within their linguistic communities.

AVOIDING LEARNING BY BLOCKING SEMANTIC ENCODING

Children have many mechanisms for learning that might be considered relatively passive and automatic. These mechanisms can be broadly characterized as processes for detecting statistical covariance of words and their referents, particularly across situations (Yu & Smith, 2007). Over time, it is argued, these mechanisms become efficient to the point of enabling the kind of single-trial learning that characterizes children's word learning. The only prerequisite for their operation is that children pay attention to the language-related events in their environment. How is it, then, that children fail to learn from an ignorant speaker or in the cases when labels might be ineffective communicative tools?

To form a semantic representation from a labeling event, children have to do two things. First, they have to attend to and encode the labeling event (i.e., "She called that thing a blicket."). Then, based upon that labeling event representation, they need to create a conventional semantic representation (i.e., "That thing *is* a blicket."). Presumably, children could avoid learning from ignorant speakers, then, by disrupting either of these processes. That is, children might not pay attention to ignorant speakers and thus not encode ignorant speakers' labeling events. Or children might encode ignorant speakers' labeling events but then suspend the usual processes that allow for the rapid creating of semantic representations.

We explored this question in a simple study that used the "ignorant speaker" paradigm that we used with preschoolers to show selective learning in prior work, with an added twist to the comprehension question (Sabbagh & Shafman, 2009). Half of the preschoolers were asked the standard comprehension test question that explicitly asks

about a semantic representation (i.e., "Which one of these things is the *modi*?"). The other half were asked a comprehension test question about the labeling event itself (i.e., "Which one did I say is the *modi*?"). The results were striking. When a knowledgeable speaker presented children with the words, the type of question did not affect their performance. However, when an ignorant speaker presented the words, children performed well when asked about the events but were at chance when asked about the semantic representations. That is, when taught by ignorant speakers, preschoolers correctly answered, "Which one did I say is a modi?" but were unsystematic when asked, "Which one *is* a modi?" Thus, when confronted with an ignorant speaker, children pay attention to the speaker and encode their labeling utterance, but they specifically block the processes that are associated with creating the semantic representation. These findings show that preschoolers do not ignore ignorant speakers. They attend to their utterances, and when asked about the specifics of the labeling event, they can answer accurately. What they appear to be doing, then, is blocking whatever processes usually lead to forming a conventional semantic representation based upon that labeling event.

This is interesting for several reasons. First, although we can presume that some process must be responsible for connecting labeling events with semantic representations, that process has not been characterized in the developmental literature. Some hint about what must occur might come from the adult literature on the distinction between episodic and semantic memory (Tulving, 2002). According to this model, attended events are stored in episodic memory systems associated with the hippocampal and parahippocampal regions of the medial temporal lobe. Over time, the episodic memory becomes "consolidated" into neo-cortical semantic memory systems. Perhaps children confronted with ignorant speakers form episodic memories but then do not engage the processes that usually rapidly consolidate those memories into conventional semantic representations.

It is also interesting that this strategy of forming an episodic but not a semantic representation of labels that issue from ignorant speakers might be advantageous. For instance, if the same ignorant speaker used the same label again, children might have a basis for learning something about the speaker (i.e., "She thinks this is a blicket."). Similarly, if a second speaker used the same label, children might elaborate the episodic representation to learn something about the practices of a highly circumscribed community (i.e., "They call this a blicket."). These representations are distinct from the decontextualized conventional semantic representations (i.e., "This *is* a blicket.") and thus might enable children to communicate effectively within contexts that are specified within the event representations and avoid errors within a larger community.

CONCLUSIONS AND CONNECTIONS

Children are selective word learners. Based on our work, we think children specifically avoid learning in cases in which they have reason to suspect that the word will not be a useful communicative tool, such as when the speaker is ignorant or the meaning has a low probability of being shared within children's linguistic communities. Finally, it does not seem that children are ignoring speakers in these circumstances. They are attending and encoding the labeling events, but are not engaging the processes that usually lead to semantic representations.

There are other instances of children being selective about the sources they will learn from. For instance, 2-year-olds have difficulty learning about the location of an object when they were presented with the information via videotape (Troseth, Saylor, & Archer, 2006). Similarly, infants can learn to discriminate non-native speech sounds when presented with ambient speech from a live teacher, but not from a videotaped teacher (Kuhl, 2007). Additionally, although not evidence of selective learning, per se, even very young infants are selective in their attention to potential social sources of information. For instance, 5- to 6-month-old infants direct more attention toward an individual who was previously shown speaking their language than an individual who was shown speaking a foreign language (Kinzler, Dupoux, & Spelke, 2007). These phenomena show that the roots of preschoolers' selective word learning might be found in early development.

ACKNOWLEDGMENTS

Preparation of this chapter was supported by a grant from the Social Sciences and Humanities Research Council of Canada (SSHRC) to M. A. Sabbagh. We thank Kate Harkness and Valerie Kuhlmeier for helpful comments on a previous draft.

REFERENCES

Birch, S. A. J., Akmal, N., & Frampton, K. L. (2010). Two year olds are vigilant of others' non-verbal cues to credibility. *Developmental Science, 13,* 363–369.

Hall, D. G., & Waxman, S. R. (2004). *Weaving a lexicon.* Cambridge, MA: MIT Press.

Henderson, A. M. E., & Sabbagh, M. A., & Woodward, A. L. (in press). Preschoolers' selective learning is guided by the principle of relevance. *Cognition.* http://dx.doi.org/10.1016/j.cognition.2012.10.006

Henderson, A. M. E., & Sabbagh, M. A. (2010). Parents' use of conventional and unconventional labels in conversations with their preschoolers. *Journal of Child Language, 37,* 793–816.

Jaswal, V. K., & Malone, L. S. (2007). Turning believers into skeptics: 3-year-olds' sensitivity to cues to speaker credibility. *Journal of Cognition and Development, 8,* 263–283.

Kinzler, K. D., Dupoux, E., & Spelke, E. S. (2007). The native language of social cognition. *Proceedings of the National Academy of Science USA, 104,* 12577–12580.

Koenig, M. A., Clement, F., & Harris, P. L. (2004). Trust in testimony: Children's use of true and false statements. *Psychological Science, 15,* 694–698.

Kuhl, P. K. (2007). Is speech learning "gated" by the social brain? *Developmental Science, 10,* 110–120.

Lucas, A. J., & Lewis, C. (2010). Should we trust experiments on trust? *Human Development, 53,* 167–172.

Markman, E. M. (1989). *Categorization and naming in children.* Cambridge, MA: MIT Press.

Sabbagh, M. A., & Baldwin, D. A. (2001). Learning words from knowledgeable versus ignorant speakers: Links between preschoolers' theory of mind and semantic development. *Child Development, 72,* 1054–1070.

Sabbagh, M. A., & Henderson, A. M. E. (2007). How an appreciation of conventionality shapes early word learning. *New Directions for Child and Adolescent Development, 115,* 25–37.

Sabbagh, M. A., & Shafman, D. (2009). How children block learning from ignorant speakers. *Cognition, 112,* 415–422.

Troseth, G. L., Saylor, M. M., & Archer, A. H. (2006). Young children's use of video as a source of socially relevant information *Child Development, 77,* 786–799.

Tulving, E. (2002). Episodic memory: From mind to brain. *Annual Reviews Psychology, 53,* 1–25.

Werker, J. F., Cohen, L. B., Lloyd, V., Stager, C., & Cassosola, M. (1998). Acquisition of word-object associations by 14-month-old infants. *Developmental Psychology, 34,* 1289–1309.

Yu, C., & Smith, L. B. (2007). Rapid word learning under uncertainty via cross-situational statistics. *Psychological Science, 18,* 414–420.

3.11

Culture-Gene Coevolutionary Theory and Children's Selective Social Learning

MACIEJ CHUDEK, PATRICIA BROSSEAU-LIARD,
SUSAN BIRCH, AND JOSEPH HENRICH

Humans have an unusual ability to socially learn complex, arbitrary information—we learn from others how to build kayaks, write papers, and fold them into airplanes. These social learning capacities made possible the accumulation of complex, culturally transmitted technologies we now rely on and likely underlie our capacity for large-scale cooperation (Chudek & Henrich, 2011). Evolutionary and developmental insights into children's social learning have great potential for cross-fertilization. Evolutionary theories can generate and integrate developmental hypotheses, while developmental investigations test and inform evolutionary theory. However, this intersection is also rich with potential for spurious storytelling. Developing *good* accounts of the evolution of the development of social learning is a real challenge.

Why does our social cognition develop as it does? Why do young minds possess the specific cognitive mechanisms that they do, not some other set? What is hard about answering these questions is that it is so easy. For any aspect of social cognition, one can easily generate tens of plausible evolutionary stories about how it helped our ancestors survive (really, try it with a friend). Unfortunately, the meager traces left by the past make most evolutionary stories impossible to either verify or refute.

To generate verifiable ultimate hypotheses, theorists face the much harder challenge of deducing past adaptations a priori, without reference to modern social cognition. This can sometimes be accomplished by starting from physical evidence of our species' history and reasoning forward by way of explicit, typically mathematical, arguments grounded strictly in evolutionary theory. The resulting ultimate theories can generate precise, falsifiable, a priori predictions about modern cognition. Though they remain hard to definitively verify as explanations for any single social-cognitive-developmental effect, these hypotheses are tested by their ability to integrate a broad spectrum of evidence under the umbrella of very few assumptions about the ancient past. For example, evolutionary models of optimal conformity rates for social learners (e.g., Boyd & Richerson, 1985, among others) agree not only with human behavior (Efferson, Lalive, Richerson, McElreath, & Lubell, 2008; Toelch, Bruce, Meeus, & Reader, 2010) but also social learning in rats (Galef & Whiskin, 2008) and fish (Pike & Laland, 2010).

Here we review Culture-Gene Coevolutionary (CGC) theory (e.g., Boyd & Richerson, 1985; Mesoudi, 2009; Richerson & Boyd, 2005), which, taking just this tack, predicted in advance several recent findings on the development of social cognition. We briefly describe the evolutionary dynamics that ground CGC, then review the predictions that these dynamics entail for the development of social cognition and their fit to recent findings.

Evolved Cumulative Cultural Learning and the Development of Social Cognition

Though some cultural learning—that is, the social transmission of behaviors from one individual to another—is present in other species, only humans learn faithfully enough that culture accumulates and gradually generates complex behaviors, such as baking and origami. This, along with other evidence (e.g., see Richerson & Boyd, 2005), suggests that sophisticated, metabolically expensive brains capable of cumulative cultural learning are selected against (i.e., genetic mutants with more sophisticated brains have fewer surviving offspring) until a species' cultural repertoire (i.e., the cultural knowhow transmitted between generations) provides a substantial fitness advantage. Once this threshold is passed,[1] culture accumulates and its fitness consequences grow exponentially—a positive feedback that generates strong genetic selection for brains better at cultural learning.

Since culture changes much faster than genes, direct genetic adaptations for better cultural learning must exploit cues that reliably distinguish better from worse cultural models across social groups and generations. CGC theorists have outlined several ecological cues that any highly cultural species should exploit. In particular, "model biases"—features of cultural models (i.e., other individuals) that reliably indicate bearers of better (i.e., more fitness-enhancing) cultural knowledge—imply phenotypic predictions about the development of social cognition. These predictions can be divided into two classes: "Relative model biases" help learners identify models possessing knowledge relevant to them (i.e., it applies to their age, sex, social, or cultural group), and "absolute model biases" help identify models whose cultural knowledge is just better (e.g., more accurate or useful).

Next, we will briefly explain the logic of each prediction and its fit to recent evidence. Some predictions will seem quite obvious to readers fortunate enough to have already studied modern human children, but remember: the test of ultimate theories is not how well they explain any one effect (that is easy), it is how easily they account for a vast range of modern phenomena, even retrospectively obvious ones, by reasoning forward from an ancestral state where they did not exist, invoking as few assumptions as possible.

Relative Model Bias: Age

Sometimes different behaviors are more fitness enhancing for human juveniles (e.g., acting cute) than for adults (e.g., sexual courtship). Consequently, selection will consistently favor cultural learners who discriminate potential models by age over learners less sensitive to model age, particularly favoring a disposition to learn from "slightly older" models (Henrich & Gil-White, 2001). Consistent with this simple

prediction, young children do seem to assess the age of cultural models: They prefer older models unless they have proven unreliable (Jaswal & Neely, 2006) but younger models in domains relevant to young people (e.g., toys: VanderBorght & Jaswal, 2009); and they are more likely to learn preferences (Shutts, Banaji, & Spelke, 2010) and a variety of other behaviors (see Hilmert, Kulik, & Christenfeld, 2006) from similarly aged models.

Relative Model Bias: Self-Similarity (Including Sex)

Sexual and social divisions of labor are common in contemporary foraging societies. Divisions present in ancestral societies would have favored learners who prefer learning from models who are most "like them" (e.g., same sex, same social group, etc.) (Henrich & Gil-White, 2001; Henrich & McElreath, 2003). Evidence that children preferentially learn from self-similar, particularly same-sex models, is decades old (e.g., Rosekrans, 1967; Wolf, 1973) and recent work has shown that they preferentially acquire same-sex models' preferences (Shutts et al., 2010). Moreover, children (Gottfried & Katz, 1977) and adults (e.g., Hilmert et al., 2006) seem particularly disposed to learn from those who share their existing beliefs.

Relative Model Bias: Ethnicity (Including Language and Accent)

The use of fitness-neutral cues to distinguish cultural groups (e.g., body markings, accent; sometimes called *ethnicity*) is a natural consequence of cultural learning (McElreath, Boyd, & Richerson, 2003). Another consequence is plentiful "coordination dilemmas"—situations where it is better to behave like your group members (e.g., norms, etiquette, morals). Together these lend selective advantage to young learners who prefer learning from their coethnics.

Five- to 6-month-olds prefer looking at individuals with familiar accents, 10-month-olds prefer accepting toys from and eating food associated with linguistic coethnics, while 5-year-olds prefer them as playmates (Kinzler, Dupoux, & Spelke, 2007; Kinzler, Shutts, DeJesus, & Spelke, 2009; Shutts, Kinzler, McKee, & Spelke, 2009). Four- to 5-year-olds preferentially trust novel object functions demonstrated by a native-sounding speaker who speaks only nonsense syllables over a non-native-sounding speaker (Kinzler, Corriveau, & Harris, 2010). Five-year-olds also make potent social inductions on the basis of ethnic labels (Diesendruck & HaLevi, 2006).

---

[1] For an account of when and why our ancestors in particular passed this threshold, see Richerson and Boyd (2005).

Absolute Model Bias: Skill

A young mind that can perceive skill[2] differences between potential models can make wiser learning decisions. For instance, young learners might infer the better hunter by who throws further. Termed "skill bias," CGC theorists predicted that cultural learners will exploit perceptible skill differences (Henrich & Gil-White, 2001; Henrich & McElreath, 2003).

Recent investigations have repeatedly demonstrated that children who witness obvious skill differences prefer learning novel object labels (e.g., Koenig & Harris, 2005; Scofield & Behrend, 2008) and functions (e.g., Birch, Vauthier, & Bloom, 2008) from more accurate models, even after a 1-week delay (Corriveau & Harris, 2009b), even when only the more skilled model is a stranger (Corriveau & Harris, 2009a; for a review, see Gelman, 2009). Children also seem sensitive to models' skill at predicting objects' nonobvious causal properties (Sobel & Corriveau, 2010). Young children also prefer learning from more confident cultural models (Birch, Akmal, & Frampton, 2010; Jaswal & Malone, 2007; Sabbagh & Baldwin, 2001), potentially exploiting the model's own assessment of his or her skill.

Absolute Model Bias: Success

Skill differences are often opaque, especially in the limited time learners have to make a decision. For instance, though the relative quality of two adults' diets may be apparent after several years, young learners must choose what to eat for dinner tonight. The cumulative consequences of skill, termed "success" (e.g., a fat belly, fine ornamentation, good outcomes in life), are often readily apparent, even when the mechanisms that generated them are not (Boyd & Richerson, 1985; Henrich & Gil-White, 2001; Henrich & McElreath, 2003). Interestingly, a sensitivity to cues to success may even explain why both North American (Olson, Banaji, Dweck, & Spelke, 2006) and Japanese (Olson, Dunham, Dweck, Spelke, & Banaji, 2008) 5- to 7-year-olds report liking and judging individuals as nicer who have experienced seemingly random, or at least unexplained, positive outcomes as well as members of groups that experience more positive outcomes.

Absolute Model Bias: Prestige

The trappings of success vary across time and societies; for example, a fat belly carries different implications now than it did once. However, one feature is reliably shared by quality cultural models everywhere: Other learners also prefer to learn from them. Henrich and Gil-White (2001) predicted a cultural species would possess a disposition to prefer learning from whomever others are learning from, termed "prestige bias."

Young children prefer learning from models bystanders have previously watched, smiled at, and agreed with (Fusaro & Harris, 2008); however, such explicit agreement could also cue a model's ethnicity (i.e., her membership in the same socially demarked group as the child, her kin, and her peers), her prior accuracy, or how common (rather than accurate) her opinions are. Our own recent work (Chudek, Heller, Birch, & Henrich, 2011) specifically tested the unique effects of prestige by demonstrating that children prefer learning from adult models bystanders have merely preferentially attended to (i.e., no endorsement or positive affect). Moreover, this effect seems domain sensitive; adults watched by bystanders while using tools are preferentially trusted for tool-use techniques but not food preferences.

Overview

Humans are undeniably a highly cultural species. For instance, children trust the testimony of adults over their own perception (Jaswal & Markman, 2007; Topál, Gergely, Miklosi, Erdohegyi, & Csibra, 2008) and imitate adults' obviously redundant actions (Lyons, Young, & Keil, 2007), even when accuracy is incentivized (Jaswal, 2010). CGC predicts which phenotypes—that is, individuals' actual judgments and behaviors—are robustly selected for in a species dependent on cultural learning.

Unlike psychological theories that specify mechanistic explanations for particular behavioral phenomena, CGC refers to the set of predictions derived by reasoning about how selective pressures shaped our cultural species. Though one could generate many proximate theories to account for these same effects, CGC is unique in simultaneously predicting this entire broad set of empirical phenomena from a simple core insight. Though many of these predictions rest on subtle mathematical arguments about natural selection, we verbally summarized their logic earlier and synthesized the developmental evidence they integrate.

CGC reasoning, which unfolded in isolation from developmental research, fits well with recent developmental findings. Far from competing with or contradicting proximate explanations, a priori

---

[2] By "skill" we just mean "whatever behavior produces higher fitness on average."

ultimate theories like CGC are consistent with most cognitive mechanisms proposed by developmental psychologists and can complement and help conceptually organize the diverse findings emerging from developmental investigations of social cognition. They answer a differed kind of question: Rather than explaining how cognitive mechanisms influence children's behavior, they help us understand why these particular mechanisms should exist in the first place. They are also an excellent source of generativity; that is, they suggest previously unconsidered phenomena—such as prestige bias—worthy of empirical study and proximate explanation. We therefore propose CGC theory as a useful framework for organizing and understanding the rapidly emerging mix of developmental insights into children's selective social learning.

REFERENCES

Birch, S. A. J., Akmal, N., & Frampton, K. L. (2010). Two year olds are vigilant of others' non verbal cues to credibility. *Developmental Science, 13*(2), 363–369.

Birch, S. A. J., Vauthier, S. A., & Bloom, P. (2008). Three- and four-year-olds spontaneously use others' past performance to guide their learning. *Cognition, 107*(3), 1018–1034.

Boyd, R., & Richerson, P. J. (1985). *Culture and the evolutionary process.* Chicago, IL: University of Chicago Press.

Chudek, M., & Henrich, J. (2011). Culture-Gene Coevolution, norm-psychology and the emergence of human prosociality. *Trends in Cognitive Science, 15*(5), 218–226.

Chudek, M., Heller, S., Birch, S., & Henrich, J. (2011). Prestige-biased cultural learning: bystander's differential attention to potential models influences children's learning. *Evolution and Human Behavior, 33*(1), 46–56.

Corriveau, K., & Harris, P. L. (2009a). Choosing your informant: Weighing familiarity and recent accuracy. *Developmental Science, 12*(3), 426–437.

Corriveau, K., & Harris, P. L. (2009b). Preschoolers continue to trust a more accurate informant 1 week after exposure to accuracy information. *Developmental Science, 12*(1), 188–193.

Diesendruck, G., & HaLevi, H. (2006). The role of language, appearance, and culture in children's social category based induction. *Child Development, 77*(3), 539–553.

Efferson, C., Lalive, R., Richerson, P. J., McElreath, R., & Lubell, M. (2008). Conformists and mavericks: The empirics of frequency-dependent cultural transmission. *Evolution and Human Behavior, 29*(1), 56–64.

Fusaro, M., & Harris, P. (2008). Children assess informant reliability using bystanders' non verbal cues. *Developmental Science, 11*(5), 771–777.

Galef, B., & Whiskin, E. (2008). Conformity in Norway rats? *Animal Behaviour, 75*(6), 2035–2039.

Gelman, S. (2009). Learning from others: Children's construction of concepts. *Annual Review of Psychology, 60*, 115.

Gottfried, A., & Katz, P. (1977). Influence of belief, race, and sex similarities between child observers and models on attitudes and observational learning. *Child Development, 48*(4), 1395–1400.

Henrich, J., & Gil-White, F. (2001). The evolution of prestige: Freely conferred deference as a mechanism for enhancing the benefits of cultural transmission. *Evolution and Human Behavior, 22*(3), 165–196.

Henrich, J., & McElreath, R. (2003). The evolution of cultural evolution. *Evolutionary Anthropology: Issues, News, and Reviews, 12*(3), 123–135.

Hilmert, C., Kulik, J., & Christenfeld, N. (2006). Positive and negative opinion modeling: The influence of another's similarity and dissimilarity. *Journal of Personality and Social Psychology, 90*(3), 440–452.

Jaswal, V. (2010). Believing what you're told: Young children's trust in unexpected testimony about the physical world. *Cognitive Psychology, 61*(3), 248–272.

Jaswal, V., & Malone, L. (2007). Turning believers into skeptics: 3-year-olds' sensitivity to cues to speaker credibility. *Journal of Cognition and Development, 8*(3), 263–283.

Jaswal, V., & Markman, E. (2007). Looks aren't everything: 24-month-olds' willingness to accept unexpected labels. *Journal of Cognition and Development, 8*(1), 93–111.

Jaswal, V., & Neely, L. (2006). Adults don't always know best. *Psychological Science, 17*(9), 757.

Kinzler, K. D., Corriveau, K., & Harris, P. (2010). Children's selective trust in native accented speakers. *Developmental Science, 14*(1), 106–111.

Kinzler, K. D., Dupoux, E., & Spelke, E. S. (2007). The native language of social cognition. *Proceedings of the National Academy of Sciences USA, 104*(30), 12577–12580.

Kinzler, K. D., Shutts, K., DeJesus, J., & Spelke, E. (2009). Accent trumps race in guiding children's social preferences. *Social Cognition, 27*(4), 623–634.

Koenig, M., & Harris, P. (2005). Preschoolers mistrust ignorant and inaccurate speakers. *Child Development, 76*(6), 1261–1277.

Lyons, D., Young, A., & Keil, F. (2007). The hidden structure of overimitation. *Proceedings of the National Academy of Sciences USA, 104*(50), 19751.

McElreath, R., Boyd, R., & Richerson, P. J. (2003). Shared norms and the evolution of ethnic markers. *Current Anthropology, 44*(1), 122–129.

Mesoudi, A. (2009). How cultural evolutionary theory can inform social psychology and vice versa. *Psychological Review, 116*(4), 929–952.

Olson, K., Banaji, M., Dweck, C., & Spelke, E. (2006). Children's biased evaluations of lucky versus unlucky people and their social groups. *Psychological Science, 17*(10), 845.

Olson, K., Dunham, Y., Dweck, C., Spelke, E., & Banaji, M. (2008). Judgments of the lucky across development and culture. *Journal of Personality and Social Psychology, 94*(5), 757.

Pike, T. W., & Laland, K. N. (2010). Conformist learning in nine-spined sticklebacks' foraging decisions. *Biology Letters, 6*(4), 466–468.

Richerson, P., & Boyd, R. (2005). *Not by genes alone: How culture transformed human evolution.* Chicago, IL: University of Chicago Press.

Rosekrans, M. (1967). Imitation in children as a function of perceived similarity to a social model and vicarious reinforcement. *Journal of Personality and Social Psychology, 7*(3), 307–315.

Sabbagh, M., & Baldwin, D. (2001). Learning words from knowledgeable versus ignorant speakers: Links between preschoolers' theory of mind and semantic development. *Child Development, 72*(4), 1054–1070.

Scofield, J., & Behrend, D. (2008). Learning words from reliable and unreliable speakers. *Cognitive Development, 23*(2), 278–290.

Shutts, K., Banaji, M., & Spelke, E. (2010). Social categories guide young children's preferences for novel objects. *Developmental Science, 13*(4), 599–610.

Shutts, K., Kinzler, K., McKee, C., & Spelke, E. (2009). Social information guides infants' selection of foods. *Journal of Cognition and Development, 10*(1), 1–17.

Sobel, D., & Corriveau, K. (2010). Children monitor individuals' expertise for word learning. *Child Development, 81*(2), 669–679.

Toelch, U., Bruce, M. J., Meeus, M. T. H., & Reader, S. M. (2010). Humans copy rapidly increasing choices in a multiarmed bandit problem. *Evolution and Human Behavior, 31*(5), 326–333.

Topál, J., Gergely, G., Miklosi, A., Erdohegyi, A., & Csibra, G. (2008). Infants' perseverative search errors are induced by pragmatic misinterpretation. *Science, 321*(5897), 1831.

VanderBorght, M., & Jaswal, V. (2009). Who knows best? Preschoolers sometimes prefer child informants over adult informants. *Infant and Child Development, 18*(1), 61–71.

Wolf, T. (1973). Effects of live modeled sex-inappropriate play behavior in a naturalistic setting. *Developmental Psychology, 9*(1), 120–123.

3.12

How Causal Learning Helps Us Understand Other People and How Other People Help Us Learn About Causes

Probabilistic Models and the Development of Social Cognition

ALISON GOPNIK, ELIZABETH SEIVER, AND DAPHNA BUCHSBAUM

Since the emergence of Theory of Mind research some 25 years ago, it has been a commonplace that understanding how other people function is crucially important for social life. Figuring out how perceptions lead to beliefs, or how intentions cause actions, can help us to make predictions about what people will do and to design ways to get them to do what we want. Developmental psychologists have charted the changes in children's causal understanding of the mind, and they have begun to extend this work to children's causal understanding of the social world more generally—their understanding of intelligence and effort, in-groups and out-groups, race and gender, and even good and evil.

Many researchers have suggested that our adult social knowledge is like a set of intuitive everyday theories—coherent, abstract causal representations that, much like scientific theories, allow us to make new predictions about the world around us and to act to change that world. Children develop and revise these theories in much the same way that scientists do. This "theory theory" has been articulated both in developmental and social psychology, though the similar ideas in the two fields have rather surprisingly only come together recently (see, e.g., Ames et al., 2001; Carey, 1985; Chiu, Hong, & Dweck, 1997; Gopnik & Meltzoff, 1997; Gopnik & Wellman, 1992; Wellman & Gelman, 1992).

Typically, research on the development of these intuitive social theories has examined when particular kinds of social knowledge emerge. But there is a deeper question to ask, not just when but why and how? Why do these changes take place? How is it possible for children to develop an increasingly accurate view of the social world, especially since the social world is even more subject to cultural and historical variation than the physical world? And then there is an even deeper question. The fundamental assumption of cognitive science is that we can understand the brain as a kind of computer designed by evolution and programmed by experience—though a computer far more powerful than any we know of now. What kinds of computations could underlie the remarkable human capacity for social learning specifically?

In the past we did not have the right tools for a computational account of intuitive theories in adults or their development in children. This reflected a deeper theoretical tension at the heart of developmental cognitive science. Children— even infants—have abstract, structured representations of the world, including intuitive theories of the mind and other people more generally. At the same time, children learn in prodigious amounts. They transform their representations of other people based on concrete experiences—the contingent, probabilistic evidence they see about what people do. How do children infer abstract psychological and social structure from the concrete contingencies of human action?

Until recently, the theoretical and computational possibilities on offer have not given a satisfying answer to this question. Connectionist theories allowed learning but denied that there are abstract representations; nativist theories allowed representation but denied that there is substantive learning. Although Piaget famously suggested "constructivism" as a middle path, he offered little detail about how constructivist processes might work.

This problem is particularly vivid and relevant for social cognition. One might be able to provide an associationist account of relatively concrete kinds of knowledge like our ability to recognize objects or perform simple motor tasks. Or you might be able to justify a nativist account of such universally similar cognitive abilities as our ability to perceive three-dimensional spatial structure or to use syntax. But social cognition is one of the best examples of knowledge that is at once highly abstract and structured and highly variable across contexts and cultures.

Fortunately, over the past 10 years, researchers in philosophy of science and machine learning have started to explain how theories, including theories of other people, can be represented and changed through probabilistic models and Bayesian learning techniques (Glymour, 2001; Griffiths & Tenenbaum, 2007; Griffiths, Chater, Kemp, Perfors, & Tenenbaum, 2010; Pearl, 2000, Spirtes, Glymour, & Scheines, 1993). This framework promises a computationally precise developmental cognitive science that can integrate structure and learning.

Probabilistic causal models and Bayesian learning formalize the processes we are all familiar with as practicing scientists. As scientists we analyze the probabilistic, statistical patterns in the evidence; we perform experiments; and we use the data from these two sources to infer what causes what and to test and revise our theories. These ideas began in the philosophy of science as a way of saying mathematically how we can best make causal inferences from these kinds of evidence. But they can also help us understand how the mind actually does make these inferences.

In fact, over the past 10 years developmental and cognitive researchers have shown that adults and children actually can solve the problem of causal learning, in general, using implicit probabilistic models (e.g., Gopnik et al., 2004; Gopnik & Schulz, 2007; Gopnik & Tenenbaum, 2007; Lu et al., 2008; Sloman, 2005 for recent reviews see Gopnik 2012; Gopnik & Wellman, 2012). They use statistical evidence and experiments to infer causal structure in a Bayesian way. But almost all of these experiments have focused on physical causality. Researchers have only recently started to apply these ideas to psychological and social causality.

In our lab we have begun to use these ideas to explore some basic questions in social psychology. First, where do our explanations of human action come from? In particular, when do we think that a person's actions are the result of her long-lasting individual personality traits, and when do we think, instead, that those actions are caused by her immediate situation? Forty years of research in social psychology have shown that these attributions have important consequences for how we act and how we treat other people (e.g., Levy & Dweck, 1998). In fact, these attributions can literally be a matter of life and death. For example, did the Abu Ghraib guards torture because they were particularly sadistic people or because of isolation, stress, and a toxic institutional structure?

Western adults show a strong bias, sometimes called "the fundamental attribution error," to answer questions like these by referring to traits rather than situations (Jones & Harris, 1967; Kelley, 1967; Ross, 1977). People from other cultures show much less of a trait bias (Morris & Peng, 1994). Although this bias has been the focus of research in adult social psychology, we know very little about how or why trait attributions and biases develop in the first place. We know something about the "when"—the general consensus in the literature has been that children do not spontaneously explain actions in terms of traits or use those traits to make new predictions until they are about 7 years old—but we do not know why they start to do so (Alvarez, Ruble, & Bolger, 2001; Peevers & Secord, 1973; Rholes & Ruble, 1984; Shimizu, 2000).

An old idea is that we might infer traits based on consistent statistical patterns of behavior (Kelley, 1967). For example, if we see that Josie consistently takes risks across many situations while Anna is consistently risk averse, we may conclude that Josie and Anna's actions are caused by some internal personality trait rather than an external situation.

Probabilistic causal models let us formalize these inferences; they tell us just what sorts of causal inferences we should draw from statistical patterns like these (see Gopnik et al., 2004, Gopnik & Schulz, 2007). Bayesian versions of probabilistic models have an additional advantage: They can explain how our prior knowledge, the knowledge we have accumulated in the past, can interact with the new evidence we observe at a particular time to shape our inferences (Griffiths & Tenenbaum, 2007). We wanted to explore whether these causal learning processes might explain the emergence of trait attributions, in general, and the Western reliance on traits in particular (Seiver, Gopnik, & Goodman, 2012).

We showed 4-year-olds, who do not yet use trait explanations spontaneously, different patterns of contingency between people, situations, and actions. Anna and Josie are little dolls that can play on a miniature trampoline and bicycle. We showed half the children that Anna happily goes on the trampoline and leaps on the bicycle three out of four times, but Josie can only bring herself to get on the trampoline and bicycle one out of four times. We showed the other half of the children that Anna and Josie both bounce on the trampoline three out of four times but only dare approach the bicycle one out of four times. The events are the same, but the statistical patterns are different. If children are making causal inferences in a Bayesian way, they should conclude that the actions are more likely to be caused by traits in the first condition, and by situations in the second.

Then we asked the children to explain why Anna and Josie acted the way they did and to predict what they would do in a new situation. In the first condition, children explained the character's actions in terms of traits (e.g., "She's brave" or "She knows how to ride a bike"), and they predicted that she would continue to be brave in new situations—she would go off the diving board, too. The second group said the children acted that way because of situations—the trampoline was safe and the bicycle was dangerous, and this was also reflected in their predictions. So the pattern of probabilistic covariation led the children to prefer one type of explanation and prediction to the other.

Bayesian inferences depend on two factors, however: the evidence you see and your prior belief in the probability of the hypotheses under consideration. The 4-year-olds in our experiment weighed the evidence equally in the two conditions, which suggested that they initially thought that trait and situation attributions were equally likely. But 6-year-olds already showed a bias toward traits. They did take the evidence into account, but they consistently thought trait explanations were more likely than situation explanations, even when the immediate evidence did not support this. This would make sense, however, if between 4 and 6, children found consistently more support for trait than situation hypotheses, both directly in their observations of what people do and indirectly in the information they receive from others. Such a pattern of evidence would lead to a stronger prior probability for trait rather than situation hypotheses. To explore this possibility, we are testing children in China, who may have less strong evidence for traits than American children.

The attribution literature concerns high-level explanations for human action. But before we can explain actions, we have to identify them. Although this might seem simple, in fact, inferring intentional goal-directed actions from a continuous stream of movements is challenging (Baldwin, Andersson, Saffran, & Meyer, 2008). This difficulty is apparent in the literature on imitation; sometimes children "overimitate," including all the details of a complex adult action (Lyons, Young, & Keil, 2007), and sometimes they only imitate the parts of that action that are relevant to the particular outcome (Gergely, Bekkering, & Király, 2002; Williamson, Meltzoff, & Markman, 2008). Why and how do children choose one analysis of action over another?

In another series of studies, we have shown that children can use statistical information to analyze and imitate actions as well as to explain them (Buchsbaum, Gopnik, Griffiths, & Shafto, 2011). We showed 4-year-old children five sequences of three actions each on a toy (e.g., the experimenter would squish it, then shake it, and then roll it). Some of these sequences, but not others, led to the toy playing music. Children could either imitate all the actions they saw or just choose a subset of the most effective actions. A Bayesian model worked out the probability that different sequences would cause the machine to go, given the patterns of evidence. The children's behavior fit this model well. When the evidence suggested that an action sequence was more likely to produce the effect, they were more likely to produce that sequence, even if they had never seen it in isolation. So children's imitation looked like a rational attempt to use the evidence to make sense of the actions they saw. Imitation, a major engine of social development, reflects a kind of probabilistic causal inference.

A last twist to this study makes an important point, however. In one condition the experimenter acted inept, as if she did not know anything about how the machine worked. In that case the children relied on the evidence. But in another condition the experimenter told the children that she was showing them how the machine worked—and then showed them exactly the same sequence of actions. In that pedagogical condition children were much more likely to overimitate, mimicking everything the experimenter did. So children made different causal inferences depending on the social context.

These studies suggest that there is a two-way interaction between causal learning and social knowledge. Children clearly use causal inference to draw important conclusions about the social world around them. At the same time their knowledge of the social world may itself shape the kinds of inferences they make, as in the contrast between the pedagogical teacher and the inept demonstrator. In a way that Piaget would have appreciated, this back and forth between what we already know about people and what we learn about them lets us slowly but surely make progress in understanding the complexities of social life. The new computational tools of probabilistic models and Bayesian inference can let us understand this learning in a deeper way.

ACKNOWLEDGMENTS

This research was supported by the J.S. McDonnell Causal Learning Collaborative. We thank Adrienne Wente for invaluable assistance.

REFERENCES

Alvarez, J. M., Ruble, D. N., & Bolger, N. (2001). Trait understanding or evaluative reasoning? An analysis of children's behavioral predictions. *Child Development, 72*(5), 1409–1425.

Ames, D. R., Knowles, E. D., Rosati, A. D., Morris, M. W., Kalish, W. C., & Gopnik, A. (2001). The social folk theorist: Insights from social and cultural psychology on the contents and contexts of folk theorizing. In B. Malle, L. Moses, & D. Baldwin (Eds.), *Intentions and intentionality: Foundations of social cognition* (pp. 287–307). Cambridge, MA: MIT Press.

Baldwin, D., Andersson, A., Saffran, J., & Meyer, M. (2008). Segmenting dynamic human action via statistical structure. *Cognition, 106*(3), 1382–1407.

Buchsbaum, D., Gopnik, A., Griffiths, T. L., & Shafto, P. (2011). Children's imitation of causal action sequences is influenced by statistical and pedagogical evidence. *Cognition, 120*(3), 331–340.

Carey, S. (1985). *Conceptual change in childhood.* Cambridge, MA: MIT Press. Press/Bradford Books.

Chiu, C. Y., Hong, Y. Y., & Dweck, C. S. (1997). Lay dispositionism and implicit theories of personality. *Journal of Personality and Social Psychology, 73*(1), 19–30.

Gergely, G., Bekkering, H., & Király, I. (2002). Rational imitation in preverbal infants. *Nature, 415*(6873), 755.

Glymour, C. N. (2001). *The mind's arrows: Bayes nets and graphical causal models in psychology.* Cambridge, MA: MIT Press.

Gopnik, A. (2012). Scientific thinking in very young children: Theoretical advances, empirical discoveries and policy implications. *Science, 28 September 2012*, 1623–1627.

Gopnik, A., Glymour, C., Sobel, D. M., Schulz, L. E., Kushnir, T., & Danks, D. (2004). A theory of causal learning in children: causal maps and Bayes nets. *Psychological Review, 111*(1), 3–32.

Gopnik, A., & Meltzoff, A. (1997). *Words, thoughts and theories.* Cambridge, MA: MIT Press.

Gopnik, A. & Schulz, L. (Eds.) (2007). *Causal learning: Psychology, philosophy, and computation.* Oxford University Press.

Gopnik, A., & Tenenbaum, J. (2007). Bayesian networks, Bayesian learning and cognitive development. *Developmental Science (Special section on Bayesian and Bayes-Net approaches to development), 10*(3), 281–287.

Gopnik, A., & Wellman, H. M. (1992). Why the child's theory of mind really is a theory. *Mind and Language, 7*(1–2), 145–171.

Gopnik, A., & Wellman, H. M. (2012). Reconstructing constructivism: Causal models, Bayesian learning mechanisms, and the theory theory. *Psychological Bulletin, 138*(6), 1085–1108. doi: 10.1037/a0028044 1085–1108

Griffiths, T. L, Chater, N., Kemp, C., Perfors, A., & Tenenbaum, J. B. (2010). Probabilistic models of cognition: Exploring representations and inductive biases. *Trends in Cognitive Sciences, 14*(8), 357–364.

Griffiths, T. L., & Tenenbaum, Joshua, B. (2007). Two proposals for causal crammar. In A. Gopnik & L. Schulz (Eds.), *Causal learning psychology, philosophy, and computation* (p. 323). New York: Oxford University Press.

Jones, E. E., & Harris, V. A. (1967). The attribution of attitudes. *Journal of Experimental Social Psychology, 3*(1), 1–24.

Kelley, H. H. (1967). Attribution theory in social psychology. In D. Levine (Ed.), *Nebraska symposium on motivation* (Vol. 15, pp. 192–238). Lincoln: University of Nebraska.

Levy, S. R., & Dweck, C. S. (1998). Trait- versus process-focused social judgment. *Social Cognition, 16*(1), 151–172.

Lu, H., Yuille, A. L., Liljeholm, M., Cheng, P. W., & Holyoak, K. J. (2008). Bayesian generic priors for causal learning. *Psychological Review, 115*(4), 955–984.

Lyons, D. E., Young, A. G., & Keil, F. C. (2007). The hidden structure of overimitation. *Proceedings of the National Academy of Sciences USA, 104*, 19751–19756.

Morris, M. W., & Peng, K. (1994). Culture and cause: American and Chinese attributions for social and physical events. *Journal of Personality and Social Psychology, 67*, 949–971.

Pearl, J. (2000). *Causality.* Cambridge, England: Cambridge University Press.

Peevers, B. H., & Secord, P. F. (1973). Developmental changes in attribution of descriptive concepts to persons. *Journal of Personality and Social Psychology, 27,* 120–128.

Rholes, W. S., & Ruble, D. N. (1984). Children's understanding of dispositional characteristics of others. *Child Development, 55,* 550–560.

Ross, L. (1977). The intuitive psychologist and his shortcomings: Distortions in the attribution process. In L. Berkowitz (Ed.), *Advances in experimental social psychology* (Vol. 10, pp. 173–220). New York: Academic Press.

Seiver, E., Gopnik, A., & Goodman, N. (2012). Did she jump because she was the big sister or because the trampoline was safe? Causal inference and the development of social attribution. *Child Development, on-line publication* 24 SEP 2012 DOI: 10.1111/j.1467–8624.2012.01865.x

Shimizu, Y. (2000). Development of trait inference: Do young children understand the causal relation of trait, motive, and behavior? *Japanese Journal of Educational Psychology, 48*(3), 255–266.

Sloman, S. A. (2005). *Causal models: How people think about the world and its alternatives.* New York: Oxford University Press.

Spirtes, P., Glymour, C., & Scheines, R. (1993). *Causation, prediction, and search.* (2nd ed.). New York: Springer-Verlag.

Wellman, H. M., & Gelman, S. A. (1992). Cognitive development: Foundational theories of core domains. *Annual Review of Psychology, 43,* 337–375.

Williamson, R. A., Meltzoff, A. N., & Markman, E. M. (2008). Prior experiences and perceived efficacy influence 3-year-olds' imitation. *Developmental Psychology, 44*(1), 275–285.

3.13

How Children Learn From and About People

The Fundamental Link Between Social Cognition and Statistical Evidence

TAMAR KUSHNIR

People are a critical source of information for young children. Vygotsky (1962, 1978) notably argued that children acquire abstract, conceptual knowledge through social transmission, as evidenced by their ability to demonstrate new knowledge in the context of social interaction prior to attaining individual mastery. Classic and contemporary research in this tradition (Bronfenbrenner, 1979; Cole, 1971; Rogoff, 2003) has confirmed that much of what children learn about the world can be directly attributed to their social environment. However, these sociocultural theories lack a unified account of *how* children use social evidence to learn. In particular, they do not address Vygotsky's original aim: to understand the role of social information in the development of rich, abstract conceptual knowledge.

A more fruitful approach has been to focus on causal knowledge as the foundation of conceptual development, and causal learning as the process underlying conceptual change (Gopnik et al., 2004; Wellman & Gelman, 1992). New discoveries show that children recruit impressive statistical inference abilities in causal learning; they use probabilities to compute the magnitude and direction of causal effects, and systematically integrate patterns of evidence across observations and actions (Bonawitz et al., 2010; Kushnir & Gopnik, 2005; Schulz, Gopnik, & Glymour, 2007). Moreover, children do not evaluate statistical evidence in a vacuum; they consider how new evidence fits with their existing knowledge, and they revise old beliefs only as evidence mounts against them (Kushnir & Gopnik, 2007; Schulz, Bonawitz, & Griffiths, 2007; Sobel, Tenenbaum, & Gopnik, 2004). Finally, statistical evidence motivates children's own actions and explanations, and children's exploratory actions in turn generate new statistical evidence (Legare, 2012; Schulz & Bonawitz, 2007; Schulz, Hooppell, & Jenkins, 2008). Together, these findings demonstrate that young children have "scientist-like" abilities to build causal knowledge. However, the role of social information in this learning process is unknown and unaddressed.

Here I propose a fundamental link between social and causal learning through children's developing social cognition. More precisely, they link through children's burgeoning understanding of the causes of human actions. Actions provide a special type of statistical evidence critical to causal learning; they are often necessary for disentangling causal directionality and distinguishing between causal relations and spurious associations. In the theoretical framework described earlier, only the most minimal assumptions about the causes of actions are necessary for causal learning (in brief, they are intentional and manipulative, but see Gopnik et al., 2004 for more details). In reality, however, young children's intuitive causal knowledge of actions is far from minimal; in a few short years they come to understand actions as motivated by goals and desires, constrained by knowledge and beliefs, and much more (Wellman, 1990). The increasing sophistication of children's knowledge of others may play no role in causal learning at all. It may even be a distraction; reasoning about agents' mental states might interfere with making simple connections between actions and causal outcomes. Here I suggest the opposite: Rather than being irrelevant or distracting, children's developing social cognition is vitally important to causal learning. I propose that young children can—and always do—evaluate statistical evidence from human actions in relation to the actions' psychological qualities. Importantly, considering both social and statistical aspects of

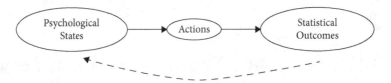

FIGURE 3.13.1: A schematic model of the proposed link between actions as psychologically caused and actions as source of statistical evidence. Learning *from* people (the existing causal arrows in the forward direction) involves using knowledge of psychological states for causal learning. Learning *about* people (a backward inference, as indicated by the dotted line) involves using statistical evidence to learn about a psychological cause.

actions allows children to acquire knowledge *from* and *about* people simultaneously.

Figure 3.13.1 shows a schematic model of this link. Children appreciate that actions are psychologically caused and that actions cause particular patterns of statistical evidence. Combining these understandings (linking through actions) leads to predictions about learning in both directions. The first prediction is that children recruit knowledge of psychological states to learn about physical causes. The second, and perhaps less intuitive prediction, is that children recruit statistical inference abilities to learn about psychological causes. In the remainder of the chapter, I describe two studies that provide support for each of these predictions. I conclude by briefly introducing further intriguing (but untested) implications of this proposal. In particular, I suggest this link allows statistical evidence to be meaningfully integrated with other accounts of social transmission such as imitation, natural pedagogical, and trust in testimony.

LEARNING FROM PEOPLE: CHILDREN USE PSYCHOLOGICAL KNOWLEDGE TO LEARN A PHYSICAL CAUSE

By the time children are 3 years old they understand that intentional acts are knowledge driven: Actors can be knowledgeable or ignorant (Lutz & Keil, 2002), and situations may or may not allow the deployment of knowledge (e.g., if the actor is acting blindly or otherwise constrained; Gergely, Bekkering, & Kiraály, 2002). Research shows that young children consider these psychological states when evaluating social and linguistic information (Baldwin & Moses, 2001; Jaswal & Neely, 2006; Koenig & Harris, 2005; Sabbagh & Baldwin, 2001). What about actions? Even accidental acts, or acts born of ignorance, have causal consequences. Thus, when engaged in causal learning, children could very well ignore psychological factors such as knowledge and focus instead on statistical outcomes. Indirect evidence from children's imitation

of causal sequences suggests otherwise (Gergely et al., 2002; Lyons, Young, & Keil, 2007; Meltzoff, 1995). Kushnir, Wellman, and Gelman (2008) attempted to provide a more direct test.

Across three groups of children, Kushnir et al. (2008) varied two psychological constraints: whether a source was knowledgeable or ignorant about a novel toy (an epistemic constraint) and also whether the source was permitted to use that knowledge in performing an action (a situational constraint). Three- and 4-year-olds saw two puppets. One had expert knowledge of the toy (i.e., "Squirrel knows all about the toy. He knows which blocks make it go"), and the other had no knowledge about the toy (i.e., "Monkey has never seen the toy before. He doesn't know which blocks make it go"). Children were then randomly assigned to one of three conditions: (1) the *puppets picked* their own blocks from a large pile, (2) the *child picked* two blocks and handed one to each puppet, or (3) the *puppets picked while blindfolded*. Then, in all conditions, the two puppets placed their blocks on the toy at the same time, activating the toy's musical light. Critically, the actions themselves were unconstrained, equally intentional, and equally associated with the effect, satisfying the minimal criteria to have special statistical properties for causal learning (Gopnik et al., 2004). If children use only these minimal criteria, then they should not prefer one block over the other as the true cause.

The results (Fig. 3.13.2) show that 3- and 4-year-old children used their knowledge of both epistemic and situational psychological constraints in their causal learning from actions. When asked, "Which block made the toy go?" children reliably chose the knowledgeable puppet's block only in the *Puppets Pick* condition. Importantly, children understood that even the knowledgeable puppet was subject to situational constraints; when the child chose the blocks, or the puppets chose while blindfolded, children responded at chance.

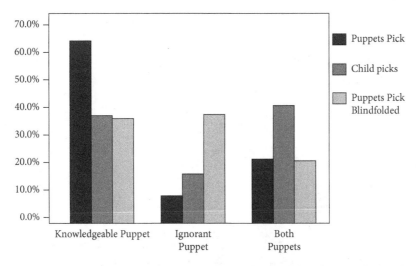

FIGURE 3.13.2: Results of Kushnir et al (2008). The percentage of preschoolers choosing the knowledgeable puppets block, the ignorant puppet's block, or both blocks in response to the question "Which block made the toy go?" across the three conditions.

These findings demonstrate that 3- and 4-year-olds recruit their emerging social cognition to evaluate the informativeness of statistical evidence from actions. Many open questions remain about the extent of this ability, including the way it interacts with varying degrees of statistical evidence, the types of social cognitive knowledge that children can recruit for causal learning, and whether developmental differences in social cognition are systematically related to causal learning through this process.

LEARNING ABOUT PEOPLE: CHILDREN USE STATISTICAL EVIDENCE TO LEARN A PSYCHOLOGICAL CAUSE

Humans acting intentionally—in accordance with their own internal motivations—have the ability to dramatically change statistical sequences of events. This key insight is precisely what makes actions so powerful for causal learning, and, as previously stated, young children share this insight (Gopnik et al., 2004; Schulz et al., 2007). Here I claim an extension of this insight when it combines with real-world social cognition: that recognizing when actions are statistically nonrandom might allow children to learn about the psychological states of agents. Of course, children might well learn about psychological states solely from psychological cues that accompany actions—eye gaze, reaching, facial expressions, affect, verbalizations, and so on—without regard for their statistical regularity or irregularity. Put another way, it is possible that

children separately use social information inherent in actions for social learning, and statistical information for causal learning. The previous example (Kushnir et al., 2008) already suggests that this is not always the case, at least not for learning physical causes. In this example, we examine the link in the other direction and ask whether children can use statistical evidence to learn about a psychological cause.

Kushnir, Xu, and Wellman (2010) investigated whether preschoolers and toddlers use a particular type of statistical evidence—evidence of nonrandom sampling—to learn about an individual's preference. We first showed 3- and 4-year-olds a puppet ("Squirrel") who selected five toys of the same type from a box (e.g., red foam circles). We varied the proportion of toys in the box across three groups of children. In the first group, 18% of the toys were of the selected type and 82% were of an alternative type (e.g., blue foam flowers). In the second group, 50% were of the selected type. In the final group, 100% were of the selected type. After they saw the selection, we asked children to give the puppet "the toy that he likes" out of three possible choices: the selected type (red circles), the alternative type (blue flowers), or a novel type (yellow cylinders). Critically, intentional and affective cues that generally signal preference were identical across conditions, as were associative cues (outcome consistency). Thus, if children infer preferences from psychological and/or associative cues alone, children should give Squirrel his selected object in all three conditions. However, if

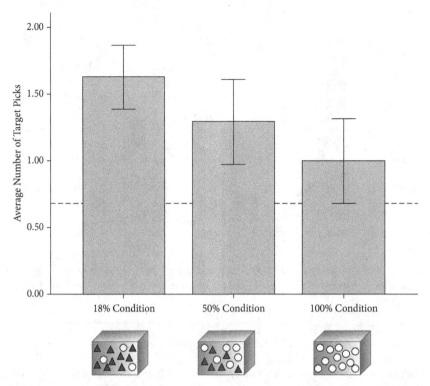

FIGURE 3.13.3: Results of Kushnir et al. (2010), Experiment 1. Average number of times (maximum = 2) that preschoolers chose to give Squirrel the target toy in each condition. The conditions varied in the percentage of target toys (18%, 50%, or 100%) in the box from which Squirrel sampled five target toys. The error bars represent 95% confidence intervals around the means.

children consider whether the sequence of actions shows evidence of nonrandom sampling, then the stronger the statistical evidence, the more likely they should be to infer a preference.

The results (Fig. 3.13.3) show that indeed preschoolers were most likely to infer a preference for the selected object when it was in the minority of objects in the box (18% condition), slightly less likely when the proportions were equal (50% condition), and least likely when it was the only object in the box (100% condition). A modified replication with 20-month-olds showed the same pattern of results. Infants (N = 48; M = 20.23 months; age range = 19–24 months) saw a female experimenter select five toys of one type out of a box containing a minority of that type (18%) or a majority of that type (82%). Again, social cues were constant and positive across conditions. Nonetheless, infants only inferred a preference when the selected toy was in the minority.

These findings show that preschoolers and infants use statistical evidence from actions to learn about a psychological cause. This initial demonstration leaves many open questions for future research on how statistical evidence interacts with other behavioral and effective cues, and how it plays a role in social learning more generally.

CONCLUSIONS

This chapter began with the assertion that people are a critical source of information for young children, and that this widely held belief might have a more precise formulation in the context of causal learning from human actions. As shown in the two examples provided, very young children consider the social qualities of actions simultaneously with their special statistical qualities. This impressive ability to learn *from* and *about* people simultaneously suggests a mechanism for rapid early learning of abstract, conceptual knowledge through social experience.

More generally, the Vygotskian ideas that motivated this investigation have received a lot of recent attention. A growing body of work has given new strength to the claim that social experience is fundamental to learning. Notably, this includes mechanisms of social transmission that clearly influence early causal learning:

the ability to imitate goals (Gergely et al., 2002; Lyons, Young, & Keil, 2002; Meltzoff, 1995); the ability to read ostensive, communicative cues ("natural pedagogy"; Csibra & Gergely, 2009); and the ability to selectively trust others' verbal testimony (Harris et al., in press; Keil, 2010). Considering these abilities separately, however, undermines their potential as mechanisms for acquiring abstract knowledge. Imitation supports learning of complex action sequences and recruits social cognition, but it does not address generalization. Natural pedagogy builds abstract learning into imitative learning by positing that explicit ostensive cues are signals to general knowledge, but it does not address what sorts of abstract knowledge children might acquire in nonostensive contexts. Selective trust in testimony, trust that can be based on a broad range of developing social intuitions, is a powerful mechanism for learning social and linguistic concepts. However, it might have very different implications for learning when concrete evidence of causal relations conflicts with evidence from testimony. Lastly, all of these accounts make predictions about how children learn from people, but not how they learn about them—arguably the most important and early emerging set of conceptual ideas. The link discussed here can be used to unify these approaches and, critically, to integrate them with statistical inference mechanisms already known to drive causal learning. Thus, it opens up an exciting new avenue for future research.

REFERENCES

Csibra, G., & Gergely, G. (2009). Natural pedagogy. *Trends in Cognitive Sciences, 13*(4), 148–153.

Cole, M. (1971). *The cultural context of learning and thinking.* New York: Basic Books.

Baldwin, D., & Moses, L. (2001). Links between social understanding and early word learning: Challenges to current accounts. *Social Development, 10*(3), 309–329.

Bonawitz, E. B., Ferranti, D., Gopnik, A., Meltzoff, A. Woodward, J., & Schulz, L. E. (2010). Just do it? Toddlers' ability to integrate prediction and action in causal inference. *Cognition, 115*, 104–117.

Bronfenbrenner, U. (1979). *The ecology of human development: Experiments by nature and design.* Cambridge, MA: Harvard University Press.

Gergely, G., Bekkering, H., & Király, I. (2002). Rational imitation in preverbal infants. *Nature, 415*, 755.

Gopnik, A., Glymour, C., Sobel, D., Schulz, L. E., Kushnir, T., & Danks, D. (2004). A theory of causal learning in children: Causal maps and Bayes nets. *Psychological Review, 111*(1), 3–32.

Jaswal, V., & Neely, L. (2006). Adults don't always know best: Preschoolers use past reliability over age when learning new words. *Psychological Science, 17*, 757–758.

Keil, F. C. (2010). The feasibility of folk science. *Cognitive Science, 34*(5), 826–862.

Koenig, M. A. & Harris, P. L. (2005). Preschoolers mistrust ignorant and inaccurate speakers. *Child Development, 76*, 1261–1277.

Kushnir, T., & Gopnik, A. (2005). Children infer causal strength from probabilities and interventions. *Psychological Science, 16*, 678–683.

Kushnir, T., & Gopnik, A. (2007). Conditional probability versus spatial contiguity in causal learning: Preschoolers use new contingency evidence to overcome prior spatial assumptions. *Developmental Psychology, 44*, 186–196.

Kushnir, T., Wellman, H. M., & Gelman, S. A. (2008). The role of preschoolers' social understanding in evaluating the informativeness of causal interventions. *Cognition, 107*(3), 1084–1092.

Kushnir, T., Xu, F., & Wellman, H. M. (2010). Young children use statistical sampling to infer the preferences of other people. *Psychological Science, 21*, 1134–1140.

Legare, C. H. (2012). Exploring explanation: Explaining inconsistent information guides hypothesis-testing behavior in young children. *Child Development, 83*(1), 173–185

Lutz, D., & Keil, F. (2002). Early understanding of the division of cognitive labor. *Child Development, 73*, 1073–1084.

Lyons, D. E., Young, A. G., & Keil, F. C. (2007). The hidden structure of overimitation. *Proceedings of the National Academy of Sciences USA, 104*, 19751–19756.

Meltzoff, A. (1995). Understanding the intentions of others: Re-enactment of intended acts by 18-month-old children. *Developmental Psychology, 31*, 838–850.

Rogoff, B. (2003). *The cultural nature of human development.* New York: Oxford University Press.

Sabbagh, M., & Baldwin, D. (2001). Learning words from knowledgeable versus ignorant speakers: Links between preschoolers' theory of mind and semantic development. *Child Development, 72*, 1054–1070.

Schulz, L. E., & Bonawitz, E. B. (2007) Serious fun: Preschoolers engage in more exploratory play when evidence is confounded. *Developmental Psychology, 43*, 1045–1050.

Schulz, L. E., Bonawitz, E. B., & Griffiths, T. (2007). Can being scared make your tummyache? Naive theories, ambiguous evidence and preschoolers' causal inferences. *Developmental Psychology, 43*(5), 1124–1139.

Schulz, L. E., Gopnik, A., & Glymour, C. (2007). Preschool children learn about causal structure from conditional interventions. *Developmental Science, 10*, 322–332.

Schulz, L. E., Hooppell, K., & Jenkins, A. (2008). Judicious imitation: Young children imitate deterministic actions exactly, stochastic actions more variably. *Child Development, 79*, 395–410.

Sobel, D. M., Tenenbaum, J. B., & Gopnik, A. (2004). Children's causal inferences from indirect evidence: Backwards blocking and Bayesian reasoning in preschoolers. *Cognitive Science, 28*, 303–333.

Vygotsky, L. (1962). *Thought and language.* Cambridge, MA: MIT Press.

Vygotsky, L. S. (1978). *Mind in society: The development of higher psychological processes.* Cambridge, MA: Harvard University Press.

Wellman, H. M. (1990). *The child's theory of mind.* Cambridge, MA: MIT Press.

Wellman, H. M., & Gelman, S. A. (1992). Cognitive development: Foundational theories of core domains. *Annual Review of Psychology, 43*, 337–375.

3.14

Children Learn From and About Variability Between People

DAVID LIU AND KIMBERLY E. VANDERBILT

Humans are the most social of all species. We have rich and complex social lives supported by an array of social-cognitive abilities and concepts to understand, predict, and explain each other's actions, thoughts, and emotions. How do children begin to grasp the many social understandings possessed by adults? Certainly there are some domain-specific innate endowments to jumpstart development, but children must also learn about people from their encounters with the social world (Wellman & Gelman, 1998). One view is that social-conceptual development involves the improvement of informal theories to better account for collected data on people (Gopnik & Wellman, 1992). If this view is correct, the nature of children's developing social cognition should reflect the nature of the data children collect about people. Yet students of social cognition have paid little attention to the specific nature of the data children use to develop their informal theories of people. In the current chapter, we explore one aspect of children's data on people: the incredible variability between individuals.

People are a varied bunch. Some smile at the mention of mustard, but others grimace. Some people can quickly change a flat tire, but others have no idea. A child learning about people has to recognize and learn from this rampant variability in people's actions. Although people are not the only entities that behave variably, we suggest that variability is a particularly dominant feature of people and their actions. Indeed, many have argued that human uniqueness includes having an incredible flexibility in thought and behavior (see, e.g., Hermer-Vazquez, Spelke, & Katsnelson, 1999; Tomasello, 1999). Therefore, children observe people behaving in a variety of different ways. We propose that this large variance in children's data on people shapes specific developmental trends in several areas of social cognition. In developing an understanding of people, children learn from and about variability between individuals.

CHILDREN LEARN FROM VARIABILITY BETWEEN INDIVIDUALS

Across domains, observation and encoding of variability in the actions of entities motivates children to seek explanations. Consider two children, Cody and Eva, who repeatedly drop their cups off their highchair. Cody observes that all of his cups shatter (his parents are not the most safety conscious), but Eva observes that only some of her cups shatter. Because the cups in Eva's world are not as consistent and predictable, she is more motivated to construct theories to explain why some cups shatter but some do not (Wellman & Liu, 2007). People behave more like the cups in Eva's world than the cups in Cody's world, and as such, children are prompted early to explain the inconsistent actions of people.

Children Who Encounter More Variability Learn Earlier

If Cody observes that everyone smiles at the sight of mustard, but Eva observes that only some people smile, Eva would be more motivated to construct concepts to understand why. Previous studies have shown that variability or inconsistency from an established expectation prompts causal explanatory reasoning (Legare, Gelman, & Wellman, 2010; Weiner, 1985), but these studies did not precisely test our specific claim here. These studies examined situations in which one encounters data inconsistent with an already learned expectation, whereas our claim involves situations in which one is learning from inconsistent versus consistent data from the start. Nevertheless, we find support from these previous studies, as it would only take a few encounters with events to establish expectations, even from the start.

Concepts Associated With Greater Variability Are Learned Earlier

Some social concepts are associated with greater variability than other social concepts, and children should be motivated to understand concepts with greater variability earlier in development. As shown in several studies, and confirmed in a meta-analysis, children develop an understanding that different individuals can have different desires roughly a year before they understand that different individuals can have different beliefs (see Wellman & Liu, 2004). For instance, 2-year-olds recognize that someone who likes a different food than them will choose a different snack, but they do not recognize that someone who thinks an object is in a different location than them will look in a different location (Wellman & Liu, 2004). Explanations for why children understand the subjectivity of desires before the subjectivity of beliefs include the additional need to understand representations for beliefs (Perner, 1991; Wellman & Liu, 2004) and the recruitment of different neural systems (Liu, Meltzoff, & Wellman, 2009). We propose that another contributing factor is the different degrees of variability data for desires and beliefs. That is, children encounter greater variability between individuals on desires than variability between individuals on beliefs.

There are several reasons for greater variability in children's data on people's desires than their data on people's beliefs. First, young children are more likely to have their own desires overtly contrasted than their own beliefs. Every day, infants and toddlers are thwarted from getting what they want. They reach for things that are taken away from them. They do things that bring smiles to their faces, but not to their parents'. Adults are always blocking them from their goals. However, it is much less apparent to infants and toddlers when they have contrasting beliefs with others about the identity or location of things. This is partly because it is easier for adults to nonverbally communicate their desires to infants and toddlers (with reaches, facial expressions, and movements toward) than one's beliefs (which rely more heavily on linguistic communication). In addition, children might hear adults talk more about contrasting desires than contrasting beliefs.

Second, there might simply be greater variability between individuals in people's desires than people's beliefs, and children's database reflects this state of reality. Direct measurements of the average variability of the population's desires and the average variability of the population's beliefs are probably impossible, as the contents of people's desires and beliefs are near infinite and rarely overlap. Thus, we considered a proxy measure. From 5 million digitized books (roughly 70% in English), Google created a database of all 1-grams to 5-grams (five-word phrases) and how often each n-gram appeared in print each year (Michel et al., 2011). We searched the 4-gram database between 1900 and 2000 for the following phrases: "different people want different," "different people like different," "different people believe different," "different people know different," and "different people think different/differently" (in preliminary analysis, we observed that "different people think differently" is a phrasing often found for think, but not for the other verbs). In searching for these 4-grams, we left the contents of desires and beliefs open ended to sidestep the issue of nonoverlapping contents. As shown in Figure 3.14.1, we found that references in print to individual differences in desires (want and like) exceeded references in print to individual differences in beliefs (believe, know, and think). Furthermore, this pattern occurred across decades, which bolsters against the possibility of the pattern being an isolated publishing trend at some moment in history.

Explaining the developmental sequence of children's abilities and concepts is fundamental to understanding cognitive development (Flavell, 1971). Here we propose that part of what drives the developmental ordering of children's social conceptual insights is the degree of variability in the data associated with each social concept. In addition to desires and beliefs, other patterns of developmental sequences are also likely influenced by different degrees of variability for different social concepts.

CHILDREN LEARN ABOUT VARIABILITY BETWEEN INDIVIDUALS

In the previous section we argued that children's causal explanatory learning is prompted by differences between individuals. As a consequence, children are primed to recognize differences between individuals. For instance, as children develop an understanding of dispositional traits, they might be able to judge, in comparison, which of two people is more selfish before they start attributing this trait to isolated individuals. They might be able to decide, in comparison, which of two informants is more trustworthy before they become skilled at deciding whether to trust isolated informants.

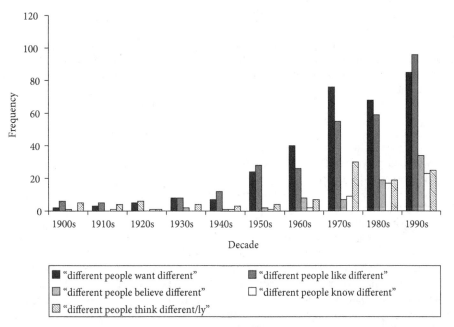

FIGURE 3.14.1: The frequency of each 4-gram per decade in the Google digitized books corpus. Overall increase in absolute frequency reflects the fact that more books from recent decades have been digitized. The key comparison is relative frequency of desire 4-grams (want and like) versus belief 4-grams (believe, know, and think) per decade.

Because variability between individuals is a particularly dominant feature of children's data on people, their initial, nascent theories of people are constructed to differentiate between individuals.

Our approach assumes that children's developing social concepts do not function in an all-or-none manner. Instead, children initially develop a nascent understanding that is just enough to reason about differences between individuals and only later learn to use that social concept to reason about isolated individuals. The development from a nascent to a more complete understanding of concepts includes higher functional maturity (Flavell, 1971), stronger activation of representations (Munakata, McClelland, Johnson, & Siegler, 1997), and mastery and selection of strategies (Siegler, 1981).

Recognizing Differences Between Individuals Before Attribution to Individuals

Our hypothesis is that across a wide variety of social concepts children's initial understanding allows them to differentiate between individuals, but it is not sufficiently advanced to allow children to reason about isolated individuals. Thus, at first, children should be better at contrasting between two people than reasoning about a single person. We recently conducted several studies to test this prediction in different social domains.

Traits

Previous research has shown that children younger than 6 years do not use a person's trait-relevant behavior to predict consistency in future behavior (e.g., Liu, Gelman, & Wellman, 2007). In a recent study, we presented to 4-year-olds trait-relevant stories with pairs of characters or a single character (Liu, unpublished data). In the pairs condition, children heard stories of two characters behaving in contrasting ways (e.g., one boy does not share his lunch, but the other boy does). In the singles condition, children heard stories of a single character behaving in a trait-relevant way twice (e.g., one boy does not share his lunch on two occasions). The results showed that 4-year-olds were more likely to predict trait-consistent behaviors in the pairs condition (70%) than in the singles condition (50%).

Knowledge

Around 3 years of age, children begin to understand that a person's knowledge or ignorance depends on her perceptual access to relevant information (Pillow, 1989). We tested whether 3-year-olds would be better at judging knowledge-ignorance between two individuals than judging the knowledge-ignorance of a single individual. In the pairs condition, children were told about a boy who saw inside a nondescript container and a boy who had not seen inside. In the singles condition, children were told only about a boy who had not seen inside. As with traits, the 3-year-olds were better at judging knowledge-ignorance in the pairs condition than the singles condition (Liu, unpublished data).

Trust

Recent research has shown that 3- and 4-year-olds are more likely to trust new labels for objects from speakers who had previously labeled objects correctly over speakers who had previously labeled objects incorrectly (Koenig & Harris, 2005). In a recent study, we explored whether 3- and 4-year-olds trust a previously inaccurate informant when the informant is not contradicted by anyone (Vanderbilt, Heyman, & Liu, unpublished data). In the pairs condition, children observed an inaccurate informant label objects incorrectly and an accurate informant label objects correctly. In the singles condition, children observed an inaccurate informant label objects incorrectly. The results showed that in the pairs condition, children trusted the inaccurate informant 20% of the time (and trusted the accurate informant 80% of the time). However, in the singles condition, children trusted the inaccurate informant 82% of the time. The children were willing to trust informants observed as having been inaccurate in the past when they were not contradicted by other informants.

These studies examined three different social concepts and involved different problem-solving situations for children. The results for each have concept- and task-specific explanations. Nevertheless, the results across all three domains show a pattern of children developing the ability to differentiate between individuals in relation to a social concept before the ability to attribute that social concept to individuals in isolation.

CONCLUSIONS

To understand children's developing concepts of people and the social world, researchers must consider the data children are collecting about people and the social world. We propose that a prominent feature of children's data on people is the variability between individuals. A consequence of constructing theories of people from variability data is the initial development of nascent theories that can only differentiate between people.

The current social-cognitive development literature is stocked with findings from paradigms that ask infants and preschool-age children to differentiate between two people. Given our observations that the ability to differentiate between people does not always accompany the mature form of a social concept, we caution against ignoring (and argue for investigation of) the further developments of these social concepts. Researchers must recognize that early nascent social cognitions are sometimes far from what will eventually support children and adults' complex social lives. For example, is 3-year-olds' selective trust of an accurate informant over an inaccurate informant related to (or anywhere near) adolescents' attempt at critical consumption of mass media? Or is infant preference for in-group over out-group members related to (or anywhere near) actual dislike or hatred of out-group members? What are the developments in between? We hope our explorations in this chapter stimulate research into the nature of the data children collect to construct their views of the world and research into developments beyond nascent abilities to differentiate between individuals.

REFERENCES

Flavell, J. H. (1971). Stage-related properties of cognitive development. *Cognitive Psychology, 2,* 421–453.

Gopnik, A., & Wellman, H. M. (1992). Why the child's theory of mind really is a theory. *Mind and Language, 7,* 145–171.

Hermer-Vazquez, L., Spelke, E. S., & Katsnelson, A. S. (1999). Sources of flexibility in human cognition: Dual-task studies of space and language. *Cognitive Psychology, 39,* 3–36.

Koenig, M. A., & Harris, P. A. (2005). Preschoolers mistrust ignorant and inaccurate speakers. *Child Development, 76,* 1261–1277.

Legare, C. H., Gelman, S. A., & Wellman, H. M. (2010). Inconsistency with prior knowledge triggers children's causal explanatory reasoning. *Child Development, 81,* 929–944.

Liu, D., Gelman, S. A., & Wellman, H. M. (2007). Components of young children's trait understanding: Behavior-to-trait inferences and trait-to-behavior predictions. *Child Development, 78,* 1543–1558.

Liu, D., Meltzoff, A. N., & Wellman, H. M. (2009). Neural correlates of belief- and desire-reasoning. *Child Development, 80,* 1163–1171.

Michel, J. B., Shen, Y. K., Aiden, A. P., Veres, A., Gray, M. K., & Pickett, J. P. (2011). Quantitative analysis of culture using millions of digitized books. *Science, 331,* 176–182.

Munakata, Y., McClelland, J. L., Johnson, M. H., & Siegler, R. S. (1997). Rethinking infant knowledge: Toward an adaptive process account of successes and failures in object permanence tasks. *Psychological Review, 104,* 686–713.

Perner, J. (1991). *Understanding the representational mind*. Cambridge, MA: MIT Press.

Pillow, B. H. (1989). Early understanding of perception as a source of knowledge. *Journal of Experimental Child Psychology, 47*, 116–129.

Siegler, R. S. (1981). Developmental sequences within and between concepts. *Monographs of the Society for Research in Child Development, 46*, 1–84.

Tomasello, M. (1999). *The cultural origins of human cognition*. Cambridge, MA: Harvard University Press.

Weiner, B. (1985). An attributional theory of achievement motivation and emotion. *Psychological Review, 92*, 548–573.

Wellman, H. M., & Gelman, S. A. (1998) Knowledge acquisition in foundational domains. In W. Damon (Series Ed.), *The handbook of child psychology*, D. Kuhn & R. Siegler (Vol. Eds.), *Cognition, perception, and language* (Vol. 2, pp. 523–573). New York: Wiley.

Wellman, H. M., & Liu, D. (2004). Scaling of theory-of-mind tasks. *Child Development, 75*, 523–541.

Wellman, H. M., & Liu, D. (2007). Causal reasoning as informed by the early development of explanations. In A. Gopnik & L. E. Schulz (Eds.), *Causal learning: Psychology, philosophy and computation* (pp. 261–279). New York: Oxford University Press.

SECTION IV

Trust and Skepticism

4.1

The Gaze of Others

PHILIPPE ROCHAT

We care how we look. This simple proposition defines us as a uniquely self-conscious species. No other animals dwell on appearance like we do. Peacocks, fish, and other butterflies use colorful self-displays to either disguise or advertise their presence to predators, competitors, or sex mates. All of this is done instinctively, the product of natural selection. In humans, however, self-presentation has arguably a profoundly different psychological meaning. It is incomparable because of the self-reflective psychology associated with it. This is what is discussed here in the perspective of development.

A trademark of all human cultures is the systematic use of self-branding devices like makeup, fashionable clothes, and complex panoplies of etiquettes and practices that mark each individual's personality and class distinction (Bourdieu, 1984; Goffman, 1959).

If we care how we look, it is primarily for social reasons, not just to please ourselves like Narcissus caught in the circularity of his self-love. We care about how we look with *others in mind* (Rochat, 2009). It is a deliberate attempt at controlling how others perceive us: how we project the self to the outside world. But it is also more than just our public appearance. It is about our reputation, the calculation of how others construe us in terms of enduring qualities such as intelligence, charm, attractiveness, or moral integrity. Etymologically, the word *reputation* does indeed derive from the Latin verb *putare*, meaning "to compute or calculate." We work hard on appearance to signal deeper qualities regarding who we are as persons.

In human affairs, we gauge the incomparable secure feeling of social affiliation or closeness: the fragile sense of belonging to our social niche by having agency and a place among others. We gauge our social affiliation via the attention, respect, and admiration of others, namely our "good" reputation. The equation is simple: good reputation = good affiliation. The struggle for recognition and the maintenance of a good reputation shapes the development of human social cognition. It is, I would argue, a major drive behind it.

SELF-CONSCIOUS PSYCHOLOGY

Human psychology is primarily self-conscious, giving particular power to the gaze of others: a *self-evaluative* power. Arguably, such power shapes much of what we construe of others (i.e., social cognition). From a very early age, it is through the gaze of others that we measure our own worth, gauging our reputation, how people respect, admire, or on the contrary tend to despise us. It is against the construal of how others see us (i.e., the evaluative gaze of others onto the self) that we measure our social affiliation, how securely accepted by others we are. Indeed, there is no more dreadful fear than the fear of being socially rejected and alienated from others (Rochat, 2009). One contemptuous look can destroy our social standing at least in our eyes if not in that of others. An admiring look, on the contrary, boosts our confidence and social well-being. This is not trivial because in human affairs, reputation is often all that matters. It explains why, for example, most people rank public speech as their greatest fear (Furmark, 2002). But where does it all start? What might account for reputation and the struggle for social recognition as cardinal features of human "self-conscious" psychology?

EMERGING SELF-CONSCIOUSNESS

For decades now, the mirror mark test has been used as an acid test of conceptualized self-awareness from both a developmental and comparative perspective (Amsterdam, 1968, 1972; Gallup, 1970). Self-directed behaviors toward a mark surreptitiously put on the face and discovered in the mirror would attest of self-concept, in other words an objectified sense of the self (but see also Mitchell,

1993; Rochat & Zahavi, 2011 for alternative views on the mirror mark test). What the individual sees in the mirror is "me," not another person, a feat that is not unique to humans since chimpanzees, orangutans, dolphins (Parker, Mitchell, & Boccia, 1995), magpies, and elephants are also reported to pass the test (Plotnick & De Waal, 2006; Prior, Schwarz, & Güntürkün, 2008).

The majority of children pass the mirror mark test by 21 months (Amsterdam, 1972; Bard, Todd, Bernier, Love, & Leavens, 2006; Bertenthal & Fisher, 1978; Lewis & Brooks-Gunn, 1979), although it depends on culture (Broesch, Callaghan, Henrich, Murphy, & Rochat, 2011). But beyond the mirror mark test and what its passing might actually mean in terms of emerging self-concept, there is an early and universal reaction to mirrors that, in my view, is most revealing of human psychology. This reaction is the typical expression of an apparent uneasiness and social discomfort associated with mirror self-experience. The same is true for seeing photographs of one's self, or hearing the recording of one's own voice. Across cultures, mirror self-experience is *uncanny*, an expression of deep puzzlement. This is evident even by adults growing up with no mirrors and who manifest "terror" when confronted for the first time with their own specular image (see Carpenter, 1976). Looking at the self in a mirror puts people, young and old, in some sort of arrested attention and puzzlement. Mirror self-experience is indeed an uncanny experience (Rochat & Zahavi, 2011).

In general, aside from the landmark passing by a majority of children of the mirror mark test from around the second birthday, mirror self-experience develops to become incrementally troubling and unsettling for the healthy child. Such development is not observed by young autistic children, impaired in their reading of others' mind (Baron-Cohen, 1995), but passing the mirror mark test (Neuman & Hill, 1978). They will remove the mark from their faces when they perceive it but do not show the signs of coyness and embarrassment so typical of nonautistic children (Hobson, 2002, p. 89). It appears that for autistic children, there is a different meaning attached to the mark they discover on their faces that they eventually touch and remove. This meaning would not entail the same kind of self-evaluation or self-critical stance in reference to the evaluative gaze of others expressed in typical children via self-conscious emotions. Autistic children's passing of the mirror test is not self-conscious proper and does not appear to entail any sense of reputation as defined earlier.

In her pioneer research on children's reactions to mirror and establishing (in parallel with Gallup, 1970) the mirror mark test, Amsterdam (1968, 1972) describes four main developmental periods unfolding between 3 and 24 months: a *first period* of mainly sociable behaviors toward the specular image. Infants between 3 and 12 months tend to treat their own image as a playmate. A *second period* is accounted for by the end of the first year in which infants appear to show enhanced curiosity regarding the nature of the specular image, touching the mirror or looking behind it. By 13 months starts a *third period* where infants show marked increase in *withdrawal behaviors*, the infant crying, hiding from, or avoiding looking at the mirror. Finally, Amsterdam accounts for a *fourth period* starting at around 14 months but peeking by 20 months when the majority of tested children demonstrate embarrassment and coy glances toward the specular image, as well as clowning. These changes index the self-reflective and ultimately the unique self-conscious psychology unfolding in human ontogeny. Such psychology is the product of a complex interplay of cognitive and affective progress that take place during this early period of child development (Amsterdam & Levitt, 1980), something that Darwin already inferred observing his own child, long before the recent wave of experimental works around the mirror mark test.

In his book *The Expression of the Emotions in Man and Animals*, Darwin (1872/1965) is struck by the unique and selective human crimsoning of the face, a region of the body that is most conspicuous to others. He writes: "Blushing is the most peculiar and the most human of all expressions" (p. 309).

Observing blushing in his son from approximately 3 years of age, and not prior, Darwin highlights the mental states that seem to induce human blushing: "It is not the simple act of reflecting on our own appearance, but the thinking what others think of us, which excites a blush. In absolute solitude the most sensitive person would be quite indifferent about his appearance. We feel blame or disapprobation more acutely than approbation; and consequently depreciatory remarks or ridicule, whether of our appearance or conduct, causes us to blush much more readily than does praise" (p. 325). These observations capture something fundamental and distinctive about humans, a unique motivation behind their social cognition: the exacerbated quest for approbation and affiliation with others, the unmatched fear of being rejected by others (see Rochat, 2009).

As I will suggest next, this is likely the by-product of childhood evolution, in particular the prolonged immaturity and protracted dependence of the human child.

EVOLUTIONARY CONTEXT OF HUMAN SELF-CONSCIOUS PSYCHOLOGY

Compared to other primate species, humans are born too soon, greatly immature and markedly dependent on others to survive. As a species, we are both "precocious" (born early) and "altricial" (in need of extended intensive care from others to survive; see Gould, 1979). It is useful, even indispensable not to lose track of this basic context when thinking about the origins of human self-conscious psychology, in particular the human exacerbated need to gain the recognition of others.

The human precocious birth and "external gestation" (Montagu, 1961) evolved under the combined pressure of a proportionally larger brain and the narrowing of the female's birth canal that is associated with the emergence of bipedal locomotion (Konner, 2010; Trevarthan, 1987). The narrowing of the birth canal in human evolution led to a precocious birth and, in turn, shaped the unique ways we are brought up and cared for over a uniquely protracted period of dependency (human prolonged immaturity, see Bruner, 1972). It is also probably what contributed to our unique self-conscious and reputation psychology that gives radically new self-evaluative meanings to the gaze of others.

HUMAN EXISTENTIAL CONUNDRUM

The prolonged immaturity and dependence on the care of others that characterize human childhood gave rise also to a unique existential conundrum: the conflicting pressures of maintaining proximity with those dispensing the indispensable care, and a growing, insatiable need for infants to roam the world in independence of others, away from the secure base of the mother or other attachment figures.

All healthy children are faced with this basic existential conundrum that is particularly exacerbated in humans. Such a conundrum enters the psychological landscape of the child from around *8 months of age* on average, the typical onset of independent locomotion that is operationally defined as the child's ability to creep or crawl a distance of 4 feet in 1 minute (Benson, 1993; Bertenthal & Campos, 1990). Coincidently, and this is at the crux of my argument here, it is at the same point in development that infants are known to show first signs of stranger's and separation anxiety (the eighth month "anguish" described by René Spitz, 1965), as well as first signs of joint attention with social partners (Scaife & Bruner, 1975).

In joint attention, children engage others in their object exploration, checking back and forth whether others are attuned to and in visual alignment with their own object of exploration (Tomasello, 1995). Although rarely thought of in this way, joint attention is probably the basic process by which children resolve the "proximity maintenance versus independent roaming" conundrum. With joint attention, children de facto incorporate the gaze of others, hence self-recognition, into their own free roaming and object exploration. They manage, at a distance, to be alone but together, "alone in the presence of someone" to coin Winnicott (1968, pp. 47–48), who construes such frame of mind as a major achievement in human development.

Construed in this way, joint attention would be, in part at least, the expression of a deliberate attempt by the child at controlling the gaze of others and maintaining recognition via objects while irresistibly drawn toward roaming the world away from the close proximity of caretakers (the child's secure base according to Bowlby, 1969/1982 and other attachment theorists).

Via joint attention, children thus gain *tele-control* (control at a distance) of others' attention. In this development, the gaze of others now conveys new, evaluative meanings about the self. It is through the gaze of others that infants start to gauge their social place and situation: how much attention and recognition they command from others while physically separated from them as they are pushed toward exploring larger portions of the world on their own.

It is interesting to note that in starting to gauge their social place and situation at a distance, via the monitoring of others' gaze, children are helped and probably guided in their behavior by what amounts to a unique feature of the human eye.

Compared to all other primate species, the anatomy of the human eye evolved a uniquely high contrast between iris and sclera (white part of the eye), making gaze direction particularly public and conspicuous to others (Kobayashi & Kohshima, 1997). In primate evolution, such a feature appears to be highly correlated with social complexity, the relative size of the cortical frontal lobe, as well as the relative mobility of eyes in their sockets, independently of head movements.

This evolution accompanies an apparent change in the function and meaning of gaze as a social signal (Emery, 2000). For humans, it correlates with a unique propensity toward "gaze grooming," a search for eye contacts and looking into each other's eyes as an expression of mutual affiliation (Kobayashi & Hashiya, 2011).

The 2-year-old running toward a cliff or a busy road, despite the mother's insistent screams and invectives to stop, is probing his place and recognition in the mind of significant others. The mother screaming and running toward the child is indeed, for the child, a measure of her attention and care toward the self, an attention that children from 8 months of age never seem to have enough. As succinctly captured by Montgomery (1989), a child about to jump into the swimming pool and screaming, "Watch me! Watch me!" is "not just pleading for attention, but for existence itself."

This, I propose, is the basic script at the root of human unique struggle for social recognition. It is also what might be at the origins of our unique propensity to experience shame and guilt, in other words to blush the way we blush as described by Darwin. Shame and guilt are indeed cardinal spin offs of the self-conscious psychology emerging during the second year and blossoming by the third, when children begin to objectify themselves through the evaluative gaze of others. Together, shame and guilt as well as their polar opposites (pride and innocence) become major emotional experiences that drive the development of social cognition (what we understand and construe of others as evaluators of the self).

In general, shame, guilt, and pride demonstrate the primacy of self-evaluation through the gaze of others, a process that might be at the origins of the moral and ethical stance children develop in the preschool years (e.g., explicit sense of "fairness"), particularly from the time they begin to claim possession on objects with expletives like "That's mine!," once again around 21 months (Rochat, 2009, 2011; Tomasello, 1998), when the majority of children also pass the mirror mark test with combined embarrassment.

Self-conscious emotions, in particular shame and guilt, are distinct for subtle and intricate reasons that I discuss next because they are particularly illuminating of the *human self-conscious psychology* emerging by the end of the second year: the "looking-glass self" psychology first proposed over a century ago by sociologist Charles Orton Cooley (1902). As Cooley writes: "The thing that moves us to pride or shame is not the mere mechanical reflection of ourselves, but an imputed sentiment, the imagined effect of this reflection upon another's mind" (p. 183).

SHAME AND GUILT

"Shame is all that we would like to hide and that we cannot bury," writes Levinas (1935/2003, see discussion pp. 63–65). Its polar opposite, pride, is about praises, positive feelings about the self and its accomplishments. It is about the pleasure and public expression of being positively judged by others, having control of social proximity, and being recognized. The exact inverse is true for shame.

Shame, like pride, can be experienced both directly and indirectly, via the shame (or pride) of others as in the case of an individual experiencing shame but also "shaming" a family and those carrying the same name. Adolescents, for example, are particularly prone to be shamed by their parents, a painful experience mediated by them. As a psychological process, shame as opposed to pride is therefore a negative, anhedonistic, deeply unpleasant human experience that has the particular characteristic of *befalling upon us*. No one enjoys being shamed. It is fundamentally involuntary, like blushing or yawning: It happens when it happens, automatically and against our will, befalling upon us as the cone of a searchlight trapping an escapee. It arises from the public display of what we would prefer to conceal, pertaining to the self or close affiliates of the self (e.g., family or friends).

The source of shame is more often than not objective, in the sense that it can be associated with an event or a situation that is recognizable not only by the shamed person but also presumably by those surrounding that person: the absence of cloth on the shamed individual caught naked by lusting eyes, or the adolescent dreading being seen by peers with his mother whether she wears a flowery hat or is too publicly demonstrative of her protective love.

Interestingly, the contrast between guilt and shame illuminates the psychological nature and subjective intricacies of human self-conscious emotions, all becoming explicit by the third year of life, including blushing, as observed by Darwin.

Guilt, in contrast to shame, captures a painful experience that might befall upon the individual, either directly or indirectly (via other people), but that is not necessarily objective in the sense that its cause or audience can be very elusive or in one's imagination. Anthropologist Ruth Benedict in her classic 1946 book on Japanese culture (*The Chrysanthemum and the Sword*) captures something fundamental that specifies the social experience of shame in contrast to guilt. She makes the following observation:

> A man is shamed either by being openly ridiculed and rejected or fantasizing to himself that he has been made ridiculous. In either case it is a potent sanction. But it requires an audience or at least a man's fantasy of an audience. Guilt does not. (…) a man may suffer from guilt though no man knows of his misdeed and a man's feeling of guilt may actually be relieved by confessing his sin. (Benedict, 1946/2005, p. 223)

Benedict's contrast between shame and guilt is conceptually, as well as ontologically, important. It helps specifying the basic psychology behind it, hence why there is a distinct name for such human experience. A key hint of the psychology behind shame revealed in contrast to guilt is the fact that we can *feel guilty of a crime that goes unnoticed*. Not with shame, as shame depends on the "objective" observations of others (quoted from Ian Buruma's foreword to Benedict's 1946/2005 book). This is a subtle yet significant and highly revealing difference.

It is interesting that shame entails primarily the testimony of an objectified audience with an evaluative (negative) gaze on the self. This potential dread becomes part of what children know about others as potential judges. Interestingly, shame stands for a dreadful experience that cannot be alleviated with a confession. Once shamed, always shamed. Contrary to guilt, there tends to be no redemption to shame, as suggested by Benedict (see earlier quote). It is part of our human nature that we can forget shame, tame it, live with it, and eventually let the painful experience fade, but we cannot get redeemed from it via public disclosure. Aside from the fact that guilt can arise outside of the witnessing and testimony of an audience, in contrast to shame, innocence (the opposite of guilt) can be reclaimed through confession or payback toward whom might have been offended, whether it is via fines, prison time, or other time-outs for children.

As a fundamental psychological dimension, shame reveals the motivational tensions underlying the way we relate and understand others (i.e., our social cognition). Shame cannot be that easily reversed or repaid, and pride (the opposite of shame) cannot be easily reclaimed once lost. Once shamed, there is nothing to confess, because the causes are out there in the open, not much to be hidden (my nudity, my mother's ugly hat). With shame, in contrast to guilt, there is nothing to be regained and not much room for changes. One has to live and cope with it, like the shame of being the one who survived death camp, poignantly described by Primo Levi (1969) and corroborated by many other deportation survivors.

Children start facing, dealing, and ultimately struggling with all these social contingencies from the time they begin to recognize themselves in mirrors, but in particular when they start to objectify themselves through the gaze of others—when they recognize not only that what they see in the mirror is their own reflection, but that it is also what others actually can see: the source of potential judgments and more or less valued recognition of the own person (Rochat, 2003, 2009). This opens a whole new, specifically human line of social-cognitive development.

SUMMARY AND CONCLUSION

Human psychology is ontologically self-conscious. At its core there is an exacerbated care for reputation. This psychology defines us as a species and becomes explicit by the end of the second year with the expression of self-conscious emotions such as shame or pride. From this point on, children not only demonstrate evidence of recognizing themselves in a mirror, a feat evident in other animals, but they also show apparent emotional weariness and self-consciousness. As a human trademark, mirror self-experience changes status, becoming construed in reference to the evaluative gaze of others.

Human self-conscious psychology cannot be thought of independently of the particular evolution of childhood, an evolution that led toward a prolonged immaturity and the incomparably protracted social dependence of the human young. As a by-product of this evolution, the gaze of others gained unique power as a social signal: the power to assess and reflect self-worth. This evolution also led us to become the shameful and guilt-prone species we are, always under the spell of the evaluative gaze of others.

Reputation and the struggle for recognition are staple expressions of our basic need for social affiliation. I suggested that from at least 2–3 years of age and all through the life span, it shapes, orients, and drives much of what we know about others, in particular the power of their judgment on the self.

REFERENCES

Amsterdam, B. K. (1968). *Mirror behavior in children under two years of age.* Unpublished Ph.D.

dissertation, University of North Carolina. Order No. 6901569, University Microfilms, Ann Arbor, MI.

Amsterdam, B. (1972). Mirror self-image reactions before age two. *Developmental Psychobiology, 5,* 297–305.

Amsterdam, B. K., & Greenberg, L. G. (1977). Self-conscious behavior of infants. *Develpmental Psychobiology, 10,* 1–6 .

Amsterdam, B. K., & Levitt, M. (1980). Consciousness of self and painful self-consciousness. *Psychoanalytic Study of the Child, 35,* 67–83.

Bard, K. A., Todd, B. K., Bernier, C., Love, J., & Leavens, D. A. (2006). Self-awareness in human and chimpanzee infants: What is measured and what is meant by the mark and mirror test? *Infancy, 9*(2), 191–219.

Baron-Cohen, S. (1995). *Mindblindness: An essay on autism and theory of mind.* Cambridge, MA: MIT Press.

Benedict, R. (2005). *The chrysanthemum and the sword: Patterns of Japanese culture.* New York: Houghton-Mifflin. [Original work published in 1946].

Benson, J. B. (1993). Season of birth and onset of locomotion: Theoretical and methodological implications. *Infant Behavior and Development, 16*(1), 69–81.

Bertenthal, B., & Campos, J. J. (1990). A systems approach to the organizing effects of self-produced locomotion during infancy. In C. Rovee-Collier & L. P. Lipsitt (Eds.), *Advances in infancy research* (Vol. 6, pp. 1–60). Norwood, NJ: Ablex.

Bertenthal, B., & Fisher, K. (1978). Development of self-recognition in the infant. *Developmental Psychology, 14,* 44–50.

Bourdieu, P. (1984). *Distinction: A social critique of the judgment of taste.* Cambridge, MA: Harvard University Press.

Bowlby, J. (1982). *Attachment and loss.* New York: Basic Books. [Original work published in 1969].

Broesch, T., Callaghan, T., Henrich, J., Murphy, C., & Rochat, P. (2011). Cultural variations in children's mirror self-recognition. *Journal of Cross Cultural Psychology.*

Bruner, J. (1972). Nature and uses of immaturity. *American Psychologist. 27*(8): 687–708.

Carpenter, E. (1976). The tribal terror of self-awareness. In P. Hockings (Ed.), *Principles of visual anthropology* (pp. xx–xx). Berlin: Walter de Gruyter GmbH & Co.

Cooley, C. O. (1902). *Human nature and the social order.* New York: Charles Scribner's Sons.

Darwin, C. (1965). *The expression of the emotions in man and animals.* Chicago, IL: Chicago University Press. [Original work published in 1872].

Emery, N. J. (2000). The eyes have it: The neuro-ethology, function and evolution of social gaze. *Neuroscience and Biobehavioral Reviews, 24,* 581–604.

Furmark, T. (2002). Social phobia: Overview of community surveys. *Acta Psychiatrica Scandinavica, 105*(2), 84–93.

Gallup, G. G. (1970). Chimpanzees: Self-recognition. *Science, 167,* 86–87.

Goffman, E. (1959). *The presentation of self in everyday life.* New York: Doubleday.

Gould, S.J. (1977). *Ontogeny and phylogeny.* Cambridge, MA: Harvard University Press.

Hobson, R. P. (2002) *The cradle of thought.* London: Pan Macmillan.

Kagan, J. (1981). *The second year: The emergence of self-awareness.* Cambridge, MA: Harvard University Press.

Kobayashi, H. & Hashiya, K. (2011). The gaze that grooms: Contribution of social factors to the evolution of primate eye morphology. *Evolution and Human Behavior, 32,* 157–165.

Kobayashi, H. & Kohshima, S. (1997). Unique morphology of the human eye. *Nature, 387,* 767–768.

Konner, M. (2010). *The evolution of childhood.* Cambridge, MA: Harvard University Press.

Levi, P. (1969). *The truce* (La tregua), London: Abacus.

Levinas, E. (1935/2003). *On escape.* Stanford, CA: Stanford University Press.

Lewis, M., & Brooks-Gunn, J. (1979). *Social cognition and the acquisition of self.* New York: Plenum Press.

Lewis, M., & Ramsay, D. (2004). Development of self-recognition, personal pronoun use, and pretend play during the 2nd year. *Child Development, 75*(6), 1821–1831.

Lewis, M., Sullivan, M., Stanger, C., & Weiss, M. (1989). Self development and self-conscious emotions. *Child Development, 60*(1), 146–156.

Mitchell, R. W. (1993). Mental models of mirror-self-recognition: Two theories. *New Ideas in Psychology,* 11/3, 295–325.

Montgomery, M. R. (1989) *Saying goodbye: A memoir for two fathers.* New York: Random House.

Montagu, A. (1961). Neonatal and infant immaturity in man. *Journal of the American Medical Association, 178*(23), 56–57.

Neuman, C. J., & Hill, S. D. (1978). Self-recognition and stimulus preference in autistic children. *Developmental Psychobiology, 11,* 6, 571–578.

Parker, S. T., Mitchell, R. W., & Boccia, M. L. (1995). *Self-awareness in animals and humans: Developmental perspectives.* Cambridge, England: Cambridge University Press.

Plotnik, J., & de Waal, F. B. M. (2006). Self-recognition in an Asian elephant. *Proceedings of the National Academy of Sciences USA, 103*(45), 17053–17057.

Prior, H., Schwarz, A., & Güntürkün, O. (2008). Mirror-induced behavior in the magpie (*Pica pica*): Evidence of self-recognition. *PLoS/Biology, 6*(8), e202.

Rochat, P. (2003). Five levels of self-awareness as they unfold early in life. *Consciousness and Cognition, 12*(4), 717–731.

Rochat, P. (2009) *Others in mind—The social origin of self-consciousness.* New York: Cambridge University Press.

Rochat, P. (2011). Possession and morality in early development. *New Directions in Child and Adolescent Development, 2011*(132), 23–38.

Scaife, M., & Bruner, J. S. (1975). The capacity for joint visual attention in the infant. *Nature, 253,* 265–266.

Spitz, R. A. (1965). *The first year of life: A psychoanalytic study of normal and deviant development of object relations.* New York: Basic Books.

Tomasello, M. (1995). Joint attention as social cognition. In C. J. Moore & P. Dunham (Eds.), *Joint attention: Its origins and role in development* (pp. 103–130). Hillsdale, NJ: Erlbaum.

Tomasello, M. (1998). One child early talk about possession. In J. Newman (Ed.), *The linguistic of giving* (pp. xx–xx). Amsterdam, The Netherlands: John Benjamins.

Trevarthan, W. R. (1987). *Human birth: An evolutionary perspective.* Hawthorne, NY: Aldine de Gruyter.

Williams, D., & Happe, F. (2009). Pre-conceptual aspects of self-awareness in autism spectrum disorder: The case of action monitoring. *Journal of Autism and Developmental Disorders, 39,* 251–259.

Winnicott, D. (1968). Playing: Its theoretical status in the clinical situation. *International Journal of Psychoanalysis, 49,* 38–52.

4.2

Empathy Deficits in Autism and Psychopaths

Mirror Opposites?

SIMON BARON-COHEN

Empathy can be defined as having two separable components: a cognitive component (the ability to recognize someone else's thoughts, intentions, and feelings) and an affective component (the drive to respond to someone else's thoughts and feelings with an appropriate emotion) (Baron-Cohen, 2003; Davis, 1994). Two different neurodevelopmental conditions involve empathy deficits: autism (Baron-Cohen, 1995; Frith, 1989) and psychopathy (Blair et al., 2005). So why do they not result in a similar outcome? If they both share low empathy, why do people with autism tend to avoid other people, struggle with relationships, and show a commitment to honesty and truth (Baron-Cohen, 2008b), whereas psychopaths often hurt other people, and manipulate and deceive others (Baron-Cohen, 2011)?

The answer to this riddle may lie in the two "fractions" of empathy. The thesis is that while people with autism have well-established difficulties in theory of mind (the cognitive component of empathy) alongside intact affective empathy, psychopaths have intact theory of mind but impaired affective empathy (Blair, 1999; Blair et al., 1996). Put otherwise, people with autism have trouble keeping track of others' intentions, beliefs, knowledge, desires, and emotions but still get upset when they hear of someone's suffering, while psychopaths find it easy to mind read others and do so to their own advantage but do not *care* about others' thoughts and feelings.

So if in psychopaths cognitive empathy is intact while affective empathy is impaired, and if in autism the profile is the opposite way around, could this explain the differences we observe in their behavior? Certainly it is a parsimonious explanation for why "zero degrees of empathy" can result in cruelty in psychopaths on the one hand, and social withdrawal and confusion in

people with autism. But can it explain the other big difference between these two groups: that people with autism often show high levels of morality, while psychopaths are by and large amoral?

The psychologist Jon Haidt (2012) has a valuable analysis of morality. He identifies five universal, foundational principles that guide our judgment of good and bad, and therefore our behavior in relation to how to treat others. These are (1) caring for others, (2) fairness and justice, (3) loyalty toward one's group, (4) respect for authority, and (5) purity. These he argues are the evolved foundations of morality because some of these can be observed in other primates and even mammals. For example, monkeys and apes who care for dependent infants act in ways to protect the vulnerable, just like humans do (the "care" principle); wolves and other "pack" animals act in ways to keep the group cohesive (the "loyalty" principle), and primates who live in social hierarchies show a keen sensitivity for how to treat those in a higher social rank to themselves (the "authority/respect" principle).

But back to people with autism and psychopaths: Why do the former often show high levels of morality—to the point of becoming whistle-blowers when they perceive others as breaking the rules—while the latter show high levels of amorality? Is this difference too a consequence of the way their empathy fractionates? I will argue that four out of five of Haidt's moral principles seem to presuppose intact affective empathy, independent of whether cognitive empathy is intact or impaired. First, consider the summary chart in Figure 4.2.1.

How might a psychopath fare on Haidt's five moral principles? We know it is almost diagnostic that a psychopath would be able to hurt an elderly person (so no "care" principle), cheat someone out of their fair share (so no "justice" principle),

Haidt's 5 Moral Foundations	Psychopath	Borderline	Autism
1. Care			√
2. Fairness/Justice			√
3. In-group/Loyalty			√
4. Respect for Authority			√
5. Purity	√	√	√
Cognitive Empathy	√		x
Affective Empathy	x	x	√
Strong Systemizing			√

FIGURE 4.2.1: Why people with autism are moral and caring, and psychopaths are not. √ = clearly present; x = clearly impaired.

and even be willing to pretend to be loyal to the company while making a deal with their competitor (so no "loyalty" principle). We also know they would not give a damn about respect for elders or those who have spent their lives working to get to a higher position (so no "respect" principle) (Cleckley, 1976; Hare et al., 1990). Indeed, the only moral principle that may be intact in psychopaths is the "purity" one: Like all of us, they may feel certain foods or actions are clean and pure, and others are dirty and disgusting. How have psychopaths ended up lacking four out of five of Haidt's universal moral foundations?

Before we answer this question, let's just work through the same moral checklist with someone with autism or Asperger syndrome in mind. For some people it will come as a surprise—given the "mindblindness" theory of autism—that many people with Asperger syndrome show high levels of care for others (Attwood, 1997). They look after their ageing parents, their pets (some even take in dozens of lost or injured animals), and many are devoted parents to their own children and show care toward the sick in their community. In addition, they give to or work for charities that provide care to those less fortunate than themselves. So the "care" principle is often well developed in autism and Asperger syndrome. Equally, many people with Asperger syndrome become passionate lobbyists for social change toward greater social justice, campaigning and protesting and marshaling their political arguments for concepts such as equality, fairness, and justice, feeling outrage for those who are unjustly interned, for example, and compassion for their plight (Baron-Cohen, 2008a). This suggests the "fairness/justice" principle is also well developed in autism spectrum conditions.

And the same is true of their feelings of loyalty. They are often described as the most loyal of employees, recognizing that betrayal is immoral

and the importance of sticking with your team, whether as a football supporter or as a member of a group. So the "group/loyalty" seems to be intact, too. People with Asperger syndrome also show keen attention to social hierarchy, not just their own position within it but a close scrutiny of those at the top, wanting their leaders to prove they deserve our respect by behaving consistently, honestly, and ethically (Baron-Cohen, 2003). So the "respect for authority" moral principle is intact, too. Finally, people with autism spectrum conditions can be as picky as anyone about what they consider is "pure" enough to put into their bodies or what in their mind constitutes spiritual purity. In that respect, the "purity" principle is a fundamental part of their morality.

What immediately strikes one, looking at Figure 4.2.1, is that an impairment in cognitive empathy does not seem to affect one's capacity to be a good moral citizen (providing affective empathy is intact), whereas an impairment in affective empathy appears to be able to wipe out four out of five of our moral principles (irrespective of whether cognitive empathy is intact). How could this be?

The answer comes from looking at a third medical condition, that of borderline personality disorder. Some 80% of patients with this disorder tragically suffered abuse or neglect in early childhood, such that they missed out on the opportunity to experience affection and a secure attachment relationship with a caregiver (Fonagy, 2000). As adults they find it hard to trust others in intimate relationships and can break off relationships impulsively and within seconds as their anger flares up. They can lash out at others in a way that suggests they do not care what the impact of their actions and words are on others. During one of these rages, their affective empathy shuts down, although they appear to have intact cognitive empathy in terms of being able to recognize facial expressions, for example. Patients with borderline personality disorder illustrate that one way in which affective empathy can fail to develop normally is after a lack of the *experience of care* in infancy and early childhood (Bowlby, 1969). They contrast with psychopaths whose callousness seems to have a strong genetic element (Viding et al., 2005) and who may *not* have suffered neglect or abuse in childhood. Like psychopaths, however, patients with borderline personality disorder may lose four of the five moral foundations: During an angry outburst they may stop caring for their children (the "care" principle), for others less fortunate than themselves (the "justice/fairness" principle), or for the needs of their group (the "group/loyalty" principle), and they may not respect their elders/seniors (the "respect/authority" principle). Like all human beings, they are likely to nevertheless have views on what constitutes purity in terms of actions, thoughts, foods, and so on (the "purity" principle).

This suggests that whether one loses one's affective empathy as a result of early neglect/abuse, as a result of genetic influences, or both, the loss of affective empathy can erode four out of five fundamental moral foundations. And it helps answer the puzzle as to why people with autism (who typically have experienced a caring environment and who do not have the genetic makeup of psychopaths) can end up both as caring and moral, despite their difficulties in cognitive empathy/mind reading.

For people with autism, their intact morality has a second cast iron platform: their strong systemizing. Systemizing is the drive to analyze or build a system, defined as anything that is lawful (Baron-Cohen, 2003). Systems include machines (which operate on mechanical rules) or natural phenomena such as plants (which follow the laws of biology and ecology), but systems can also be abstract (such as music or math), collectible (e.g., a system for how to organize your DVDs at home), or even social (like a legal system). People with autism are strong systemizers, typically becoming highly focused ("obsessed") with particular systems (Baron-Cohen, 2008b). Perhaps because of their difficulties with cognitive empathy, they rely even more on systemizing to understand the social world, wanting people to be consistent and to follow rules. These can include rules of morality. This drive to understand the system in all its exquisite detail, and in a black-and-white, binary fashion, is not just an advantage when it comes to figuring out gadgets, building Lego structures, and piecing together train timetables or the names of every dinosaur (just some of the "obsessions" that develop in autism) but can also lead to a strong moral code.[1]

This leads to several conclusions. First, low empathy comes in at least two varieties: low cognitive empathy and low affective empathy. People with autism show the former and psychopaths show the latter.[2] Second, low affective empathy can leave the person capable of hurting another person, while low cognitive empathy typically just leaves the person confused by others and needing to avoid others. Third, low cognitive empathy alone does not leave the person uncaring or unemotional towards the plight of others, and nor does it affect their moral development. In contrast, low affective empathy (whether for genetic and/or environmental reasons) can undermine a person's moral development. Finally, fourth, people with autism are likely to end up with an intact moral code not just because they have intact affective empathy, but also because they have a strong drive to systemize. The study of atypical groups in the population can teach us about the importance of different factors in typical development, and vice versa (Cicchetti, 1984).

---

[1] As an aside, some women with Asperger syndrome sometimes argue they are not strong systemizers because they were awful at math. But the systemizing theory does not propose that people with autism or Asperger syndrome should be good at or understand *all* systems, since it is the nature of systemizing that one latches onto just one system at a time to understand it deeply. For some people it may be math, but for others it may be physics, horse riding, cooking, map collecting, or any other system.

[2] I claim that people with Asperger syndrome or autism have intact affective empathy, and like all such claims, this should be qualified with the phrase "on average." That means there may be some individuals with Asperger syndrome or autism who have both impaired cognitive and affective empathy. The prediction would then be that this subgroup alone might be at risk of hurting others. But my clinical experience of adults with Asperger syndrome is that the majority of them have intact affective empathy and a strong moral conscience. It should also be borne in mind that individuals can have more than one diagnosis, and certainly I have met people with both Asperger syndrome and borderline personality disorder.

REFERENCES

Attwood, T. (1997). *Asperger's syndrome*. London: Jessica Kingsley.

Baron-Cohen, S. (1995). *Mindblindness: An essay on autism and theory of mind*. Cambridge, MA: MIT Press/Bradford Books.

Baron-Cohen, S. (2003). *The essential difference: Men, women and the extreme male brain*. London: Penguin.

Baron-Cohen, S. (2008a). *Autism and Asperger syndrome*. Oxford, England: Oxford University Press.

Baron-Cohen, S. (2008b). Autism, hypersystemizing, and truth. *Quarterly Journal of Experimental Psychology, 61*, 64–75.

Baron-Cohen, S. (2011). *Zero degrees of empathy (The science of evil)*. London: Penguin.

Blair, J., Sellars, C., (1996). Theory of mind in the psychopath. *Journal of Forensic Psychiatry, 7*, 15–25.

Blair, R. J. R. (1999). Responsiveness to distress cues in the child with psychopathic tendencies. *Personality and Individual Differences, 27*, 135–145.

Blair, R. J. R., Mitchell, D., (2005). *The psychopath: Emotion and the brain*. Oxford, England: Blackwell.

Bowlby, J. (1969). *Attachment*. London: Hogarth Press.

Cicchetti, D. (1984). The emergence of developmental psychopathology. *Child Development, 55*, 1–7.

Cleckley, H. M. (1976). *The mask of sanity: An attempt to clarify some issues about the so-called psychopathic personality*. St Louis, MO: Mosby.

Davis, M. H. (1994). *Empathy: A social psychological approach*. Boulder, CO: Westview Press.

Fonagy, P. (2000). Attachment and borderline personality disorder. *Journal of the American Psychoanalytical Association, 48*, 1129–1146; discussion 1175–1187.

Frith, U. (1989). *Autism: Explaining the enigma*. Oxford, England: Basil Blackwell.

Haidt, J. (2012). *The righteous mind*. New York: Pantheon.

Hare, R. D., Hakstian, T. J., (1990). The Revised Psychopathy Checklist: Reliability and factor structure. *Psychological Assessment* 2: 338–341.

Viding, E., Blair, R. J., Moffitt, T. E., & Plomin, R. (2005). Evidence for substantial genetic risk for psychopathy in 7-year-olds. *Journal of Child Psychology and Psychiatry, 46*, 592–597.

4.3

Status Seeking

The Importance of Roles in Early Social Cognition

CHARLES W. KALISH

What do children want? Although Freud may not have asked this question directly, his implicit answer shaped a dominant perspective on social cognitive development. Children are little egoists. They want gratification of their intrinsic, individual drives and desires. To turn these egoists into social beings requires significant effort, external force, and to some degree, distortion of basic psychological processes. Freud's perspective also fit with a particular evolutionary view of the competitive, individual basis of human nature. The asocial view of childhood has been challenged, both from within evolutionary biology, where social adaptations may be cooperative as well as competitive (Sober & Wilson, 1998), and by sociocultural perspectives on development (Tomasello, 1999). Something of the individual egoist persists, though, in our study of children's social cognition. We may not view children (solely) as selfish maximizers anymore, but our theories of social cognition often suggest they see themselves and others in this way. The point of this chapter is to illustrate the value of an alternative set of constructs and perspectives on social cognition. The core concept is that of social status. Children understand themselves and other people in terms of positions within a social structure. What do children want (and want to know about)? Status.

In common usage, "status" connotes possession of privilege or power. Status is often conceptualized with respect to a dominance hierarchy in which those with lower status defer to those with higher status. Although some kinds of dominance may involve status, status is broader than dominance. The broad sense is clear in Searle's theory of status functions (Searle, 1995). For Searle, the core of status is the designation of "counting as." For X to have status A means that there is some context in which X "counts as" A. "Counting as" is an ascribed property, subjective in the sense that

things only have status because people decide or believe they do. Thus, status is distinct from affordances or utilities (e.g., X works well as an A). For example, consider the status of being a doctor. A doctor may have many intrinsic qualities, certain skills or knowledge (e.g., of medicine), and historical properties (e.g., has attended medical school). However, being a doctor, having the status, does not consist of possessing any of those properties. What makes someone a doctor is the agreement of others that the person counts as one. The intrinsic properties may affect the assignment of status (we will not deem someone a doctor who has not attended medical school), but they do not constitute status.

What good is status? Ex hypothesi somebody could have all the skills, knowledge, and training of a doctor but not be one because the status is unrecognized. Conversely, lacking characteristic abilities is not inconsistent with being a doctor (e.g., What do you call the person who graduated at the bottom of his class in medical school?). Who would you want treating your illness? Status is no guarantee. However, whose care will your insurance company reimburse? Whose prescription will your pharmacy fill? The person with status. Searle notes that the implications of status are purely normative. Having status means people ought to treat the person as a doctor, and the doctor ought to behave as one. Status carries with it rights and duties. Doctors are allowed to do certain things (e.g., write prescriptions, bill insurance companies), and they are obligated to do certain others (e.g., respect patient confidentiality). Learning about the status of "doctor" provides a set of normative expectations. What the status of doctor is "good for" is knowing how a doctor is obligated to behave and how others are obligated to behave with respect to one.

The doctor example illustrates one class of status: social roles. "Doctor" is a particularly clear case because there are formal statements of criteria for achieving the status, and regulations laying out powers and permissions. Other social roles are more informal. For example, what rights and obligations are due to someone filling the role of "father"? Norms of appropriate behavior are often vague, contested, and variable. So, too, are the criteria for status assignment. In nontraditional families, or cases of sperm donation, it is not always clear who "counts as" a father. There are many kinds of status besides social roles. The clearest cases are regulated actions, such as traffic laws (what counts as a "full stop") and rules of games (what counts as a "touchdown"; see Rakoczy, 2008). As with social roles, there is likely a continuum from formal to informal statuses for actions. Object functions are another large class of statuses (what counts as a "hammer"). For Searle, the most interesting class of status is linguistic (what counts as the word for dog) because such status assignments serve as the basis for other statuses (because "promise" has the meaning it does, saying "I promise" conveys the status of having promised). Ownership is another, perhaps paradigmatic example (what counts as "mine"; Kalish & Anderson, 2011).

Status is particularly interesting in the context of social cognitive development for at least two reasons. First, the phenomena that are most centrally social are all statuses. Searle argues that all social constructions and institutions are statuses. Second, status cognition is ineluctably social.

The statuses discussed earlier are characterized as social conventions within social domain theory (Turiel, 1983). As conventions, statuses are kinds of social agreements; they are arrangements to organize interpersonal interactions. As such, status requires more than one person. The minimal case is something like a promise between two people (see Astington, 1988; Mant & Perner, 1988 on children's understanding of promising). More generally, Tomasello and his colleagues have explored the ways that statuses may emerge from shared intentions in interpersonal interactions (Tomasello, 2009). How and when children understand the interpersonal conditions of status assignments are still very much open questions (Kalish & Cornelius, 2007; Kalish, Weissman, & Bernstein, 2000; Kim & Kalish, 2009). The key point, however, is that statuses are social objects. My promise to you does not consist in your having a particular belief (e.g., that I promised), nor in my having a particular belief, or even in us both independently having those beliefs. Rather, something like shared belief is necessary.

Although the paradigmatic examples of statuses, and the ones of concern in this chapter, are conventions, it is at least possible to conceive of something like "natural" status (Kalish, 2005). Research in moral development confirms that quite young children share the intuition with many adults that moral status does not depend on people's beliefs or intentions (Turiel, 1983). That is, theft is wrong regardless of whether anyone knows it.[1] Regardless of whether a status is discovered or invented, it is always the case that any causal consequences depend on people recognizing it: The causal effects of status "run through" intentional causal chains. The classic error in this regard is Piaget's example of immanent justice (Jose, 1990). Immanent justice is the belief that (at least some) consequences of having status are not mind dependent. The thief will get sick or suffer some unlucky fate, regardless of whether anyone knows about his transgression. In some sense, then, the key developmental question regarding status is when children appreciate its exclusively mind-dependent effects (Kalish, 1998). Interestingly, it is not clear that adults see the consequences of moral transgressions as mind dependent (Raman & Winer, 2004), and such beliefs seem culturally dependent (e.g., the concept of karma). It is unclear whether we should say that many people lack the concept of status, or whether they think that moral violations involve something besides or in addition to status.

There are interesting and important developmental questions relating to children's understanding of the sources and consequences of status. Framing questions in these terms may unite some currently diverse lines of developmental research (Kalish & Sabbagh, 2007). For example, questions about the role of creator's intent in determining object function can be recast in terms of how objects come to count as one kind rather than another. However, for the remainder of this chapter, I would like to turn to a different set of status implications. Having described status in general, the focus now turns to a specific class of statuses: social roles.

The core meaning of status is how you ought to use or behave toward some thing or person, and how some thing or person ought to work for

---

[1] Note that this is not to say that the beliefs and intentions of the violator do not matter. To judge that "intentionally taking something that does not belong to you" counts as theft does involve consideration of mental states. However, whether such an act counts as theft may not depend on what anyone thinks.

(function) or behave toward you. A social role is a set of these kinds of normative expectations for a class of persons (Linton, 1936). To inhabit a social role is to possess a set of rights and duties. To understand a social role is to know what is permitted to and required of someone in the role. Although there has been some attention to role concepts within social cognitive development (Watson, 1984), by and large children's conceptions of social categories have not been construed in these terms. This is a serious omission. Social roles are an important and distinctive perspective on social categories and may be especially important and distinctive early in development.

Role expectations have been a major focus of research on the development of gender concepts. It is well known that children (and adults) see gender in normative terms: Boys and girls are allowed and required to do different things (Blakemore, 2003). For example, playing with dolls is an appropriate behavior for a girl but a kind of violation for a boy. Gender norms present something of a puzzle for developmental accounts; what is it that gives gender this normative force? Typically the answer is located in social sanctions (society punishes gender-inconsistent behavior) or in identity construction (if one's self-concept depends on gender, then challenges to gendered expectations are threatening; for review, see Martin, Ruble, & Szkrybalo, 2002). Thus, some special feature or significance of gender explains gender roles. An alternative perspective, though, is that role expectations are central to most, if not all, social categories; the cognitive function of social categories is to provide normative expectations.

Preschool-aged children are quick to associate norms with social categories. For example, they expect members of novel social categories to share rights and duties, more so than preferences or emotional reactions (Kalish & Lawson, 2008). Normative properties generalize from one category member to another. Young children are somewhat less willing to generalize norms in the context of particular individuals, and they are more likely to generalize norms than psychological states within categories (Kalish, 2012). While school-aged children and adults often expect social categories to be organized around, and predictive of, psychological qualities (e.g., traits), young children may be most attentive to rights and duties. In particular, this work with novel social categories illustrates that experience with social sanction and identity relevance are not necessary for the attribution of normative significance to social categories.

Role concepts fit well with the theory that scripts organize early social cognition (Nelson, Gruendel, Franklin, & Barten, 1988). Though scripts are often characterized as simple empirical generalizations of observed co-occurrences (Gopnik & Wellman, 1994), there is more to them than that. Scripts encode normative, not just statistical, expectations. The restaurant script tells us more than just that customers typically give their order to waiters, who then bring the food. Such interactions are constitutive of the roles of "customer" or "waiter." To "count as" a customer in this context just is to have a normative way of interacting with people who "count as" waiters. It might be possible to learn regular patterns of social interactions as bare probabilities, but many suspect people rarely do so (Gilbert, 1992; Kalish & Sabbagh, 2007). If customers typically give their orders to waiters (in a particular kind of restaurant), then the representation encoded in a script is that this is proper, normatively expected behavior. The converse holds as well; if some behavior is normatively expected, then it is statistically expected. People tend to do what they are supposed to. For adults, this expectation is based on a kind of rationality assumption. If young children really adhere to something like immanent justice, they may see a more direct connection between roles and behaviors. Note that these representations need not involve attributions of personalities or traits: We do not conclude that waiters particularly like being ordered about by customers, nor that customers are "bossy" just by fulfilling their role expectations.

Recognizing the link to scripts highlights an important feature of roles: They are typically interdefined. Learning the role of doctor involves learning how doctors are obligated/allowed to interact with people in other roles, such as nurses, patients, and pharmacists. The same relation holds with less formal roles, such as the pragmatics governing interactions between participants in a dialogue. Tomasello (2009) argues that this kind of mutual constitution provides children with powerful learning opportunities. By construing a social interaction in terms of "my role" and "your role," the child acquires a kind of third-party view of the interaction. Understanding my role depends on understanding yours because I have to know what you expect of me and what I can expect of you. So, for example, by being a patient a child learns something about what it is to be a doctor. Thinking about how these roles are coordinated, what part each person plays, also provides a more generalized, nonegocentric view of the interaction.

By learning the patient role, the child learns something of the script or context "visits to the doctor."

The general point of a status-based approach is that the social world has an essentially normative structure. Much of what children have to learn is how they and others ought to behave. The empirical hypothesis is that children are motivated to seek out this information and to represent social actors and objects in term of norms. One important class of status concerns social roles.

Research on social cognition has often been motivated by a desire to understand the origins of various errors or evils. We know that principles of category learning can result in *stereotypes*: generalizations from a few individuals to all members of a social category. *Prejudice*, ascription of value or valence to social categories, may develop from representations of in-group/out-group distinctions. Thinking about social status leads directly to *discrimination*: the assignment of differential rights and obligations based on social category. While young children may be prone to stereotyping, and hold some prejudiced attitudes, they may be particularly likely to discriminate. From the status perspective, making discriminatory judgments is what social cognition is all about.

REFERENCES

Astington, J. W. (1988). Promises: Words or deeds? *First Language, 8*, 259–270.

Blakemore, J. E. O. (2003). Children's beliefs about violating gender norms: Boys shouldn't look like girls, and girls shouldn't act like boys. *Sex Roles, 48*, 411.

Gilbert, M. (1992). *On social facts*. Princeton, NJ: Princeton University Press.

Gopnik, A., & Wellman, H. M. (1994). The theory theory. In L. A. Hirschfeld & S. A. Gelman (Eds.), *Mapping the mind: Domain specificity in cognition and culture* (pp. 257–293). New York: Cambridge University Press.

Jose, P. E. (1990). Just-world reasoning in children's immanent justice judgments. *Child development, 61*, 1024–1033.

Kalish, C. W. (1998). Reasons and causes: Children's understanding of conformity to social rules and physical laws. *Child Development, 69*, 706–720.

Kalish, C. W. (2005). Becoming status conscious: Children's appreciation of social reality. *Philosophical Explorations, 8*, 245–263.

Kalish, C. W. (2012). Generalizing norms and preferences within social categories and individuals. *Developmental Psychology, 48*, 1133–1143.

Kalish, C. W., & Anderson, C. D. (2011). Ownership as a social status. In O. Friedman & H. Ross (Eds.), *Children's ownership. new directions in child and adolescent development, 132*, 65–77.

Kalish, C. W., & Cornelius, R. (2007). What is to be done? Children's ascriptions of conventional obligations. *Child Development, 78*, 859–878.

Kalish, C. W., & Lawson, C. A. (2008). Development of social category representations: Early appreciation of roles and deontic relations. *Child Development, 79*, 577–593.

Kalish, C. W., & Sabbagh, M. A. (Eds.) (2007). Conventionality in cognitive development: How children acquire shared representations in language, thought, and action. *New Directions in Child and Adolescent Development, 115*.

Kalish, C. W., Weissman, M., & Bernstein, D. (2000). Taking decisions seriously: Young children's understanding of conventional truth. *Child Development, 71*, 1289–1308.

Kim, S., & Kalish, C. W. (2009). Children's ascriptions of property rights with changes of ownership. *Cognitive Development, 24*(3), 322–336.

Linton, R. (1936). *The study of man: An introduction* (Student's ed.). New York: D. Appleton-Century.

Mant, C. M., & Perner, J. (1988). The childs understanding of commitment. *Developmental Psychology, 24*, 343–351.

Martin, C. L., Ruble, D. N., & Szkrybalo, J. (2002). Cognitive theories of early gender development. *Psychological Bulletin, 128*, 903–933.

Nelson, K., Gruendel, J. M., Franklin, M. B., & Barten, S. S. (1988). At morning it's lunchtime: A scriptal view of children's dialogue. In M. Franklin & S Barten (Eds.), *Child language: A reader* (pp. 263). New York: Oxford University Press.

Rakoczy, H. (2008). Taking fiction seriously: Young children understand the normative structure of joint pretence games. *Developmental Psychology, 44*, 1195–1201.

Raman, L., & Winer, G. A. (2004). Evidence of more immanent justice responding in adults than children: A challenge to traditional developmental theories. *British Journal of Developmental Psychology, 22*, 255–274.

Searle, J. R. (1995). *The construction of social reality*. New York: Free Press.

Sober, E., & Wilson, D. S. (1998). *Unto others: The evolution and psychology of unselfish behavior*. Cambridge, MA: Harvard University Press.

Tomasello, M. (1999). The human adaptation for culture. *Annual Review of Anthropology, 28*, 509–529.

Tomasello, M. (2009). *Why we cooperate*. Cambridge, MA: MIT Press.

Turiel, E. (1983). *The development of social knowledge: Morality and convention*. New York: Cambridge University Press.

Watson, M. W. (1984). Development of social role understanding. *Developmental Review, 4*, 192–213.

4.4

Reputation Is Everything

ALEX W. SHAW, VIVIAN LI, AND KRISTINA R. OLSON

From corporate boardrooms and urban street corners to high schools and courtrooms, it is hard to find a place where people are not obsessed with their reputation (Anderson, 1984; Deephouse, 2000). *Reputation*, as used here, refers to people's beliefs about and positive or negative evaluations of a person, based on directly or indirectly gathered social information (De Cremer & Sedikides, 2008). Because people's status and opportunities often depend on their reputation, individuals try to improve their reputation by modifying their speech and actions to make others view them favorably (Baumeister, 1982). For corporations and public figures, reputation management is a multi-million-dollar industry—public relations firms spend countless hours attempting to manipulate and improve the reputation of their clients (Gray & Balmer, 1998). Normal folks act as their own public relations agents, engaging in conscious efforts to verbally modify others' impressions of them: boasting, exaggerating, and self-promoting (Baumeister, 1982). People can also implicitly change their behavior to improve their reputation with others: correcting their bad habits, behaving more prosocially, and committing fewer immoral acts when others are watching (Jones & Pittman, 1982; Latane, 1970; Leary & Kowalski, 1990). Interestingly, people do not even need to be in the presence of others for reputational concerns to be salient. Rather, people can be unconsciously influenced even by perceived cues that they are being watched—the mere presence of a picture of eyes in a background is enough to make people more generous (Haley & Fessler, 2005).

Despite the importance of promoting one's reputation in our society, we are still unsure how and when human beings ontogenetically develop an understanding of reputation. Here we focus on children's understanding of their own reputation, but at the end of this chapter we will speculate on the challenges that children may encounter when trying to develop a sense of others' reputations.

WHEN DO REPUTATIONAL CONCERNS BEGIN TO INFLUENCE CHILDREN'S BEHAVIOR?

There are at least two different ways that children can try to improve their reputation: They can consciously promote themselves to others through intentional actions and speech, or they can be implicitly influenced by the actual or perceived presence of others, leading to unconscious behavior change in service of their reputation. What little research has been done on children's understanding of reputational concerns has focused mainly on the former aspect—what children understand about how one can self-promote through verbally expressing one's good points or downplaying one's bad points. Explicitly engaging in self-promotion to increase one's reputation might be hard to understand because it requires not only knowing that other agents form impressions about oneself but also knowing that one can modify these impressions, an understanding of what things one should do or say to improve these impressions, and a motivation to do so (Banerjee, 2002; Hill & Pillow, 2006). This complexity predicts that concerns with one's reputation should emerge relatively late. We will review some of the literature regarding children's use of explicit self-promotion strategies and then discuss some of our lab's recent work that investigates young children's more implicit concerns with their own reputations.

Children, by age 8, use self-promotional strategies in order to ingratiate themselves to others and avoid negative evaluations; this demonstrates some understanding that they can influence others' impressions of them. Aloise-Young (1993) demonstrated that 8-year-old children, but not younger children, provide socially desirable information to another child when attempting to get that child to pick them as a partner in a game—children provided more information about their ability to win when they were attempting to gain a partner for the game. Children of the same age also advise third parties to provide others with information that fits with the desires of their audience—knowing that one should provide different information to impress an athlete than one would use to impress an intellectual (Banerjee, 2002). These examples demonstrate that at age 8, children understand their reputations are malleable in the minds of others, and they know that selectively providing information about themselves can make them appear socially desirable to others. Additionally, 8-year-old children appear to know not to express socially undesirable preferences publicly, indicating some desire to affect their own reputation—they inhibit in-group favoritism and out-group prejudice more when their judgments would be made public than when they could make these judgments in private (Rutland, Cameron, Milne, & McGeorge, 2005).

These results seem to suggest that children do not understand the idea of intentional self-promotion until about age 8. While children may not know how to use strategies of self-promotion themselves before this age, younger children may still implicitly modify their own behavior in order to appear favorably to others.

We know that adults often modify their behavior in order to appear more generous than they are, but it is unclear whether children do this. Although adults are generous in anonymous interactions with others (Batson, 1991), they often appear more concerned with gaining a reputation as a generous person than with truly being generous or fair (Dana, Weber, & Kuang, 2007). Adults are substantially more generous when they are observed by others than when they are not (Reis & Gruzen, 1976) and will especially increase their generosity to others if they expect that others will know they have given money and will have a chance to reciprocate (Barclay & Willer, 2007). Additionally, adults feel much less compelled to share money with others if they can do so without *appearing* ungenerous—looking fair to others can be more important than being fair to others (Dana et al., 2007). These results indicate that adults are at least partially driven to be generous in order to appear favorable to others. Although there has been a lot of work demonstrating that children can be both generous and fair (for review, see Hook & Cook, 1979; Warneken & Tomasello, 2009), there has been very little work investigating whether some of their generosity is influenced by reputational incentives.

Our preliminary results suggest that children's generosity is partially motivated by reputation. In one study we investigate whether children will change their sharing behavior based on whether the recipient of their sharing can see what they decide (Leimgruber, Shaw, Santos, & Olson, 2012). Five-year-old children are randomly assigned to be a decider or a receiver. The decider gets to decide how many rewards the other child will receive, but she will always get the same reward regardless of how much she decides to give. On some of these trials the decisions are public, and on others the decisions are private. Our results suggest that children's generosity is heavily dependent on whether the decision is made public. When their decision is public, children are very prosocial, but when their decision is made privately, they are antisocial—giving other children the fewest possible rewards. This result suggests that children's tendency to be generous may be partially influenced by wanting to appear generous to others.

Adults also demonstrate concerns with reputation in their desire to get credit for their ideas. We constantly exchange ideas with one another and dislike those who take other people's ideas without giving credit—there are norms and even laws that explicitly forbid taking another person's idea without permission (for review, see Park, 2003). Individuals gain resources and social favor based on the quality of their ideas—for example, in coining theories that explain how the world works, generating novel solutions to problems, or coming up with jokes that make others laugh (Miller, 2000). Adults may seek credit for their ideas to establish a reputation as a creative individual who makes intellectual contributions (Goodenough & Decker, 2009). Thus, if children object to plagiarism and seek credit for their ideas, this may reveal that they are concerned with their reputation.

Children do seem concerned with individuals taking undue credit for ideas that are not their own, suggesting children may value the reputation that one garners through their creative ideas. Children dislike those who take others' ideas by age 5—negatively evaluating those who plagiarized other people's work relative to those who produced unique work, revealing that children negatively evaluate those who intentionally take others' ideas (Olson & Shaw, 2011). Additionally, Barnes and Olson (2009) found that children of the same age object to an individual stealing their ideas as well, responding negatively to an experimenter plagiarizing their story. These authors had children make up stories and then tell their stories to the experimenter. The experimenter then retold each child's story to a confederate (who admired the story) and either gave the child credit for the story or failed to give credit for the story. The authors found that 5-year-old children wanted credit for their stories; when they were not given credit for their story, they looked upset and lodged objections such as "She's stealing my story." From other work, we know that children clearly think that ideas are valuable objects that can be owned (Shaw, Li, & Olson, 2012) and that they value ideas over effort by the time they are 6-years-old (Li, Shaw, & Olson, in press). Giving credit to others for ideas may be important to children because ideas indicate something about one's creativity or underlying abilities, and children, like adults, may dislike when others falsely indicate they have some ability that they in fact lack. These objections to others stealing ideas can be taken as evidence that children understand the importance of ideas to their reputation; they dislike that someone is taking away their credit as a creative storyteller.

In sum, children appear to have some implicit understanding of reputational concerns by as early as age 5 years. Past research on children's self-promotional strategies underestimates young children's (below age 8) capacity to modify their behavior in order to influence others' impressions of them. Children are sensitive to reputational concerns in their sharing, being generous when the recipients of their generosity will know their decisions, but being much less generous when their decisions are made privately. Children are also concerned with getting credit for their ideas, perhaps because they want to gain a positive reputation as a creative person. Children want to make themselves look good in the eyes of others, implicitly behaving as though they recognize the old public relations adage: Reputation is everything.

FUTURE DIRECTIONS FOR UNDERSTANDING HOW REPUTATIONAL CONCERNS FUNCTION

Now that we know that even young children care about their reputation, the next step for our research will be to begin investigating what function these reputational concerns serve. There are least two broad classes of reasons for people to promote their reputation to others: to avoid being excluded for being ungenerous or being seen as a defector (Panchanathan & Boyd, 2004) and to seek out opportunities to promote their social status (Bird & Smith, 2005). Although these two motivations will often predict the same behavior,

this is not always the case. For example, if a person was walking down the street with friends and saw a homeless person several blocks down, a motivation to avoid looking ungenerous would predict the person might lead the group across the street, pretending she did not notice the homeless person, whereas a motivation to promote one's social status would predict that the individual would lead the group directly toward the homeless person, making a scene of generously donating several dollars in front of her friends.

While people's behavior is likely influenced by both of these tendencies, understanding when and why each motivation is active will likely allow for more effective interventions. In some situations, parents, teachers, or policy makers may want to motivate people by making it clear that others can be exposed as a defector if they act in a selfish or ungenerous manner. For example, when trying to ensure regulation on Wall Street, it is probably best to emphasize increased transparency and accountability so that individuals understand that if they selfishly try to earn profits at others' expense (i.e., if they defect) they will be discovered, punished, and ostracized accordingly. In our own work, this would map onto the discovery that children were only generous when they could be discovered as a defector (Leimgruber et al., 2012) and other work of ours which suggests that children are considerably more willing to be unfair when they will not appear unfair (Shaw, Montinari, Piovesan, Olson, Gino, & Norton, in press). Clearly children were motivated to not be seen as a defector. However, the incentive of avoiding being seen as a defector will not always produce the most desirable behavior. In other situations, individuals might instead want to emphasize that people have the opportunity to demonstrate their creativity and generosity. For example, when trying to increase the production of good ideas at a board meeting, it might be better to emphasize that there is a clear relationship between the quality of one's ideas and possible advancement in the company than to establish that one will be punished for not contributing ideas (defection). In our own work children sought out credit for their creative ideas when there was no risk of being seen as a defector (Barnes & Olson, 2009). Clearly, different strategies are needed depending on one's goals, and policy makers will only be able to design efficient socially desirable programs if they understand how to motivate the behavior in question.

In addition to the question of what function these reputational concerns serve, future work might investigate how children think about *others'* reputations and whether they properly discount others' impression management strategies. For example, do children understand that a person who gives anonymously is likely to be more generous than someone who gives to others only when other people are watching? To form accurate impressions of others, children must learn to discriminate between people's genuine selves from the selves they present to others. This task is made even more difficult by the fact that people must form impressions of others based not only on direct experience but also on indirect information (e.g., gossip). This means that children must learn not only to interpret an individual's behavior but also interpret others' words of praise and condemnation about that individual in forming their own impressions about her. How children weigh these different types of information is not known. We look forward to discovering how children's understanding of reputation develops into the complex system available to teenagers and adults—the kind of system that allows high school bullies to track who is tough and who is a wimp, NBA coaches to assess who is a team player and who is a selfish ball hog, and others to navigate everyday life in which people try their best to make sure others do not get an accurate impression of who they really are.

REFERENCES

Aloise-Young, P. A. (1993). The development of self-presentation: Self-promotion in 6- to 10-year-old children. *Social Cognition, 11,* 201–222.

Anderson, E. (1984). The code of the streets. *Atlantic Monthly, 5,* 81–94.

Banerjee, R. (2002). Audience effects on self-presentation in childhood. *Social Development, 11,* 487–507.

Barclay, P., & Willer, R. (2007). Partner choice creates competitive altruism in humans. *Proceedings from the Royal Society, B, 272,* 749–753.

Barnes, J. L., & Olson, K. R. (2009, October). *Storytelling and ownership: Children's conceptions of intellectual property.* Poster presented at the Cognitive Development Society Meeting, San Antonio, TX.

Batson, D. (1991). *The altruism question: Toward a social social-psychology answer.* Hillsdale, NJ: Erlbaum.

Baumeister, R. F. (1982). A self-presentational view of social phenomena. *Psychological Bulletin, 91,* 3–26.

Bird, R. B., & Smith, E. A. (2005) Signaling theory, strategic interaction, and symbolic capital. *Current Anthropology, 46,* 221–248.

Dana, J., Weber, R. A., & Kuang, X. (2007). Exploiting moral wiggle room: Experiments demonstrating an illusory preference for fairness. *Economic Theory, 33,* 67–80.

De Cremer, D., & Sedikides, C. (2008) Reputational implications of fairness for personal and relational self-esteem. *Basic and Applied Social Psychology, 30,* 66–75.

Deephouse, D. L. (2000). Media reputation as a strategic resource: An integration of mass communication and resource-based theories. *Journal of Management, 26,* 1091–1112.

Goodenough, O., & Decker, G. (2009). Why do good people steal intellectual property? In M. Freeman & O. Goodenough (Eds.), *Law, mind, and brain* (pp. 345–372). London: Ashgate.

Gray, E. R., & Balmer, J. M. T. (1998). Managing corporate image and corporate reputation. *Long Range Planning, 31,* 695–702.

Haley, K. J., & Fessler, D. M. T. (2005). Nobody's watching? Subtle cues affect generosity in an anonymous economic game. *Evolution and Human Behavior, 26,* 245–256.

Hill, V., & Pillow, B. H. (2006). Children's understanding of reputations. *Journal of Genetic Psychology, 167,* 137–157.

Hook, J., & Cook, T. D. (1979). Equity theory and the cognitive ability of children. *Psychological Bulletin, 86,* 429–445.

Jones, E. E., & Pittman, T. S. (1982). Towards a general theory of strategic self- presentation. In J. Suls (Ed.), *Psychological perspectives on the self* (Vol. 1, pp. 231–262). Hillsdale, NJ: Erlbaum.

Latane, B. (1970). Field studies of altruistic compliance. *Representative Research in Social Psychology, 1,* 49–61.

Leary, M. R., & Kowalski, R. M. (1990). Impression management: A literature review and two-component model. *Psychological Bulletin, 107,* 34–47.

Leimgruber, K. L., Shaw, A., Santos, L. R., & Olson, K. R. (2012). Young children are more generous when others are aware of their actions. *PLoS One, 7,* e48292.

Li, V., Shaw, A., & Olson, K. R. (in press). Children value ideas over effort. *Cognition.*

Miller, G. (2000). *The mating mind.* New York: Doubleday.

Olson, K. R., & Shaw, A. (2011). "No fair, copycat!" What children's response to plagiarism tells us about their understanding of ideas. *Developmental Science, 14,* 431–439.

Panchanathan, K., & Boyd, R. (2004). Indirect reciprocity can stabilize cooperation without the second-order free rider problem. *Nature, 432,* 499–502.

Park, C. (2003). In other (people's) words: Plagiarism by university students—literature and lessons. *Assessment and Evaluation in Higher Education, 28,* 471–488.

Reis, H. T., & Gruzen, J. (1976). On mediating equity, equality, and self-interest: The role of self-presentation in social exchange. *Journal of Experimental Social Psychology, 12,* 487–503.

Rutland, A., Cameron, L., Milne, A., & McGeorge, P. (2005) Social norms and self- presenta-tion: Children's implicit and explicit intergroup attitudes. *Child Development, 76,* 451–466.

Shaw, A., Li, V., & Olson, K. R. (2012). Children apply principles of physical ownership to ideas. *Cognitive Science, 36,* 1383–1403.

Shaw, A., Montinari, N., Piovesan, M., Olson, K. R., Gino, F., & Norton, M. I. (in press). Children develop a veil of fairness. *Journal of Experimental Psychology: General.*

Warneken, F., & Tomasello, M. (2009). Varieties of altruism in children and chimpanzees. *Trends in Cognitive Sciences, 13,* 397–402.

4.5

Understanding Expertise

The Contribution of Social and Nonsocial Cognitive Processes to Social Judgments

JUDITH H. DANOVITCH

Children's understanding of the world around them is dynamic and constantly changing as new information is acquired and more sophisticated reasoning skills emerge. Although great progress has been made in understanding the course of social and cognitive development since Piaget and others began empirical research into children's developing epistemological concepts, the research literature has tended to focus on relatively isolated skills or closely related sets of skills. For example, we now know a great deal about executive function or attachment, but discussion of how these areas of development relate to each other is often speculative and rarely the objective of empirical research. However, in reality, many of a child's daily social interactions and activities rely on combinations of different social and cognitive reasoning skills. To illustrate this idea, I present new findings regarding children's understanding of expertise that demonstrate how seemingly unrelated sets of social and cognitive processes may interact synergistically over the course of development to produce more powerful means of reasoning about the social world.

THINKING ABOUT EXPERTS

In contrast to lay intuitions that children are simple-minded when it comes to social reasoning, research has shown that even young children think in sophisticated ways about other people's thoughts and knowledge. Children as young as age 2 are sensitive to the fact that some people are more reliable information sources than others (e.g., Birch, Akmal, & Frampton, 2010) and, by age 3, children rely more on sources who have previously shown themselves to be accurate and knowledgeable (e.g., Koenig, Clement, & Harris, 2004). Children also understand the limits of

knowledge and education. They know that being smart or having studied many subjects does not translate into knowing everything there is to know about the world and, in fact, 7- and 8-year-olds indicate that intelligence of the "academic" variety does not necessarily translate into making good decisions in other domains, such as morality (Danovitch & Keil, 2007).

Children not only understand who is a reliable source of information, but they also display an intuitive awareness of other people's expertise and the fact that different people know different things, known as the division of cognitive labor. One of the first demonstrations of this understanding in young children involved a task where children were asked whether a doctor or a mechanic would know more about the answer to a particular question (Lutz & Keil, 2002). Three-year-olds consistently stated that the doctor would be better at answering questions about the human body and that the mechanic would be better at answering questions about cars and their parts. This finding may have been driven by semantic associations or by children's exposure to these familiar experts firsthand (although it is arguable how much exposure young children are likely to have to mechanics). More dramatically though, slightly older children also chose the appropriate expert for questions about topics that had no obvious connection to the human body or vehicles (confirmed through analyses of semantic associations) and often drastically departed from these categories. For example, 4- and 5-year-olds indicated that a doctor would know more about why plants need sunlight to grow and a mechanic would know more about how a yo-yo works. The researchers attributed this surprisingly sophisticated understanding to children's emerging intuitions that phenomena that seem quite disparate on the surface, such as the workings of cars and yo-yos, are linked by deeper sets of underlying causal principles. Thus, even though they may not be familiar with "biology" as an academic discipline, children intuitively infer that a doctor is actually an expert on biology and therefore he is more likely to know about other living things besides humans, even including plants.

There is also evidence that by age 4 children can generate accurate assumptions about unfamiliar experts that they are unlikely to have encountered before, such as experts on eagles, bicycles, and dogs (Koenig & Jaswal, 2011; Lutz & Keil, 2002). By the beginning of elementary school, children begin to reason more flexibly about domains of expertise. They understand that expertise can be driven by an individual's goals (Danovitch & Keil, 2004), and eventually they come to appreciate ways of clustering knowledge in other people's minds that correspond to a range of academic disciplines, from evolutionary biology to cognitive psychology to economics (Keil, Stein, Webb, Billings, & Rozenblit, 2008). In addition to drawing accurate inferences about what an expert is likely to know, children in elementary school become sensitive to "imposters" whose domain of expertise is implausible, such as an expert who knows only about dogs with red collars (Keil, 2010).

Taken together, these findings suggest an early emerging penchant for understanding expertise that cannot be attributed solely to semantic associations, previous firsthand experience with an expert, or explicit instruction. Critically, many of the experts described in these studies and their topics of expertise are not familiar to children (e.g., an expert who knows why bubble wrap keeps glass from breaking), yet children are able to answer questions about them correctly. This is particularly surprising in light of the fact that children in the same age range have difficulty with other aspects of social cognition, such as understanding subjectivity (Carpendale & Chandler, 1996) and conflicting desires (Choe, Keil, & Bloom, 2005). Some of this difficulty can be attributed to the fact that children are still solidifying their understanding that other people have different thoughts and beliefs than themselves, known as a Theory of Mind. How is it that children who exhibit a relatively fragile Theory of Mind are still able to draw specific and accurate inferences about another person's expertise?

EXPLANATIONS FOR CHILDREN'S UNDERSTANDING

Two contrasting processes may be invoked to explain young children's aptitude at identifying and reasoning about expert knowledge. The first process consists of social reasoning. Children are intrinsically motivated to interact with the people they encounter and they rely on other people to provide information that they cannot obtain on their own (see Harris, 2007). It is strange and potentially embarrassing for an adult to assume that a conversational partner is knowledgeable about or interested in a topic when they actually are not, and such a mistake can occasionally have serious consequences. The repercussions of misreading another person's mind are also apparent among individuals with autism, who frequently make precisely these kinds of mistakes and can have difficulty maintaining social exchanges despite being motivated to do so. It is in a young child's best interest to pay attention to what other people know and to draw correct inferences about expert knowledge as a means of navigating the social world. Thus, one account of children's understanding of the division of cognitive labor is that it is essentially a by-product of other emerging social cognitive skills. These skills are critical for children's successful social interactions by allowing them to comprehend what other people know.

A second contrasting account of children's understanding of expertise reframes the question of inferring another person's knowledge as a question of understanding categories of information. From this perspective, evaluating an individual's expertise is accomplished by identifying the overarching categories that encompass the objects or phenomena in question. For example, to answer a question about apples, you should consult an expert on eagles, and not an expert on bicycles, because both eagles and plants belong to the category of living things. Indeed, when evaluating expert knowledge, there is evidence that younger children rely on simple schemas for causal patterns that are unique to different domains (Keil et al., 2008). These schemas may explain how children initially make correct judgments about unfamiliar domains of expertise, such as molecular biology or physics, long before they are introduced to these disciplines in formal educational settings. Critically, in this account, the specific body of knowledge associated with an expert is secondary to the place that that knowledge occupies in the hierarchy of categories and concepts that exist in the world. If categorical structure is more central to understanding expertise than the features of an individual source, then presumably children would draw the exact same judgments about domains of expertise if the information came from a nonhuman source, such as a book or a computer.

New findings from my lab suggest that children's developing ability to determine what an expert knows depends on both of these processes. In a study of 46 preschool children ages 3 through 5, we administered an expert knowledge task where children decide whether an eagle or a bicycle expert is better suited to answering each of 24 questions (Exp 2., Lutz & Keil, 2002). Children also completed three classic measures of understanding false beliefs (change of location, unexpected identity, and unexpected contents; see Wellman, Cross, & Watson, 2001) and a categorization task where they had to match drawings of 24 different objects to a drawing of either an eagle or a bicycle. The objects in the categorization task corresponded to the key term in each of the expert knowledge questions; for example, an apple corresponded to the question "Who knows more about why apples are sweet?" The false-belief tasks served as an indicator of children's Theory of Mind development—a social cognitive process, and the categorization tasks measured children's ability to categorize objects with the eagle or bicycle, potentially by deciding whether each object is a living or nonliving thing.

Children's responses on the expert knowledge task closely replicated Lutz and Keil's original results, with children's performance improving steadily with age. Moreover, even after controlling for the effects of age, children's accuracy assigning each question to the appropriate expert was significantly associated with both false-belief understanding and categorization ability. These findings are provocative in that they suggest that understanding the division of cognitive labor in terms of expert knowledge requires *both* theory of mind and the ability to categorize objects in the world. More important, these results suggest that although each of these abilities is necessary to achieve a full-fledged understanding of expertise, neither one is sufficient on its own: Children who had only mastered one of the component skills typically did not perform as well on the expert knowledge task as children who had mastered both.

Although these findings suggest potential developmental pathways for an emerging understanding of the division of cognitive labor, this question needs to be explored from additional perspectives in order to elaborate on the mechanisms at work. First, it is noteworthy that there are individual differences among children of similar ages in reasoning about expert knowledge. It would be valuable to further explore the basis for these individual differences and whether they correspond to different levels of functioning in other situations where children must assess the nature of another person's knowledge, such as deciding whether to trust an individual's testimony (e.g., Koenig et al., 2004) or detecting bias (e.g., Mills & Keil, 2005). Similarly, more empirical data are needed about the trajectory of these skills over the course of childhood. For example, do children with less well developed Theory of Mind skills exhibit less sophisticated ways of reasoning about expertise, such as relying more on topic-based clusters, when they enter elementary school? Longitudinal data could thus reveal how the emergence of specific social and cognitive skills affects different types of social judgments over the course of development.

INSIGHTS FROM AUTISM

Clinical settings also potentially offer insights into the contributions of social and nonsocial cognitive processes to understanding expertise. Children with social or cognitive impairments exhibit intuitions and behaviors that might reveal the quality and quantity of influence that different skills and competencies contribute to the identification of information sources. For instance, high-functioning children with autism spectrum disorders often have intact verbal and categorization skills (Gastgeb, Strauss, & Minshew, 2006; Tager-Flusberg, 1985), yet they may still be severely impaired in terms of social functioning (Klin, Saulnier, et al., 2007). If an understanding of expertise can be achieved solely through nonsocial cognitive reasoning abilities such as object categorization, then children with autism may prove to be surprisingly adept at discerning what an expert is likely to know.

Another potentially informative characteristic of autism spectrum disorders is that a large percentage of children with high-functioning autism and Asperger's syndrome develop circumscribed interests about a particular topic (see Klin, Danovitch, et al., 2007). These interests typically dominate much of the child's daily activities and conversations, and in some cases the topic of interest can be quite unusual or esoteric, such as an interest in washing machines or tsunamis. Although no empirical research exists into the direct effect of circumscribed interests on social interactions, there is anecdotal evidence that autistic individuals with circumscribed interests have difficulty determining whether people they encounter are interested in hearing about their topic of interest or whether conversational partners are even capable of understanding what the individual is saying.

Nevertheless, the factual nature of a circumscribed interest requires that at some point the individual with autism obtain information about the topic from a source (i.e., a child is unlikely to implicitly learn the geographic distributions of 100 different species of snakes). How children with autism initially obtain information about their circumscribed interest remains unknown. Do they utilize expert testimony obtained from other people, books, or Web sites? If so, do they seek out information from appropriate and reliable sources, or do they do they look for it in a more haphazard fashion? The answer to these questions can potentially inform our understanding of typical development by showing how information-seeking behaviors develop in the absence or near absence of social reasoning skills. If children with autism who have normative IQs and who are highly motivated to seek out information about a topic still show impairments when determining where to go for the information they seek, this would suggest that social cognition plays a pivotal role that cannot be circumvented. Conversely, it is possible that individuals with autism can rely on their intact nonsocial cognitive skills to compensate for their social impairments in this situation and consequently draw accurate inferences about the division of cognitive labor in others' minds.

CONCLUSIONS

As I propose here, understanding expertise is an example of a seemingly social judgment—determining what an expert knows—that may actually depend on recognizing the structure of nonsocial information in the world in addition to the ability to judge the contents of other minds. The case of understanding expertise illustrates how complex social interactions can require combinations of skills that may develop in relative isolation but come together synergistically to allow children to make more sophisticated judgments. The relative importance of each skill and whether strength in one skill area can compensate for weakness in or the absence of another, as may be true for individuals with autism, remains an open question. This question has potentially important implications not only for understanding typical patterns of development but also for therapeutic interventions. For example, clinicians could capitalize on an atypically developing child's strengths in an unaffected domain to enable them to improve their reasoning in affected domains.

This approach to evaluating the development of complex social judgments may also prove useful for elucidating the development of other behaviors that potentially rely on integrating nonsocial cognitive processes, such as causal reasoning and conceptual understanding, in order to fully appreciate another person's thoughts and behaviors. For instance, child and adult inferences about ownership and property may be influenced by both the instrumental aspects of property, such as the affordances provided by a specific piece of property, and the social signals conveyed by property, such as social status (see Dittmar, 1991). In summary, it is essential that we not ignore the *cognitive* component of *social cognition*. As research into the development of social cognition continues to expand and enlighten, we must remain aware of the ways in which nonsocial cognitive processes may influence, and perhaps provide the foundation for, the development of social cognitive abilities.

ACKNOWLEDGEMENTS

Thank you to Kimberly Fenn and Nicholaus Noles for helpful comments on a previous draft.

REFERENCES

Birch, S. A. J., Akmal, N., & Frampton, K. L. (2010). Two-year-olds are vigilant of others' nonverbal cues to credibility. *Developmental Science, 13*, 363–369.

Carpendale, J. I., & Chandler, M. J. (1996). On the distinction between false belief understanding and subscribing to an interpretive theory of mind. *Child Development, 67*, 1686–1706.

Choe, K. S., Keil, F. C., & Bloom, P. (2005). Children's understanding of the Ulysses conflict. *Developmental Science, 8*, 387–392.

Danovitch, J. H., & Keil, F. C. (2004). Should you ask a fisherman or a biologist? Developmental shifts in ways of clustering knowledge. *Child Development, 75*, 918–931

Danovitch, J. H., & Keil, F. C. (2007). Choosing between hearts and minds: Children's understanding of moral advisors. *Cognitive Development, 22*, 110–123.

Dittmar, H. (1991). Meanings of material possessions as reflections of identity: Gender and social-material position in society. *Journal of Social Behavior and Personality, 6*, 165–186.

Gastgeb, H. Z., Strauss, M. S., & Minshew, N. J. (2006). Do individuals with autism process categories differently? The effect of typicality and development. *Child Development, 77*, 1717–1729.

Harris, P. (2007). Trust. *Developmental Science, 10*, 135–138

Lutz, D., & Keil, F. C. (2002). Early understanding of the division of cognitive labor. *Child Development, 73*, 1073–1084.

Mills, C. M., & Keil, F. C. (2005). The development of cynicism. *Psychological Science, 16*, 385–390.

Keil, F. C. (2010). The feasibility of folk science. *Cognitive Science, 34*, 826–862.

Keil, F. C., Stein, C. M., Webb, L., Billings, V., & Rozenblit, L. (2008). Discerning the division of cognitive labor: An emerging understanding of how knowledge is clustered in other minds. *Cognitive Science, 32*, 259–300.

Klin, A., Danovitch, J. H., Merz, A. B., Dohrmann, E., & Volkmar, F. R. (2007). Circumscribed interests in higher-functioning individuals with autism spectrum disorders: An exploratory study and a theory. *Research and Practice for Persons with Severe Disabilities, 32*, 89–100.

Klin A., Saulnier, C. A., Sparrow S. S., Cicchetti, D. V., Volkmar, F. R., & Lord, C. (2007). Social and communication abilities and disabilities in higher functioning individuals with autism spectrum disorders: The vineland and the ADOS. *Journal of Autism and Developmental Disorders, 37*, 748–759.

Koenig, M. A., Clément, F., & Harris, P. L. (2004). Trust in testimony: Children's use of true and false statements. *Psychological Science, 10*, 694–698.

Koenig, M. A., & Jaswal, V. K. (2011). Characterizing children's expectations about expertise and incompetence: Halo or pitchfork effects? *Child Development, 82*(5), 1634–1637.

Tager-Flusberg, H. (1985). Basic level and super-ordinate level categorization by autistic, mentally retarded, and normal children. *Journal of Experimental Child Psychology, 40*, 450–469.

Wellman, H., Cross, D., & Watson, J. (2001). Meta-analysis of theory-of-mind development: The truth about false belief. *Child Development, 72*, 655–684.

4.6

Respectful Deference

Conformity Revisited

PAUL L. HARRIS AND KATHLEEN H. CORRIVEAU

The Asch paradigm has often been used to measure "conformity" among adults. We have recently created a child-friendly version that has produced similar results, with 3- to 4-year-olds deferring to a majority on about 25% of trials. However, the finding that Asian American preschoolers defer at higher rates, particularly if they are first- rather than second-generation Asian Americans, has led us to reflect on how young children growing up in different cultures (even within the same country) are encouraged to weigh two potentially conflicting sources of information: their own judgments as compared to the testimony of others. Asian American children are more inclined to respectful deference when presented with claims that contradict their own judgment. Because the Asian American children that we studied attend secular schools, presumably watch similar television programs, and sample the same broader culture outside the home, we suggest that variation in rates of conformity—or deference—may be attributable to cross-cultural variation in parenting style and the environment at home. Some parents acknowledge and accept individual differences in opinions and beliefs, whereas others emphasize respect for collectively agreed-on knowledge and standards of behavior. More generally, we argue that deferential receptivity is an important strategy for cultural learning and should not be negatively construed as simple conformism.

JUDGING FOR YOURSELF VERSUS LISTENING TO OTHERS

In a classic series of studies, Solomon Asch (1956) asked adults to weigh two distinct sources of information: their own perceptual judgment and the reports made by other people. The task was a relatively simple match-to-sample task in which participants were asked to say which line from a set of three matched a target line. Left to their own devices, adults accurately picked out the matching line. Yet when they made their selection in the wake of several other people who had all agreed on a different choice, they were quite often swayed by this consensus. On about one third of the trials, they agreed with the consensus, effectively making a "mistake" that they would not ordinarily make.

In this chapter, we discuss three related issues. First, the experiments described by Asch were conducted with adults and we know little about how children respond in the same situation. Yet the setup devised by Asch offers a simple and powerful technique for probing how children weigh their own perceptual judgment as compared to the claims made by other people. Accordingly, we report recent findings in which the judgments of preschool children were assessed. Second, Asch and indeed most subsequent commentators have conceptualized the task as one in which participants choose either to stick to their own independent perceptual judgment or to "conform" to the alternative judgment made by others. From this perspective, the normative or expected response is an autonomous and perceptually correct judgment, whereas the tendency to conform is a deviant and surprising error. We argue that this stance oversimplifies the dilemma that participants face. It is more fruitful to think of participants as weighing two distinct sources of information. Finally, we ask how far cultures differ in the relative weight that they attach to those two sources of information.

Testing Young Children

As part of a broader program of research on the extent to which young children revise their own independent judgments depending on the claims that adults make (Harris & Corriveau, 2011), we devised an analogue of the Asch paradigm suitable for preschoolers (Corriveau & Harris, 2010). Children were shown a set of three strips of foamboard (varying by 10% in height) and asked to choose the "big one." Pretests established that 3- and 4-year-olds could make such judgments without error. In subsequent test trials, children made the same judgments after having watched a short video clip in which they saw three adults indicate a different strip as the biggest—all three adults picked out the medium-sized strip on some trials and the shortest on others.

We found that preschoolers "conformed" to the adult consensus on about one quarter of the trials. Evidence of conformity on these trials was strong because children who failed to choose the biggest strip chose either the medium-sized or the smallest strip, depending on what the consensus had indicated moments before. However, two other pieces of evidence suggested that children were doing something more than simply yielding to social pressure. First, at the end of the experiment children were invited to say whether the adults (in the video) had been "good" or "not so good" at answering the questions. As compared to children who never conformed, children who conformed on one or more trials were more likely to judge the adults to be good at answering the questions. Second, when children were asked to say which line the adult consensus had picked out on a given trial, children who had sometimes conformed were likely to say that the consensus had picked out the correct strip. By implication, conformist children were not saying to themselves: "These adults have made a bizarre judgment but let me quietly go along with it." Rather, as compared to the nonconformist children, they were quite positive in their appraisal of the adult consensus.

We sought to make sense of these findings in the following way. Although the Asch paradigm appears to create an extreme dilemma, its key elements are seen in most judgments. In particular, faced with any given judgment call, we can consult our own autonomous knowledge base or seek guidance from others. Admittedly, when asked to make a very simple perceptual judgment, we rarely consult others. However, in appraising a wine, a movie, or a restaurant, there is nothing unusual about taking note of the judgments made by others—we do it routinely. The Asch line task is very simple, so it is tempting to conclude that individuals should be very confident of their own judgments. Yet that simplicity is a double-edged sword. Even if its simplicity bolsters confidence in one's own conclusion, that same simplicity makes it unlikely that other people have made a mistake.

Hence, when the consensus does not align with one's own conclusion, it is likely to provoke doubts about that conclusion.

Accordingly, we concluded that children were not just conforming to social pressure. They were showing "respectful deference." They entertained the possibility that the consensus had provided accurate information. This interpretation fits well with the two observations made earlier. Children who sometimes agreed with the consensus were prone to say that its members were very good at answering the questions and had identified the biggest line correctly even if they had not actually done so.

This is not to say that children who displayed respectful deference were fully convinced. When subsequently given a more practical task of selecting the biggest strip in order to build a bridge across a toy river, children did so without error—there was no sign of persistent deference (Corriveau & Harris, 2010). Nevertheless, immediately after the consensus gave its judgment, some children did defer.

Cultural Variation

In the two studies just described, the rate of conformity was greater among Asian American children as compared to European American children (40% versus 18%, respectively). Although we had not predicted this outcome, it proved to be consistent with prior findings with adults. Replications of the original Asch paradigm have revealed considerable cross-national variation in the frequency of conformist responses. In a meta-analysis of those replications, Bond and Smith (1996) found a robust relationship between the frequency of conformity and the level of collectivism established in survey studies of cross-national variation in values (e.g., Hofstede, 1983). Replication studies conducted in countries where collectivism is pronounced revealed a stronger tendency toward conformist responses than the level reported by Asch and subsequent investigators in the United States. In particular, studies conducted in East Asian cultures such as Hong Kong and Japan revealed a greater conformist bias.

The parallels between the pattern that we found for preschoolers and the pattern previously established with adults gave us confidence that the cross-cultural variation that we had observed was likely to be robust. More immediately, the parallels between children and adults strengthened our confidence in the way that we had interpreted the developmental findings. It makes sense that cultures might vary in the extent to which they nurture respectful deference.

Socialization for Respectful Deference?

Recent research on children's Theory of Mind points to intriguing differences between Chinese and American preschoolers in the way that they gradually construct an understanding of how people's beliefs vary (Wellman, Fang, Lui, Zhu, & Liu, 2006). Chinese preschoolers find it easier to grasp that someone else may not know something that they themselves know (e.g., the contents of a closed container) than to understand that someone might hold, and indeed act on, a belief that they themselves do not share (e.g., concerning the whereabouts of a lost object). Surprisingly, this developmental progression is reversed among US preschoolers: They are better at recognizing how people diverge in their beliefs than at recognizing that one person may know something that another is ignorant of.

In follow-up research, Shahaeian, Peterson, Slaughter, and Wellman (2011) have shown that a similar difference emerges when Australian and Iranian children are compared. Iranian children are better at acknowledging another person's ignorance than at recognizing how people diverge in their beliefs, whereas Australian children show the reverse pattern. Thus, the developmental sequence for Chinese and Iranian children is equivalent but different from the developmental sequence for American and Australian children, who are equivalent to one another.

A plausible interpretation of this variation is that knowledge and its acquisition is construed differently in different cultures: as a set of external observable facts that everyone—provided they have access to those facts—will acknowledge, or alternatively as a set of opinions that people affirm independent from one another. Stated differently, Chinese and Iranian preschoolers are led to construe beliefs as knowledge involving a definite mind-to-world fit, whereas American and Australian preschoolers are led to conceive of beliefs along the same lines as desires and opinions: as individualized and subjective.

How might such a difference arise? We know that patterns of family discourse impact children's developing understanding of mind (Harris, de Rosnay, & Pons, 2005). In particular, exposure to conversation about mental states facilitates children's understanding of beliefs (Meins & Ferneyhough, 1999; Ruffman, Slade, & Crowe, 2002; Taumoepeau & Ruffman, 2006; 2008). Recent evidence shows that European American mothers talk considerably more with their children about cognitive states—knowing and thinking—than

do Chinese American immigrant mothers, even when allowances are made for maternal education (Doan & Wang, 2010). Moreover, European American mothers are more likely to modulate their assertions than Chinese American mothers. For example, they are more likely to include words like "might," "maybe," "perhaps," "possibly," and so forth when making assertions. Such modulation is consistent with the idea that European American mothers are more prone to signal the provisional or personal nature of their assertions as compared to Chinese American mothers. In sum, although further research is needed to establish the link, it is plausible that European American preschoolers conceptualize beliefs as personalized claims more readily than Chinese American preschoolers because they are often involved in family conversations where individualized assertions are voiced and marked as such. More generally, it is plausible that European American preschoolers are less prone to respectful deference than Asian American preschoolers because they regard other people's assertions as expressions of opinion rather than as statements of agreed fact.

Cross-Generational Variation

If the differences between European American children and Asian American children can be traced to early socialization practices, especially variation in family discourse, we can ask whether such differences persist across generations of immigrants or become attenuated following migration and settlement. To answer this question, Kim, Song, Corriveau, and Harris (2011) repeated the study described earlier with two key changes. First, three different groups of preschoolers (ranging from 3 to 5 years of age) were tested: Caucasian American children; first-generation Asian American children; and second-generation Asian American children. Second, half the children made their judgment publicly, as in the previous study of Corriveau and Harris (2010), but the remaining children made their judgment privately, with the experimenter concealed behind a screen.

Two main findings emerged from these data. First, we replicated the difference in the rate of deference between Caucasian American and Asian American preschoolers found in Corriveau and Harris (2010). Although cultural variation was modest when children made private judgments, it was marked when they made public judgments. All of the first-generation Asian American children, approximately 60% of the second-generation Asian American children, and just over 25% of the Caucasian American children deferred at least once in the public setting. We also found that the Asian American mothers with a more authoritarian parenting style had children who were prone to defer at least once. Arguably, the parenting style of Asian American mothers becomes less authoritarian with increasing integration into US culture. In future research, we plan to compare the discourse of first- and second-generation Asian American mothers to see whether second-generation parents are more similar to US parents in terms of the frequency with which they talk about cognitive states and modulate their assertions.

The assumption that children learn best by making their own autonomous judgments seems plausible and is often emphasized in Western educational settings. On the other hand, the transmission of human culture is clearly facilitated when children are willing to learn from others (Harris, 2012). Recent findings on children's imitation offer persuasive evidence of children's natural receptivity in this respect. Introduced to an unfamiliar apparatus and given a demonstration of how to operate it—for example, shown a technique for extracting an attractive object housed inside the apparatus—children readily adopt the demonstrated technique. Strikingly, they follow the demonstrator's technique even if, left to their own devices, they adopt a different and indeed a more efficient technique (Lyons, Damrosch, Lin, Simeone, & Keil, 2011; Lyons, Young, & Keil, 2007; Nielsen & Tomaselli, 2010). Moreover, shown different techniques by different individuals, they reproduce the technique of whichever demonstrator remains present (Nielsen & Blank, 2011). This type of deferential imitation is not found in chimpanzees (Horner & Whiten, 2005), implying that it is a distinctive feature of human cultural learning. Indeed, the tendency toward such overimitation has been found in various cultural settings: in North America, in Europe, and among Kalahari Bushmen children. Such deferential imitation closely resembles the pattern just described for children's perceptual judgments.

As we have seen, children will set aside their own perceptual judgments in the wake of guidance from an adult. We conclude that "respectful deference," even at the increased rate displayed by Asian American children, should not be automatically viewed as problematic. Even if autonomous judgment is valued in the United States, current evidence strongly suggests that respectful deference has promoted cultural learning for millennia in the human species.

REFERENCES

Asch, S. E. (1956). Studies of independence and conformity. A minority of one against a unanimous majority. *Psychological Monographs, 70* (9, Whole No. 416).

Bond, R., & Smith, P. B. (1996). Culture and conformity: A meta-analysis of studies using Asch's (1952b, 1956) line judgment task. *Psychological Bulletin, 119,* 111–137.

Corriveau, K. H., & Harris, P. L. (2010). Preschoolers (sometimes) defer to the majority in making simple perceptual judgments. *Developmental Psychology, 46,* 437–445.

Doan, S. N., & Wang, Q. (2010). Maternal discussions of mental states and behaviors: Relations to emotion situation knowledge in European American and immigrant Chinese children. *Child Development, 81,* 1490–1503.

Harris, P. L. (2012). *Trusting what you're told: How children learn from others.* Cambridge, MA: Belknap Press/Harvard University Press.

Harris, P. L., & Corriveau, K. H. (2011). Young children's selective trust in informants. *Philosophical Transactions of the Royal Society B, 366,* 1179–1187.

Harris, P. L., de Rosnay, M., & Pons, F. (2005). Language and children's understanding of mental states. *Current Directions in Psychological Science, 14,* 69–73.

Kim, E., Song, G., Corriveau, K. H., & Harris, P. L. (2011, March 31–April 2). *Cultural differences in children's deference to authority.* Poster presented at the Biennial Meeting of the Society for Research in Child Development, Montreal, Canada.

Lyons, D. E., Damrosch, D. H., Lin, J. K., Simeone, D. M., & Keil, F. C. (2011). The scope and limits of overimitation in the transmission of artifact culture. *Philosophical Transactions of the Royal Society B, 366,* 1158–1167.

Lyons, D. E., Young, A. G., & Keil, F. C. (2007). The hidden structure of overimitation. *Proceedings of the National Academy of Sciences USA, 104,* 19751–19756.

Hofstede, G. (1983). Dimensions of national cultures in fifty countries and three regions. In J. Deregowski, S. Dziurawiec, & R. Annis (Eds.), *Explications in cross-cultural psychology* (pp. 335–355). Lisse, The Netherlands: Swets & Zeitlinger.

Horner, V., & Whiten, A. (2005). Causal knowledge and imitation/emulation switching in chimpanzees (Pan troglodytes) and children (Homo sapiens). *Animal Cognition, 8,* 164–181.

Meins, E., & Ferneyhough, C. (1999). Linguistic acquisitional style and mentalising development: The role of maternal mind-mindedness. *Cognitive Development, 14,* 363–380.

Nielsen, M., & Blank, C. (2011). Imitation in young children: When who gets copied is more important than what gets copied. *Developmental Psychology, 47*, 1050–1053.

Nielsen, M., & Tomaselli, K. (2010). Overimitation in Kalahari Bushman children and the origins of human cultural cognition. *Psychological Science, 21*, 729–736.

Ruffman, T., Slade, L., & Crowe, E. (2002). The relationship between children's and mother's mental state language and theory of mind understanding. *Child Development, 73*, 734–751.

Shahaeian, A., Peterson, C. C., Slaughter, V., & Wellman, H. M. (2011). Culture and the sequence of steps in theory of mind development. *Developmental Psychology, 47*, 1239–1247.

Taumoepeau, M., & Ruffman, T. (2006). Mother and infant talk about mental states relates to desire language and emotion understanding. *Child Development, 77*, 465–481.

Taumoepeau, M., & Ruffman, T. (2008). Stepping-stones to others' minds: Maternal talk relates to child mental state language and emotion understanding at 15, 24, and 33 months. *Child Development, 79*, 284–302.

Wellman, H. M, Fang, F., Liu, D., Zhu, L., & Liu, G. (2006). Scaling of theory-of-mind understandings in Chinese children. *Psychological Science, 17*, 1075–1081.

4.7

Children's Understanding of Unreliability

Evidence for a Negativity Bias

MELISSA A. KOENIG AND SABINE DOEBEL

One central function of language is the communication of new information to others (Tomasello, 2009; Williams, 2002). This very basic idea—that a speaker can tell someone else about a situation because she was in it, while her hearer was not—highlights the presence of an epistemic advantage that any given person can have over another. These epistemic differences can occur as very local and temporary differences between people in terms of their access to information in the immediate environment, as well as more profound and lasting differences between experts or specialists in some particular domain of knowledge. Such epistemic differences among people have two important implications for children: (a) they stand to gain immensely from the communication of others who have an epistemic advantage; and (b) they are vulnerable to misinformation due to this broad dependency on others for information, which may reduce, cancel, or even reverse these gains.

There is reason to think that humans have a set of cognitive mechanisms to ensure that communication remains advantageous despite such risks (Sperber et al., 2010). One set of mechanisms concerns *how* young children decide to trust or mistrust an informant. We examine the proposition that young children may be generally cost oriented in such decisions—they weigh negative aspects of a person's competence more heavily than positive ones, as do adults. We suggest here that young children's avoidance of incompetent sources may reflect a "negativity bias" or a "positive-negative asymmetry" (Baumeister, Bratslavsky, Finkenauer, & Vohs, 2001; Peeters & Czapinski, 1990; Rozin & Royzman, 2001; Vaish, Grossmann, & Woodward, 2008). For example, among adults, negative information typically carries more weight than good information about a person (e.g., Peeters & Czapinski, 1990; Vonk, 1996) and children's memory for morally negative actions is often better than their memory for positive actions (Kinzler & Shutts, 2008). After a brief review, we consider several recent studies of children's selective learning that indicate an asymmetry between positive and negative information about a speaker's competence, discuss how this asymmetry may change with development, and end by considering the specific implications of this pattern of findings.

Children show considerable sophistication in their efforts to evaluate people as potential sources of information. Not only do children prefer to learn from reliable over less reliable individuals (Birch, Vauthier, & Bloom, 2008; Jaswal & Neely, 2006; Koenig & Harris, 2005; Sabbagh & Baldwin, 2001), they form enduring profiles of an informant's prior accuracy and continue to use this information when evaluating new testimony after a week has passed (Corriveau & Harris, 2009a). The ability to use an individual's epistemic reliability to guide learning and imitation appears to be an early emerging competence (Birch, Akmal, & Frampton, 2010; Chow, Poulin-Dubois, & Lewis, 2008; Koenig & Woodward, 2010; Poulin-Dubois & Chow, 2009). Infants and young children take into account the circumstances that affect a speaker's ability to demonstrate competence, such as limited information access (Koenig & Echols, 2003; Kushnir, Wellman, & Gelman, 2008; Nurmsoo & Robinson, 2009; Poulin-Dubois & Chow, 2009), and preschoolers have been shown to forgive past inaccuracy when appropriate (Nurmsoo & Robinson, 2009; Robinson & Nurmsoo, 2009). By age 4, children monitor the relative magnitude of a person's errors in certain domains (i.e., estimates of quantity) and assess incorrect information for "how wrong" it is (Einav & Robinson, 2010). In the context of a simple game, children of this age verbally protest when they see others follow rules that were provided by a previously inaccurate source (Rakoczy, Warneken, & Tomasello, 2009). Furthermore, children are capable of revising their judgments in light of new evidence bearing on an individual's reliability (Scofield & Behrend, 2008) and by 4 years of age monitor the relative frequency of errors made by two informants (Pasquini, Corriveau, Koenig, & Harris, 2007).

This line of research thus documents a general competence that infants and young children display when learning from others and indicates an impressive range of cues used to make these selective judgments. However, there are important questions concerning when, how, or under what conditions children demonstrate selective learning. Children's preference for a more accurate or reliable source may be driven by a desire to avoid learning from an incompetent source, a positive bias to approach a more accurate or unmarked source, or some combination of the two. Recent experiments directly address this ambiguity, either by single-speaker designs or by pitting positively and negatively marked sources against neutral ones, rather than against each other.

In research by Koenig and Jaswal (2011), children were presented with two informants, one of whom was an expert about dogs and one who was less expert about dogs. Crucially, the individual who was less expert about dogs did not commit errors, nor was she ignorant about them; she was a neutral informant who was simply less knowledgeable compared to the expert. After being told that the dog expert "works at an animal hospital, works with dogs all the time, and knows more about dogs than anyone I know," children saw the expert label a series of dogs using breed names (e.g., "That's a Basenji dog") and the nonexpert describe a perceptually obvious feature of the dog (e.g., "That's a brown dog"). During the test phase, children were divided into two conditions and the expert and nonexpert used contrasting novel breed names for pictures of new dogs or labels for novel artifacts. We found that children who could remember which informant was the dog expert preferred her over the novice when learning the breed names of dogs, but they displayed no such preference when the two informants presented artifact labels. In other words, we found no evidence for an overgeneralized trust or "halo effect" toward the dog expert. Consistent with research by Keil and colleagues (see Keil, 2006 for a review), children's deference toward a dog expert was limited to the domain of dogs. This suggests that children's preference for information is often constrained by their evaluation of whether the information is relevant to the speaker's reliability

rather than driven by a more primitive appeal toward competent individuals.

In a follow-up experiment, the same basic procedure was used to investigate whether children would expect *incompetence* to generalize across domains. Children were first told about an informant who was specifically limited in her dog knowledge: "Jenny spends time with other kinds of animals but when she was a girl, Jenny didn't have any dogs and she doesn't have any now either. Jenny knows less about dogs than anyone I know." The inexpert speaker then mislabeled a series of dogs (e.g., "Basenji cat"), whereas the other speaker made neutral comments about them (e.g., "That's a nice one. I like that one."). The neutral comments were worded in terms of preferences to provide the children with no information about her accuracy. We found that children who could identify the person who did not know much about dogs preferred the neutral source for *both* dog and artifact labels. In contrast to the domain-specific trust of an expert in the first study, when children found an individual to be incompetent, they avoided her across domains (in favor of a weak or neutral informant). In sum, children gave a conservative, domain-specific treatment to expertise relative to the domain-general mistrust given to an incompetent source. Young children may not decide to trust or mistrust by simply taking into account all of the relevant information they have about a person; instead, judgments to mistrust may form and function quite differently than judgments to trust.

Such findings are in line with evidence from Corriveau, Meints, and Harris (2009), who found that when 3-year-old children were presented with a previously accurate informant and one who made neutral comments (i.e., "Look at that one"), they treated them as equally good informants, suggesting that being accurate did not confer any special status to a potential informant. In marked contrast, 3-year-olds systematically avoided an inaccurate informant in favor of both an accurate source and a neutral one. Similarly, 3-year-olds consistently avoided an informant who had erred just once in the past (Pasquini et al., 2007), whereas 4-year-olds proved selective across all informant contrasts, including one between an accurate and neutral source (Corriveau et al., 2009). Indeed, as we suggest later, it may be that younger children are especially moved to avoid unfamiliar speakers who make even a single error.

The potency of errors for young learners can be seen in research where children are confronted with a single speaker who is inaccurate (Ganea,

Koenig, & Gordon-Millet, 2011; Koenig & Echols, 2003; Koenig & Woodward, 2010). For example, in research by Koenig and Woodward (2010), 24-month-old children interacted with a speaker who accurately or inaccurately labeled familiar objects, and who subsequently presented children with a new word-object pairing. Findings across several experiments indicated that although toddlers attended to the inaccurate speaker, word learning was less robust when new terms were provided by a previously inaccurate speaker than by an accurate speaker. When children's memory for the word trained by the inaccurate source was later tested by a second speaker or taxed by a brief delay period, children failed to systematically select the target object. In fact, toddlers modulated their learning from an inaccurate source after only three instances of misnaming. This finding is consistent with research by Sabbagh and colleagues (Sabbagh & Shafman, 2009; Sabbagh, Wdowiak, & Ottaway, 2003). Sabbagh and Shafman (2009) found that 4-year-old children, shortly after hearing novel words from ignorant speakers, gave correct responses to questions about the labeling episode (i.e., "Which one did I say is the blicket?") but not to standard comprehension questions (i.e., "Which one is the blicket?"). When the children were tested again after a brief delay, their memories for the ignorant speaker's labeling episode also declined rapidly. Taken together, these findings demonstrate that while children attend to and encode their experiences with unreliable speakers, the formation of stable semantic representations are compromised by only a few signs of the speaker's ignorance or incompetence.

Given that an early and acute sensitivity to negative behavior is well documented in the sociomoral domain (Mumme & Fernald, 2003; Vaish, Carpenter, & Tomasello, 2010), we recently investigated whether preschoolers would show differential learning from individuals who behaved in ways consistent or inconsistent with sociomoral norms, such as helping a friend retrieve a toy or deliberately ripping a friend's artwork (Doebel & Koenig, in press). To make clear inferences about which of two informants children were motivated to avoid or prefer, participants were shown four video clips of a main character being consistently nice or mean to a peer, along with four clips of a neutral character spending time with a peer (e.g., in parallel play). On four subsequent test trials, children were given the opportunity to ask for and endorse the testimony of one of the two actors who provided discrepant labels for a novel object. After the test phase, children were asked who knew more, and whom they would prefer to play with.

Several findings indicate that children were particularly moved by the behavior displayed by the immoral agent relative to the moral one (see also Mascaro & Sperber, 2009). Children were more accurate in identifying which of two informants was "nicer" in the immoral condition. On test trials, while children did not prefer the testimony of the moral informant over the neutral informant, they systematically rejected the testimony of the previously immoral informant in favor of that of the neutral actor. Furthermore, they were more likely to prefer and judge the neutral informant as more knowledgeable when she was contrasted with an immoral agent, whereas no discrimination was evident between the moral and neutral agents. Such findings are consistent with other research on early social cognition demonstrating that children require fewer examples of negative behaviors to infer negative traits about other people than they do positive behaviors to infer positive traits (e.g., Aloise, 1993), and their memory for individuals who have done negative things (e.g., stolen cookies) is better than their memory for individuals who have done positive things (e.g., shared cookies) (Kinzler & Shutts, 2008). Children have been shown to use a person's prior accuracy to make inferences about sociomoral behavior (Brosseau-Liard & Birch, 2010); however, whether such inferences were moved by accuracy or inaccuracy information (or both) remains an open question. It may be that being able to track negative information about an individual is more useful than tracking positive information, especially insofar as such information permits inferences that allow one to avoid various kinds of harm.

Based on this brief review, we tentatively suggest that a negativity bias might characterize or underlie children's early decisions about whom to *mistrust*. When determining the extent to which children believe the claims of another, examples of when someone has been wrong may be weighted more heavily than examples of when they have been right.

To be clear, our claim is not that children are unaffected by positive information. Children's reasoning about traits has shown a "positivity bias" whereby children expect individuals who exhibit positive behaviors to have other positive attributes (Boseovski, 2010; Heyman & Giles, 2004). Indeed, we speculate that the negativity effects discussed here participate in a more general positive-negative asymmetry. On one side, there may be a basic positivity bias that reflects children's tendency to approach, learn about, and discover new objects and people, unless unfavorably marked. Infants bring a ready disposition to learn from others (G. Csibra & G. Gergely, 2006), especially their spoken messages (Jaswal, 2010; Jaswal, Croft, Setia, & Cole, 2010), and positive attitudes toward familiar caregivers likely guide younger children's selective learning (Corriveau & Harris, 2009b). On the other side, this bias may be allied with a strongly marked, subjective sensitivity for negative stimuli. Infants reject and correct mistaken labels by 16 months (Koenig & Echols, 2003), young children adjust their epistemic trust in an informant on the basis of minimal information (Corriveau & Harris, 2009b; Koenig & Woodward, 2010), and draw broad inferences about the incompetence of mistaken sources (Koenig & Jaswal, in press). Studies that investigate positive and negative information independently, and in different domains, are needed to gain insight into when and how children demonstrate negativity or positivity biases.

Although much research on valence effects stresses their affective character, some cognitive researchers have called attention to informational negativity effects and the complexity of negative information (Cacioppo & Berntson, 1994; Peeters & Czapinski, 1990). For example, adults spend more time looking at negative than at positive stimuli (Fiske, 1980) and other cases of the bias exist in adult memory, information processing, and neurological processing (see Baumeister et al., 2001). In line with the possibility that inaccurate messages carry greater informational complexity and require more cognitive effort for children, it will be important to investigate whether young children spend more time processing inaccurate messages, look longer at unreliable than reliable sources, and whether children's long-term memory for the identity of the source is best supported by the presence of negative information.

The negativity bias has often been thought to serve the evolutionarily adaptive purpose of supporting safe exploration of the environment while appropriately avoiding threatening situations (Cacioppo & Berntson, 1994; Kanouse & Hanson, 1972; Rozin & Royzman, 2001). Thus, an early expression of the negativity bias in testimony may be part of a built-in evolutionary mechanism given the adaptive advantage of a naive pedagogical stance (Csibra & Gergely, 2009; Gergely, Egyed, & Király, 2007) and vigilance toward mistaken information (Sperber, 2006). Just as negative facial expressions (such as anger) may cause defensive responses in infants (Mumme & Fernald, 2003), it could be that messages that conflict with early semantic knowledge cause greater arousal, impaired memory, and slower habituation (Koenig & Echols, 2003). The fact that vervet monkeys learn to ignore alarm calls from a consistently unreliable signaler lends further support to this general idea (Cheney & Seyfarth, 1988).

Alternatively, the presence of a positive-negative asymmetry in the domain of testimony may depend on children's early experience with speakers and the messages they share with their children. As infants acquire a rudimentary vocabulary, this allows them in turn to identify and interpret the simple claims that parents direct to their children. Because obvious inaccuracy in communication is the exception rather than the rule—especially in the case of early adult–child communication—perhaps infants begin to experience many, perhaps well-rehearsed, plain truths about the objects and events in their immediate environment (Williams, 2002). As infants encounter more and more of these accurate claims, what may have begun as a neutral starting point in terms of expectations concerning speaker accuracy starts to shift closer to a positive setting, becoming an experience-based expectation of accuracy. That is, a default setting of trust may be built up on the basis of prior encounters with accurate messages or "plain truths," and this may be a framework the child brings to new encounters with unfamiliar informants. This disproportionate experience of accurate claims may be part of what makes inaccurate messages particularly salient and demanding of more attention and resources, resulting in an early bias based on an experience-based asymmetry between accuracy and inaccuracy.

Speculatively, just as early expectations of accuracy may be based on the shared plain truths that recur in their conversations with adults, the bias may become less potent as the composition of messages adults direct to children becomes more diversified. Recall, for example, that 4-year-olds monitored informants for both accuracy and inaccuracy and trusted an accurate informant over a neutral one (Corriveau et al., 2009). Similarly, in Pasquini et al. (2007), 4-year-olds preferred to learn from someone who was 75% accurate, in spite of her mistake, over one who was rarely accurate. These documented age changes raise the intriguing possibility that children come to appreciate, as adults present an increasingly sophisticated set of messages (i.e., hypothetical statements, new forms of humor, nonliteral language), the ways in which both speakers and types of messages vary in accuracy, resulting in a decreased reliance on a simple assumption of accuracy. To the extent that simple baseline expectations are reduced over time, the negativity bias may become less marked with age (although we expect some level of vigilance toward inaccuracy to persist over the life span).

The foregoing review and proposal, while speculative, suggests as a fruitful avenue for research further investigation of how the valence of the information factors into children's evaluation of an informant's testimony, and under which circumstances one should expect a negativity bias in selective trust. Important questions remain concerning how positivity and negativity biases interact, how children's use of negative information compares to adults when deciding to trust, and how children's relative sensitivity to one or the other kind of information may vary depending on the domain of information (e.g., moral information, factual claims) and unreliability cue (ignorance, inaccuracy, immorality), as well as the degree of sophistication a child has attained in her understanding of the multifarious nature of messages.

REFERENCES

Aloise, P. A. (1993). Trait confirmation and disconfirmation: The development of attribution biases. *Journal of Experimental Child Psychology*, *55*(2), 177–193.

Baumeister, R. F., Bratslavsky, E., Finkenauer, C., & Vohs, K. D. (2001). Bad is stronger than good. *Review of General Psychology*, *5*(4), 323–370.

Birch, S. A., Akmal, N., & Frampton, K. L. (2010). Two-year-olds are vigilant of others' non-verbal cues to credibility. *Developmental Science*, *13*(2), 363–369.

Birch, S. A., Vauthier, S. A., & Bloom, P. (2008). Three-and four-year-olds spontaneously use others' past performance to guide their learning. *Cognition*, *107*(3), 1018–1034.

Boseovski, J. J. (2010). Evidence for "rose-colored classes": An examination of the positivity bias in young children's personality judgments. *Child Development Perspectives*, *4*(3), 212–218.

Brosseau-Liard, P., & Birch, S. (2010). "I bet you know more and are nicer too!" What children infer from others' accuracy. *Developmental Science*, *13*(5), 772–778.

Cacioppo, J. T., & Berntson, G. G. (1994). Relationship between attitudes and evaluative space: A critical review, with emphasis on the separability of positive and negative substrates. *Psychological Bulletin*, *115*(3), 401–423.

Cheney, D. L., & Seyfarth, R. M. (1988). Assessment of meaning and the detection of unreliable signals by vervet monkeys. *Animal Behaviour*, *36*(2), 477–486.

Chow, V., Poulin-Dubois, D., & Lewis, J. (2008). To see or not to see: Infants prefer to follow the gaze of a reliable looker. *Developmental Science*, *11*(5), 761–770.

Corriveau, K., & Harris, P. L. (2009a). Preschoolers continue to trust a more accurate informant 1 week after exposure to accuracy information. *Developmental Science*, *12*(1), 188–193.

Corriveau, K., & Harris, P. L. (2009b). Choosing your informant: Weighing familiarity and recent accuracy. *Developmental Science*, *12*(3), 426–437.

Corriveau, K. H., Meints, K., & Harris, P. L. (2009). Early tracking of informant accuracy and inaccuracy. *British Journal of Developmental Psychology*, *27*(2), 331–342.

Csibra, G., & Gergely, G. (2006). Social learning and social cognition: The case for pedagogy. *Processes of change in brain and cognitive development. Attention and performance*, *XXI*.

Csibra, G., & Gergely, G. (2009). Natural pedagogy. *Trends in Cognitive Sciences*, *13*(4), 148–153.

Doebel, S., & Koenig, M. A., (in press). Children's use of moral behavior in selective trust: Discrimination versus learning. *Developmental Psychology*.

Einav, S., & Robinson, E. (2010). Children's sensitivity to error magnitude when evaluating informants. *Cognitive Development*, *25*(3), 218–232.

Fiske, S. T. (1980). Attention and weight in person perception: The impact of negative and extreme behavior. *Journal of Personality and Social Psychology*, *38*(6), 889–906.

Ganea, P. A., Koenig, M. A., & Gordon-Millet, K. (2011). Changing your mind about things unseen: Toddlers' sensitivity to prior reliability. *Journal of Experimental Child Psychology*, *109*(4), 445–453.

Gergely, G., Egyed, K., & Király, I. (2007). On pedagogy. *Developmental Science*, *10*(1), 139–146.

Heyman, G. D., & Giles, J. W. (2004). Valence effects in reasoning about evaluative traits. *Merrill-Palmer Quarterly*, *50*(1), 86–110.

Jaswal, V. K., Croft, A. C., Setia, A. R., & Cole, C. A. (2010). Young children have a specific, highly robust bias to trust testimony. *Psychological Science*, *21*(10), 1541–1547.

Jaswal, V. K., & Neely, L. A. (2006). Adults don't always know best. *Psychological Science*, *17*(9), 757–758.

Kanouse, D. E., & Hanson, L. R. (1972). Negativity in evaluations. In E. E. Jones, D. E. Kanouse, H. H. Kelley, R. E. Nisbett, S. Valins, & B. Weiner (Eds.), *Attribution: Perceiving the causes of behavior* (pp. 47–62). Morristown, NJ: General Learning Press.

Keil, F. (2006). Doubt, deference, and deliberation: Understanding and using the division of cognitive labor. In J. Hawthorne & T. Gendler (Eds.), *Oxford studies in epistemology* (pp. 143–166). New York: Oxford University Press.

Kinzler, K. D., & Shutts, K. (2008). Memory for "mean" over "nice": The influence of threat on children's face memory. *Cognition, 107*(2), 775–783.

Koenig, M. A., & Echols, C. H. (2003). Infants' understanding of false labeling events: The referential roles of words and the speakers who use them. *Cognition, 87*(3), 179–208.

Koenig, M. A., & Harris, P. L. (2005). Preschoolers mistrust ignorant and inaccurate speakers. *Child Development, 76*(6), 1261–1277.

Koenig, M. A., & Jaswal, V. K. (2011). Characterizing children's expectations about expertise and incompetence: Halo or pitchfork effects? *Child Development, 82*(5), 1634–1647.

Koenig, M. A., & Woodward, A. (2010). Sensitivity of 24-month-olds to the prior inaccuracy of the source: Possible mechanisms. *Developmental Psychology, 46*(4), 815–826.

Kushnir, T., Wellman, H. M., & Gelman, S. A. (2008). The role of preschoolers' social understanding in evaluating the informativeness of causal interventions. *Cognition, 107*(3), 1084–1092.

Mascaro, O. & Sperber, D. (2009). The moral, epistemic, and mindreading components of children's vigilance towards deception. *Cognition, 112*(3), 367–380.

Mumme, D. L., & Fernald, A. (2003). The infant as onlooker: Learning from emotional reactions observed in a television scenario. *Child Development, 74*(1), 221–237.

Nurmsoo, E., & Robinson, E. J. (2009). Children's trust in previously inaccurate informants who were well or poorly informed: When past errors can be excused. *Child Development, 80*(1), 23–27.

Pasquini, E., Corriveau, K., Koenig, M., & Harris, P. (2007). Preschoolers monitor the relative accuracy of informants. *Developmental Psychology, 43*(5), 1216–1226.

Peeters, G., & Czapinski, J. (1990). Positive-negative asymmetry in evaluations: The distinction between affective and informational negativity effects. *European Review of Social Psychology, 1*(1), 33–60.

Poulin-Dubois, D., & Chow, V. (2009). The effect of a looker's past reliability on infants' reasoning about beliefs. *Developmental Psychology, 45*(6), 1576–1582.

Rakoczy, H., Warneken, F., & Tomasello, M. (2009). Young children's selective learning of rule games from reliable and unreliable models. *Cognitive Development, 24*(1), 61–69.

Robinson, E., & Nurmsoo, E. (2009). When do children learn from unreliable speakers? *Cognitive Development, 24*(1), 16–22.

Rozin, P., & Royzman, E. B. (2001). Negativity bias, negativity dominance, and contagion. *Personality and Social Psychology Review, 5*(4), 296.

Sabbagh, M., & Shafman, D. (2009). How children block learning from ignorant speakers. *Cognition, 112*(3), 415–422.

Sabbagh, M., Wdowiak, S. D., & Ottaway, J. M. (2003). Do word learners ignore ignorant speakers? *Journal of Child Language, 30*(04), 905–924.

Sabbagh, M. A., & Baldwin, D. A. (2001). Learning words from knowledgeable versus ignorant speakers: Links between preschoolers' theory of mind and semantic development. *Child Development, 72*(4), 1054–1070.

Scofield, J., & Behrend, D. A. (2008). Learning words from reliable and unreliable speakers. *Cognitive Development, 23*(2), 278–290.

Sperber, D. (2006). An evolutionary perspective on testimony and argumentation. *Biological and Cultural Bases of Human Inference*, 177–189.

Sperber, D., Clement, F., Mascaro, O., Mercier, H., Origgi D., & Wilson, D. (2010). Epistemic vigilance. *Mind and Language, 25*(4), 359–393.

Tomasello, M. (2009). *Why we co-operate*. Cambridge, MA: MIT Press.

Vaish, A., Carpenter, M., & Tomasello, M. (2010). Young children selectively avoid helping people with harmful intentions. *Child Development, 81*(6), 1661–1669.

Vaish, A., Grossmann, T., & Woodward, A. (2008). Not all emotions are created equal: The negativity bias in social-emotional development. *Psychological Bulletin, 134*(3), 383.

Vonk, R. (1996). Negativity and potency effects in impression formation. *European Journal of Social Psychology, 26*(6), 851–865.

Williams, B. (2002). *Truth and truthfulness*. Princeton, NJ: Princeton University Press.

4.8

Biased to Believe

VIKRAM K. JASWAL

Young children have a well-deserved reputation for credulity. They really seem to believe much of what they are told—from the mundane (this four-legged animal is called a "dog") to the normally unobservable (people have lungs) to the incredible (dinosaurs the size of trucks used to roam the earth). At first, this may seem like a pretty unremarkable observation. After all, children (and adults) have to accept some of what they hear on faith in order to learn about things that are beyond their own experience. But what makes children's credulity quite remarkable is how utterly deep and resilient it is. In fact, my colleagues and I have found that the bias to trust testimony[1] is so strong that many young children cannot help but believe what they are told, even when it conflicts with their firsthand experience and even when there is an incentive for responding skeptically.

In one study, we asked how toddlers would resolve a conflict between a physical event they witnessed and an adult's report about that event (Jaswal, 2010). We used an apparatus modeled after Hood (1995), consisting of a large wooden frame with three chimneys affixed above three cups. Each chimney was connected with a tube to a nonadjacent cup such that the left-most chimney, for example, might be connected to the middle cup, the middle chimney to the right cup, and so on. In this study, the tubes were clear and the cups were opaque.

Thirty-month-olds watched as an experimenter dropped a goldfish cracker into one of the chimneys. Because the tubes were clear, they could see the cracker as it traveled through a particular tube until it disappeared into one of

the opaque cups (at which point, they no longer had visual access to the cracker). When they were asked where the cracker was, children almost always accurately identified the cup into which they had seen it disappear. Next, an adult sitting next to them, who had seen the very same event, claimed that it was in a different (incorrect) cup. This testimony was offered as an assertion, not as a correction or imperative. For example, if a child had initially indicated a cup with bear stickers on it (each cup had several stickers of a particular animal on it), the adult simply said, "It's in the dog cup." Children were allowed to search for the cracker until they found it. If they found it in the first cup they looked in, they got to eat it; if not, it was put away.

On the very first trial, about half of the children first searched in the cup mentioned by the adult, even though it was not where they had just seen the cracker disappear, where they had just said it was, or where they had just heard it land (the cracker made a sound as it fell into a cup). This is, perhaps, not surprising given that it was an unfamiliar game with an unfamiliar adult.

What was surprising was that the same sequence of events was repeated five more times, and many children continued to look for the goldfish cracker where the adult claimed it was. Given that they never found (or got to eat) the cracker by searching there, one might have expected them to become more skeptical as the game went on. But they did not: On the first three trials, children searched the cup indicated by the adult, on average, 50% of the time, and on the last three trials, they did so 60% of the time. In fact, one quarter of the children were deferential on five or six of the six trials. (On the opposite end of the continuum, about one quarter ignored the adult on most of the trials, a point to which we will return later.)

It is important to note that children had not simply forgotten which opaque cup they had seen

[1] "Testimony" here is simply used to refer to information conveyed through language (Harris, 2002). Philosophical definitions of testimony can be much broader (e.g., street signs, historical texts; Coady, 1992), but this chapter will focus on verbal testimony.

the cracker fall into. On those trials where they first searched the (empty) cup mentioned by the adult, their second search tended to be to the correct cup rather than the other empty one. Thus, the adult's erroneous testimony had not overwritten the children's memory for the event.

It is also important to note that their repeated deference was unlikely to be the result of mere compliance. First, as parents (and developmental psychologists) can attest, young children are not known for their compliance (e.g., Landauer, Carlsmith, & Lepper, 1970). Second, we conducted an additional study in which the procedure was similar, but this time, both the tubes and cups into which the object fell were clear (in the earlier described study, the tubes were clear but the cups were opaque). We reasoned that if social pressure alone were responsible for children's behavior, they would continue to be deferential even when the adult's testimony was obviously wrong. Results were clear: When children heard the adult claim an object had fallen into a cup they could see was empty, they nearly always ignored that testimony. Thus, compliance alone cannot explain why many children in the earlier study so frequently deferred to the adult's testimony.

The explanation we favor is that many children genuinely believed that they would find the cracker where the adult said it was. The source of this belief was a robust, default bias children have to trust what they are told. The bias is robust in the sense that it can operate even when it competes with other compelling interests, such as obtaining a tasty treat. It operates by default in the sense that it does not require any special conditions to be triggered.

The notion that children are biased to trust testimony is, of course, not a new one. The Scottish philosopher Thomas Reid (1764/2003), for example, posited a *principle of credulity*, "a disposition to confide in the veracity of others, and to believe what they tell us" (p. 194). Reid suggested that children become less credulous as they experience "deceit and falsehood" over the course of development, but the tendency to believe remains strong even in adulthood.

One elegant experimental demonstration of this comes from a study by Gilbert and his colleagues (1990). Adults were presented with a novel proposition (in written form), which they learned to be true or false. Crucially, this information was provided while the participants were completing a secondary task. The hypothesis was that if propositions are, by default, accepted as true, then "unaccepting" them should take cognitive effort

that might not be available given the demands of the secondary task.

And this was exactly what Gilbert and colleagues (1990) found. When adults were asked to remember whether a given proposition was true or false, there was a marked asymmetry in their errors: They were more likely to misremember as true something that was said to be false than to misremember as false something that was said to be true. (There was no such asymmetry when adults did not have to simultaneously complete the secondary task.) Thus, although the average adult may be better able than the average preschooler to inhibit the bias to trust testimony, the bias itself is always present.

When a bias is invoked as an explanation for children's (or adults') behavior, at least two questions need to be addressed. First, do the benefits of having the bias outweigh the costs? In the case of a bias to trust testimony, the answer is clearly "yes." As alluded to earlier, much of what we need or want to know can only be learned from what other people tell us. Furthermore, we simply do not have the time or ability to verify most testimony. For example, how many of us could prove to ourselves that the President was at Camp David this weekend, or that dinosaurs roamed the earth 60 million years ago? Fortunately, we are generally safe in trusting testimony because people normally say what they believe to be true (e.g., Grice, 1975). Of course, for a variety of reasons, including error, ignorance, and deception, people do sometimes say things that are wrong; having a bias to believe means that we will occasionally be misled. But this is a relatively rare occurrence.

A second important question concerns where such a bias would come from. One possibility is that what we have been calling a bias to believe testimony actually reflects a much more general, undifferentiated tendency to trust other people. For example, when I go to the bank, I not only trust that the teller will truthfully testify to my balance but also that she or he will safeguard my personal information and return my driver's license at the end of the transaction. As Baier (1986) pointed out, children's total dependence on their caregivers leaves them little choice but to trust that those around them will behave in helpful (or at least benign) ways: They "can make suspicious, futile, self-protective moves against the powerful adults in their world...But surviving infants will usually have shown some trust, enough to accept offered nourishment, enough not to attempt to prevent such close approach" (p. 241).

From the chimney study described earlier, it is clear that many children will continue to believe what they are told even after being misled several times (see also, e.g., Mascaro & Sperber, 2009). To address the specificity question, in a recent study, we asked whether children would be as likely to continue to trust another, nontestimonial method of conveying the same (false) information (Jaswal, Croft, Setia, & Cole, 2010). If they are, then a general stance of trust toward others may be sufficient to explain their willingness to believe what they are told. If, however, children's trust in testimony is more resilient, this would suggest that a more specific bias is at work.

On each of eight trials, 3-year-olds saw an adult place two cups (say, a red cup and a blue cup) upside down on a tray. They watched as she hid a sticker under one of the cups, though a screen prevented them from seeing which one. One group of 3-year-olds heard the adult say that the sticker was under the red cup when she had actually placed it under the blue one. This was our "testimony" condition. A second group of children saw the adult carefully and unambiguously place an arrow on the red (empty) cup without saying anything. This was our "arrow" condition. Children were invited to search for the sticker, and if they found it in the first cup they looked under, they got to keep it. Otherwise, the adult got to keep it. Before the first trial, as she was introducing the game, the adult made it clear that she wanted to keep as many stickers as she could, and twice during the study, children were told (by a third party) that the adult was being "tricky."

On the very first trial, children in both conditions looked for the sticker under the empty cup mentioned or marked by the adult. This presumably reflects a (quite reasonable) expectation that when adults offer information, they will do so in a helpful, conventional manner—in this case, by using words or an arrow to indicate where something is rather than where it is not. (It is interesting that none of the children inferred from the adult's stated desire to collect as many stickers as possible that they should be wary of information she provided. But this was presumably an unfamiliar situation, and so children may not have initially understood that it was a competitive game.)

On later trials, however, children in the two conditions behaved very differently. Those in the arrow condition quickly learned to look under the cup that the adult had *not* marked with an arrow. In essence, they had learned that if they wanted the sticker, they could not interpret the arrow in the conventional way. But those in the testimony condition continued to search in the empty cup where the adult claimed the sticker was, even

though this meant that they never found (or got to keep) any stickers. In fact, over half of the children in the testimony condition were misled on all eight trials; just 6% of those in the arrow condition were misled as often. (All children were given all the stickers at the end of the study.)

Children's difficulty in the testimony condition relative to the arrow one suggests that, in addition to whatever undifferentiated trust in others they may have, they have a specific bias to trust what people tell them. As for the source of this bias, there are two extreme positions. On the one hand, Reid (1764/2003) suggested that credulity is an "original principle" of human nature, not something that is learned. On the other, Hume (1748/2004) held that we learn to trust testimony from the accumulation of evidence that what people say is normally true. My own position is somewhat of a middle ground. Some baseline level of trust would seem to be required to get language acquisition started (e.g., Coady, 1992). To learn vocabulary, for example, children have to be receptive to the words people use when referring to things. But this initial trust could be undifferentiated; it need not be specific to language or testimony. The specific bias to trust testimony could emerge out of the more generic trust, as children repeatedly experience the correspondence between what they are told and what is the case.

One reason to suspect that the specific bias to trust testimony is learned is that children also have a robust bias to trust at least one other ubiquitous and usually veridical form of communication. Couillard and Woodward (1999) found that 3-year-olds have difficulty *not* searching where they see someone point. They argued that by the age of 3 years, children have been reinforced repeatedly for searching locations to which people point. Not searching there requires them to inhibit this highly practiced response. Although one could argue that both testimony and pointing are privileged from the start, it may be more parsimonious to suggest that same well-understood learning mechanisms are responsible for both. Presumably, with enough practice and reinforcement, children could also develop a robust expectation about the veridicality of, for example, arrows.

Children's bias to believe what they are told is strong, but it is obviously not inviolable. There was variability in both the chimney task and the sticker game, with some children never or only occasionally trusting the adult's testimony. Some of our current work focuses on trying to understand the sources of these individual differences. For example, we found that as children gain confidence in a given belief, they are more likely to ignore testimony that conflicts with that belief (Jaswal, 2010; see also Tamis-LeMonda et al., 2008). Additionally, preliminary evidence suggests that those children who are better able to inhibit a prepotent response are also more likely to respond skeptically to misleading testimony (Jaswal et al., 2011).

That young children are generally willing to believe what they are told is probably not news to most people, but the depth and resilience of their trust in testimony is surprising. A robust bias ensures that they will be able to take advantage of their culture's accumulated knowledge and expertise, much of it transmitted through spoken language. Characterizing this bias represents a first step toward understanding why it can be so difficult for children (and adults) to achieve a healthy balance between belief and skepticism.

REFERENCES

Baier, A. (1986). Trust and anti-trust. *Ethics, 96,* 231–260.

Coady, C. A. J. (1992). *Testimony: A philosophical study.* New York: Oxford University Press.

Couillard, N. L., & Woodward, A. L. (1999). Children's comprehension of deceptive points. *British Journal of Developmental Psychology, 17,* 515–521.

Gilbert, D. T., Krull, D. S., & Malone, P. S. (1990). Unbelieving the unbelievable: Some problems in the rejection of false information. *Journal of Personality and Social Psychology, 59,* 601–613.

Grice, H. P. (1975). Logic and conversation. In P. Cole & J. L. Morgan (Eds.), *Syntax and semantics, Vol. 3. Speech acts* (pp. 41–58). New York: Academic Press.

Harris, P. L. (2002). What do children learn from testimony? In P. Carruthers, S. Stich, & M. Siegal (Eds.), *The cognitive basis of science* (pp. 316–334).

Cambridge, England: Cambridge University Press.

Hood, B. M. (1995). Gravity rules for 2- to 4-year-olds? *Cognitive Development, 10,* 577–598.

Hume, D. (2004). *An enquiry concerning human understanding.* New York: Dover. [Original work published in 1748].

Jaswal, V. K. (2010). Believing what you're told: Young children's trust in unexpected testimony about the physical world. *Cognitive Psychology, 61,* 248–272.

Jaswal, V. K., Croft, A. C., Setia, A. R., & Cole, C. A. (2010). Young children have a specific, highly robust bias to trust testimony. *Psychological Science, 21,* 1541–1547.

Jaswal, V. K., Perez-Edgar, K., Kondrad, R., Palmquist, C., Cole, C., Cole, C., & Kreafle, J.,. (2011, April). *Young children's trust in misleading testimony: Individual differences in age, inhibitory control, and temperament.* Paper presented at the biennial meeting of the Society for Research in Child Development, Montreal, Canada.

Landauer, T. K., Carlsmith, J. M., & Lepper, M. (1970). Experimental analysis of the factors determining obedience of four-year-old children to adult females. *Child Development, 41,* 601–611.

Mascaro, O., & Sperber, D. (2009). The moral, epistemic, and mind- reading components of children's vigilance towards deception. *Cognition, 112,* 367–380.

Reid, T. (2003). *An inquiry into the human mind on the principles of common sense* (D.R. Brookes, Ed.). University Park, PA: Penn State Press. [Original work published in 1764].

Tamis-LeMonda, C. S., Adolph, K. E., Lobo, S. A., Karasik, L. B., Ishak, S., & Dimitropoulou, K. A. (2008). When infants take mothers' advice: 18-month-olds integrate perceptual and social information to guide motor actions. *Developmental Psychology, 44,* 734–746.

4.9

Food as a Unique Domain in Social Cognition

JULIE LUMENG

Children are naturally reluctant to sample new foods, a phenomenon that has been termed "food neophobia" (Pliner & Hobden, 1992). Food neophobia seems to increase during the second year of life and is believed to be adaptive, in that it prevents the child from ingesting substances that are potentially poisonous or have little nutritional value (Cashdan, 1994). The second year of life is when mobility has increased but mouthing behavior has not yet entirely disappeared, and a natural reluctance to eat unfamiliar foods would therefore presumably be particularly protective during this age range. Food neophobia is also particularly important for omnivores. Unlike other animals whose dietary repertoire is extremely limited, after weaning, human beings have the somewhat overwhelming task of identifying which of a myriad of items in their environment are edible, safe, and nutritious (Rozin, 1976).

Although food neophobia is presumably protective in early childhood, it can quickly become a challenge. In a modern environment in which children's access to poisonous plants is relatively limited, this behavioral predilection translates into the young child regularly refusing new foods that are presented, much to the parent's frustration. In fact, it requires about 10 exposures to a new food before the child will readily accept it (Birch & Marlin, 1982; Sullivan & Birch, 1999), and most parents do not persist this long (Carruth, Ziegler, Gordon, & Barr, 2004). Overcoming food neophobia also appears to have a critical window in development in early childhood; liking for a new food is more likely to be acquired in early childhood as opposed to later childhood (Cooke & Wardle, 2005; Skinner, Carruth, Bounds, & Ziegler, 2002). In summary, overcoming food neophobia is a central goal of early childhood nutrition and feeding.

To this end, a substantial amount of work has focused upon methods to overcome children's reluctance to sample a new food. Much of this work has focused on the powerful role of modeling on shaping both children's willingness to sample a new food, as well as, once the food is tasted, their liking for it. In this literature on eating behavior, the child has frequently been conceptualized as a bit of a "blank slate" that will readily model his or her behavior after a well-intentioned adult modeling great pleasure over the taste of brussels sprouts. As any parent knows, however, simply eating vegetables in front of a child and exclaiming that they are delicious has a somewhat limited effect on both the child's willingness to eat the vegetable, as well as his or her liking for the vegetable. In fact, modeling seems to become less effective in shaping food preferences and eating behavior as children grow out of infancy (Harper & Sanders, 1975; Hendy & Raudenbush, 2000). In addition, if parental modeling were highly effective in shaping a young child's food preferences, one would hypothesize that there would be a high correlation between the food preferences of a parent and child, but this is not the case (Pliner & Pelchat, 1986; Rozin, 1991).

In the context of the present childhood obesity epidemic (Ogden, Carroll, Curtin, Lamb, & Flegal, 2010), there has been increased interest in the last two decades regarding how to effectively shape children's eating behavior. Many of the randomized controlled trials testing expensive and intense behavioral interventions for obesity (Summerbell et al., 2003), as well as practice guidelines from major professional organizations impacting children's health (Barlow & Committee, 2007), have included parental modeling as a major focus. The evidence, however, for the effect of modeling on children's eating behavior is somewhat weak.

Modeling has long been recognized as shaping food selection among animals (Galef & Whiskin, 1997). The literature supporting a role for modeling in food choice among children dates back to 1938, when Duncker first reported a significant role for maternal modeling in shaping food selection (Duncker, 1938). A series of subsequent studies reported similar effects of modeling on children's eating behavior (Addessi, Galloway, Visalberghi, & Birch, 2005; Birch, 1980; Brody & Stoneman, 1981; Galef, 1989; Harper & Sanders, 1975; Hendy, 2002; Hendy & Raudenbush, 2000; Rozin, 1976; Rozin & Kennel, 1983; Rozin & Schiller, 1980).

Simultaneously, however, a growing body of literature has presented a more nuanced view of the development of children's social cognitions. Infants as young as 12 months of age can use adults' emotional reactions to guide their own affective responses and the amount of time they spend examining a novel toy (Moses, Baldwin, Rosicky, & Tidball, 2001). This suggests a developmentally early-emerging ability to attend to and use the affective responses of others when guiding one's response to novel objects. Children also have a developing ability to appreciate that adults can experience different sensations or feelings from themselves. (Bretheron & Beeghly, 1982). Children as young as 18 months are able to recognize that an adult can have a different food preference than themselves and act upon that information (offering the adult broccoli instead of goldfish crackers) (Repacholi & Gopnik, 1997). Other work has also shown that children as young as age 2 years are able to recognize shared and nonshared preferences (Fawcett & Markson, 2010). As young as age 3 years, children recognize that adults can be unreliable informants, providing incorrect information about a stimulus (Clement, Koenig, & Harris, 2004; Koenig & Harris, 2005). By age 4 years, children will modify their own behavior and choices based on their understanding of whether the adult is reliable (Koenig & Harris, 2005). These findings raise questions about the literature on the purportedly robust effect of adult modeling on children's food choices. Specifically, if one imagines a parent trying to persuade their 4-year-old child to eat spinach, the literature on adult modeling of eating behavior would suggest that the adult simply eating the spinach in front of the child, expressing great pleasure and enjoyment, should effectively persuade the child to eat the spinach. The research in the development of children's social cognitions, however, would suggest a different outcome. Specifically, the child is well aware that the adult likes different foods (like spinach) than the child. In addition, the child is very able to understand that the information that

the adult is providing (that the spinach is delicious) may well be unreliable. Logically, then, it would make sense that the adult modeling would not be very effective in persuading the child to eat the spinach (and particularly so as the child grows older). This limited efficacy of modeling is indeed what seems to be experienced by many parents.

A second issue regards characteristics of the model. Age of the model may be one salient characteristic. Although adults modeling eating novel foods is a remarkably effective method of persuading children to eat those foods (Addessi et al., 2005; Harper & Sanders, 1975), peers have also been identified as quite effective models. Children will imitate the observed food selections of a same-age or older peer (Brody & Stoneman, 1981; Duncker, 1938), peers can influence children to sample novel foods (Hendy, 2002), and peers can shift food preferences (Birch, 1980). Some literature has suggested that child models are more effective than adult models in shaping children's food selection and liking (Duncker, 1938; Hendy & Raudenbush, 2000; Shutts, Banaji, & Spelke, 2010). We recently also tested this directly by showing 3- and 4-year-old children a set of four photographs of a model eating an unseen and unidentifiable food from a spoon. Some of the food-eating models were adults, and some were children. The child participants were asked to select which of the photographs showed the model eating the food they would like to have for a snack. When child models were pitted directly against adult models, the child participants regularly selected the child model. On a practical level to most parents, this finding makes intuitive sense. In addition, advertisers clearly grasp this, since commercials for junk food targeted to children nearly always feature child models enjoying the sugared cereal or hamburger and not adults.

However, the literature on social cognition presents a different picture. Specifically, children generally identify adults as more knowledgeable than children (Taylor, Cartwright, & Bowden, 1991) and, all things being equal, are more likely to rely on information provided by adults than by children (Jaswal & Neely, 2006). Children are also attuned to the idea that adults with different areas of expertise may have different types of knowledge (Lutz & Keil, 2002). The fact that children seem to model their eating behavior after other children, and not after adults, would suggest that children perceive other children as more "expert" in food selection than adults. Indeed, in word learning, when adults are identified as unreliable, children prefer information provided by their peers over the adult (Jaswal & Neely, 2006). One might not necessarily predict this. Since food selection is a risky endeavor (a single incorrect choice could realistically lead to a fatal poisoning), one would hypothesize that children would be more apt to follow the lead of an adult with decades of experience selecting food from the environment. Instead, the child follows the lead of the peer 3-year-old. It is possible that children may have a predilection to model food selection after peers who are more biologically similar to themselves, as this would be adaptive. Specifically, children have quite different nutritional needs than adults (e.g., higher dietary fat content, higher caloric density, differences in micronutrients such as iron). Alternatively, children's predilection to model their eating behavior after other children (as opposed to adults) may be driven by similarities in taste preferences; it is well documented that compared to adults, children have a preference for greater intensity sweet and sour (Desor, 1987; Desor, Greene, & Maller, 1975; Liem & Mennella, 2003) .

The idea that children understand food differently than nonfood stimuli has also been proposed previously in work indicating that children are likely to categorize food by color, and nonfoods by shape (Macario, 1991). We recently found support for the hypothesis that children use social information differently to make a choice about a food, as compared to a nonfood item (Lumeng, Cardinal, Jankowski, Kaciroti, & Gelman, 2008). The manner in which they would use it differently was difficult to predict based on the conflicting literatures described earlier. Specifically, children may be more skeptical consumers of information provided by an unreliable adult when the stimulus is food, as compared to when it was a nonfood item. Alternatively, they may more indiscriminately trust information provided by an adult about a food, as compared to a nonfood item, even when they recognize that the adult is an unreliable informant. This may occur because food selection is somewhat fraught with potential peril. Regardless of whether the adult likes different foods from the child, the child may be particularly apt to trust the adult's direction regarding food choice (as compared to choices about nonfoods) because though the adult's direction may not lead to the most palatable foods, the adult will at least point to safe foods. In contrast, when the stimulus is a nonfood item, safety is generally not an issue. Indeed, in our experiment the pattern of findings was consistent with the latter, and not former, hypothesis. Specifically, children were more apt to simply trust the adult's direction regarding

a food stimulus, as compared to a nonfood stimulus, even when they identified the adult as providing unreliable information about the desirability of the food or nonfood stimulus.

Given that food selection is a very high-risk enterprise (the wrong choice could lead to death), it is rather remarkable that children do not have an early-developing ability to accurately select safe foods from the environment. Rather, their ability to choose safe and edible foods in very early childhood is apparently *entirely* dependent on social learning from others. Given their dependence on social learning about food for survival, one might expect to observe nuanced and rapidly developing social cognitions specifically in relation to food. Children do not, however, seem to evidence their highest level of social cognition in the food domain. For example, children are remarkably less skeptical consumers of adult-provided information when the information is about food, as compared to a nonfood item, while also being apt to model their eating behavior after other children, as opposed to other adults, even when they recognize that adults are more knowledgeable and experienced than children. In short, contrary to what one might expect, children's ability to inform their choices based on their social cognitions seems to be weaker for food, as opposed to nonfood items. In summary, food is a unique and important domain in which to study social cognitive development because while children evidence nuanced understanding of the reliability of others as models, they often seem to not apply these social cognitions when the stimulus is a food. Understanding this apparent paradox has the potential to inform the study of social cognitive development in general, while also having substantial practical implications related to the development of currently much-needed interventions to shape children's eating behavior and food selection.

REFERENCES

Addessi, E., Galloway, A. T., Visalberghi, E., & Birch, L. L. (2005). Specific social influences on the acceptance of novel foods in 2–5-year-old children. *Appetite, 45*(3), 264–271.

Barlow, S., & Expert Committee. (2007). Expert Committee Recommendations regarding the prevention, assessment, and treatment of child and adolescent overweight and obesity: Summary report. *Pediatrics, 120*(Suppl. 4), S164–S192.

Birch, L. (1980). Effects of peer models' food choices and eating behaviors on preschoolers' food preferences. *Child Development, 51,* 489–496.

Birch, L., & Marlin, D. (1982). I don't like it; I never tried it: Effects of exposure on two-year-old children's food preferences. *Appetite, 3*(4), 353–360.

Bretheron, I., & Beeghly, M. (1982). Talking about internal states: The acquisition of an explicit theory of mind. *Developmental Psychology, 18,* 906–921.

Brody, G., & Stoneman, Z. (1981). Selective imitation of same-age, older, and younger peer models. *Child Development, 52,* 717–720.

Carruth, B. R., Ziegler, P. J., Gordon, A., & Barr, S. I. (2004). Prevalence of picky eaters among infants and toddlers and their caregivers' decisions about offering a new food. *Journal of the American Dietetic Association, 104,* 57–64.

Cashdan, E. (1994). A sensitive period for learning about food. *Human Nature, 5*(3), 279–291.

Clement, F., Koenig, M., & Harris, P. (2004). The ontogenesis of trust. *Mind and Language, 19,* 360–379.

Cooke, L., & Wardle, J. (2005). Age and gender differences in children's food preferences. *British Journal of Nutrition, 93,* 741–746.

Desor, J. (1987). Longitudinal changes in sweet preferences in humans. *Physiology and Behavior, 39,* 639–641.

Desor, J., Greene, L., & Maller, O. (1975). Preferences for sweet and salty in 9- to 15-year-old adult humans. *Science, 190*(4215), 686–687.

Duncker, K. (1938). Experimental modification of children's food preferences through social suggestion. *Journal of Abnormal Child Psychology, 33,* 490–507.

Fawcett, C., & Markson, L. (2010). Children reason about shared preferences. *Developmental Psychology, 46,* 299–309.

Galef, G. B. (1989). Enduring social enhancement of rats' preferences for the palatable and piquant. *Appetite, 13*(2), 81–92.

Galef, B. G., Jr., & Whiskin, E. E. (1997). Effects of social and asocial learning on longevity of food-preference traditions. *Animal Behaviour, 53,* 1313–1322.

Harper, L. V., & Sanders, K. M. (1975). The effect of adults' eating on young children's acceptance of unfamiliar foods. *Journal of Experimental Child Psychology, 20,* 206–214.

Hendy, H. (2002). Effectiveness of trained peer models to encourage food acceptance in preschool children. *Appetite, 39,* 217–225.

Hendy, H. M., & Raudenbush, B. (2000). Effectiveness of teacher modeling to encourage food acceptance in preschool children. *Appetite, 34,* 61–76.

Jaswal, V., & Neely, L. (2006). Adults don't always know best: Preschoolers use past reliability over age when learning new words. *Psychological Science, 17,* 757–758.

Koenig, M. A., & Harris, P. L. (2005). Preschoolers mistrust ignorant and inaccurate speakers. *Child Development, 76*(6), 1261–1277.

Liem, D., & Mennella, J. (2003). Heightened sour preferences during childhood. *Chemical Senses, 28,* 173–180.

Lumeng, J. C., Cardinal, T. M., Jankowski, M., Kaciroti, N., & Gelman, S. A. (2008). Children's use of adult testimony to guide food selection. *Appetite, 51,* 302–310.

Lutz, D., & Keil, F. (2002). Early understanding of the division of cognitive labor. *Child Development, 73,* 1073–1084.

Macario, J. F. (1991). Young children's use of color classification: Foods and canonically colored objects. *Cognitive Development, 6,* 17–46.

Moses, L. J., Baldwin, D. A., Rosicky, J. G., & Tidball, G. (2001). Evidence for referential understanding in the emotions domain at twelve and eighteen months. *Child Development, 72*(3), 718–735.

Ogden, C. L., Carroll, M. D., Curtin, L. R., Lamb, M. M., & Flegal, K. M. (2010). Prevalence of high body mass index in US children and adolescents, 2007–2008. *Journal of the American Medical Association, 303*(3), 242–249.

Pliner, P., & Hobden, K. (1992). Development of a scale to measure the trait of food neophobia in humans. *Appetite, 19,* 105–120.

Pliner, P., & Pelchat, M. (1986). Similarities in food preferences between children and their siblings and parents. *Appetite, 7*(4), 333–342.

Repacholi, B. M., & Gopnik, A. (1997). Early reasoning about desires: Evidence from 14- to 18-month-olds. *Developmental Psychology, 33,* 12–21.

Rozin, P. (1976). *The selection of food by rats, humans, and other animals.* New York: Academic Press.

Rozin, P. (1991). Family resemblance in food and other domains: The family paradox and the role of parental congruence. *Appetite, 16,* 93–102.

Rozin, P., & Kennel, K. (1983). Acquired preferences for piquant foods by chimpanzees. *Appetite, 4*(2), 69–77.

Rozin, P., & Schiller, D. (1980). The nature and preference for chili pepper by humans. *Motivation and Emotion, 4,* 77–101.

Shutts, K., Banaji, M. R., & Spelke, E. S. (2010). Social categories guide young children's preferences for novel objects. *Developmental Science, 13*(4), 599–610.

Skinner, J., Carruth, B., Bounds, W., & Ziegler, P. (2002). Children's food preferences: A longitudinal analysis.

Journal of the American Dietetic Association, 102, 1638–1647.

Sullivan, S., & Birch, L. (1999). Pass the sugar, pass the salt: Experience dictates preference. *Developmental Psychology, 26,* 546–551.

Summerbell, C., Ashton, V., Campbell, K., Edmunds, L., Kelly, S., & Waters, E. (2003). Interventions for treating obesity in children. *Cochrane Database of Systematic Reviews, 4.* CD001872.

Taylor, M., Cartwright, B., & Bowden, T. (1991). Perspective taking and theory of mind: Do children predict interpretive diversity as a function of differences in observers' knowledge? *Child Development, 62,* 1334–1351.

SECTION V ────────────

Us and Them

5.1

What Is Group Psychology?

Adaptations for Mapping Shared Intentional Stances

DAVID PIETRASZEWSKI

Collections of people can do things that collections of most other things cannot. They can join together and coordinate their actions against the interests of others, come to each other's aid, work together to extract benefits that would otherwise be inaccessible, and create benefits that would otherwise not exist. This makes collections of people incredibly powerful and incredibly unique. Furthermore, unique dynamics emerge when more than two people interact over time which are not readily reducible to the dyadic level (Harcourt, 1988). For example, the status between people can change even if they do not directly interact. If you and I are allies, and X hurts me, then your relationship with respect to X changes even though you and X did not interact at all.

In order for you and I (and X) to anticipate and reason about these changes, sophisticated and selective inferences are necessary. To the extent that unique dynamics and properties characterize multiperson coordination and cooperation, the mind must contain psychological structures built around and for such dynamics. These can be referred to as coalitional psychology.

The function of coalitional psychology is to (1) infer the actual and potential alliance relationships between people, (2) generate expectations of how those individuals are likely to act and react, and (3) initiate and engage in these alliance relationships. Accomplishing these tasks in an ecologically valid context requires cue-based structures for detecting coalitional affiliation as well as coalitional inference, expectation, and motivational systems. These systems embody the deep structure or "social grammar" of multi-person cooperation dynamics (such as the indirect consequences described in the example above) and operate by tracking and modifying the intentional stances of others. In this framework, intentional stances

can be thought of as how much a particular agent values another agent and are factored into expectations of who will come to whose aid, who will take whose side in a conflict, who will help whom, and so on.

The central premise of this chapter is that many "group" phenomena—race, lexically marked ethnic kinds, minimal groups—can be understood as the output of this coalitional psychology. Recent findings in multiple labs are converging on this idea, and the remainder of this chapter will survey these findings. These results suggest that thinking about the basic functions of psychological structures—such as the functions of coalitional psychology—offers new ways to look at old problems and clear directions for future research.

FUNCTION 1: INFER THE ACTUAL AND POTENTIAL ALLIANCE RELATIONSHIPS BETWEEN PEOPLE

Visual Markers

For decades, one of the most robust findings in adult social psychology had been the primacy of race as a dimension of person perception—that people immediately notice, encode, and store in memory the race of the people that they encounter. Years of research on implicit racial categorization suggested that race is a pre-primed, context-insensitive, and experimentally immutable social category. But, in fact, a growing number of studies now demonstrate that race is neither a primary dimension of person perception, nor is it immutable, but is instead a readily modifiable consequence of cognitive structures designed to keep track of social alliances (an experimental validation of the idea that racial features are otherwise arbitrary dimensions that gain their meaning through social dynamics; Sidanius & Pratto, 1999, 2012).

Tracking alliances requires psychological structures which monitor for actual events of coordination, cooperation, and competition, and keep track of who is doing what to whom. It also requires tracking anything that might predict these kinds of relationships ahead of time. This may include many different things (including shared knowledge, differential proximity, and so on), but would also include any otherwise arbitrary feature of the world that tends to co-occur with coalitional behaviors. Coalitional psychology would pick up on these features and treat them as probabilistic cues for coalitional expectations (e.g., shared intentional stances).

In the case of race, in a world in which certain physical features are correlated with affiliation patterns, coalitional psychology will pick up on those physical features and use them to generate expectations about how people are likely to get along. However, coalitional alliances are also dynamic (I may be on X's team today but on your team tomorrow). This means that coalitional psychology must not only attend to newly diagnostic cues but also abandon the use of previously diagnostic cues. If categorization by race is in fact a consequence of this coalition tracking, then this predicts that a context in which race is no longer coalitionally predictive should reduce categorization by race.

This is precisely what has been found, both in antagonistic contexts in which race is not predictive of who has an antagonistic stance toward whom (Kurzban, Tooby, & Cosmides, 2001) and also in cooperative contexts in which race is not predictive of who cooperates with whom (Pietraszewski, 2009; Pietraszewski, Cosmides, & Tooby, under review). This exact experimental manipulation has little to no impact on participants' categorization by sex, meaning that these results cannot be driven by limited attentional resources. That information about who is on whose side reduces categorization by race suggests that race is a consequence of coalitional psychology, and that sex is not. That race—a previously diagnostic coalitional cue—is so quickly abandoned for more diagnostic cues suggests that coalitional psychology is constantly searching for socially predictive cues.

Recent developmental evidence provides converging support of this account (e.g., Bigler, Jones, & Lobliner, 1997; Rhodes, this volume). The Bigler studies are particularly powerful because they demonstrate what happens to arbitrary visual similarities when they become associated with coalitional cues in a real-world situation. In an experimental condition, teachers gave elementary school students two different shirt colors to wear in class for 4 weeks. Teachers used the shirt colors as much as possible in social interactions: in seating arrangements and class decorations, in addressing students, when granting permission, and so on. In a control condition, teachers interacted with the students without regard to shirt color. Perceptions of in- and out-group variability, peer preferences, and actual helping behavior all demonstrated the engagement of coalitional psychology in the experimental condition, but not in the control: Children framed the context in terms of an in-group and out-group, saw less variability within each group, and were biased toward their own group. Moreover, in a second experimental condition shirt color was assigned based on a permanent biological trait: hair color. There were no differences between the two experimental conditions; that one dimension of similarity was initially random whereas one was based on a biological trait did not matter. What causes a particular shared dimension to engage coalitional psychology is how it used socially, not whether it is permanent or biological.

There is also an elegant demonstration of this last point in adults. Using the same implicit measures of social categorization used to study race, Sack (2005) presented all participants with the same set of visual stimuli—some people who had very obvious wine-stain birthmarks on their faces and some who did not. The explanation of the marks was manipulated between subjects. Some were told that these were biological genetic mutations, whereas others were told that they were volitionally acquired when joining a group. In the biological condition there was no implicit categorization by mark, but in the social group condition there was strong categorization.

Taken as a whole, these studies in both children and adults suggest (1) that certain preexisting visually marked categories like race behave as if they are instances of coalitional representations; (2) novel visual dimensions will be treated as markers of coalition membership, but only if they correlate with alliance patterns; and (3) visual salience and biological permanence are not sufficient to engage coalitional psychology.

Lexical Markers

Linguistic communication sets up an opportunity to communicate and learn about coalitional events or structures in the absence of direct experience. Therefore, when someone refers to a collection of people with a label, one possible inference is that this label refers to a coalitional unit. This means that a lexical label applied to a person or collection of people should be considered a candidate for marking a coalitional group, or more precisely, should probabilistically engage coalitional inferences and expectations. Recently, Baron and colleagues (Baron, Dunham, Banaji, & Carey, in press) have demonstrated that applying a lexical label in this ways engages coalitional inferences in preschoolers and adults.

Of course, coalitions are not the only type of human "kinds," and therefore not every lexical marker applied to a collection of individuals will refer to a coalitional unit. Language or residency groups, for instance, seem to have their own set of associations and expectations (Hirschfeld and Gelman, 1997) and accents in particular have been hypothesized and shown to be distinct from coalitional psychology (Pietraszewski & Schwartz, 2006; Pietraszewski & Schwartz, under review). While these other "kinds" are not treated as coalitions, this does not preclude the possibility that these "kinds" could evoke certain default coalitional expectations under the right circumstances.

[handwritten margin note: wouldn't have expected that]

[handwritten margin note: ?]

Shared Opinions as Coordination Signals

Coordination is a prerequisite for cooperation. If two people are allied with one another, or have overlapping interests, they are likely to assess a situation in a similar way. This relationship between shared assessment and cooperation out in the world can lead to cognitive structures that treat these assessments as intrinsic cues of intentional stance and therefore coalitional affiliation. In fact, recent evidence (Pietraszewski, Curry, Bang-Peterson, Cosmides, & Tooby, under review) suggests that shared political opinions are sufficient to engage coalitional psychology in adults.

FUNCTION 2: GENERATE EXPECTATIONS OF HOW INDIVIDUALS ARE LIKELY TO ACT AND REACT

Maintaining an up-to-date representation of the social world and predicting the outcome of future interactions requires the deployment of inferences and expectations once coalitional cues have been detected. These modify intentional stance representations according to the social grammar of coalitional dynamics. What these inferences are, how they are deployed in response to coalitional cues, and how they form coherent and selective

expectations is still largely unexplored. However, a few preliminary investigations have been done.

Pietraszewski and German (2013) examined the inferences responsible for anticipating how people will react to events in which they are not involved. These should be highly sensitive to coalitional relationship status and should selectively modify intentional stances, but not other states. Preschoolers and adults were shown a conflict between two characters and were then asked to indicate who would be angry in response to the conflict, including uninvolved characters. All participants expected this intentional stance to extend to the uninvolved allies of the characters, but not to their acquaintances. In a control condition involving spinning on playground equipment, participants were asked to indicate who would be dizzy. Participants did not extend this (nonintentional) internal state to any of the uninvolved characters; neither to the allies nor to the acquaintances. This suggests that these inferences selectively extend intentional stances and therefore cannot be as a simple as "if A and B are allies, A and B will always feel the same thing." Baron and colleagues (in press) have demonstrated a similar finding. In response to a lexically marked collection of agents, children will extend an expectation of mean behavior to other agents who also share that label, but they will not extend other behaviors such as eating versus not eating. While preliminary, these studies demonstrate that coalitional cues selectively modify intentional stance expectations in ways consistent with coalitional dynamics. *[handwritten: but don't extend to other behaviors]*

FUNCTION 3: INITIATE AND ENGAGE IN ALLIANCE RELATIONSHIPS

Decades of research demonstrate that intergroup biases form over arbitrary similarities and differences (the minimal group paradigm and its variants). In fact, randomly drawing numbers from a jar is sufficient to induce these effects (Locksley, Ortiz, & Hepburn, 1980). Given that arbitrary differences are not sufficient to engage coalition tracking, why are people using arbitrary differences as a reason for being biased?

This is an instance where being clear about function is critical. Human beings make their living by cooperating, not by watching others cooperate. Initiating and engaging in cooperative relationships require fundamentally different motivational and behavioral repertoires than does keeping track of them. In the real world, mutually represented shared properties are a substrate over which actual cooperative relationships can be formed. Coalitional psychology should therefore frame arbitrary similarities as an opportunity to establish a cooperative relationship. This will require signaling interest in a cooperative relationship and probing for the receptivity to this in others. This can be accomplished through motivational and valuation structures which direct the differential allocation of resources along that shared dimension and by inducing and signaling positive regard for those who are similar along that dimension. *— similar interests*

Historically, group psychology grew out a framework which supposed that groups are formed around the rational assessment of conflicts of interest. Minimal group results were so devoid of apparent logic in this respect that they entirely changed the study of group psychology. Theoretical accounts arose which posited that shared identities are intrinsically valued in and of themselves in order to explain these effects (social identity theory: Tajfel & Turner, 1986; self-categorization theory: Turner, Hogg, Oakes, Reicher, & Wetherell, 1987). More recent studies from Yamagishi and others (e.g., Yamagishi, Jin, & Kiyonari, 1999) demonstrate that minimal group biases are instead yoked to the expectation of future reciprocation. Things that might disrupt this possibility—such as expecting your allocation to come from someone other than a minimal in-group member—cause minimal group effects to go away.

There is ongoing debate about whether the intrinsic value of social identities versus expected payoffs are truly driving these effects. But this debate is unnecessary—both can be true. That minimal group effects represent the output of a psychology whose function is to initiate and engage in cooperative alliances provides a coherent account of why otherwise arbitrary similarities are assigned a positive valuation and why any resource allocation in such a context is yoked to an expectation of future returns.

Finally, this view—that the mind is designed to expend effort and upfront cost to look for and signal coordination—suggests a broader approach to the psychology underlying minimal groups. Initiating coalitional alliances along particular dimensions in the real world requires sifting the social world for dimensions along which you and your social interests will do well. This "constructive" first-person aspect of coalitional psychology is probably one of the most important and yet least studied aspects of social cognition.

CONCLUSION

Many important phenomena in social and developmental psychology can be understood as manifestations of a common set of cognitive structures: a coalitional psychology. The functions of this coalition psychology is to (1) infer the actual and potential alliance relationships between people, (2) generate expectations of how those individuals are likely to act and react, and (3) initiate and engage in these alliance relationships. How these basic functions are carried out is still largely unknown. However, recent breakthroughs in studies of children and adults are offering the first glimpses of a structure and logic that promises to be a sophisticated and complicated—but also succinct and complete—model of human group psychology.

REFERENCES

Baron, A. S., Dunham, Y., Banaji, M. R., & Carey, S. (in press). Constraints on the acquisition of social category concepts. Journal of Cognition and Development.

Bigler, R. S., Jones, L. C., & Lobliner, D. B. (1997). Social categorization and the formation of intergroup attitudes in children. *Child Development*, 68, 530–543.

Harcourt, A. H. (1988). Alliances in contests and social intelligence. In R. W. Byrne, & A. Whiten (Eds.), *Machiavellian intelligence* (pp. 132–152). New York: Oxford University Press.

Hirschfeld, L. A., & Gelman, S. A. (1997). What young children think about the relationship between language variation and social difference. *Cognitive Development*, 12, 213–238.

Kurzban, R., Tooby, J., & Cosmides, L. (2001). Can race be erased? Coalitional computation and social categorization. *Proceedings of the National Academy of Sciences USA*, 98, 15387–15392.

Locksley, A., Ortiz, V., & Hepburn, C. (1980). Social categorization and discriminatory behavior: Extinguishing the minimal intergroup discrimination effect. *Journal of Personality and Social Psychology*, 39, 773–783.

Pietraszewski, D. (2009). Erasing race with cooperation: Evidence that race is a consequence of coalitional inferences. Unpublished Ph.D. dissertation, University of California, Santa Barbara.

Pietraszewski, D., & German, T. C. (2013). Coalitional psychology on the playground: Reasoning about indirect social consequences in preschoolers and adults. *Cognition, 126*, 352–363.

Pietraszewski, D., & Schwartz, A. (2006, June). Is accent a dedicated dimension of agent representation? Poster presented at the Human Behavior and Evolution Society, Philadelphia, PA.

Sack, J. D. (2005). The effect of social essentialism on categorization and induction. *Dissertation Abstracts International*, 66, 3469.

Sidanius, J., & Pratto, F. (1999). Social dominance: An intergroup theory of *social hierarchy and oppression*. New York: Cambridge University Press.

Sidanius, J., & Pratto, F. (2012). Social dominance theory. In P. A. M. Van Lange, A. W. Kruglanski, & E. T. Higgins (Eds.), *Handbook of theories of social psychology* (Vol. 2, pp.418–438). Thousand Oaks, CA: Sage.

Tajfel, H., & Turner, J.C. (1986). The social identity theory of intergroup behavior. In S. Worchel & W. G. Austin (Eds.), *Psychology of intergroup relations* (pp.7–24). Chicago, IL: Nelson-Hall.

Turner, J. C., Hogg, M. A., Oakes, P. J., Reicher, S. D., & Wetherell, M. S. (1987). *Rediscovering the social group: A self-categorization theory*. Oxford, England: Blackwell.

Yamagishi, T.,, Jin, N., & Kiyonari, T. (1999). Bounded generalized reciprocity: Ingroup boasting and ingroup favoritism. *Advances in Group Processes*, 16, 161–197.

5.2

The Conceptual Structure of Social Categories

The Social Allegiance Hypothesis

MARJORIE RHODES

Social categorization plays a critical role in early social cognition, influencing memory (Shutts & Kinzler, 2007), social inferences (Diesendruck & HaLevi, 2006), preferences (Kinzler, Dupoux, & Spelke, 2007), and behavior (Rhodes & Brickman, 2008). The early emergence of these category effects is particularly noteworthy given the great amount of variability in social categorization. People are categorized in numerous ways (e.g., based on gender, race, personality, interests, language, religion, sports teams, hair color, height; Bigler & Liben, 2007), and these categories vary in the extent to which they are informative beyond the criteria used to define them. For example, gender categories have implications for a range of inferences about biological, social, and psychological properties (Taylor, Rhodes, & Gelman, 2009); in contrast, categories based on hair color are relatively uninformative.

To make sense of this variability, when children confront a new way of categorizing people, they must distinguish categories that capture fundamental information about identity from those that are less informative. This chapter presents a proposal regarding the conceptual framework that children rely on to solve this problem. This proposal—referred to as the social allegiance hypothesis—asserts that children attribute special status to cooperative social allegiances, such that they view categories that are defined by distinct allegiances as informative, fundamental components of identity. Evidence supporting the social allegiance hypothesis will be reviewed, including evidence that children view cooperative allegiances as (a) fundamental and informative components of identity, (b) determining unique moral obligations, and (c) conferring membership in social kinds. Subsequently, the process by which allegiance information could contribute to social categorization across development will be discussed, and the social allegiance hypothesis will be compared to several theoretical alternatives.

EVIDENCE OF THE CONCEPTUAL STATUS OF COOPERATIVE SOCIAL ALLEGIANCES

The work summarized here involves preschool-age children (ranging in age from 3 to 6 years). The preschool years provide an opportunity to examine children's earliest beliefs about social categories, before exposure to formalized schooling or to a great deal of group-based experiences. In all of this work, children are introduced to novel categories of people. The novel categories are marked visually (by shirt color) and are given novel labels ("Flurps" and "Zazes"). While holding these perceptual features constant, different conditions vary the extent to which the categories are described as reflecting distinct cooperative allegiances.

Children View Cooperative Allegiances as Fundamental and Informative

Rhodes and Brickman (2011) provide evidence that children view groups defined by distinct allegiances as fundamental and informative components of identity. In this work, children were introduced to two novel categories. In some conditions, the groups reflected distinct allegiances; each group was engaged in within-group cooperative activities directed toward a goal, and the goals of the two groups were mutually exclusive (e.g., each group wanted to get a resource, and there was only enough for one group to succeed). Thus, these categories marked groups of people with distinct allegiances. In other conditions, the groups were described as engaging in identical behaviors, but there was enough of the resource for both groups. Thus, the groups had a shared (non-mutually exclusive) goal, and the categories did not reflect patterns of distinct allegiances (i.e., having an allegiance to one group did not mean that one could not also have an allegiance to the other group).

Describing the groups as marking distinct allegiances dramatically influenced preschoolers' inferences. Children in the distinct allegiances conditions viewed category membership as stable (i.e., as a permanent, unchangeable component of identity), whereas children in the non-distinct allegiances conditions did not. Also, children in the distinct allegiances conditions viewed category membership as playing an explanatory role in individual behavior. For example, in response to the question, "Why should a Flurp share toys with another Flurp?" children in the distinct allegiances conditions responded by referencing category membership (e.g., "Because they are both Flurps.") In contrast, children in the non-distinct allegiances conditions referenced general social obligations (e.g., "Because it is nice").

Children in the distinct allegiances conditions were also more likely to predict that category membership would constrain individual behavior. Children in these conditions responded that group members should help members of their own group (not members of the other group), and that it might be acceptable to harm a member of the other group (but not a member of one's own group). In contrast, children in the non-distinct allegiances condition relied on categories to guide their inferences in a much narrower manner; they responded that individuals should help their own group but could also help the other group, and they said that it was unacceptable to harm, regardless of group membership.

Children View Cooperative Allegiances as Determining Unique Moral Obligations

Recent work suggests that preschoolers also use cooperative allegiances to understand moral obligations, such that they view moral prohibitions against harming as applying more strongly among members of the same allegiance-based group (Rhodes, in press; Rhodes & Chalik, in press). For example, when preschoolers were asked to predict when harmful actions (e.g., stealing a toy, hitting, social exclusion) would occur, preschoolers expected harm to occur more often between members of different allegiance groups than

between members of the same group. Children also explained moral infractions that occurred across group lines by appealing to group membership (e.g., "Why did a Zaz steal a toy from a Flurp?" "Because he's a Zaz, but he's a Flurp...They're not the same kind"), whereas they explained moral infractions that occurred within groups by appealing to individual moral shortcomings (e.g., "Why did a Zaz steal a toy from a Zaz?" "Because he's a very mean boy"). Also, on an implicit evaluation task, preschoolers evaluated harmful actions that occurred among members of the same group more harshly than harmful actions that occurred between members of different groups.

Children View Cooperative Allegiances as Conferring Membership in Social Kinds

Another recent set of studies (Rhodes, Brickman, & Gelman, 2009) examined whether children use cooperative allegiances as a basis for categorization. This work used a "switched-at-birth" method (Hirschfeld, 1995). Children were introduced to two novel groups, were told that a baby was born to parents from one group but raised by parents from another, and were asked to predict the category membership, physical properties, and novel behavioral properties of the adopted child. Thus, children must determine whether membership in a novel social kind is determined by birth (and thus should match the birth parents) or by participation in activities with the adoptive family (and thus should match the adoptive parents). Across conditions, this study varied whether the novel groups were defined by patterns of distinct allegiances (i.e., cooperative allegiances working toward group-specific goals), or in control conditions, by distinct social practices (i.e., as groups with different customs and preferences).

Figure 5.2.1 presents the probabilities of adoptive parent predictions, separately by condition and property type. There were four key findings. First, children expected the child to take on the category membership of the adoptive parents, indicating that they viewed kind identity as determined by participation in a social group (instead of by birth). Second, children made these inferences more strongly when the groups were defined by distinct allegiances, as compared to by distinct social practices, indicating that they viewed cooperative experiences as particularly important types of social experiences for determining category membership. Third, only when the groups were defined by distinct allegiances, children used

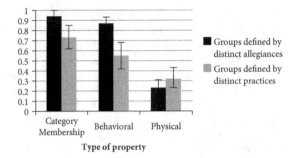

FIGURE 5.2.1: Probabilities with 95% confidence intervals of adoptive parent predictions (Rhodes et al., 2009).

the categories to make inferences about novel behavioral properties. Fourth, although children expected category membership and behavioral properties to be determined by the adoptive parents, they expected physical properties to be determined by birth. Interestingly, children made differentiated predictions about physical properties and category membership even in a follow-up condition in which the two groups differed in skin color. Thus, children predicted that individuals would have the skin color of the birth parents but the category membership of the adoptive parents. Together, these data suggest that children prefer to base categorization decisions on participation in a cooperative allegiance, rather than on birth or physical features.

COOPERATIVE ALLEGIANCES AND THE DEVELOPMENT OF SOCIAL CATEGORIZATION

The studies summarized earlier document that children view allegiance patterns as indicating fundamental and informative social categories. How could attributing special conceptual status to social allegiances contribute to the development of social categorization? Cosmides and colleagues (2003) have proposed that because allegiances are often not directly observable, people track observable markers that predict allegiance patterns, which can include categorical indicators like race, language, religion, and so on, depending on one's environment. Building on this work, the social allegiance hypothesis predicts that the development of social categorization proceeds as children identify particular markers as predictors of social allegiances in their environment, and then come to view those markers as informative criteria for categorization. Within this framework, the development of social categorization is dependent on particular types of input and is flexible across time and contexts.

COMPARISON TO THEORETICAL ALTERNATIVES

Domain-General Accounts

Domain-general accounts of categorization emphasize the role of general features—such as perceptual similarity and labeling—to account for why children view some categories as more informative than others (see Sloutsky & Fisher, 2008). In the research reviewed here, these features (e.g., perceptual markers, linguistic labels) were held constant across conditions. Thus, differences in general category salience cannot explain why children viewed the novel categories as more informative when distinct allegiances were emphasized. Nevertheless, these features undoubtedly play an important role by allowing children to track and recognize category members. Thus, the features identified by domain-general accounts contribute to the development of social categorization—by facilitating category learning and recognition—yet cannot fully explain why children view some categories as more informative than others.

Prepared Categories

Prepared categories proposals suggest that children are predisposed to view certain social categories (e.g., gender, race, ethnicity, linguistic groups) as fundamental and informative (Gil-White, 2001; Kinzler et al., 2007). From this perspective, children are prepared to see particular categories as meaningful because these categories served critical organizing roles in human societies throughout the course of human cognitive evolution. In contrast, the social allegiance proposal does not require that any particular categories be prepared for; instead, categories take on significance if they are experienced as markers of allegiance patterns in one's environment.

Yet some blending of the prepared categories and social allegiances proposals is possible. For example, children may be predisposed to view some categories as informative (e.g., gender and age, due to their special significance in organizing patterns of human reproduction), whereas other categories (e.g., race) may take on significance through the processes described by the social allegiance proposal (cf. Kurzban, Tooby, & Cosmides, 2001). This distinction maps on to patterns of developmental and cross-cultural variability in social categorization. For example, Rhodes and Gelman (2009) found that preschoolers view gender categories as fundamental, even in communities where adults have more flexible gender beliefs, suggesting that the effects of cultural input on children's beliefs about gender may be limited. Yet they also found that children view race as fundamental only later in childhood, and only in some cultural contexts, suggesting that racial categories depend on a more protracted and input-dependent developmental process.

Social Essentialism

Social essentialism suggests that the development of social categorization is guided by beliefs that categories are defined by intrinsic, stable qualities (the category "essence"; Gelman, 2003). In some descriptions, this essence has been described as determined by birth (Hirschfeld, 1995). Thus, just as children assume that a tiger is a tiger because it inherited a "tiger essence," children also assume that a person is Irish, for example, because he inherited an "Irish essence" (Atran, 1990). On this account, children will construe categories that fit their essentialist intuitions (e.g., those in which membership appears to pass from parents to children) as fundamental and informative social kinds.

The data described earlier from Rhodes et al. (2009) are inconsistent with the proposal that young children view social category memberships as necessarily determined by birth. Yet there are several ways that the social allegiance proposal and social essentialism might be integrated. For example, other accounts of social essentialism assert that essentialism may not require the belief that membership is determined by birth (Gelman & Hirschfeld, 1999); rather, people may think broadly about how the essence is acquired. Thus, one possibility is that individuals believe that participating in cooperative allegiances is a process by which individuals obtain the category essence. From this perspective, the social allegiance hypothesis and social essentialism speak to different components of social categorization: Children attend to allegiance patterns to identify informative categories, but once these categories are identified, children represent them in an essentialist manner. Alternately, social essentialism and the social allegiance hypotheses might apply to different categories. For example, social essentialism may best describe the ways that children represent some categories (e.g., gender categories) and the social allegiance proposal may best describe how they represent other categories (e.g., team memberships, cultural groups).

CONCLUSIONS

Understanding the development of social categorization has been a challenge for cognitive and developmental psychologists. Theoretical accounts must describe a conceptual system that is flexible enough to allow for great variability in social categorization across contexts and historical time, yet constrained enough to allow for the rapid acquisition of social categories in early childhood. The social allegiance hypothesis fits both of these criteria. Thus, a promising area for future work will be to examine how attention to cooperative allegiances drives the development of social categorization across childhood.

REFERENCES

Atran, S. (1990). *Cognitive foundations of natural history*. New York: Cambridge University Press.

Bigler, R. S., & Liben, L. S. (2007). Developmental intergroup theory. *Current Directions in Psychological Science, 16*, 162–166.

Cosmides, L., Tooby, J., & Kurzban, R. (2003). Perceptions of race. *Trends in Cognitive Sciences, 7*, 173–179.

Diesendruck, G., & HaLevi, H. (2006). The role of language, appearance, and culture in children's social category-based induction. *Child Development, 77*, 539–553.

Gelman, S. A. (2003). *The essential child: Origins of essentialism in everyday thought*. New York: Oxford University Press.

Gelman, S. A., & Hirschfeld, L. A. (1999). How biological is essentialism? In D. L. Medin & S. Atran (Eds.), *Folkbiology* (pp. 403–446). Cambridge, MA: MIT Press.

Gil-White, F. J. (2001). Are ethnic groups biological "species" to the human brain? *Current Anthropology, 42*, 515–554.

Hirschfeld, L. A. (1995). Do children have a theory of race? *Cognition, 54*, 209–252.

Kinzler, K. D., Dupoux, E., & Spelke, E. S. (2007). The native language of social cognition. *Proceedings of the National Academy of Sciences USA, 104*, 12577–12580.

Kurzban, R., Tooby, J., & Cosmides, L. (2001). Can race be erased? Coalitional computation and social categorization. *Proceedings of the National Academy of Sciences USA, 98*, 15387–15392.

Rhodes, M. (in press). Naïve theories of social groups. *Child Development.*

Rhodes, M., & Brickman, D. (2008). Preschoolers' responses to social comparisons involving relative failure. *Psychological Science, 19*, 969–972.

Rhodes, M., & Brickman, D. (2011). The influence of competition on children's social categories. *Journal of Cognition and Development, 12*, 194–221.

Rhodes, M., Brickman, D., & Gelman, S. A. (2009, April). Beliefs about birth, race, and coalitions in preschoolers' concepts of social categories. In A. Baron & M. Rhodes (Chairs), *Psychological constraints on social categorization and inductive inference.* Symposium conducted at the Biennial Meeting of the Society for Research in Child Development, Denver, CO.

Rhodes, M., & Chalik, L. (in press). Social categories as markers of intrinsic interpersonal obligations. *Psychological Science.*

Rhodes, M., & Gelman, S.A. (2009). A developmental examination of the conceptual structure of animal, artifact, and human social categories across two cultural contexts. *Cognitive Psychology, 59*, 244–274.

Shutts, K., & Kinzler, K. (2007). An ambiguous-race illusion in children's face memory. *Psychological Science, 18*, 763–767.

Sloutsky, V. M., & Fisher, A. V. (2008). Attentional learning and flexible induction: How mundane mechanisms give rise to smart behaviors. *Child Development, 79*, 639–651.

Taylor, M., Rhodes, M., & Gelman, S.A. (2009). Boys will be boys, cows will be cows: Children's essentialist reasoning about human gender and animal development. *Child Development, 79*, 1270–1287.

5.3

Essentialism

The Development of a Simple, But Potentially Dangerous, Idea

GIL DIESENDRUCK

We hate *them*. Not always, not all of us, not all of them. But the ease with which people—mature, educated, generally well-intending—can develop negative attitudes toward a different group of people is remarkable. Pick a group of people who know each other, call half of them "the blues" and the other half "the reds," and let them go on with their regular activities. Come back a few days later. Chances are "the blues" and "the reds" are bunching up together, telling stories about the other, favoring their own, and hindering the other. This would be quite harmless if it were only an intriguing social psychological game. These processes, however, have parallels in real life with appalling consequences.

For centuries, European empires extracted Africans from their native lands and took them across the ocean in inhumane conditions to live as slaves. In the space of a few years in the 1940s, Nazi Germany advocated and carried out the extermination of millions of Jews. In the space of 3 months in 1994, Rwandan Hutu extremists killed close to a million Rwandan Tutsis. In these latter two cases, as in many other examples of ethnic cleansing, individuals performed these atrocities on their neighbors, coworkers, patients, clients, pupils, and teachers. How could this have been? What were the psychological processes that allowed a human being to subjugate or exterminate another? What justified picking up a machete and executing an acquaintance? There are numerous attempts at answering this question. In this chapter I will discuss only one: the perpetrators' belief that the natural order of the world made their acts legitimate. Specifically, the belief that perpetrators and victims were intrinsically, fundamentally, and incommensurably different from each other. In jargon, the belief that *we* and *them* are essentially different kinds of people.

ESSENCES AS EXCUSES

The Nazis were notorious for exploiting the potential of "essentialization" for encouraging Germans to persecute Jews. Goebbels's Propaganda Ministry produced films in which Jews were portrayed as having extremely negative characteristics, and this belief was supported by "scientific evidence" for them being inherently and inevitably inferior beings. Jews were a different species—a most malignant and contaminating species—and as such it was justified to annihilate them.

Modern social psychological studies demonstrate that Goebbels's strategy is indeed effective. Correlational and experimental studies reveal that social essentialism is linked to people's difficulty with switching frames of mind (Chao, Cher, Roisman, & Hong, 2007), stereotypes (Bastian & Haslam, 2006; Levy, Stroessner, & Dweck, 1998), prejudice (Prentice & Miller, 2007), dehumanization (Leyens et al., 2003), disinterest in intergroup interaction (Williams & Eberhardt, 2008), and justifications for social stratification (Yzerbyt, Corneille, & Estrada, 2001). In fact, simply telling people that certain group differences (e.g., between men and women) are grounded on intrinsic, biologically based facts, led them to endorse discriminatory practices (Morton, Postmes, Haslam, & Hornsey, 2009; see also Keller, 2005). In short, if "they" are essentially different from "us," then inequality is permissible, prejudice acceptable, and intergroup interaction pointless. In a sense, in the minds of its holders, essentialism provides a convincing *explanation* for social differences.

Crucially, it seems that people do not need propaganda films to develop essentialist beliefs (Rothbart & Taylor, 1992). Adults in India essentialize caste (Mahalingam, 2003), in Mongolia ethnicity (Gil-White, 2001), and in Western countries race (Haslam, Rothschild, & Ernst, 2000).

At the sociological level, each of these cultures has unique structures and narratives for justifying social order. At the psychological level, these variations create minimal diversity in adults' tendency to essentialize social groups.

In fact, children as young as 5 years of age manifest essentialist-like beliefs. North American children believe that one's biological sex determines preferences irrespective of the social input people receive (Taylor, 1996), that one's race is determined by one's biological parents (Hirschfeld, 1996), and that gender categories correspond to objective partitions of the natural world (Rhodes & Gelman, 2009). Analogous notions are expressed by 5- to 6-year-olds in Madagascar (Astuti, Solomon, & Carey, 2004) and Israel (Diesendruck, Goldfein-Elbaz, Rhodes, Gelman, & Neumark, in press), with regard to ethnic groups. This cross-cultural prevalence and developmental early emergence of social essentialism begs the question of how it emerges. Why is it that adults and children around the world come to converge on this belief?

Broadly speaking, there are three kinds of explanations for why a belief may be early emerging and found cross-culturally: (a) reality calls for it, (b) we are all taught it from early on, or (c) we are all born with it. For the past 5 years, my students and I have been examining these possibilities with respect to social essentialism. Our strategy has been to tackle this issue via cross-cultural and developmental studies. Our conclusion so far is that reality has very little to do with how children create and conceive of social categories, and that while instruction may reinforce essentialism, it does not create it from scratch. Essentialism seems to be an intuitive belief about social reality, with instruction serving to direct children toward the culturally relevant social categories on which to apply it. Now to the evidence.

WHAT'S IN A NAME?

One of the basic means by which reality could dictate how we form categories is by packaging members of categories in tightly similar groups, visually distinctive from members of other groups. It arguably works for how we differentiate between cats and dogs, and thus perhaps it also works for how we differentiate between Black and White people. If this were the case, then seeing two people who look alike should be sufficient to lead children to treat them as members of the same category. For instance, children should assume that if person A has property P, then similar-looking person B has it, too. Studies have shown that perceptual

similarity is not sufficient to drive children's inferences about animals or people (Gelman, 2003). We wanted to see whether it even contributes.

In a series of studies, we investigated this question among Israeli secular kindergarteners (Diesendruck & HaLevi, 2006). In a typical trial, an experimenter showed children pictures of two characters—for example, a Jewish-looking boy and an Arab-looking boy—and labeled their category membership (e.g., "He is a Jew/Arab") and a contrastive personality trait (e.g., "He is nice/mean"). A variety of other social categories and personality traits were also used. Furthermore, the experimenter told children about a unique psychological characteristic of each of the characters (e.g., their favorite game). The experimenter then showed children a third character who belonged to the same category as one of the initial characters but had the same personality trait as the other. Children were asked to decide whose psychological characteristic this third character shared. One of the main findings of this study was that children drew their inferences based on the ethnic membership of the characters, indicating that already by age 5, Israeli children regard it as a most inductively powerful category.

The second study, however, was the most revealing about the role of visual similarity. In that study, all three characters looked alike, and thus children could not rely on perceptual similarity to draw inferences. The main finding here was that children responded exactly as they did in the first study. In other words, the fact that two ethnicity members looked alike in the first study did not contribute at all to the inductive power of ethnicity. All that mattered was their category names: two of them were "Jews," and the other an "Arab."

The idea that names have a substantive role in the way children conceive of categories has been widely supported in the developmental literature (see for reviews, Waxman, 2010; Xu, 2010). But what exactly do names do? One idea is that by applying the same name to seemingly disparate individuals we imply that there is some reality to that category (Carey, 1995). In this sense, naming may cause essentialization. An alternative idea is that naming has a more moderate role; it marks the boundaries of categories and denotes relevant categories for discourse (Sperber, 1996). In this vein, names do not create essentialism in a vacuum but instead exploit fertile grounds. In particular, labels may be effective triggers of essentialism only when applied to a priori potent

[handwritten margin notes: "prove it with other categories!" at top; "prior category experience?" at left]

categories, and only for children already inclined to essentialize these categories.

To address this latter hypothesis, we embarked on an investigation of kindergarten, second-grade, and sixth-grade Israeli children from three cultural subgroups: secular Jews, modern-orthodox Zionist Jews, and Muslim Arabs. In a set of studies, we used a similar induction task to the one described earlier (Birnbaum, Deeb, Segall, Ben-Eliyahu, & Diesendruck, 2010). Only this time, we gave children a more difficult choice for drawing their inferences; namely, they had to decide between two alternative social categories (e.g., gender or social status vs. ethnicity). Moreover, for half of the children we labeled the social category membership of the characters in a triad, whereas for the other half of the children we did not. Our main findings were that by sixth grade, almost all children systematically drew inferences based on ethnicity. However, in second grade—and remarkably in kindergarten as well—only one group of children did so: modern-orthodox Zionist Jews. Importantly, these second graders and kindergarteners relied on ethnicity only when it was explicitly labeled. When children were not provided with the labels, and the only kind of information they had to go by for making their decisions was the perceptual similarity between the characters, then none of the second-grade or kindergarten groups systematically inferred by ethnicity. In fact, there was no correlation between children's capacity to recognize the category a character belonged to and their tendency to draw inferences based on it.

Thus again, what impacted children's tendency to rely on a category for drawing inferences was not the physical attributes of the category members. Rather, it was their category membership as marked by a label. Crucially, this was the case only for ethnic categories—for example, not for gender or social status—and only for a particular sector of children—modern-Orthodox Zionist Jews. This category specificity of the effect of labels intimates that children are relying on more than what is made available to them in the task. Namely, children are relying on their underlying concepts about the categories. Importantly, the finding that often times children drew inferences based on ethnicity even though they were incapable of visually identifying Jews or Arabs indicates that their ethnic concepts were abstract; they did not derive from detailed knowledge. The sector specificity of this effect reinforces the aforementioned conclusion, by indicating that labeling emphasizes ethnic

essentialism not on all children, but rather only on those who might be already susceptible to such a belief. In brief, labeling is not enough to lead *any* child to essentialize *any* social category.

Why are modern-Orthodox Zionist Jewish children susceptible to ethnic essentialism? One possibility is that these children may be absorbing their parents' political ideology. Within the Israeli political spectrum, modern-Orthodox Zionist Jews tend toward the right wing, rejecting a two-state solution for the Israeli-Palestinian conflict. In a current study, we are indeed finding correlations between parents' endorsement of right-wing statements and their children's scores in various ethnic essentialism measures (Segall & Diesendruck, 2011). Moreover, there are differences in how parents talk to their children about ethnicity, consistent with the group differences vis-à-vis essentialism described earlier. A second possibility is that religious beliefs per se may endorse essentialist beliefs. In a study among secular and religious Jewish children, we found that the more children believed that God was the creator of social categories, the more essentialist they were about social categories (Diesendruck & Haber, 2009).

Taken together, these findings indicate that essentialism does not derive from bottom-up processes, insofar as there is nothing in a category itself that makes children essentialize it. Rather, cultural factors affect this process. But what exactly does culture do?

CULTURE PROVIDES CONTENT, NOT FORM

On the one hand, the sheer fact that different social categories are essentialized in different cultures intimates that culture plays a fundamental role in social essentialism. On the other hand, the finding that people in all cultures studied *do* essentialize suggests that the tendency to essentialize *some* social category may be universal. We believe our developmental findings shed light on these seemingly disparate possibilities.

I will focus on two sets of data here. One set comes from the induction studies across three Israeli sectors mentioned earlier (Birnbaum et al., 2010). Recall that in those studies, children's task was to decide which among a number of social or personality categories was a better source for inferring people's characteristics. In other words, that task provided an estimate of the *relative* essentialist status of ethnicity. The other set comes from studies on similar sectors, as well as two groups of "integrated" children, which I will dis-cuss later (Deeb, Segall, Birnbaum, Ben-Eliyahu, & Diesendruck, 2011). The essentialism measure here was quite different. It involved a series of direct questions about the extent to which Jews and Arabs constitute essentially different kinds of people. For instance, children were asked, "To what extent do Jews and Arabs differ in the way they think/what they like/what they have inside their bodies?" "Is it possible for an Arab to become a Jew?" and "Is it possible for a Jewish mother to give birth to an Arab child?" (see Diesendruck & Haber, 2009, for the questions). In short, the ques-tionnaire asked exclusively about ethnicity and thus provided an estimate of children's *absolute* ethnic essentialism.

What we found is that the tendency to draw inferences based on ethnicity—instead of based on other social or personality categories—*increased* with age, from kindergarten to sixth grade. In turn, children's absolute ethnic essentialism scores *decreased* across these same ages. What seems to be going on is that by kindergarten, Israeli child-ren are highly essentialist about ethnicity. But in fact they seem to be highly essentialist about other social categories as well—as shown by the work of Hirschfeld (1996) on race, and Taylor (1996) and Rhodes & Gelman (2009) on gender." As they mature, two processes take place. First, they acquire more knowledge about ethnicity and realize that some of their preconceived essential-ist notions about ethnicity may not be true. For instance, they may learn that there are ways for an Arab to become Jewish. Consequently, abso-lute ethnic essentialism decreases. At the same time, children learn to discriminate the cultural relevance of the various social categories available in their particular society. Israeli children learn that ethnicity is a more relevant category than gender, social status, or niceness and thus is *the* category that one should conceive of essentialisti-cally. As a result of this realization, relative eth-nic essentialism increases. A recent study more directly confirmed these developmental pro-cesses (Diesendruck, Birnbaum, Deeb, & Segall, in press).

What the earlier account implies is that essen-tialism per se may not be taught, but instead it is a default conceptualization of social groups. As I noted earlier, Israeli kindergarteners essential-ize ethnicity even though they cannot systemat-ically recognize what Jews and Arabs look like. As Medin and Ortony (1989) conjectured, essen-tialism is a conceptualization devoid of details—a "placeholder" belief—held by people in the absence of specific knowledge of what the essence might be. By chronically labeling relevant catego-ries, cultures identify for the child the categories onto which such placeholder notions should be attached (see also Bigler & Liben, 2007). In some cases, cultures can go further and reinforce these notions, by providing ideological information consistent with an essentialist construal.

CAN ESSENTIALISM BE UNDONE?

A theoretically interesting and practically impor-tant implication of these conclusions is that essentialism toward a particular category may be undone. To recapitulate: Essentialism is not an inevitable imposition of social reality, and its targeting of ethnicity, for instance, is largely due to cultural input. Thus, what if instead of being exposed to political and religious ideology endors-ing an essentialization of ethnicity, young Israeli children were to be exposed to a radically differ-ent experience of ethnicity? What if knowledge of a different kind was to supplant the placeholder belief?

To answer this question, we investigated child-ren from four groups: secular Jewish and Muslim Arab children attending regular public schools, and secular and Arab children attending inte-grated schools (again, kindergarteners, second graders, and sixth graders; Deeb et al., 2011). Whereas in the regular schools, all pupils were either Jewish or Arab and the curricula focused either on Jewish or Arab traditions, in the inte-grated schools, pupils were both Jewish and Arab and the curricula included traditions and values from both cultures. Children performed a num-ber of tasks, but here I will mention only two.

In the first task, children were told a simple story about a boy looking for his dog, which was lost in a park. During his searches, the boy encoun-ters four different adults, each characterized by a different set of social categories explicitly labeled (e.g., one is described as a "Jewish religious rich woman"). After hearing the story, children were asked to recount it. We did not expect children to remember all the social category information about all four characters in the story. But that was exactly our goal. We wanted to see *which* social category information children stored and consid-ered relevant to recount, and which children did it. The second task was the absolute ethnic essen-tialism questionnaire described earlier.

What we found in the first task was that chil-dren from the integrated schools were *more* likely than children from the regular schools to recount the ethnicity of the characters in the story. Second, we found that children from the integrated schools were *less* essentialist than children from the regular schools. In fact, we found that the *more* a child mentioned ethnicity in his or her recount of the story, the *lower* was his or her essentialism score. Finally, we found that in kindergarten, children from all four groups had an equivalent high level of essentialism. For those attending the integrated schools, essentialism dropped significantly by second grade. For those in the regular schools, it took 4 more years for this to occur.

These findings corroborate our conclusions from the earlier studies. They show that not only is category salience an unreliable predictor of the tendency to essentialize a category, but under certain circumstances, it may be even negatively related to it. Furthermore, again we see that the youngest children tested were the most essentialist vis-à-vis ethnicity in absolute terms. That is, independently of their home environment, 5-year-old Jewish and Arab children in Israel start off highly essentialist about ethnicity. With learning, essentialism drops; and if the learning occurs in the context of integrated, institutionalized, and collaborative settings, then essentialism drops quite fast.

There is a popular belief that if we do not talk about people's race or ethnicity, then children will not "see" race or ethnicity—they will be "color blind"—and thus they will not be racist either. The problem with this sort of blindness is that by not informing children about race or ethnicity, we leave them with empty concepts. Empty social concepts are the cognitive niche of essentialism. Our findings in the integrated schools indicate that in such contexts, knowledge about ethnicity dispels, rather than creates, essentialism.

FINAL THOUGHTS

In his attempt to understand the Rwandan genocide, Phillip Gourevitch writes: "Mass violence…must be conceived as the means toward achieving a new order, and although the idea behind that new order may be criminal and objectively very stupid, it must also be *compellingly simple and at the same time absolute.* The ideology of genocide is all of those things, and in Rwanda it went by the name of Hutu Power" (Gourevitch, 1998, pp. 17–18, my emphases). Essentialism is precisely this kind of idea. It is absolute by definition and so simple that even 5-year-olds get it. Recognizing that some of the worst human atrocities may be founded on basic and arguably intuitive ways of conceiving of the social world is certainly not very comforting. Ignoring this, however, only distances us even more from remedying essentialism's potential dangers.

ACKNOWLEDGMENTS
Gil Diesendruck is a faculty member of the Department of Psychology and the Gonda Brain Research Center at Bar-Ilan University, Israel. The writing of this chapter, as well as much of the research described in it, were funded by grant no. 621/05 from the Israel Science Foundation, and by a Bar-Ilan University Rector's grant, to Gil Diesendruck.

REFERENCES
Astuti, R., Solomon, G. E., & Carey, S. (2004). Constraints on conceptual development. *Monographs of the Society for Research in Child Development, 69* (Serial No. 277).

Bastian, B., & Haslam, N. (2006). Psychological essentialism and stereotype endorsement. *Journal of Experimental Social Psychology, 42*, 228–235.

Bigler, R. S., & Liben, L. S. (2007). Developmental intergroup theory: Explaining and reducing children's social stereotyping and prejudice. *Current Directions in Psychological Science, 16*, 162–166.

Birnbaum, D., Deeb, I., Segall, G., Ben-Eliyahu, A., & Diesendruck, G. (2010). The development of social essentialism: The case of Israeli children's inferences about Jews and Arabs. *Child Development, 81*, 757–777.

Carey, S. (1995). On the origin of causal understanding. In D. Sperber, D. Premack, & A.J. Premack (Eds.), *Causal cognition: A multi-disciplinary debate* (pp. 268–308). Oxford, England: Oxford University Press.

Chao, M. M., Cher, J., Roisman, G. I., & Hong, Y. (2007). Essentializing race: Implications for bicultural individual's cognitive and physiological reactivity. *Psychological Science, 18*, 341–348.

Deeb, I., Segall, G., Birnbaum, D., Ben-Eliyahu, A., & Diesendruck, G. (2011). Seeing isn't believing: The effect of contact on children's essentialist beliefs about ethnic categories. *Journal of Personality and Social Psychology, 101*(6), 1139–1156.

Diesendruck, G., Birnbaum, D., Deeb, I., & Segall, G. (in press). Learning *what* is essential: Relative and absolute changes in children's beliefs about the heritability of ethnicity. *Journal of Cognition and Development.*

Diesendruck, G., Goldfein-Elbaz, R., Rhodes M., Gelman, S., & Neumark, N. (in press).Cross-cultural differences in children's beliefs about the objectivity of social categories. *Child Development.*

Diesendruck, G., & Haber, L. (2009). God's categories: The effect of religiosity on children's teleological and essentialist beliefs about categories. *Cognition, 110,* 100–114.

Diesendruck, G., & HaLevi, H. (2006). The role of language, appearance, and culture in children's social category based induction. *Child Development, 77,* 539–553.

Gelman, S. A. (2003). *The essential child: Origins of essentialism in everyday thought.* New York: Oxford University Press.

Gil-White, F. J. (2001). Are ethnic groups biological "species" to the human brain? Essentialism in our cognition of some social categories. *Current Anthropology, 42,* 515–554.

Gourevitch, P. (1998). *We wish to inform you that tomorrow we will be killed with our families.* New York: Farrar, Straus, & Giroux.

Haslam, N., Rothschild, L., & Ernst, D. (2000). Essentialist beliefs about social categories. *British Journal of Social Psychology, 39,* 113–127.

Hirschfeld, L. A. (1996). *Race in the making.* Cambridge, MA: MIT Press.

Keller, J. (2005). In genes we trust: The biological component of psychological essentialism and its relationship to mechanisms of motivated social cognition. *Journal of Personality and Social Psychology, 88,* 686–702.

Levy, S. R., Stroessner, S. J., & Dweck, C. S. (1998). Stereotype formation and endorsement: The role of implicit theories. *Journal of Personality and Social Psychology, 74,* 1421–1436.

Leyens, J., Cortes, B., Demoulin, S., Dovidio, J. F., Fiske, S. T., Gaunt, R., . . . Vaes, J. (2003). Emotional prejudice, essentialism, and nationalism. *European Journal of Social Psychology, 33,* 703–717.

Mahalingam, R. (2003). Essentialism, culture, and power: Representations of social class. *Journal of Social Issues, 59,* 733–749.

Medin, D. L., & Ortony, A. (1989). Psychological essentialism. In S. Vosniadou & A. Ortony (Eds.), *Similarity and analogical processing* (pp. 179–195). New York: Cambridge University Press.

Morton, T. A., Postmes, T., Haslam, S. A., & Hornsey, M. J. (2009). Theorizing gender in the face of social change: Is there anything essential about essentialism? *Journal of Personality and Social Psychology, 96,* 653–664.

Prentice, D. A., & Miller, D. T. (2007). Psychological essentialism of human categories. *Current Directions in Psychological Science, 16,* 202–206.

Rhodes, M., & Gelman, S. A. (2009). A development examination of the conceptual structure of animal, artifact, and human social categories across two cultural contexts. *Cognitive Psychology, 59,* 244–274.

Rothbart, M., & Taylor, M. (1992). Category labels and social reality: Do we view social categories as natural kinds. In G. R. Semin & K. Fiedler (Eds.), *Language, interaction, and social cognition* (pp. 11–36). Thousand Oaks, CA: Sage.

Segall, G., & Diesendruck, G. (2011). *The language of essentialism.* Poster presented at the Biennial Meeting of the Society for Research in Child Development. Montreal: Canada.

Sperber, D. (1996). *Explaining culture: A naturalistic approach.* Cambridge, England: Blackwell.

Taylor, M. (1996). The development of children's beliefs about social and biological aspects of gender differences. *Child Development, 67,* 1555–1571.

Waxman, S. R. (2010). Names will never hurt me? Naming and the development of racial and gender categories in preschool-aged children. *European Journal of Social Psychology, 40,* 593–610.

Williams, M. J., & Eberhardt, J. L. (2008). Biological conceptions of race and the motivation to cross racial boundaries. *Journal of Personality and Social Psychology, 94,* 1033–1047.

Xu, F. (2010). Count nouns, sortal concepts, and the nature of early words. In J. Pelletier (Ed.), *Kinds, things, and stuff: New directions in cognitive science* (pp. 191–206). New York: Oxford University Press.

Yzerbyt, V., Corneille, O., & Estrada, C. (2001). The interplay of subjective essentialism and entitativity in the formation of stereotypes. *Personality and Social Psychology Review, 5,* 141–155.

5.4

Generic Statements, Causal Attributions, and Children's Naive Theories

ANDREI CIMPIAN

Generic statements express generalizations about *entire categories* (e.g., "*Birds* lay eggs," "*Boys* like sports") and are thus a powerful means of transmitting and acquiring information. Above and beyond their role in information transfer, however, generic statements shape children's causal inferences about the generalizations they express. In this chapter, I trace the influence of this process on children's theories about the natural and social world, as well as on their motivation and performance in achievement contexts.

The ability to divide the world into discrete categories (e.g., chairs, dogs, teenagers) is a key feature of human cognition because it allows us to conceive of indefinite numbers of distinct individuals as being equivalent in some respects—as being the same kind of thing. This assumed equivalence reduces the informational complexity of our environments and, crucially, facilitates broad generalizations across individuals in a category. Such category-wide generalizations are pervasive in everyday thought and behavior. For example, every time people assume that it is safe to sit on a chair they have never used before or to approach a stranger's dog, they are relying on category-wide, or *generic*, generalizations about chairs and dogs, respectively (i.e., that chairs are sturdy and that dogs are friendly).

Given the central role of these generic generalizations in our cognitive lives, it is natural to ask how they are formed or acquired in childhood. Undoubtedly, children's own interactions with the world are a source. Seeing a particular dog's friendly behavior, for instance, would provide a child with some grounds for extending this feature to the category *dog* as a whole. However, despite children's apparent willingness to make projections of this sort (e.g., Gelman & Markman, 1986; Xu & Tenenbaum, 2007), inductive generalizations are by necessity uncertain, insofar as any

set of observations can support an infinite number of alternative generalizations with equal legitimacy (e.g., furry, four-legged things are friendly; Goodman, 1965).

GENERIC STATEMENTS CONVEY CATEGORY-WIDE CONTENT KNOWLEDGE AND SHAPE CAUSAL THEORIES

The uncertainty that is inherent in generalizing from firsthand evidence is, by comparison, negligible when children acquire generic facts from other people. In fact, *generic statements* (or generics) such as "Dogs are friendly" provide the most transparent means of learning generic generalizations because they unambiguously signal that a particular property (e.g., friendliness) applies to an entire kind (e.g., dogs; Carlson & Pelletier, 1995). Not only do generic statements have the right semantics to convey category-wide generalizations, but they are also (1) common in child-directed speech, accounting for approximately 4% of all utterances addressed to preschool-age children in everyday contexts (Gelman, Goetz, Sarnecka, & Flukes, 2008) and (2) comprehensible to children as young as 2 or 3 years of age (e.g., Cimpian & Markman, 2008; Cimpian, Meltzer, & Markman, 2011; Gelman & Raman, 2003). This evidence suggests that generic statements may be a substantial source of knowledge about categories for young children.

However, the impact of generic statements on children's conceptual systems is not limited to the transmission of generic facts. Generics also shape children's inferences about the *causal source* of the novel generic facts conveyed, leading children to view these facts as inherent and natural—as direct by-products of membership in the relevant categories. It is important to note that the causal attributions generated for a fact are part and parcel of how that fact is understood. For example, attributing dogs' friendliness to the biology of their species frames it as a deeper, more essential (Gelman, 2003) feature than attributing it to some external cause such as their typical rearing conditions. In other words, how a new feature is integrated into the network of causal relationships pertinent to a concept determines how the feature is ultimately understood (e.g., Ahn, Kim, Lassaline, & Dennis, 2000; Murphy & Medin, 1985). The evidence reviewed next suggests that generic statements influence this process such that the novel facts they convey are, at least under certain circumstances, understood to be relatively deep, essential, and central to the category rather than superficial and peripheral.

For example, when 4- and 5-year-old children were presented with generic statements about novel properties of natural kinds (e.g., "Dolphins have a lot of fat under their skin"), the children often inferred that these properties must be enabling some important life-sustaining process (e.g., keeping warm: "'cause they dive deep, and deep is cold, and it's warm with big bellies") and are thus an essential aspect of the biology of these kinds (Cimpian & Markman, 2009). In contrast, when the same novel properties were introduced via a nongeneric statement about an individual (e.g., "She [a dolphin] has a lot of fat under her skin"), they were typically attributed to prior, often accidental, causes (e.g., overeating: "probably because it probably ate too much food"). A separate study established that children's use of the generic versus nongeneric linguistic information was not automatic but rather flexible and context sensitive: When the properties were ones children knew to be generic, presenting them in generic (e.g., "Apples have seeds inside") or nongeneric (e.g., "This apple has seeds inside") statements had no effect on children's causal attributions. It was only when the properties were novel that the generic versus nongeneric phrasing (e.g., "Apples have ovules inside" vs. "This apple has ovules inside") caused children's attributions, and thus their understanding of these novel properties, to diverge.

Along the same lines, when 5-year-olds were presented with generic statements about features of unfamiliar *artifact* kinds (e.g., "Ludinos have a bent tip"), they typically explained these features in terms of their supposed functions (e.g., "because to pour stuff out"; Cimpian & Cadena, 2010). Children's responses in a follow-up experiment indicated that they also believed these features to be a part of the artifacts' intentional design (e.g., ludinos were made with a bent tip), further reinforcing the conclusion that generically conveyed information becomes part of the category core. Importantly, when the same properties were introduced via nongeneric statements (e.g., "This ludino has a bent tip"), children's attributions gravitated toward accidental causes instead (e.g., "'cause something stepped on it"). Thus, the essentialist understanding children demonstrated for the generic versions of these properties could not have been a trivial consequence of the content of the properties per se.

Strikingly, generic language leads to the same types of essentialist inferences when it conveys information about social others. In Cimpian and Markman's (2011) studies, for example, children often attributed novel abilities introduced via generic statements (e.g., "Boys/girls are really good at a game called *gorp*") to the inherent traits of the relevant social categories (e.g., "because girls are really, really smart" or "'cause boys grow up fast"). When introduced generically, novel biological properties of social others (e.g., "Boys/girls have something called *fibrinogen* in their blood") were also attributed to inherent traits (e.g., "because they're sensitive"), or else they were thought to enable vital biological functions (e.g., "'cause it can help their blood"). Children's causal inferences diverged again from this pattern when the same information was presented in nongeneric format: The novel abilities were ascribed to the effort of the individual who was said to possess them (e.g., "because he practiced a lot of times"), while the novel biological properties were often thought to be due to an illness or some external agent (e.g., "maybe the bunny bite her"). In sum, children tend to assume that socially relevant information learned from generic statements describes deep, stable, inherent aspects of other people's biological and psychological makeup.

One might wonder, however, if children's talk of deep, inherent causes truly reflects their essentialized understanding of the facts learned from generic statements, or if it may simply be a side effect of having to explain a feature of an entire category. On this alternative view, being asked to explain a new feature of a category (e.g., why boys are good at gorp) might automatically trigger talk about other category-wide features, many of which are inherent and deep (e.g., boys grow up fast); however, such responses would not speak to children's understanding of this new feature per se. To test whether generic language truly shapes children's theories about the information learned, Cimpian and Erickson (2012) introduced novel information in either generic or nongeneric format but then asked children to explain the same nongeneric instantiation of this information. For example, although the information about gorp game ability was introduced in generic statements to half the children and in nongeneric statements to the other half, the experimenter went on to show *all* participants a picture of a single child, tell them that this child was also good at the gorp game, and ask them why they think that is. Thus, the children in the generic and nongeneric conditions were asked to explain exactly the same (nongeneric) fact about a single child. As predicted, their understanding of this child's ability was shaped by how the ability had been originally introduced, such that children who learned about this ability from generic statements were significantly more likely to essentialize it. This result provides further evidence for the role of generic statements in the development of children's theories.

It is important to note, however, that the essentializing effect of generic language is not deterministic. Framing a new fact generically is not by itself sufficient to lead to attributions to deep causes. (After all, generic statements can also express facts that do not have a deep causal connection with their kinds, as in "Barns are red"; Prasada & Dillingham, 2006.) Among the additional factors that affect children's causal inferences about linguistically conveyed generic generalizations, two are particularly noteworthy: the nature of the *categories* that the generalizations are about and the content of the *properties* being generalized (Cimpian & Markman, 2011). Especially in the social domain, there is much variability in the extent to which categories are essentialized—that is, in the extent to which they are thought to reflect deep, natural distinctions (e.g., men vs. women) versus more arbitrary or superficial groupings (e.g., Lady Gaga fans vs. Britney Spears fans; see Prentice & Miller, 2007). Categories that are relatively superficial are less likely to support inferences to deep, inherent causes. For example, because Lady Gaga fans are not typically conceptualized as having biological characteristics that distinguish them from fans of other pop stars, it may be less plausible to attribute some new generic fact about them to their biology. Analogously, there is variability in the extent to which properties are compatible with inferences to deep causes. For example, although success at some activity may plausibly be construed as the

external manifestation of underlying traits or talents (e.g., Dweck, 1999), other properties may not lend themselves to such attributions—for example, properties that seem temporary or accidental (e.g., being dirty; Cimpian & Markman, 2008; Gelman, 1988). Four- and five-year-olds' causal inferences are sensitive to both the nature of the categories and the content of the properties introduced via generic statements (Cimpian & Markman, 2011; Experiments 3 and 4), illustrating the flexibility of young children's causal learning mechanisms.

CONSEQUENCES FOR CHILDREN'S ACHIEVEMENT

In the remainder of this chapter, I review recent evidence that exposure to generic statements affects children's achievement-related theories and, consequently, their attitudes and behaviors in achievement settings. Children's theories about what it takes to succeed undoubtedly influence their ability to do well in school: Those who believe that success is a matter of possessing an inherent trait or talent (*entity* theorists) are often at a disadvantage relative to those who believe that success is a matter of effort and strategies (*incremental* theorists), especially when the material is challenging (e.g., Blackwell, Trzesniewski, & Dweck, 2007; Mueller & Dweck, 1998). Because generic language about ability typically leads children to infer that the source of the relevant ability is a trait (e.g., being smart or talented; Cimpian & Markman, 2011), it is possible that it would also induce the maladaptive feelings and behaviors associated with an entity theory. That is, children might worry about how much of this supposed trait they possess and thus become less likely to enjoy what they are doing; they may avoid challenges so that they can look competent and thus prove that they have the requisite traits; they may have strong negative reactions to mistakes or failures because such negative outcomes imply lack of talent; and so on. By promoting trait attributions, then, generic language may ultimately impair children's motivation and performance.

To test whether generics affect motivation, Cimpian (2010) asked 4- to 7-year-old children to play a novel game called *gorp*, in which they pretended to make different things out of paper. Critically, half of the children heard generic statements about gorp ability (e.g., "Girls/boys are really good at the gorp game"), while the other half heard nongeneric statements (e.g., "There's a girl/boy who is really good at the gorp game"). Children's motivation was assessed with a broad set of questions that probed, among other things, their perceived competence, their liking for the game, their emotional reactions, and their strategies for fixing mistakes (see Cimpian, Arce, Markman, & Dweck, 2007). In line with our prediction, generic language was clearly detrimental to children's motivation. Relative to children in the nongeneric condition, those who were exposed to generics felt less happy and less competent, liked the game less, were less persistent, and so on. Also noteworthy was the fact that generic language impaired motivation regardless of whether it conveyed negative or positive associations between the game and children's own group. That is, hearing generic sentences about the high ability of one's group (a positive association) led to lower motivation scores, just as did hearing generic sentences about the high ability of the outgroup (an implied negative association, as when a girl hears that boys are good at gorp). Although counterintuitive, the detrimental effect of generic statements about the high ability of one's own group is to be expected if, as we argued, these statements promote entity attributions to stable underlying traits. The inference that an inherent talent is the causal source of one's performance is likely to change the whole tenor of the activity, putting children under a spotlight and raising the question of whether they in fact have what it takes to succeed. Our data suggest that this charged atmosphere, which is responsible for the detrimental effect on children's motivation, is as likely to arise when one's group is said to possess the requisite talents as when one's group is inferred not to possess them.

Generic statements about ability affect not only children's attitudes toward a task but also their very ability to perform it. In a recent study, we taught 4- to 7-year-old children how to play the *Finding game*, a novel task consisting of multiple trials in which children had to find a complex target shape among a set of alternatives (Cimpian, Mu, & Erickson, 2012). Children played a baseline round, after which they heard either generic ("Boys/girls are really good at the Finding game") or nongeneric ("There's a boy/girl who is really good at the Finding game") statements about ability at this game. They were then asked to play a test round. The results were compelling: Although the generic and nongeneric groups were identical in their ability to find the target shapes at baseline, children exposed to generic language performed significantly worse in the test round than children exposed to nongeneric language. Also, as in Cimpian (2010), the generic statements about

the high ability of one's own gender seemed to be as damaging as the generic statements about the high ability of the other gender. Thus, even a modest amount of generic language, coming from a person with whom children were unfamiliar, was sufficient to induce a maladaptive way of thinking about an unfamiliar task, which in turn led children to perform worse than they would have otherwise. In children's daily lives, where children have more of a rapport with the people providing such input and the tasks have higher stakes, the negative effect of exposure to generic statements may be even greater.

These findings also speak to children's vulnerability to stereotype information such as that expressed by generic statements about ability. Although the threatening effect of familiar societal stereotypes (e.g., about gender and math) has been documented in children around this age (Ambady, Shih, Kim, & Pittinsky, 2001), this is the first study to show that exposure to a few sentences conveying an *entirely novel* stereotype is likely to have a similarly debilitating effect on children's achievement. It is important to note that, in contrast to Ambady et al. (2001), the positive stereotypes set up by the generic statements in our study caused children to perform worse, not better. As explained earlier, this counterintuitive result is in fact predicted by our argument that generic statements induce entity-like beliefs that in turn interfere with children's ability to focus constructively on the task at hand. Moreover, this finding is compatible with the adult literature on the consequences of activating familiar positive stereotypes: Briefly, whether positive stereotypes debilitate or facilitate performance appears to depend on the manner of their activation. When they are activated indirectly and subtly (e.g., by subliminally priming participants with words associated with the positively stereotyped identity), positive stereotypes often boost confidence and improve performance (e.g., Ambady et al., 2001; Shih, Ambady, Richeson, Fujita, & Gray, 2002; Shih, Pittinsky, & Ambady, 1999). However, when they are activated directly and blatantly (e.g., by telling Asian American participants that the examination they are about to take was designed to test the stereotype that Asians are good at math), positive stereotypes often cause participants to worry about whether they will live up to these stereotypes, which actually impairs their performance (e.g., Brown & Josephs, 1999; Cheryan & Bodenhausen, 2000; Shih et al., 2002; see also Baumeister, Hamilton, & Tice, 1985).

Since our generic statements express the stereotype information quite directly, their negative effect on performance is entirely consistent with the pattern that emerges from this literature.

In the studies described so far, children's beliefs and behaviors were assessed in the context of the specific activities about which they had heard generic statements (Cimpian, 2010; Cimpian & Markman, 2011; Cimpian et al., 2012). It is possible, however, that exposure to generic language about abilities has broader effects on children's theories about achievement. Specifically, the more generic statements children hear, the more likely they may be to *generalize* a trait-based conception of abilities to domains they have *never* heard described in generic language. This hypothesis was tested in a two-part study with 4- and 5-year-olds (Cimpian, Bian, & Sutherland, unpublished data). The first part consisted of a series of questions about familiar activities (e.g., riding a bike). Half of the children were asked these questions in generic form (e.g., "Are girls good at riding a bike?"), while the other half were asked the same questions in nongeneric form, about a child they were familiar with (e.g., "Is Julie good at riding a bike?"). The goal of this phase was to prime, or activate, the explanatory framework associated with generic statements of ability. That is, when repeatedly asked whether boys or girls are good at various activities, the thoughts of children in the generic condition may be repeatedly drawn to the *traits* that would be needed to succeed in these activities. This trait-based explanatory framework may then "spill over" and be applied to other, novel activities as well. In the second part, we tested for the predicted generalization effect by asking children whether effort is needed for success in several novel activities. This test phase, which was *identical* across the generic and nongeneric conditions, consisted of introducing several novel abilities in the context of a single individual (e.g., "This girl is really good at a game called *gorp*") and then measuring to what extent children thought that effort was important to the development of these novel abilities (e.g., "Does this girl have to practice this game, or is she just good at it?"). Our results were sobering: The children who had simply been asked whether boys or girls are good at various familiar activities were significantly less likely to endorse the importance of effort during the generalization test than children who were asked the nongeneric versions of these questions. Arguably, children in the generic condition were primed by the questions in the first part to privilege traits over effort

as the causal source of one's abilities. The fact that even relatively little exposure to generic language may be sufficient to induce these general, and rather troubling, changes in children's beliefs speaks to the power of this linguistic cue.

CONCLUSION

Generic statements give direct, unambiguous expression to people's knowledge about categories. As such, they are an ideal means of learning about the world. Their influence, however, extends beyond the acquisition of content knowledge. The evidence reviewed here suggests that generic statements are also a major influence on children's causal theories, with potential consequences for their achievement.

ACKNOWLEDGMENTS

The research described in this chapter was supported by a Koppitz fellowship from the American Psychological Foundation, research funds from the University of Illinois, and Spencer Foundation grant 201100111. Many thanks to Joe Robinson, Cindy Fisher, and Vikram Jaswal for their helpful comments on previous drafts of this chapter.

REFERENCES

Ambady, N., Shih, M., Kim, A., & Pittinsky, T. L. (2001). Stereotype susceptibility in children: Effects of identity activation on quantitative performance. *Psychological Science, 12*(5), 385–390.

Ahn, W., Kim, N. S., Lassaline, M. E., & Dennis, M. J. (2000). Causal status as a determinant of feature centrality. *Cognitive Psychology, 41*, 361–416.

Baumeister, R. F., Hamilton, J. C., & Tice, D. M. (1985). Public versus private expectancy of success: Confidence booster or performance pressure? *Journal of Personality and Social Psychology, 48*(6), 1447–1457.

Blackwell, L. A., Trzesniewski, K. H., & Dweck, C. S. (2007). Theories of intelligence and achievement across the junior high school transition: A longitudinal study and an intervention. *Child Development, 78*, 246–263.

Brown, R. P., & Josephs, R. A. (1999). A burden of proof: Stereotype relevance and gender differences in math performance. *Journal of Personality and Social Psychology, 76*, 246–257.

Carlson, G. N., & Pelletier, F. J. (Eds.). (1995). *The generic book*. Chicago, IL: Chicago University Press.

Cheryan, S., & Bodenhausen, G. V. (2000). When positive stereotypes threaten intellectual performance: The psychological hazards of "model minority" status. *Psychological Science, 11*(5), 399–402.

Cimpian, A. (2010). The impact of generic language about ability on children's achievement motivation. *Developmental Psychology, 46*(5), 1333–1340.

Cimpian, A., Arce, H. C., Markman, E. M., & Dweck, C. S. (2007). Subtle linguistic cues affect children's motivation. *Psychological Science, 18*(4), 314–316.

Cimpian, A., & Cadena, C. (2010). Why are *dunkels* sticky? Preschoolers infer functionality and intentional creation for artifact properties learned from generic language. *Cognition, 117*(1), 62–68.

Cimpian, A., & Erickson, L. C. (2012). The effect of generic statements on children's causal attributions: Questions of mechanism. *Developmental Psychology, 48*(1), 159–170.

Cimpian, A., & Markman, E. M. (2008). Preschool children's use of cues to generic meaning. *Cognition, 107*(1), 19–53.

Cimpian, A., & Markman, E. M. (2009). Information learned from generic language becomes central to children's biological concepts: Evidence from their open-ended explanations. *Cognition, 113*(1), 14–25.

Cimpian, A., & Markman, E. M. (2011). The generic/nongeneric distinction influences how children interpret new information about social others. *Child Development, 82*(2), 471–492.

Cimpian, A., Meltzer, T. J., & Markman, E. M. (2011). Preschoolers' use of morphosyntactic cues to identify generic sentences: Indefinite singular noun phrases, tense, and aspect. *Child Development, 82*(5), 1561–1578.

Cimpian, A., Mu, Y., & Erickson, L. C. (2012). Who is good at this game? Linking an activity to a social category undermines children's achievement. *Psychological Science, 23*(5), 533–541.

Dweck, C. S. (1999). *Self-theories: Their role in motivation, personality, and development.* Philadelphia, PA: Psychology Press.

Gelman, S. A. (2003). *The essential child: Origins of essentialism in everyday thought.* London: Oxford University Press.

Gelman, S. A. (1988). The development of induction within natural kind and artifact categories. *Cognitive Psychology, 20*, 65–95.

Gelman, S. A., Goetz, P. J., Sarnecka, B. W., & Flukes, J. (2008). Generic language in parent-child conversations. *Language Learning and Development, 4*, 1–31.

Gelman, S. A., & Markman, E. M. (1986). Categories and induction in young children. *Cognition, 23*, 183–209.

Gelman, S. A., & Raman, L. (2003). Preschool children use linguistic form class and pragmatic cues to interpret generics. *Child Development, 74*, 308–325.

Goodman, N. (1965). *Fact, fiction, and forecast.* Indianapolis, IN: Bobbs-Merrill.

Mueller, C., & Dweck, C. S. (1998). Praise for intelligence can undermine children's motivation and performance. *Journal of Personality and Social Psychology, 75*, 33–52.

Murphy, G. L., & Medin, D. L. (1985). The role of theories in conceptual coherence. *Psychological Review, 92*, 289–316.

Prasada, S., & Dillingham, E. M. (2006). Principled and statistical connections in common sense conception. *Cognition, 99*, 73–112.

Prentice, D. A., & Miller, D. T. (2007). Psychological essentialism of human categories. *Current Directions in Psychological Science, 16*, 202–206.

Shih, M., Ambady, N., Richeson, J. A., Fujita, K., & Gray, H. M. (2002). Stereotype performance boosts: The impact of self-relevance and the manner of stereotype activation. *Journal of Personality and Social Psychology, 83*(3), 638–647.

Shih, M., Pittinsky, T. L., & Ambady, N. (1999). Stereotype susceptibility: Identity salience and shifts in quantitative performance. *Psychological Science, 10*(1), 80–83.

Xu, F., & Tenenbaum, J. B. (2007). Word learning as Bayesian inference. *Psychological Review, 114*(2), 245–272.

5.5

From Categories to Exemplars (and Back Again)

YARROW DUNHAM AND JULIANE DEGNER

The psychological study of the development of prejudice is now some 80 years old. At this point, perhaps its least controversial conclusion is that prejudice emerges quite early, certainly by age 4 or 5 in the context of race in North American settings (e.g. Aboud, 1988). The interest of these findings—and the surprise they often elicit in educators and parents—stems from the assumption that *prejudice* (the affective or attitudinal dimension of intergroup bias) produces *discrimination* (the behavioral dimension). Put differently, attitudes are assumed to be causal players, the "under the hood" psychological entity that drives behavior (e.g., Allport, 1935). And certainly it is generally the case that those with more negative intergroup attitudes do discriminate more (e.g., Ajzen & Fishbein, 1977; Greenwald, Poehlman, Uhlmann, & Banaji, 2009).

But what do we know about how prejudice and discrimination relate to one another in childhood? When assessed with traditional verbal measures, children between the ages of 5 and 7 show the strongest prejudice observed across the life span (a claim recently validated meta-analytically; Raabe & Beelmann, 2011). Thus, we have every reason to predict that children in this age range would engage in highly discriminatory behavior, indeed, in the *most* discriminatory behavior that we observe across the life span. Do they? While the question of whether children in the preschool years discriminate *at all* is still somewhat open, it seems clear that they do not discriminate *a lot*. Studies tend to find at most low levels of discrimination, and they further suggest that what is observed cannot be securely attributed to race. That is, the importance of race is reduced when other, most notably socioeconomic factors, are statistically controlled for (Graham, Cohen, Zbikowski, & Secrist, 1998; Kupersmidt, DeRosier, & Patterson, 1995; Singleton & Asher,

1979). Thus, the cautious conclusion is that while children do care about some things that are *correlated* with race (for example, cues associated with poverty), at least in the preschool to early elementary school ages, *race itself* exerts little influence on their behavioral tendencies in the real ecology of a playground or classroom.

How troubling should we consider this disconnect between attitudes and behavior? Certainly if we survey the field, we will find that failures to find attitude-behavior correspondence are nearly as common as successes, an observation that has produced its share of hand-wringing (e.g., Wicker, 1969). In response, the field has generated some convincing reasons for the apparent disconnect, as well as some strategies to overcome it. Most prominently in the domain of prejudice, attitudes and behavior might not line up if individuals are reluctant to report on their true attitudes, for example because admissions of prejudice carry social costs. But of course younger children *do* express prejudice at extremely high rates (for example, expressing preference for their racial in-group on about 80% of trials; Dunham, Baron, & Banaji, 2006), making it implausible that they are greatly influenced by social norms against its expression (which is not to say they are never influenced by such norms; see Rutland, Cameron, Milne, & McGeorgoe, 2005). Relatedly, social psychologists have suggested that even those who consciously hold little prejudice may have (if only inadvertently) internalized negative representations of out-groups, and that it is this "implicit" form of attitude that drives much discriminatory behavior (e.g., Fazio, Sanbonmatsu, Powell, & Kardes, 1986). If this contention is correct, it raises the possibility that children tend not to discriminate because they have not yet acquired implicit biases. But this possibility also fails to pass empirical muster: Certainly by early elementary school, children show implicit biases every bit as strong as their adult counterparts (reviewed in Dunham, Baron, & Banaji, 2008).

Thus, children show strong prejudice at both the explicit and implicit level, but these attitudes do not reliably manifest themselves in behavior. How can this "attitude-behavior gap" be closed? Here we begin with careful consideration of the constructs themselves. Stereotypes and prejudices are at their core *category-level* phenomena. That is, they say nothing about individuals-*qua-individuals*, only about individuals-*qua-exemplars* of specific categories. This is just to say that stereotypes and prejudices are about groups and their members (e.g., semantic associations between groups and traits; Greenwald et al., 2002). Perhaps this seems obvious, but we belabor the point because it brings into focus an important gap between the attitude and its behavioral manifestation, a gap that may be particularly crucial in early childhood.

A potential instance of discrimination is an *interpersonal interaction*, and as such it is first and foremost an interaction with an *individual*. Take it as a given that this individual falls under the scope of a negatively evaluated category. But that category-level evaluation is not *inherent* in the individual; to do any work, it must actually be activated in the course of the interaction. And here is the gap that we mean to highlight. We suggest that children acquire negative evaluations of social categories (qua categories) well before those categories are routinely brought to bear in the course of social interaction. In a sense, the prejudice floats above the fray, exerting causal influence only when the context makes the categories particularly salient, leading to their activation and subsequent application.

By way of example, consider the familiar case of LaPiere (1934), who found that restaurant and hotel proprietors in the early 1930s overwhelmingly rejected a written entreaty to accept a Chinese couple as customers, but even more overwhelmingly accepted them without visible malice or even hesitancy when they actually visited unannounced. While certainly many factors could make responses to a letter and to an actual encounter diverge, we focus here on just one, concerning the extent to which the category is operative in the potential discriminator's mind. The in-person encounter is with a couple that is, among other things, neatly dressed, kind looking, elderly, and Chinese. Whether, in the midst of these factors, the couple's "Chineseness" is activated, and if so whether it is strong enough to override the other factors present in the actual interaction (being well dressed; being in the company of a White American; being elderly), become the operative questions. By contrast, a written entreaty to accept "a Chinese couple" is explicitly at the level of a (named, stigmatized) category. The reader cannot but have their concept of "Chinese" activated, and especially in the absence of other salient competitors, stereotypes associated with the Chinese will involve themselves in the generation of a behavioral response.

Thus, negative attitudes toward one category are but one force among many, and they will not necessarily win out when pitted against other factors, such as additional attitudes or contextual cues. However, we are also pointing out that a category-level representation can only affect an individual when that individual is in fact actually placed into the category in the moment of the interaction. The category must be active to exert its influence at all, to even be one of the causal forces influencing behavior.

Even in adults, category activation is no sure thing. For example, while there is evidence that in some cases both adults and elementary school children automatically categorize race and gender (as shown, for example, by memory confusion paradigms: Bennett & Sani, 2003; Taylor, Fiske, Etcoff, & Ruderman, 1978), it is by no means the case that such categorization is inevitable. For example, when placed under cognitive load, adults failed to encode the race of a woman they viewed on a video screen, as evidenced by the lack of stereotype-based intrusions into a subsequent word completion task, suggesting that category application requires mental resources (Gilbert & Hixon, 1991), even in adults, who have learned and probably overlearned racial categories. And this gives us every reason to think that category application will be even less sure in children, for whom racial categories are not yet firmly established. In a recent study, we found that 5-year-olds correctly assigned a racial label to photographs of Black, White, and Asian children only about 65% of the time, which just exceeds chance performance but speaks of a surprisingly fragile mapping between category labels and perceptual features (despite stimuli that, through their use of highly representative racial exemplars, likely make the category boundary artificially clear; indeed, adults were near ceiling on this same task).

Thus, one reason a category might not be deployed by children is that it is still fragile and poorly integrated with diagnostic perceptual cues. But even once children *can* categorize with a high degree of accuracy, there remain further reasons why children might be less likely to actually do it. Consider the range of social categories adults can apply with a high degree of accuracy. Among these, they only *automatically* deploy a limited set (e.g., race and gender, and even those not in all cases, as we discussed earlier). This suggests that only categories that are deeply ingrained and culturally reinforced will be brought to bear habitually, with others requiring more effort and/ or more contextual cues to initiate their deployment. Children might, then, go through a period of having racial categories but not deploying them unless the context provides strong cues suggesting they are relevant.

Our consideration of this question has led us to suspect that many of the most common assessments of prejudice provide just this sort of relevance cue. That is, they strongly encourage activation of racial categories. Take, for example, the family of methods derived from the Clark Doll Task (Clark & Clark, 1939), in which contrasting "minimal pairs" of individuals are presented, and children are asked to say who they like better, would prefer to play with, and so on, in a forced-choice manner. The pairs are designed to be as closely matched as possible on dimensions other than race (e.g., typically only same-gender pairs are employed; the faces are matched on age, attractiveness, and clothing; and when drawings are used only a few prototypical cues such as skin color or hair type vary), and multiple trials are presented sequentially. The sequential presentation of minimal pairs that differ most prominently (or even exclusively) along a racial dimension is nothing if not a powerful way to make that dimension salient. Thus, the methodology strongly encourages the activation of racial categories and their attendant evaluations—a category-based stereotype or prejudice. Imagine contrasting prejudice assessed through this "minimal pairs" methodology with a task in which individuals are presented one at a time, and ratings of each individual are made on a continuous dimension of liking that is independent of ratings of other targets. Here, while race varies across individuals, other factors do as well, like gender, attractiveness, clothing, hair style, and so on. While care is needed to ensure that across the entire stimulus set attractiveness and other

factors are equated, this task differs in that the child is free to direct his or her attention toward whatever factors are most naturally salient to him or her. To the extent that race is among them, it should affect preferences, but if race is influential only when the context makes it salient, we should see considerably weaker preferences on such a task.

We recently explored this possibility in 5- and 7-year-old children (Dunham, unpublished data). As expected, when presented with a minimal pairs methodology, both 5- and 7-year-olds robustly preferred the White in-group, choosing the same race peer almost 70% of the time. However, in a single-target rating task, 5-year-olds showed no evidence whatsoever of in-race preferences, while 7-year-olds showed a statistically significant but still weak preference for their racial in-group. That is, when individuals are presented *qua individuals*, freely varying along a number of dimensions, the ubiquitous finding of in-race preference in young children disappears. At risk of repetition: When the situation does not make a racial category salient, the category-level evaluation will not necessarily be active, and so it will not influence how an individual is evaluated.

What about when attitudes are assessed at the implicit level? As with adults, the most widely used measure of implicit attitudes in children is the Implicit Association Test (IAT; Greenwald, McGhee, & Schwarz, 1998). Multiple investigators have now found that, when measured with the IAT, racial preferences appear in adult-like forms from as early as they can reliably be measured (for a review, see Olson & Dunham, 2010). But the IAT is first and foremost a category-based preference measure, in that it involves the explicit categorization of individuals into named groups (e.g., faces are explicitly classified by race). This is by no means a weakness of the measure, which was specifically designed to measure category-based evaluations. However, it cannot thereby answer the question of whether that negative category-level evaluation affects how an individual is evaluated in vivo (again, remember the instructive case of LaPiere's Chinese couple). One can contrast the IAT with methods such as evaluative priming, in which faces of individuals (varying in race) precede words or pictures that must be categorized by valence, and the question becomes whether faces of a certain race facilitate responding, for example, whether Black faces facilitate responding to negative targets. Note that because no explicit categorization is involved, we would expect an influence of racial category only if the participant sponta-neously brings that category to bear. And indeed, when assessed in this manner, participants appear "less prejudiced," at least when we consider the proportion of a participant pool who manifest pro-White, anti-Black implicit bias in the United States. However, if some other aspect of the proce-dure makes racial categories salient (for example, being told you will be asked to recall how many individuals fell into each racial category), then both families of measures produce similar rates of bias (Olson & Fazio, 2003).

Bringing it back to development, the argu-ment we are pursuing here suggests that while category-based assessments will reveal ear-ly-emerging implicit preference, assessments that measure the evaluation of *individuals* (who happen to be members of a given category) will only reveal race-based implicit preferences later in develop-ment. This is exactly what was found in a study of White German and Dutch children's implicit attitudes toward Turkish immigrants (Degner & Wentura, 2010). While children between 9 and 15 all showed a uniform degree of pro-White bias on the IAT, when measured in an evaluative priming paradigm there was a linear increase in the strength of preference with age, with the youngest children showing no evidence of in-group preference at all. Of course, measures differ in many ways, but to more accurately peg the difference to explicit use of categories, Degner and Wentura followed the lead of Olson and Fazio (2003) described earlier by asking children to categorize each prime by race immediately after responding to the target picture that followed it. With this manipulation, their younger participants now showed robust implicit bias on the priming measure as well, sug-gesting that just as with adults, category activation is the key factor driving the presence of implicit bias, but that "baseline" category activation levels are lower in children than in adults.

Of course, caution must be taken when com-paring these results to the more familiar case of race in America. Could these results depend on the European context, in which Turkish immi-grants might be both more perceptually similar (to children's White majority in-group) and less familiar than African Americans in the United States? To answer this question, in a recent study we measured White elementary school child-ren's implicit race preferences toward African Americans using both the IAT and the Affect Misattribution Procedure (AMP; Payne, Cheng, Govorun, & Stewart, 2004), a priming-based methodology that depends for positive results on different stimuli arousing different degrees of pos-itive and negative affect but that does not include any explicit categorization. Replicating prior work, both 6- and 9-year-old children showed robust implicit preferences for White over Black when measured with the IAT. However, only 9-year-olds showed implicit White over Black preference when measured with the AMP. Thus, when evalu-ating the categories themselves, 6-year-olds show a pro-White implicit preference, but when exposed to faces of Black and White children, these same children's responses did not appear to be affected by race (Dunham, unpublished data).

We interpret this pattern of results as show-ing that children acquire a *category-level* evalua-tion of named social categories such as race well before they make habitual use of that category in the course of a routine social encounter (related suggestions can be found in Hirschfeld, 1996 and Quintana, 1998, although they do not draw out the implications in the same way). This means that in most such encounters, the causal path-way by which the attitude could influence behav-ior is not present—either because the child has not yet learned to apply the category accurately, or because, despite having learned how to apply it, the child does not yet do so automatically. In either of these cases, the category-level evaluation sits idly by, doing no work at all, because the inter-action partner has not actually been categorized into the relevant group. Of course, many questions remain. Most prominently, what leads to the even-tual automatization of category application? Is it simply a case of more experience, or are there spe-cific forms of cultural input that lead to this out-come and explain why some but not all categories become so automatic? Documenting the path to automaticity, and the cultural inputs that support it, is therefore a primary future research goal.

Another critical piece of the puzzle involves assessing how different forms of attitude affect children's behavior. Our claim entails the strong prediction that, at least in younger children, exemplar-level measures like priming will be better predictors of discrimination than will category-level measures like the IAT, because they measure the spontaneous application of the racial categories. Despite the practical challenges of measuring discriminatory behavior in children, this central prediction of our proposal needs to be investigated.

Our main contribution is to note that an attitude toward a group is not the same thing as an attitude toward an individual who happens to be a member of that group. To equate those two is to presume an additional cognitive step, the step from category *possession* to category *application*. We believe this step is a later developmental attainment, and its absence in early childhood may well explain the apparent disconnect between attitudes and behavior in young children. This conceptual point has a practical sibling: Researchers must carefully consider whether the methods they choose provide leverage on the research questions they are pursuing. Some measurement techniques necessarily implicate categories and their attendant evaluations, or provide a strong contextual push in that direction. Others include tacit assumptions about whether these same categories are active during tasks of varying subtlety, or they seek to measure that activation directly. These differences in methods parallel differences in substantive theoretical and empirical claims regarding how categories become guides to behavior. We hope researchers will keep the distinctions firmly in mind and choose methods that match their substantive research goals.

REFERENCES

Aboud, F. E. (1988). *Children and prejudice*. Oxford, England: Basil Blackwell.

Ajzen, I., & Fishbein, M. (1977). Attitude–behavior relations: A theoretical analysis and review of empirical research. *Psychological Bulletin, 84*, 888–918.

Allport, G. W. (1935). Attitudes. In C. Murchison (Ed.), *A handbook of social psychology* (pp. 789–994). Worcester, MA: Clark University Press.

Bennett, M., & Sani, F. (2003). The role of target gender and race in children's encoding of category-neutral person information. *British Journal of Developmental Psychology, 21*, 99–112.

Clark, K. B., & Clark, M.K. (1939). The development of consciousness of self and the emergence of racial identification in negro preschool children. *Psychological Bulletin, 10*, 591–599

Degner, J., & Wentura, D. (2010). Automatic prejudice in childhood and early adolescence. *Journal of Personality and Social Psychology. 98*, 356–374.

Dunham, Y., Baron, A. S., & Banaji, M. R. (2006). From American city to Japanese village: A cross-cultural investigation of implicit race attitudes. *Child Development, 77*, 1268–1281.

Dunham, Y., Baron, A.S., & Banaji, M.R. (2008). The development of implicit intergroup cognition. *Trends in Cognitive Sciences, 12*(7), 248–253.

Fazio, R. H., Sanbonmatsu, D. M., Powell, M. C., & Kardes, F. R. (1986). On the automatic activation of attitudes. *Journal of Personality and Social Psychology, 50*, 229–238.

Gilbert, D. T., & Hixon, H. J. (1991). The trouble of thinking: Activation and application of stereotypic beliefs. *Journal of Personality and Social Psychology, 60*(4), 509–517.

Graham, J. A., Cohen, R., Zbikowski, S. M., & Secrist, M. E. (1998). A longitudinal investigation of race and sex as factors in children's classroom friendship choices. *Child Study Journal, 28*(4), 245–267.

Greenwald, A. G., McGhee, D. E., & Schwartz, J. L. K. (1998). Measuring individual differences in implicit cognition: The implicit association test. *Journal of Personality and Social Psychology, 74*(6), 1464–1480.

Greenwald, A. G., Banaji, M. R., Rudman, L. A., Farnham, S. D., Nosek, B. A., & Mellott, D. S. (2002). A unified theory of implicit attitudes, stereotypes, self-esteem, and self-concept. *Psychological Review, 109*, 3–25.

Greenwald, A. G., Poehlman, T. A., Uhlmann, E., & Banaji, M. R. (2009). Understanding and using the Implicit Association Test: III. Meta-analysis of predictive validity. *Journal of Personality and Social Psychology, 97*, 17–41.

Hirschfeld, L. A. (1996). *Race in the making: Cognition, culture, and the child's construction of human kinds*. Cambridge, MA: MIT Press.

Raabe, T., & Beelmann, A. (2011). Development of ethnic, racial, and national prejudice in childhood and adolescence: A multinational meta-analysis of age differences. *Child Development, 82*(6), 1715–1737.

Kupersmidt, J. B., DeRosier, M. E., & Patterson, C. P. (1995). Similarity as the basis for children's friendships: The roles of sociometric status, aggressive and withdrawn behavior, academic achievement and demographic characteristics. *Journal of Social and Personal Relationships, 12*(3), 439–452.

LaPiere, R. T. (1934). Attitudes vs. actions. *Social Forces, 13*(2), 230–237.

Rutland, A., Cameron, L., Milne, A., & McGeorge, P. (2005). Social norms and self-presentation: Children's implicit and explicit intergroup attitudes. *Child Development, 76*(2), 451–466.

Olson, K. R., & Dunham, Y. D. (2010). The development of implicit social cognition. In B. Gawronski & B. Keith Payne (Eds.), *Handbook of implicit social cognition: Measurement, theory, and applications* (pp. 241–254). New York: Guilford Press.

Olson, M. A., & Fazio, R. H. (2003). Relations between implicit measures of prejudice: What are we measuring? *Psychological Science, 14*(6), 636–639.

Quintana, S. M. (1998). Children's developmental understanding of ethnicity and race. *Applied and Preventive Psychology, 7*, 27–45.

Singleton, L. C., & Asher, S. R. (1979). Racial integration and children's peer preferences: An investigation of developmental and cohort differences. *Child Development, 50*, 936–941.

Taylor, S. E., Fiske, S. T., Etcoff, N. L., & Ruderman, A. J. (1978). Categorical and contextual bases of person memory and stereotyping. *Journal of Personality and Social Psychology 36*(7), 778–793.

Wicker, A. W. (1969). Attitudes versus actions: The relationship between verbal and overt behavioral responses to attitude objects. *Journal of Social Issues, 25*, 41–78.

5.6

Bridging the Gap Between Preference and Evaluation During the First Few Years of Life

ANDREW SCOTT BARON

Evaluative preferences are a cornerstone of human life. Judgments of good and bad mediate behavior, influencing daily decisions from which fruits and vegetables to purchase from a local store, to the friendships people form, and, of course, to the editorial decision to publish this manuscript. In addition to guiding behavior, evaluative judgments influence explicit and implicit cognitive processes, including the encoding and retrieval of memories, leading to stronger memories for negative information relative to positive information (Aloise, 1993; Ito, Larsen, Smith, & Cacioppo, 1998; Rozin & Royzman, 2001). Representations of good and bad also shape moral intuition. The positive and negative intentions and outcomes of one's actions are carefully weighed when determining responsibility, praise, and punishment (Cushman, Young, & Hauser, 2006; Haidt, 2001). The ubiquity of evaluative judgments is underscored by its domain generality as they extend across explicit and implicit levels of processing and across ontological barriers, including people, animals, and artifacts (Bargh, Chaiken, Govender, & Pratto, 1992).

Understanding the psychology of evaluation is perhaps most important in the social domain of intergroup cognition, where such evaluations widely lead to intergroup conflict, discrimination, and prejudice (Devine, 1989; Greenwald, Poehlman, Uhlmann, & Banaji, 2009). On measures of explicit intergroup bias, children as young as 3 years begin to exhibit positive and negative social group evaluations (Patterson & Bigler, 2006). A rich body of work has detailed similar findings illustrating own-group preference across many social groups, including those based on gender, class, age, ethnicity, race, language, and religion (see Bigler & Liben, 2007, for a review). An emerging body of research has utilized new methodologies to focus on the development of *implicitly* represented intergroup evaluations as well. For example, Baron and colleagues demonstrated that unconscious race attitudes are present by age 6, revealing a positive evaluation of in-group members relative to out-group members (Baron & Banaji, 2006, 2009; Dunham, Baron, & Banaji, 2008; Rutland, Cameron, Milne, & McGeorge, 2005). More recently, this finding has been extended to 3- and 4-year-olds (Cvencek, Greenwald, & Meltzoff, 2011). Much of this work has also suggested that children may be equipped with an automatic tendency to prefer the in-group by the fourth or fifth year of life. Collectively, this work illustrates that intergroup evaluations of this age are not restricted to a single category and instead reflect a more generalized system of social evaluation that is an important part of children's early social cognition.

The robust presence of explicit and implicit representations of intergroup evaluation so early in development point to its emergence within the first few years of life, well before an age when children are exposed to the attitudes of peers, teachers, or the media and likely well before children begin to explicitly identify with others as an in-group member or as an out-group member. This chapter will trace evidence for the early emergence of intergroup preference and suggest that these preferences may initially not be evaluative at all. One candidate mechanism by which these representations may acquire evaluative content over the first few years of life will be proposed. Specifically, it will be suggested that such positive and negative evaluations may emerge as a by-product of two distinct cognitive processes: perceptual fluency (a familiarity bias) and children's developmentally emerging explanatory frameworks (an attribution bias).

FOUNDATIONS OF INTERGROUP EVALUATION IN INFANCY: PREFERENCE WITHOUT EVALUATION

As preschoolers already exhibit positive and negative intergroup evaluations on both explicit and implicit levels of analysis, researchers have turned to infancy to identify the roots of intergroup evaluation. Surprisingly, such work has suggested that by 3 months of age infants exhibit preferences for a variety of social categories. For example, research has demonstrated that 3-month-olds exhibit a visual preference for own-race faces (Bar-Haim, Ziv, Lamy, & Hodes, 2006; Kelly et al., 2005). Visual looking-time preferences have been observed for categories of facial attractiveness and gender as well. For example, Langlois and colleagues (Langlois, Ritter, Roggman, & Vaugh, 1991) showed that infants prefer to look more at faces judged to be attractive by adults. Research by Quinn, Yahr, Kuhn, Slater, and Pascalis (2002) demonstrated that infants prefer to look at female faces relative to male faces. Work by Kinzler, Dupoux, and Spelke (2007) has provided cross-cultural demonstrations that 10-month-olds prefer to look at and even interact more with individuals who speak their native language compared with a foreign language. Collectively, this work demonstrates infants have acquired a variety of intergroup preferences within the first year of life.

The aforementioned results notwithstanding, it remains unclear whether such findings with infants are based on a genuine evaluation of one group as more positive (or negative) than another rather than a preference to look at the more familiar individual (or group member). Indeed, there is a crucial theoretical distinction here between a *familiarity preference* on the one hand and an *evaluative preference* on the other hand. Only evaluative preferences entail positive and negative content, and it is this type of contentful representation that appears to drive intergroup behavior among older children and adults. Indeed, most demonstrations of intergroup preference in infancy, including those described earlier, have revealed a mediating role for familiarity. For example, race preference is mediated by the majority race in the environment (Bar-Haim et al., 2006). Attractiveness preference is mediated by prior exposure to faces of varying degrees of attractiveness (Rubenstein, Kalakanis, & Langlois, 1999). Gender preference is mediated by the sex of the primary caregiver (Quinn et al., 2002). Speakers of a native language with a familiar accent are preferred over those with an unfamiliar accent (Kinzler et al., 2007). Clearly, familiarity plays an important role in establishing intergroup preference among infants. Whether these demonstrations of preference only capture a sense of familiarity or whether they also demonstrate social evaluation remains an open question.

Of course, infants of this age can form evaluative representations. Research has shown that infants can evaluate actions as either positive or negative (Hamlin, Wynn, & Bloom, 2007). This demonstration is important as it shows infants are capable of establishing positive and negative evaluations. Thus, while early *intergroup* preferences may lack evaluative content as suggested here, these findings imply that this absence is likely not caused by an inability to form representations with evaluative content *good* and *bad*. Although infants may be able to rely on the same sort of evaluative mechanism described by Hamlin and colleagues to support intergroup evaluation (e.g., observation of prosocial and antisocial behavior), the argument advanced here considers an entirely independent way in which evaluative preferences form. Instead, intergroup evaluations may be constructed on top of a familiarity-based preference in the absence of direct experience with one group behaving prosocially or antisocially.

AUTOMATIC PREFERENCE FOR THE FAMILIAR

A preference for the familiar appears to be automatic as even a single exposure, supraliminal or subliminal, is sufficient to establish such a preference (Zajonc, 1968). These observations have been reported across behavioral and physiological measures for a range of stimuli, including sounds, images, smells, and textures, underscoring the generality of this mechanism of preference formation. Furthermore, the roots of this bias are present early in life as newborns exhibit such preferences based on experiences in utero across every modality (DeCasper, Fifer, Oates, & Sheldon, 1987; DeCasper & Spence, 1986; Romantshik, Porter, Tillman, & Varendi, 2007; Varendi, Porter, & Winberg, 1996). That such a mechanism for establishing preference is present from birth and possibly universal across cultures suggests that it may be one such pathway for young children to establish *evaluative* preferences. At the very least, preferences rooted in familiarity may either serve as a cognitive prior to the formation of evaluative preferences, or it may serve as a potential building block for the acquisition of intergroup evaluations later in development.

MOVING FROM PREFERENCE TO EVALUATION: THE DRIVE TO EXPLAIN

Humans exhibit an intrinsic drive to explain behavior. Philosophers and cognitive scientists alike have argued that humans spontaneously engage in a variety of stances (e.g., teleological, intentional) in order to generate, accept, and justify explanations for their own and others' behavior (Dennett, 1998; Heider, 1958; Keil & Wilson, 2000; Kelley & Michela, 1980; Lombrozo & Carey, 2006; Malle, 2003). Research suggests that the explicit drive to explain one's own actions begins to emerge between 2 and 3 years of age, well after children have established a variety of familiarity-based intergroup preferences. Familiarity-based preferences shape two particular behaviors that may invite explanation: visual attention and behavioral interaction (e.g., choosing to take a toy from a member of the familiar group over the unfamiliar/less familiar group). The proposal offered here suggests that once children become motivated to explain their own behavior they begin to ascribe positive attributions to the groups that currently receive their greater attention. In other words, children begin to justify their selective interaction in terms of attributing a positive evaluation to that group (e.g., "I attend more to this group *because* this group is good") and a negative evaluation to the other group (e.g., "I chose not to take the toy offered by that group *because* they must not be nice").

Accordingly, the construction of such an explanation for selective intergroup attention will then serve to reinforce the newly created evaluation. Specifically, research shows that once a child (or adult) forms an evaluation of an individual or group, recall and recognition of congruent information are facilitated (Devine, Hirt, & Gehrke, 1990; Stangor & McMillan, 2002). Therefore, children may be more likely to notice when individuals from familiar groups engage in positive behaviors and when individuals from less familiar groups engage in negative behaviors. In addition to a confirmation bias, research has demonstrated that memory for expectancy-congruent behavior is stronger than memory for expectancy-incongruent behavior. Therefore, once children establish a positive (or negative evaluation) of a social group, enhanced memory for consistent behaviors should be observed. As such, a confirmation bias and an expectancy congruency bias may collectively serve to reinforce children's emerging evaluative intergroup preferences, filling a central gap in the transition from a familiarity-driven preference observed among infants to the evaluative intergroup preferences observed among preschoolers and older children.

SUPPORTED PREDICTIONS

Several predictions follow from the argument that a developmentally emerging explanatory framework leads to positive attributions of familiar groups and to negative attributions of unfamiliar groups. First, whereas infants may exhibit evaluations for select individuals and social groups (e.g., those observed to engage in prosocial or antisocial behaviors), once toddlers begin to adopt an explanatory stance toward their own behavior, familiar groups will automatically be encoded as good and unfamiliar groups as bad. Second, the encoding of familiar groups as good and unfamiliar (or less familiar) groups as bad will be supported and enriched via confirmation and expectancy congruency biases. Indeed, while this claim may always apply when a social group is evaluated, the implication here is that these perceptual biases should be observed much earlier in development than previously demonstrated. Third, early intergroup evaluations will be sensitive to the degree of visual familiarity children have with members of different social groups. Specifically, children from homogeneous environments will show a stronger positivity bias toward familiar groups compared with children from heterogeneous environments who have decidedly more exposure to other groups. In addition, within environments where there is little to no out-group exposure, in-group positivity will likely emerge prior to out-group negativity as the child's behaviors inviting explanation will be predicated almost exclusively in terms of selective interaction with the familiar in-group. Thus, the asymmetry in the reported development of in-group and out-group attitudes (e.g., Aboud, 2003) may likely be shaped by the amount of exposure children have had to out-group members and not as the result of a particular cognitive limitation to form negative intergroup evaluations.

CONCLUSION

Understanding the origins of intergroup evaluation promises to open new avenues to shape intergroup behavior. Research suggests that the seeds of intergroup bias are planted surprisingly early and, at least on implicit measures, appear to undergo little change in magnitude across development (Baron & Banaji, 2006, 2009). However, there is a gaping hole in the literature between 1- and 3-year-olds. On measures of explicit and implicit intergroup bias, 3-year-olds reveal positive and negative evaluations. The consensus from work with infants is that they have at least established preferences for familiar social groups. Between the first and third year of life children transition from a preference rooted in familiarity to one that entails positive and negative evaluative content. The argument put forth here suggests that as toddlers begin to adopt explicit explanatory stances, they will seek to justify their selective intergroup behavior. Those groups of people with whom the child is more familiar will subsequently be perceived as more *positive* than or as *better* than other (less familiar) groups. This initial attribution will then be reinforced through perceptual biases that facilitate the identification and recall of evaluatively consistent behaviors among group members. This proposal will hopefully shed light on one potential mechanism by which intergroup evaluation unfolds and spark specific questions for future research to examine.

REFERENCES

Aboud, F. (2003). The formation of in-group favoritism and out-group prejudice in young children: Are they distinct attitudes? *Developmental Psychology, 39*(1), 48–60.

Allport, G. (1954). *The nature of prejudice*: Addison-Wesley.

Aloise, P.A. (1993). Trait confirmation and disconfirmation: The development of attribution biases. *Journal of Experimental Child Psychology, 55*(2), 177–193.

Bargh, J.A., Chaiken, S., Govender, R., & Pratto, F. (1992). The generality of the automatic attitude activation effect. *Journal of Personality and Social Psychology, 62*(6), 893–912.

Bar-Haim, Y., Ziv, T., Lamy, D., & Hodes, R.M. (2006). Nature and nurture in own-race face processing. *Psychological Science, 17*(2), 159–163.

Baron, A. S., & Banaji, M. R. (2006). The development of implicit attitudes: Evidence of race evaluations from ages 6 and 10 and adulthood. *Psychological Science, 17*(1), 53–58.

Baron, A. S., & Banaji, M. R. (2009). Evidence of system justification in young children. *Social and Personality Psychology Compass, 3*(6), 918–926.

Bigler, R. S., & Liben, L. S. (2006). A developmental intergroup theory of social stereotypes and prejudice. In R. V. Kail (Ed.), *Advances in child development and behavior* (Vol. 34, pp. 39–89). San Diego, CA: Elsevier.

Cushman, F., Young, L., & Hauser, M. (2006). The role of conscious reasoning and intuition in moral judgment: Testing three principles of harm. *Psychological Science, 17*(12), 1082–1089.

Cvencek, D., Geenwald, A. G., & Meltzoff, A. (2011). Measuring implicit attitudes of 4-year-olds: The Preschool Implicit Association Test. *Journal of Experimental Child Psychology, 109*(2), 187–200.

DeCasper, A. J., Fifer, W. P., Oates, J., & Sheldon, S. (1987). Of human bonding: Newborns prefer their mothers' voices. In *Cognitive development in infancy.* (pp. 111–118). Hillsdale, NJ: Erlbaum.

DeCasper, A. J., & Spence, M. J. (1986). Prenatal maternal speech influences newborns' perception of speech sounds. *Infant Behavior and Development, 9*(2), 133–150.

Dennett, D. C. (1987). *The intentional stance.* Cambridge, MA: MIT Press.

Devine, P. G. (1989). Stereotypes and prejudice: Their automatic and controlled components. *Journal of Personality and Social Psychology, 56*, 5–18.

Devine, P., Hirt, E., & Gehrke, E. (1990). Diagnostic and confirmation strategies in trait hypothesis testing. *Journal of Personality and Social Psychology, 58*(6), 952–963.

Dunham, Y., Baron, A. S., & Banaji, M. R. (2008). The development of implicit intergroup cognition. *Trends in Cognitive Sciences, 12*(7), 248–253.

Greenwald, A. G., Poehlman, T. A., Uhlmann, E. L., & Banaji, M. R. (2009). Understanding and using the Implicit Association Test: III. Meta-analysis of predictive validity. *Journal of Personality and Social Psychology, 97*(1), 17–41.

Haidt, J. (2001). The emotional dog and its rational tail: A social intuitionist approach to moral judgment. *Psychological Review, 108*(4), 814–834.

Hamlin, J. K., Wynn, K., & Bloom, P. (2007). Social evaluation in preverbal infants. *Nature, 450*(7169), 557–559.

Heider, F. (1958). *The psychology of interpersonal relations.* New York: Wiley.

Ito, T. A., Larsen, J. T., Smith, N. K., & Cacioppo, J. T. (1998). Negative information weighs more heavily on the brain: The negativity bias in evaluative categorizations. *Journal of Personality and Social Psychology, 75*(4), 887–900.

Keil, F. C., & Wilson, R. A. (2000). *Explanation and cognition.* Cambridge, MA: MIT Press.

Kelley, H. H., & Michela, J. L. (1980). Attribution theory and research. *Annual Review of Psychology, 31*, 457–501.

Kelly, D. J., Quinn, P. C., Slater, A. M., Lee, K., Gibson, A., Smith, M., ... Pascalis, O. (2005). Three-month-olds, but not newborns, prefer own-race faces. *Developmental Science, 8*(6), F31–F36.

Kinzler, K. D., Dupoux, E., & Spelke, E. S. (2007). The native language of social cognition. *Proceedings of* the *National Academy of Sciences USA, 104*(30), 12577–12580.

Langlois, J. H., Ritter, J. M., Roggman, L. A., & Vaughn, L. S. (1991). Facial diversity and infant preferences for attractive faces. *Developmental Psychology, 27*(1), 79–84.

Lombrozo, T., & Carey, S. (2006). Functional explanation and the function of explanation. *Cognition, 99*(2), 167–204.

Malle, B. F. (2004). *How the mind explains behavior: folk explanations, meaning, and social interaction.* Cambridge, MA: MIT Press.

Patterson, M. M., & Bigler, R. S. (2006). Preschool children's attention to environmental messages about groups: Social categorization and the origins of intergroup bias. *Child Development, 77*(4), 847–860.

Quinn, P., Yahr, J., Kuhn, A., Slater, A., & Pascalis, O. (2002). Representation of the gender of human faces by infants: A preference for female. *Perception, 31*(9), 1109–1121.

Romantshik O., Porter R. H., Tillmann V., & Varendi, H. (2007). Preliminary evidence of a sensitive period for olfactory learning by human newborns. *Acta Pædiatrica, 96*(3), 372–376.

Rozin, P., & Royzman, E. B. (2001). Negativity bias, negativity dominance, and contagion. *Personality and Social Psychology Review, 5*(4), 296–320.

Rubenstein, A. J., Kalakanis, L., & Langlois, J. H. (1999). Infant preferences for attractive faces: A cognitive explanation. *Developmental Psychology, 35*(3), 848–855.

Rutland, A., Cameron, L., Milne, A., & McGeorge, P. (2005). Social norms and self-presentation: Children's implicit and explicit intergroup attitudes. *Child Development, 76*(2), 451–466.

Stangor, C., & McMillan, D. (1992). Memory for expectancy-congruent and expectancy-incongruent information: A review of the social and social developmental literatures. *Psychological Bulletin, 111*(1), 42–61.

Varendi, H., Porter, R. H., & Winberg, J. (1996). Attractiveness of amniotic fluid odor: Evidence of prenatal olfactory learning? *Acta Paediatrica, 85*(10), 1223–1227.

Zajonc, R. B. (1968). Attitudinal effects of mere exposure. *Journal of Personality and Social Psychology, 9*(2), 1–27.

5.7

On the Developmental Origins of Differential Responding to Social Category Information

PAUL C. QUINN, GIZELLE ANZURES, KANG LEE, OLIVIER PASCALIS, ALAN SLATER, AND JAMES W. TANAKA

Historically, the ability to parse the world into categories was considered to be a late developmental achievement dependent on language and instruction (e.g., Leach, 1964). However, during the 1990s, evidence began to accumulate that quite young infants display abilities to form category representations for natural and artifactual object classes from perceptual experience (reviewed in Quinn, 2011). In a typical study, infants in the age range between 3 to 4 months are presented with multiple instances from a common category (i.e., realistic, photographic visual images) and then presented with a novel instance of the familiar category paired with a novel instance from a novel category. A category representation for the familiarized class is inferred if infants generalize responsiveness (as measured in looking time) to the novel instance from the familiarized class and display preferential responsiveness to the novel instance from the novel class. Thus, for example, infants presented with visual images of cats will generalize to novel cats but respond differentially to birds, dogs, and horses; and infants presented with visual images of horses will generalize to novel horses but respond differentially to cats, giraffes, and zebras. Similar results have been obtained with furniture classes where infants have been shown to form category representations for chairs that exclude exemplars of couches, beds, and tables, and for couches that exclude exemplars of chairs, beds, and tables.

The significance of the infant object categorization work lies in the fact that it tells us that infants are not experiencing the world as an undifferentiated bunch of grapes. Rather, young infants possess abilities to divide objects based on surface appearance into perceptual clusters that later come to have conceptual significance for children and adults. The knowledge-rich representations of children and adults can thus be viewed as informational enrichments of the category representations formed by infants based on perceptual experience. By this view, the more abstract knowledge that is acquired subsequently through language and instruction about different object classes (i.e., the knowledge that cats give birth to kittens, have cat DNA, and are labeled as "cat") can be incorporated into the category representations formed by infants, thereby enriching these representations to the point that they come to have the inductive potential of the more mature concepts of children and adults.

AN EXPERIENCE-BASED ASYMMETRY IN YOUNG INFANTS' REPRESENTATION OF FEMALE VERSUS MALE FACES

Given the positive evidence of categorization by infants for object classes and the emerging literature on the development of social cognition (e.g., Striano & Reid, 2008), it seemed a natural transition to investigate how infants would represent people and their social category attributes (e.g., gender, race, attractiveness, and emotion information in faces). In one of our initial studies, 3- to 4-month-olds presented with female or male faces and tested with female versus male faces displayed an asymmetrical pattern of responding: Infants familiarized with female faces did not display a subsequent preference for male faces; however, infants familiarized with male faces showed an ensuing preference for female faces (Quinn, Yahr, Kuhn, Slater, & Pascalis, 2002). The basis for the asymmetry became clear in a follow-up study investigating infant spontaneous visual preference for pairings of female versus male faces presented without prior familiarization. The infants preferred female over male faces, a preference that makes the categorization asymmetry understandable: When familiarized with female faces, a spontaneous preference for female faces and novel category preference for male faces would interfere with each other and produce a null preference; however, when familiarized with male faces, a spontaneous preference for female faces and novel category preference for female faces would work in concert and produce a robust preference for female faces.

Left open is the question of why infants prefer female over male faces. After initial control studies showed that the preference was not attributable to lower level psychophysical variables such as differential attractiveness, hair length, or cosmetic usage, we began to wonder whether the higher order cognitive variable of familiarity might be at work. In particular, all of the infants in the Quinn et al. (2002) studies described thus far were reared with female primary caregivers. This suggests the possibility that looking at faces in the social domain by infants might be driven by the following rule: Look more at whomever looks more like the caregiver. A straightforward test of this hypothesis would be to investigate whether the spontaneous preference for female versus male faces is reversed in a population of infants reared by male caregivers. While the base rate of that population is small, we did manage to test eight such infants, and remarkably, seven of the eight preferred male over female faces (Quinn, 2003; Quinn et al., 2002). These results indicate that representation of information about human faces is influenced by the gender of the primary caregiver and, more generally, that infant performance in the laboratory is influenced by experiences occurring prior to arrival at the laboratory.

DIFFERENTIAL EXPERIENCE AND A PREFERENCE FOR SAME- OVER OTHER-RACE FACES

The next question we sought to answer was whether the effect of differential experience with gender on visual preference could be extended to race/ethnicity information. Specifically, we asked whether early differential experience with same- versus other-race faces would lead to an acquired preference for same- versus other-race faces. The major findings were that while 3-month-old Caucasian infants reared in Caucasian families and exposed to predominantly Caucasian faces preferred Caucasian faces over African, Asian, and Pakistani faces (Kelly et al., 2005), 3-month-old Chinese infants reared in Chinese families and exposed almost exclusively to Chinese faces preferred Chinese faces over African, Caucasian, and

Pakistani faces (Kelly, Liu, et al., 2007). These outcomes complement those of Bar-Haim, Ziv, Lamy, and Hodes (2006), who reported same-race preferences in 3-month-old Caucasian versus African infants exposed primarily to own-race faces, but no differential preference in a sample of African infants who were exposed to both Caucasian and African faces. It is also worth noting that both the same-race preference and female preference were not observed in newborns (Kelly et al., 2005; Quinn et al., 2008). Taken together, the evidence supports the notion of an unspecified face representation at birth, which is shaped by the faces observed within the visual environment during the initial months of development, thereby becoming tuned to own-race faces and the gender of the primary caregiver.

REPRESENTATION OF FEMALE AND OWN-RACE FACES AT THE LEVEL OF INDIVIDUALS VERSUS REPRESENTATION OF MALE AND OTHER-RACE FACES AT THE LEVEL OF CATEGORY

With the findings thus far described demonstrating that the visual preferences of infants for the social categories of gender and race are affected by differential experience with these classes, one can ask whether other processing differences between the categories might be observed. That is, if differential experience leads to increased visual attention for the more frequently experienced category, might one also observe deeper encoding for the more frequently experienced category? In the case of gender, although the exemplars of the female versus male categories were shown to be discriminable for 3- to 4-month-olds, when the infants were presented with a category of female faces, they subsequently preferred a novel over familiar female face; however, when presented with a category of male faces, there was no differential preference for a novel over familiar male face (Quinn et al., 2002). In the case of race, whereas 3-month-old Caucasian infants exposed predominantly to Caucasian faces performed as well on a recognition memory task (i.e., familiarization with one face, and preference test between that face and a novel face) involving either own- or other-race faces, 9-month-old Caucasian infants demonstrated recognition memory only for Caucasian faces (Kelly, Quinn, et al., 2007). Likewise, Chinese infants exposed almost exclusively to Chinese faces recognized both own- and other-race faces at 3 months; however, over the next 6 months, the ability to recognize own-race faces was retained, whereas the capacity to individuate other-race faces was reduced, demonstrating a pattern of perceptual narrowing (Kelly et al., 2009). This recognition advantage and its time course of development have also been observed for human infants viewing same- versus other-species of faces, such as humans versus monkeys (Pascalis, de Haan, & Nelson, 2002). All of the results suggest that experience with faces in the first half-year of life narrows infants' face representation from a general to a specific one that is tuned to the individual instances of frequently encountered face categories.

A POSSIBLE RELATION BETWEEN VISUAL ATTENTION, RECOGNITION, AND SCANNING

The proposed link between visual attention and recognition memory for more frequently experienced categories receives additional support from a recent eye-tracking study of Chinese infants between 4 and 9 months of age exposed primarily to Chinese faces (Liu et al., 2011). Over the age range tested, there was a gradual decrement in fixation time on the internal features of other-race faces and maintenance of fixation time on the internal features of same-race faces. As noted earlier, a preference for same-race faces based on differential experience results in greater visual attention to such faces, which in turn increases the likelihood that they will be processed at a deeper (i.e., subordinate) level. The eye-tracking findings add to this account by suggesting that lesser experience with other-race faces may bring about decreases in looking time to the internal features of such faces, which in turn increase the likelihood that the faces will be processed at a more summary category level (i.e., Caucasian). In other words, if infants gradually come to spend less time fixating on the internal features of other-race faces, and there is important identifying information associated with those internal features, then it stands to reason that the infants would become less skilled at individuating other-race faces from one another.

CATEGORIZATION OF SAME-RACE FACES VERSUS CATEGORICAL PERCEPTION OF OTHER-RACE FACES

Further evidence for tuning into social category information in faces is evident in a study that investigated how infants between 6 and 9 months of age respond to race categories (Anzures, Quinn, Pascalis, Slater, & Lee, 2010). In particular, 9-month-old Caucasians differentiated categories of female Caucasian and Asian faces (i.e., they generalized to novel instances of the familiarized race category and responded differentially to novel instances of the novel race category), whereas 6-month-old Caucasians did not. The 6-month-olds showed differential responsiveness to Caucasian faces after familiarization with Asian faces, but no such increase in looking at Asian faces after familiarization with Caucasian faces. This pattern of responsiveness is consistent with the idea that 6-month-old performance in the racial categorization task was influenced by the spontaneous preference for own-race faces. Infants' spontaneous preference for own-race faces could have contributed to the observed increase in looking at own-race faces after familiarization with other-race faces, and it would have interfered with increased looking at the less preferred other-race faces after familiarization with own-race faces.

The findings of Anzures et al. (2010) suggest that younger infants' racial categorization may be influenced by a spontaneous preference for the category of faces with which they have the most experience, whereas older infants are able to separate categories of own- versus other-race faces. There was also an important sense in which even the older infants' representations for same- and other-race faces were not the same. Specifically, at 9 months of age, same-race faces were discriminated, suggesting that they were *categorized* (where a category refers to a grouping together of discriminably different entities that are responded to equivalently). By contrast, at the same age, other-race faces were not discriminated, suggesting that they were represented through *categorical perception* (where the perception is of similar exemplars that are difficult to discriminate). This pattern of results in turn implies that own- and other-race faces are, by 9 months, represented by different category structures.

TUNING INTO GENDER AND RACE INFORMATION IN FACES BY INFANTS: WHAT ARE THE LONGER TERM DEVELOPMENTAL CONSEQUENCES?

One can ask whether there are longer term developmental consequences of the differential responding that infants display for gender and race categories. Consider the case of processing faces by race. The lesser visual attention, decline in recognition memory, and categorical perception of other-race faces observed in infants appears to foreshadow race-based social preference in children (Kinzler, Shutts, DeJesus, & Spelke, 2009) and the well-known other-race effect (lesser discrimination of other-race faces compared with own-race faces) observed in both children (e.g., Goodman et al., 2007) and adults (Meissner & Brigham, 2001). For gender, the female preference in infants may work in concert with same-sex friendships in girls leading to an own-gender recognition advantage in females that is present as early as 8 years of age, and a female preference in infants may be interfered with by same-sex friendships in boys leading to own-gender recognition advantages in males that are manifested relatively later by 14 years of age (Ge et al., 2008; Wright & Sladden, 2003).

Whether the effects we have reported with infants also provide the initial starting point for stereotypic beliefs and prejudicial behavior is a more tenuous connection, but it should be noted that stereotyping and prejudice are evident by the age of 4 and are most likely to be observed in instances where there are salient perceptual differences among groups, as there are between the genders and between the races (reviewed in Bigler & Liben, 2007). Moreover, as we described earlier, the category representations formed by infants for generic object classes may serve as perceptual placeholders for the beliefs that come to be associated with these categories during childhood, and the argument has been advanced that a mechanism of this nature can be used to account for how physically attractive faces preferred by infants come to be attributed with positive characteristics by children (Ramsey, Langlois, Hoss, Rubenstein, & Griffin, 2004). We should also mention that a link has been made between face recognition and prejudice: In particular, individuation training on other-race faces reduces implicit racial bias in adults (LeBrecht, Pierce, Tarr, & Tanaka, 2009).

This view emphasizes the overlap between perceptual and social categories (cf. Hirschfeld, 1996). Just as objects belonging to the perceptual category of "bird" share the visual features of two feet, wings, and a beak, people belonging to the "social" category of female have thinner face contours and higher cheekbone features, and members of the "social" category of Caucasian have lighter skin color, thinner lips, and narrower nose features relative to African and Asian individuals. Given the strong perceptual information that facilitates the formation of these "social" categories, it

should not be surprising that they are among the first categories formed by infants. Moreover, just as generic object categories that start out as perceptual become more conceptual, face categories that start out as perceptual may become more social when we assign socially meaningful properties to the categories (e.g., "aggressive," "trustworthy"). In this manner, social category distinctions marked by salient perceptual differences are also likely the ones that will promote the generation and maintenance of stereotypes. Overall, data on individual differences in performance on social category preference and recognition tasks in infants and how they correlate with stereotypic beliefs, intergroup attitudes, and prejudicial behaviors in children and adults are needed to further understand the degree of developmental continuity in social category processing.

It is noteworthy to us that infants directed their attention to the more *familiar* gender and race, a finding that fits well with data showing that infants prefer mother over stranger in studies assessing responsiveness to face identity (Bushnell, 2001). It is also consistent with the finding that infants extract emotion information from faces more readily when the faces depicting the emotion are portrayed by familiar individuals (Kahana-Kalman & Walker-Andrews, 2001). In addition, familiarity preferences for gender and race in infants are in accord with the report that physically abused children perceive anger in emotionally ambiguous faces more often than children who have not been abused (Pollak & Kistler, 2002). The familiarity rule that infants seem to follow when processing various social attributes from faces contrasts with the *novelty* rule that infants seem to follow when processing information about generic nonface objects (Fantz, 1964). The contrast raises the interesting possibility that infant looking is directed by two different systems of motivation: a social system that directs infants to form attachment relationships with familiar objects and a nonsocial system that directs infants to explore the properties of novel objects in their environment. This suggestion fits well with our understanding of the brain connections between face and emotion-processing areas (Schultz, 2005). It also harkens back to the idea that infant behavior is organized by complementary systems for attachment security and exploration-based mastery of the environment (Bowlby, 1988) and is further consistent with the notion that the mechanisms which underlie the processing of objects versus people may not be completely overlapping (e.g., Neisser, 1994).

CONCLUDING SUMMARY

This chapter has reviewed a set of recent research studies that have been investigating how infants' face processing is tuned by experience with different classes of faces early in development. The research reveals that different degrees of exposure to gender and race categories impact how infants (1) organize faces into different social groupings and (2) attend to and recognize individual faces within these general classes. In particular, early in development, infants may process a broad range of faces from different races and genders with equal facility. As infants develop and are selectively exposed to a limited number of face categories (i.e., one's own race and the gender of the primary caregiver), they come to demonstrate certain processing differences for those predominantly experienced categories relative to categories of lesser experience (i.e., increased visual attention, superior recognition, and categorization as opposed to categorical perception). Current investigations are exploring possible longer term developmental consequences of infants' initial differential responding to social categories, including how such responding contributes to the emergence of social biases, stereotyping, and prejudicial belief systems in children and adults.

ACKNOWLEDGMENT

This research was supported by National Institutes of Health grant HD-46526. The authors thank Mahzarin Banaji for helpful comments.

REFERENCES

Anzures, G., Quinn, P. C., Pascalis, O., Slater, A. M., & Lee, K. (2010). Categorization, categorical perception, and asymmetry in infants' representation of face race. *Developmental Science*, 13, 553–564.

Bar-Haim, Y., Ziv, T., Lamy, D., & Hodes, R. M. (2006). Nature and nurture in own-race face processing. *Psychological Science*, 17, 159–163.

Bigler, R. S., & Liben, L. S. (2007). Developmental intergroup theory: Explaining and reducing children's social stereotyping and prejudice. *Current Directions in Psychological Science*, 16, 162–166.

Bowlby, J. (1988). *A secure base*. New York: Basic Books.

Bushnell, I. W. R. (2001). Mother's face recognition in newborn infants: Learning and memory. *Infant and Child Development*, 10, 67–74.

Fantz, R. L. (1964). Visual experience in infants: Decreased attention to familiar patterns relative to novel ones. *Science*, 164, 668–670.

Ge, L., Anzures, G., Wang, Z., Kelly, D. J., Pascalis, O., Quinn, P. C.,…Lee, K. (2008). An inner-face advantage in children's recognition of familiar peers. *Journal of Experimental Child Psychology*, 101, 124–136.

Goodman, G. S., Sayfan, L., Lee, J. S., Sandhei, M., Walle-Olsen, A., Magnussen, S.,…Arredondo, P. (2007). The development of memory for own- and other-race faces. *Journal of Experimental Child Psychology*, 98, 233–242.

Hirschfeld, L. A. (1996). *Race in the making: Cognition, culture, and the child's construction of human kinds*. Cambridge, MA: MIT Press.

Kahana-Kalman, R., & Walker-Andrews, A. S. (2001). The role of person familiarity in young infants' perception of emotional expressions. *Child Development*, 72, 352–369.

Kelly, D. J., Liu, S., Ge, L., Quinn, P. C., Slater, A. M., Lee, K.,…Pascalis, O. (2007). Cross-race preferences for same-race faces extend beyond the African versus Caucasian contrast in 3-month-old infants. *Infancy*, 11, 87–95.

Kelly, D. J., Liu, S., Lee, K., Quinn, P. C., Pascalis, O., Slater, A. M., & Ge, L. (2009). Development of the other-race effect in infancy: Evidence towards universality? *Journal of Experimental Child Psychology*, 104, 105–114.

Kelly, D. J., Quinn, P. C., Slater, A. M., Lee, K., Ge, L., & Pascalis, O. (2007). The other-race effect develops during infancy: Evidence of perceptual narrowing. *Psychological Science*, 18, 1084–1089.

Kelly, D. J., Quinn, P. C., Slater, A. M., Lee, K., Gibson, A., Smith, M., Ge, L., & Pascalis, O. (2005). FAST TRACK REPORT: Three-month-olds, but not newborns, prefer own-race faces. *Developmental Science*, 8, F31–F36.

Kinzler, K. D., Shutts, K., DeJesus, J., & Spelke, E. S. (2009). Accent trumps race in guiding children's social preferences. *Social Cognition*, 27, 623–634.

Leach, E. (1964). Anthropological aspects of language: Animal categories and verbal abuse. In E. H. Lenneberg (Ed.), *New directions in the study of language* (pp. 23–63). Cambridge, MA: MIT Press.

Lebrecht, S., Pierce, L. J., Tarr, M. J., & Tanaka, J. W. (2009). Perceptual other-race training reduces implicit racial bias. *PLoS One*, 4(1), e4215.

Liu, S., Quinn, P. C., Wheeler, A., Xiao, N., Ge, L., & Lee, K. (2011). Similarity and difference in the processing of same- and other-race faces as revealed by eye-tracking in 4- to 9-month-old infants. *Journal of Experimental Child Psychology*, 108, 180–189.

Meissner, C. A., & Brigham, J. C. (2001). Thirty years of investigating the own-race bias in memory for faces: A meta-analytic review. *Psychology, Public Policy, and Law*, 7, 3–35.

Neisser, U. (1994). Multiple systems: A new approach to cognitive theory. *European Journal of Cognitive Psychology*, 6, 225–241.

Pascalis, O., de Haan, M., & Nelson, C. A. (2002). Is face processing species-specific during the first year of life? *Science, 296,* 1321–1323.

Pollak, S. D., & Kistler, D. J. (2002). Early experience is associated with the development of categorical representations for facial expressions of emotion. *Proceedings of the National Academy of Sciences USA, 99,* 9072–9076.

Quinn, P. C. (2003, April). Why do young infants prefer female faces? In M. S. Strauss (Organizer), *Development of facial expertise in infancy.* Symposium conducted at the meeting of the Society for Research in Child Development, Tampa, FL.

Quinn, P. C. (2011). Born to categorize. In U. Goswami (Ed.), *Blackwell handbook of childhood cognitive development* (2nd ed., pp. 129–147). Oxford, England: Blackwell.

Quinn, P. C., Uttley, L., Lee, K., Gibson, A., Smith, M., Slater, A. M., & Pascalis, O. (2008). Infant preference for female faces occurs for same- but not other-race faces. *Journal of Neuropsychology* [Special Issue on Face Processing], *2,* 15–26.

Quinn, P. C., Yahr, J., Kuhn, A., Slater, A. M., & Pascalis, O. (2002). Representation of the gender of human faces by infants: A preference for female. *Perception, 31,* 1109–1121.

Schultz, R. T. (2005). Developmental deficits in social perception in autism: The role of the amygdala and fusiform face area. *International Journal of Developmental Neuroscience, 23,* 125–141.

Striano, T., & Reid, V. M. (2008). *Social cognition: Development, neuroscience and autism.* Oxford, England: Wiley-Blackwell.

Ramsey, J. L., Langlois, J. H., Hoss, R. A., Rubenstein, A. J., & Griffin, A. (2004). Origins of a stereotype: Categorization of facial attractiveness by 6-month-old infants. *Developmental Science, 7,* 201–211.

Wright, D. B., & Sladden, B. (2003). An own gender bias and the importance of hair in face recognition. *Acta Psychologica, 114,* 101–114.

5.8

Building a Better Bridge

SANDRA WAXMAN

An essential developmental task facing infants and young children from across the world's communities is to identify key individuals (e.g., their family pet, a favorite sippy cup), to form *concepts* that capture commonalities among the individuals they encounter (e.g., dog, cup), and to learn *words* to express them (e.g., "Magic," "dog," "cup"). There is now considerable evidence that even before infants take their first steps, their conceptual and linguistic systems are powerfully linked. What this means is that the concepts infants form are shaped not only by the objects they encounter and events they witness but also by the words that accompany them.

Most of the developmental evidence documenting this link between naming and concepts derives from investigations focused on categories of *objects* (e.g., dog, animal). More recently, researchers have considered the role of language in young children's categorization and reasoning about *people*. This work, which has revealed some intriguing parallels that showcase the power of language—and naming in particular—in the early establishment and use of social categories and object categories alike, provides a strong initial footing as we begin to build a bridge that will bring fundamental issues in object categorization into serious contact with issues in social categorization. At the same time, however, it is now apparent that the current blueprint for this bridge is far too narrow. If we are to build a bridge that is sufficiently strong to describe, predict, and explain the development of social categories like those based on race, ethnicity, or gender; how these are shaped by experience; and how they gain inductive force, it is essential that we broaden its footings to include infants and young children raised in a more diverse set of circumstances that reflect more fully the range of human social experience.

WORDS AND OBJECT CATEGORIES

The developmental evidence on naming and object categorization reveals that from infancy, naming has powerful conceptual consequences (see Waxman and Gelman, 2009 for a brief review). In the eloquent words of Roger Brown (1958), words serve as invitations to form categories. Recent work reveals that even before they begin to produce any words on their own, naming facilitates the formation of object categories and supports the use of these categories in reasoning about objects. For example, Waxman and Markow (1995) presented infants with several distinctly *different* toy objects (e.g., a dog, a duck, a bird), all members of the *same* object category (e.g., animal). Infants' ability to detect the category-based commonality among these individuals was influenced powerfully by naming. All infants saw the very same sets of objects; for all infants, an experimenter called attention to each object as she offered it to the infant. For infants in the No Word control condition, she said, "See what I have?" But for infants in the Word condition, she introduced each object in conjunction with the same novel word (e.g., "See the *fauna*?"). Infants in the Word condition detected the commonality among the distinct individuals; those in the No Word condition did not. This facilitative effect of words has now been documented in infants as young as 3 and 6 months of age.

Moreover, this "invitation" has considerable conceptual force, directing infants' subsequent attention to new objects, even if they have yet to be named. In addition, providing a category name promotes infants' and young children's *use* of that category as an inductive base. For example, if they discover a new property of one individual (e.g., it makes a particular noise when it is shaken), they are more likely to expect that this property will also be true of another member of the category, if that category has been named (Graham, Kilbreath, & Welder, 2004).

IMPLICATIONS FOR SOCIAL CATEGORIES

Of course, fundamental cognitive processes like categorization and inductive inference are not engaged uniquely by *objects*. We also make strong and abiding inferences about *people*. From a developmental perspective, the key question is how these social categories develop and whether they have the inductive strength to guide children's expectations about the behaviors and intentions of others. This is especially compelling because it is clear that the content of our social categories, especially those based on race and ethnicity, are not innately given but are instead social constructions tuned by experience and learning. In fact, although the belief that the social world is comprised of distinct *kinds of people*, partitioned on the basis of race and ethnicity, enjoys scant scientific support, it is held deeply and universally and carries serious consequences: Racial and ethnic categories function essentially as "natural kinds," and like other natural kinds, they support strong inferences about members of those categories, including inferences about the capacities, intentions, and behaviors of individuals that we will never encounter in our direct experience.

How do these socially constructed social categories develop? Does naming promote the establishment of social categories and support their use, for better or worse, as an inductive base? Certainly, this claim has been with respect to adults. As Gordon Allport observed, category labels "act as shrieking sirens...deafening us to all finer discriminations that we might otherwise perceive" (Allport, 1954, p. 179). Although it is unlikely that category labels deafen us entirely to distinctions among individuals, the power of social category names cannot be denied.

But what about young children? We know that infants and preschool-aged children *notice* a range of physical features that will become correlated with social categories (e.g., skin color, hair length, native language, type of dress) and use these features to distinguish between individuals. Importantly, however, there is little evidence that they *use* physical features like these to predict the behaviors of others—unless social categories are highlighted explicitly (Patterson & Bigler, 2006).

This raises a chorus of crucial questions. How, in the natural course of development, do social categories like these become highlighted? How do children move beyond noticing that individual people vary along certain dimensions (e.g., skin color, native language, or accent) and begin to establish distinct *kinds of people*? How do these social categories gain inductive force?

WORDS AND SOCIAL CATEGORIES

Together with others in the field, I have recently begun to address these questions (Waxman, 2010). To do so, I have adapted a standard cognitive task—the "category-based induction" task—to examine how 3- and 4-year-olds establish categories of *people* and use these categories to support inferences about others. In this task, an experiment introduces a child to a picture of one individual (e.g., a White woman). Children complete this task with a range of different individuals (e.g., a White woman, a Black man, etc.). She then teaches the child a novel property of that individual—one that cannot be observed from perceptual inspection (e.g., "See this one? This one loves to play a game called *zaggit*").[1] We then ask how broadly the child is willing to extend that property to other individuals.

On the one hand, the results are reassuring: Children overwhelmingly used the broad category *person* as an inductive base. They judged that the novel property could be extended equally to other people, regardless of their race or gender. (Children did not tend to extend the property to nonhuman animals or artifacts.) This tells us that in the absence of evidence to do otherwise, preschoolers use the broad category *people* to guide their expectations about the behaviors and dispositions of others.

But how do children begin to partition this broad and inductively rich category into distinct *kinds of people*? Here, we found a powerful role for naming: Providing a novel category name for the target individual highlighted that individual's membership within a distinct *kind of person* (based on race or gender) and licensed the use of that *kind of person* as an inductive base when reasoning about the preferences of others. More specifically, we found that if we introduced the target individual (e.g., a White woman) as a member of a named social category (e.g., "This one is

---

[1] We introduced novel properties because if we had introduced familiar properties (e.g., likes to eat *ice cream*), children's performance might very well have been influenced by their existing expectations and observations (e.g., that most people, and even some nonhuman animals, like to eat ice cream).

a *Wayshan*"),[2] they no longer extended the property (e.g., "loves to play a game called *zaggit*") equally across all people. Instead, they were now *more likely* to extend it to other individuals from the same social category (either race or gender) as the target individual. Importantly, in this task *only* the target individual was named, although the novel name was applied only to a single individual (the target), the influence of this name extended beyond that individual. It guided children's expectations of other—and unnamed—individuals presented at test.

What this suggests is that naming is instrumental in the establishment and use of social categories (e.g., Diesendruck & HaLevi, 2006; Patterson & Bigler, 2006; Rhodes & Gelman, 2009). Naming supports the belief that social categories are natural kinds, and that individual members of these kinds have commonalities that surpass our direct observation.

BUILDING THE BRIDGE

This work, together with other work in this volume, reveals fundamental parallels underlying the establishment of *kinds of objects* and *kinds of people*. In particular, category naming appears to provide key structural support for connecting the rich research traditions in our categorization and reasoning about *objects* and about *people*. However, the bridge is still shaky, not only because construction has only recently begun but, more importantly, because its grounding is precipitously narrow. After all, the social categories that we form, and the inductive potential that these categories ultimately hold, are highly inflected by our experience with members of our own social group and others. This includes our direct interactions, observed interactions, and the information that we glean from the comments and behaviors of others. Because the breadth of social experiences available within different communities varies widely, and because the social categories we form are shaped by this kind of experience, it is surprising to find that with only a few noteworthy exceptions, the bridge that we are currently building rests predominantly upon evidence from White children raised by White, middle-class parents in predominantly White, urban, Western communities.

If our goal is to build a bridge that is sufficiently strong to describe, predict, and explain the origins of social categories like race and ethnicity, how they are shaped by experience, and how they gain inductive force, we must consider the developmental trajectories of infants and young children raised in a more diverse set of circumstances that reflect more fully the range of human social experience. Therefore, in what follows, I outline several issues that underscore the importance of broadening the empirical base.

CHILDREN WHO ARE MEMBERS OF MINORITY GROUPS MAY ESTABLISH CATEGORIES BASED ON RACE OR ETHNICITY EARLIER THAN THOSE FROM THE MAJORITY

The existing evidence suggests that social categories based on race and ethnicity may emerge later than those based on gender (Rhodes & Gelman, 2009; Waxman, 2010). However, this developmental pattern may be a consequence of the fact that the developmental evidence thus far involves predominantly members of the majority culture. It is quite plausible that, by dint of their experience, children from minority groups will establish racial and ethnic categories earlier than their majority-culture counterparts, especially because the contrast (both implicit and explicit) between their own in-group and the majority is likely more tangible, and the consequences of category membership more apparent.

VARIATIONS IN EXPERIENCE MAY MATTER MORE IN CARVING OUT SOCIAL CATEGORIES BASED ON RACE AND ETHNICITY THAN THOSE BASED ON GENDER

Across cultures, categories based on race, ethnicity, and gender are tenaciously held and readily imbued with inductive force. But variations in experience may matter more for racial and ethnic categories than for gender categories. In contrast to the convergence in gender categorization across cultures (male vs. female), there is considerable variation in the particular racial and ethnic categories identified within a culture, and variation in the criteria for membership in those categories. For example, the "one-drop rule" was accepted as the criterion for classifying an individual as African American in some—but not all—US states; the federal criterion for classifying

---

[2] We introduced novel words (e.g., "Wayshan") because, by definition, these have no a priori meaning for the child and therefore permit us to examine the effects of naming, independent of any potential confounds related to their familiarity with known social category names.

an individual as a Menominee Indian is currently 25% Menominee blood ancestry.

From a developmental perspective, gender-based distinctions may emerge early for several different *kinds* of reasons. First, consider experience. With rare exception, infants and young children observe and interact with both males and females on a daily basis. But their exposure to members of distinct racial and ethnic groups varies widely. Some children grow up with little or no firsthand exposure to members of racial or ethnic groups other than their own. Others are raised in more diverse communities; in some diverse communities, individuals from different racial groups participate jointly in the social milieu, but in others, children are exposed to individuals from different racial groups within the context of sharply segregated communities. This variation in experience is likely to have significant impact on the social categories children carve out and the valence that these will hold.

Second, at least some of the consequences of gender category assignment are quite explicit (e.g., gender-specific initiations in traditional cultures; gender-specific restrooms, toys, clothing, and behavioral norms in the Western industrialized world). Third, there are cognitive factors that favor the acquisition of binary distinctions (like gender) over graded distinctions (like race and ethnicity) within categories. Finally, we name the gender-based categories ubiquitously in the input to young children, mentioning gender categories like "boy" and "girl" more explicitly—and less self-consciously—than racial- or ethnic-based distinctions. For example, teachers typically address their classrooms using gender names ("Boys and girls, I want you line up quietly for gym"). In contrast, there is a clear prohibition against invoking racial or ethnic names in such circumstances ("Whites, Blacks, Hispanics, and Asians, please settle down"). The same is true in addressing adults (e.g., "Men and women of the Class of 2013").

WHAT IS THE SCOPE OF CHILDREN'S INITIAL RACIAL AND ETHNIC CATEGORIES, AND HOW ARE THESE SHAPED BY EXPERIENCE?

Do children initially make a binary partition, distinguishing their own "in-group" from all others? For example, do White children use "non-White" as an inductive base, grouping together individuals that are Black, Hispanic, Asian, or Native American, or do they carve out more specific categories? How is this process mediated by membership in a racial minority? For example, do Native American children in the United States initially make a binary distinction (native or nonnative), or do they initially carve out more specific groupings among nonnative individuals? Also at issue is whether children, like adults, make finer partitions within their "own" social category than in others? Such distinctions are, of course, shaped by experience. For example, in New York City, and particularly in the Black community, a distinction is drawn between Blacks of African versus Caribbean descent, but this distinction is barely noticed in most White communities. This raises the question of how factors such as native language, dialect, or behavioral practices contribute to the establishment of such distinctions.

HOW DO CHILDREN INTEGRATE THE RANGE OF CORRELATED CHARACTERISTICS THAT CONSTITUTE SOCIAL CATEGORY MEMBERSHIP?

Researchers have tended to focus on a single physical feature (e.g., skin color, native language). Infants become sensitive to features like these early, and their sensitivity is tuned by their experience (Kinzler, Shutts, Dejesus, & Spelke, 2009; Sangrigoli & de Schonen, 2004). But although physical features like these may serve as entry points, the racial and ethnic categories that we ultimately form tend not to be reduced to such features alone. Instead, in the natural course of social experience, variations in physical features, coupled with variation in native language, dialect or speech register, and cultural practices, are all part and parcel of the "diversity" experience. How do these come together as children carve out distinct *kinds of people* and their valences?

HOW DO WE DECIDE WHICH CATEGORY SERVES AS THE APPROPRIATE INDUCTIVE BASE?

If any individual is a member of many social categories (e.g., woman, African American, physician, grandmother), then how do we determine the range of extension for a given property applied to a given individual? The answer will likely depend upon the property in question, the social category in question, and the child's experiences with a range of social groups.

In closing, the object categories and social categories that children carve out, and the inductive power with which they are imbued, are shaped not only by the diversity of objects and people that they observe but by how these are marked in their language. This finding, coupled with other work reported in this volume, begins to connect decades of work in cognitive and social development. But the bridge that we are now building is precarious: It rests on far too narrow an empirical base. To advance our theories of development and to promote positive social and educational outcomes for children growing up in the diverse kinds of social environments that constitute the human experience, we must now revise the blueprint to rest upon a broader set of footings.

REFERENCES

Allport, G. (1954). *The nature of prejudice*. Reading, MA: Addison-Wesley.

Brown, R. (1958). *Words and things*. Glenview, IL: Free Press.

Diesendruck, G., & HaLevi, H. (2006). The role of language, appearance, and culture in children's social category-based induction. *Child Development, 77*, 539–553.

Graham, S. A., Kilbreath, C. S., & Welder, A. N. (2004). Thirteen-month-olds rely on shared labels and shape similarity for inductive inferences. *Child Development, 75*, 409–427.

Kinzler, K. D., Shutts, K., DeJesus, J., & Spelke, E. S. (2009). Accent trumps race in guiding children's social preferences. *Social Cognition, 27*, 623–634.

Patterson, M. M., & Bigler, R. S. (2006). Preschool children's attention to environmental messages about groups: Social categorization and the origins of intergroup bias. *Child Development, 77*, 847–860.

Rhodes, M., & Gelman, S. A. (2009). A developmental examination of the conceptual structure of animal, artifact, and human social categories across two cultural contexts. *Cognitive Psychology, 59*, 244–274.

Sangrigoli, S., & de Schonen, S. (2004). Effect of visual experience on face processing: A developmental study of inversion & non-native effects. *Developmental Science, 7*, 74–87.

Waxman, S. (2010). Names will never hurt me? Naming and the development of racial and gender categories in preschool-aged children. *European Journal of Social Psychology, 40*(4), 593–610.

Waxman, S. R., & Gelman, S. A. (2009). Early word-learning entails reference, not merely associations. *Trends in Cognitive Sciences, 13*(6), 258–263.

Waxman, S. R., & Markow, D. B. (1995). Words as invitations to form categories: Evidence from 12- to 13-month-olds. *Cognitive Psychology, 29*, 257–302.

5.9

Is Gender Special?

KRISTIN SHUTTS

Humans are capable of categorizing people according to many dimensions, including age, athletic team affiliation, gender, occupation, race, and religion. Recognized social distinctions can also vary significantly from one culture to another. For example, whether one is a Hutu or a Tutsi is relevant in Rwanda, but not in Israel. The range and flexibility of social categorization across different contexts have led some to posit that the human propensity for social categorization may arise from a set of general mechanisms. Applied to the development of social categories in children, this might mean that humans come into the world able to divide the social world any which way. Certain distinctions could rise to prominence due to environmental influences (e.g., labeling by adults, de facto segregation), but the same processes account for the emergence of all social categories (Bigler & Liben, 2007).

The proposition that children and adults possess a general, flexible capacity for learning about social categories has received considerable empirical support in developmental and social psychology. Additionally, general-purpose social categorization is a parsimonious and satisfying way to account for the diversity of social categories across time and place. But is a general learning account the right way to think about the development of all social categories? Or are children predisposed to classify their social world according to some dimensions?

I would like to propose that gender is a social category whose development and prominence might be supported by a special cognitive system. Unlike many other human category distinctions (e.g., Catholics and Protestants; Packers and Vikings fans; Blacks and Whites), males and females exist in nearly every society. Moreover, being able to classify others according to gender is relevant to at least one important activity of our species: namely, reproduction. For these reasons,

evolutionary psychologists have suggested that humans evolved cognitive machinery dedicated to gender categorization (Cosmides, Tooby, & Kurzban, 2003). As evidence in favor of this proposal, researchers point to experiments showing that gender encoding—unlike, race encoding—is automatic and difficult to suppress in adults (Kurzban, Tooby, & Cosmides, 2001).

Most adults have had extensive opportunities to learn about males and females and practice gender categorization. Do creatures with less social experience also consider gender? Indeed, young infants classify novel faces by gender when tested with looking-time procedures (Quinn, Yahr, Kuhn, Slater, & Pascalis, 2002) and most 2-year-old children can label and sort photographs of themselves and others according to gender (Weinraub et al., 1984). Children not only detect gender at an early age, but they also use gender to guide inferences and social evaluations (see Ruble, Martin, & Berenbaum, 2006). Perhaps the most robust and reliable phenomenon in the gender development literature is children's early tendency to prefer others who match their own gender. Children as young as 2 years of age display gender segregation in naturalistic settings (Maccoby & Jacklin, 1987) and preschoolers demonstrate own-gender favoritism in controlled laboratory settings (Martin, 1989; Shutts, Roben, & Spelke, in press).

It is important to note that children detect, make inferences, and develop preferences based on other social category distinctions as well. However, gender appears unique in its early emergence and influence on young children. Studies that directly compare young children's use of gender to another social category marked by visual information—namely, race—make this point most clearly. For example, when asked to select potential friends from photograph pairs consisting of either a boy and girl or a White and Black child, 3- and 4-year-old children showed reliable *but evolutionarily wouldn't that allow us to survive?*

we all find gender everything

preferences for children of their own gender but chose randomly between same- and other-race photographs (Abel & Sahinkaya, 1962; Shutts et al., in press).[1] Additionally, after seeing novel objects and endorsed by pairs of people who differed either by gender or by race, 3-year-old children modeled their own choices of items after those of same-gender children; participants' use of race was less reliable (Shutts, Banaji, & Spelke, 2010). Outside the domain of preferences, studies focused on children's social concepts indicate that young children view gender distinctions as more objectively determined and inductively powerful than racial categories (Rhodes & Gelman, 2009; Waxman, 2010).

The similarity of children's gender-based social preferences both within and across cultures also underscores the power of gender, especially when viewed in comparison to variation in children's race-based social preferences. For example, both boys and girls from different racial groups and communities in Africa, Europe, North America, and South America show robust in-group favoritism on tasks designed to measure gender attitudes (e.g., De Guzman, Gustavo, Ontai, Koller, & Knight, 2004; Maccoby & Jacklin, 1987; Shutts, Kinzler, Katz, Tredoux, & Spelke, 2011; Yee & Brown, 1994). In-group favoritism based on race, however, is noticeably absent in some groups of children. For example, White children in Europe, North America, Oceania, and South Africa tend to prefer members of their own racial group over other groups; but, children from other racial and ethnic groups (e.g., Black children in the U.S. and South Africa) do not tend to exhibit racial in-group favoritism (Aboud, 1988; Shutts, Kinzler, et al., 2011). In-group preferences based on gender seem to emerge across varied contexts, while racial preferences seem more sensitive to cultural factors. This idea is consonant with social dominance theory, which describes gender as a universal distinction and classifies race as one of many "arbitrary-set" categories that depend on sociocultural factors (Sidanius & Pratto, 2001).

Does the fact that young children classify others based on gender, and initially care more about gender than about race, provide sufficient evidence to support the claim that children are predisposed to divide the social world into males versus females? No. The obvious alternative explanation for the early emergence and resilience of gender is that environments provide children with information that gender is a critical distinction. Such information could include language (e.g., labels and gendered pronouns), the promotion of gendered appearances (e.g., clothing, haircuts), and encouraged participation in gender-specific activities (e.g., toys marketed primarily to members of one gender; different restrooms for boys and girls). Any or all of these factors could account for why gender is such a salient and meaningful category for young children.

The long literature on "core knowledge" about aspects of the physical world (Spelke, 2004) provides guidance for research strategies that could shed light on whether humans are predisposed to consider gender categories (as well as other dimensions, of course). One suggestion is to study gender categorization and social preferences in creatures that have limited experience in the social world, namely, young infants. If young infants use gender information to guide their affiliation preferences and inferences about other individuals, this might suggest that children are predisposed to consider gender categories.

A second suggestion is to compare gender development in children whose environments lack specific properties that could contribute to the prominence of gender categories. This could include children who grow up in linguistic environments without gendered pronouns (e.g., Mandarin), as well as children being raised in gender-neutral environments. For example, with the help of the Bucharest Early Intervention Project, my colleagues and I recently examined gender preferences in institutionalized children who had spent their infant and preschool years with limited exposure to gender distinctions. Boys and girls living in the institution were given identical haircuts, wore the same clothing, had minimal access to toys and play activities, and interacted (minimally) with adult females only. Despite this, both boys and girls in our sample showed significant preferences for unfamiliar children of their own gender (Shutts, Spelke, & Nelson, unpublished data). These findings suggest that gender-based, in-group favoritism can emerge without significant early exposure to highly visible gender contrasts, as well as without early participation in social environments that are explicitly organized by gender.

An additional suggestion for future research on whether gender is a privileged category is to identify unique signature patterns of gender categories

[1] The children in these studies were White and came from racially homogenous environments, but studies of children in more racially diverse settings corroborate the basic findings (e.g., Kircher & Furby, 1971; Stevenson & Stevenson, 1960).

in adults and test for those signatures in infants, animals raised under controlled conditions, and people living in varied cultures and environments. Again, this strategy has proven useful in identifying and understanding other potential cases of core knowledge in humans (Spelke, 2004). In the case of numerical cognition, for example, studies provide evidence for common systems underlying numerical representations in infants, nonhuman animals, and adults (Feigenson, Dehaene, & Spelke, 2004).

CONCLUSIONS

Humans—including those who have only been around for a handful of years—attend to a number of different social categories. An individual encountered on the street is not viewed simply as a person, but rather as female, Asian, and a Packers fan. Studies suggest, however, that gender may be a special category: Very young children classify people by gender early in development (Weinraub et al., 1984); preschoolers use gender to guide their selection of social partners (Maccoby & Jacklin, 1987; Martin, 1989); and adults encode gender in an automatic and mandatory fashion (Kurzban et al., 2001). In contrast, very young preschoolers do not seem to exhibit robust racial bias (Abel & Sahinkaya, 1962; Shutts et al., in press), and adults ignore racial group membership in the face of competing social alliance information (Kurzban et al., 2001).

As reviewed herein, there are important directions for future research on the origins of gender categorization. Although the question of whether humans are predisposed to consider gender as a meaningful distinction remains unanswered, psychologists are well situated to provide answers in the near future. Researchers have made significant advances in behavioral methods for testing infants' social preferences in recent years (see Chapter 5.12). Moreover, noninvasive tools for assessing cognitive processes over development (e.g., event-related potentials [ERPs], near-infrared spectroscopy [NIRS]) may also prove helpful in studies of social categories and preferences. Additionally, researchers who specialize in studies of nonhuman animals have also become interested in the emergence of social categories and intergroup biases (e.g., Mahajan et al., 2011). Because studies of nonhuman animals offer opportunities for controlled rearing, such research may provide particularly useful in understanding factors supporting the emergence of different social categories. The availability of new methods, together with increased cross talk

between developmental and social psychologists, makes the present moment an exciting and fruitful time to be studying social categorization and intergroup preferences in children.

REFERENCES

Abel, H., & Sahinkaya, R. (1962). Emergence of sex and race friendship preferences. *Child Development*, 33, 939–943.

Aboud, F. (1988). *Children and prejudice*. Cambridge, MA: Basil Blackwell.

Bigler, R., & Liben, L. (2007). Developmental intergroup theory: Explaining and reducing children's social stereotyping and prejudice. *Current Directions in Psychological Science*, 16, 162–166.

Cosmides, L., Tooby, J., & Kurzban, R. (2003). Perceptions of race. *Trends in Cognitive Sciences*, 7, 173–178.

De Guzman, M. R. T., Gustavo, C., Ontai, L. L., Koller, S. H., & Knight, G. P. (2004). Gender and age differences in Brazilian children's friendship nominations and peers sociometric ratings. *Sex Roles*, 51, 217–225.

Feigenson, L., Dehaene, S., & Spelke, E. (2004). Core systems of number. *Trends in Cognitive Sciences*, 8, 307–314.

Kircher, M., & Furby, L. (1971). Racial preferences in young children. *Child Development*, 42, 2076–2078.

Kurzban, R., Tooby, J., & Cosmides, L. (2001). Can race be erased? Coalitional computation and social categorization. *Proceedings of the National Academy of Sciences USA*, 98, 15387–15392.

Maccoby, E. E., & Jacklin, C. N. (1987). Gender segregation in childhood. In E. H. Reese (Ed.), *Advances in child development and behavior* (Vol. 20, pp. 239–287). New York: Academic Press.

Mahajan, N., Martinez, M. A., Gutierrez, N. L., Diesendruck, G., Banaji, M. R., & Santos, L. R. (2011). The evolution of intergroup bias: Perceptions and attitudes in rhesus macaques. *Journal of Personality and Social Psychology*, 100, 387–405.

Martin, C. L. (1989). Children's use of gender-related information in making social judgments. *Developmental Psychology*, 25, 80–88.

Quinn, P. C., Yahr, J., Kuhn, A., Slater, A., & Pascalis, O. (2002). Representation of the gender of human faces by infants: a preference for female. *Perception*, 31, 1109–1121.

Rhodes, M., & Gelman, S. (2009). A developmental examination of the conceptual structure of animal, artifact, and human social categories across two cultural contexts. *Cognitive Psychology*, 59, 244–274.

Ruble, D. N., Martin, C. L., & Berenbaum, S. A. (2006). Gender development. In W. Damon & N.

Eisenberg (Eds.), *Handbook of child psychology* (6th ed., Vol. 3, pp. 858–931). New York: Wiley.

Sidanius, J., & Pratto, F. (2001). *Social dominance: An intergroup theory of social hierarchy and oppression.* Cambridge, England: Cambridge University Press.

Shutts, K., Banaji, M. R., & Spelke, E. S. (2010). Social categories guide young children's preferences for novel objects. *Developmental Science, 13,* 559–610.

Shutts, K., Kinzler, K. D., Katz, R., Tredoux. C., & Spelke, E. S. (2011). Race preferences in children: Insights from South Africa. *Developmental Science, 14,* 1238–1291.

Shutts, K., Roben, C.K.P., & Spelke, E.S. (in press). Children's use of social categories in thinking about people and social relationships. *Journal of Cognition and Development.*

Spelke, E. S. (2004). Core knowledge. In N. Kanwisher & J. Duncan (Eds.), *Attention and performance: Functional neuroimaging of visual cognition* (Vol. 20, pp. 29–56). Oxford, England: Oxford University Press.

Stevenson, H. W., & Stevenson, N. G. (1960). Social interaction in an interracial nursery school. *Genetic Psychology Monographs, 61,* 37–75.

Waxman, S. (2010). Names will never hurt me? Naming and the development of racial and gender categories in preschool-aged children. *European Journal of Social Psychology, 40,* 593–610.

Weinraub, M., Clemens, L. P., Sockloff, A., Ethridge, T., Gracely, E., & Myers, B. (1984). The development of sex role stereotypes in the third year: Relationships to gender labeling, gender identity, sex-typed toy preference, and family characteristics. *Child Development, 55,* 1493–1509.

Yee, M., & Brown, R. (1994). The development of gender differentiation in young children. *British Journal of Social Psychology, 33,* 183–196.

5.10

Does Your Infant Say the Words "Girl" and "Boy"?

How Gender Labels Matter in Early Gender Development

KRISTINA M. ZOSULS, DIANE N. RUBLE, CATHERINE TAMIS-LEMONDA, AND CAROL LYNN MARTIN

When did you first realize that you were a girl or a boy? This simple question turns out not to be so simple to answer. It is also a more important question to understanding many aspects of children's early behaviors than one might assume. When children first label themselves as "girl" or "boy," this milestone typically represents children's first identification with a social group and plays an important role in how children think and feel about themselves, how they behave, and how they interact with and perceive others. In this chapter, we discuss surprising findings from our research on children's emergent identification with a gender category.

Children begin the process of learning gender categories and identifying with the categories "boy" or "girl" earlier than many assume. Even more significantly, this early self-categorization has consequences for children's behavior. The findings we describe challenge both popular and academic conceptions of early gender-stereotyped behaviors being exclusively driven by "innate" or biological forces or parent socialization. Our research has additionally discovered that children's initial awareness of gender categories is influenced by the gender attitudes that characterize the cultures and subcultures children inhabit. Thus, the cultural context can affect the timing of children's emergent knowledge about gender categories in unforeseen ways.

GENDER AS A SOCIAL CATEGORY

Although gender categories and gender identity are linked to biological processes, they are also *social* categories, associated with socially constructed, shared, and understood norms for behavior. As such, being a girl or a boy involves belonging to a social category and acquiring knowledge of the traits and behaviors associated with that category. Knowing that one

is a girl or a boy also entails developing a range of feelings and thoughts associated with having that identity. This knowledge and the feelings related to belonging to a gender category hold consequences for the behaviors and interests of girls and boys throughout childhood and into adulthood. In fact, the initial emergence of this knowledge, in the form of a *basic gender identity* (i.e., the sense of oneself as a girl or a boy), might be seen as a developmental milestone that changes the way that children orient themselves toward their social world and shapes the way that they behave.

THEORETICAL BACKGROUND

According to the *self-socialization perspective*, built on Kohlberg's (1966) cognitive developmental theory and encompassed in a number of theories that emphasize active construction in relation to social category identification—*gender schema theories* (e.g., Bem, 1981; Martin & Halverson, 1981), *cognitive-developmental theories* (Kohlberg, 1966; Ruble, 1994), intrapsychic theories of self-socialization (Tobin et al., 2010), and *social categorization theories* (Bigler, Jones, & Lobliner, 1997; Tajfel & Turner, 1986; see Liben & Bigler, 2002, and Ruble, Martin, & Berenbaum, 2006, for reviews of these different theoretical perspectives)—children's emergent knowledge about and identification with a gender group is associated with changes in their interest in and orientation toward gender.

Children construct gender identities based on their social experiences and observations and develop behaviors consistent with their understandings of what it means to be a boy or a girl. In other words, once a girl becomes aware that she is a girl, she will show greater interest in girls and become more motivated to look like a girl (e.g., wear pink frilly dresses) and do things that girls do (e.g., play with dolls). Given that children exhibit some gender-stereotyped interests early in development, when they are barely talking, some theorists argue that the role of gender cognitions in the development of gender-stereotyped attributes has been overstated (Bandura & Bussey, 2004), whereas others continue to maintain that cognitions play an important role in gender development (Martin, Ruble, & Szkrybalo, 2002, 2004). To address this debate, in our research we have asked: When do children learn about gender categories and when do they first develop a gender identity? Do gender-stereotyped interests and behaviors parallel the development of this knowledge?

THE SIGNIFICANCE OF GENDER LABELS

Children receive information about gender from many different sources and in many different ways. For instance, the colors blue and pink are visually salient markers of gender for children, indicating that the social world is divided into two categories: male and female. One of the most fundamental ways in which gender distinctions are made apparent is through the use of gender labels. Gender labels such as *boy* and *girl* not only highlight gender as an important category for viewing others but also serve as a basis for self-categorization or identity. *Gender labeling*, or children's ability to understand and correctly use gender labels to refer to themselves and others, signals an advance in children's awareness of gender categories and ability to use gender category information deliberately (e.g., Fagot & Leinbach, 1993). Toddlers' budding vocabularies provide a fascinating window onto the concepts that very young children are learning, and the use of gender labels, such as *girl*, *boy*, *lady*, and *man*, may represent a first indication that children understand that people can be categorized along gender lines.

When young children use words, they are also expressing their conceptual knowledge (Bloom, 1993). In fact, word learning and conceptual development are closely interconnected; children begin to use words for the categories they learn and, in turn, the use of those words supports further acquisition of knowledge about those categories (Nelson, 2005; Waxman & Lidz, 2006). Labels for categories also have a powerful effect on how children view social categories and respond to members of different social groups (Gelman, 2009). Thus, when a 2-year-old boy can point to himself and other boys and say "boy," this word is more than a name or just another word in his growing vocabulary. The production of this word

signifies that this child has some understanding that he belongs to a social group called "boys." This child's mental representation of this category is likely to be quite simple (e.g., "Boys have short hair and like to play with cars") and even idiosyncratic (e.g., "Boys like to play Scrabble" because an older brother likes the game), but it nonetheless serves as an initial representation and guide for what it means to be a boy.

THE DEVELOPMENT OF GENDER LABELING

Given this link between labels and category knowledge, we decided to look at children's language development as a way to investigate when children begin to understand gender categories and develop a basic gender identity. We used data from biweekly diaries of the language development of 76 children to investigate the timing of the emergence of gender labels (Zosuls et al., 2009). Specifically, mothers were provided with a packet of language inventories to use for note taking and to refer to during biweekly phone interviews with a researcher, who probed mothers about their children's language comprehension and production. The researchers created rich language diaries documenting the children's language development from 10 months to 21 months. We were particularly interested in coding two aspects of these diaries: flexible production (i.e., spontaneous word use across multiple contexts) of gender labels (i.e., *girl*, *boy*, *lady*, *man*, *woman*, *guy*) and self-labeling (i.e., calling oneself *girl* or *boy*). By 17 months, only a quarter of the children had flexibly produced a gender label, but by 21 months, a majority (68%) of the children had flexibly produced a gender label, and most children were using more than one label. This development of gender labeling in the 6 months or so before children turn 2 years old coincides with a time period during which children exhibit rapid gains in their vocabulary production (i.e., the "vocabulary spurt"; e.g., Bloom, 1973), which is also associated with advances in children's object categorization (e.g., Booth & Waxman, 2002; Nazzi & Gopnik, 2001). Thus, it stands to reason that this might also be a time during which children become aware of one of the most pervasive and significant social categories: gender. We further investigated the developmental timing of children's acquisition of their first and subsequent gender labels. These analyses revealed that children produced their second label 2–3 weeks following production of their first label. Interestingly, even controlling for children's general language development and the fact that there were no significant gender differences in key indicators of general language development, girls achieved their first and second gender labels significantly earlier than boys. This gender difference is consistent with some other studies indicating that girls are more precocious in their gender category knowledge (Poulin-Dubois, Serbin, & Derbyshire, 1998; Serbin, Poulin-Dubois, Colburne, Sen, & Eichstedt, 2001) and other aspects of gender development, such as the preference for same-gender playmates (LaFreniere, Strayer, & Gauthier, 1984). The reasons for this precocity are not clear, but they deserve further investigation.

We were also interested in children's self-labeling specifically, and we coded the diaries for instances in which parents explicitly stated that children used gender labels to refer to or describe themselves in simple sentences (i.e., phrases containing more than one word). Only about a fifth (17%) of the children had self-labeled by the time that they were 21 months. This measure was very conservative and likely underestimated considerably the number of children who could self-label, as parents were not specifically probed for their children's self-labeling and this code required that children put words together (e.g., "me girl"). Nonetheless, this analysis revealed that before the age of 2, children may begin to acquire a gender identity.

THE CONSEQUENCES OF GENDER LABELING FOR GENDER-STEREOTYPED BEHAVIORS

From a theoretical perspective, our research has shown that children's categorization of self and others is consequential in terms of the development of gender-typed behaviors. In the same study described earlier (Zosuls et al., 2009), we also coded for the amount of time children spent playing (alone) with a set of male and female gender-stereotyped and neutral toys at 17 and 21 months. At both ages, boys and girls were more similar than different in their toy preferences. For example, girls and boys both spent the most time playing with a kitchen/tea set, and the doll was the second most played with toy by both genders. Thus, gender differences at this young age were not very apparent. Nonetheless, there were gender differences in play with the two most highly stereotyped toys: a doll and a truck. Specifically, boys played more than girls with the truck at both 17 and 21 months, and girls played more with the doll than boys at 21 months. Since we were particularly interested in studying whether gender

category knowledge motivates children to change their behaviors to be more consistent with stereotypes for their gender, we tested whether gender labeling was associated with *increases* in gender-typed play from 17 to 21 months. Children who knew more gender labels, children who knew both the labels boy and girl, and children who had self-labeled showed significantly greater increases in gender-typed play over the course of the 4 months. In sum, our results indicated that gender category knowledge is associated with growth in children's stereotyped play behaviors at an age in development when children had previously been thought to not yet understand gender categories.

GENDER DEVELOPMENT IN CHILDREN FROM ETHNICALLY DIVERSE BACKGROUNDS

In a subsequent research study, we investigated gender labeling and gender-stereotyped play among 195 24-month-old children from three ethnic groups in New York City: African Americans, Mexican immigrants, and Dominican immigrants (Zosuls, 2009). We assessed children's knowledge of child gender labels (i.e., knowing *boy* and *girl*) and self-labeling through maternal reports and assessed children's gender-typed play with a set of gender-stereotyped and neutral toys. Assessment of play was based on a more fine-grained analysis than used previously, in which we coded not only *what* toys children chose for play but also *how* they engaged with those toys (i.e., types of play). Gender differences in types of play fell into the stereotypically feminine category of "social" play (cuddling the doll, having the doll talk on the phone) and a stereotypically masculine "motion" category reflecting an interest in things that move (pushing the truck, opening and closing the doll's eyes). Moreover, consistent with the previous findings, children who knew child gender labels and who self-labeled engaged in significantly greater levels of gender-typed play, although this relation was only significant among girls. A possible reason that this relation was not found among boys is that fewer boys knew gender labels, a finding that is consistent with our previous results indicating greater precocity in gender labeling among girls. Three main messages are supported by these findings. First, children's gender-typed behaviors extend to the *types of play* children exhibit with toys, not just the toys they select for play. Second, the development of these forms of play, at least in part, may be the result of gender category knowledge. Finally, the developmental process, in which children's acquisition of gender knowledge appears related to children's gender-typed behaviors, seems to be generalizable across ethnic groups, although the age at which labels are acquired may be influenced by other factors.

CONTEXTUAL INFLUENCES ON THE EMERGENCE OF GENDER LABELING

Does the initial construction of gender identity occur earlier in sociocultural contexts in which gender is more salient or traditional? Although our research suggests that gender labeling may develop before 24 months and is connected gender-typed play, sociocultural influences on these aspects of gender development remain unexplored.

In the same study described earlier using the ethnically diverse sample, we additionally assessed two forms of mothers' gender-related attitudes: gender role attitudes (i.e., concerning marital roles and child rearing) and attitudes about children's counterstereotypic behaviors (i.e., conforming to norms about girls' and boys' behaviors). One limitation to the small body of research on the role of parents' gender attitudes on children's gender development is that studies have typically assessed parents' gender-role attitudes but have not investigated attitudes that more directly assess how they respond to their children's everyday behaviors. Thus, we were interested in understanding how these two forms of attitudes appear in mothers of different backgrounds and, most centrally, how these attitudes are related to children's gender development.

Patterns of mothers' gender role attitudes were consistent with some of the literature and stereotypes of African Americans and Latinos; African Americans held the least traditional gender role attitudes, and the most recent Latino immigrant group, Mexicans, held the most traditional attitudes. In contrast, this pattern was essentially reversed among mothers of boys in the case of attitudes about children's counterstereotypic behaviors. Compared to Latino mothers, African American mothers expressed the least degree of tolerance for counterstereotypic behaviors among their sons.

Our principal goal was to investigate the links between mothers' gender-related attitudes and the emergence of children's gender labeling. We felt that gender role attitudes, as those assessed in previous studies (e.g., Fagot & Leinbach, 1989; Weinraub et al., 1984), might be more likely to reflect a range of parent behaviors that make gender distinctions more salient (e.g., household division of labor) and thus support the acquisition of gender category knowledge (i.e., gender labeling), while parents' attitudes about children's counterstereotypic behaviors should have more direct implications for the encouragement of gender-typed behaviors. Indeed, mothers' gender role attitudes were significantly related to children's knowledge of child gender labels. That is, mothers with more traditional gender role attitudes had children who had greater gender category knowledge. On the other hand, no associations were found between mothers' attitudes about counterstereotypic behaviors and children's gender labeling. It will be interesting in future research to examine directly the underlying processes that may link different kinds of parental gender attitudes to different aspects and phases of gender development.

CONCLUSIONS

The studies described in this chapter underscore the idea that early in development—even before the age of 2—children develop an awareness of the importance and relevance of their membership in social groups. The novel methodological approaches used in our research, namely the use of children's language development and detailed observations of children's play, provide a window onto the early emergence and processes involved in children's developing awareness of gender categories and identification with a gender group. Furthermore, the extension of our research to different ethnic groups highlights the ways in which the social context influences the timing and nature of early social identities. Showing that children's initial knowledge about or identification with gender can occur at different ages, depending on sociocultural context, and can set in motion a sequence of other changes provides powerful support for self-socialization perspectives.

REFERENCES

Bandura, A., & Bussey, K. (2004). On broadening the cognitive, motivational, and sociocultural scope of theorizing about gender development and functioning: Comment on Martin, Ruble, and Szkrybalo (2002). *Psychological Bulletin, 130(5)*, 691–701.

Bem, S. L. (1981). Gender schema theory: A cognitive account of sex typing. *Psychological Review, 88*, 354–364.

Bigler, R. S., Jones, L. C., & Lobliner, D. B. (1997). Social categorization and the formation of intergroup attitudes in children. *Child Development, 68*, 530–543.

Bloom, L. (1973). *One word at a time: The use of single word utterances before syntax.* The Hague, The Netherlands: Mouton.

Bloom, L. (1993). *The transition from infancy to language: Acquiring the power of expression.* Cambridge, England: Cambridge University Press.

Booth, A. E., & Waxman, S. (2002). Object names and object functions serve as cues to categories for infants. *Developmental Psychology, 38*, 948–957.

Fagot, B., & Leinbach, M. D. (1989). The young child's gender schema: Environmental input, internal organisation. *Child Development, 60*, 663–672.

Fagot, B., & Leinbach, M. D. (1993). Gender-role development in young children: From discrimination to labeling. *Developmental Review, 13*, 205–224.

Gelman, S. A. (2009). Learning from others: Children's construction of concepts. *Annual Review of Psychology, 60*, 115–140.

Kohlberg, L. (1966). A cognitive-developmental analysis of children's sex-role concepts and attitudes. In E. E. Maccoby (Ed.), *The development of sex differences* (pp. 82–173). Stanford, CA: Stanford University Press.

LaFreniere, P., Strayer, F. F., & Gauthier, R. (1984). The emergence of same-sex affiliative preferences among preschool peers: A developmental/ ecological perspective. *Child Development, 55*, 1958–1965.

Liben, S. L., & Bigler, R. S. (2002). The developmental course of gender differentiation: Conceptualizing, measuring and evaluating constructs and pathways. *Monographs of the Society for Research in Child Development, 67*(2, Serial No. 269), 1–147.

Martin, C. L., & Halverson, C. (1981). A schematic processing model of sex typing and stereotyping in children. *Child Development, 52*, 1119–1134.

Martin, C. L., Ruble, D. N., & Szkrybalo, J. (2002). Cognitive theories of early gender development. *Psychological Bulletin, 128*, 903–933.

Martin, C. L., Ruble, D. N., & Szkrybalo, J. (2004). Recognizing the centrality of gender identity and stereotype knowledge in gender development and moving toward theoretical integration: Reply to Bandura and Bussey (2004). *Psychological Bulletin, 130*, 702–710.

Nazzi, T., & Gopnik, A. (2001). Linguistic and cognitive abilities in infancy: When does language become a tool for categorization? *Cognition, 80*, B11–B20.

Nelson, K. (2005). Cognitive functions of language in early childhood. In B. D. Homer & C. S. Tamis-LeMonda (Eds.), *The development of social cognition* (pp.7–28). Mahwah, NJ: Erlbaum.

Poulin-Dubois, D., Serbin, L. A., & Derbyshire, A. (1998). Toddlers' intermodal and verbal knowledge about gender. *Merrill-Palmer Quarterly, 44*, 338–354.

Ruble, D. N. (1994). A phase model of transitions: Cognitive and motivational consequences. In M. Zanna (Ed.), *Advances in experimental social psychology, 26*, 163–214.

Ruble, D. N., Martin, C. L., & Berenbaum, S. A. (2006). Gender development. In N. Eisenberg, W. Damon, & R. M. Lerner (Eds.), *Handbook of child psychology: Vol. 3. Social, emotional, and personality development* (6th ed., pp. 858–932). Hoboken, NJ: Wiley.

Serbin, L. A., Poulin-Dubois, D., Colburne, K. A., Sen, M. G., & Eichstedt, J. A. (2001). Gender stereotyping in infancy: Visual preferences for and knowledge of gender-stereotyped toys in the second year. *International Journal of Behavioral Development, 25*(1), 7–15.

Tajfel, H., & Turner, J. C. (1986). The social identity theory of intergroup behavior. In S. Worchel & W. G. Austin (Eds.), *Psychology of intergroup relations* (2nd ed., pp. 7–24). Chicago, IL: Nelson-Hall.

Tobin, D. D., Menon, M., Menon, M., Spatta, B. C., Hodges, E. V., & Perry, D. G. (2010). The intrapsychics of gender: A model of self-socialization. *Psychological Review, 117*, 601–622.

Waxman, S. R., & Lidz, J. (2006). Early word learning. In D. Kuhn & R. Siegler (Eds.), *Handbook of child psychology: Cognition, perception and language* (6th ed., pp. 299–336). New York: Wiley.

Weinraub, M., Clemens, L. P., Sockloff, A., Etheridge, R., Gracely, E., & Myers, B. (1984). The development of sex role stereotypes in the third year: Relationships to gender labeling, gender identity, sex-typed toy preferences, and family characteristics. *Child Development, 55*, 1493–1503.

Zosuls, K. M. (2009). *Gender development in African American, Dominican, and Mexican immigrant toddlers: Self socialization in three cultural contexts.* Unpublished Ph.D. dissertation, New York University, New York, NY.

Zosuls, K. M., Ruble, D. N., Tamis-LeMonda, C. S., Shrout, P. E., Bornstein, M. H., & Greulich, F. K. (2009). The acquisition of gender labels in infancy: Implications for sex-typed play. *Developmental Psychology, 45*, 688–701.

5.11

Bringing the Cognitive and the Social Together

How Gender Detectives and Gender Enforcers Shape Children's Gender Development

CINDY FAITH MILLER,* CAROL LYNN MARTIN,*
RICHARD A. FABES, AND LAURA D. HANISH

At age 6, Mia enjoys wearing dresses and has long hair she often wears in a ponytail. Mia's closest friends are two girls from her class, and they enjoy playing dress-up and house and take gymnastics together after school. Mia's father is a coach and he has been teaching her to play soccer. When Mia grows up, she wants to be a teacher because she wants to help people.

Like many children, Mia appears to be gender typical in most of her interests and behaviors. Why has Mia adopted interests that are consistent with cultural gender stereotypes? How did Mia develop beliefs that girls like to play dress up or that girls like to play with girls? Gender colors our lives in obvious ways (e.g., Mia's liking of girls) but also in more subtle ways. For instance, imagine that a new videogame comes on the market. Will Mia try it out? If she likes the game, will she recommend it to her friends? The answers to these questions will be influenced by Mia's gender-related social cognitions. If Mia's same-sex friends tell her they like the game, she may assume that it would appeal to other girls, like her, and will likely try it out. If she likes the game, she probably will expect that others like her—that is, girls—will like the game and will recommend it to them, but she probably will not recommend it to boys. As illustrated, Mia's decisions will be guided by the influence of her peers, her gender-stereotyped beliefs, and her own experiences playing the game.

In this chapter, we introduce a conceptual model that considers the interrelations between these cognitive, behavioral, and social influences. First, we consider the cognitive side of gender development—how children act as *gender detectives,* who form expectancies about the gender-relatedness of objects, activities, and people based on social influences and individual preferences and behaviors. But expectancies are only part of the picture; therefore, we also discuss how children's own behaviors and preferences for activities play a role in how they think and interact with others. Next, we turn to the social side of gender development and consider how one type of social agent—peers—may act as *gender enforcers* to pressure children into thinking and behaving in gender-appropriate ways. Finally, we present the challenges inherent in integrating behavioral, social, and cognitive components of gender development.

THE MANY SIDES OF GENDER DEVELOPMENT

Gender development is multidimensional. Questions about gender range from "When do children recognize that they are a girl or a boy?" to "How are girls and boys different?" Although answers to these questions have contributed to our understanding of gender development, they do not tell the whole story. To fully understand gender development, we need to understand how and whether the different aspects or components associated with gender (e.g., cognitions, behavior, social interactions) influence each other (Martin & Ruble, 2010; Martin, Ruble,

---

*The first two authors contributed equally to this paper.

& Szkrybalo, 2002). Our goal is to tell this part of the story by describing the links among gendered components, and we do this by introducing a cognitive-behavioral-social model of gender development.

Our model focuses attention on three broad interrelated components: gender cognitions (e.g., basic gender identity, stereotypes, attitudes); individual preferences and behaviors (e.g., interests, toy play); and the social environment (e.g., social observations of and interactions with peers) (see Fig. 5.11.1). A key assumption is that each component influences and is influenced by the other two components. Next we present supporting research and some of the unanswered questions that remain for each of these interrelated components.

CHILDREN AS GENDER DETECTIVES

On her first day of school, Mia sits at the lunch table eating a peanut butter and jelly sandwich. She notices that a few boys are eating peanut butter and jelly, but not one girl is. When her father picks her up from school, Mia runs up to him and exclaims, "Peanut butter and jelly is for boys! I want a turkey sandwich tomorrow!"

Everywhere Mia looks she sees cues about gender: clothes and toys are color-coded, girls and boys dress differently, and people tell her about gender stereotypes. And children are interested in these cues, so much so that they are like gender detectives—using gender-magnifying glasses to search for cues in the environment that will help them discern the categories of gender and tell them the appropriate behaviors connected with each gender. As gender detectives, children search for cues to help them form beliefs about what they should

do and how they may behave, so these beliefs play a pivotal role in gender development (Kohlberg, 1966; Martin, 2000, Martin & Halverson, 1981). Children's search of the social world allows them to identify obvious cues, such as girls having long hair or boys liking cars. But their detective work does not end there—the lens that children use to understand gender also picks up on cues in which the gender associations are quite weak (or nonexistent), and then children draw strong inferences based on these cues. For instance, over the course of only one day, Mia notices that more boys than girls at her school eat peanut butter and jelly and, even with such limited evidence, she draws the inference that peanut butter and jelly is "for boys" (Martin & Ruble, 2004).

When searching for gender cues, children give Sherlock Holmes a run for his money. They are astute, motivated observers. This is especially true when situations or people make gender categories salient for children, such as when parents say, "Good boy!" or when teachers line up students by gender. When this occurs, children's detective work kicks into high gear as they actively scan the environment in search for cues about how each gender behaves, dresses, and acts. Not surprisingly, children then have at their fingertips information they can use to guide their own behavior, as Mia showed when she determined that peanut butter and jelly is a food for boys, so she no longer wants that as her lunch. Why does it matter to Mia if she happens to be sent to school with a peanut butter and jelly sandwich? It is because, like all children, she wants to define herself by and be a good member of her social group, which motivates her to match her behavior with what she believes her gender is like (see Martin et al., 2002 for review). In this way, children become self-socializers of gender who take an active role in constructing gender knowledge (peanut butter and jelly is for boys) and

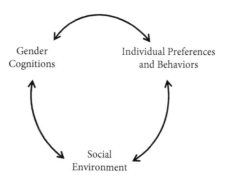

FIGURE 5.11.1: Cognitive-behavioral-social model of gender development.

use that knowledge to inform their own behavior (e.g., I am not going to eat peanut butter and jelly anymore).

Being a Gender Detective Shapes Behavior

To assess the power of gender cues on children's behavior, one method we have used in our research involves presenting novel objects or games to children and experimentally manipulating gender associations by telling them that the object is "for girls" or "for boys" (for reviews, see Martin & Dinella, 2002; Miller, Trautner, & Ruble, 2006). Studies using this method show that children prefer, explore, and remember details about toys labeled as being for their own gender group more than they do for toys labeled for the other gender group. In a study with children 4 to 6 years of age, one experimenter applied gender labels to novel toys, and a second experimenter assessed children's preferences and memory for the labels to control for demand characteristics (Martin, Eisenbud, & Rose, 1995, Study 3). Most children remembered the labels and showed a preference for same-gender toys over other-gender toys. These types of studies illustrate that children use the gender labels to form gender stereotypes, and then these stereotypes shape their behavior.

Different kinds of stereotypes may have different effects. To test this idea, we exposed kindergarten and fifth-grade children to either category stereotypes (e.g., "This is really a game for girls") or ability stereotypes (e.g., "Girls do a lot better than boys on this test") and assessed whether children performed better on the same-gender labeled task compared to the other-gender labeled task (Miller & Ruble, unpublished data). We found developmental differences: Only kindergarten girls and boys were affected by the category labels, and only kindergarten girls and fifth-grade boys were affected by the ability labels. Children's reactions to the different types of labels also depended on whether they accepted the labels, had flexible attitudes, and whether gender was salient to them. Clearly the wording of stereotypes makes a difference in whether it impacts younger or older girls and boys, showing that all stereotypes are not equal in their influence.

Being a Gender Detective Shapes Children's Social Worlds

Much attention has been given to how events in the world influence the way we think, but here we focus on the less intuitive influence of how the way we think—in this case, about gender—can shape the environment. Before Mia meets other girls, she assumes she might like them because she holds a "gender theory" that girls tend to be alike; that is, she holds an essentialist view of gender (Gelman & Taylor, 2000; Martin, 2000; Taylor, 1996). Mia also knows the societal convention that "girls play with girls" and "boys play with boys," which may guide her to play with girls over boys when given the choice. Mia's reasoning shows that children's beliefs about gender play an important role in influencing their decisions about who might be fun to interact with, and these cognitions act to initiate and maintain their social interactions. Several studies from our lab demonstrate this power of gender cognitions. When children are given short descriptions about unfamiliar girls and boys, they make decisions about how much they think they would like the children and make guesses about the children's preferences based only on knowing their gender (Martin, 1989). Furthermore, children's beliefs about what other people think about gender also influence their behavior. When children think that other people approve of same-gender peer play more than other-gender play, they spend more time interacting with same-gender peers (Martin, Fabes, Evans, & Wyman, 1999). It is important to note, however, that not all children form and use gender cognitions in the same way. We know little about why and how children vary in their gender beliefs, or why some children act on these beliefs more strongly than others. Answering these questions may better arm parents and educators with information about how to support and assist children to handle gender issues and to encourage children to develop a wide range of experiences that are not limited by gender stereotypes.

"WHAT I LIKE, OTHER GIRLS WILL LIKE"

Mia's parents were excited when Mia told them that she wanted to join the soccer team that her father was coaching. She seemed to pick up on the game quickly and began talking about her soccer experiences all the time. She also started spending more time with girls from her soccer team, even when they were not playing soccer. Mia's parents were thrilled that she was making new friends but were surprised when Mia began talking about how soccer is a "girls' sport" and that their 6-year-old neighbor, Ryan, couldn't play the game with her.

How do children's personal preferences, like Mia's interest in soccer, influence their gender development? Why would Mia assume that other girls, but not boys, will also like this activity? Why would she spend more time with girls even when she wasn't playing soccer? Answers to these questions involve assessing the impact of children's personal preferences, and, recently, theoretical models have given attention to this topic (see Liben & Bigler, 2002; Tobin et al., 2010).

"If I Like It, It Must Be a Girl Thing": How Personal Preferences Influence the Development of Stereotypes

Mia is enthusiastic about soccer and firmly believes that it's a sport "for girls." Is this because she is making the assumption that she is representative of other girls and, therefore, thinks that they will like it because she does? To test this idea requires examining whether changes occur in gender cognitions as a result of children's own preferences, and novel objects are ideal for testing this idea experimentally. We showed young children novel non-gender-typed toys and asked them how much they and other children would like the toys. They could easily answer that all other children would like the toys, but they did not. Instead, they showed gender-based reasoning: They thought that toys they liked would be liked by other children of their own gender but not necessarily by children of the other gender, again suggesting that children hold gender essentialist beliefs (Martin et al., 1995).

From such results we conclude that children use their own preferences to help them form at least preliminary stereotypes about girls' and boys' preferences. Mia might think, "If I like soccer, then it's a girl thing, and other girls probably like it too." Personal preferences also may help expand or break down stereotypes. For instance, when children understand that they have interests that do not match traditional stereotypes, this understanding may allow them to recognize variability in stereotypes. Girls who like male-typical activities tend to think that these activities are appropriate for both genders. This allows them to link their favorite activities with their beliefs and to maintain consistency between their preferences and their stereotypes (Martin & Dinella, 2012). For instance, if Mia played on an ice hockey team, she might think that ice hockey is appropriate

for boys *and for girls*, whereas many girls would stereotype this as an activity for boys. From these studies we can draw the interesting conclusion that stereotypes guide preferences (see earlier), but preferences also contribute to the formation of stereotypes (Liben & Bigler, 2002).

Birds of a Feather Flock Together: How Children's Personal Preferences Shape the Social World

It may seem obvious that, if Mia likes soccer and gymnastics, she will be brought into contact with girls since she would have other girls on her soccer and gymnastics teams. But it is less obvious whether simply having contact with other children in a sport, for instance, would lead to developing friendships. Separating what children do from whom they do it with is challenging. Does Mia begin to engage in gymnastics because she wants to interact with girls, or does interacting with girls lead her to choose to become interested in gymnastics? Based on recent research evidence, we now know that shared interests bring children together over and above children's tendency to prefer playmates of the same gender. That is, when children share similar levels of interest in gender-typed activities, they tend to form friendships (Martin et al., in press).

The few studies that have been done on these topics suggest that preferences have an impact on what children believe and with whom they interact. We do not yet understand how often children form beliefs based on their own experiences or whether these beliefs persist in the face of evidence that contradicts those beliefs.

PEERS AS GENDER ENFORCERS AND GENDER RESISTORS: INFLUENCES OF THE SOCIAL ENVIRONMENT

One day on the playground, Mia started playing with a group of children who were building a fort. One boy yelled out, "No girls allowed in our fort!" Mia stomped off and walked over to her friend, Samantha, who told her not to worry because "Only boys like to play in forts." She then invited Mia to play jump rope with her and three other girls. Mia noticed that she was the only one not wearing nail polish. When she got home from school, she asked her mother whether they could paint their nails together and whether she could have a new jump rope for her birthday.

Mia's closest friends are girls. Like Mia, children tend to make friends with children who are the same gender as themselves, and they spend most of their social time with them. Peers are powerful agents of gender socialization. Because they spend so much time in same-gender groups, girls and boys can be thought of as growing up in separate cultures in which they are exposed to the social norms, interaction styles, skills, and preferences of their own gender and receive much less exposure to the other gender.

Peers Shape Children's Beliefs

"You can't play dress-up with us—you're a boy" or the message that Mia heard of "no girls are allowed" are admonitions frequently heard on preschool playgrounds. In several of our studies our coders reported that they saw children acting as *gender enforcers*. We were curious about this and since that time we have studied these children and their influence. Gender enforcers ensure that the activities going on around them are gender appropriate for all children involved—they know the gender stereotypes and they are going to make sure that everybody abides by them. For instance, if Mia decided that she wanted to play football with the boys at recess, she might be met with resistance from both same-sex enforcers ("Why would you want to play a boys' sport?") and other-sex enforcers ("Football is only for boys, Mia!"). These interactions would then strengthen Mia's belief that football is something that is clearly not for girls.

Although informal observations illustrate the powerful influence of peers on children's gendered beliefs, many questions remain unanswered. We do not yet know whether gender enforcers' admonitions alert children to new stereotypes or strengthen preexisting stereotypes. But we suspect that a powerful force in the development of stereotypes is when gender detectives—who are searching for cues about gender—come into contact with gender enforcers, who are more than happy to provide all types of gender information. This combination likely promotes rapid learning of new stereotypes and strengthening of existing stereotypes. Simply spending time with same-sex peers at school may provide both direct teaching about and informal training in stereotyping.

Peers Shape Children's Behavior

Mia spends much of her time playing with her girlfriends, and she is influenced by her exposure to them. The time children spend with same-gender peers provides many opportunities for socialization into gender roles: Young children who spend more time with same-gender peers show increasing participation in gender-typed activities and social behaviors (e.g., boys become more aggressive; girls spend more time close to teachers). Evidence suggests that exposure to same-gender peers acts to exaggerate gender differences, and this form of socialization happens within as little as a few months' time (Martin & Fabes, 2001). Experimental evidence using novel interests also confirms that children's interests are influenced by unfamiliar same-gender peers: Mia would assume that she would prefer playing "spoodle" if suggested by a girl, rather than "blicket" if suggested by a boy (Shutts, Banaji, & Spelke, 2010).

In addition to learning about the interests and activities of one's own sex, children also learn what to avoid. For instance, some parents report that their sons who once enjoyed playing with dolls began to lose interest in them after they entered preschool. Did this happen because they were teased for their interest in dolls by their peers at school? Gender enforcers likely play a role in encouraging children to conform to stereotypes. Research in our lab has confirmed the influence of gender enforcers on one type of stereotypic behavior: children's play partner choices. Children with more exposure to gender enforcers (children identified as saying "you shouldn't play because you're a girl/boy") spend more time interacting with same-gender peers and less with other-gender peers (McGuire, Martin, Fabes, & Hanish, 2007).

Although we know that social interactions influence children's cognitions and behavior to support traditional gender roles, we have only begun to address the issue of how social interactions may work to undermine gender stereotypes and behavior. For instance, do children challenge gender stereotypes? "Fairness enforcers" or "gender resistors" may monitor other children's interactions and remind them if they are not being fair by excluding a child from play, or they may actively argue against any use of stereotypes. Recent research (Lamb, Bigler, Liben, & Green, 2009) suggests that elementary-age children can be trained to challenge instances of stereotyping and discrimination. Does exposure to these children help to undermine gender stereotypes and discrimination among peers? We do not know the answer to this question, and future research should explore the possibility that peers can act to both perpetuate and confirm stereotypes but also to resist and challenge stereotypes.

GENDER COGNITIONS, SOCIAL ENVIRONMENT, AND BEHAVIORS AS A TRANSACTIONAL MODEL

In our discussion so far, we described how Mia's gender development is influenced by the relationships between her gender cognitions (e.g., peanut butter and jelly is for boys), individual behavioral preferences (e.g., soccer), and social environment (e.g., interactions with girls). The message that we hope to convey is that gender development involves multiple components, working together in both simple and complex ways, and that these components work together over time to produce changes in behavior, thinking, and the social environment. The interrelatedness of the components becomes even more evident as we consider how these pathways interact with one another over the course of early gender development. Here we consider two examples; one concerning how gender activity preferences, beliefs, and peer relationships influence one another over the course of a year, and the other is how gender cognitions, preferences, and the social environment are interwoven in early development.

First let's consider changes occurring over the course of a year as young children in school get to know one another. What are the roles and interconnections between cognitions, the social environment, and behavior? For instance, does Mia primarily interact with girls because she consistently chooses girl playmates who then expose her to feminine-typed activities, or is it because she selects activities, such as gymnastics, that then bring her into contact with same-gender peers? Using intensive observations over the course of a year and new social network methods, we are able to, for the first time, explore the complex influences on gender development occurring within preschool classrooms (Martin et al., in press). We found evidence for both pathways. The most important contributor to gender segregation in children's play was simply that children are drawn to same-gender peers. Children may have this preference because they think same-gender peers might be more similar to themselves or more fun. Mia assuming she would like a new girl in class or approaching a girl to play before she knows her would be examples of this pathway in action. The other pathway involves being drawn into play with others because of shared interests. We found that children with shared interests in gender-typical activities began to spend more time together. And, not surprisingly, children were socialized by their peers in those encounters. Just like Mia started wearing nail polish after spending time with a group of same-sex peers, children in our study showed increasing similarity with their friends in interest in gender-typical activities as the year progressed. Importantly, we showed that peers exerted influence over children even after we took into account children's tendency to select similar peers as friends. Children's social networks also played a role in helping children develop new friendships through a process called *transitivity*: Mia likes Samantha, and this brings Samantha into contact with Mia's friend Ashley, thereby increasing Samantha's exposure to same-gender peers. As a consequence of these processes, even small preferences for selecting peers on the basis of their being the same gender or on the basis of similar interests in gender-typed activities can accumulate to produce high levels of gender segregation. Since gender segregation is a setting for increased contact and exposure to same-gender interaction styles, interests, and so on, as Mia becomes more skilled in same-gender interaction styles, she likely continues to seek out same-gender peers, and then is further socialized by time spent with those peers.

Next we consider how Mia's gender-typed beliefs develop and how these beliefs might interact with her behavior and the social environment throughout her childhood. By 2 to 3 years of age, Mia began to believe that things like dolls are "for girls" and things like trucks are "for boys." Around the same time, Mia began to show preferences for gender-typed toys (e.g., dolls) and for playing with same-gender peers. Over early and middle childhood, her environment continued to be filled with gender-stereotyped messages—from peers, parents, teachers, cartoons, television commercials, and toy stores. Consequently, Mia's preferences strengthened and her beliefs became broader and covered more domains (e.g., occupations). For Mia, like most children, a mutually interacting system develops that promotes gender typing. Based on both strong and weak (or nonexistent) cues, Mia develops beliefs about the activities and interests of boys and girls (e.g., girls like playing house and boys like playing sports), and she uses these to help her decide who she might want to interact with, even before she has a chance to assess the accuracies/inaccuracies of applying these beliefs to specific peers. Mia may decide, for instance, to approach an unfamiliar girl instead of a boy on the playground because she assumes that the girl, but not the boy, will like playing house, like she does. Is Mia accurate in her assumption? She might never know because she did not ask the boy to play with her. Instead, she approached the girl and only learned that she and her new friend like to do some of the same types of things. As children sort themselves into same-gender groups, they become increasingly socialized into gender-typed behaviors by their same-gender peers and develop the interaction styles, norms, and interests that make them increasingly comfortable with same-gender peers and increasingly uncomfortable and unfamiliar with other-gender peers. Socialization in the separate cultures also likely acts to confirm the beliefs they hold about the genders differing in many ways. For instance, when Mia scans the playground and observes boys playing baseball and football together and girls playing jump rope and house together, she feels satisfied that her original belief that girls and boys like to do different things is correct. By middle childhood, similar to many but not all children, Mia has a fully functioning and highly developed gender belief system that may be resistant to information that would challenge or disconfirm her beliefs. Although there are similarities in processes underlying gender development, not all children develop such gender-differentiated belief systems. Children vary in their beliefs depending on a variety of factors including their developmental stage, social and family contexts, and life experiences (Fabes, Martin, & Hanish, 2004, Martin & Halverson, 1981; Taylor, Rhodes, & Gelman, 2009). Much more attention needs to be given to why differing patterns arise within and between the genders.

In this chapter, we illustrated how cognitive, social, and behavioral forces act to shape and constrain the development of gender. We illustrated how children both learn and resist gender stereotypes and how small initial differences have the potential to grow and be magnified into larger differences. In some people's minds, these differences are so extreme that males and females are portrayed as coming from different planets or of being different species. In modern society, this view is not accurate or useful. Mia likely benefits from interacting with same-sex peers and developing feminine skills and attributes, but it is also important for Mia to be exposed to a wider range of peer influences and opportunities. The ultimate goal of our research is to uncover answers that will help us strive for a society where men and women and boys and girls live, work, and play together as one group instead of two.

ACKNOWLEDGMENTS

Support for the authors was provided in part by grants from the National Institute of Child Health and Human Development (1 R01 HD45816-01A1), the Cowden Endowment, and the T. Denny Sanford Foundation. We are grateful to Diane Ruble for comments on an earlier draft.

REFERENCES

Fabes, R. A., Martin, C. L., & Hanish, L. D. (2004). The next 50 years: Considering gender as a context for understanding young children's peer relationships. *Merrill Palmer Quarterly, 50,* 260–273.

Gelman, S. A., & Taylor, M. G. (2000). Gender essentialism in cognitive development. In P. H. Miller & E. Kofsky Scholnick (Eds.), *Toward a feminist developmental psychology* (pp. 169–190). Florence, KY: Taylor & Frances.

Kohlberg, L. A. (1966). A cognitive-developmental analysis of children's sex role concepts and attitudes. In E. E. Maccoby (Ed.), *The development of sex differences* (pp. 82–173). Stanford, CA: Stanford University Press.

Lamb, L. M., Bigler, R. S., Liben, L. S., & Green, V. A. (2009). Teaching children to confront peers' sexist remarks: Implications for theories of gender development and educational practice. *Sex Roles, 61,* 361–382.

Liben, L. S., & Bigler, R. S. (2002). The developmental course of gender differentiation. In W. Overton (Ed.), *Monographs of the Society for Research in Child Development* (Vol. 67 no. 2, pp. vii–147). Boston, MA: Blackwell.

Martin, C. L. (1989). Children's use of gender-related information in making social judgments. *Developmental Psychology, 25,* 80–88.

Martin, C. L. (2000). Cognitive theories of gender development. In T. Eckes & H. M. Trautner (Eds.), *The developmental social psychology of gender* (pp. 91–121). Mahwah, NJ: Erlbaum.

Martin, C. L., & Dinella, L. (2002). Children's gender cognitions, the social environment, and sex differences in the cognitive domain. In A. McGillicuddy-De Lisi & R. De Lisi (Eds.), *Biology, society, and behavior: The development of sex differences in cognition* (pp. 207–239). Westport, CO: Ablex.

Martin, C. L., & Dinella, L. (2012). Congruence between gender stereotypes and activity preference in self-identified tomboys and nontomboys. *Archives of Sexual Behavior, 41,* 599–610.

Martin, C. L., Eisenbud, L., & Rose, H. (1995). Children's gender-based reasoning about toys. *Child Development, 66,* 1453–1471.

Martin, C. L., & Fabes, R. A. (2001). The stability and consequences of young children's same-sex peer interactions. *Developmental Psychology, 37,* 431–446.

Martin, C. L., Fabes, R. A., Evans, S. M., & Wyman, H. (1999). Social cognition on the playground: Children's beliefs about playing with girls versus boys and their relations to sex segregated play. *Journal of Social and Personal Relationships, 16,* 751–771.

Martin, C. L., & Halverson, C. (1981). A schematic processing model of sex typing and stereotyping in children. *Child Development, 52,* 1119–1134.

Martin, C. L., Kornienko, O., Schaefer, D. R., Hanish, L. D., Fabes, R. A., & Goble, P. M. (in press). The role of sex of peers and gender-typed activities in young children's peer affiliative networks: A longitudinal analysis of selection and influence. *Child Development.*

Martin, C. L., & Ruble, D. N. (2004). Children's search for gender cues: Cognitive perspectives on gender development. *Current Directions in Psychological Science, 13,* 67–70.

Martin, C. L., & Ruble, D. N. (2010). Patterns of gender development. *Annual Review of Psychology, 61,* 12.11–12.29.

Martin, C. L., Ruble, D. N., & Szkrybalo, J. (2002). Cognitive theories of early gender development. *Psychological Bulletin, 128,* 903–933.

McGuire, J., Martin, C. L., Fabes, R. A., & Hanish, L. D. (March, 2007). *The role of "gender enforcers" in young children's peer interactions.* Presented at the Society for Research in Child Development, Boston, MA.

Miller, C. F., Trautner, H. M., & Ruble, D. N. (2006). The role of gender stereotypes in children's preferences and behavior. In L. Balter & C. S. Tamis-LeMonda (Eds.), *Child psychology: A handbook of contemporary issues* (2nd ed., pp. 293–323). New York: Psychology Press.

Shutts, K., Banaji, M. R., & Spelke, E. S. (2010). Social categories guide young children's preferences for novel objects. *Developmental Science, 13,* 599–610.

Taylor, M. G. (1996). The development of children's beliefs about social and biological aspects of gender differences. *Child Development, 67,* 1555–1571.

Taylor, M. G., Rhodes, M., & Gelman, S. A. (2009). Boys will be boys; cows will be cows: Children's essentialist reasoning about gender categories and animal species. *Child Development, 80,* 461–481.

Tobin, D. D., Menon, M., Menon, M., Spatta, B. C., Hodges, E. V. E., & Perry, D. G. (2010). The intrapsychics of gender: A model of self-socialization. *Psychological Review, 117,* 601–622.

5.12

The Development of Language as a Social Category

KATHERINE D. KINZLER

Although there are infinite ways in which we might divide the social world, social and developmental psychologists often converge in identifying three primary variables for person perception: gender, race, and age. Here I argue that language provides a critical and potentially primary way in which children evaluate the social world. Before they speak, infants prefer to interact with individuals who share their native language. Older children selectively learn from and prefer native-accented speakers of their native language as friends. Preferences based on accent do not hinge exclusively on preferences for intelligible speech, and early language-based social preferences surpass those based on race. Social reasoning about language as a marker of group membership may have origins in cognitive evolution, and discussion of language as a social category has both theoretical implications for how we conceptualize the nature of early social cognition more generally and also practical implications for law and public policy that protect against accent discrimination.

A classic story told to introductory psychology classes is as follows: A woman moves into a new apartment building. Amidst the chaos of moving, she encounters a new neighbor. Later, she cannot recall what the neighbor looked like, except she remembers that the neighbor was a middle-aged White woman. The lesson, of course, is that psychologists observe that race, gender, and age are prominent for person perception. These variables can be automatically and effortlessly encoded by a perceiver who does not remember other individuating information about the person he or she just saw (e.g., Brewer, 1988). Developmental psychologists, too, find that children attend to gender, race, and age remarkably early in development. Infants' patterns of visual attention reflect

attention to these variables, and children express selective social preferences based on a novel individual's social category membership.

In the current chapter I argue that language provides a critical and potentially primary social category by which we evaluate novel individuals. With a few notable exceptions, language as a social category has been a somewhat neglected area of study by modern social and developmental psychologists (Gluszek & Dovidio, 2010). Here I review research from adults (largely from the fields of socio- and psycholinguistics) providing evidence that the way an individual speaks plays a large role in guiding others' attitudes toward that person. Moreover, though children's remarkable early language abilities are well known, we know less about the development of children's reasoning about language as a social category. I present evidence that beginning in infancy, children evaluate others based on their language and accent, and that early social preferences based on accent surpass those based on race. Finally, I conclude with suggestions for needed future research.

ACCENT ATTITUDES

Adults evaluate others based on their speech. From one perspective, some forms of linguistic evaluation could be seen as veridical. Given how difficult a nonnative accent is to master past childhood, accent could be used as an honest signal of an individual's native origins. Indeed, accent is used as a cue to nationality and regional origin (Labov, 2006). Nonetheless, social meaning is derived from accent in many ways, including those that harness stereotypes about groups of individuals and apply them to a novel individual. Originating with seminal studies conducted by Lambert and colleagues in the 1960s (e.g., Lambert, Hodgson, Gardner, & Fillenbaum, 1960), a field of research investigating "accent attitudes" emerged. Though too broad a literature to adequately review here (for a review, see Giles & Billings, 2004), this research finds that adults make myriad judgments of others based on their language, dialect, or accent. Often studies employ a matched guised technique, whereby a naïve participant will evaluate the same individual speaking in two different languages or accents as having robustly different personalities and physical attributes. Adults sometimes prefer individuals who speak in their native accent or dialect, and sometimes prefer individuals who speak what they consider to be a high-status or "prestige" dialect. Adults who speak what may considered to be a nonstandard accent or dialect themselves can express linguistic insecurity about their own speech.

Recently, a few notable studies have addressed the importance of accent in guiding person perception. Gluszek and Dovidio (2010) underscore the importance of accent in social evaluation, and how speaking with a nonnative accent can be stigmatized. Rakic, Steffens, and Mummendey (2011) find that using a "who said what" paradigm (Taylor, Fiske, Etcoff, & Ruderman, 1978), participants categorize others' ethnic identities via their accent. This categorization based on auditory input is more powerful than categorization based on visual cues to ethnicity. Nonetheless, we know little about the affective and cognitive consequences of categorizing others by their accent, and how language-based social categorization emerges and develops during childhood. The development of language-based social reasoning provides the focus of the remainder of the chapter.

THE DEVELOPMENT OF LANGUAGE-BASED SOCIAL EVALUATION

Young infants demonstrate remarkable linguistic abilities and preferences for familiar speech. Beginning at birth, newborns prefer the sound of their mother's language, which they heard while in the womb (Mehler et al., 1988). In recent research (Kinzler, Dupoux, & Spelke, 2007), colleagues and I observed that infants' earliest preferences for native speech extend to preferences for native *speakers*. In one study, 5- to 6-month-old infants were shown movies of two individuals who both smiled at the infant, and then spoke in either the infants' native language (English) or a foreign language (Spanish). Speakers were bilingual speakers of English and Spanish, so that way we could control across infants any extraneous preferences. During a subsequent test trial, infants looked longer at the person who

previously spoke to them in English rather than in Spanish. In a following study, we presented 10-month-old infants in the United States and France with videos of a speaker of English and a speaker of French, who each spoke and then each held out a toy, silently and in synchrony, for the infant to grasp. Just at the moment at which the two actors' toys disappeared from screen, two "real" toys emerged, giving the illusion that they came from the screen. Infants preferentially chose the toy that was offered by the native speaker, providing evidence that even in the first year of life, prior to speaking themselves, infants selectively choose interactions with native speakers.

Children's favor for native speakers of their native language does not diminish throughout early childhood. Preschool-age children selectively trust the testimony of native-accented speakers when learning the function of novel objects (Kinzler, Corriveau, & Harris, 2011). Children also begin to make inferences about others based on their language—for instance, they report that individuals who speak in their native language are more likely to be of a familiar racial group or live in a familiar dwelling (Hirschfeld & Gelman, 1997).

Though the evidence for children's early preferences for native-accented speech is compelling, one might question whether preferences for native-accented speech are particularly important, or whether they reflect more domain-general preferences for familiar social entities (e.g., Cameron, Alvarez, Ruble, & Fuligni, 2001). Two classes of findings in particular suggest that children's social responses to language reflect reasoning that goes beyond preferences for the familiar. First, social preferences for native-accented speech are not exclusively based on preferences for more intelligible speech. Children's sociolinguistic judgments about native versus foreign speakers are observed when both native and foreign languages are filtered such that neither is intelligible (Hirschfeld & Gelman, 1997). Similarly, children's social preferences based on accent are just as robust as those based on language, even when children understand the foreign-accented speech (Kinzler, Shutts, DeJesus, & Spelke, 2009). And children's trust in the testimony of native-accented over foreign-accented speakers persists even when both individuals speak only in nonsense speech (Kinzler et al., 2011). Thus, though preferences for more familiar or more intelligible speech may underlie part of children's early language-based social reasoning, this does not tell the whole story of children's early reasoning about others based on their language.

Second, from infancy throughout early childhood, accent and language trump race in guiding children's early social preferences. Though infants look longer at individuals of a familiar race (e.g., Bar-Haim, Ziv, Lamy, & Hodes, 2006), they do not selectively reach for toys offered by familiar-race individuals, when tested with the methods that have yielded positive past results based on language (Kinzler & Spelke, 2011). By the late preschool years, children often express clear race-based social preferences. Nonetheless, though White children in the United States often express preferences for own-race individuals, these preferences are eclipsed by preferences for accent. In one study (Kinzler et al., 2009), 5- to 6-year-old White monolingual English-speaking children demonstrated social preferences for Black children who spoke in an American accent of English, compared to White children who spoke in French-accented English. Thus—at least early in childhood—children's social evaluation about others based on their accent can trump their race-based social reasoning (see also Kinzler & Dautel, 2012).

EVOLUTIONARY HYPOTHESES

Why does language trump race in guiding young children's social preferences? Evolutionary analyses provide one lens by which we might evaluate potential priorities in children's earliest social preferences. Prior to the onset of long-distance migration, neighboring groups in ancient times did not likely differ in skin color. Evolutionary psychologists have thus argued that we may not have evolved to see race *per se* as a meaningful social category. Rather, humans might have evolved to monitor patterns of coalition more generally, and race is then plugged in to that system in modern, racially stratified societies (Cosmides, Tooby, & Kurzban, 2003; Kurzban, Tooby, & Cosmides, 2001). Though infants can perceive perceptual differences in skin color, race may gain its potency as a social category in modern times only insofar as children have exposure to, and experience with, a world in which race is a good cue to coalition membership. In contrast, cognitive evolution may have favored attention to language as an important social marker. Given the speed with which language can evolve over a short period of time, language and dialect may have been a reliable marker of coalition membership throughout our evolutionary history, as they are today (Cohen,

2012; Henrich & Henrich, 2007; McElreath, Boyd, & Richerson, 2003).

LOOKING FORWARD

The research discussed earlier demonstrates children's early and robust social preferences for native speakers of their native language, yet most of these studies focus on children who are monolingual learners of their society's majority language. This is not a representative sample of children, given that most children grow up in bilingual or multilingual environments (Werker & Byers-Heinlein, 2008). To fully understand the development of children's reasoning about language as a social category, research with children in diverse linguistic environments is particularly critical. In one study with school-aged multilingual children in South Africa, we observed both a preference for native speech versus foreign speech (in this case, Xhosa vs. French) and also a preference for speakers of a high-status language over children's first language (English vs. Xhosa) (Kinzler, Shutts, & Spelke, 2012). Similarly, by first grade, child speakers of Hawaiian Creole prefer what was considered "standard" English to Creole (Day, 1980).

Relatedly, future research might investigate the developmental time course of accent attitudes across childhood. Much of the literature with adults discusses a preference for speech that conveys status or other social meaning about a group of speakers. Research with infants and young children provides evidence of children's early preferences for native speakers. Presumably, infants' early preferences for native speech and older children's and adults' preferences for high-status speech recruit two different processes. Understanding how these two phenomena interrelate across development will be particularly important.

Finally, just as accent as a social category has been neglected by research on human social groups, so too has it been neglected by the law (Matsuda, 1991). Fortunately, US law protects against discrimination based on gender, age, and race. Though language-based stereotypes and social evaluation have potential consequences for employment (Lippi-Green, 1997), accent is not a protected category in the United States. I am optimistic that future research on children and adults' reasoning about language as a social category might encourage efforts by policy makers to construct policy that acknowledges the potency of accent-based social evaluation and its potential implications for social bias and discrimination.

REFERENCES

Bar-Haim, Y., Ziv, T., Lamy, D., & Hodes, R. (2006). Nature and nurture in own-race face processing. *Psychological Science, 17*, 159–163.

Brewer, M. B. (1988). A dual process model of impression formation. In T. K Srull & R. S. Wyer (Eds.), *Advances in social cognition* (Vol. 1, pp. 1–36). Hillsdale, NJ: Erlbaum.

Cameron, J. A., Alvarez, J. M., Ruble, D. N., & Fuligni, A. J. (2001). Children's lay theories about ingroups and outgroups: Reconceptualizing research on prejudice. *Personality and Social Psychology Review, 5*, 118–128.

Cohen, E. (2012). The evolution of tag-based cooperation in humans: the case for accent. *Current Anthropology, 53*, 588–616

Cosmides, L., Tooby, J., & Kurzban, R. (2003). Perceptions of race. *Trends in Cognitive Sciences, 7*, 173–178.

Day, R. (1980). The development of linguistic attitudes and preferences. *TESOL Quarterly, 14*, 27–37.

Giles, H., & Billings, A. (2004). Assessing language attitudes: Speaker evaluation studies. In A. Davies & C. Elder (Eds.), *Handbook of applied linguistics* (pp. 187–209). Oxford, England: Basil Blackwell.

Gluszek, A., & Dovidio, J. F. (2010). The way they speak: A social psychological perspective on the stigma of nonnative accents in communication. *Personality and Social Psychology Review, 14*, 214–237.

Henrich, N., & Henrich, J. (2007). *Why humans cooperate: A cultural and evolutionary explanation.* Oxford, England: Oxford University Press.

Hirschfeld, L. A., & Gelman, S. A. (1997). What young children think about the relation between language variation and social difference. *Cognitive Development, 12*, 213–238.

Kinzler, K. D., & Dautel, J. (2012). Children's essentialist reasoning about language and race. *Developmental Science, 15*, 131–138.

Kinzler, K., Dupoux, E., & Spelke, E. (2007). The native language of social cognition. *Proceedings of the National Academy of Sciences USA, 104*, 12577–12580.

Kinzler, K. D., Corriveau, K. H., & Harris, P. L. (2011). Children's selective trust in native-accented speakers. *Developmental Science, 14*, 106–111.

Kinzler, K. D., Shutts, K., DeJesus, J., & Spelke, E. S. (2009). Accent trumps race in guiding children's social preferences. *Social Cognition, 27*, 623–624.

Kinzler, K. D., Shutts, K., & Spelke, E. S. (2012). Language-based social preferences among children in South Africa. *Language Learning and Development, 8*, 215–232.

Kinzler, K. D., & Spelke, E.S. (2011). Do infants show social preferences for people differing in race? *Cognition, 119, 1–9.*

Kurzban, R., Tooby, J., & Cosmides, L. (2001). Can race be erased? Coalitional computation and social categorization. *Proceedings of the National Academy of Sciences USA, 98*, 15387–15392.

Labov, W. (2006). *The social stratification of English in New York City* (2nd ed.). New York: Cambridge University Press.

Lambert, W. E., Hodgson, R. C., Gardner, R. C., & Fillenbaum, S. (1960). Evaluational reactions to spoken languages. *Journal of Abnormal and Social Psychology, 60*, 44–51.

Lippi-Green, R. (1997). *English with an accent: Language, ideology, and discrimination in the United States.* New York: Routledge.

Matsuda, M. J. (1991). Voices of America: Accent, antidiscrimination law, and a jurisprudence for the last reconstruction. *Yale Law Journal, 100*, 1329–1467

McElreath, R., Boyd, R., & Richerson, P. J. (2003). Shared norms and the evolution of ethnic markers. *Current Anthropology, 44*, 122–129.

Mehler, J., Jusczyk, P., Lambertz, G., Halsted, N., Bertoncini, J., & Amiel-Tison, C. (1988). A precursor of language acquisition in young infants. *Cognition, 29*, 143–178.

Rakic, T., Steffens, M. C., & Mummendey, A. (2011). Blinded by the accent! The minor role of looks in ethnic categorization. *Journal of Personality and Social Psychology, 100*, 16–29.

Taylor, S. E., Fiske, S. T., Etcoff, N. L., & Ruderman, A. J. (1978). Categorical and contextual bases of person memory and stereotyping. *Journal of Personality and Social Psychology, 36*, 778–793.

Werker, J. F., & Byers–Heinlein, K. (2008). The youngest bilinguals: First steps in perception and comprehension of language. *Trends in Cognitive Sciences, 12*, 144–151.

5.13

The Study of Lay Theories

A Piece of the Puzzle for Understanding Prejudice

SHERI R. LEVY, LUISA RAMÍREZ, LISA ROSENTHAL, AND
DINA M. KARAFANTIS

"Lay" theories are the theories that people use in their everyday life. Lay theories are often communicated by popular sayings or proverbs such as *Madruga y verás, trabaja y tendrás* (proverb from Colombia: *Wake up early and you will see, work and you will have*; proverb from the United States: *The early bird catches the worm*), which parents may use to coax their children to work harder on tasks they value (known as the Protestant work ethic, suggesting that hard work leads to success; e.g., Ramírez, Levy, Velilla, & Hughes, 2010). Lay theories not only serve people's epistemic needs to understand and make predictions about their social world but also serve their social needs to form and maintain relationships as well as psychological needs to feel in control and good about themselves (e.g., Levy, Chiu, & Hong, 2006). People additionally benefit from the perception that their theories represent the "correct" social reality; unlike scientists, most lay people do not test their theories for accuracy (e.g., Heider, 1958).

At the same time, people's lay theories also can have positive or negative consequences for those they are trying to understand. Decades of findings from cognitive, cultural, developmental, and social psychological research involving children, adolescents, and adults across numerous cultures indicate that lay theories are powerful predictors of greater or weaker prejudice, stereotyping, and discrimination toward numerous groups (gay men, overweight persons, people living with AIDS, poor persons, socially stigmatized racial/ethnic groups, women; Hong, Levy, & Chiu, 2001). In some of these studies, lay theories are even more powerful predictors than relevant cognitive and personality variables (e.g., Levy, Stroessner, & Dweck, 1998).

To address how lay theories foster prejudice or tolerance toward social groups, we have adopted an integrative social-developmental perspective (e.g., Levy, West, & Ramírez, 2005). The perspective considers an enduring social psychological question about how contexts shape people's judgments and behavior with an enduring developmental question about how the accumulation of experience influences people's judgments and behaviors. Our findings suggest that age, context (e.g., culture), and social status (e.g., racial/ethnic group) are key determinants of if and when a prominent lay theory relates to prejudice or tolerance (e.g., Levy et al., 2005; Levy, West, Ramírez, & Karafantis, 2006; Ramírez et al., 2010; Rosenthal, Levy, & Moyer, 2011).

Starting in childhood, people learn their culture's lay theories and how to apply them to their observations and experiences with groups (e.g., Dweck, 1999). People may learn that certain lay theories can serve as justification for prejudice, justifying socially unacceptable views. People do not necessarily adopt a lay theory to support their prejudice, per se, but prejudice can be part of the associative network of beliefs connected to one's lay theory. For example, some people use the Protestant work ethic (PWE), the belief that hard work leads to success, to motivate themselves and others to work hard to achieve success, even despite barriers and challenges; at the same time, PWE can be linked to Western cultural values emphasizing personal responsibility such that some people (particularly advantaged group members) may use PWE to justify the denial of social services to disadvantaged groups, through the suggestion that their disadvantage is the result of their laziness.

The cultural transmission of lay theories such as PWE reflect an associated meaning mechanism in which a lay theory is linked to other beliefs within the relevant cultural context, which make it possible in this example for PWE to have a justifier-of-inequality implication in Western cultures. The notion of an associated meaning mechanism derives from the long-standing social psychological literature indicating that the same construct can be perceived differently by different people or in different contexts (e.g., Bruner, 1957; Turner & Oakes, 1997). Lewin (1951) noted that children hold a narrow view of the implications of their actions but gain a broader view with experience, which applied to PWE suggests that people in some contexts could acquire a growing understanding of PWE's implications with age and experience. In short, lay people are presumed to accumulate and refine their understandings of prevalent lay theories such as PWE through cultural or personal experience and personal relevance such that PWE has more than one intergroup implication as part of its associative network (e.g., Levy et al., 2005; Rosenthal, Levy, et al., 2011; see Crandall & Martinez, 1996). This suggests that adults are likely to be familiar with several potential intergroup implications of a lay theory, but children (or adults less familiar with the culture or environment) might view a theory primarily through only one intergroup implication.

Much of the work on the implications of lay theories for judging groups of people has examined children ages 10 and older because by age 10, children have mastered relevant social-cognitive skills such as perceiving similarities across different groups and differences within the same group (e.g., Aboud, 1988). While 10-year-olds may have a sufficiently sophisticated understanding of groups, warranting comparing their responses to those of adults, 10-year-olds nonetheless do not yet have a full understanding of (and perhaps only have a budding interest in) the inner workings of their culture, including economics and politics.

People's level of agreement with different lay theories is rather easily measured by researchers; children, adolescents, and adults evaluate their current level of agreement with the simple, straightforward statements reflecting each lay theory (e.g., Kelly, 1955). Studies in which people's lay theories are temporarily made salient (e.g., through reading an article supporting that lay theory) provide similar findings as when the lay theories are measured by self-report, suggesting that lay theories

play a causal role in people's social attitudes (e.g., Levy, West, et al., 2006).

PROTESTANT WORK ETHIC

In the remainder of this chapter, we highlight some relevant findings on PWE, a prominent lay theory in numerous countries (e.g., Canada, England, New Zealand, the United States), which as already noted appears to have at least two intergroup implications: one for prejudice and one for tolerance (see Furnham et al., 1993; Rosenthal, Levy, et al., 2011). To foreshadow, the tolerant implication of PWE seems to exist across age, cultural, and social status groups, whereas the intolerant implication seems to be culturally bound with children in those cultures first learning the tolerant implication and later learning the intolerant implication.

As one example of the tolerant implication, in the United States, PWE is often referred to as the "American Dream," with the egalitarian idea that people from all social categories have equal potential to succeed through hard work—referred to as "PWE-Equalizer." Here is a quote from an adult participant in one of our studies illustrating how she sees her world through the lens of PWE-Equalizer: "*Anyone can succeed—look at Oprah Winfrey and others who came from nothing and made it big. America is the land of opportunity.*" Children likely learn PWE-Equalizer through hearing such rags-to-riches stories as well as through other classic stories such as *The Little Engine That Could*. This is a story of a little engine who, through diligent effort, was able to reach a valued outcome that appeared insurmountable. Children of all groups are likely motivated to endorse PWE-Equalizer because it gives them a sense of control over their future while revealing a positive pathway (effort) to success (e.g., see McClelland, Atkinson, Clark, & Lowell, 1953, regarding achievement motive). Indeed, among African American and European American children (ages 10 to 15), PWE positively relates to beliefs in social equality (Levy, West, et al., 2006; Ramírez et al., 2010).

At the same time, scholars have long argued that a belief in PWE contributes to negative evaluations of disadvantaged groups in the United States such as poor persons and African Americans through the notion that disadvantaged persons deserve their disadvantage for not working hard enough—referred to as "PWE-Justifier" (e.g., Levy et al., 2005, see Crandall, 2000). Here is a quote from an adult participant in one of our studies illustrating how she sees her world through the lens of PWE-Justifier: "*a poor person on the street who is begging for money…hasn't worked hard to succeed, and therefore has suffered the consequences.*" As children reach adolescence in the United States, they are expected to be increasingly exposed to others using PWE in this way—to argue that disadvantaged group members are to blame for their disadvantage. Adolescence is a critical developmental period with changes in social identities and roles (e.g., Ruble, 1994), and adolescents are likely increasingly aware of and exposed to cultural teachings in which prejudice is linked to attributions of personal responsibility and controllability. As educational and career prospects are increasingly being evaluated in adolescence, it may be that advantaged group members are more motivated to take personal credit for their own (or their group's) accomplishments and seek ways to deny efforts at increasing representation of disadvantaged groups' in education and work settings (affirmative action policies); hence, advantaged adolescents may be particularly likely to make or be receptive to a connection between PWE and American individualism of blaming the disadvantaged. Because PWE-related arguments are part of the social milieu, we would expect all late adolescents to be knowledgeable about both PWE-Equalizer and PWE-Justifier and use whichever one is most salient or personally relevant in a particular context or life period.

A series of studies with different age groups in the United States supported these conjectures. For example, participants in one study aimed at testing the effects of PWE were randomly assigned to one of two experimental conditions, which involved reading a brief pro-PWE or anti-PWE induction article, with each article describing the same allegedly credible and extensive psychological research; however, the articles differed in that they concluded that the findings either supported or opposed PWE. In this study, we found that the pro-PWE article facilitated greater beliefs in egalitarianism among the 10- and 15-year-olds, who assumedly construe PWE in terms of its egalitarian implication, compared to the 21-year-olds, who presumably are also familiar with PWE's inequality-justifying associations (Levy, West, et al., 2006). In another study with college students only, we tested whether one way in which the justifier-of-inequality implication arises is through exposure to others using PWE to justify inequality, as in the argument that disadvantaged groups and group members are to blame for their

disadvantage and that they could pull themselves out of their dire situation through effort. All college student participants were instructed to engage in a thought exercise but were randomly assigned to one of two conditions. Half of the participants were asked to think and write about instances of others using "people who work hard succeed" in support of their arguments (justification condition), whereas the other half of participants were asked to think and write about what "people who work hard succeed" means (definition or control condition). As expected, participants asked to think about past instances of others using PWE in support of their arguments generated examples of blaming people for their misfortune and additionally made less egalitarian responses (reported less support for social equality and donated less money to a homeless shelter) compared to participants in the definition or control condition (Levy, West, et al., 2006). Moreover, findings across studies suggest that the shift in PWE's meaning toward intolerance begins in late adolescence (ages 16–18), which is also when adolescents begin to compete with others for educational and work placement.

Although with experience, all adults may have greater knowledge of and exposure to PWE-Justifier than do children, as noted earlier, PWE-Justifier should be most relevant to advantaged group members in that it justifies their advantaged place in society (see Rosenthal, London, Levy, Lobel, & Herrera-Alcazar, 2011). Accordingly, European American adults have been found to generally endorse PWE-Justifier more than African American adults do (Levy et al., 2010).

Following from the assumption that people refine their understanding of certain lay theories such as PWE through cultural experience, PWE should not accumulate the same implications in all environments. In less individualistic cultures where attributions of individual responsibility and controllability are less ubiquitous, PWE should be less likely to take on the justifier-of-inequality implication; instead, PWE is expected to function through its equalizer implication (Ramírez et al., 2010; Rosenthal, Levy, et al., 2011; see Crandall & Martinez, 1996). We tested this conjecture in Colombia, where people's beliefs about work have historically had strong ties to Catholicism, with work thought to represent punishment rather than a pathway to prestige; because of this, Colombians are encouraged to accept their disadvantage as a means to salvation and therefore are not directly blamed for their disadvantage. As hypothesized, PWE was consistently related to egalitarianism among Mestizo children, adolescents, and adults who represent the majority group in Colombia, which contrasts with developmental findings with European Americans (Ramírez et al., 2010).

As further evidence that culture plays a contributing role to PWE's intergroup implications, a recent meta-analysis of PWE's relation to prejudice (Rosenthal, Levy, et al., 2011), which involved a systematic, statistical review of 37 past published and unpublished studies across the previous 40 years, indicated that PWE is more strongly related to prejudice toward racial/ethnic minorities, poor persons, sexual minorities, and women in Western countries (Canada, England, New Zealand, the United States) than in non-Western countries (e.g., India, Jamaica, and Singapore). In other words, the justifier-of-inequality implication of PWE appeared to be more prevalent in Western versus non-Western countries. Taken together, these findings suggest that sociocultural experiences shape the intergroup implications of PWE.

CONCLUSION

In conclusion, like trained scientists, ordinary people need theories to help them maneuver their way through their social world. While lay theories serve epistemic, social, and psychological needs for people, lay theories are also powerful social filters with nontrivial effects on perceptions, judgments, and responses to others. Our integrative social-developmental perspective suggests that lay people's characteristics (age, culture, social status) interact with the environments in which people are nested to affect lay theory use in particular contexts and over time. Research suggests that PWE can be akin to a double-sided coin with two intergroup implications that depend upon lay people's age, context, and personal needs. Research on PWE also suggests that prejudice can develop, at least partially, through adopting a lay theory that originally has egalitarian implications. All in all, the study of prevalent lay theories such as PWE has uncovered a piece of the puzzle for understanding prejudice.

REFERENCES

Aboud, F. E. (1988). *Children and prejudice*. New York: Blackwell.

Bruner, J. S. (1957). Going beyond the information given. In J. S. Bruner, E. Brunswick, L. Festinger, F. Heider, K. F. Muenzinger, C. E. Osgood, et al. (Eds.), *Contemporary approaches to cognition* (pp. 41–69). Cambridge, MA: Harvard University Press.

Crandall, C. S. (2000). Ideology and ideologies of stigma: The justification of stigmatization. In T. F. Heatherton, R. E. Kleck, M. R. Hebl & J. G. Hull (Eds.), *The social psychology of stigma* (pp. 126–150). New York: Guilford Press.

Crandall, C. S., & Martinez, R. (1996). Culture, ideology, and antifat attitudes. *Personality and Social Psychology Bulletin, 22*, 1165–1176.

Dweck, C. S. (1999). *Self-theories: Their role in motivation, personality, and development*. Philadelphia, PA: Psychology Press.

Furnham, A., Bond, M., Heaven, P., Hilton, D., Lobel, T., Masters, J., ...Daalen, H. V. (1993). A comparison of Protestant work ethic beliefs in thirteen nations. *Journal of Social Psychology, 133*, 185–197.

Heider, F. (1958). *The psychology of interpersonal relations*. New York: Wiley.

Hong, Y. Y., Levy, S. R., & Chiu, C. Y. (2001). The contribution of the lay theories approach to the study of groups. *Personality and Social Psychology Review, 5*, 98–106. doi: 10.1207/S15327957PSPR0502_1.

Kelly, G. A. (1955). *The psychology of personal constructs*. New York: Norton.

Levy, S. R., Chiu, C. Y., & Hong, Y. Y. (2006). Lay theories and intergroup relations. *Group Processes and Intergroup Relations, 9*, 5–24. doi: 10.1177/1368430206059855.

Levy, S. R., Freitas, A. L., Mendoza-Denton, R., Kugelmaas, H., & Rosenthal, L. (2010). When sociopolitical events strike cultural beliefs: Divergent impact of Hurricane Katrina on African Americans' and European Americans' endorsement of the Protestant work ethic. *Basic and Applied Social Psychology, 32*, 1–10. doi: 10.1080/01973533.2010.495673

Levy, S. R., Stroessner, S. J., & Dweck, C. S. (1998). Stereotype formation and endorsement: The role of implicit theories. *Journal of Personality and Social Psychology, 74*, 1421–1436.

Levy, S. R., West, T., & Ramírez, L. (2005). Lay theories and intergroup relations: A social developmental perspective. *European Review of Social Psychology, 16*, 189–220. doi: 10.1080/10463280500397234

Levy, S. R., West, T., Ramírez, L., & Karafantis, D. M. (2006).The Protestant work ethic: A lay theory with dual intergroup implications. *Group Processes and Intergroup Relations, 9*, 95–115. doi: 10.1177/1368430206059874

Lewin, K. (1951). *Field theory in social science: Selected theoretical papers*. New York: Harpers.

McClelland, D. C., Atkinson, J. W., Clark, R. A., & Lowell, E. L. (1953). *The achievement motive*. East Norwalk, CT: Appleton-Century-Crofts.

Ramírez, L., Levy, S. R., Velilla, E., & Hughes, J. M. (2010). Considering the roles of culture and social status: The Protestant work ethic and egalitarianism. *Revista Latinoamericana de Psicología, 42,* 381–390.

Rosenthal, L., Levy, S. R., & Moyer, A. (2011). Protestant work ethic's relation to intergroup and policy attitudes: A meta-analytic review. *European Journal of Social Psychology,* doi: 10.1002/ejsp.832

Rosenthal, L., London, B., Levy, S. R., Lobel, M., & Herrera-Alcazar, A. (2011). The relation between the Protestant work ethic and undergraduate women's perceived identity compatibility in nontraditional majors, *Analyses of Social Issues and Public Policy.* doi: 10.1111/j.1530-2415.2011.01264.x

Ruble, D. N. (1994). A phase model of transitions: Cognitive and motivational consequences. In M. Zanna (Ed.), *Advances in experimental social psychology* (pp. 163–214). New York: Academic Press.

Turner, J. C., & Oakes, P. J. (1997) The socially structured mind. In C. McGarty & S. A. Haslam (Eds.), *The message of social psychology* (pp. 355–373). Oxford, England: Blackwell.

5.14

Social Acumen

Its Role in Constructing Group Identity and Attitudes

DREW NESDALE

Children can explicitly differentiate among people based on overt physical cues (e.g., skin color, language) by 3 to 4 years of age. Soon afterward, they identify their own ethnic group membership and thereafter they reveal increasingly strong in-group bias (greater liking for in-group over out-groups), up to 6 to 7 years of age. Beyond this age, however, the pattern diverges. For many children, their in-group bias gradually declines during middle childhood, whereas, for others, their in-group bias may stabilize or even increase. These changes may reflect changes in in-group liking, out-group liking, or both, although children tend to maintain a greater preference for their in-group over any out-group (Nesdale, 2001). While these findings indicate that children's attitudes do not follow a simple linear trajectory, they also show that their in-group and out-group preferences are not perfectly coordinated. Together, the findings represent a considerable challenge for researchers seeking to explain them.

I will briefly outline the central tenets of one approach, *social identity development theory* (SIDT; Nesdale, 2007a), that was designed to account for the development of children's group attitudes, especially their intergroup prejudice (i.e., attitudes of dislike or hatred toward members of out-groups). I will also describe a new construct, social acumen, that enhances the theory and extends our understanding of children's group-based identities and attitudes.

SOCIAL IDENTITY DEVELOPMENT THEORY

Social identity development theory (SIDT; Nesdale, 2007a) was founded on research indicating that, from the commencement of schooling, middle childhood is increasingly marked by children's involvement in social groups or cliques

and that much of their social interaction during this period takes place in the context of these groups (Rubin, Bukowski, & Parker (1998). These findings are consistent with the view that children have a fundamental need to be accepted and to belong (Baumeister & Leary, 1995), and that group memberships are an integral part of their self-concepts (Bennett & Sani, 2008).

On this basis, SIDT proposes that the development of negative intergroup attitudes (i.e., intergroup prejudice) is the end point of a process that involves four sequential phases: undifferentiated (typically, up to 2–3 years), ethnic awareness (beyond 2–3 years), ethnic preference (after acquisition of ethnic awareness and identification with a particular ethnic group), and ethnic prejudice (typically, after 6–7 years, but only in some, not necessarily all, children). These phases vary primarily in terms of the social motivations, attitudes and behaviors that characterize them, and the events that precipitate changes from one phase to the next. Of particular relevance to the present discussion are the ethnic preference and ethnic prejudice phases.

The *ethnic preference* phase is instigated by the child's identification with a particular ethnic group. It mainly involves a focus on, and concern for, children's continuing membership of their *in-group*, as well as the positive distinctiveness of the in-group, in comparison with other groups. On this basis, children who are in the ethnic preference phase will always like their own group and prefer it to other groups, who will be liked less and seen as possessing less positive qualities, compared with the in-group. Given the importance of group membership to children, the group has the potential to exert a considerable influence on group members. For example, children are likely to be motivated to maintain, if not enhance, the status of their group, to conform to whatever expectations that the group holds concerning the appropriate attitudes, beliefs, and behaviors to be displayed by group members (i.e., group norms), and to defend the group should it be threatened by others.

In addition, however, it is proposed that *some*, but *not all*, children's attitudes toward members of an out-group may change from mere ethnic preference to *ethnic prejudice* (i.e., feel dislike or hatred, rather than merely greater preference, for the in-group), under particular circumstances. These include whether children highly identify with their in-group, and/or out-group prejudice is a norm held by members of the in-group, and/or the in-group is threatened by members of the out-group.

One implication from this approach is that prejudice toward particular ethnic out-groups does not emerge in all children as a matter of course. Instead, whether children display ethnic prejudice is dependent upon their unique social situation, rather than their particular age or specific cognitive abilities. That is, it depends upon their group identification and the intergroup context.

RESEARCH SUPPORT FOR SOCIAL IDENTITY DEVELOPMENT THEORY

Research shows that, certainly by school age, children seek to be members of social groups, and that they tend to like, and see themselves as similar to, in-group compared with out-group members (Nesdale, Durkin, Maass, & Griffiths, 2004, 2005). Children will even like their in-group more than an out-group when the in-group has lower status than the out-group, especially if they perceive little possibility of changing groups (Nesdale & Flesser, 2001). Children also derive at least some of their sense of self-worth from their group memberships (Bennett & Sani, 2008).

There is also evidence that children reveal a strong bias toward their in-group when they are required to make choices, indicate preferences, or allocate rewards between the in-group and an out-group, and that they display in-group positivity versus out-group negativity in their trait attributions (see Nesdale, 2001). Perhaps unsurprisingly, they are also motivated to enhance and defend the status of their group (Ojala & Nesdale, 2010). Furthermore, children who are rejected by their peer group display heightened state anxiety, decreased self-esteem, enhanced risk-taking, and a tendency toward antisocial behavior, from as young as 6 years (Nesdale, 2008).

While the preceding findings illuminate the *ethnic preference* phase, there is also evidence that, in addition to their preference for their in-group, children can also come to dislike or hate a particular out-group (i.e., *ethnic prejudice* phase). This attitude is revealed when in-group members are highly identified with the in-group, and/or when the in-group has a norm or expectation that endorses negative attitudes toward (particular) out-groups, and/or when in-group members perceive that the standing of their group is being threatened by an out-group (Nesdale, Durkin, Maass, & Griffiths, 2005; Nesdale, Maass, Durkin, & Griffiths, 2005).

Overall, the preceding findings indicate that peer group membership is exceedingly important to children. Indeed, it appears that if there is the possibility of being accepted and included in a group, most children will seek to be included. Moreover, once group membership is achieved, the evidence indicates that the peer group has the potential to exert a considerable influence on group members' attitudes, beliefs, and behaviors toward both in-group and out-group members.

However, it is important to emphasize that the effect of social group identification on children's group attitudes is neither automatic nor unthinking. The fact that a child has identified with a particular group does not imply that she or he will thereafter blindly follow the explicit and implicit dictates of the group. Rather, as children increase in age, they learn that their social world is comprised of an array of significant individuals and groups, each with particular demands and expectations (e.g., parents, teachers, older siblings, their classmates, other peers), of which their in-group is only one. Furthermore, they come to understand that they need to make judgments and decisions about the attitudes, beliefs, and behaviors to be displayed in particular social contexts involving these significant others, at particular times. Thus, children's attitudes and behaviors are increasingly likely to be influenced by their developing *social acumen*, as they increase in age.

SOCIAL ACUMEN AND ITS EFFECTS ON CHILDREN'S IN-GROUP AND OUT-GROUP ATTITUDES

Social acumen is somewhat analogous to business acumen but, in the context of middle childhood, refers to children's accumulating knowledge of how the social system works, their strategic awareness of how to use this information to their advantage, and their skill in making it happen (Nesdale, 2004, 2010; Nesdale & Dalton, 2011; Nesdale & Lawson, 2011). Social acumen is founded upon children's early and continuing social monitoring of other children and their social interactions, as well as their own interactions with other children (Nesdale, 2007a). Based on these experiences, children begin to develop the three core aspects of social acumen; that is, social knowledge, social intelligence, and social competence.

Social knowledge refers to information that is shared by the majority of the children in the immediate social context (e.g., what are the generally acceptable and unacceptable types and modes of play, how to make friends and keep them, what you have to do to become, and remain, a group member, which behaviors lead to exclusion, etc.) but also includes knowledge concerning the demands and expectations of significant others (e.g., older siblings, parents, teachers). Moreover, social knowledge encompasses children's strategic awareness of how to use this information to their advantage, including to the benefit of significant others (e.g., in-group members).

Social intelligence or perceptiveness refers to social cognitive attributes or skills that enhance and contribute to their social knowledge, such as accurate person perception and social flexibility (e.g., able to tell whether others lie, able to accommodate to new situations and people, able to persuade others to get wishes carried out, able to guess the feelings of others).

Social competence refers to children's abilities or skills at putting the preceding knowledge and understanding to work in engaging positively and effectively in social interactions with others (e.g., able to initiate and maintain positive relationships, able to communicate effectively, able to coordinate actions and feelings with others).

Social acumen develops over time, beginning when children first come into contact with other children, but expanding and elaborating more quickly when the child begins playschool, preschool and, particularly, elementary school. However, while I would anticipate that children, by the end of middle childhood, would have a relatively sophisticated social acumen compared with younger children, it is also likely that there would be variability in the social acumen of children of a similar age, and that children's social acumen would continue to increase with age and experience.

EFFECTS OF SOCIAL ACUMEN ON INTRA- AND INTERGROUP ATTITUDES

It is plausible that children's developing social acumen would have an increasing influence upon their social attitudes, beliefs, and behaviors, including their choice of groups with whom to identify. Thus, whereas children almost invariably like out-groups less than their in-group (Nesdale, 2007b), children, by school age, actually like their in-group less when it has low versus high status, and they would prefer to move to a high-status group (Nesdale & Flesser, 2001), presumably because they know of the advantages associated with high-status groups (e.g., popularity, control of resources, influence).

In addition, given the importance of group acceptance and belonging to children, it is unsurprising that research has shown that children do not necessarily think less of their group if it has a norm of exclusion versus inclusion toward nonmembers and out-groups, and that they express attitudes that are consistent with their group norm (Nesdale, Maass, et al., 2005), even when it conflicts with an individual value or disposition. For example, children will suspend their own tendencies toward emotional empathy for ethnic minority group members if that tendency conflicts with a group norm of exclusion (Nesdale, Griffiths, Durkin, & Maass, 2005).

However, presumably because children, as they increase in age, are increasingly aware that negative intergroup attitudes and behaviors are considered to be unacceptable and inappropriate by adults (Rutland, Cameron, Milne, & McGeorge, 2005), their out-group attitudes and behavior intentions are likely to become less negative with increasing age (Nesdale, Maass, et al., 2005; Nesdale, Maass, Kiesner, Durkin, & Griffiths, 2008), especially when under the surveillance of adults (Rutland et al., 2005).

In a similar vein, research has shown that when a child is subject to, for example, a group norm (e.g., exclusion of out-group members) that is contrary to a school norm (e.g., inclusion of out-group members), the latter did not extinguish the impact of the in-group norm. Instead, the group norm and school norm effects were independent of each other. The children's out-group attitudes reflected their in-group norms, although less so with increasing age, whereas the school norm increased the positivity of out-group attitudes, at both ages (Nesdale & Lawson, 2011). Presumably, the children responded affirmatively to both norms because of the perceived importance of both groups to them; that is, they recognized that it would be wise to respond affirmatively to both sources of influence so as not to run afoul of either source. Interestingly, in this and a later study (Nesdale & Dalton, 2011), although the children conformed to the exclusionary in-group norm, they actually liked the in-group less, especially with increasing age.

CONCLUSION

Children's intra- and intergroup attitudes are significantly influenced by their identification with a particular group. At the same time, research indicates that children's attitudes are not blindly group dependent. Rather, with increasing age, children's identification with particular groups, and their endorsement of group attitudes, is increasingly influenced by their developing social acumen; that is, their understanding of the social context and how this knowledge can be used to their best advantage. Importantly, the new social acumen construct serves to increase our understanding of how children's in-group bias may vary (i.e., increase, stabilize, decrease) during middle childhood via its impact on their in-group and/or out-group attitudes. Finally, supporting this approach, our recent research has shown that social acumen can be measured, that children differ in the extent of it, and that social acumen is a significant predictor of out-group attitudes (Nesdale, 2010). Social acumen promises to play an important role in children's attitudes and behavior.

REFERENCES

Baumeister, R. F., & Leary, M. R. (1995). The need to belong: Desire for interpersonal attachment as a fundamental human motivation. *Psychological Bulletin, 117*, 497–529.

Bennett, M., & Sani, F. (2008). Children's subjective identification with social groups: A group reference effect approach. *British Journal of Developmental Psychology, 26*, 381–387.

Nesdale, D. (2001). Development of prejudice in children. In M. Augoustinos & K. Reynolds (Eds.), *Understanding prejudice, racism, and social conflict* (pp. 57–72). London: Sage.

Nesdale, D. (2004, 19–21 February). *Social acumen and ethnic prejudice in children.* Paper presented at Nag's Head Conference on Children and Race: Development, Cognitions, Affect, and Stereotypes, Boca Raton, FL.

Nesdale, D. (2007a). The development of ethnic prejudice in early childhood: Theories and research. In O. Saracho & B. Spodek (Eds.), *Contemporary perspectives on social learning in early childhood education* (pp.213–240). Charlotte, NC: Information Age Publishing.

Nesdale, D. (2007b). Children's perceptions of social groups. In J. A. Zebrowski (Ed.), *New research on social perception* (pp.1–46). Hauppauge, NY: Nova Science.

Nesdale, D. (2008). Peer group rejection and children's intergroup prejudice: Experimental studies. In M. Killen & S. Levy (Eds.), *Intergroup attitudes and relations in childhood through adulthood* (pp. 32–46). Oxford, England: Oxford University Press.

Nesdale, D. (2010, July). *Children and social groups: Accounting for the age effect.* Paper presented at EASP meeting, Developmental Perspectives on Intergroup Prejudice, Lisbon, Portugal.

Nesdale, D., & Dalton, D. (2011). Effect of social group norms and school norms on children's intergroup prejudice. *British Journal of Developmental Psychology, 29*(4), 895–909.

Nesdale, D., Durkin, K., Maass, A., & Griffiths, J. (2004). Group status, out-group ethnicity, and children's ethnic attitudes. *Journal of Applied Developmental Psychology, 25*, 237–251.

Nesdale, D., Durkin, K., & Maass, A., & Griffiths, J. (2005). Threat, group identification, and children's ethnic prejudice. *Social Development, 14*, 189–205.

Nesdale, D., & Flesser, D. (2001). Social identity and the development of children's group attitudes. *Child Development, 72*(9), 506–517.

Nesdale, D., Griffiths, J., Durkin, K., & Maass, A. (2005). Empathy, group norms and children's ethnic attitudes. *Journal of Applied Developmental Psychology, 26*, 623–637.

Nesdale, D., & Lawson, M. J. (2011). Social groups and children's intergroup attitudes: Can school norms moderate the effects of social group norms? *Child Development, 82*(5), 1594–1606.

Nesdale, D., Maass, A., Durkin, K., & Griffiths, J. (2005). Group norms, threat, and children's racial prejudice. *Child Development, 76*(3), 652–663.

Nesdale, D., Maass, A., Kiesner, J., Durkin, K., & Griffiths, J. (2008). Effects of group norms on children's bullying intentions. *Social Development, 17*, 889–907.

Ojala, K. (2007). Group belongingness and intra- and intergroup processes in children. PhD dissertation, Griffith University, Queensland, Australia.

Rubin, K., Bukowski, W., & Parker, J. G. (1998). Peer interactions, relationships and groups. In N. Eisenberg (Ed.), *Handbook of child psychology: Vol 3. Social emotional and personality development* (5th ed., pp. 619–700). New York: Wiley.

Rutland, A., Cameron, L., Milne, A., & McGeorge, P. (2005). Social norms and self-presentation: Children's implicit and explicit intergroup attitudes. *Child Development, 76*, 451–466.

5.15

Understanding and Reducing Social Stereotyping and Prejudice Among Children

REBECCA S. BIGLER

Social stereotyping and prejudice are pressing social problems for humanity; they contribute to war, aggression, oppression, and injustice. Importantly, stereotyping and prejudice have origins in childhood. Decades of research indicate that many children, even among those as young as 3 years of age, endorse social stereotypes and prejudices. Thus, the developmental study of intergroup biases constitutes an important area of psychological research.

I was a graduate student at the Pennsylvania State University when I encountered the work of psychologists interested in intergroup relations, including Muzafer Sherif, Gordon Allport, and Henri Tafjel. I was impressed and inspired by their efforts to delineate the causal factors involved in the development of intergroup biases and to generate clear empirical evidence of their operation. As a developmental student working under the supervision of Lynn Liben, I was disappointed, however, by the level of theoretical and empirical attention to developmental issues. I thus began a 25-year effort, involving many wonderful student collaborators and continuous input from Lynn Liben, to use experimental methodologies to (a) examine the roles of environmental and organismic factors in the formation of children's in-group biases and (b) develop effective strategies for reducing social stereotyping and prejudice among children.

In this chapter, I briefly outline the nature of my experimental research and describe four broad results stemming from this work that I consider especially important. I then suggest ways in which these results might usefully inform future psychological exploration of the causes of intergroup bias, and social and educational policies related to the treatment of social groups within children's environments.

EXPERIMENTAL PARADIGMS

Identifying Causal Mechanism of Social Stereotyping and Prejudice

It is difficult to identify the causes of stereotyping and prejudice with respect to particular social groups (e.g., race, gender) because children are exposed to myriad potential causes (e.g., symbolic and live models, operant condition, explicit and implicit messages about groups) well before even their first birthday. Influenced by the Sheriffs' Robber's Cave study and Jane Eliiot's classic demonstration of "blue-eyed/brown-eyed" bias filmed for television, I therefore sought to use a novel group paradigm to examine the causal factors related to intergroup bias among children (e.g., Bigler, 1995; Bigler, Brown, & Markell, 2001; Bigler, Jones, & Lobliner, 1997; Brown & Bigler, 2002). In a typical study, participants are 6- to 11-year-old summer-school students who are unacquainted with each other when school begins. They are initially given tasks measuring factors (e.g., cognitive-developmental level, self-esteem) hypothesized to affect intergroup attitudes. Novel groups are then created, usually by assigning children to wear different colored tee shirts. Characteristics of the groups (e.g., proportional size, purported traits) and their treatment within the classroom (e.g., labeling, segregation) are manipulated. After several weeks, children's intergroup attitudes are assessed using a battery of attitudinal and behavioral measures.

Reducing Social Stereotyping and Prejudice

Hundreds of activities and programs aimed at reducing children's social stereotyping and prejudice exist. Unfortunately, relatively few are based on psychological theory or have ever been empirically evaluated. In my work, I have sought to provide rigorous tests of theoretically derived manipulations aimed at reducing children's social stereotyping and prejudice (e.g., Bigler & Liben, 1990, 1992; Hughes, Bigler, & Levy, 2007; Lamb, Bigler, Liben, & Green, 2009; Pahlke, Bigler, & Green, 2010; Weisgram & Bigler, 2007). In a typical study, participants are 6- to 11-year-old students attending school or summer programs who are randomly assigned to receive one of two (or more) instructional programs that differ only in the targeting of a single, narrow skill (e.g., multiple classification skill) or experience (e.g., exposure to information about discrimination) hypothesized to reduce stereotyping and prejudice. Children are initially given tasks measuring individual differences hypothesized to affect reaction to lessons (e.g., cognitive skills) and intergroup attitudes. A battery of attitudinal (and occasionally behavioral) measures is then given immediately following the conclusion of the lessons and again several weeks or months later.

FOUR BROAD RESEARCH FINDINGS

Children Are Predisposed to Develop and Maintain Social Stereotypes and Prejudice

At the broadest level, my own empirical work, as well as that of many others, indicates that children have a proclivity to develop in-group biases. Children are adept at categorization, and once a particular basis for sorting individuals becomes psychologically salient, children readily develop stereotypes and prejudices favoring their in-group. For example, even preschool-age children who were members of novel, minimal "red" and "blue" groups showed some forms of in-group bias when their teachers used the groups to label and organize the classroom (Patterson & Bigler, 2006). Effects generated by our typical experimental paradigm are small in size and indicate the presence of in-group favoritism rather than out-group derogation. They are remarkable, however, in that children show these biases despite having a wealth of opportunities (e.g., several weeks of interaction with actual in-group and out-group members) to disconfirm their inaccurate generalizations. In sum, the establishment of psychologically salient social groups constitutes a risk that children will develop stereotypes and biases, in part because of a host of constructive processes that children bring to understanding their social world (see Bigler & Liben, 2006, 2007).

With respect to intervention, my own—and other researchers'—work suggests that once children have developed beliefs about the traits, activities, and roles associated with particular social groups (i.e., stereotypes) and affective responses to groups (i.e., prejudices), these views are difficult to modify (see Bigler, 1999, for review of racial attitude interventions). My collaborators and I have conducted a number of interventions aimed at reducing children's stereotyping and prejudice that failed to produce statistically significant differences between experimental and control groups and—at least in part as a result of their ineffectiveness—have gone unpublished. Our experiences have taught us that children very frequently fail to (a) attend to, (b) comprehend, (c) remember, or (d) believe the veracity of authority figures' messages that contradict their own strongly held attitudes and beliefs. For example, in response to being told about a female firefighter, some children claim to have heard about a male firefighter, and in response to being told that "anyone—a boy or a girl—can have a pink ___ [backpack, umbrella, shirt]," some children insist that the instructor is mistaken and steadfastly refuse to relinquish the belief that only girls can possess pink items.

Among these failures, we have also identified a number of strategies that appear to reliably reduce stereotyping and prejudice among children. As a general rule, effective counterstereotypic messages are explicit rather than implicit (Bigler & Liben, 1990, 1992). That is, the instructor should clearly state the new view to be adopted (e.g., "Both men and women can be firefighters") rather than rely on children to infer such principles from symbolic models (e.g., a story featuring a female firefighter). In addition, effective interventions typically require children to practice—overtly—the expression of desired beliefs and behaviors (e.g., Bigler, 1990; Lamb et al., 2009), thereby promoting internalization and allowing instructors to monitor children's processing of intervention messages. Even in these best-case scenarios, however, our intervention programs often produce statistically significant rather than practically significant changes (see Bigler & Liben, 1990). That is, stereotyping and prejudice are mitigated somewhat but not eliminated. To date, I know of no single, highly effective means to obviate social stereotyping and prejudice, especially among strongly biased children. In the case of stereotyping and prejudice, it may well be that an ounce of prevention is worth a pound of cure.

Environmental Conditions Shape Children's Stereotyping and Prejudice

Children's in-group biases are not inevitable; we have generated clear evidence that in-group biases develop in response to certain environmental conditions (Bigler et al. 1997; Patterson & Bigler, 2006). For example, when placed in perceptually salient, dichotomous novel groups (e.g., "reds" and "blues") for many weeks, most children show no in-group bias whatsoever when these groups are ignored by their classroom teachers (Bigler et al., 1997). According to my work, two powerful environmental factors that facilitate stereotyping and prejudice are adults' explicit and implicit use of the social groups. Those children placed in perceptually salient, dichotomous novel groups whose teachers used the groups to (a) label children (e.g., "Good morning, reds and blues") or (b) organize environments (e.g., segregated children by group membership, even in the absence of labeling) developed in-group biases (see Bigler & Liben, 2006, 2007). I argue that any perceptually salient human attribute (e.g., eye color, hair color, handedness, height) would readily be adopted by children as a basis for stereotyping and prejudice were adults to label and use the category routinely.

In sum, I argue that evolution has led to a flexible cognitive system that motivates and equips children to infer—from environmental cues—which particular social groups (i.e., bases of classification) are important (and which are *not*) from among the many possible bases of social grouping available within a given context (Bigler & Liben, 2006, 2007). Thus, there is reason to be optimistic about the possibility that gender, racial, and other intergroup biases might be eradicated with careful attention to messages that are given to children about such groups (discussed in the next section).

Cognitive Abilities Interact With Environments to Shape Stereotypes and Prejudice

Although social conditions affect children's in-group biases, so, too, do the cognitive skills and proclivities that children bring to understanding their social worlds. That is, knowledge of cognitive development is vital to predicting children's in-group attitudes and behavior. So, for example, research indicates that young children tend to focus on perceptually salient attributes in person-perception tasks. As a consequence, perceptually salient features such as race, gender, age, and attractiveness are much more likely to become the basis of their stereotypes and prejudices than perceptually indistinct features (e.g., some nationalities and political affiliations; e.g., Bigler, 1995; Rutland, 1999).

Cognitive development similarly affects children's response to interventions aimed at reducing stereotyping and prejudice. Although many laypersons intuitively expect children's intergroup views to be highly malleable, several cognitive characteristics of young children appear to constrain their responsive to counterstereotypic messages. For example, young children, who lack the ability to grasp individuals' simultaneous membership in nonoverlapping groups (e.g., "women" and "firefighters"), are especially likely to distort or forget counterstereotypic depictions (e.g., female firefighters; see Bigler & Liben, 1990, 1992).

Modest Personal and Group Views Are Linked to Reduced Stereotyping and Prejudice

One individual difference that has consistently predicted in-group biases within our novel group studies is self-esteem; those children with higher global self-esteem show greater in-group biases than their peers with lower global self-esteem (Bigler et al., 1997). Consistent with other theorists' views (Aboud, 1988), it appears that children project their positive self-views onto those of the in-groups (Patterson, Bigler, & Swann, 2009). That is, in contrast to the popular notion that the endorsement of intergroup biases serves to inflate self-esteem, it appears that high self-esteem promotes intergroup bias.

Based on the finding that intergroup biases are founded on excessively positive views of the in-group, one possible form of intervention involves exposing children to information about the shortcomings of their in-group. Indeed, it has long been argued that children who are members of stigmatized group members (e.g., African Americans, females, overweight individuals) show lower levels of intergroup bias because societal messages have made them well aware of their in-groups' negative characteristics. Children who are members of privileged groups might, therefore, show lower levels of intergroup bias as a result of learning about their in-groups' history of discriminatory behaviors toward a particular out-group. Results from recent studies indicate that learning about historical forms of racism (Hughes et al., 2007) and sexism (Pahlke et al., 2010; Weisgram & Bigler, 2007) can produce decreases in social stereotyping and prejudice on the basis of race and gender, respectively. In sum, children are likely to endorse fewer stereotypes and prejudices when their views of the self and in-group acknowledge both positive and negative qualities.

IMPLICATIONS

Although novel group paradigms have been useful for generating new information about the causes of stereotyping and prejudice, there is much left to learn. There remain, for example, important questions about the interaction of environmental conditions and children's cognitive proclivities in shaping their intergroup attitudes. For example, children are able to detect correlations among attributes (traits, roles) and social groups under at least some circumstances. The process of detecting correlations is likely to be influenced by cognitive abilities, group properties (perceptual salience, proportional size), self-views and self-serving biases, and attitudinal schemata (e.g., existing views of groups). Additional research is needed to understand these complex interactions. Similarly, important questions about intervention programming remain unanswered. For example, little is known about the potential positive and negative consequences of directly addressing issues of social inequality and discrimination with children.

Despite the remaining unknowns, societies committed to providing children with environments that promote positive intergroup relations might usefully draw on psychological research to guide social, educational, and legal policy. Findings from my novel group paradigm suggest that the psychological salience of particular social groups for children will increase to the extent that societies call attention to groups by, for example, labeling them routinely and presenting conditions, such as segregation, that convey the importance of group membership. Importantly, most of the factors that serve to make social groups psychologically salient are under social control. Laws, for example, constrain adults' use of some social categories to label children (e.g., federal law forbids routinely labeling children's race in classrooms) and might be extended to others (e.g., forbidding routine labeling of gender). Laws have also been used to govern the degree of racial and gender segregation within schools. Indeed, the legislative system in the United States has a history of demanding changes in adults' intergroup behavior, even when the majority of the population was against such changes (e.g., *Brown v. the Board of Education*, Title IX) and, according to many theorists (Allport, 1954), such legislation is a powerful causal agent of personal prejudice reduction. It is my hope that psychological research will continue to provide valuable information to legal and other institutions in the service of social justice and equality.

REFERENCES

Aboud, F. (1988). *Children and prejudice*. London: Blackwell.

Allport, G. W. (1954). *The nature of prejudice*. Cambridge, MA: Perseus Books.

Bigler, R. S. (1995). The role of classification skill in moderating environmental influences on children's gender stereotyping: A study of the functional use of gender in the classroom. *Child Development*, 66, 1072–1087.

Bigler, R. S. (1999). The use of multicultural curricula and materials to counter racism in children. *Journal of Social Issues*, 55, 687–705.

Bigler, R. S., Brown, C. S., & Markell, M. (2001). When groups are not created equal: Effects of group status on the formation of intergroup attitudes in children. *Child Development*, 72, 1151–1162.

Bigler, R. S., Jones, L. C., & Lobliner, D. B. (1997). Social categorization and the formation of intergroup attitudes in children. *Child Development*, 68, 530–543.

Bigler, R. S., & Liben, L. S. (1990). The role of attitudes and intervention in gender-schematic processing. *Child Development*, 61, 1440–1452.

Bigler, R. S., & Liben, L. S. (1992). Cognitive mechanisms in children's gender stereotyping: Theoretical and educational implications of a cognitive-based intervention. *Child Development*, 63, 1351–1363.

Bigler, R. S., & Liben, L. S. (2006). A developmental intergroup theory of social stereotypes and prejudice. In R. V. Kail (Ed.), *Advances in child development and behavior* (Vol. 34, pp. 39–89). San Diego, CA: Elsevier.

Bigler, R. S., & Liben, L. S. (2007). Developmental intergroup theory: Explaining and reducing children's social stereotyping and prejudice. *Current Directions in Psychological Science*, 16, 162–166.

Brown, C. S., & Bigler, R. S. (2002). Effects of minority status in the classroom on children's intergroup attitudes. *Journal of Experimental Child Psychology*, 83, 77–110.

Hughes, J. M., Bigler, R. S., & Levy, S. (2007). Consequences of learning about racism among European American and African American children. *Child Development*, 78, 1689–1705.

Lamb, L., Bigler, R. S., Liben, L. S., & Green, V. A. (2009). Teaching children to confront peers' sexist remarks: Implications for theories of gender development and educational practice. *Sex Roles: A Journal of Research, 61*, 361–382.

Pahlke, E., Bigler, R. S., & Green, V. A. (2010). Effects of learning about historical gender discrimination on middle school-aged children's occupational judgments and aspirations. *Journal of Early Adolescence, 30,* 854–894.

Patterson, M. M., & Bigler, R. S. (2006). Preschool children's attention to environmental messages about groups: Social categorization and the origins of intergroup bias. *Child Development, 77,* 847–860.

Rutland, A. (1999). The development of national prejudice, in-group favouritism and self-stereotypes in British children. *British Journal of Social Psychology, 38,* 55–70.

Weisgram, E. S., & Bigler, R. S. (2007). Effects of learning about gender discrimination on adolescent girls' attitudes toward and interest in science. *Psychology of Women Quarterly, 31,* 262–269.

5.16

What Are They Thinking?

The Mystery of Young Children's Thoughts on Race

FRANCES E. ABOUD

Children are curious and appreciative of differences. So said Gordon Allport in his book on *The Nature of Prejudice* (1954). So believed most of us. The assumption was that young children between 3 and 7 years were open and curious and in this way would learn about the world. Once learned, attitudes would soon crystallize or become hardened and unchangeable. If you could get to them early enough, it was reasoned, you could feed their curiosity with positive information about minorities. The optimistic view was that psychologists, educators, and parents had an opportunity to promote intergroup harmony and respectful attitudes toward ethnic minorities. But reality turned out to be different.

The children of 4, 5, and 6 years in my early research were not curious about my picture books of Native Indian or Black people. Even after my introductory remarks designed to make the story exciting, they repeatedly chose to read or listen to stories about White children (Aboud, 1977). Their curiosity was narrow in scope; it was about the socially approved White children, whether they themselves were White, Native Indian, or Black. Our belief that young children are curious about ethnic diversity was a myth.

White children also appeared to be not very appreciative of visible differences in skin color or hair texture. Assigning positive and negative evaluations to pictures or photos of peers from their own and other ethnic groups, children attach more negative and fewer positive evaluations to out-group than in-group peers. Not that they were hateful. Rather, they were much more appreciative of similarities. So the gap between their own group and another group of children was wide. They held strong biases favoring Whites.

Another myth I uncovered in my work was that children learned prejudice from their parents. We now know that the influence parents have on their children is overrated. My own research and that of many others since (Aboud & Doyle, 1996; Katz & Kofkin, 1997) has shown no discernible correlation between a young child's attitudes and those of the parents. Children think their ethnic attitudes are similar, but they are not. Children also think their friends hold similar ethnic attitudes, but they are no more similar than a randomly selected classmate's. Even more baffling was the finding by Branch and Newcombe (1986) that young children of Black parents who were actively involved in the civil rights movement and affirmative action were themselves pro-White, rating White people more positively than Black people. They missed the intended message regarding Black pride and instead picked up the unintended message that empowered people line up with the powerful ethnic group. Children appeared to be tuning into an ambient radio frequency—societal noise—rather than their parents' personal message.

Fortunately, young children are open and speak their mind. At least in Canada where I work, political correctness did not stop young children from voicing their opinions or negative evaluations of out-groups. Yet they were also unconcerned about playing with children who looked different whenever there were opportunities to do so. As with the research of others, my child participants appeared to have a disconnect between their negative evaluations of visible minorities and their willingness to interact (e.g., Aboud, Mendelson, & Purdy, 2003; Bar-Tal, 1996). The problem was specifically with their social cognitions. If they had no opportunity to play with an ethnically mixed group of children, their rather uncurious and fixed cognitions might dominate their repertoire. The problem was most evident with White majority children whose life experiences tended to be homogeneously in-group. Arousing children's curiosity and appreciation of visible minority differences became a challenge. Storybooks with lots of colored pictures were the medium of choice for a variety of reasons. Storybooks have the dual function of promoting literacy and social cognition. They afford teachers and parents a role to play in promoting respect for diversity. Many caregivers are anxious about saying the wrong thing, about even raising the topic of race with young children who behaved as if they were color-blind, but obviously were not. Storybooks that heaped on the positive attributes made the task easier. If children learned prejudice from adults, we assumed they would just as easily learn respect. However, the task was unexpectedly difficult.

We tried a number of different kinds of storybooks. Some were about two Black friends who shared exciting escapades and had loving and generous families. The stories provided positive evaluations of the young characters: friendly, smart, strong, helpful. In other words, the characters possessed all the positive evaluations one typically finds in a measure of attitudes. We hoped children would identify with the story characters and discover their positive attributes and individual differences. However, the children we read to did not change their attitudes. They remained steadfastly negative toward Blacks.

We then tried stories of cross-ethnic relationships. Two girl friends were so close that they decided to swap families for an evening; two boys at sea saved endangered animals. Another was about a Black girl whose father was White; the confused remarks of passersby generated enlightening father–daughter discussions. We modified the stories to suit our purposes so they exemplified close relationships, usually friendships, the children exhibited positive attributes, engaged in exciting adventures together, and their parents expressed approval. In other words, the stories depicted attractive young children, along with all the qualities necessary for harmonious contact (Allport, 1954) and all the qualities one wanted in a friend (Aboud et al., 2003). We avoided folktales, historical fiction, and heart-breaking tales of runaway slaves in favor of current real-life people with whom one could identify and become friends. Such storybooks are difficult to find on the market so we have commissioned writers and illustrators to create some.

Reading four cross-ethnic friendship stories produced some success (Aboud, 2002; Johnson & Aboud, in press). Children of 7 years became somewhat more positive toward Blacks without changing their attitude toward Whites. However, younger children of 5 and 6 years did not. They were still negative toward Blacks. Their recall of counterstereotype information about the story characters was over 90%, so the lack of change could not be attributed to poor recall. Many liked the Black story characters, but not any other Black people. Some were open about their evaluations, saying, "Those children can't be friends because they look different," "I don't like her hair," or "I don't like his skin or his clothes."

Another surprise emerged when we asked children about the attitudes of the young women who read the stories. On the basis of her photo alone, before she read the four stories, they thought she would evaluate Whites positively and Blacks negatively. This was consistent with our own and others' research showing that children assume adults are biased in favor of Whites (e.g., Aboud & Doyle, 1996). After hearing her read four stories about cross-ethnic friends, only the 7-year-olds changed their inferred evaluations, thinking now she might be somewhat positive to Blacks. The younger children continued to infer that she possessed negative attitudes. What were they thinking? Why would she have chosen four books about people who were unlikeable? The intended antibias message was lost in the unintended message that adults are biased. Perhaps adults needed to be more explicit about their attitudes and why they chose to read books about cross-ethnic friends.

A Black adult reading such books should not need to be so explicit. Children might infer that she would possess positive attitudes toward Blacks. In fact, many researchers have noted the experimenter-race effect, which refers to children minimizing their stated prejudice in the presence of an out-group experimenter. The effect demonstrates how sensitive children are to an adult's race such that they modify their own expressed attitudes to avoid her disapproval. However, the young White participants in our studies assumed the Black adult reading to them held attitudes similar to the White adult, namely positive to Whites and negative to Blacks. One norm fits all?

These findings raised questions about why it was so easy for children to learn bias and so difficult to unlearn bias and adopt more respectful attitudes. Other researchers have reported similar findings with young children. Wham, Barnhart, and Cook (1996) had teachers and parents of kindergarten children read them books on diversity with no impact on attitudes. Persson and

Musher-Eizenman (2003) showed diversity videos with little benefit. Kowalski (1998) assessed children's attitudes toward Japanese people after their kindergarten teacher helped them exchange photos, artwork, and stories with a sister school in Japan for a year. The program had no discernible effect on their attitudes toward Japanese people (see a review of these and other interventions in Aboud, Tredoux, Tropp, Brown, Niens, & Noor, 2012).

Older children's attitudes, on the other hand, appear to be less crystallized, not more. Their attitudes have been easier to influence—with storybooks, videos, and class lessons about discrimination. They may become more particular about their friends, selecting in-group over out-group friends increasingly with age. But their social cognitions are more flexible. The 7- and 8-year-olds in our research were receptive to the antibias message from the stories and from the White in-group adult who read them.

When first integrating the empirical research on the acquisition and development of children's ethnic attitudes, I noticed how inadequate was learning theory's explanation. Children's attitudes toward visible minorities did not develop gradually as predicted; bias appeared rather quickly around 4 or 5 years of age. After 7 or 8 years, attitudes moderated. Some researchers feel that this is entirely due to children's awareness that prejudice is disapproved and their reluctance to express negative views when tested. My view is that attitudes moderate as social-cognitive developments take place. They moderate as children acquire additional attitudes that I called counterbias because they run counter to what is considered bias. Counterbias attitudes, namely negative evaluations of one's in-group and positive evaluations of an out-group, increase dramatically after 7 years, while biased attitudes remain. At this age, children also understand the unfairness of prejudice and discrimination. So maturity is more than simply conforming to social norms of political correctness. It is a qualitatively different way of seeing oneself and others as Piaget predicted (Piaget & Weil, 1951).

One important principle emerging from this research is that seemingly inconsistent attitudes are additive, not subtractive. With age, children add counterbias attitudes on to their biased ones. The biased evaluations do not appear to drop out. There may be fewer situations that elicit biased evaluations, and older children may choose not to use them when reasoned thoughts are able to guide judgments and actions. But if overlearned, they may remain in memory for many years. By implication, efforts such as ours to modify children's attitudes succeed not by helping children to unlearn biases but to learn new counterbiases and seek situations that strengthen them.

A second principle is that young White children are focused on their in-group attachment. This orientation may come from children's observation that the social rules are set by Whites and from their motivation to learn the rules necessary for approval and belonging. There are indeed many rules to learn and the consequences of breaking them are isolation and humiliation from teachers and peers. So stories about minority-only children may be ineffective because there is no in-group peer with whom to identify. Stories about an in-group peer with an out-group friend may overcome this constraint. By implication, attempts to modify young children's out-group attitudes need to keep in mind that their primary focus is on a favorable in-group.

A third principle is that there are developmental constraints to learning. Whatever modeling, reward, rehearsal, and rationale is provided to young children, it needs to be tailored to their age-related mindset. At least two cognitive constraints conspire to work against our antibias message. One is that young children are egocentric and believe that their bias is correct. The second is that they believe all people think as they do. Consequently, an antibias message is incorrect and anyone who espouses it is a nonnormative outlier. Their way of thinking may be tied to biological maturation, but this is not to say prejudice is inborn or in one's genes. These constraints start to disappear by 8 years.

A measure of role-taking and reconciling differences demonstrates how cognitively mature are 8-year-olds compared to 5-year-olds (Aboud, 1981). We ask children to place pictures of people from different ethnic groups on a 60-cm board closer to the front of the board the more liked and farther away the less liked. Then comes the role-taking task where the child is shown a photo of another person and asked to take that person's role and line up the pictures according to that person' preferences. Children start to make sense with this task around 5 years. In other words, they acknowledge that a Chinese person would like a Chinese friend over a White, and a Black person a Black friend. But the ability to reconcile these differences comes later. Here is the reconciliation test question: Are both of you right or is someone wrong? Five-year-olds say that two different sets of preferences cannot both be right; most often, the other person is wrong. "Do anyone's preferences need to be changed?" we ask. Five-year-olds change the Black or Chinese child's preferences to match their own. Eight- and nine-year-olds show greater reconciliation skills by answering that the two different sets of preferences are both right. They can even provide a justification for why both are valid, namely people can like whomever they want, maybe they have friends like that. When asked whether anyone's preferences need to be changed, they are more likely to change their own, not to match the other's but to show more respect for differences. They can even justify why a White in-group person might prefer Black or Chinese people. This could be the critical social cognition that opens children's thought processes to antibias messages. When we present 5-year-olds with the logical explanation underlying reconciliation, they are more receptive to the antibias message in the storybooks. The flexibility that comes with an ability to reconcile differences opens a child's mind to different yet equally right ways to be.

The take-home message here is that we are still trying to understand why young children are less receptive than expected to our antibias messages. Starting with some basic evidence of how children evaluate different ethnic groups, we have uncovered an unexpected resistance among the youngest ones to change. They appear to distort and dismiss our antibias messages. The inadequacy of learning theory and our conventional view of children as curious and open to new ideas led to our search for a more cognitive and developmental framework. Piaget and Kohlberg provided helpful insights into how and why social cognition develops, but we are still searching for the conditions that facilitate attitude change. The task is not simply about understanding how to modify children's racial attitudes; it is about facilitating change for the better in all aspects of our life.

REFERENCES

Aboud, F. E. (1977). Interest in ethnic information: A cross-cultural developmental study. *Canadian Journal of Behavioural Science, 9*, 134–146.

Aboud, F. E. (1981). Egocentrism, conformity, and agreeing to disagree. *Developmental Psychology, 17*, 791–799.

Aboud, F. E. (2002, June). *Antibias messages and prejudice reduction in young children*. Symposium talk at the Society for the Psychological Study of Social Issues, Toronto, Canada.

Aboud, F. E., & Doyle, A. B. (1996). Parental and peer influences on children's racial attitudes. *International Journal of Intercultural Relations, 20*, 371–383.

Aboud, F. E., Mendelson, M. J., & Purdy, K. T. (2003). Cross-race peer relations and friendship quality. *International Journal of Behavioral Development, 27*(2), 165–173.

Aboud, F. E., Tredoux, C., Tropp, L. R., Brown, C. S., Niens, U., & Noor, N. M. (2012). Interventions to reduce prejudice and enhance inclusion and respect for ethnic differences in early childhood: a systematic review. *Developmental Review, 32,* 307–336.

Allport, G. W. (1954). *The nature of prejudice.* Reading, MA: Addison Wesley.

Bar-Tal, D. (1996). Development of social categories and stereotypes in early childhood: The case of "the Arab" concept formation, stereotype and attitudes by Jewish children in Israel. *International Journal of Intercultural Relations, 20*, 341–370.

Branch, C. W., & Newcombe, N. (1986). Racial attitude development among young Black children as a function of parental attitudes: A longitudinal and cross-sectional study. *Child Development, 57*, 712–721.

Johnson, P.J., & Aboud, F. E. (in press). Modifying ethnic attitudes in young children: The impact of communicator race and message strength. *International Journal of Behavioral Development*

Katz, P. A., & Kofkin, J. A. (1997) Race, gender, and young children. In S. S.Luthar, J. A. Burack, D. Cicchetti, & J. Weisz (Eds.), *Developmental psychopathology: perspectives on adjustment, risk, and disorder* (pp. 51–74). New York: Cambridge University Press.

Kowalski, K. (1998). The impact of vicarious exposure to diversity on preschoolers' ethnic/racial attitudes. *Early Child Development and Care, 146*, 41–51.

Persson, A., & Musher-Eizenman, D. R. (2003). The impact of a prejudice-prevention television program on young children's ideas about race. *Early Childhood Research Quarterly, 18*, 530–546.

Piaget, J., & Weil, A. M. (1951). The development in children of the idea of the homeland and of relations to other countries. *International Social Science Journal, 3*, 561–578.

Wham, M. A., Barnhart, J., & Cook, G. (1996). Enhancing multicultural awareness through storybook reading experience. *Journal of Research and Development in Education, 30*, 1–9.

5.17

How Do Children Learn to Actively Control Their Explicit Prejudice?

ADAM RUTLAND

Most psychologists believe that awareness of social categories is necessary for a child to fully understand his or her social world. Moreover, psychologists have long suggested that prejudice may originate from the ability to categorize the social world (e.g., Allport, 1954; Tajfel, 1978). Indeed, research suggests that early in development, children identify with social groups and that this identification has the potential to result in favoritism toward their group (i.e., in-group bias) or even prejudice toward those from other groups (i.e., negative evaluations of out-groups) (see Aboud, 1988; Killen & Rutland, 2011; Levy & Killen, 2008).

However, recent research suggests that these explicit intergroup prejudices are not inevitably the result of either a child's socialization or cognitive architecture. In this chapter we show how explicit intergroup prejudices are highly dependent on a child's active recursive reasoning about mental states and group norms (i.e., expectations about interactions between groups). This social reasoning requires an understanding of group norms about expressing explicit bias toward different types of groups and also the ability to understand other people's mental states and their attitudes or beliefs about social relationships ("Theory of Social Mind").

In this chapter, it will be contended that children actively regulate their explicit intergroup attitudes in order to manipulate the impressions of them held by valued others within their social group, and they do not simply produce or inhibit certain behaviors in accordance with societal rules. The aim of this chapter is to explain how children learn to control their explicit intergroup prejudice, when accountable to an audience, as they develop recursive reasoning about others' mental states and group norms.

We have conducted research suggesting that children's control of their prejudice requires an understanding of social norms about expressing explicit bias toward different types of groups (see Rutland, Killen, & Abrams, 2010). In turn, developing this understanding involves children acquiring certain social or moral knowledge, and social-cognitive skills, especially the ability to understand other people's mental states and their attitudes or beliefs about social relationships (see Abrams & Rutland, 2008; Killen, Rutland, & Jampol, 2008). The control of explicit ethnic bias by attending to norms of one's group that condemn explicit prejudice is likely to involve recursive reasoning about mental states, since the child is concerned about the way he or she is seen in the mind of important others.

Recursive social reasoning initially involves what developmental psychologists call "Theory of Mind" (ToM), namely the capacity to impute mental states or understand that others have beliefs, desires, and intentions that are different from one's own. Research shows children from approximately 5 years of age engage in such recursive mental state reasoning about false beliefs (i.e., understand that one person may have a false belief about another person's belief). This second-order false belief understanding, however, is known to develop well into middle childhood (Baron-Cohen, O'Riordan, Stone, Jones, & Plaisted, 1999). From around 6–7 years of age children can understand false beliefs about social, not just physical, stimuli and begin to understand about false emotions as well as false beliefs (Harris, Johnson, Hutton, Andrews, & Cooke, 1989).

Importantly, from approximately 7 years of age children develop an understanding of other people's minds and emotions that arise in *social relationships* (i.e., "Theory of Social Mind" [ToSM]). Given this, it is not surprising that with increasing age children anticipate other group members' viewpoints on expressing explicit prejudice toward other groups or peers within their own group (Abrams, Rutland, & Cameron, 2003; Abrams, Rutland, Ferrell, & Pelletier, 2008; Abrams, Rutland, Pelletier, & Ferrell, 2009). Abrams et al. (2009) measured children's ToSM by examining their ability to distinguish their own feelings about a character from the feelings of a peer who does not share the same information about that character. This requires an ability to use information about the prior social relationship between two peers to make an inference about their feelings toward one another, independently of the child's own knowledge and feelings about that peer. Abrams and colleagues (2009) found that understanding of group dynamics and norms (i.e., who will be accepted and rejected by the group) was related to the development of better social perspective-taking ability as measured by the ToSM task. Moreover, children with advanced ToSM were able to use this information to inform their prejudiced judgments of individual peer group members.

ToSM may also be important to children's ability to understand group norms about showing explicit intergroup bias and their self-presentation of explicit intergroup bias (Rutland, 2004; Rutland, Cameron, Milne, & McGeorge, 2005). This form of self-control or self-presentation is more than the ability to produce and inhibit certain thoughts or behaviors in accordance with societal rules (Bandura, 1986); rather, it is a mechanism by which children actively regulate their social attitudes in order to manipulate the impressions of them held by valued others in their group (Leary, 1996; Schlenker, 1980). In support of this argument, research indicates that school-age children, with advanced mental state understanding capacity, have the ability to understand self-presentational motives and by approximately 8 years of age can provide spontaneous explanations for complex self-presentational behavior (Banerjee & Yuill, 1999a, 1999b; Bennett & Yeeles, 1990).

GROUP NORMS AND THE CONTROL OF EXPLICIT BIAS

Is the control or self-presentation of explicit bias in childhood simply a matter of developing advanced mental state understanding or ToSM? Recent research suggests not (e.g., FitzRoy & Rutland, 2010). The process of controlling explicit biases is also likely to depend on whether a child understands that his or her group normally acts

according to moral principles (e.g., fairness). In particular, group norms about showing explicit biases affect the self-presentation of young children's explicit attitudes and their exclusion judgments of individual children within their peer group (Abrams, Rutland, Cameron, & Ferrell, 2007; FitzRoy & Rutland, 2010; Rutland et al., 2005). For example, Abrams and colleagues (2007) manipulated children's *accountability* to their own group (i.e., a summer school), in the sense that their actions were visible and may have had to be defended or could have been criticized. They were told that other children and adults in their summer school would see their answers to all the questions at the end of the study, thus making salient their own group's norm about whether to explicitly exclude or include individuals.

Summer schools in England are not comparable to a North American sleep-away summer camp, since they are nonresidential schemes that provide sports and other activities for children drawn from a variety of schools in the local area. Typically, children attend for 1 or 2 weeks, or a few days each week during the 6-week summer vacation period. The mix of children changes daily and according to the activities they pursue. These schools therefore provide a relatively "minimal" group membership with no particular history of close interpersonal relationships but with sufficient meaning and value that children evaluate their own summer school positively relative to others. In this context, then, showing explicit bias in favor of your own group and excluding individuals because they contravene the norms of your group was understood as legitimate and tolerated. Abrams and colleagues found that increasing accountability to the peer group facilitated children's desire to defend their group norms, increased their exclusion of disloyal (i.e., socially deviant or counter normative) children within their own group, and resulted in explicit intergroup bias.

Another recent study we conducted found increasing accountability actually decreased explicit intergroup bias. This study, Rutland et al. (Study 1, 2005), was conducted in the sensitive context of interracial relations in Britain, where strong social norms exist about not showing explicit racial biases. This study assessed 5- to 16-year-old White British majority status children's personal norms about ethnic exclusion, by describing to them an imaginary situation involving a group of White majority status children excluding a minority status child and asking them about how right or wrong was this racial exclusion.

Rutland and colleagues found that children who showed evidence of a stronger personal norm against racial exclusion demonstrated lower explicit prejudice toward those from a different racial group. In contrast, children with a weaker personal norm about racial exclusion (i.e., they thought the racial exclusion was relatively less bad) only inhibited their prejudice when the contrary social norm of their own White British majority status group was made highly salient by increasing their accountability to this group. An increase in accountability was achieved by making the children think their answers were being recorded on video and could be shown to other children and adults from their own racial group.

We are showing here that when White British majority status children who have the potential to show racial prejudice because they have relatively weak personal norm are made accountable to their own group, they "put the brakes upon their prejudices. They do not act them out—or they act them out only up to a certain point. Something stops the logical progression somewhere" (Allport, 1954, p. 332). Writing in the United States during the 1950s, Allport described a few examples of such situations when adults attempt to control their racial prejudice. The study described earlier by Rutland and colleagues (2005) suggests that children also at times show such explicit prejudice control. Nonetheless, little is known about the "something" that Allport said helps stop the development of explicit prejudice, especially among children who are known to show intergroup bias at an early age.

PROCESSES UNDERLYING THE CONTROL OF EXPLICIT PREJUDICE

To address how White majority status children control their explicit prejudice, we examined important affective and social-cognitive processes involved in the inhibition of ethnic prejudice (FitzRoy & Rutland, 2010). This research revealed that *both* children's ToSM and their understanding of their group's social norm about showing explicit bias moderated how their explicit ethnic bias changed when made accountable (in a similar way to the previous study by Abrams et al., 2007).

In contrast to previous studies (e.g., Rutland et al., 2005) that have assessed children's personal norm about showing ethnic exclusion, FitzRoy and Rutland (2010) examined their awareness of their own group's social norm about showing ethnic prejudice. Then they manipulated children's accountability to their own ethnic group, so it was either relatively low (i.e., only a researcher from the child's own ethnic group was present) or it was relatively high (i.e., a researcher from the child's own ethnic group was present and the children thought their answers would be shown to classmates and teachers from the child's ethnic group). In Study 2, FitzRoy and Rutland (2010) found children with high ToSM scores showed little ethnic bias irrespective of the level of public accountability. They also found that when children were not aware their own group held an anti-prejudice norm, their ethnic bias was unaffected by manipulating public accountability. However, when children understood their group held an anti-prejudice norm, children with low ToSM scores significantly decreased their ethnic bias when public accountability was made relatively higher.

The key finding here is that children with low ToSM scores, who were not able to readily or easily attend to the norms of their group about not showing ethnic bias, only controlled their explicit bias when they had some awareness that their own group would not show ethnic bias and this norm was made salient by increasing their accountability to their group. This study for the first time revealed that children's ToSM and awareness of their own group's norm together are important processes in how they learn to control their explicit ethnic bias. These findings go beyond previous research showing that children control their prejudice by highlighting how social-cognitive and normative processes combine during the process of ethnic bias control in childhood (Abrams & Rutland, 2008; Nesdale, 2004; Rutland et al., 2005).

What other factors encourage people to control their explicit ethnic attitudes? Research with adults suggests social emotions (e.g., guilt and embarrassment) might be important. Therefore, FitzRoy and Rutland (Study 1) also considered whether children's propensity to show embarrassment influenced their level of explicit ethnic bias when being made accountable to their own ethnic group. They measured children's self-attribution of embarrassment by presenting a child with a hypothetical scenario involving a rule violation that included the child being responsible for a younger friend. The children with high social emotions were more likely to say they would feel embarrassed in this situation.

It was found that 8- to 9-year-old children's propensity to show embarrassment moderated their ability to control explicit ethnic bias. The ethnic attitudes of the younger children

(6–7 years old), who overall showed little tendency to attribute social emotions, were as expected unaffected by the public accountability manipulation. Also as predicted, we found that 8- to 9-year-old children with a higher individual propensity to attribute embarrassment were unaffected by the public accountability manipulation. In contrast, 8- to 9-year-olds with a low individual propensity to show social emotions controlled their ethnic intergroup bias when public accountability was increased. Arguably, these children under low accountability did not establish that they and their group would feel social emotions (e.g., embarrassment) when expressing explicit ethnic bias and only did so when made highly accountable to their own group.

Children's social emotions (i.e., their ability to show embarrassment) acted in a similar way as ToSM in enabling children to control their explicit bias. Children low in both social emotions and ToSM suppressed their bias when made accountable to their group. These findings suggest that children's understanding of social emotions and ToSM are interrelated. Namely, children who show the ability to understand others' mental states about emotions within social relationships are more likely to feel social emotions like embarrassment. Indeed, previous research has suggested that the attribution of social emotions such as embarrassment is associated with recursive cognitions about others' mental states and second-order mental state understanding (Banerjee, 2002). The studies conducted by FitzRoy and Rutland (2010) suggest a child's developing capacity to understand his or her social emotions and beliefs, and how they might be different or the same as others' social emotions and beliefs, is important if the child is to control his or her intergroup bias. This type of recursive reasoning about emotions and mental states in group contexts arguably offers the child the potential to frame his or her group attitudes to create a positive image among members of the child's own group (i.e., engage in self-presentation).

It is worth noting that such recursive social reasoning may not always result in low explicit bias, since children's control of their explicit attitudes toward social groups depends on the specific norms children perceive to be held by their own group to which they are most often accountable. Explicit prejudice control also appears to depend on when children develop enough social knowledge to the extent that they know whether their group will or will not tolerate explicit bias against an out-group.

Typically, group norms in North American and European societies condemn explicit *racial* or *ethnic* prejudice, and subsequently children's self-presentation of these attitudes results in the control of prejudice. In contrast, the story can be very different when considering social norms and explicit attitudes toward social groups based upon categories other than race or ethnicity. For example, take prejudice based upon the social category of nationality. Pro-bias norms regarding other nationalities have been found before in studies with White European children in either Britain (e.g., Abrams et al., 2003; Rutland, 1999) or the Netherlands (e.g., Verkuyten, 2001). Therefore, unsurprisingly, Rutland et al. (2005–Study 2) found that 10- to 12-year-old White British children *increased* their explicit national bias when they thought they were accountable to their own group, which held a norm that such explicit bias was tolerable. These studies show that the self-presentation process can also operate to promote explicit biases in attitude domains other than race (e.g., nationality, gender or school group).

To conclude, the research described herein demonstrates that children will not inevitably show explicit intergroup prejudice, either because they passively absorb others' attitudes or because it automatically results from their social categorization of the world. Instead, research suggests children's attitudes are a product of their recursive social reasoning about mental states and group norms.

ACKNOWLEDGMENTS

Thanks to my collaborators who worked with me on the research described in this chapter: Dominic Abrams, Lindsey Cameron, Sarah FitzRoy, Alan Milne, Peter McGeorge, and Jennifer Ferrell. Thanks also to Melanie Killen, who commented on drafts of this chapter.

REFERENCES

Aboud, F. E. (1988). *Children and prejudice* Oxford, England: Blackwell.

Abrams, D., & Rutland, A. (2008). The development of subjective group dynamics. In S. Levy & M. Killen (Eds.), *Intergroup attitudes and relations in childhood through adulthood* (pp. 47–65). Oxford, England: Oxford University Press.

Abrams, D., Rutland, A., & Cameron, L. (2003). The development of subjective group dynamics: Children's judgments of normative and deviant in-group and out-group individuals. *Child Development, 74,* 1840–1856.

Abrams, D., Rutland, A., Cameron, L., & Ferrell, J. M. (2007). Older but wilier: Ingroup accountability and the development of subjective group dynamics. *Developmental Psychology, 43*(1), 134–148.

Abrams, D., Rutland, A., Ferrell, J. M., & Pelletier, J. (2008). Children's judgments of disloyal and immoral peer behavior: Subjective group dynamics in minimal intergroup contexts. *Child Development, 79*(2), 444–461.

Abrams, D., Rutland, A., Pelletier, J., & Ferrell, J. (2009). Children's group nous: understanding and applying peer exclusion within and between groups. *Child Development, 80*, 224–243.

Allport, G. W. (1954). *The nature of prejudice.* New York: Doubleday Anchor Books.

Bandura, A. (1986). *Social foundations of thought and action: A social cognitive theory.* Englewood Cliffs, NJ: Prentice-Hall.

Banerjee, R. (2002). Audience effects on self-presentation in childhood. *Social Development, 11*, 487–507.

Banerjee, R., & Yuill, N. (1999a). Children's explanations of self-presentational behaviour. *European Journal of Social Psychology, 29*, 105–111.

Banerjee, R., & Yuill, N. (1999b). Children's understanding of self-presentational display rules: Associations with mental-state understanding. *British Journal of Developmental Psychology, 17*, 111–124.

Baron-Cohen, S., O'Riordan, M., Stone, V., Jones, R., & Plaisted, K. (1999). Recognition of faux pas by normally developing children and children with Asperger syndrome or high-functioning autism. *Journal of Autism and Developmental Disorders, 29*(5), 407–418.

Bennett, M., & Yeeles, C. (1990). Children's understanding of the self-presentational strategies of ingratiation and self-promotion. *European Journal of Social Psychology, 20*, 455–461.

FitzRoy, S., & Rutland, A. (2010). Learning to control ethnic intergroup bias in childhood. *European Journal of Social Psychology, 40*, 679–693.

Harris, P., Johnson, C. N., Hutton, D., Andrews, G., & Cooke, T. (1989). Young children's theory of mind and emotion. *Cognition and Emotion, 3*, 379–400.

Killen, M., & Rutland, A. (2011). *Children and social exclusion: Morality, prejudice and group identity.* Oxford, England: Wiley-Blackwell.

Killen, M., Rutland, A., & Jampol, N. (2008). Social exclusion in middle childhood and early adolescence. In K. H. Rubin, W. Bukowski & B. Laurenson (Eds.), *Handbook of peer interactions, relationships and groups* (pp. 249–266). New York: Guilford Press.

Leary, M. R. (1996). *Self-presentation: Impression management and interpersonal behaviour.* Boulder, CO: Westview Press.

Levy, S., & Killen, M. (2008). *Intergroup attitudes and relations in childhood through adulthood.* Oxford, England: Oxford University Press.

Nesdale, D. (2004). Social identity processes and children's ethnic prejudice. In M. Bennett & F. Sani (Eds.), *The development of the social self* (pp. 219–245). Hove, England: Sage.

Rutland, A. (1999). The development of national prejudice, ingroup favouritism and self stereotypes in British children. *British Journal of Social Psychology, 38*, 55–70.

Rutland, A. (2004). The development and self-regulation of intergroup attitudes in children. In M. Bennett & F. Sani (Eds.), *The development of the social self* (pp. 247–265). East Sussex, England: Psychology Press.

Rutland, A., Cameron, L., Milne, A., & McGeorge, P. (2005). Social norms and self-presentation: Children's implicit and explicit intergroup attitudes. *Child Development, 76*(2), 451–466.

Rutland, A., Killen, M., & Abrams, D. (2010). A new social-cognitive developmental perspective on prejudice: The interplay between morality and group identity. *Perspectives on Psychological Science, 5*, 279–291.

Schlenker, B. R. (1980). Impression management: The self-concept, social identity, and interpersonal relations. Monterey, CA: Brooks/Cole.

Tajfel, H. (1978). Social categorization, social identity and social comparison. In H. Tajfel (Ed.), *Differentiation between social groups: Studies in the social psychology of intergroup relations* (pp. 61–76). London: Academic Press.

Verkuyten, M. (2001). National identification and intergroup evaluations in Dutch children. *British Journal of Developmental Psychology, 19*(4), 559.

SECTION VI —————————

Good and Evil

6.1

What Primates Can Tell Us About the Surprising Nature of Human Choice

LAURIE R. SANTOS AND LOUISA C. EGAN BRAD

Psychologists interested in the nature of human social cognition face a problem that other scientists do not. A physicist studying the nature of a black hole does not have to worry about his own intuitive notion of what it *means* to be a black hole. Likewise, a molecular biologist has no personal phenomenology associated with the protein she is studying. Psychologists, however, do not have this luxury. Psychologists often find themselves probing into phenomena that they themselves *intuitively experience*: things like choices, preferences, and attitudes. The study of human social cognition necessitates poking about into phenomena that we—as experiencers of our own human cognition—think we know about intimately. Although psychological scientists have developed an impressive number of creative tools for studying these psychological phenomena in unbiased, objective ways (e.g., Bargh, 2006; Greenwald & Banaji, 1995), the fact that people *experience* their own psychological processes can make the study of human social cognition a tricky sort of enterprise, particularly when it comes to convincing people about the verity of our sometimes-unintuitive empirical results. This is especially true in cases where our objective empirical findings about how a particular process actually works directly conflict with our own subjective experience of how that process *seems* to work.

One area in which this tension between subjective experience and empirical findings has become particularly salient is in the study of human choice behavior. As humans, our lives are intimately defined by the choices we make each day. Our choices determine big things like where to live and work, as well as innumerable smaller issues like what shirt to wear, which cereal box to purchase, and exactly how to word a sentence in an e-mail. We also tend to have a very salient phenomenology associated with the act of making

choices. Most of the time, we feel as though our choices satisfy a number of reasonable criteria: We think our choices are free (they are made of our own volition and not dictated by outside circumstances), deliberate (they result from our own initiative and intentions), and rational (they are executed in ways that are meant to satisfy our stable preferences). Unfortunately, recent social psychological research suggests that most of our decisions do not work this way. Indeed, a growing body of work suggests that many aspects of human choice violate our subjective intuitions about how choice works. First, a growing body of empirical work suggests our choices are often less free than we think. A variety of new findings suggest that human choice is affected by a number of (often irrelevant) contextual factors (e.g., Kahneman, Slovic, & Tversky, 1982). Second, our choices are not always as salient to us as they feel. Psychologists have learned that we do not represent the content of our choices nearly as well as we feel we do (e.g., Johansson, Hall, Sikstrom, & Olsson, 2005). Finally, the road from preferences to choices does not seem to be a one-way street; instead, researchers have found that our preferences can be manipulated by the act of choosing (e.g., Ariely & Norton, 2008; Harmon-Jones & Mills, 1999).

Such findings pose a real threat to our intuitive idea of what it means to be a human acting on the basis of a free and rational will. But some of the most daunting empirical insights into the nature of human choice have not come from studying *humans*. Over the last few years, researchers have begun to gain insights into the nature and origins of human choice by turning to our closest living evolutionary relatives: nonhuman primates. Such work has revealed that many surprising aspects of human choice appear to be shared fairly broadly across the primate order. Indeed, some of the most counterintuitive aspects of human choice appear to be more evolutionarily ancient than we thought. Here, we review two of the most counterintuitive aspects of our own choices and discuss why understanding the evolutionary origins of these counterintuitive features can provide insights into how human choice really works.

THE CONSEQUENCES OF CHOOSING: HOW OUR DECISIONS LEAD OUR PREFERENCES ASTRAY

Imagine you have been asked to take part in a consumer rating study. You are presented with an array of different kinds of household items and asked to rate how much you like each of these items by marking a line on an eight-point scale. After rating all the different items, the experimenter running the study tells you that you will be able to take one of the items home at the end of the experiment. You are then allowed to choose between two of the objects that you have rated about equally. After deliberating for a bit, you make your choice and are given your item.

Intuitively, this sort of choice situation seems pretty straightforward. It is easy to imagine rating a set of items on the basis of our preferences and then choosing one of two possible items. What is unintuitive, however, is what happens to our preferences *after* we make our choice. Instinctively, one might assume that our preferences are stable features of our psychology, and thus nothing about them should change after making one little decision. To explore whether this intuitive model is accurate, Brehm (1956) presented people with this very situation and looked at what happened to people's preference ratings after they made their choice. Interestingly, he found that people's preferences after their choice were not the same as they were before the choice—people changed their preferences to match their decision. Specifically, participants rated the item they had chosen more highly than they had originally, and they rated the rejected item lower than in their original ratings. Although people fail to realize it, the act of choosing against an item seems to have consequences—choosing changes our future preferences by altering them to better fit with our decision, even in cases in which the decision itself is arbitrary (see also Sharot, Velasquez, & Dolan, 2010).

In the 50 years since Brehm's original observations, researchers have seen countless examples of these choice-induced preference changes in action (see review in Egan, Bloom, & Santos, 2010; Harmon-Jones & Mills, 1999). Until recently, however, little work had explored the origins of this strange tendency. Could it be that this process is a fundamental aspect of the way we make decisions? Or is this phenomenon instead more experience-dependent, one that emerges from the kinds of complex decisions we make over our life course? To get at this issue, we (Egan, Santos, & Bloom, 2007) explored whether choice-induced preference change is exhibited in a population that lacks experience with human choices: brown capuchin monkeys (*Cebus apella*). Capuchin monkeys are a small New World primate that last shared a common ancestor with humans approximately 35 million years ago. As such, they represent one of our evolutionarily distant relatives, and are thus a perfect population in which to study the evolutionary origins of choice-induced preference changes.

To explore whether monkeys' preferences are affected by their decisions, we adapted Brehm's famous choice task for use with our nonverbal capuchin subjects. We first found a set of objects for the monkeys to choose between: different-colored M&Ms candies. We then allowed our monkeys to make a choice between two M&Ms of different colors—let's say red and blue—and then tested how this choice affected monkeys' preference for the color they chose against. To test this, we gave the monkeys a second choice between an M&M of the color they rejected and another M&M of a third color (e.g., green). We found that monkeys' preference for the rejected M&M changed after making a choice against it. Monkeys reliably preferred the novel colored M&M color over the rejected color, suggesting that choosing against an item might change the monkeys' preferences as well. Importantly, we found that such preference changes do not occur in cases in which the monkeys *themselves* are not involved in the choice. In a control condition in which the experimenter made the choice for the monkey, our subjects did not show any subsequent preference changes, suggesting that it is the act of choosing that causes the monkeys to alter their future preferences.

The capuchin results provide striking evidence that choice-induced preference changes are not an evolutionarily recent phenomenon. In particular, these findings suggest that members of a species that lacks experience with the complex choices of humans still demonstrate an identical process of altering their preferences to fit with their decisions. In this way, the primate findings provide important insight into our understanding of human choice processes. Finding qualitatively similar biases in a distantly related monkey species demonstrates that this counterintuitive aspect of human choice behavior seems to be a very basic process, a part of our psychological machinery that evolved long ago and thus may be an integral part of how our decisions operate.

THE CREDULITY OF CHOICE: WHEN THE RESULTS OF OUR CHOICES ARE NOT WHAT THEY SEEM

Another intuitive aspect of our choices that has come under recent empirical fire is the extent to which we have insight into the preferences that bear on our choices. Instinctively, it seems obvious that we *know* what we prefer and what we do not. However, recent empirical work has called even this basic intuition into question (see Ariely & Norton, 2008 for a review). In a recent demonstration, Johansson and colleagues (2005) presented people with two photographs of women's faces and asked them to choose the one that was more attractive. After people made their choice, the experimenter removed the rejected photo and then asked participants to describe why they chose the photo they did, giving them a second chance to look at the chosen photo. Through a bit of sleight of hand, the experimenter sometimes replaced the chosen photo with the rejected one. This means that when participants began their explanation, they were unknowingly looking at the photo they had rejected, not the one they had selected. Surprisingly, the majority of participants did not notice the switch, suggesting that people fail to remember which photograph they actually preferred. In this and other studies (e.g., Hall et al., 2010), people seem oblivious to choices they have made just moments before.

In addition to not noticing what we have chosen, we are also more susceptible than we realize to feeling as though we have made a choice when in fact our "choice" was actually predetermined (Nisbett & Wilson, 1977). In one recent example, Sharot and colleagues (2010) gave participants a cover story in which they were told about the possibility of making subliminal choices. She then presented them with an arbitrary choice between two strings of symbols that participants were led to believe was in fact a true "subliminal" choice between different vacation options that were masked behind the string. After choosing one of the two strings (presumably randomly), people

were then shown a particular vacation option that was meant to be what was behind the masked string. Participants not only bought into this manipulation, but even more surprisingly, they showed choice-induced preference changes after their manipulated choice. Specifically, in line with the Brehm (1956) effects discussed earlier, participants decreased their rating of vacation options that they believed they had chosen against.

In this way, people seem to be oblivious to the preferences that guide their choices. Indeed, people seem so blind to these manipulations that they allow illusions of choice to affect their future preferences. But could this counterintuitive feature of human choice also represent a basic, evolutionarily preserved aspect of human choice behavior? To get at this issue, we (Egan et al., 2010) decided to see whether capuchin monkeys could be similarly misled about the nature of their own choices and preferences. First, we developed a situation in which we could convince our capuchin subjects that they had made a real choice in cases in which they actually had no freedom to exercise a choice. We capitalized on an enrichment game that our subjects play in which pieces of food are placed into a bin filled with wood shavings. The monkeys are allowed to search the bin and retrieve whichever food rewards they choose before being asked to leave the testing enclosure. Typically, monkeys will retrieve some but not all of the food, suggesting that they see this foraging game as a chance to make a choice about which foods they really want. In our study, we set up a "rigged" version of this foraging game; although it seemed to the monkeys that they had a choice over which of two possible foods to retrieve, the experimenter had surreptitiously rigged their choice by placing only one kind of food in the bin. More specifically, although it looked to the monkeys as though the experimenter had hidden pieces of two different kinds of food in the bin, in reality only one piece of food was available for them to find. In this way, when the monkeys foraged for the hidden food, they were forced to find a specific kind of food, despite the fact that it appeared as though they should have a choice. After monkeys underwent this foraging choice illusion, we then gave them a true choice between the kind of food they thought they left behind and a novel kind of food. In this subsequent choice, the monkeys had full visual access to both options and made their choice freely. In accordance with the results from human participants (Sharot et al., 2010), our capuchin subjects continued avoiding the kind of food they thought they had chosen against. These results suggest that like people, capuchins may not fully grasp the nature of their own preferences and can thus become blind to the content of their past choices. Moreover, these results suggest that capuchins update their preferences after their choices even in cases where the choices themselves are not actually real decisions.

CONCLUSIONS: TAKING AN EVOLUTIONARY APPROACH TO CHOICE

Despite a lifetime of making choices, our intuitions seem to tell us little about how human decision making actually works. As reviewed earlier, recent work in social psychology suggests that real human decision making violates a number of maxims we believe our choices obey. First, we do not seem to know the preferences that guide our decision making and can fall prey to the illusion that we have made a choice even in cases where we had no freedom to make one. Second, our choices appear to shape our preferences more than we realize. Even the simple act of making one decision can alter the way we think about the options involved in that decision. Finally, we experience choice-based preference changes not just in cases of real decisions; recent work suggests that even the illusion of a choice can shape the way our future preferences work. In all these ways, the real psychological processes that constitute our choices and preferences violate many of our intuitions about how our decisions actually work.

Perhaps even more surprisingly, these irrational choice process are not unique to our species. Our findings with capuchin monkeys suggest that nonhuman primate choice falls short in the same ways as human choice does. Like humans, monkeys allow their arbitrary choices to affect their future preferences. In addition, monkeys appear equally susceptible to illusions that they are free to choose; they too can be convinced that they made a choice in cases in which their hands were forced. In this way, the psychological processes that are foreign to our own intuitions appear to be central not just to our own decision making but to the choices of other primates as well. This pattern of results suggests our own biased choice strategies result from a long evolutionary history.

The discovery that human choice biases are shared across the primate order provides several important insights both into how these processes work and how they evolved. First, observing qualitatively similar choice biases in human and nonhuman primates provides an important hint that these biases are incredibly robust. Capuchins and humans face strikingly different kinds of decisions and have different levels of cognitive complexity, yet both species demonstrate qualitatively similar decision-making processes. In this way, the capuchin findings suggest that human choice biases are likely to be deeply ingrained and fundamental to the way we make decisions. Moreover, the capuchin results hint that our own choice processes may be more impervious to explicit knowledge or top-down strategies than we would like to admit (see Lakshminarayanan and Santos, 2011 for more discussion of this issue).

The comparative study of choice processes also provides some clarity about the evolutionary history of these surprising processes. At first glance, the choice biases we have reviewed might appear to be rather poor strategies from an evolutionary perspective. Changing one's preferences to match one's decisions and forgetting the content of one's choices both appear to be relatively disadvantageous cognitive processes. Nevertheless, our capuchin studies suggest that such biased mechanisms have survived 35 million years of selection pressures, forces that surely would have selected against these mechanisms if they were indeed detrimental. In this way, the comparative work reviewed here hints that our choice biases may not be as detrimental as we might think. Indeed, it is possible that such biases may even be adaptive under some circumstances (see Lakshminarayanan & Santos, 2011) or result from some greater process that is itself adaptive.

The surprises we have encountered about the nature of our own choice processes are an important lesson in the problems of introspection more broadly. Luckily, psychologists have developed an amazing empirical tool-kit for objectively exploring the psychological mechanisms that make us who we are. The answers we have obtained sometimes shock us but are exceedingly valuable for a richer representation of how our preferences and decisions operate. As we are products of our evolutionary history, an understanding of similar processes in our close primate relatives provides yet another tool that can help us to advance our understanding of our own selves.

REFERENCES

Ariely, D., & Norton, M. I. (2008). How actions create—not just reveal—preferences. *Trends in Cognitive Sciences*, 12, 13–16.

Bargh, J. A. (Ed.). (2006). *Social psychology and the unconscious: The automaticity of higher mental processes*. Philadelphia, PA: Psychology Press.

Brehm, J. W. (1956). Postdecision changes in the desirability of alternatives. *Journal of Abnormal and Social Psychology, 52*, 384–389.

Egan, L. C., Bloom, P., & Santos, L. R. (2010). Choice-induced preferences in the absence of choice: Evidence from a blind two choice paradigm with young children and capuchin monkeys. *Journal of Experimental Social Psychology, 46*, 204–207.

Egan, L. C., Santos, L. R., & Bloom, P. (2007). The origins of cognitive dissonance: Evidence from children and monkeys. *Psychological Science, 18*, 978–983.

Hall, L., Johansson, P., Tärning, B., Sikström, S., & Deutgen, T. (2010). Magic at the marketplace: Choice blindness for the taste of jam and the smell of tea. *Cognition, 17*, 54–61.

Greenwald, A. G., & Banaji, M. R. (1995). Implicit social cognition: Attitudes, self-esteem, and stereotypes. *Psychological Review, 102*, 4–27.

Harmon-Jones, E., & Mills, J. (1999). *Cognitive dissonance: Progress on a pivotal theory in social psychology*. Washington, DC: American Psychological Association.

Johansson, P., Hall, L., Sikstrom, S., & Olsson, A. (2005). Failure to detect mismatches between intention and outcome in a simple decision task. *Science, 310*, 116–119.

Kahneman, D., Slovic, P., & Tversky, A. (Eds.). (1982). *Judgment under uncertainty: Heuristics and Biases*. Cambridge, England: Cambridge University Press.

Lakshminarayanan, V. and Santos, L. R. (2011). The evolution of our preferences: Insights from nonhuman primates. In R. Dolan & T. Sharot (Eds.) *Neuroscience of Preference and Choice: Cognitive and Neural Mechanisms*. NewYork: Academic Press 75-93.

Nisbett, R., & Wilson, T. (1977). Telling more than we can know: Verbal reports on mental processes. *Psychological Review, 84*, 231–259.

Sharot, T., Velasquez, C. M., & Dolan, R. J. (2010). Do decisions shape preference? Evidence from blind choice. *Psychological Science, 21*, 1231–1235.

6.2

Horrible Children

The Limits of Natural Morality

PAUL BLOOM

Thomas Hobbes argued that man "must be naturally wicked...he is vicious because he does not know virtue." Without government to restrain us, we would exist in a state of total war. Our lives would be "solitary, poor, nasty, brutish, and short." This view has been endorsed and developed by prominent psychologists, such as Sigmund Freud, who argue that morality must be imposed from above. It is the task of society, and particularly of parents, to transform babies from little psychopaths into civilized beings who experience empathy, guilt, and shame and who are sensitive to the demands of fairness and justice.

There is now considerable evidence that this is mistaken. Some degree of sociality, of concern for others, perhaps even of morality, is part of human nature. This insight comes from many disciplines. Evolutionary theorists have discovered the adaptive logic behind altruistic behavior toward those we are related to and those we frequently interact with. Social psychologists and social neuroscientists have found specialized psychological and neural mechanisms that underlie empathy and compassion. Research from behavioral economics suggests that people are motivated by concerns such as fairness, equity, and reciprocity, not merely self-interest. And there is anecdotal and experimental evidence that other primates possess at least some of these social and moral capacities.

Some of the most striking findings come from the field of child development (see Bloom, 2011, for review). Like many other animals, human babies are sensitive to the pain of other members of their species; they find it aversive to see or hear others suffer. As soon as they are able to, they often try to assuage this suffering—1-year-olds soothe others in distress by stroking and touching or by handing over a bottle or toy. And when toddlers are put into a situation in which an adult is struggling to get something done, like opening a cabinet door with his hands full, they tend to spontaneously help, even without any prompting, encouragement, or reward.

Some of my own research has explored early-emerging moral evaluation (see also Chapter 1.5). In our studies, we show babies one-act morality plays. For instance, a character struggles to get up a hill, and either a second character pushes him up or a third character pushes him down. Children and babies are sensitive to the difference between the helper and the hinderer. If you ask toddlers at 19 months of age, "Who is the nice guy?" and "Who is the mean guy?" they point to the helper as the nice guy, and the hinderer as the mean guy. Six-month-olds prefer to reach for the helper over the hinderer, and 3-month-olds prefer to look at the helper. Twenty-one-month-olds tend to reward the helper and punish the hinderer, and 8-month-olds prefer someone who rewards a helper (by adult lights, a just response) to one who punishes a helper (an unjust response).

There are few Hobbesians left in psychology. Many scholars would now endorse the position of Hobbes's critic, Jean-Jacques Rousseau, who defended the notion of the Noble Savage. For Rousseau, the state of nature would not be total war; rather "uncorrupted morals" would prevail. We are essentially kind and moral beings. This view has been defended in recent books by prominent scholars such as Frans de Waal (*The Age of Empathy*) and Dacher Keltner (*Born to Be Good*). Keltner and his colleagues begin the introduction of the recently published collection *The Compassionate Instinct* on a triumphant note: "We are witnessing a revolution in the scientific understanding of human nature" (Keltner, Smith, & Marsh, 2010, p. 5).

In this brief chapter, I want to mount a counterrevolution. I agree that humans possess inborn tendencies toward kindness and compassion, and possess a surprisingly rich moral sense. But these are constrained in important ways. Our sociality and morality naturally extend toward those who are close to us, to those we see as family, and to those who fall into our social groups. We have no natural affinity for the rest of humanity. Rousseau is correct, then, when it comes to the family and the community. But Hobbes is right for everyone else. We are Noble Savages at home, nasty and brutish elsewhere.

There is an evolutionary logic to this distinction. Our social instincts have evolved to help us deal with those that we are in continued interaction with, in part to cope with situations in which selfish short-term desires must be suppressed for maximum gain. Our ancestors who were inclined to help others, to be gratified by the help of others, and motivated to punish those who defect, would have out-reproduced those without these sentiments, and this is why we possess these sentiments today. But the same logic of natural selection dictates that these altruistic and moralizing impulses should be *parochial*—there is a strong reproductive benefit to being biased to favor friends and family, and one would expect this to be incorporated as part of any innate moral sense. (Imagine a mother who made no distinction between the hunger of her own baby and the hunger of another baby, and think of her reproductive success relative to one who loved her own baby the most.)

So far, this is uncontroversial. One does not need to do a scientific study to know that people give *some* moral and emotional priority to family and friends and neighbors—we care about them more and we feel more of a moral obligation toward them. But I would like to explore two stronger claims about the limitations of human kindness.

First, *We choose sides early on*. Children and even babies are highly prone to categorize the world into Us versus Them—and to favor Us (see Olson & Dweck, 2009, for review). This begins with a simple preference for the familiar. A baby would rather look at her mother's face than the face of a stranger and would rather listen to her mother's voice than the voice of a stranger. Babies prefer to listen to their native language. Babies who are raised in White households prefer to look at White people; those raised in Black households prefer to look at Black people. Young children

prefer to imitate and learn from and associate with those who look like them and who speak the same language.

The most striking example of the child's eagerness to engage in Us/Them categorization comes from studies building on Henri Taijfel's classic work on "minimal groups." There are now several studies finding that it is fairly easy to get young children to favor their own group over others, even when the groups are formed in the most minimal and arbitrary of ways, such as children in a classrroom being randomly assigned red versus blue t-shirts (see Dunham, Baron, & Banaji, 2008 for review).

Now, these distinctions are all subtle—they pertain to subgroups of Us. A red t-shirt child might give more money to a red t-shirt than to a blue t-shirt child, but both children are thought of as classmates and will typically elicit a positive emotional response. Compare this to our reaction to strangers. Around the age of 9 months, as children's mobility increases, they show what is called "stranger anxiety," where they are terrified by new people. Children come to partially subdue this response in the months that follow, but some degree of xenophobia never goes away and seems to capture a universal default. The second claim, then, is that *We have no natural affinity toward strangers*. Toward them, we are Hobbesian.

This is most apparent in small-scale societies. Jared Diamond talks about hunter-gatherer societies in Papua New Guinea and notes: "To venture out of one's territory to meet other humans, even if they lived only a few miles away, was equivalent to suicide." Margaret Mead was famously romantic about the lifestyles of these communities, viewing them as morally superior in many regards to modern societies. But in an interview, she was blunt about their feelings toward strangers: "Most primitive tribes feel that if you run across one of these subhumans from a rival group in the forest, the most appropriate thing to do is bludgeon him to death." We do manage to overcome this extreme parochialism—human groups do eventually come to cooperate, trade, and intermarry—but our natural default is to hate and fear strangers.

Strangers are also often disgusting. This is an observation made by Charles Darwin, always an honest observer of his own reactions: "In Tierra del Fuego a native touched with his fingers some cold preserved meat which I was eating at our bivouac, and plainly showed utter disgust at its softness; whilst I felt utter disgust at my food being touched by a naked savage, though his hands did not appear dirty." People from out-groups often inspire disgust. There is a logic to this—one candidate for the evolutionary function of disgust is disease avoidance, and strangers carry disease. Disgust toward strangers might be terrible morality, but it was excellent epidemiology.

Plainly, most modern humans are better than this. Contemporary humans override these feelings toward strangers. When one flies into a strange airport, the odds of being bludgeoned to death at the arrival gate are relatively low. Indeed, many of us care about strangers in faraway lands, sometimes to the extent that we give up resources that could be used for our friends and family, such as money and even blood. We possess abstract moral notions of equality and freedom for all; we see racism and sexism as evil; we reject slavery and genocide; we try to love our enemies. Of course, our actions typically fall short, often far short, of our moral principles, but these principles do shape, in a substantial way, the world that we live in. But none of this is natural. These ideas and actions are the products of culture; they do not come naturally and are not present in young children.

One can test this claim using the tools of behavioral economics. One of the main findings of that field is that, when playing simple economic games, people apply norms of fairness and reciprocity to anonymous strangers, even at a cost to themselves. These methods can be extended developmentally and cross-culturally to explore the emergence of these moral norms. Consider the Dictator Game. In a typical study, subjects are told that they will play with a stranger who will never know their identity. They are then given a sum of money and told that they can give as much of the money as they want to the stranger. If people are selfish maximizers, the solution is obvious: Why give money to a stranger? But most people do give, and the average gift is between 20% and 30%, with some studies finding considerably more.

The usual interpretation is that this giving reflects an egalitarian impulse; the subject feels that it is wrong to have so much more than this other person. Some scholars are skeptical, however. People are often generous in the real world, but our kindness is toward those we love, or those who approach us for help, or those who we believe are in need—not to anonymous strangers. (If you found two ten dollar bills in the street, would you hand one of them over the next stranger you saw?) One alternative—supported by experimental evidence (e.g., List, 2007)—is that the giving

behavior is in part due to demand characteristics; it is motivated by a desire to be seen as doing the right thing, as being a good person in front of the experimenter, and not out of an interest in the welfare of the stranger.

Still, regardless of the precise psychological mechanism, the adults in these studies *do* give up resources for strangers, which is decidedly non-Hobbesian. The critical question, for our purposes, is whether this is the product of culture or whether it reflects some inborn proclivities.

This question has been addressed in various developmental studies, including an important article by Ernst Fehr and his colleagues (2008), titled "Egalitarianism in Young Children." They tested 229 Swiss children, from 3 to 8 years, on a series of economic games. Instead of money, they used candies, such as Smarties. Children were told that their decisions would affect other children whom they did not know and who do not know them. Each game had an *in-group* condition, where the other children were said to come from the same playschool, kindergarten, or school and an *out-group* condition, where the other children were said to come from a different community.

Consider the in-group condition first. One of the games was a simple Dictator Game: The child was given two candies and had the option of (a) keeping one and giving the other away or (b) keeping both. In this condition, the 7- and 8-year-olds were generous. About half of them gave away a candy. But the younger children were less giving—only about 20% of the 5- and 6-years-olds gave away a candy, and only about 10% of the 3- and 4-year-olds did so.

It is not clear how to interpret this trend. Maybe fairness matters less to the older children. Alternatively, the youngest children may have the same equity/kindness/fairness impulse as the older ones, but they also really like candies, and, unlike the 7- and 8-year-olds, cannot overcome their self-interest. Their appetite overwhelms their altruism. A second game avoids this conflict. Here the child gets to choose between either (a) getting a candy and giving the other person a candy or (b) getting a candy and giving the other person nothing. Here one can be altruistic (and fair, and egalitarian) without having to override self-interest.

The 7- and 8-year-olds did as one would expect: About 80% gave away a candy. For the younger children, however, only about half did. That is, about half of the children in the younger age groups chose not to give away a candy to a stranger even at no cost to themselves.

What about the out-group condition? When they were dealing with a child from a different community, children were even less nice. Fewer than 30% of the children in any of the age groups gave in the Dictator Condition; in fact, the proportion *drops* with age, with few of the older children giving up their candy for a strange other. And in the No-cost condition, all of the children, including the 7- and 8-year-olds, were largely indifferent to the fate of the stranger, choosing to give at a rate of 15%–20% less than in the in-group condition.

Fehr et al. write, "These results indicate that human egalitarianism and parochialism have deep developmental roots." (p.1079). But while the results do indicate early roots of parochialism—since the in-group/out-group difference applies at every age—there is no evidence for egalitarianism in children younger than 7 years.

Consider also the recent report by Joseph Henrich and colleagues (Henrich et al., 2010) looking at performances in economic games, including the Dictator Game, across 15 diverse populations. It turns out the high generosity found in adults in behavioral economic studies in the industrialist West is an outlier—most people in the world are far less altruistic. Henrich et al. find that the propensity to behave kindly to strangers is strongest in large-scale communities with market economies, where such norms are essential to the smooth functioning of trade. They conclude that this propensity is a consequence of the modern culture, not human nature.

The development work of Fehr et al. and the cross-cultural work of Henrich et al. support the two main claims in this chapter: *We choose sides early on* and *We have no natural affinity toward strangers*. Richard Dawkins was right, then, when he said at the start of his book *The Selfish Gene*, "Be warned that if you wish, as I do, to build a society in which individuals cooperate generously and unselfishly toward a common good, you can expect little help from biological nature." Or as a character in a Kingsley Amis novel once put it, "It was no wonder that people were so horrible when they started life as children."

REFERENCES

Bloom, P. (2011). Moral nativism and moral psychology. In M. Mikulincer& P. R. Shaver (Eds.), *The social psychology of morality: Exploring the causes of good and evil* (pp. 71–90). Washington, DC: American Psychological Association.

Dunham, Y., Baron, A. S., & Banaji, M. R. (2008). The development of implicit intergroup cognition. *Trends in Cognitive Sciences, 12,* 248–253.

Fehr, E., Bernhard, H., & Rockenbach B. (2008). Egalitarianism in young children. *Nature, 454,* 1079–1084.

Henrich, J., Ensminger, J., McElreath, R., Barr, A., Barrett, C., Bolyanatz, A.,…Ziker, J. (2010). Markets, religion, community size, and the evolution of fairness and punishment. *Science, 327,* 1480–1484.

Keltner, D., Smith, J. A., & Marsh, J. (2010). Introduction. In D. Keltner, J. A. Smith, & J. Marsh, J. (Eds.) *The compassionate instinct* (pp. 5–7) .New York: Norton.

List, J. A. (2007).On the interpretation of giving in dictator games. *Journal of Political Economy, 115,* 482–494.

Olson, K. R., & Dweck, C. S. (2009). Social cognitive development: A new look. *Child Development Perspectives, 3,* 60–65.

6.3

Young Children's Moral and Social-Conventional Understanding

JUDITH G. SMETANA

The study of human development involves an understanding of how children acquire the skills and abilities necessary to function adequately within their culture. An important aspect of this is that children must acquire knowledge of the moral standards and conventional rules and customs of their society or social group (Maccoby, 2007). It is typically assumed that moral and social rules are acquired through socialization—that is, that parents, teachers, and other adults shape children's values and beliefs by serving as role models, praising children for their good behavior, and punishing them when they disobey. Thus, successful socialization is often measured by children's internalization and compliance with the rules and values of their society.

In contrast, my colleagues and I (see Nucci, 2001; Smetana, 2006, 2011; Turiel, 1983, 2002) view children as active agents in their own development. We have shown that the social and moral rules of society are not merely reproduced but rather are *constructed* through development. Our claim is that through dynamic and constructive processes, children develop an understanding of *morality*, or individuals' prescriptive judgments of how individuals ought to behave toward others, based on concepts of welfare (harm), fairness, and rights. These are seen as different from *social conventions*, or the arbitrary, consensually agreed-on social norms (for example, manners and etiquette) that structure social interactions in different social contexts. These are distinct types of social knowledge that follow different developmental pathways.

DISTINCTIONS IN YOUNG CHILDREN'S MORAL AND CONVENTIONAL CONCEPTS

Our claim is that even young children are able to identify moral rules and transgressions as distinct from those pertaining to social conventions. To test this claim, and in the context of interviews, we ask young children to make judgments about familiar, everyday, hypothetical transgressions, depicted in pictures. For instance, moral transgressions might pertain to hitting or teasing another child or taking away their toys, whereas social-conventional transgressions might include not saying "please," using fingers to eat ice cream, or not following preschool rules like where one sits during story time or whether children put toys away in the expected place. The interview questions usually involve yes/no responses, but the questions tap some very sophisticated notions about the criteria that define morality, drawn from moral philosophy and extensive psychological research.

For instance, to assess whether children grasp that moral violations are *generalizably wrong* (whereas social conventions are relative to specific social contexts), we ask whether hypothetical acts are wrong across different contexts (at home or at school or, for older children, "here" or in another country). We also ask children to evaluate whether different transgressions would be wrong even if there were no rule or if the teacher did not see the violation. The expectation is that moral acts will be viewed as wrong regardless of whether there are rules or whether an authority says so, respectively, whereas social conventions should be seen as wrong only if there are rules or an authority says that it is so. Furthermore, to determine whether children view conventional but not moral rules as alterable, we ask children whether it would be permissible for teachers to change the rule (for instance, to make hitting permissible). We also ask children to rate the severity of different rule violations and how much punishment the transgressor deserves.

One of the startling findings from this research is that children distinguish between these different types of transgressions as early as age 3 and more completely by age 4 (Killen & Smetana, 1999; Nucci & Turiel, 1978; Smetana, 1981, 1985; Smetana & Braeges, 1990; Smetana, Schlagman, & Adams, 1993; Smetana et al., 1999, 2012). The well-replicated results are that preschool children generally treat moral transgressions as more generalizably wrong, more independent of rules and authority, more serious, and more deserving of punishment than social-conventional transgressions. They also treat moral rules as less alterable—and more important—than conventional rules. Distinctions in moral and social judgments are not restricted to American children. Although the specific conventions vary in different cultures, similar results have been obtained among very young children in China (Yau & Smetana, 2003) and Colombia (Ardila-Rey & Killen, 2001), and among older children in a wide range of cultures across nearly all continents. Differentiations between moral and conventional judgments also have been found in atypically developing children, including young children with autism (Blair, 1996) and preschool children who have experienced maltreatment, including physical abuse and neglect (Smetana et al., 1999). It is also notable that even at very young ages, children in different cultures treat a set of issues (for instance, about clothing and food preferences) as personal, up to the individual, and beyond the boundaries of conventional regulation and moral concern (Killen & Smetana, 1999; Nucci, 1981; Nucci & Weber, 1995; Yau & Smetana, 2003). Young children hold to the belief that some personal choices should be up to them, even when adults assert to the contrary, a pattern that we have not observed in reference to moral and conventional events.

This research does not mean that preschool children are capable of making mature moral judgments. Rather, their evaluations can be seen as initial, rudimentary, but important steps in moral judgment development. Young children's moral judgments are limited in several respects. First, young children apply moral concepts only to familiar, everyday events but not to those that are unfamiliar or more abstract (Davidson, Turiel, & Black, 1983). Preschool children also show a better understanding of concrete moral violations, for instance, those involving physical harm rather than psychological harm or unfair resource distribution (Smetana et al., 1993). By middle childhood, moral evaluations are extended in these ways. As children develop, they also incorporate more psychological elements in their moral thinking, leading to more

flexible moral concepts. For instance, by 5 years of age, children refer to mental states, intentions, and their own or others' emotions when discussing moral conflicts (Wainryb, Brehl, & Matwin, 2005). They also begin to understand that others may have different moral beliefs than their own (Flavell, Mumme, Green, & Flavell, 1992; Wainryb & Ford, 1998), and they are able to consider both intentions and outcomes in making moral evaluations (Zelazo, Helwig, & Lau, 1996). Although it is often assumed that an understanding of others' mental states (referred to as "theory of mind") is necessary for more mature moral judgments, our research has shown that the development of moral evaluations and theory of mind are reciprocal, transactional processes (Smetana, Jambon, Conry-Murray, & Sturge-Apple, 2012).

Finally, not all social events can be categorized as strictly moral or conventional; they may involve overlapping moral, conventional, pragmatic, or prudential (pertaining to comfort, safety, or harm to the self) concerns. Young children are unable to recognize or coordinate multiple components in their judgments; this ability develops during the elementary school years and continues to develop during adolescence (Smetana, 2006).

SOCIAL EXPERIENCES AND DEVELOPMENTAL PROCESSES

How does this understanding of moral and conventional concepts develop? Rather than proceeding through "top-down" (or innate) processes, we hypothesize that moral judgments develop "from the bottom up." Children appear to be born with a capacity for empathy and reciprocity; this makes good evolutionary sense, as individuals in all cultures must learn to get along with others. But children are not born with an understanding of specific rules and values. Morality is not given; it develops. That is, children attempt to understand their social world and make meaning out of their social interactions. Moral and social knowledge develop as children strive to understand the meaning of acts and regularities in the environment. For instance, children have ample experiences, as victims and observers, of the harm or unfairness caused by others' moral transgressions. Children generalize from these experiences to construct prescriptive moral judgments. Parents' reasoning, behaviors, and responses to transgressions play an important role in children's moral development, but not because they mold children's responses. Parents facilitate moral understanding by providing information about the social world and about the harm or unfairness caused by moral transgressions. For instance, adult responses that point out how moral violations affect others or that ask children to take the other's perspective (e.g., "Look what you did—how do you think he feels when you hit him?") help children to understand the consequences of their acts for others' welfare or rights. These kinds of responses, along with children's direct experiences, are important sources of moral development.

In contrast, conventional interactions develop from social interactions that highlight the rules, sanctions, and regularities that are appropriate in different social contexts. In other words, moral judgments develop from an understanding of acts, whereas social conventions develop from an understanding of rules and regularities in different social contexts. Interactions regarding personal issues tacitly acknowledge children's opportunities for preferences and choices (Nucci & Weber, 1995).

These claims have been supported by numerous observational studies of naturalistic social interactions in different contexts such as at home, in school, and on playgrounds. Studies have examined both *who* responds (adults, such as parents and teachers, or children) and the specific ways they respond to different types of transgressions (see Smetana, 1995, 2006 for reviews). These studies confirm that social interactions in the context of moral and conventional transgressions differ qualitatively. The claim that children construct moral and social-conventional knowledge through their social experiences also has been supported by experimental studies that vary the features of moral and conventional acts and then examine children's judgments and justifications under these different conditions (Helwig, Zelazo, & Wilson, 2001; Smetana, 1985; Zelazo et al., 1996).

Furthermore, there are individual differences according to children's temperament in the rate at which preschool children acquire moral understanding. A recent 1-year longitudinal study of preschoolers (Smetana et al., 2012) showed that children who were higher in effortful control, a precursor of executive control and part of an inhibitive system of behavior, were slower to develop an understanding that moral rules are not alterable and that moral transgressions are wrong regardless of whether there are rules prohibiting the behavior. Although this finding is counterintuitive, we speculate that because these children misbehave less often, they have less experience—and thus gain less input—about moral rules. In contrast, children who were higher in the temperamental dimension of surgency (which is associated with extraversion, positive affect and also impulsivity) understood at earlier ages that moral transgressions are generalizably wrong and more deserving of punishment. Thus, this study suggests that different dispositional characteristics influence children's interactions, and hence their acquisition of moral and social concepts. Although there may be differences in how quickly young children acquire different moral concepts, most children understand these concepts by the end of the preschool years.

In addition, emotional responses are clearly part of children's social interactions that influence the development of moral and conventional judgments. Children's experiences of moral events can be highly emotional and affectively laden. Research has shown that children make connections between different emotions and different types of events, which become part of their cognitive representations and differentiation of moral and conventional events (see Arsenio, Gold, & Adams, 2006 for a review). A currently popular view in much of psychology is that individuals respond to social events in primarily emotional, intuitive, and automated ways and that they rarely engage in reflective reasoning. In this view, reasoning (judgments) is seen as distinct from affect. In the social domain view, though, children, adolescents, and adults are active, volitional beings who seek to make sense of their social surroundings and interactions. Emotions are part of those social interactions. Moral judgments are not "cold-blooded" or devoid of emotion; rather, emotions are deeply embedded in social reasoning. Studying adult judgments does not take into consideration the developmental processes from which they arise. My research suggests that children first form their ideas through thought and reflection, although later, simple judgments may seem to occur in an automatic way. It is clear that even adults struggle to make complex moral decisions and to coordinate moral and nonmoral concerns in their reasoning.

I have focused here primarily on the development of young children's moral and social concepts. As noted previously, these judgments are only the first, tentative steps on the long, winding road to mature moral and social cognition, which includes the ability to think about a variety of moral issues, including civil liberties, discrimination, rights, inclusion and exclusion in social groups, and tolerance and respect for others.

REFERENCES

Ardila-Rey, A., & Killen, M. (2001). Colombian preschool children's judgments about autonomy and conflict resolution in the classroom setting. *International Journal of Behavioral Development, 25*, 246–255.

Arsenio, W. F., Gold, J., & Adams, E. (2006). Children's conceptions and displays of moral emotions. In M. Killen & J. G. Smetana (Eds.), *Handbook of moral development* (pp. 581–609). Mahwah, NJ: Erlbaum.

Blair, R. J. R. (1996). Morality in the autistic child. *Journal of Autism and Developmental Disorders, 26*, 571–579.

Davidson, P., Turiel, E., & Black, A. (1983). The effect of stimulus familiarity on the use of criteria and justifications in children's social reasoning. *British Journal of Developmental Psychology, 1*, 49–65.

Flavell, J. H., Mumme, D. L., Green, F. L., & Flavell, E. R. (1992). Young children's understanding of different types of beliefs. *Child Development, 63*, 960–977.

Helwig, C. C., Zelazo, P. D., & Wilson, M. (2001). Children's judgments of psychological harm in normal and noncanonical situations. *Child Development, 72*, 66–81.

Killen, M., & Smetana, J. G. (1999). Social interactions in preschool classrooms and the development of young children's conceptions of the personal. *Child Development, 70*, 486–501.

Maccoby, E. E. (2007). Historical overview of socialization theory and research. In J. E. Grusec & P. D. Hastings (Eds.), *Handbook of socialization: Theory and research* (pp. 13–41). New York: Guilford Press.

Nucci, L. (1981). The development of personal concepts: A domain distinct from moral or societal concepts. *Child Development, 52*, 114–121.

Nucci, L. (2001). *Education in the moral domain.* Cambridge, England: Cambridge University Press.

Nucci, L. P., & Turiel, E. (1978). Social interactions and the development of social concepts in preschool children. *Child Development, 49*, 400–407.

Nucci, L. P., & Weber, E. K. (1995). Social interactions in the home and the development of young children's conceptions of the personal. *Child Development, 66*, 1438–1452.

Smetana, J. G. (1981). Preschool children's conceptions of moral and social rules. *Child Development, 52*, 1333–1336.

Smetana, J. G. (1985). Preschool children's conceptions of transgressions: The effects of varying moral and conventional domain-related attributes. *Developmental Psychology, 21*, 18–29.

Smetana, J. G. (1995). Morality in context: Abstractions, ambiguities, and applications. In R. Vasta (Ed.), *Annals of child development* (Vol. 10, pp. 83–130). London: Jessica Kingsley.

Smetana, J. G. (2006). Social-cognitive domain theory: Consistencies and variations in children's moral and social judgments. In M. Killen & J. G. Smetana (Eds.), *Handbook of moral development* (pp. 119–153). Mahwah, NJ: Erlbaum.

Smetana, J. G. (2011). *Adolescents, families, and social development: How teens construct their worlds.* Sussex, England: Wiley-Blackwell.

Smetana, J. G., & Braeges, J. L. (1990). The development of toddlers' moral and conventional judgments. *Merrill-Palmer Quarterly, 36*, 329–346.

Smetana, J. G., Jambon, M., Conry-Murray, C., & Sturge-Apple, M. (2012). Reciprocal assocations between young children's moral judgments and their developing theory of mind. *Developmental Psychology, 48*, 1144–1155.

Smetana, J. G., Rote, W. M., Jambon, M., Tasopoulos-Chan, M., Villalobos, M., & Comer, J. (2012). Developmental changes and individual differences in young children's moral judgments. *Child Development, 83*(2), 683–696.

Smetana, J. G., Schlagman, N., & Adams, P. (1993). Preschoolers' judgments about hypothetical and actual transgressions. *Child Development, 64*, 202–214.

Smetana, J. G., Toth, S., Cicchetti, D., Bruce, J., Kane, P., & Daddis, C. (1999). Maltreated and nonmaltreated preschoolers' conceptions of hypothetical and actual moral transgressions. *Developmental Psychology, 35*, 269–281.

Turiel, E. (1983). *The development of social knowledge: Morality and convention.* Cambridge, England: Cambridge University Press.

Turiel, E. (2002). *The culture of morality: Social development, context, and conflict.* New York: Cambridge University Press.

Wainryb, C., Brehl, B., & Matwin, S. (2005). Being hurt and hurting others: Children's narrative accounts and moral judgments of their own interpersonal conflicts. *Monographs of the Society for Research in Child Development, 70* (3).

Wainryb, C., & Ford, S. (1998). Young children's evaluations of acts based on beliefs different from their own. *Merrill-Palmer Quarterly, 44*, 484–503.

Yau, J., & Smetana, J. G. (2003). Conceptions of moral, social-conventional, and personal events among Chinese preschoolers in Hong Kong. *Child Development, 74*, 647–658.

Zelazo, P. D., Helwig, C. C., & Lau, A. (1996). Intention, act, and outcome in behavioral prediction and moral judgment. *Child Development, 67*, 2478–2492.

6.4

The Origin of Children's Appreciation of Ownership Rights

KAREN R. NEARY AND ORI FRIEDMAN

People are permitted to use remarkably few of the many objects they encounter. Though they can make relatively free use of their own belongings, they are barred from using objects belonging to others, and they can make only limited use of public property. It is forbidden to drink a stranger's coffee, write in a book displayed in a shop, or paint murals on the wall of an elementary school without permission. Disregarding the limits imposed by ownership leads to social conflicts. Thieves take others' property, vandals destroy it, and both are subject to punishment and scorn for these actions. Hence, recognizing ownership rights is crucial for socially appropriate behavior.

Appreciating ownership rights, then, is important for children's social cognitive development. It might be expected that young children's appreciation of ownership rights is very limited. Young children frequently quarrel over objects (e.g., Ross & Conant, 1992; Shantz, 1987), and such conflicts plausibly arise because children have little appreciation of owners' rights. When Billy and Sally fight over her crayon, Billy might insist on using it because he does not know that Sally's ownership entitles her to decide whether he can use it. He might even realize that Sally is normally entitled to exclude nonowners from her crayon but nonetheless judge that his urgent need for the crayon trumps her ownership.

Moreover, learning about ownership rights should be difficult. Ownership rights are invisible and abstract. In looking at an owned object, one cannot see which privileges or rights are conferred to the owner of the object (Jackendoff, 1992, Chapter 3; Snare, 1972). Even if it is observed that the object is typically used by the owner and not by other people, these observations do not necessarily warrant the conclusion that the owner has rights over the object[1]; rather than concerning the actual use of property, ownership instead concerns deontic rules about permitted use.

Furthermore, young children are often faced with situations where owners' rights are disregarded or downplayed. Accounts of ownership rights typically claim that owners are entitled to use their property and to decide whether others are permitted to use their property (e.g., Snare, 1972). Yet parents sometimes forbid children from playing with their own toys, forbid children from using their toys in certain ways, confiscate children's toys, and insist that children share their toys with others. These violations of ownership rights are not rare: Ross (1996) observed naturally occurring disputes over objects between pairs of siblings aged 2 and 4. In one common type of dispute, one sibling played with a toy that belonged to the other, who wanted it back. When intervening in these disputes, parents did not consistently support owners and were as likely to instead side with nonowners. It is difficult to see how these parental interventions could help children appreciate ownership rights. On the contrary, parents' frequent support for nonowners might lead children to

---

[1] For example, suppose that a child repeatedly observes that her father and mother wear their own clothes and not each other's clothing. The child may learn generalizations like "Mommy wears her green shirt, and Daddy does not." But this generalization only implies that it would be *unusual* for her father to wear the shirt, not that it would be wrong for him to do so. Moreover, even if the child came to believe that her father should not wear the shirt, the child would also have to come to view the wrongness as arising from ownership (e.g., the shirt belongs to Mommy) and not from some other factor (e.g., the shirt is for females only).

have a weak conception of ownership rights and to view these rights as easily overridden by competing principles of entitlement.

Hence, there are several reasons to believe that young children should have a limited appreciation of ownership rights, only gaining this understanding in later years (for empirical evidence broadly consistent with this view, see Kim & Kalish, 2009, and Rossano, Rakoczy, & Tomasello, 2011). However intuitive, we believe that this view is incorrect and gets the developmental picture *backward*. We suggest that young children appreciate ownership rights and in some sense value these rights more than adults do. This view has surprising implications about the developmental origins of ownership rights and the function of parental input regarding ownership.

The impetus for our view is an additional finding from Ross's (1996) observational study. Even though parents did not consistently support owners over nonowners, the disputes were mostly won by owners nonetheless. This finding is striking. It suggests that children uphold ownership rights, and even maintain these rights in opposition to parental input. This interpretation of the finding contradicts the view that children have little appreciation of ownership, and it also contradicts the intuitive view that children's understanding of ownership rights is strongly influenced by parental input. If young children are initially ignorant of ownership rights and gradually come to learn about them from their parents, we might expect children's views of ownership rights to mirror those of their parents or be weaker. Opposite to this, children appeared to give ownership more priority than did their parents.

However, other interpretations of Ross's (1996) findings are possible. First, owners' success in the disputes might not have resulted because children appreciate ownership rights. Instead, owners might have won because they were more emotionally connected to the toys than were nonowners and therefore more motivated to fight for their toys. Sally might fight harder for her crayon than Billy does, because she cares about the crayon more. Likewise, Billy may relinquish the crayon because of Sally's persistence and not because he knows or cares that it is hers. Second, parents' interventions in the disputes might not reflect their actual beliefs about the importance of ownership rights. Parents might be motivated to end disputes between children, and they may often feel that the easiest way to end disputes is by leaving toys with their current possessors.

We have recently conducted experiments to provide more decisive evidence about whether preschoolers value ownership, and whether they do so more than adults. Preschoolers and adults were shown scenarios in which two characters are embroiled in a dispute over an object, and then they judged who should win the dispute. Because preschoolers and adults were spectators, they occupied the same position relative to the dispute and could not be influenced by factors inherent to occupying a particular position within it.

In one experiment, participants watched scenarios in which one character was using an object, but the owner of the object also wanted it. For instance, a boy was using a crayon and needed it to finish making a birthday card. However, the crayon belonged to a girl, who also wanted to use it. When asked which character should get to use the crayon, children aged 3 to 5 mostly chose the owner (girl in this example), while adults mostly chose the character already using the crayon (boy in this example). Similar findings were obtained in a second experiment on 3- to 7-year-olds and adults, in which the owner wanted the possessor to stop using it (without wanting to use it herself). Children at all ages sided with the owner and said that the possessor should stop using the crayon, while adults were no likelier to side with the owner than the nonowner. The same pattern of findings also emerged in a third experiment on 4-year-olds and adults, in which the scenarios were about adult characters and objects more valuable than crayons (i.e., a cell phone and a shovel).

The experiments also included conditions where the object did not belong to either of the disputants, but to their school. For instance, a boy was using a crayon and needed it to finish making a birthday card, but a girl also wanted to use the crayon. Here, children and adults responded more similarly, favoring the boy over the girl. These findings show that children view current use and need as compelling principles entitling continued use of an object, but they happen to give more priority to ownership rights. The findings also demonstrate that children in the ownership condition do not just favor the girl because they feel she deserves a turn to use the crayon. Instead, their judgments depend on whether she owns the crayon.

The findings from these experiments suggest that young children value ownership and give it more priority than adults do when reasoning about ownership disputes. Why do children support owners' rights? This is puzzling if children learn about the importance of ownership from adults, because our findings suggest that adults do not strongly support owners' rights. Moreover, Ross's (1996) observations suggest that adults' weak support for ownership is manifest in their interventions in children's disputes over objects. If children began without an appreciation of ownership rights, and then acquired some appreciation from adults, then children might be expected to give *less* priority to owners' rights than adults. However, it could be that children learn about ownership from adults, without their beliefs about ownership rights coming to mirror those of adults. While adults might have a nuanced sense of when ownership rights should be given priority, children might initially acquire a simple ownership "theory" to cover all situations. For instance, children might come to believe that owners should be supported in *all* disputes with nonowners. On this account, adults' appreciation of ownership is flexible, while children's is rigid.

To examine whether children rigidly uphold ownership rights, we considered situations in which siding against an owner would be more compelling. We felt it might be especially compelling to disregard ownership rights in situations where it is necessary to prevent harm. This intuition may be reflected in Plato's *Republic*—early on Socrates suggests it would be wrong to return weapons to a "man not in his right mind" (Plato, 1871). Presumably, the weapons should not be returned because the owner is likely to inflict harm with them. To consider a more mundane example, although permission is typically required before borrowing a neighbor's garden hose, it is acceptable to use the hose without permission if it is needed to help extinguish a dangerous fire.

We conducted two further studies examining 3- to 5-year-olds' and adults' judgments about such situations, where ownership rights are pitted against the duty to prevent harm. In one study, participants watched a scenario in which a boy wanted to use a net to save a dog stuck in a swimming pool, but a girl did not want him to use the net. Adults and children aged 4 and older said the girl should use the net to save the dog, and they did so regardless of whether the net belonged to the boy or to neither character; their responses did not depend on ownership. Three-year-olds were more likely to favor the girl when she owned the net than otherwise, but their responses did not depart from chance in either condition. In other words, they did not rigidly uphold owners' rights.

Similar findings were obtained in a second study, which featured scenarios loosely based on the example from Plato's *Republic*. In one scenario,

a boy held a baseball bat, but a girl wanted to take it to break a school window. Adults and 5-year-olds claimed the boy should not let the girl have the bat, responding this way regardless of whether it belonged to the girl or to neither character; 3- and 4-year-olds were more likely to side with the girl when she owned the bat than otherwise, but not at rates exceeding chance. So again, even the younger children did not rigidly uphold owners' rights.

These findings suggest developmental changes in judgments about whether it is acceptable to disregard ownership rights to prevent harm. But the findings do not support the view that children rigidly support owners' rights in all situations. Even 3-year-olds show some flexibility in considering whether ownership rights should be upheld. Of course, this does not decisively rule out the possibility that children initially learn an "always support owners" rule. Perhaps children initially acquire such an inflexible rule (perhaps at age 2), and then subsequently learn that ownership rights should be disregarded when this is necessary to prevent harm. However, this account leaves open many questions. It does not explain how children initially come to learn that ownership is important, a puzzling question given children's exposure to considerable evidence suggesting that ownership rights can be disregarded. This view also does not explain why children manage to learn that ownership should be disregarded to prevent harm, while somehow failing to acquire the adult view that in some instance a nonowner in the midst of using an object should be permitted to use it, even against the owners' wishes.

Regardless, we believe a simpler explanation is possible for why children support ownership rights. Rather than *learning* about ownership rights and their importance, children's appreciation of ownership rights might be a natural consequence of their having a sense of people's personal rights. Consider the actions people are permitted to take with regard to themselves and with regard to one another. If Sally wants to put a sticker on her own hand, then she may; however, Billy will only be permitted to put a sticker on Sally's hand if she consents. An approximate account for these intuitions is that Sally is entitled to determine what happens to herself, including her hand. To the extent that other people determine the state of her hand (especially in ways not consistent with her plausible goals or desires), they interfere with this entitlement. If Billy puts the sticker on Sally's hand without her permission, he (rather than she) determines the state of her hand.

This example concerns Sally's hand and her personal (or bodily) rights. However, nothing would change if the example instead concerned an object belonging to Sally, such as her backpack. Sally can put a sticker on her backpack if she wishes, while Billy can only put the sticker on her backpack if she consents. Here, an approximate account for this intuition is that Sally is entitled to determine what happens to her property. Even if this particular formulation of the principle is not quite right, the broader point is that there is a striking parallel between the personal rights that concern Sally's hand and the property rights that concern her backpack (Humphrey, 1992, p. 143). We believe this parallel is not a coincidence but results because people's notions of ownership rights are *extensions* of their notions of personal rights. This view may explain how young children come to appreciate ownership rights, and it may also help explain why people conceive of ownership rights at all.

It is plausible that infants have some appreciation of personal rights. On seeing an actor attempt to fulfill a goal such as climbing a hill, infants differentiate between agents who help the actor fulfill the goal (e.g., by pushing the actor up the hill) from those who interfere with the goal (e.g., by pushing the actor down the hill) (Kuhlmeier, Wynn, & Bloom, 2003) and prefer "helpers" over "hinderers" (Hamlin, Wynn, & Bloom, 2007). Although it is uncertain how infants construe such situations, the findings are at least consistent with the possibility that they possess a rudimentary notion of personal rights. For instance, infants might assume that agents are entitled to control their actions, and that it is wrong for others to interfere with this control.

If infants (or young children) possess such a basic notion of personal rights, we believe they do not need to learn a *new* set of rights to reason about ownership. At most, they need to extend their notions of personal rights so that these also apply to property.[2] On this view, young children's appreciation of ownership rights is not hindered by parental input that should make learning about these rights difficult because this appreciation does not depend on parental input; it more likely depends on children possessing some notion of personal rights.

Nonetheless, adult input about ownership might serve an important function. It might help children appreciate that there are social situations where owners are expected to disregard their entitlement to control their property. If a neighborhood friend asks to borrow an egg (needed to bake a cake), ownership principles do not obligate the owner of the egg to grant the request. But it would be very odd, and socially inappropriate, to deny the request without providing some excuse. This is why adults encourage children to share—to help children understand social expectations, and particularly those applying to friends and family members.

Such social expectations differ considerably across contexts. Children might be expected to share candy with a friend, but they would not be expected to share their birthday presents in the same way (i.e., because candy is given rather than lent). Nor would they be expected to share anything with an unfamiliar adult. Hence, parental input might be needed to teach children about the expectations specific to various relations and to help remind children about the nature of the current social situation (e.g., "Billy is a *friend*. We share with friends."). It is worth noting, though, that such social expectations are not limited to owned objects; they influence personal rights as well. Strictly, one is permitted to decline a friend's request for help moving a desk. But again, there is an expectation that the request will be fulfilled, unless one provides a reason or excuse that it cannot.

In sum, we propose that children may have an appreciation of ownership rights from early in development, and that their understanding of ownership rights might not depend on adult input. Instead, children might come to understand ownership by extending existing notions of personal rights to owned property. In this view, the chief function of adult input about ownership is to weaken it, by helping children appreciate that there are situations where social obligations require owners to share their property. If this view is correct, then children's frequent disputes over objects cannot result from children lacking an appreciation of ownership. Disputes might instead occur because nonowners have difficulty overcoming their desires for others' property, and

---

[2] This theory is similar in some regards to accounts claiming that children come to a notion of ownership rights by extending their sense of self or bodily agency onto objects (e.g., Humphrey, 1992, Chapter 18; Rochat, 2009), but there is a crucial difference. These other accounts claim that children's appreciation of ownership arises from their own first-person sense of self or agency. However, the current account claims that ownership is an extension of children's notion of *people's* personal rights. This notion of personal rights applies as much to others as to oneself.

because owners fail to appreciate their social obligation to share.

REFERENCES

Hamlin, J. K., Wynn, K., & Bloom, P. (2007). Social evaluation by preverbal infants. *Nature, 450*, 557–559.

Humphrey, N. (1992). *A history of the mind: Evolution and the birth of consciousness.* New York: Simon & Schuster.

Jackendoff, R. S. (1992). *Languages of the mind: Essays on mental representation.* Cambridge, MA: MIT Press.

Kim, S., & Kalish, C.W. (2009). Children's ascriptions of property rights with changes of ownership. *Cognitive Development, 24*, 322–336.

Kuhlmeier, V., Wynn, K., & Bloom, P. (2003). Attribution of dispositional states by 12-month-olds. *Psychological Science, 14*, 402–408.

Plato. (1871). The republic. In *The dialogues of Plato, Vol. 2.* (B. Jowett, Trans.). London: MacMillian.

Ross, H. S. (1996). Negotiating principles of entitlement in sibling property disputes. *Developmental Psychology, 32*, 90–101.

Ross, H. S., & Conant, C. L. (1992). The social structure of early conflict: Interaction, relationships, and alliances. In C. Shantz & W. W. Hartup (Eds.), *Conflict in child and adolescent development* (pp. 153–185). Cambridge, England: Cambridge University Press.

Rossano, F., Rakoczy, H., & Tomasello, M. (2011). Young children's understanding of violations of property rights. *Cognition, 121*(2), 219–227.

Shantz, C. U. (1987). Conflicts between children. *Child Development, 58*, 283–305.

Snare, F. (1972). The concept of property. *American Philosophical Quarterly, 9*, 200–206.

6.5

Becoming a Moral Relativist

Children's Moral Conceptions of Honesty and Dishonesty in Different Sociocultural Contexts

KANG LEE AND ANGELA EVANS

Is honesty always right and dishonesty always wrong? To many parents, the answer to this question seems obvious. This sentiment is also shared by a group of philosophers called deontologists (Bok, 1978; Kant, 1949; Krupfer, 1982; St. Augustine, 1952). Deontologists believe that dishonesty always entails negative moral values and thus should be eschewed in all circumstances. Perhaps due to such presumptions, moral development research in the past was devoted to understanding how children define what a lie is (Bussey, 1992; Peterson, 1995; Peterson, Peterson, & Seeto, 1983; Piaget, 1932; Siegal & Peterson, 1998; Strichartz & Burton, 1990; Wimmer, Gruber, & Perner, 1984). Little was known until the late 1990s about whether children agree with deontologists that honesty is always right and lying is always wrong.

Developmental research in the last two decades has completely overturned the predominant deontological view. Evidence to date suggests that both children and adults hold a utilitarian view of honesty (Bentham, 1843; Mill, 1869; Sweetser, 1987), believing that the moral value of honesty and dishonesty depends on the situation. In some situations, dishonesty is evaluated negatively and honesty positively. However, in other situations, honesty is viewed as morally wrong and dishonesty as morally right. There are at least four situations where, with increased age, children reject the deontological view and embrace the utilitarian view.

The first situation involves politeness, where blunt honesty may be hurtful but dishonesty, or more precisely white lie-telling, avoids it. A typical scenario is when an individual receives an undesirable gift from a well-meaning gift giver. Typically, in such situations adults allow the need

to be polite and to avoid hurting others to override the need to be truthful. For this reason, adults not only endorse white lies (Lee & Ross, 1997) but also tell them regularly (DePaulo & Bell, 1996; DePaulo & Kashy, 1998). Although children tend to give negative ratings to white lies (e.g., Heyman, Sweet, & Lee, 2009), beginning from 4 years of age, their ratings of white lies are not as negative as those given to antisocial lies (Bussey, 1999). By the end of the elementary school years, children's ratings of white lies even become positive (Walper & Valtin, 1992) and are affected by additional situational factors (Ma, Xu, Heyman, & Lee, 2010).

For example, Ma et al. (2010) found that older Chinese children (11-year-olds) consider the consequence of misinformation for the listener when deciding whether a white lie or the blunt truth is morally acceptable. When the consequence of misinformation is high (e.g., likely negative future implications), white lie-telling was viewed more negatively and blunt truth-telling more positively, even though the blunt truth may hurt the listener's feelings (e.g., telling a friend that her painting, intended for a future competition, is of poor quality). In contrast, when the consequence of misinformation is low (e.g., minimal to no negative future implications), children favor white lie-telling over blunt truth-telling (e.g., telling a gift giver about liking an undesirable gift). It should be noted that children and adults alike still consider false statements lies and truthful statements truths in politeness situations (Bussey, 1992; Ma et al., 2010; Xu, Luo, Fu, & Lee, 2009). Thus, these findings suggest that with age, children become increasingly utilitarian in their moral valuations of honesty and dishonesty; however, their concept of what constitutes a lie or the truth remains unaffected by situational factors. In addition to the early development of a utilitarian moral evaluation of lies told in politeness situations, young children readily tell white lies themselves (Talwar & Lee, 2002; Talwar, Murphy, & Lee, 2007; Xu, Bao, Fu, Talwar, & Lee, 2010). Moreover, Xu, Bao, Fu, Talwar, and Lee (2010) found a positive relation between children's moral evaluation of white lie-telling and their actual behavior.

A second situation where children have been shown to hold a utilitarian view of honesty is the modesty situation. In this situation, individuals are expected to show humility by refraining from acknowledging their good deeds or personal achievements. This social expectation of modesty is more emphasized in East Asian than Western cultures (Sun, 2004). Existing developmental studies have found a robust cross-cultural modesty effect (Fu et al., 2010; Fu, Lee, Cameron, & Xu, 2001; Heyman, Itakura, & Lee, 2010; Lee, Cameron, Xu, Fu, & Board, 1997; Lee, Xu, Fu, Cameron, & Chen, 2001) with East Asians (mainland Chinese, Taiwanese, Japanese, and Korean), from 7 years onward, giving increasingly less positive ratings to individuals who tell the truth about their own prosocial behavior (e.g., tidying up a messy classroom) and increasingly less negative ratings to individuals who lie about it (the ratings become positive at age 11). In contrast, North Americans consistently give the former positive, and the latter negative moral ratings. Children's justifications have consistently shown marked cross-cultural differences: Western children typically refer to the need to be honest and are often puzzled as to why people would lie about their own prosocial behavior, while East Asian children, with increased age, typically refer to the need to be modest, the virtue of humility, and the potential negative consequences of public immodesty.

Lee (2000) proposed that the cross-cultural modesty effect is driven by the East Asian cultures' emphasis on group cohesion and harmony, which is promoted by humility and undermined by immodesty, particularly when modesty or immodesty is displayed in public. One candidate for this common cultural structure is the stronger emphasis on collectivism than individualism in the East Asian cultures. Collectivism promotes community-oriented activities such as prioritizing goals and interests of a collective, emphasizing duty to community, and basing personal identity on group harmony and achievements (Hofstede, 1980, 1991; Triandis, 1995). In contrast, individualism focuses on individual rights, emphasizes the interests of self and immediate family, and bases personal identity on individual accomplishments. Although the exact nature of these two constructs remains controversial, data suggest that these constructs capture critical structural differences between Eastern and Western cultures (see Oyserman, Coon, & Kemmelmeier, 2002 for a meta-analysis).

Recent evidence supports the collectivism hypothesis proposed by Lee (2000). Fu et al. (2010) and Heyman et al. (2010) found that Chinese and Japanese elementary school children judge telling the truth about one's good deeds in public to be less positive than doing so in private. The public-private distinction regarding modesty is important because the social expectations about modesty in the Eastern Asian societies mainly regulate how individuals should communicate positive information about themselves in front of a group. When American children evaluate similar scenarios depicting lie- or truth-telling about one's good deeds (Heyman et al., 2010), the public-private distinction makes little impact on their moral evaluations in a modesty situation; they tend to favor honesty and disfavor dishonesty.

A third situation that also calls for the utilitarian approach to the moral valuation of honesty and dishonesty is concerned with whether individuals' truthful and untruthful communication will benefit or harm a group to which they belong (collective situation). Individuals in any society belong to a multitude of groups (e.g., school, peer group, sports team, country). Sometimes, the group goal or interest may collide with the need to be truthful. Should the collective good override honesty? In the adult literature, untruthful statements told purportedly for the benefit of a collective are called "blue lies" (Barnes, 1994; Klockars, 1984). It is not unusual to observe blue lies in adult society. For example, police officers have been found to give false statements in the name of justice against an accused (hence the term "blue lie"). Recently, Fu, Xu, Cameron, Heyman, and Lee (2007) asked 7-, 9-, and 11-year-old Chinese and Canadian children to rate stories where the protagonists were faced with a moral dilemma: either lie- or truth-telling would harm oneself but help one's group (e.g., lying to conceal one's sickness to help one's team win a singing competition). Chinese children rated the lie-for-group behavior less negatively, and the truth-for-group behavior more positively, than European-Canadian children. Furthermore, those Chinese children who rated another's lie-for-group behavior less negatively were themselves more inclined to tell an actual lie to help their school team in an interschool chess competition (Fu et al., 2008).

However, there are two caveats regarding children's moral evaluations of honest and dishonest statements made in the collective situation. One is that blue lies must serve a legitimate social purpose. When children are asked to evaluate individuals who are lying to cover up their group's antisocial behaviors (e.g., cheating in a team competition), Chinese children at all ages, like their American counterparts, judge such lies highly negatively (Sweet, Heyman, Fu, & Lee, 2010). Another caveat is that the nature of the group for which children may consider dishonesty to be justified must be an entity that they value, which is illustrated by a recent study by Fu et al. (unpublished data). Fu et al. presented participants from 7 to 17 years of age moral dilemmas in which story characters must decide to tell a lie or the truth to help a group. The nature of the group varied from more immediate to more distant, such as one's class, one's school, or one's country. Before 11 years of age lying or truth-telling for one's class is rated more positively than for the other two larger groups. However, with increased age, lying or truth-telling for one's school becomes the most important, and then after 13 years of age, lying or truth-telling for one's country is rated most positively. Thus, with development, children's moral conception of honesty and dishonesty changes depending not only on whether honesty or dishonesty serves one's group but also which group it serves.

The fourth situation in which utilitarian moral evaluations of honesty and dishonesty are made is when an individual's self-interest is at stake. Beginning at an early age, children make clear distinctions between the types of self-interests that a lie or the truth serves to protect or enhance. While younger Western children, particularly those 7 years of age and under, tend to generally evaluate truth-telling positively and lying negatively, when there is a legitimate self-interest (e.g., needing time to prepare for an exam) that conflicts with the need to be truthful, older children in the West tend to give positive moral evaluations to lying for oneself or a friend (Fu et al., 2007; Sweet et al., 2010). More important, unlike Chinese children who favor truth-telling or lying for a collective, children in the West generally favor truth-telling or lying for an individual (self or a friend) as long as it serves to protect or enhance the individual's legitimate self-interest.

In contrast, children in all cultures from preschool years onward condemn dishonest statements to conceal antisocial behaviors and condone truth-telling to confess one's own antisocial behavior (e.g., Bussey, 1992; Heyman et al., 2010; Lee et al., 1997). Interestingly, when it comes to reporting about another's transgressions, children in the West make a distinction between telling the truth about another's major versus minor transgression (no study with children in other cultures has been conducted). The former is concerned with transgressions that render harm to others, whereas the latter is concerned with violations of rules that are arbitrarily laid down by authority figures (Helwig & Turiel, 2002; Turiel, 2002). In terms of major transgressions, children from preschool years onward evaluate telling the truth as highly positive (Ingram & Bering, 2010; Chiu Loke et al., 2011 Piaget, 1932). Younger children similarly rate reporting minor transgressions positively. However, with increased age, children become increasingly wary of reporting minor transgressions, as they consider it tattling. This age-related change suggests that with age, children become aware that the moral value of honesty, even about a transgression, is not absolute but is also determined by situational factors. One of the main factors that may have affected their moral judgments about tattling is their concern of potential interpersonal consequences to the person who reports, the person who receives the report, and the person about whom the report is made. Piaget (1932) even suggested that this concern reflects the development of a sense of equality and reciprocity at the expense of submission to adult authority, or more specifically, at the expense of honesty to the adult authority.

In summary, the developmental evidence obtained mainly in the last two decades clearly suggests that children may initially act like a deontologist who deems all forms of lies morally wrong and truths morally right, regardless of what purpose lies and truths serve and in what circumstances. A few years after their entrance to elementary school, children begin to acquire a utilitarian view about the morality of honesty and dishonesty. By as early as 11 years of age, children's moral judgments of honesty and dishonesty are determined largely by situations. To them, as to adults, there is no longer a straightforward answer to the question of whether honesty or dishonesty is morally right or wrong. Rather, the answer to this question is now determined by whether and to what extent lying or truth-telling serves a prosocial purpose. In turn, whether a statement is deemed to serve a prosocial purpose depends on the situation.

As made clear by this review of the literature, a multitude of situations make honesty morally questionable and dishonesty acceptable. These situations are concerned with whether lies or truths serve the purpose of politeness or modesty, or the interests of a collective or an individual.

Also, as made clear by this review, the cultural context in which children are socialized plays an important role in children's moral evaluations of honesty and dishonesty. Truths may be deemed morally right and lies may be morally wrong in one cultural context, but the reverse in another. For example, lies intended to be modest and to help a collective are considered morally acceptable by East Asian children, but not by children in the West. It must be emphasized that East Asian children are not alone in holding a utilitarian view. Western children also hold a utilitarian view in situations when ones needs to be polite or legitimate individual interests are at stake. In the latter situation, Western children are more inclined to view dishonesty as morally right if it serves an individual's interest, which is opposed by East Asian children. One of the major sources of these cross-cultural differences is likely the socialization of different social and moral norms that children are exposed to (Helwig & Turiel, 2002; Turiel, 2002). This suggestion is supported by the fact that children from the East and the West tend to be similar in their moral judgments of honesty and dishonesty initially, which is largely deontological. With increased age, they become utilitarian in their own unique ways, depending on the culture in which they are socialized.

The existing findings regarding children's moral judgments of honesty and dishonesty have profound implications for current theories about moral development in general. They directly challenge the universality assumption of moral development (Kohlberg, 1964; see Rest, 1986) and add to the growing evidence which supports the notion that moral development is culturally specified (see Shweder et al., 2006). Furthermore, cross-cultural differences aside, the existing evidence also suggests that children may start with deontological and universally similar moral notions about right and wrong, but with increased socialization, become more utilitarian and even morally relativist. A relativist view of moral development would suggest that children

not only differ in their general moral outlooks because they are from different cultures, but they also differ in their application of moral principles in different situations within a particular culture because moral principles are in and of themselves relative. Being a moral relativist obviously poses a tremendous challenge to children as they must be highly sensitive to situational factors and flexible in selecting and applying moral principles accordingly. The existing evidence suggests that by at least early adolescence children are already quite sophisticated moral relativists (see Killen & Smetana, 2006).

ACKNOWLEDGMENTS

The preparation of this manuscript was supported by grants to the first author from the National Institutes of Health (R01 HD 048962 & R01 HD047290) and the Social Sciences and Humanities Research Council of Canada.

REFERENCES

Augustine, St. (1952). *Treaties on various issues.* Washington, DC: Catholic University of America Press.

Barnes, J. A. (1994). *A pack of lies: Towards a sociology of lying.* Cambridge, England: Cambridge University Press.

Bentham, J. (1843). *The works of Jeremy Bentham* (Vol. 5). Edinburgh, Scotland: William Trait.

Bok, S. (1978). *Lying: Moral choice in public and private life.* New York: Random House.

Bussey, K. (1992). Lying and truthfulness: Children's definitions, standards, and evaluative reactions. *Child Development, 63,* 129–137.

Bussey, K. (1999). Children's categorization and evaluation of different types of lies and truths. *Child Development, 70,* 1338–1347.

Chiu Loke, I., Heyman, G. D., Forgie, J., McCarthy, A., & Lee, K. (2011). Children's moral evaluations of reporting on the transgressions of peers: Age-related changes in evaluations of tattling. *Developmental Psychology, 47*(6), 1757–1762.

DePaulo, B. M., & Bell, K. L. (1996). Truth and investment: Lies are told to those who care. *Journal of Personality and Social Psychology, 71,* 703–716.

DePaulo, B. M., & Kashy, D. A. (1998). Everyday lies in close and casual relationships. *Journal of Personality and Social Psychology, 74,* 63–79.

Fu, G., Brunet, M. K., Lv, Y., Ding, X., Heyman, G. D., Cameron, C. A., & Lee, K. (2010). Chinese Children's moral evaluation of lies and truths: Roles of context and parental individualism-collectivism tendencies. *Infant and Child Development, 19,* 498–515.

Fu. G., Evans, A. D., Wang, L., & Lee, K. (2008). Lying in the name of collective good: A developmental study. *Developmental Science, 11*, 495–503.

Fu, G., Lee, K., Cameron, C. A., & Xu, F. (2001). Chinese and Canadian adults' categorization and evaluation of lie- and truth-telling about pro- and anti-social behaviors. *Journal of Cross Cultural Psychology, 32*, 740–747.

Fu, G., Xu, F., Cameron, C. A., Heyman, G., & Lee, K. (2007). Cross-cultural differences in children's choices, categorizations, and evaluations of truths and lies. *Developmental Psychology, 43*, 278–293.

Helwig, C. C., & Turiel, E. (2002). Children's social and moral reasoning. In P. K. Smith & C. H. Hart (Eds.), *Blackwell handbook of childhood social development* (pp. 476–490). Malden, MA: Blackwell.

Heyman, G., Itakura, S., & Lee, K. (2010). Japanese and American children's reasoning about accepting credit for prosocial behavior. *Social Development, 20*(1), 171–184.

Heyman, G. D., Sweet, M. A., & Lee, K. (2009). Children's reasoning about lie-telling and truth-telling in politeness contexts. *Social Development, 18*, 728–746.

Hofstede, G. (1980). *Culture's consequences: International differences in work-related values.* Beverly Hills, CA: Sage.

Hofstede, G. (1991) *Cultures and organizations: Software of the mind.* London: McGraw-Hill.

Ingram, G. P. D., & Bering, J. M. (2010), Children's tattling: The reporting of everyday norm violations in preschool settings. *Child Development, 81*, 945–957.

Kant, I. (1949). On a supposed right to lie from altruistic motives. In L. W. Beck (Ed.), *Critique of practical reason and other writings* (pp. 346–350). Chicago, IL: University of Chicago Press.

Killen, M., & Smetana, J. G. (Eds.). (2006). *Handbook of moral development.* Mahwah, NJ: Erlbaum.

Klockars, C. B. (1984). Blue lies and police placebos: The moralities of police lying. *American Behavioral Scientist, 27*(4), 529–544.

Kohlberg, L. (1964). Development of moral character and moral ideology. In M. L. Hoffman & L. W. Hoffman (Eds.), *Review of child development research* (Vol. 1, pp. 381–431). New York: Russell Sage.

Krupfer, J. (1982). The moral presumption against lying. *Review of Metaphysics, 36*, 103–126.

Lee, K. (2000). The development of lying: How children do deceptive things with words. In J. W. Astington (Ed.), *Minds in the making* (pp. 177–196). Oxford, England: Blackwell.

Lee, K., Cameron, C. A., Xu, F., Fu, G, & Board, J. (1997). Chinese and Canadian children's evalua-

tions of lying and truth-telling. *Child Development, 64*, 924–924.

Lee, K., & Ross, H. (1997). The concept of lying in adolescents and young adults: Testing Sweetser's folkloristic model. *Merrill-Palmer Quarterly, 43*, 255–270.

Lee, K., Xu, F., Fu, G., Cameron, C. A., & Chen, S. (2001). Taiwan and mainland Chinese and Canadian children's categorization and evaluation of lie- and truth-telling: A modesty effect. *British Journal of Developmental Psychology, 19*, 525–542.

Ma, F., Xu, F., Heyman, G.D., & Lee, K. (2010). Chinese children's evaluations of white lies: Weighing the consequences for recipients. *Journal of Experimental Child Psychology, 108*(2), 308–321.

Mill, J. S. (1869). *On liberty.* London: Longman, Roberts & Green.

Oyserman, D., Coon, H. M., & Kemmelmeier, M. (2002). Rethinking individualism and collectivism: Evaluation of theoretical assumptions and meta-analysis. *Psychological Bulletin, 128*, 3–72.

Peterson, C. C. (1995). The role of perceived intention of deceiver in children's and adult's concepts of lying. *British Journal of Developmental Psychology, 13*, 237–260.

Peterson, C. C., Peterson, J. L., & Seeto, D. (1983). Developmental changes in ideas about lying. *Child Development, 54*, 1529–1535.

Piaget, J. (1932). *The moral judgment of the child* (M. Gabain, Trans.). New York: The Free Press.

Rest, J. R. (1986). *Moral development: Advances in research and theory.* New York: Praeger.

Shweder, R. A., Goodnow, J., Hatano, G., Levine, R., Markus, H., & Miller, P. (2006). The cultural psychology of development: One mind, many mentalities. In W. Damon (Ed.), *Handbook of child psychology* (6th ed., pp. 719–779). New York: Wiley.

Siegal, M., & Peterson, C. C. (1998). Pre-schoolers' understanding of lies and innocent and negligent mistakes. *Developmental Psychology, 34*, 332–341.

Strichartz, A. F., & Burton, R. V. (1990). Lies and truth: A study of the development of the concept. *Child Development, 61*, 211–220.

Sun, L. J. (2004). *The deep structure of the Chinese culture.* Guilin, China: Guanxi Normal University Press.

Sweet, M., Heyman, G., Fu, G., & Lee, K. (2010). Are there limits to collectivism? Culture and children's reasoning about lying to conceal a group transgression. *Infant and Child Development, 19*, 422–442.

Sweetser, E. E. (1987). The definition of lie: An examination of the folk models underlying a semantic prototype. In D. Holland (Ed.), *Cultural models in language and thought* (pp. 43–66). New York: Cambridge University Press.

Talwar, V., & Lee, K. (2002). Emergence of white-lie telling in children between 3 and 7 years of age. *Merrill-Palmer Quarterly, 48,* 160–181.

Talwar, V., Murphy, S., & Lee, K. (2007). White lie-telling in children for politeness purposes. *International Journal of Behavioral Development, 31,* 1–11.

Triandis, H. C. (1995). *Individualism and collectivism.* Boulder, CO: Westview Press.

Turiel, E. (2002). *The culture of morality: Social development, context, and conflict.* Cambridge, England: Cambridge University Press.

Walper, S., & Valtin, R. (1992). Children's understanding of white lies. In W. Winter (Series Ed.) & R. J. Watts, S. Ide, & K. Ehlich (Vol. Eds.), Politeness in language: Studies in history, theory and practice (pp. 231–251). *Trends in Linguistics: Studies and Monographs, 59.* Berlin: Mouton de Gruyte.

Wimmer, H., Gruber, S., & Perner, J. (1984). Young children's conception of lying: Lexical realism— moral subjectivism. *Journal of Experimental Child Psychology, 37,* 1–30.

Xu, F., Bao, X., Fu, G., Talwar, V., & Lee, K. (2010). Lying and truth-telling in children: From concept to action. *Child Development, 81,* 581–596.

Xu, F., Luo, Y. C., Fu, G., & Lee, K. (2009). Children's and adults' conceptualization and evaluation of lying and truth-telling. *Infant and Child Development, 18,* 307–322.

6.6

The Origins of the Prosocial Ape

Insights From Comparative Studies of Social Preferences

JOAN B. SILK

In 1960, Jane Goodall observed chimpanzees use tools to fish for termites. When she informed her mentor, Louis Leakey, of her findings, he dashed off a telegram: "Now we must redefine 'tool,' redefine 'man,' or accept chimpanzees as humans." Over the course of the last 50 years, we have continued to narrow the gap between humans and other primates. Each time we identify a trait that distinguishes humans from other primates—language, culture, warfare, Theory of Mind—we confront Leakey's dictum. Vervet monkeys use referential signals; capuchin monkeys, chimpanzees, and orangutans develop cultural traditions; chimpanzees systematically eliminate members of neighboring communities; and macaques have some understanding of others' knowledge and intentions. Much of what makes us human we have inherited from our primate ancestors.

Finding out that humans are not unique does not mean that humans and other primates are the same. In each domain, from tool use to Theory of Mind, there are consequential differences between humans and other primates. For example, chimpanzees seem to understand something of others' goals and intentions, but not their beliefs, and this limits their ability to deceive and manipulate others to their own advantage. Vervet monkeys can signal the presence of a particular kind of predator, but they cannot communicate about what happened in the past or is likely to occur in the future. Social learning occurs in many species, but there is little evidence of cumulative cultural change.

There is now considerable interest in another set of human traits that seems to set us apart from other species. It turns out that humans are not only unusually smart apes, we are also exceptionally cooperative ones. Food sharing and division of labor are fundamental features of all human societies. We hold open doors for strangers, pay our taxes, contribute to charity, keep promises, and punish violators of social norms. We have a strong preference for fair outcomes and an aversion to inequity. To the surprise of most economists, people are not just motivated by their own material gains (Fehr & Fischbacher, 2003). Behavioral economic experiments conducted in a wide range of societies around the world indicate that most people in most places voluntarily incur material costs to secure outcomes that provide benefits to others (Henrich et al., 2010). In these experiments, subjects interact with strangers in anonymous one-shot interactions, reducing the motivation to cooperate for reputational benefits or subsequent reciprocity. Prosocial behavior is motivated at least in part by empathy (Batson, Ahmad, Powell, & Stocks, 2008) and concern for the welfare of others (other-regarding preferences).

How and why did we get to be such altruistic creatures? As with language and tool use, it is clear that humans did not invent altruism. Altruistic behavior occurs in a wide range of organisms. Self-sacrifical altruism occurs in slime molds, single-celled organisms that congregate into a multicellular mass when food supplies run low. Some cells in the mass form a stalk and do not reproduce, while cells positioned at the upper end of the stalk form reproductive spores (Queller, Ponte, Bozzaro, & Strassmann, 2003). Diseased worker bees permanently remove themselves from their colonies, effectively committing suicide, to avoid infecting other group members (Rueppel, Hayworth, & Ross, 2010). Dolphins form stable alliances with unrelated males to control access to receptive females (Möller, Beheregaray, Harcourt, & Krützen, 2001). And so on.

It is less clear whether the social preferences that underlie altruistic behavior in humans have equally deep roots. Altruistic behavior is not necessarily the product of other-regarding preferences. The mechanisms that motivate altruism in chimpanzees are unlikely to be the same as the mechanisms that lead to self-sacrificial altruism in one-celled slime molds or honey bees. But as the phylogenetic distance between species declines, it becomes more plausible that common mechanisms are at work. Thus, de Waal (2009) contends: "Behaviorally speaking, the difference between a human and an ape jumping into the water to save another isn't that great. Motivationally speaking, the difference can't be that great, either" (p. 107).

But there can be important motivational differences in closely related species. We know, for example, that bonobos are substantially more tolerant during feeding than chimpanzees, and the two species have quite different endocrine responses to stressful events (Wobber et al., 2010). These two species are more closely related to one another than either is to humans. Moreover, behaviors that seem very similar on the surface may have very different meanings to the animals themselves. A chimpanzee might allow another individual to take part of his kill because he feels sympathy for the other's hunger, because he worries that the other might try to take the entire carcass by force, or because he has received meat from the other on the previous day. Thus, it is possible that other-regarding preferences evolved or became greatly elaborated after humans diverged from the last common ancestor 5–7 million years ago.

Ambiguity about the motives underlying altruistic behavior in other primates has prompted a series of experiments that are designed to determine whether chimpanzees and other primates take advantage of opportunities to provide benefits to others. These experiments can be divided into two basic categories. In one set of experiments subjects are presented with two options that have different payoffs for themselves and their partners; their choices reflect their underlying social preferences. In another set of experiments, one subject is given the opportunity to help another individual complete a task and obtain a goal; its willingness to provide help is a measure of its altruistic predispositions. Surprisingly, the results from these two sets of experiments have led to very different conclusions about chimpanzees' social preferences.

In the Prosocial Game, actors are presented with a choice between two options (Silk et al., 2005). One option delivers a food reward to the actor and an identical food reward to another individual in an adjacent enclosure. The other option delivers a food reward to the actor and nothing to the other individual. Actors might prefer the 1/1 option because they have prepotent biases toward larger numbers of rewards (regardless of the distribution), so a control condition is included in which no potential recipient is present to receive rewards. Actors and recipients are members of the same social group, can see one another, and can see the distribution of rewards.

Actors' choices in the Prosocial Game provide insights about their social preferences. If individuals are concerned about the welfare of others, they are expected to prefer the 1/1 option over the 1/0 option, and their preference for the prosocial option is expected to be stronger when another individual is present (test condition) than when the actor is alone (control condition). Alternatively, if individuals view potential recipients as rivals or competitors, they may be motivated to deprive them of resources. If so, they are expected to prefer the 1/0 option over the 1/1 option, and their preference for the selfish option is expected to be stronger in the test condition than in the control condition. Finally, if actors are indifferent to the welfare of others, they are expected to choose at random, and their choices in the control and test condition will not differ.

The Prosocial Game and several closely related variants have now been played with chimpanzees from four different populations using a number of different experimental apparatuses (Jensen, Hare, Call, & Tomasello, 2006; Silk et al., 2005; Vonk et al., 2008; Yamamoto & Tanaka, 2010). In all of these studies, chimpanzees were just as likely to choose the 1/1 option in the control condition as in the test condition. There is good reason to believe that the chimpanzees knew how the apparatuses worked and were attending to the payoff options. Nonetheless, they did not consistently distinguish between the control and test conditions. Thus, this set of experiments provides no evidence that chimpanzees are concerned for the welfare of others.

In the other set of experiments, one subject is given the opportunity to help another individual complete a task and obtain a goal; its willingness to provide help is a measure of its altruistic predispositions. These instrumental helping experiments were designed to determine whether the chimpanzees were more likely to act when help was needed than in an otherwise comparable situation in which help was not needed. The first instrumental helping experiments were conducted with young chimpanzees that were paired with their human caretaker in several different task situations. The chimpanzees helped the caretaker retrieve out-of-reach objects more in the test condition than in the control condition, but they did not meet this criterion for several other kinds of tasks, such as helping the experimenter avoid a physical obstacle (Warneken & Tomasello, 2006). In subsequent experiments, chimpanzees also helped unfamiliar humans obtain an out-of-reach object (Warneken, Hare, Melis, Hanus, & Tomasello, 2007). Moreover, chimpanzees assisted familiar chimpanzees who needed help to gain access to a locked room (Warneken et al., 2007), obtain a tool needed to complete a task (Yamamoto, Humle, & Tanaka, 2009), or gain access to a food reward (Melis et al., 2010). In these experiments, actors were most likely to give help when recipients requested their assistance.

Thus, these two sets of experiments generated quite different conclusions about chimpanzees' predisposition to provide benefits to others. The results from the prosocial games suggested that chimpanzees were indifferent to the welfare of others, while the instrumental helping experiments suggested that chimpanzees were motivated to provide help to others. When experimental findings produce such disparate results, there is a strong tendency to find fault with one set of findings and downplay their importance.

In a welcome departure from tradition, nearly everyone who has participated in these experiments has avoided this temptation. Instead, there has been earnest effort to figure out why chimpanzees behave one way in one set of experiments and a different way in another set of experiments. Many possibilities have been raised (e.g., prosocial preferences are muted in the Prosocial Game because food is perceived as a zero-sum resource; actors were unaware that their partners desired food rewards; actors focus on the rewards for themselves and are oblivious to the rewards for others). But none of these explanations is theoretically compelling and none seems compatible with the full range of evidence. So the puzzle remains unresolved.

I think that the answer may have been hiding in plain view: The actual level of prosocial responses is surprisingly similar across both sets of studies. For example, in the Prosocial Game, actors chose the prosocial (1/1) option 49%–58% of the time when recipients were present (Silk et al., 2005). In the most closely matched instrumental helping task, actors helped others gain access to food rewards 40%–50% of the time (Melis et al., 2010).

Chimpanzees returned out-of-reach objects to their caretakers about 53% of the time (Warneken & Tomasello, 2006) and retrieved objects for unfamiliar experimenters 38%–54% of the time in two different versions of an instrumental helping task (Warneken et al., 2007). Chimpanzees provided tools to their partners on 59% of trials on average, and mother-offspring dyads were more helpful than unrelated dyads (Yamamoto et al., 2009). There are also some experiments of *both* kinds (food distribution and instrumental helping) that have yielded even higher levels of helpful behavior (e.g., Jensen et al., 2006, Experiment 1; Warneken et al., 2007, Experiment 3; Yamamoto et al., Experiment 2).

What should we make of the fact that chimpanzees help about half the time in these experiments? We might be impressed that they help so often, and claim strong continuities between the altruistic predispositions of humans and other primates. On the other hand, we might be surprised that they do not help more. After all, in these experiments, help is very cheap and recipients clearly want rewards. In addition, the chimpanzees are paired with members of their social groups with whom they have long-term relationships. Nonetheless, chimpanzees effectively flip a coin each time they are presented with the opportunity to help. By comparison, in an anonymous version of the Prosocial Game, 3- to 4-year-old children chose the prosocial option about 65% of the time, and 7- to 8-year-old children chose the prosocial option nearly 80% of the time (Fehr, Bernhard, & Rockenbach, 2008).

What conclusions can we draw about the motives that underlie chimpanzees' prosocial behavior? This is a case where negative findings are more informative than positive findings. The *absence* of prosocial behavior in these experiments provides strong evidence that chimpanzees lack other-regarding preferences, but the *presence* of prosocial behavior is harder to interpret. Chimpanzees might help their partners because they are concerned about their welfare. However, it is also possible that helpful behavior is a form of reciprocal altruism (Silk et al., 2005), which is motivated by selfish preferences. Because the chimpanzees have been paired with group members that they interact with on a daily basis, they might be motivated to help those who have helped them in the past and might be able to help them again in the future. Although opportunities for immediate reciprocity were limited in most of these experiments, chimpanzees may keep track of favors given and received over substantial time periods and across multiple currencies (Gomes & Boesch, 2009; Gomes, Mundry, & Boesch, 2008).

There is an important gap between the extent of prosocial behavior among humans and other primates, but we do not yet know how wide or deep the gap in the motivations that underlie altruistic behavior may be. We share biases in favor of kin and reciprocating partners. But humans have evolved cultural, cognitive, emotional, and motivational traits that enable us to greatly expand the complexity of our cooperative social relationships, extend the boundaries of concern to strangers, and develop moral sentiments that counter the strong pull of self-interest. Comparative studies, which reveal both the similarities and differences between humans and other primates, provide valuable insight about how and why we were launched on this distinctive evolutionary trajectory.

REFERENCES

Batson, C. D., Ahmad, N., Powell, A. A., & Stocks, E. L. (2008). Prosocial motivation. In J. Shah & W. Gardner (Eds.), *Handbook of motivational science* (pp. 135–149). New York: Guilford Press.

De Waal, F. B. M. (2009). *The age of empathy.* New York: Harmony Books.

Fehr, E., Bernhard, H., & Rockenbach, B. (2008). Egalitarianism in young children. *Nature, 454,* 1079–1084.

Fehr, E., & Fischbacher, U. (2003). The nature of human altruism. *Nature, 425,* 785–791.

Gomes, C. M., & Boesch, C. (2009). Wild chimpanzees exchange meat for sex on a long-term basis. *PloS One, 4,* e5116.

Gomes, C. M., Mundry, R., & Boesch, C. (2008). Long-term reciprocation of grooming in wild West African chimpanzees. *Proceedings of the Royal Society, B, 276,* 699–706

Henrich, J., Ensminger, J., McElreath, R., Barr, A., Barrett, C., Bolyanatz, A.,…Ziker, J. (2010). Markets, religion, community size, and the evolution of fairness and punishment. *Science, 327,* 1480–1484.

Jensen, K., Hare, B., Call, J., & Tomasello, M. (2006). What's in it for me? Self-regard precludes altruism and spite in chimpanzees. *Proceedings of the Royal Society, B, 273,* 1013–1021.

Melis, A. P., Warneken, F., Jensen, K., Schneider, A., Call, J., & Tomasello, M. (2010). Chimpanzees help conspecifics obtain food and non-food items. *Proceedings of the Royal Society, B,* doi: 10.1098/rspb.2010.1735.

Möller, L. M., Beheregaray, L. B., Harcourt, R. G., & Krützen, M. (2001). Alliance membership and kinship in wild male bottlenose dolphins (*Tursiops aduncus*) of southeastern Australia. *Proceedings of the Royal Society, B, 268,* 1941–1947.

Queller, D. C., Ponte, E., Bozzaro, S., & Strassmann, J. E. (2003). Single-gene greenbeard effects in the social amoeba *Dictyostelium discoideum. Science, 299,* 105–106.

Rueppel, O., Hayworth, M. K., & Ross, N. P. (2010). Altruistic self-removal of health-compromised honey bee workers from their hive. *Journal of Evolutionary Biology, 23,* 1538–1546.

Silk, J., Brosnan, S. F., Vonk, J., Henrich, J., Povinelli, D. J., Shapiro, S.,…Mascaro, J. (2005). Chimpanzees are indifferent to the welfare of unrelated group members. *Nature, 437,* 1357–1359.

Vonk, J., Brosnan, S., Silk, J. B., Henrich, J., Schapiro, S., Richardson, A.,…Povinelli, D. J. (2008). Chimpanzees do not take advantage of very low cost opportunities to deliver food to unrelated group members. *Animal Behaviour, 75,* 1757–1770.

Yamamoto, S., & Tanaka, M. (2010). The influence of kin relationship and reciprocal context on chimpanzees' other-regarding preferences. *Animal Behaviour, 79*(3), 595–602.

by chimpanzees and young children. *PLoS Biology, 5,* 1414–1420.

Warneken, F., & Tomasello, M. (2006). Altruistic helping in human infants and young chimpanzees. *Science, 311,* 1301–1303.

Wobber, V., Hare, B., Maboto, J., Lison, S., Wrangham, R., & Ellison, P. T. (2010). Differential changes in steroid hormones before competition in bonobos and chimpanzees. *Proceedings of the National Academy of Sciences USA, 107,* 12457–12462.

Yamamoto, S., & Tanaka, M. (2010). The influence of kin relationship and reciprocal context on chimpanzees' other-regarding preferences. *Animal Behaviour, 79,* 595–602.

Yamamoto, S., Humle, T., & Tanaka, M. (2009). Chimpanzees help each other upon request. *PloS One, 4,* e7416.

6.7

Cooperation, Behavioral Diversity, and Inequity Responses

SARAH F. BROSNAN AND LYDIA M. HOPPER

Do I care what you got? Such social comparison seems natural; after all, natural selection is about relative, rather than absolute, fitness. Moreover, several species, including both humans and other animals, are known to contrast their current outcomes with prior ones, and to pay attention to the identity and skill of partners from whom they can learn information. Despite this, only some species make social comparisons, and even in these species, only in some circumstances. This raises questions of why there is such a spotty distribution across the animal kingdom and what this means for the function of the behavior. In fact, evidence accruing in primates, as well as some other species, strongly suggests that inequity ties in to the degree to which a species cooperates. However, there are effects of the social and ecological contexts that must also be considered. In this chapter, we consider the emerging theoretical context for inequity responses and consider where research should be focused in the future.

For individuals in species that regularly interact with others, there are myriad opportunities to obtain information from these interactions. Such information can range from basic facts about the other individual's status or physical condition to more complex social learning about the environment to the acquisition of new skills. One area that has remained neglected until recently is whether individuals from species other than humans can also use others' outcomes to inform their interpretation of their own outcomes. In other words, is your preferred piece of fruit somewhat less delightful if another individual got a bigger or better one? We know other species contrast their current to former outcomes (Tinklepaugh, 1928) and change their perception based on framing (Chen, Lakshminarayanan, & Santos, 2006), but do they envy others' outcomes? Recent evidence indicates that yes, in some circumstances, individuals' perceptions of their own reward can be altered based on comparisons with the outcomes of others.

Over the last 7 years, evidence has accumulated showing that in some contexts, monkeys and apes judge their outcomes based on those of others (Brosnan, 2006). In experiments, pairs have to each complete a task in order to receive a food reward. Sometimes the focal subject's rewards are the same as their partner's, but in some cases their partner receives superior rewards. In the latter instance subjects are far more likely to reject rewards than when they and their partner received the same, lower value reward. Critically, subjects also differentiate between their partner getting a better reward and the presence of better rewards which neither individual receives. They refuse more often in the former case, again indicating that this is a social comparison of one's own reward to that of another, rather than a contrast between one's current reward and another that is visible and thus potentially available.

But of course the story is more complicated than this, and this is where it becomes so interesting. The response to inequity is highly variable at every level. Some individuals show strong responses, while others show none at all, indicating that a variety of factors surrounding the expression of the behavior are important in shaping its manifestation. Moreover, different species respond differently, indicating that the response is not a homology within the primates, but the result of specific selective pressures that operate independently of the shared primate characteristics. Finally, although the evolutionary perspective is beginning to take shape, very little is known about the ontogeny of the behavior, or how it is connected with other behaviors within the species' repertoires. We first discuss what our current knowledge suggests with respect to the response, following which we speculate on further implications.

The response to inequity is very susceptible to the social, environmental, and experimental contexts. We know that not all individuals respond, and of course it is very likely that responses vary even within the same individual, depending on context. To give an example, studies using the same protocol among chimpanzees have been conducted now by two different research groups at three different sites and indicate a high degree of variability, even within the same facility (Bräuer, Call, & Tomasello, 2009; Brosnan, Schiff, & de Waal, 2005; Brosnan, Talbot, Ahlgren, Lambeth, & Schapiro, 2010). On the surface, these groups are similar—group housed, living in multimale, multifemale, indoor/outdoor conditions with extensive enrichment and opportunities for social interaction—yet the responses to inequity vary substantially. Dominance rank appears, in some situations, although apparently not all, to influence behavior. More dominant individuals, not surprisingly, react more strongly to outcomes that are not as good as their less dominant partner's. Moreover, the sex of the individuals involved, and the groups in which they live, may affect outcomes, again in some, but not all, situations. When there is a difference, males are more likely to react to less good outcomes than are females and, at least at one facility, individuals from a longer term, more stable group reacted less often to such outcomes than those from an otherwise equally sized and provisioned group. Finally, it may be that the spatial relationship between the individuals affects outcomes, with individuals responding primarily when tested within the same enclosure, with the possibility for physical contact, rather than separated by a barrier.

In none of these cases are the differences surprising. After all, one expects such a reaction from more dominant individuals, who are accustomed to receiving better outcomes and lack any social reason to suppress a response. What is surprising, however, is that these factors do not appear to cause consistent differences across different groups or contexts. This may simply be an issue of insufficient sample size; even with more than three dozen chimpanzees, there is certainly room for improvement. However, it may also reflect underlying mechanisms and interactions, or individual differences, which are as yet unknown. In particular, we believe that any response that is so essentially grounded in social interactions will be heavily influenced by the relationships of the individuals involved. We predict that individuals' responses to inequity will vary across different social configurations, and potentially across different life history stages, for instance, varying responses with respect to changing dominance rank or other relationships (Brosnan, 2011; Chapter 1.6, this volume). Ongoing research is aimed at addressing these predictions by investigating the various roles of individuals' relationships, personalities, rank, sex, and so on, as well as the interactions among them, on chimpanzees' responses.

It also appears to matter what sort of inequity is involved. For instance, while there is good evidence that individuals respond to differences in outcomes, there is as yet no evidence that they respond to differences in procedure (Brosnan, Talbot, et al., 2010; van Wolkenten, Brosnan, & de Waal, 2007). Thus, primates do not seem to pay attention to the degree of effort involved, or whether their partner had a more efficient procedure (e.g., fewer time delays). Of course, one caveat to this is that the lack of a behavioral response is not the same thing as a failure to notice a difference. Therefore, we need to investigate other contexts related to the procedure and the reward distribution to verify that these omissions are not due to disinterest. In either case, however, it is intriguing that outcomes (food rewards) cause more robust behavioral reactions than procedures, such as effort. One possibility is that it is difficult for one individual to judge the degree of effort expended by another. Another possibility is that there are cognitive limits on how much information can be processed, setting a cap on comparative abilities. Future studies can help to figure out which of these, or other, hypotheses provide the best explanation.

The issue of whether behavioral responses actually measure understanding is particularly relevant in the study of prosocial behavior. Such studies are in themselves related to inequity, as they investigate whether individuals alter their behavior to benefit others (whether there is a cost to the actor). Despite little experimental evidence for prosocial behavior in these studies (Silk et al., 2005; Vonk et al., 2008, although see Horner et al., 2011), which has been interpreted as a lack of prosocial behavior, chimpanzees do notice such discrepancies. In one study, chimpanzees were more likely to refuse good rewards if their partners got worse ones, although they still preferred getting less than a partner the least; they were about three times more likely to refuse the worse reward if their partner got a better one than to refuse the better reward if their partner got a worse one (Brosnan et al., 2010). This reaction occurred among the same colony, and some of the same individuals, who had previously shown no evidence of prosocial behavior (Silk et al., 2005; van Wolkenten et al., 2007). Of course, such a response may not actually indicate prosocial behavior (for instance, it may be due to fear of future retribution), but it nonetheless indicates that they recognize when others receive outcomes that are not as good as their own. Therefore, future studies are needed to investigate which contexts elicit such behavioral responses and to attempt to tease apart how well these behavioral responses reflect actual recognition of and displeasure regarding the experienced inequity.

To consider the final piece of variability, we have recently compared responses from a number of different apes and New World monkey species in an effort to understand the phylogenetic distribution of responses to inequity. We find that this response is not consistent across the primate lineage and thus does not seem to reflect a homology (Brosnan, 2011). However, this still leaves open the question of what factor is related to the behavior. Considering first the apes, chimpanzees show responses to inequity in at least some contexts (Bräuer et al., 2009; Brosnan et al., 2005, 2010), while orangutans do not (Bräuer et al., 2009; Brosnan, Flemming, Talbot, Mayo, & Stoinski, 2011). Bonobos and gorillas remain questionable. Bonobos in one study failed to reach statistical significance, but their refusal rate nonetheless doubled (from approximately 10% to 20%) between the control and inequity conditions (Bräuer et al., 2009). Gorillas seem to pay attention to inequities in social behavior (van Leeuwen, Zimmermann, & Davila Ross, 2010), but no similar study has been done using food rewards. Thus, the data from the apes show that this is not a homology among the hominoids, and possibly not among the African apes. Moreover, having a large encephalization quotient is not sufficient to respond to inequity. However, we cannot rule out two other relevant features: the degree of cooperation among nonkin and sociality. Data from monkeys help to answer this question.

Capuchin monkeys do show social contrast, refusing rewards when their partners receive better ones (Brosnan & de Waal, 2003; Fletcher, 2008; van Wolkenten et al., 2007). However, the closely related (confamilial) squirrel monkey does not (Talbot, Freeman, Williams, & Brosnan, 2011).

In fact, the squirrel monkey seems to respond more strongly to individual contrast, or what they themselves were offered previously, than social comparison. In these studies, they increased their rates of refusal if a better reward was offered than what was ultimately given to them, but seeing a social partner receive a better reward did not alter their behavior. Squirrel monkeys, like capuchins, live in large social groups, ruling out sociality as the critical feature; however, they do not cooperate to nearly the degree of capuchins, nor are they as encephalized. Further supporting this, macaques, another monkey species that shows social cooperation with non-kin, also responds negatively to inequity (Massen et al., 2012). Thus, among the species that have been tested, the inequity response maps most closely on to the prevalence of cooperation among nonkin within the social group: species that cooperate frequently, such as in group hunts and other coalitions and alliances related to social support, respond to inequity, while those that cooperate rarely do not.

More intriguingly, among species that are interdependent, such as the cooperatively breeding callitrichids, there is apparently no response to inequity between partners in a mated pair (at least in tamarins; Neiworth, Johnson, Whillock, Greenberg, & Brown, 2009). These individuals continue to take less good rewards despite their partners' superior ones. Despite the fact that these species are inherently cooperative in their social structure, this finding supports the previous work linking cooperation and sensitivity to inequity. We previously hypothesized that individuals are sensitive to inequity in species in which finding a new partner was an easy way to minimize the costs of cooperation; if one partner dominated the outcomes of a cooperative interaction, then it was best to find a new one (Brosnan, 2011). On the other hand, the calculus differs for interdependent species. In these species, the costs of responding to a slight inequity are far outweighed by the costs of changing partners. Not only are new partnerships time consuming to form, but in most cases there would be a loss of reproductive potential as well, as both parents are required to successfully rear the existing offspring. Thus, while it may make sense for a chimpanzee male to find a new partner with whom to hunt, as neither giving up an opportunity to hunt nor finding a new partner is particularly costly, for a tamarin, the costs of changing partners are likely prohibitive for all but the most extreme inequity. These data again indicate a link between social comparison and another important area of study for social cognition: prosocial behavior. The callitrichids are more prosocial than many other monkey species, and it has been hypothesized that this is due to their interdependent nature as cooperative breeders (Hrdy, 2009; van Schaik, & Burkart, 2010). Thus, the nature of the social environment appears to have played a critical role in shaping many features of social cognition, including how individuals respond to inequitable outcomes (Brosnan, 2011).

Although social cognition and development are often considered outside of an explicitly evolutionary context, the negative response to inequity corresponds extremely well with the ideas of natural selection; after all, natural selection is about relative, rather than absolute, fitness. In evolutionary terms, it does not matter how much you gain overall; what matters is that you gain enough to outdo (that is, out-reproduce) others. This is, of course, something of an oversimplification; nonetheless, it emphasizes the relative nature of selection and the ensuing high likelihood that a behavior that promotes relative well-being would be supported. In fact, among species that routinely cooperate outside of kin relationships, the benefits for finding a partner who provides the best outcomes are quite large. Simply increasing one's gains is not enough if one's partner is increasing their own faster. This also emphasizes the need to study behavior at multiple levels, in this case at the level of natural selection and also at the level of the individual animal's behavior. The ultimate function of the behavior may be completely dissociated from the way the behavior manifests as a cognitive mechanism. Misunderstanding the different levels involved can lead to unnecessary disagreements in the literature.

We have considered the immediate context and evolutionary time, but there is one more important time period, that of ontogeny. This is by far the least well studied in the case of inequity, both in humans and in other primates, but may be particularly important for understanding the interactions between inherited predispositions and social influence. Thus, despite the lack of developmental data outside of humans (e.g., Sloane, Baillargeon, & Premack, 2012), we provide a brief speculation here. In experimental games in which they have to divide sums of money between themselves and others (e.g., the Dictator and Ultimatum games), children make and accept smaller offers than do adults (Harbaugh, Krause, & Liday, 2002) and show increasing preferences for equity with age (Fehr, Bernhard, & Rockenbach, 2008;

Gummerum, Hanoch, Keller, Parsons, & Hummel, 2010). Even though young children appear to have difficulty verbalizing feelings of inequity, more recent evidence has emerged revealing that 3-year-olds show reactions to receiving less than their partner (LoBue, Nishida, Chiong, DeLoache, & Haidt, 2009) and, even from 12 months old, infants recognize "unfair" third-party distributions despite being unable to respond to them (Geraci & Surian, 2011). Thus, understanding this interaction in human infants and children, as well as other juvenile primates (for whom no data currently exist), will be very useful in understanding the development, as well as evolution, of the reaction. Future research, with both humans and primates, will help to elucidate the extent to which the development of an understanding of fairness is culturally driven, through parental and societal influence, and/or linked with the development of Theory of Mind and verbal reasoning (e.g., Takagishi, Kameshima, Schug, Koizumi, & Yamagishi, 2010, see Chapter 6.2). Given the fact that many primate species show responses to inequity, it seems premature to assume that Theory of Mind is a requirement, as simpler mechanisms may facilitate such responses.

Of course, the reaction to inequity does not exist in a vacuum and it is likely to affect, and be affected by, a wide range of behaviors and circumstances. For instance, it is interesting to speculate about how behaviors such as punishment, executive functioning, including self-control, and altruism are related to social comparison (Brosnan, 2011; Melis, Altrichter, & Tomasello, 2013). Social comparison also represents a component of social learning, another obvious factor to consider in relation to inequity responses, as it also involves the assessment of others' actions and outcomes, explicitly or implicitly. Theoretical models of social learning strategies have identified potential circumstances "when" animals should follow the behavior of others, as well as "what" and "who" they should copy (Laland, 2004). Only more recently, however, have these mechanisms and strategies been tested empirically (e.g. Hopper, 2010; Horner, Proctor, Bonnie, Whiten, & de Waal, 2010; Pike & Laland, 2010), revealing that both humans and other animals are indeed sensitive to the wider social setting in which learning occurs. Furthermore, it is likely that the social and environmental factors that influence social learning are analogous to those that have been shown to affect inequity responses. For example, the social learning strategy of "copy the majority" (Laland,

2004; Rendell et al., 2010) may apply to choosing a cooperative partner. A useful rule of thumb may be to select partners chosen most frequently by other group members, but this of course will be mediated by individual factors (Hopper & Whiten, 2012) and group dynamics (Hopper, Schapiro, Lambeth, & Brosnan, 2011).

One of the most exciting aspects of social cognition is the recent explosion of comparative data that help us to better understand the function and evolution of behavior, in both humans and other species. Social comparison offers a relatively new approach, but one that has begun to expand rapidly, in large part thanks to the powerful nature of the comparative method in uncovering evolutionary function. In the case of the inequity response, much of this understanding is due to its intrinsic variation. Although variation is sometimes lamented as problematic, the differences between individuals provide a window on which factors affect behavior, which leads to more nuanced understandings of both evolution and development. In particular, although we continue to refine our understanding of the relationship between cooperation and the response to inequity, the current evidence strongly indicates that they are closely related and may have coevolved due to the influence of inequity on cooperation. As we begin to better understand how this behavior relates to others, such as social learning, rather than viewing the phenomenon in a vacuum, we will better understand the complex interactions that affect human behavior and place it firmly within the evolutionary context.

REFERENCES

Bräuer, J., Call, J., & Tomasello, M. (2009). Are apes inequity averse? New data on the token-exchange paradigm. *American Journal of Primatology*, 7, 175–181.

Brosnan, S. F. (2006). Nonhuman species' reactions to inequity and their implications for fairness. *Social Justice Research*, 19, 153–185.

Brosnan, S. F. (2011). A hypothesis of the co-evolution of inequity and cooperation. *Frontiers in Decision Neuroscience*, 5, 43.

Brosnan, S. F., & de Waal, F. B. M. (2003). Monkeys reject unequal pay. *Nature*, 425, 297–299.

Brosnan, S. F., Flemming, T., Talbot, C., Mayo, L., & Stoinski, T. (2011). Responses to inequity in orangutans. *Folia Primatologica*, 82, 56–70.

Brosnan, S. F., Schiff, H. C., & de Waal, F. B. M. (2005). Tolerance for inequity may increase with social closeness in chimpanzees. *Proceedings of the Royal Society of London B*, 1560, 253–258.

Brosnan, S. F., Talbot, C., Ahlgren, M., Lambeth, S. P., & Schapiro, S. J. (2010). Mechanisms underlying the response to inequity in chimpanzees, Pan troglodytes. *Animal Behavior*, 79, 1229–1237.

Chen, M. K., Lakshminarayanan, V., & Santos, L. R. (2006). How basic are behavioral biases? Evidence from capuchin monkey trading behavior. *Journal of Political Economy*, 114(3), 517–537.

Fehr, E., Bernhard, H., & Rockenbach, B. (2008). Egalitarianism in young children. *Nature*, 454, 1079–1083.

Fletcher, G. E. (2008). Attending to the outcome of others: Disadvantageous inequity aversion in male capuchin monkeys (Cebus apella). *American Journal of Primatology*, 70, 901–905.

Geraci, A., & Surian, L. (2011). The developmental roots of fairness: Infants' reactions to equal and unequal distributions of resources. *Developmental Science*, 14(5), 1012–1020.Gummerum, M., Hanoch, Y., Keller, M., Parsons, K., & Hummel, A. (2010). Preschoolers' allocations in the dictator game: the role of moral emotions. *Journal of Economic Psychology*, 31, 25–34.

Harbaugh, W., Krause, K., & Liday, S. G., Jr. (2002). *Bargaining by children*. University of Oregon Economics Working Paper No. 2002–4.

Hopper, L. M. (2010). "Ghost" experiments and the dissection of social learning in humans and animals. *Biological Reviews*, 85, 685–701.

Hopper, L. M., Schapiro, S. J., Lambeth, S. P., & Brosnan, S. F. (2011). Chimpanzees' socially maintained food preferences indicate both conservatism and conformity. *Animal Behavior*, 81, 1195–1202.

Hopper, L. M., & Whiten, A. (2012). The evolutionary and comparative psychology of social learning and culture. In J. Vonk & T. K. Shackelford (Eds.), *The Oxford handbook of comparative evolutionary psychology* (pp. 451–473). Oxford, England: Oxford University Press.

Horner, V., Carter, J. D., Suchak, M., & de Waal, F. B. M. (2011). Spontaneous prosocial choice by chimpanzees. *Proceedings of the National Academy of Sciences USA*. doi: 10.1073/pnas.1111088108.

Horner, V., Proctor, D., Bonnie, K. E., Whiten, A., & de Waal, F. B. (2010). Prestige affects cultural learning in chimpanzees. *PLoS ONE*, 5(5), e10625.

Hrdy, S. B. (2009). *Mothers and others: The evolutionary origins of mutual understanding*. Cambridge, MA: Harvard University Press.

Laland, K. N. (2004). Social learning strategies. Learning and Behavior, 32(1), 4–14.

LoBue, V., Nishida, T., Chiong, C., DeLoache, J. S., & Haidt, J. (2009). When getting something good is bad: Even three-year-olds react to inequality. *Social Development*, 20(1), 154–170.

Massen, J. J. M., van den Berg, L. M., Spruijt, B. M., & Sterck, E. H. M. (2012). Inequity aversion in relation to effort and relationship quality in long-tailed macaques (*Macaca fascicularis*). *American Journal of Primatology. 74*, 145–156.

Melis, A. P., Altrichter, K., & Tomasello, M. (2013). Allocation of resources to collaborators and free-riders in 3-year-olds. *Journal of Experimental Child Psychology, 114*, 364–370.

Neiworth, J. J., Johnson, E. T., Whillock, K., Greenberg, J., & Brown, V. (2009). Is a sense of inequity an ancestral primate trait? Testing social inequity in cotton top tamarins (*Saguinus oedipus*). *Journal of Comparative Psychology, 123*(1), 10–17.

Pike, T. W., & Laland, K. N. (2010). Conformist learning in nine-spined sticklebacks' foraging decisions. *Biology Letters, 6*, 525–528.

Rendell, L., Boyd, R., Cownden, D., Enquist, M., Eriksson, K., Feldman, M. W., Fogarty, L., Ghirlanda, S., Lillicrap, T., & Laland, K. N. (2010). Why copy others? Insights from the social learning strategies tournament. *Science, 328*, 208–213.

Silk, J. B., Brosnan, S. F., Vonk, J., Henrich, J., Povinelli, D. J., Richardson, A. S.,…Schapiro, S. J. (2005). Chimpanzees are indifferent to the welfare of unrelated group members. *Nature, 437*, 1357–1359.

Sloane, S., Baillaregeon, R., & Premack, D. (2012). Do infants have a sense of fairness? *Psychological Science, 23*(2), 196–204.

Takagishi, H., Kameshima, S., Schug, J., Koizumi, M., & Yamagishi, T. (2010). Theory of mind enhances preference for fairness. *Journal of Experimental Child Psychology, 105*, 130–137.

Talbot, C., Freeman, H. D., Williams, L. E., & Brosnan, S. F. (2011). Squirrel monkeys' response to inequitable outcomes indicates evolutionary convergence within the primates. *Biology Letters, 7*(5), 680–682.

Tinklepaugh, O. L. (1928). An experimental study of representative factors in monkeys. *Journal of Comparative Psychology, 8*, 197–236.

van Leeuwen, E., Zimmermann, E., & Davila Ross, M. (2010). Responding to inequities: gorillas try to maintain their competitive advantage during play fights. *Biology Letters, 7*(1), 39–42.

van Schaik C. P., & Burkart, J. (2010). Mind the gap: cooperative breeding and the evolution of our unique features. In P. M. Kappeler, & J. B. Silk (Eds.), *Mind the gap: Tracing the origins of human universals* (pp. 477–497). Heidelberg, Germany: Springer.

van Wolkenten, M., Brosnan, S. F., & de Waal, F. B. M. (2007). Inequity responses in monkeys modified by effort. *Proceedings of the National Academy of Sciences USA, 104*(47), 18854–18859.

Vonk, J., Brosnan, S. F., Silk, J. B., Henrich, J., Richardson, A. S., Lambeth, S. P. & Povinelli, D. J. (2008). Chimpanzees do not take advantage of very low cost opportunities to deliver food to unrelated group members. *Animal Behaviour, 75*(5), 1757–1770.

6.8

Morality, Intentionality, and Exclusion

How Children Navigate the Social World

KELLY LYNN MULVEY, ALINE HITTI, AND MELANIE KILLEN

From an early age, children develop a strong sense of fairness and justice. Young children share resources when they do not directly benefit personally, and they evaluate transgressions that involve harm to others as unfair. Yet prejudicial attitudes and bias toward others exist early, which interfere with children's application of moral judgments to social situations, and particularly so in contexts that involve complexity or ambiguity. In this essay, we will discuss the role of intentionality in children's social evaluations about intergroup and interpersonal encounters with peers. We propose that the gap between children's moral judgments and their display of social biases can be best explained by examining children's ability to differentiate their own perspective from that of a group's perspective, to recognize when group goals may be at odds with moral principles, and to understand that others may not have access to the same information that the self has (theory of mind) and specifically in contexts that are morally relevant.

Differentiating one's own perspective from the group's viewpoint involves understanding group dynamics, which manifest in intergroup encounters. Intergroup encounters are those in which an individual identifies with a group and views other groups as having an out-group status. A phenomenon well documented in social psychology and recently examined in developmental psychology is in-group bias, which is when children favor the in-group more than the out-group (Banaji, Baron, Dunham, & Olson, 2008; Bennett & Sani, 2008b). In-group bias can lead to out-group negativity, which may manifest as prejudice, or unfair treatment toward others. Thus, children's group identity bears on the application of morality in social situations involving intergroup relationships. (Rutland, Killen, & Abrams, 2010). From our theoretical perspective, social conflicts involved in intergroup encounters reflect both societal knowledge (how groups work, or group dynamics) as well as moral knowledge (fair treatment of others). Recognizing when group goals challenge moral beliefs is a complex developmental process (Killen & Rutland, 2011).

Understanding how children attribute intentions to others involves studying children's mental state ability, and, for the purpose of this paper, in morally relevant interpersonal peer encounters. In the context of interpersonal exchanges, researchers have demonstrated that peer interactions contribute to children's acquisition of social cognitive skills, including theory of mind (Carpendale & Lewis, 2006), folk beliefs (Gelman, 2009), emotional knowledge and moral judgments (Malti, Gasser, & Buchmann, 2009), and their understanding of friendship and fair distribution (Dunn, Cutting, & Demetriou, 2000). In our theoretical framework, these connections reflect the intersection of psychological knowledge (understanding intentionality), on the one hand, and moral judgment, on the other hand. Attributing mental states of others has been the hallmark of theory of mind research.

Interpersonal peer exchanges involving attributions of blame and negative intentions to others provide a direct test of theory of mind competence and moral judgment (Killen, Mulvey, Richardson, Jampol, & Woodward, 2011; Lagattuta, 2005; Smetana, Jambon, Conry-Murray, & Sturge-Apple, 2011). Understanding children's social cognitive development in terms of group identity and theory of mind competence will, then, provide insight into why it is that children's attitudes reflect prejudicial and negative attributional biases in intergroup and interpersonal social encounters, even though they also maintain beliefs about fairness and equal treatment.

Traditional Constructs		
Moral	**Societal**	**Psychological**
• Fairness • Harm • Equal Treatment	• Conventions • Customs • Traditions	• Personal Choice
Extensions		
Moral	**Societal**	**Psychological**

• Prejudice
• Wrongfulness of
  Discrimination
• Unfair Bias
	• Group Functioning
	• Group Norms
	• Group Identity
		• Autonomy
		• Perspective-taking
		• Attribution of
		  Intentions

FIGURE 6.8.1: Foundational Constructs and Current Extensions of Social Domain Theory.

Thus, our central thesis is that research on social cognitive development provides a partial explanation of the discrepancy between moral development and the emergence of prejudice and negative bias toward others. This viewpoint is in contrast to theories in which children who fail to display moral behavior do so out of extreme selfish desires, greed, or psychopathology. While psychopathological behavior exists, it reflects a small proportion of the population. Our theory is a normative one, designed to explain apparent discrepancies in children's behavior that are due to social cognitive challenges rather than personality deficiencies. While immersed in their social worlds, children must regularly make attributions of intentions, judge the emotional states of others, and discern what beliefs and desires other individuals and groups hold.

What makes our proposition novel is that we focus on the connections between moral judgments, intentionality applied to others, and decisions to exclude peers based on group membership, such as gender, race, and ethnicity, by using a social domain model of development, drawing upon the moral, societal, and psychological domains. Our two proposals are that (1) conflicts stemming from social exclusion reflect concerns for fairness (moral), which must be balanced with group identification (societal), and the traditions that accompany these group memberships, and (2) conflicts pertaining to the attributions of intentions, which are frequent sources of social antagonism among peers, reflect the assignment of blame (moral) and theory of mind errors (psychological). We will chart out these types of

social cognitive conflicts as well as the ways they extend social domain theory, see Figure 6.8.1 and propose that investigations to understand these conflicts will shed light on how children understand exclusion, bias, and prejudice.

SOCIAL COGNITIVE DOMAINS OF KNOWLEDGE

To explain our thesis, we need to identify what we know about children's social cognitive differentiations when making social decisions. Extensive research drawn from social domain theory reveals that children differentiate in their reasoning about social situations between three different conceptual domains: the moral, the societal, and the psychological (Nucci, 2001; Smetana, 2006; Turiel, 2006a). Research has shown that even very young children (3–4 years of age) distinguish between these domains when evaluating their social world. The moral domain involves fairness, justice, rights, and welfare of others; the societal domain involves socially defined rules, regulations, and customs, which can be altered and which, in their absence, do not cause direct harm to others; and the psychological domain includes understanding of personal choice (Nucci, 2001), preferences, and desires (see Smetana, 2006; Turiel, 2006b). While research examining the psychological domain has frequently focused on elements of personal choice (for instance, Nucci & Weber, 1995), conceptually, theory of mind competence, which reflects the knowledge that others may have different intentions, beliefs, and desires than oneself (Wellman & Liu, 2004), is a form of psychological understanding, even though it has only recently been analyzed this way in social domain theory (Lagattuta, Nucci, & Boascaki, 2010).

The early phases of the social domain research program focused on charting the taxonomy of the domains (Nucci, 1981; Smetana, 1984; Turiel, 1983), which involved assessing how young children evaluated prototypic transgressions in which few competing considerations existed (e.g., measuring whether children differentiated what made it wrong to hit someone for no reason from what made it wrong to call a teacher by her first name). Summarizing a large body of research, the general findings were that children as young as 3 and 4 years of age used underlying criteria (e.g., authority jurisdiction, generalizabilty, punishment avoidance) to differentiate moral and societal (conventional) rules and events in the social world (Killen & Rutland, 2011; Smetana, 2006).

Children are continually confronted with social conflicts in their daily lives, and many of these conflicts are multifaceted, involving not just one domain but multiple domains, including moral, societal, and psychological issues. In fact, moral considerations often compete with societal (conventional) or psychological ones. For example, taking turns on the swing by waiting in line could be multifaceted; the act of taking turns might be viewed as a moral issue about ensuring fairness, and the means by which fairness is ensured, that is, waiting in line, could be viewed as conventional. Whereas the evaluation of the former act is not subject to consensus (e.g., "Everyone should get a turn"), the latter rule violation is determined by the group (e.g., "If you want to pick a number instead of waiting in line, that's okay"). We use the phrase "might be viewed as a moral issue" because how individuals construe social exchanges is an empirical question warranting in-depth investigation.

Extensive empirical research has documented the validation of the use of multiple criteria for determining how children evaluate social exchanges (see Smetana, 2006, for a review). Thus, research on how children evaluate social rules has shed light on the meaning they give to morally relevant exchanges. When these exchanges are multifaceted, additional analyses, beyond domain criteria, are required. This is because evaluating an exchange that reflects multiple conceptual systems involves an analysis of the priority that one gives to different considerations.

Furthermore, evaluating complex issues, including those that cross domains, involves the attributions of intentions, such as whether the protagonist committed an act with negative or positive intentions. This is specifically important regarding morally relevant actions given that intentionality is what determines, in part, whether an individual is culpable. Research on children's social cognitive skills has focused extensively on children's misattributions of intentions, that is, when children interpret a peer's accidental transgression, for example, as negatively intended (e.g., viewing the accidental spilling of milk on someone's leg as mean and hostile). Social information processing models have documented how children who are not socially skilled often overattribute hostile intentions, referred to as the hostile attribution bias (Dodge & Rabiner, 2004). We propose that examining the attributions of intentions is a complex skill for all children, and that the normative data from theory of mind research provides a way for measuring attributions of intentions for children who are not necessarily at risk for aggression but who are navigating the social world. Thus, we aim to examine intersections between the three domains, the moral, the societal, and the psychological, as a means of better understanding how children navigate the complex social world they encounter.

INTERGROUP PREJUDICE: MORAL-SOCIETAL CONFLICTS

In this section, we describe how our social domain model provides a heuristic for investigating social conflicts that stem from prejudicial attitudes, both explicit and implicit (Banaji & Bhaskar, 2000). The argument, made by Rutland, Killen, and Abrams (2010), is that prejudice is often the result of the assertion of group identity, on the one hand (as demonstrated by social identity theory, see Tajfel & Turner, 1979), and the violation of moral principles, on the other hand, such as inequality and unfairness. To the extent that individuals become aware of this, prejudice reduction becomes feasible. In this chapter, we frame group identity as reflecting societal domain judgments, that is, attitudes that reflect the group, such as maintaining group functioning and group identity. This can be illustrated by research examining children's evaluations of social exclusion, for example, when one individual is denied participation in an activity or entry into a group. As described in the next section, exclusion research reveals conflicts between the moral and societal domains, for instance, when an individual rejects an out-group member to preserve the in-group identity (Killen & Rutland, 2011).

Societal Expectations About Group Identity

When do children and adolescents justify exclusion on the basis of group identity? Moreover, how does group identity bear on judgments about the legitimacy of exclusion? Research on social identity has demonstrated that categories such as gender, ethnicity, and race emerge early in development, with more socially defined identities, such as nationality, religion, and culture, appearing later (Bennett & Sani, 2008a). A large body of research has focused on how group identity is part of children's social development and contributes to their understanding of others, social groups, and the self (Rutland, Abrams, & Levy, 2007). These identities change in development, and this bears directly on judgments about exclusion and the fair treatment of others. In-group bias, or preference given to the in-group, has been related to out-group threat in a developmental trajectory that has been demonstrated by Nesdale and colleagues (Nesdale, 2004).

As an illustration of how explicit identification with a group is related to moral judgments, Killen and colleagues (Killen, Henning, Kelly, Crystal, & Ruck, 2007) interviewed US ethnic majority and minority children and adolescents (ages 9, 12, and 15) regarding their evaluations of social exclusion in interracial peer contexts. While all children evaluated the explicit use of group identity (race) as a reason for exclusion as wrong and unfair, children differed in their evaluations of conventional reasons for interracial exclusion (such as parental or peer influence to refrain from interracial friendship). With age, children differentiated between race-based and conventional-based exclusion. Adolescents were more likely than younger children to view race-based exclusion as wrong (and unfair), and they were also more likely to view conventional-based exclusion as legitimate (for group functioning reasons such as avoiding parental or peer discomfort).

At times children use moral reasoning to reject interracial exclusion, and at other times they draw on societal rules and conventions about how groups work to justify exclusion. While the ostensibly conventional reasons for excluding another do not explicitly involve prejudicial attitudes, it is possible that prejudices, biases, and stereotypes underlie many of these reasons. For instance, if a child evaluates exclusion of someone of another race as acceptable because of parental discomfort, the determination that such discomfort exists may

be based on stereotypic understandings about what contributes to discomfort.

In this study children's own group identity was related to their evaluations of exclusion in these scenarios, which indicates that one's own experiences influence one's judgments. For instance, ethnic minority participants also rated the occurrence of race-based exclusion as higher than did ethnic majority participants. In addition, ethnic minority participants evaluated conventional (societal) reasons condoning exclusion as more wrong than did ethnic majority children and adolescents, citing that the recipient might feel that the exclusion was race based, which could contribute to a sense of unfair rejection by the minority peer. Thus, it is possible that their evaluations of conflicts between the moral and societal domain are in part influenced by their own greater experience of exclusion due to prejudicial attitudes. Furthermore, attributions of intentions about the goal of the encounters were related to judging exclusion as wrong or legitimate.

Social Expectations About Intergroup Dynamics

Conflict between the moral and societal domains can occur when children are evaluating intergroup dynamics, which involves decisions about the in-group (for instance, excluding an in-group member who disagrees with the group) as well as exclusion of the out-group. A substantial body of research from subjective group dynamics indicates that children are less willing to include a child from their own group who deviates from the norms of the group than a child from an out-group who adheres to their own group's norms (Abrams & Rutland, 2008). Social groups are central in child development, and children often balance their loyalty to their social groups with moral judgments. One's peer group, for instance, may not always have positive intentions, make decisions with which one agrees, or hold norms that one deems morally acceptable. Thus, understanding group dynamics may be more complex psychologically than making references to conventions and traditions, as described in the previous studies. In such cases, differentiating one's own beliefs and desires from the beliefs and desires of one's own peer group is another form of conflict between the societal and moral domains.

A new line of research has examined deviance from moral and conventional (societal) norms in intergroup contexts. In one study, 9- and 13-year-olds evaluated decisions by a boys' or girls' group to exclude an in-group member because the person deviated from either moral (sharing resources) or conventional (wearing a group t-shirt) norms (Killen, Rutland, Abrams, Mulvey, & Hitti, 2012). For the moral context, children viewed exclusion of group members who deviated from their group's equality norm (e.g., by advocating for more resources for the in-group than the out-group) when their group norm was to give more to the in-group. Thus, when the in-group member was being unequal, children and adolescents viewed it as more legitimate to exclude their in-group member than when the in-group member was being equal; in-group bias was not enough to warrant keeping the member when their norm conflicted with morality. Moreover, the intentions of the deviant member constituted the source of decision making about inclusion and exclusion.

Deciding whether to give priority to group identity or group norms is challenging. As an example, people sometimes vote for someone for office because of shared identity (same gender or ethnicity). Other times, people vote for someone because of the norms they espouse (moral, conventional). When these two types of decisions come in conflict, one must decide between giving priority to group identity or to the type of norm. This type of decision generated an assessment in the study described earlier. When asked to make a more complex judgment about whom to include or exclude from their own group (boys' or girls' club), children and adolescents chose to include an opposite-gender member when that person upheld equality principles. In the context of decisions that involve both moral and societal components, in-group favoritism is not always the preferred judgment, even for 9-year-old children. This experimental paradigm sets the stage for examining a range of different types of group identities, such as those associated with ethnicity, culture, and immigrant status (see Killen et al., 2012). Examining situations where moral and psychological conflicts may arise will also help to provide further information regarding what accounts for the biases and prejudices that children express.

INTERPERSONAL ATTRIBUTIONS OF BLAME: MORAL-PSYCHOLOGICAL INTERSECTIONS

What often makes moral judgments difficult for children is the psychological knowledge required for understanding the intentions of others in interpersonal contexts, particularly in the context of assigning blame or identifying transgressors in social exchanges. Psychological knowledge is often measured using traditional theory of mind tasks, which assess whether one is able to judge another's beliefs, intentions, and desires (Wellman & Liu, 2004). While these tasks require social knowledge to the extent that one is asked to think about the information that another person has access to, they omit other social components such as ownership claims, social relationships, and victim roles. Recently, there have been several new findings demonstrating connections between moral reasoning and theory of mind (Chandler et al., 2001; Killen et al., 2011; Lagattuta, 2005; Leslie, Knobe, & Cohen, 2006; Smetana, et al., 2011; Wainryb & Brehl, 2006), including findings from researchers using neuroscience approaches (Young, Cushman, Hauser, & Saxe, 2007). It is argued that understanding about intentionality underlies both morality and theory of mind, suggesting that there must be direct links between these two forms of knowledge. Research findings provide support for the theory that young children think about the motives of others, assign blame when acts are intentional, and, at times, interpret intentionality from a moral perspective.

Following this logic, and using the social domain model, in a recent study, theory of mind and moral knowledge were investigated by measuring psychological knowledge in a morally relevant context (Killen et al., 2011). The rationale for the study was to examine children's attributions of intentions in a morally relevant context, one in which a child's desired object (a cupcake) is destroyed by an accidental transgressor (when the "cupcake owner" is out of the room, unable to observe the displacement of the desired object from a table to the trash can). Children's theory of mind knowledge was measured using traditional false-belief tasks, as well as a new task which required children to recognize that a child who committed a transgression did so because he or she held a false belief. In this study, participants aged 3–8 years were asked to evaluate the intentions of a classroom helper who accidentally threw away a cupcake owned by a child who was not present in the room during the transgression. Participants also provided their evaluation of the accidental transgressor's act (was it all right or not all right?), and whether the accidental transgressor should be punished.

The novel findings pertained to significant patterns between moral reasoning and theory of mind. First, children who failed false-belief theory of mind tasks identified the accidental transgression as more wrong than did children who passed false-belief theory of mind. Additionally, whereas children who passed false-belief theory of mind tasks indicated that the transgressor's intentions were positive, those who failed viewed the accidental transgressor's intentions as negative. Reflecting this finding, participants who exhibited false-belief theory of mind were less likely to advocate for punishment for the accidental transgressor than those who did not show false-belief theory of mind. When children weigh moral judgments, their ability to understand psychological information, such as their theory of mind ability, is implicated in their decision making, and this has extensive consequences for the development of positive interpersonal relationships. Furthermore, findings indicate that when Theory of Mind tasks are embedded in morally relevant contexts (involving a transgressor and a victim), children have greater difficulty understanding false beliefs than when theory of mind is measured in a socially removed manner, as it is traditionally measured. Thus, this new research is revealing the importance of considering intentionality and children's evaluations of the psychological knowledge of others, identifying conflicts between the moral and psychological domains. This study also demonstrates that measuring psychological knowledge using socially rich scenarios is important.

Finally, while intersections between the moral and psychological domain clearly have implications for examining intentionality, the psychological domain may bear on moral decision making more broadly. For instance, a recent study examined the relationship between psychological understanding and theory of mind abilities using the Ultimatum Game (Takagishi, Kameshima, Schug, Koizumi, & Yamagishi, 2010). In this study, it was shown that children with theory of mind were more likely to make a fair offer (defined as splitting resources equally or giving more to the other player in the game) than those without theory of mind. This study, however, employed a behavioral economics game, which is removed from the actual peer experiences of children in everyday social contexts. The research does indicate, though, that further examinations of the intersections between the moral and the psychological domain are warranted, in particular those that assess children's decisions about resource distribution and fair behavior.

CONCLUSIONS

Identifying conflicts between domains of social cognition—moral, societal, and psychological—reveals how social-cognitive development can explain, in part, the emergence of biases in both intergroup and interpersonal peer contexts. When children and adolescents make moral judgments, their knowledge of the conventions of the groups with which they identify and their ability to understand the psychological states of others, including their intentions, desires, and beliefs, come into play. We argue that knowledge of group functioning as well as group identity involves the attributions of intentions of others. When children struggle with such conflicts, they often rely on underlying prejudicial attitudes or biases in evaluating the complex situations that they encounter in their everyday lives.

Furthermore, children's experiences at times reflect intersections of all three domains. For instance, in the recent study examining children's evaluations of members who deviate from moral and societal group norms, findings show that psychological information is relevant (Killen et al., 2012). In addition to the findings described earlier, participants recognized that the group would not like a peer who deviated from their group norms (regardless of the type of norm), but participants maintained that they themselves would prefer deviant group members who advocated for the equality principles. These findings document that children reason about the decisions made by groups in complex ways and that they are able to distinguish their own beliefs from that of their group, drawing upon their psychological knowledge and skills.

Additionally, while the research on the moral and psychological domains examined how children's theory of mind abilities bear on moral judgments (Killen et al., 2011) from an interpersonal perspective, children also make attributions of intentions in intergroup contexts. Extending this paradigm to intergroup and intragroup encounters could be fruitful. For example, do children's stereotypic expectations bear on their attributions of intentions in a theory of mind context? How might children have responded if the transgressor and the victim did not share group membership and instead were members of two different ethnic groups?

Children rely upon the moral, societal, and psychological domains in making judgments and evaluations. Unraveling the complex relationship between how children interpret the intentions of individuals and groups around them, and the role that their intergroup attitudes play in these evaluations, provides insight into the conflict that exists between children's strong sense of fairness and their reliance upon stereotypes and bias in responding to the world around them. As children navigate their social world they encounter increasingly complex social situations. These situations require them to balance their own beliefs, intentions, emotions, and values with those of others around them, including those who may be part of their in-group and those who are part of different out-groups. Our proposal, then, suggests that understanding group dynamics and moral decision making should include evaluations of social-cognitive abilities, which will affect how children interpret intentionality. This line of research will enable educators to better determine how best to promote fairness reasoning to create a more just and civil society.

REFERENCES

Abrams, D., & Rutland, A. (2008). The development of subjective group dynamics. In S. R. Levy & M. Killen (Eds.), *Intergroup relations and attitudes in childhood through adulthood* (pp. 47–65). Oxford, England: Oxford University Press.

Abrams, D., Rutland, A., Pelletier, J., & Ferrell, J. M. (2009). Children's group nous: Understanding and applying peer exclusion within and between groups. *Child Development, 80*, 224–243.

Banaji, M., Baron, A. S., Dunham, Y., & Olson, K. (2008). Some experiments on the development of intergroup social cognition. In S. R. Levy & M. Killen (Eds.), *Intergroup relations: An integrative developmental and social psychological perspective* (pp. 87–104). Oxford, England: Oxford University Press.

Banaji, M. R., & Bhaskar, R. (2000). Implicit stereotypes and memory: The bounded rationality of social beliefs. In D. L. Schacter & E. Scarry (Eds.), *Memory, brain, and belief* (pp. 139–175). Cambridge, MA: Harvard University Press.

Bennett, M., & Sani, F. (2008a). Children's subjective identification with social groups. In S. Levy & M. Killen (Eds.), *Intergroup attitudes and relationships from childhood through adulthood* (pp. 19–31). Oxford, England: Oxford University Press.

Bennett, M., & Sani, F. (2008b). Children's subjective identification with social groups: A self-stereotyping approach. *Developmental Science, 11*, 69–75.

Carpendale, J., & Lewis, C. (2006). *How children develop social understanding*. Oxford, England: Blackwell.

Chandler, M. J., Sokol, B. W., & Hallett, D. (2001). Moral responsibility and the interpretive turn: Children's changing conceptions of truth and rightness. In B. F. Malle, L. J. Moses, & D. A. Baldwin (Eds.), *Intentions and intentionality: Foundations of social cognition* (pp. 345–365). Cambridge, MA: MIT Press.

Dodge, K. A., & Rabiner, D. L. (2004). Returning to roots: On social information processing and moral development. *Child Development, 75*, 1003–1008.

Dunn, J., Cutting, A. L., & Demetriou, H. (2000). Moral sensibility, understanding others, and children's friendship interactions in the preschool period. *British Journal of Developmental Psychology, 18*, 159–177.

Gelman, S. A. (2009). Learning from others: Children's construction of concepts. *Annual Review of Psychology, 60*, 115–140.

Killen, M., Henning, A., Kelly, M. C., Crystal, D., & Ruck, M. (2007). Evaluations of interracial peer encounters by majority and minority U.S. children and adolescents. *International Journal of Behavioral Development, 31*, 491–500.

Killen, M., Mulvey, K. L., Richardson, C., Jampol, N., & Woodward, A. (2011). The accidental transgressor: Morally-relevant theory of mind. *Cognition, 119*, 197–215.

Killen, M., & Rutland, A. (2011). *Children and social exclusion: Morality, prejudice, and group identity*. New York: Wiley Blackwell.

Killen, M., Rutland, A., Abrams, D., Mulvey, K. L., & Hitti, A. (2012). Development of intra- and intergroup judgments in the context of moral and social-conventional norms. *Child Development.* doi: 10.1111/cdev.12011

Lagattuta, K. H. (2005). When you shouldn't do what you want to do: Young children's understanding of desires, rules, and emotions. *Child Development, 76*, 713–733.

Lagattuta, K. H., Nucci, L., & Boascaki, S. (2010). Bridging theory of mind and the personal domain: Children's reasoning about resistance to parental control. *Child Development, 81*, 616–635.

Leslie, A., Knobe, J., & Cohen, A. (2006). Acting intentionally and the side-effect effect: Theory of mind and moral judgment. *Psychological Science, 17*, 421–427.

Malti, T., Gasser, L., & Buchmann, M. (2009). Aggressive and prosocial children's emotion attributions and moral reasoning. *Aggressive Behavior, 35*, 90–102.

Nesdale, D. (2004). Social identity processes and children's ethnic prejudice. In M. Bennett & F. Sani (Eds.),

The development of the social self (pp. 219–245). New York: Psychology Press.

Nucci, L. P. (1981). The development of personal concepts: A domain distinct from moral or societal concepts. *Child Development, 52,* 114–121.

Nucci, L. P. (2001). *Education in the moral domain.* Cambridge, England: Cambridge University Press.

Nucci, L. P., & Weber, E. K. (1995). Social interactions in the home and the development of young children's conceptions of the personal. *Child Development, 66,* 1438–1452.

Rutland, A., Abrams, D., & Levy, S. R. (2007). Extending the conversation: Transdisciplinary approaches to social identity and intergroup attitudes in children and adolescents. *International Journal of Behavioral Development, 31,* 417–418.

Rutland, A., Killen, M., & Abrams, D. (2010). A new social-cognitive developmental perspective on prejudice: The interplay between morality and group identity. *Perspectives in Psychological Science, 5,* 280–291.

Smetana, J. G. (1984). Toddlers' social interactions regarding moral and social transgressions. *Child Development, 55,* 1767–1776.

Smetana, J. G. (2006). Social-cognitive domain theory: Consistencies and variations in children's moral and social judgments. In M. Killen & J. G. Smetana (Eds.), *Handbook of moral development* (pp. 119–154). Mahwah, NJ: Erlbaum.

Smetana, J. G., Jambon, M., Conry-Murray, C., & Sturge-Apple, M. L. (2011). Reciprocal associations between young children's developing moral judgments and theory of mind. *Developmental Psychology.* doi: 10.1037/a0025891

Tajfel, H., & Turner, J. C. (1979). An integrative theory of intergroup conflict. In W. G. Austin & S. Worchel (Eds.), *The social psychology of intergroup relations* (pp. 33–47). Monterey, CA: Brooks-Cole.

Takagishi, H., Kameshima, S., Schug, J., Koizumi, M., & Yamagishi, T. (2010). Theory of mind enhances preference for fairness. *Journal of Experimental Child Psychology, 105,* 130–137.

Turiel, E. (1983). *The development of social knowledge: Morality and convention.* Cambridge, England: Cambridge University Press.

Turiel, E. (2006a). The development of morality. In N. Eisenberg, W. Damon, & R. M. Lerner (Eds.), *Handbook of child psychology: Social, emotional, and personality development* (pp. 789–857). Hoboken, NJ: Wiley.

Turiel, E. (2006b). Thought, emotions, and social interactional processes in moral development. In M. Killen & J. G. Smetana (Eds.), *Handbook of moral development* (pp. 7–35). Mahwah, NJ: Erlbaum.

Wainryb, C., & Brehl, B. A. (2006). I thought she knew that would hurt my feelings: Developing psychological knowledge and moral thinking. In R. V. Kail (Ed.), *Advances in child development and behavior* (Vol. 34, pp. 131–171). San Diego, CA: Elsevier Academic Press.

Wellman, H. M., & Liu, D. (2004). Scaling of theory-of-mind tasks. *Child Development, 75,* 502–517.

Young, L., Cushman, F. A., Hauser, M. D., & Saxe, R. (2007). The neural basis of the interaction between theory of mind and moral judgment. *Proceedings of the National Academy of Sciences USA, 104,* 8235–8240.

6.9

Converging Developments in Prosocial Behavior and Self-Other Understanding in the Second Year of Life

The Second Social-Cognitive Revolution

CELIA A. BROWNELL, SARA R. NICHOLS,
AND MARGARITA SVETLOVA

Given our everyday view of toddler-aged children as intensely possessive (e.g., "Mine!"), frequently aggressive with playmates over toys and belongings (e.g., "No!"), and singularly self-oriented and autonomy oriented (e.g., "I do it!"), it may come as some surprise that they turn out also to be cooperative, helpful, and caring, at least under some circumstances. Positive, prosocial behavior emerges early in the second year of life and develops rapidly over the ensuing 2 years, setting the stage for the extensive and sometimes remarkable prosociality of childhood and adolescence. The process begins with affiliative behavior at the close of the first year when infants begin to show, point, and give objects to their parents to share their interest or excitement. By age 3 children routinely help, comfort, and cooperate with each other as well as with adults, and they recognize some of the social and moral norms that govern such behavior. Although the earliest forms of prosocial action have not yet been thoroughly investigated and the patterns of change are not fully articulated, a basic picture of its early appearance and growth has nevertheless begun to take shape (Hay & Cook, 2007).

What mechanisms might underlie the early and foundational developments in prosocial behavior during this period of dramatic growth? It seems likely that human infants are uniquely predisposed to prosociality; however, the ability to act for and with others arises from ontogenetic processes grounded in more proximal mechanisms. Among these, we have focused on the role of early social understanding, especially

conscious self-awareness and the complementary understanding of others in relation to the self. Understanding others' goal-directed behavior, which begins to develop in the first year of life, is a necessary component, but it is not sufficient for prosocial responsiveness—knowing what another is trying to accomplish or what someone feels positively or negatively about is only half the story. To be actively prosocial, children must understand others' desires and needs in relation to their own.

By manipulating the nature or clarity of a potential recipient's need or desire and controlling key factors such as partner characteristics and communications, we have probed components of social understanding presumed to be involved in the ability to respond prosocially. We have also examined directly whether individual differences in the development of prosocial action are associated with individual differences in the development of self-other understanding.

PROSOCIAL ACTION IN RELATION TO PARTNER COMMUNICATION AND SUPPORT

One way to examine the role of social understanding in early prosocial action is to ask how much support or scaffolding of the relevant social understanding is needed for the child to produce prosocial behavior. This can be varied to mirror the range of cues and supports that toddlers experience in everyday life. At one extreme, when infants play with age mates, the child's partner possesses approximately the same level of social insight as the child herself and provides little or no structure for the child's understanding or performance. At the other end of the continuum, when infants play with actively engaged adults, the partner overtly supports and helps the child understand the situation and how to act appropriately by providing clear, sometimes exaggerated, well-timed communicative cues about the partner's own desires, needs, and feelings and encouraging the child to attend to them; by helping the child understand that she can change them for the better, and how to do so; and by conveying emotional information about the consequences of the child's actions and possibly providing positive feedback or social reinforcement for prosocial behavior. Findings from several studies using this approach, outlined later in this chapter, have shown that 1-year-olds require substantial support from a partner to behave prosocially except in simple behavioral contexts that make the partner's goals or desires transparent. Two-year-olds, in contrast, generate prosocial responses on their own, across multiple contexts and partners, largely free of external supports for social understanding and appropriate responding.

Cooperating and Comforting

To study the early development of infants' ability to cooperate outside of the regular routines and structure of parent–child play, nonverbal tasks were designed to enable two children to coordinate behavior with each other to retrieve some desirable toys (Brownell & Carriger, 1990; Brownell, Ramani, & Zerwas, 2006). We found that 12- and 18-month-old peers were unable to consider their partner's behavior relative to their own and to the dyad's common goal. The occasional successful coordinations between the 18-month-old children were largely coincidental, and many children could not cooperate with a peer even once; no 12-month-old dyad ever cooperated. One-year-olds pursued their own individual goals, failing to recognize when the peer's behavior and/or spatial position was relevant for their goals and vice versa, and often interfering with or obstructing their peers' behavior when they could have otherwise cooperated to achieve the end desired by both of them. Even when children were individually trained on the task before being presented with the cooperative version, 1-year-olds were unable to cooperate. By 24–27 months, however, toddlers readily achieved a common goal by coordinating their behavior both spatially and temporally. They monitored, accommodated to,

and even anticipated one another's actions, positioning themselves and timing their behavior relative to the peer's. By 30 months of age, they even indicated gesturally or verbally to the peer what he or she should do and when (Brownell & Carriger, 1991). This age-related change in children's ability to cooperate is quite dramatic, progressing from no apparent ability to cooperate with peers at 12 months of age, to primitive, serendipitous cooperation by 18 months, culminating in clearly collaborative behavior based on actively considering the partner's action and location in relation to one's own and to the commonly desired goal by 24–30 months.

In such nonroutine interactions without the structure and scaffolding of knowledgeable, supportive, and predictable adult partners, children must rely on their own still immature social understanding. To be able to behave in a coordinated and accommodating manner together with the peer, and to do so in light of their common goal, toddlers must be able to make sense of their peers' behavior in terms of the other's desires, intentions, and goals. Because 1-year-olds' behavior is often unpredictable and their goals, intentions, and desires are difficult to read, even for attentive parents, very young children may find it especially difficult to detect them, much less to join, accommodate to, or influence them. Peer cooperation thus puts infants' nascent social understanding to particularly stringent test. Peers may be a bit of a mystery, their intentions inscrutable, their behavior often uninterpretable.

This possibility led us to examine toddlers' understanding of their peers' emotional behavior more systematically. By 12 months of age, if not before, infants can read and use adults' emotion expressions to regulate their own behavior toward ambiguous objects and events in a phenomenon known as *social referencing*: They tend to approach objects and people toward which adults are emotionally positive and avoid those toward which adults display negative affect (Campos & Stenberg, 1981). And by 18 months of age, infants respond to adults' emotional expressions of distress appropriately with concern and sometimes even comforting (Zahn-Waxler, Radke-Yarrow, Wagner, & Chapman, 1992). However, when we tested infants with peers using parallel tasks, we found that 12- and 18-month-olds did neither of these things. Instead, they responded unpredictably to a peer's positive and negative emotions toward ambiguous toys and did not alter their play with the toys (Nichols, Svetlova, & Brownell, 2010).

In a second study, when 18-month-olds encountered an emotionally distressed peer, they rarely expressed any concern, although they were likely to become distressed themselves (Nichols, Svetlova, & Brownell, 2009). By age 2, in contrast, a peer's emotion expressions toward novel toys activated the children's play with the toys, and they exhibited empathic concern for the upset peer. Thus, 1-year-olds are somewhat stymied by peers' behavioral expressions and communications about their internal emotional states, whereas 2-year-olds are more able to interpret them and to respond appropriately.

Together, the findings from these studies suggest that infants' early social understanding as constructed in adult–child relationships remains too immature to serve peer interaction, and in particular that the challenges of prosocial responding may require that others' internal states be communicated explicitly. Adult social and communicative support for prosocial behavior may enhance children's attention to, interest in, and inferences about others' internal states and the characteristics of the objects or events toward which others behave. If so, prosocial behavior should be more likely when adults make another's needs, desires, and emotions more apparent, reducing the demand on the child for complex inferences about the other's internal states and how to alleviate them.

Sharing and Helping

To test this possibility directly, we experimentally manipulated the amount and explicitness of adult communication about others' goals and desires to determine its effect on helping and sharing in 1- and 2-year-olds. In a food-sharing task adapted from work with chimpanzees and designed to reduce the motivational cost of sharing by removing the personal sacrifice (Silk et al., 2005), 18- and 25-month-old children could choose to deliver a small snack only to themselves or to themselves and another person simultaneously. We varied whether the recipient was silent about wanting some snack or made her desire explicit (e.g., "I like crackers; I want some crackers"). When the recipient was silent, children at both ages chose randomly across multiple trials. But when the recipient communicated her desire explicitly, 25-month-olds systematically shared, whereas 18-month-olds did not, continuing to respond randomly (Brownell, Svetlova, & Nichols, 2009). Two-year-olds were thus able to infer and act on an adult's desire for a snack from the adult's

explicit verbal expressions of desire, but they could not do so when the adult was silent.

In a more naturalistic version of this task, using a variety of attractive toys instead of food, the child had an abundance of something (e.g., large set of cars) while a friendly, familiar adult playmate had none (Brownell, Iesue, Nichols, & Svetlova, in press). We again systematically varied the adult's communication, this time in a series of four progressive cues indicating her desire for some toys: (1) sighing and gazing at the toys; (2) verbalizing need, "I don't have any, I need some so I can play"; (3) reaching toward the toys with gaze alternation; and (4) making an overt request, "Can I have some?" Children were scored for when in the sequence of communicative cues they shared. Older children shared more often and did so with substantially fewer cues than did younger children. As in the previous study, 24-month-olds needed to hear the recipient's need made explicit before they shared (second cue). However, 18-month-olds shared only after the recipient made an unambiguous request for some toys (fourth cue), suggesting that they may actually have been complying rather than behaving prosocially.

Thus, children's earliest cooperation, comforting, and sharing behavior depends on adults' communications to help them understand what a potential recipient wants, needs, or feels and how to assist another. Helping behavior may be an exception to this general conclusion, however. Prior research has shown that even young 1-year-olds will spontaneously do things like open a cabinet door for an adult whose hands are full or return a pen that an adult has accidentally dropped (Warneken & Tomasello, 2007). Perhaps inferring another's goals from clearly goal-directed behavior, necessary for such helping, is easier for the young child than inferring another's emotions or desires from more subtle or ambiguous cues or actions, necessary for other forms of prosocial behavior. We examined this possibility by contrasting young children's ability to help an adult instrumentally to complete an interrupted action with their ability to help empathically by alleviating an adult's emotional distress (Svetlova, Nichols, & Brownell, 2010). In both types of task, instrumental helping and emotional helping, the child could help by giving the adult something she needed that was out of her reach. For instrumental helping the object was needed to complete a goal-directed action, for example, a clothespin to finish clipping things to a line. For emotional helping the object was needed to alleviate a negative emotion or internal state, for example, a blanket to make the adult warm when she was visibly shivering and cold.

As we had done previously, we varied the adult's communications about her internal state and what was needed to alter or alleviate it, using a fixed sequence of specific gestural, vocal, and verbal cues. The eight cues varied from nonverbal indications of need (looking about for the needed object in the instrumental tasks; facial, vocal, and postural emotion cues in the emotion tasks, e.g., "Brrrr!" with shivering and shaking) to more direct indications of need by reaching toward the object combined with gaze alternation, to an overt request as the final cue if the child had not yet helped (e.g., "Can you bring me that clothespin/blanket?").

Once more, 2-year-old children helped more often and with substantially less communicative support from the adult than did 1-year-olds. This was especially true for emotion-based helping when the adult was experiencing and communicating a negative emotional or physiological state. On the emotion-based tasks, 1-year-olds generally helped only after the adult had delivered six or more cues, including naming the specific object needed plus a direct request for help (e.g., "Can you help me?"). Older children, on the other hand, helped on average at the second cue (naming the internal state, "I'm cold") or at the third cue (verbally expressing a general need, "I need something to make me feel warm"), that is, at earlier cues with more indirect and subtle communications. Children of both ages helped more quickly on the instrumental helping tasks when the adult needed help completing an action, although there were still age differences. Younger children typically helped after the third cue (verbal expression of general need) or the fourth cue (naming the needed object, "a clothespin!") on instrumental tasks, whereas older children helped after the first (nonverbal) or second cue (name internal state).

Thus, 1-year-olds can behave prosocially in situationally obvious, goal-oriented helping situations when an adult makes it very clear what the other person needs and what can be done to mitigate the need. Two-year-olds' greater ability to infer others' needs and desires permits them to recognize another's need for help from more general information and more subtle cues and to rely less on the adult for this information and support in generating prosocial responses.

ASSOCIATIONS WITH SELF-OTHER UNDERSTANDING

As noted previously, attending to and representing others' desires and goals is necessary but not sufficient for prosocial responding. The child must also represent and consider the other's behavior, desires, and goals in relation to his or her own, which in turn requires the ability to reflect consciously and deliberately on oneself, including one's behavior and internal states. Thus, a fundamental prerequisite for the development of prosocial responsiveness is objective self-awareness, in which the child distinguishes his or her own psychological point of view on the world from that of others, understanding that others have unique perspectives on the world, including on the child herself (Hoffman, 2007; Moore, 2007; Zahn-Waxler et al., 1992). To respond helpfully to someone else's emotional distress, for example, the child must know that another's distress is unique to that person, even if the child herself is also distressed; to intervene, the child must also know that the other person may need something different from what the child herself needs when she is upset. To share with another requires that the child be able to recognize the other's need or desires in relation to his own, and that he understands that he possesses or controls something that can mitigate the other's need; if he attends only to his own desires, prosocial motivational processes will not be activated. To cooperate, children must be able to take their partner's intentions, desires, and goal-directed activity into account in concert with their own, and to adjust their own behavior accordingly by monitoring, timing, and sequencing their behavior together with the partner to attain a common goal. Based on this line of reasoning, we have directly assessed children's self-other understanding and tested for its association with prosocial behavior in several of the aforementioned studies.

Consistently across studies, children with more advanced self-other understanding also exhibited more advanced prosocial responding, even with age controlled. For example, toddlers who were more skillful in cooperating with peers could represent their own and others' actions together in symbolic play at more advanced levels (Brownell & Carriger, 1990) and were better at sharing an adult's perspective, talking about their own and others' actions and internal states, and using personal pronouns (Brownell et al., 2006). Children who produced more internal state words were more likely to share (Brownell et al., 2009) as were children with more advanced possession and ownership understanding, and they did so with lower levels of adult communicative support (Brownell et al., in press).

We believe that these convergences point to a second "social-cognitive revolution" which drives the dramatic growth in prosocial action at the end of the second year of life. Whereas the first social-cognitive revolution occurs at the end of the first year of life when infants become able to participate in joint attention and thereby achieve new competencies in communication and interaction (Carpenter, Nagell, & Tomasello, 1998; Moore & Dunham, 1995), this one occurs at the end of the second year of life when toddlers begin to generate objective, consciously accessible representations of self and others in relation to one another and to the world (Barresi & Moore, 1996; Kagan, 1981; Perner, 1991; Zelazo, 2004), an ability that underlies and makes possible the emergence of flexible, autonomous prosocial behavior outside of the envelope of adult–child interaction and across multiple partners and contexts.

We further suggest that being able to comfort, help, share, and collaborate with others based on inferred wants, needs, and goals may also represent the first instances of intentionally altering another's emotional and mental state independent of one's own. Although younger infants share objects and events with an adult to bring the adult's attention into alignment with the infant's own, prosocial behavior is meant to alter the recipient's internal state in and of itself, independent of and possibly different from the child's own. Notably, this facility is also critical for the ability to teach or instruct another. Hence, this second social-cognitive revolution at the end of the second year may also make possible the uniquely human transition from "collaborator" to "teacher" in addition to the transition from "recipient" to "donor" in prosocial exchanges.

ACKNOWLEDGMENTS

The research reported in this chapter was supported in part by grants from the National Institute of Child Health and Human Development (HD043971 and HD055283) to the first author. We thank the parents and children whose participation made this research possible, as well as the dedicated students who assisted with data collection and coding.

REFERENCES

Barresi, J., & Moore, C. (1996). Intentional relations and social understanding. *Behavioral and Brain Sciences*, *19*, 107–154.

Brownell, C., & Carriger, M. (1990). Changes in cooperation and self-other differentiation during the second year. *Child Development*, *61*, 1164–1174.

Brownell, C., & Carriger, M. (1991). Collaborations among toddler peers: Individual contributions to social contexts. In L. B. Resnick, J. M. Levine, & S. D. Teasley (Eds.), *Perspectives on socially shared cognition* (pp. 365–383). Washington, DC: American Psychological Association.

Brownell, C., Iesue, S., Nichols, S., & Svetlova, M. (in press). Mine or Yours? Development of sharing in toddlers in relation to ownership understanding. *Child Development*.

Brownell, C., Ramani, G., & Zerwas, S. (2006). Becoming a social partner with peers: Cooperation and social understanding in one- and two-year-olds. *Child Development*, *77*, 804–821.

Brownell, C., Svetlova, M., & Nichols, S. (2009). To share or not to share: When do toddlers respond to another's needs? *Infancy*, *14*, 117–130.

Campos, J., & Stenberg, C. (1981). Perception, appraisal and emotion: The onset of social referencing In M. E. Lamb & L. R. Sherrod (Eds.), *Infant social cognition* (pp. 273–314). Hillsdale, NJ: Erlbaum.

Carpenter, M., Nagell, K. & Tomasello, M. (1998). Social cognition, joint attention, and communicative competence from 9–18 months of age. *Monographs of the Society for Research in Child Development, sn 255, 63*(4).

Hay, D., & Cook, K. (2007). The transformation of prosocial behavior from infancy to childhood. In C. A. Brownell & C. B. Kopp (Eds.), *Socioemotional development in the toddler years: Transitions and transformations* (pp. 100–131). New York: Guilford Press.

Hoffman, M. (2007). The origins of empathic morality in toddlerhood. In C. A. Brownell & C. B. Kopp (Eds.), *Socioemotional development in the toddler years: Transitions and transformations* (pp. 132–145). New York: Guilford Press.

Kagan, J. (1981). *The second year: Emergence of self-awareness*. Cambridge, MA: Harvard University Press.

Moore, C. (2007). Understanding self and others in the second year. In C. A. Brownell & C. B. Kopp (Eds.), *Socioemotional development in the toddler years: Transitions and transformations* (pp. 43–65). New York: Guilford Press.

Moore, C. & Dunham, P. (1995). *Joint attention: Its origins and role in development*. Hillsdale, NJ: Erlbaum.

Nichols, S., Svetlova, M. & Brownell, C. (2009). The role of social understanding and empathic disposition in young children's responsiveness to distress in parents and peers. *Cognition, Brain, and Behavior*, *4*, 448–478.

Nichols, S. R., Svetlova, M., & Brownell, C. A. (2010). Toddlers' understanding of peers' emotions. *Journal of Genetic Psychology, 171,* 35–53.

Perner, J. (1991). *Understanding the representational mind.* Cambridge, MA: MIT Press.

Silk, J., Brosnan, S., Vonk, J., Henrich, J., Povinelli, D., Richardson, A.,…Schapiro, S. J. (2005). Chimpanzees are indifferent to the welfare of unrelated group members. *Nature, 437,* 1357–1359.

Svetlova, M., Nichols, S. R., & Brownell, C. A. (2010). Toddlers' prosocial behavior: From instrumental to empathic to altruistic helping. *Child Development, 81,* 1814–1827.

Warneken, F., & Tomasello, M. (2007). Helping and cooperation at 14 months of age. *Infancy, 11,* 271–294.

Zahn-Waxler, C., Radke-Yarrow, M., Wagner, E., & Chapman, M. (1992). Development of concern for others. *Developmental Psychology, 28,* 126–136.

Zelazo, P. (2004). The development of conscious control in childhood. *Trends in Cognitive Sciences, 8,* 12–17.

6.10

Disposition Attribution in Infancy

The Foundations of Understanding Helping and Hindering Interactions

VALERIE KUHLMEIER

The search for the foundations of human social cognition has led to an innovative research endeavor focusing on the first 2 years of life. What, if anything, do infants understand about the bustling of the people around them? How does the ability to make sense of other people develop over time, and importantly, what are the initial starting blocks of this ability? In this chapter, the specific focus is on the understanding of the intentional actions of others, and in particular, the underlying dispositions that explain those actions. The implications of this work are broad ranging, with connections not only to childhood and adult social cognition but also to the study of clinical populations (e.g., autism), comparative cognition, evolutionary psychology, moral decision making, and artificial intelligence, among others.

Research in the past 15 years has greatly advanced our understanding of what infant humans are gleaning from the endless action of the agents, human and nonhuman, around them. The action, it appears, is parsed into meaningful units (Baldwin, Baird, Saylor, & Clark, 2001) of goal-directed action (e.g., Gergely, Nadasdy, Csibra, & Biro, 1995; Woodward, 1998).

Often evidence comes from using looking-time measures, as in Woodward's (1998) seminal study in which infants witnessed an actor repeatedly reach and grasp one of two toys until they decreased their looking to a predefined criterion, indicating that they had habituated, or learned, about the event. Then, in test trials, the positions of the toys were switched, and the actor grasped either the old goal toy (which now required moving in a new direction to reach it) or the other, new toy (moving in the old direction). Infants as young as 6 months showed longer looking—registering "surprise"—to the scene in which

the person reached for and grasped the new goal toy, suggesting that when they first saw the action, they encoded it as a goal-directed, intentional action toward a specific object instead of a targetless movement in a particular direction. Using procedures like this, additional studies have shown that infants see goals even in the actions of nonhuman agents (e.g., Gergely et al., 1995; Luo & Baillargeon, 2005; Schlottmann & Ray, 2010).

At least for adults, the interpretation of goal-directed actions is aided by considering the dispositions from which the actions originate. Here, like others (e.g., Luo & Baillargeon, 2007), we define "goal" as a "particular state of affairs that an agent wants to achieve" (p. 490), whereas "disposition" refers to the "tendency or state that helps to explain *why* [italics added] an agent may choose to pursue a particular goal or engage in a particular activity" (p. 491). Thus, a *goal* in the actions modeled in Woodward (1998) may be to grasp the toy, and the *disposition* underlying the action may be a preference for that particular toy over the alternative.

My colleagues and I have recently been examining infants' ability to recognize dispositional states, particularly preference, as part of their understanding of goal-directed action (e.g., Kuhlmeier, Wynn, & Bloom, 2003; Kuhlmeier, Dunfield, Stewart, Wynn, & Bloom, unpublished data). The first task, however, was to create a scenario in which one might likely suppose that an actor had a reason to prefer one individual to another—how does one set up an infant-appropriate "reason" for an actor's positive disposition? Using previous work by Premack and Premack (1997) as a guide, we created computer-animated events depicting, for example, a square helping and triangle hindering a circle, events that by at least

12 months of age, infants see as positive and negative, respectively. We reasoned that after observing such events, infants may indeed recognize that the circle should have a positive disposition toward the helper and a negative disposition toward the hinderer. In turn, the test entailed examining whether infants would now have an expectation regarding the circle's behavior in a novel situation based on the past experiences with the helper and hinderer (see Rosati et al., 2001, for a review of tasks and scenarios used to test trait attribution in older children). The use of helping and hindering events in particular opened a window to further questions regarding disposition attribution with implications for moral and prosocial development, a topic addressed later in this review.

WHY DID THE CIRCLE APPROACH THE SQUARE?

We showed infants short movies depicting a red circle with eyes and a nose trying to climb a hill. On some attempts, a yellow square went behind the circle and pushed (helped) it up, and in others, a green triangle went in front of the circle and pushed (hindered) it down. Then, infants watched two types of test events in which the hillside was no longer present and the circle approached either the square or the triangle. We reasoned that since these test events differ only in terms of who the circle is approaching, distinguishing between the two events would require carryover of dispositional states from the hillside to these new approach events. That is, to differentiate between the two goal-directed approaches would require an assumption of the "why" underlying the goal behavior. Nine- and 12-month-old infants, but not 6-month-olds, do differentiate between the two events, looking longer at the inconsistent scene in which the circle approaches the agent who hindered it rather than helped it (Hamlin, Wynn, & Bloom, 2007; Kuhlmeier, Wynn, & Bloom, 2004; see Kuhlmeier et al., 2003, for results with simple faceless stimuli). The results suggest that by at least 9 months, infants recognize that given the experience on the hillside, the circle should be more positively predisposed toward the helper than the hinderer and thus be more likely to approach the former than the latter.

Adults, though, realize that dispositions reside within individuals. If Bob has a positive experience with Jane, for instance, he might develop the disposition of liking Jane, and might later develop certain goals associated with her, such as wanting to approach her. This sort of attribution can

become complicated, however. One must remember Bob's past experience and in some cases, devalue another person's potentially conflicting dispositions—Bob might like Jane even if, say, John does not. We have recently examined whether infants also recognize the individual specificity of dispositions (Kuhlmeier et al., unpublished data). We provided infants with information about two agents' (A and B) positive or negative interactions with a third agent (C)—do infants track the differing experiences of A and B, attribute specific dispositions toward C for each, and consider that A and B's subsequent actions toward C should, in fact, differ?

Now, infants watched movies in which a square helped one agent (e.g., a circle) as it attempted to climb a hill but also observed the square hinder another agent (e.g., a triangle). In test trials, infants saw the circle and triangle each approach the square. If infants recognize that the circle and triangle should hold different dispositions (e.g., positive and negative) toward the square due to past experiences, they should find the scene in which an agent approached its helper to be consistent, and scenes in which an agent approached its hinderer to be inconsistent, and looking time would differ between the two trials. This is exactly what was observed; 14-month-olds looked longer at events in which the agent who was hindered approached the square.

What exactly are these infants attributing to the individual characters? We suggest that infants are attributing dispositions to each of the climbers when observing the interactions in the hill environment (e.g., "The circle does not like the square," and "The triangle likes the square"). The subsequent actions in the second environment are then interpreted by tracking these individual dispositions and applying a preexisting rule such as "Agents tend to approach things they like and avoid things they don't like." Indeed, infants themselves appear to prefer agents whom they see helping others; after witnessing the square enable the circle to reach the top of the hill and the triangle hinder the circle's climb, infants as young as 9 months reach for the square more often than the triangle (Hamlin et al., 2007). Similar results are found even when using multiple types of helping and hindering events (Hamlin & Wynn, 2011).

An issue awaiting empirical study is when and how infants would determine whether particular dispositions might also be *shared* across individuals. It remains to be examined, for example, if observation of previous actions and interactions may not only provide infants with information regarding probable differences in dispositions among agents but also support assumptions of shared dispositions (e.g., if two agents are helped by a third). Additionally, it is unknown whether infants would use distributional evidence in a similar manner (e.g., if many agents appear to be positively disposed toward another agent).

ATTRIBUTING DISPOSITIONS TO HELPERS?

It may be tempting to assume that infants also attribute to the *helper* a positive disposition toward the *helped* (circle), but this remains an open question. In fact, what is known thus far is that infants do not differentiate between test movies in which the helper or hinderer approaches the circle. Kuhlmeier et al. (2003) report a control condition (designed primarily to rule out an alternative interpretation of results based on increased looking to positively valenced events) in which infants look equally when the agents approach the circle; however, this condition offers limited evidence for the current question as even adults may find it unsurprising for a hinderer to approach his former victim (perhaps to hinder again). Relatedly, it is not known whether infants expect agents to help actors who have helped the agents in the past. This type of reciprocity is still being explored. Thus, it is not entirely clear whether infants attribute either positive dispositions (e.g., preferences) to helpers toward the targets of the helping behavior, or even traits to helpers such as "helpfulness" or "generosity."

At this point, we *do* know that slightly older infants (21 months) will show elements of reciprocity in their own helping behavior. Dunfield and Kuhlmeier (2010) have recently examined whether the earliest instances of infant helping show selectivity, working from the now widely accepted proposal that one way to maintain helping between unrelated individuals is by monitoring and remembering past interactions and selectively providing aid accordingly (e.g., Trivers, 1971). By providing aid specifically to those who have helped you, the costliness of providing help to an individual who may not help back can be avoided.

Importantly, in Dunfield and Kuhlmeier (2010) particular attention was paid to whether intentions or outcomes of previous interactions with two unfamiliar adults might mediate infants' subsequent choice of one adult as the recipient of aid

(i.e., retrieving an out-of-reach object). Although traditional models of reciprocity emphasize the role of outcome monitoring (e.g., the obtainment of goods) in the identification of good social partners (e.g., Hamilton, 1964a, 1964b), others have suggested that the intentions behind an individual's previous actions may also influence reciprocity (e.g., Brosnan & de Waal, 2002; Dugatkin, 1997; Falk & Fischbacher, 2006; McCabe, Rigdon, & Smith, 2003).

Across three experiments, Dunfield and Kuhlmeier (2010) found that infants preferred to help an individual who, in a previous interaction, intended to provide a toy over one who did not, and that infants consider this positive intention even without a positive outcome (e.g., if the actor tried but failed to deliver the toy). Furthermore, it appears that infants are not solely avoiding unwilling individuals but also selectively helping those who have shown a willingness to provide. The actors the infants preferred to help were not simply "nice people" in relation to others, as all the actors were friendly (e.g., all smiled and spoke in pleasant tones). Instead, it was their willingness to provide (even if unable to) that set them apart and seemed to influence infant helping behavior. Thus, for infants, it appears that "it's the thought that counts."

Although this study was primarily designed to examine early specificity in helping behavior, it also begins to address how toddlers construe individuals who are willing to provide. There are at least two possible alternatives for the type of attribution that led to the selective helping in Dunfield and Kuhlmeier (2010). One possibility is that the infants' behavior was based on attributing to certain actors the goal to provide the toy—even if the action failed (see also Carpenter, Akhtar, & Tomasello, 1998, and Meltzoff, 1995)—which then influenced subsequent helping behavior toward these actors, perhaps through imitative mechanisms. Alternatively, it is possible that infants attributed dispositions to the actors who displayed the intention to provide, such as having a "helpful" or "generous" trait, and that this served to define them as good partners, those with whom it might be beneficial to enter into a reciprocal helping relationship.

CONCLUSIONS

Before 2 years of age, infants appear to be supplementing their reasoning about goals with at least some disposition attributions; a circle may approach a square not simply because the circle often engages in that activity but because it has a positive disposition toward the square. Disposition attribution may be only rudimentary at this age, however, as past research has suggested that young children do not have an adult-like conception of dispositions, complete with strong expectations of the consistency of dispositions over time (e.g., Kalish, 2002; Miller & Aloise, 1989; Ruble & Dweck, 1995). Additionally, it may be the case that some dispositions are more readily recognized by infants than others. In sum, though, these early instances of disposition attribution likely form the foundation for complex social cognitive reasoning in children and adults.

REFERENCES

Baldwin, D. A., Baird, J. A., Saylor, M. M., & Clark, M. A. (2001). Infants parse dynamic action. *Child Development, 72*, 708–707.

Brosnan, S. F., & de Waal, F. B. M. (2002). A proximate perspective on reciprocal altruism. *Human Nature, 13*, 129–152.

Carpenter, M., Akhtar, N., & Tomasello, M. (1998). Fourteen- through 18-month-old infants differentially imitate intentional and accidental actions. *Infant Behavior and Development, 21*, 315–330.

Dugatkin, L. A. (1997). *Cooperation among animals: An evolutionary perspective.* New York: Oxford University Press.

Dunfield, K. A., & Kuhlmeier, V. A. (2010). Intention-mediated selective helping in infancy. *Psychological Science, 21*, 523–527.

Falk, A., & Fischbacher, U. (2006). A theory of reciprocity. *Games and Economic Behaviour, 54*, 293–315.

Gergely, G., Nadasdy, Z., Csibra, G., & Biro, S. (1995). Taking the intentional stance at 12 months of age. *Cognition, 56*, 165–193.

Hamilton, W. D. (1964a). The genetical evolution of social behaviour I. *Journal of Theoretical Biology, 7*, 1–16.

Hamilton, W. D. (1964b). The genetical evolution of social behaviour II. *Journal of Theoretical Biology, 7*, 17–52.

Hamlin, J. K., Wynn, K., & Bloom, P. (2007). Social evaluation by preverbal infants. *Nature, 450*, 557–559.

Hamlin, J. K., & Wynn, K. (2011). Young infants prefer prosocial to antisocial others. *Cognitive Development, 26*, 30–39.

Kalish, C. W. (2002). Children's predictions of consistency in people's actions. *Cognition, 84*, 237–265.

Kuhlmeier, V. A., Wynn, K., & Bloom, P. (2003). Attribution of dispositional states by 12-month-olds. *Psychological Science, 14*, 402–408.

Kuhlmeier, V. A., Wynn, K., & Bloom, P. (2004, May). *Reasoning about present dispositions based on past interactions.* Paper presented at the International Conference on Infant Studies, Chicago, IL.

Luo, Y., & Baillargeon, R. (2005). Can a self-propelled box have a goal? Psychological reasoning in 5-month-old infants. *Psychological Science, 16*, 601–608.

Luo, Y., & Baillargeon, R. (2007). Do 12.5-month-old infants consider what objects others can see when interpreting their actions? *Cognition, 105*, 489–512.

McCabe, K. A., Rigdon, M. L., & Smith, V. L. (2003). Positive reciprocity and intentions in trust games. *Journal of Economic Behaviour and Organization, 52*, 267–275.

Meltzoff, A. M. (1995). Understanding the intentions of others: Re-enactments of intended acts by 18-month-old children. *Developmental Psychology, 31*, 838–850.

Miller, P. H., & Aloise, P. A. (1989). Young children's understanding of the psychological causes of behavior: A review. *Child Development, 60*, 257–285.

Premack, D., & Premack, A. J. (1997). Infants attribute value +/- to the goal-directed actions of self-propelled objects. *Journal of Cognitive Neuroscience, 9*, 848–856.

Rosati, A. D., Knowles, E. D., Kalish, C. W., Gopnik, A., Ames, D. R., & Morris, M. W. (2001). The rocky road from acts to dispositions: Insights for attribution theory from developmental research in theories of mind. In B. Malle, L. Moses, & D. Baldwin (Eds.) *Intentions and intentionality: Foundations of social cognition* (pp. 287–303). Cambridge, MA: MIT Press.

Ruble, D. N., & Dweck, C. S. (1995). Self-perceptions, person conceptions, and their development. In N. Eisenberg (Ed.), *Social development: Review of personality and social psychology* (Vol. 15, pp. 109–139). Thousand Oaks, CA: Sage.

Schlottmann, A., & Ray, E. (2010). Goal attribution to schematic animals: Do 6-month-olds perceive biological motion as animate? *Developmental Science, 13*, 1–10.

Trivers, R. L. (1971). The evolution of reciprocal altruism. *Quarterly Review of Biology, 46*, 189–226.

Woodward, A. L. (1998). Infants selectively encode the goal object of an actor's reach. *Cognition, 69*, 1–34.

6.11

What Do Children and Chimpanzees Reveal About Human Altruism?

FELIX WARNEKEN

Philosophers, psychologists, and biologists have long debated the basis of human altruistic behavior. Proponents of a Hobbesian worldview argue that altruistic behaviors mainly depend upon the acquisition of social norms which override and control our pervasive selfish nature. Conversely, followers of Rousseau support the idea that we might have basic altruistic tendencies to care about others, which do not depend on social norms alone. While it is unlikely that there is an easy solution to this perennial debate, recent advances in the behavioral sciences allow us to formulate these questions more clearly and provide the empirical evidence to address them. In this chapter, I argue that a critical task for this endeavor is to investigate the psychological mechanisms underlying altruistic behaviors and to trace their emergence in human ontogeny and phylogeny. That is, focusing solely on the mature state of altruistic behaviors in human adults cannot provide us with satisfactory answers about the origins of the cognitive and motivational processes underlying altruism. "Altruistic" is thus used in terms of the underlying psychological mechanisms: behaviors that are rooted in a motivation to provide a concrete benefit to another individual rather than oneself. This psychological view of altruism does not necessarily require that these behaviors align with views of altruism defined in terms of fitness costs and benefits at an evolutionary level of analysis. Specifically, I will summarize some of the most recent empirical findings that this psychological approach has produced, examining both early child development and comparisons with one of our closest evolutionary relatives—chimpanzees. Studies of children's helping behaviors show that humans act altruistically from a very early age, before specific socialization factors such as teaching of cultural norms could have had a major impact on their

development. Moreover, even chimpanzees on occasion act helpfully toward others—raising the possibility that humans are perhaps not as special in their psychology as one might think. These findings provide new insights—but also raise new questions—for the debate about human nature dating back to Hobbes and Rousseau.

HELPING IN HUMAN CHILDREN

Why study children? Research on adults has established that factors such as adherence to social norms and reputation formation play a major role in social life, especially when altruistic behaviors are concerned. On the other end, children are often characterized as acting based upon selfish motivations alone, not considering the welfare of others before they have acquired specific prosocial norms. Therefore, it has been proposed that socialization practices such as the internalization of social norms and rewarding appropriate behaviors are the major (and perhaps only) factors accounting for the emergence of altruistic behaviors in development. However, these claims are mainly based upon studies of school-aged children or adults who have already gone through a long socialization period. Therefore, studying young children is essential to determine whether these proposed socialization practices are actually the starting point of altruistic behaviors or, alternatively, build upon an early emerging and perhaps biological predisposition.

One of the earliest manifestations of altruistic inclinations can be found in simple helping behaviors in which one person struggles to complete a task and the child can intervene. For most of the chapter, I will focus on these "instrumental helping" behaviors because they are particularly interesting for the topic of this book: social cognition. Specifically, in order to competently help someone with an instrumental problem, the child has to have the social-cognitive capacity to represent the other person's unfulfilled goal, as well as the motivation to act on that goal. Thus, these cases of instrumental helping differ from other altruistic behaviors such as sharing (where the problem consists of a lack of resource and the intervention is to give up part of one's own) and empathic intervention (where the actor comforts a person in distress, responding to emotional needs) (Warneken & Tomasello, 2009). Thus, in instrumental helping situations, actors can use their ability to represent other people's goals to intervene on behalf of others.

Young children start to help surprisingly early, not long after their first birthday. In an initial study, we presented 18-month-old infants with 10 different situations in which an adult was having trouble achieving a goal (Warneken & Tomasello, 2006). For instance, an experimenter may be accidentally dropping clothespins while hanging towels on a line or banging helplessly into a cabinet door with a stack of magazines in his hands or not know how to open a novel box. In these kinds of situations, children displayed spontaneous, unrewarded helping behaviors in a variety of ways. Another study showed that even 14-month-old children act helpfully, although at this early age only with cognitively less demanding tasks (such as a person reaching for an object) (Warneken & Tomasello, 2007). Thus, during the second year of life, toddlers appear to become more proficient at helping with different goals (Svetlova, Nichols, & Brownell, 2010). They even seem to be able to take into account whether the helpee is knowledgeable or ignorant when choosing how to help (Buttelmann, Carpenter, & Tomasello, 2009). Taken together, these studies show that shortly after their first birthdays, human children begin to spontaneously help others, becoming more flexible in their ability to intervene in various types of situations over the second year of life.

Children are thus able to help—but what exactly motivates their helping? Perhaps importantly, helping occurs spontaneously in the parent's absence, proving that it is not due to subtle cues from the parent or obedience to parental authority (Warneken & Tomasello, 2012). Moreover, toddlers are willing to put some effort into helping, as they literally toddle over obstacles to help another person or help despite having to leave a fun game behind (Warneken, Hare, Melis, Hanus, & Tomasello, 2007; Warneken &

Tomasello, 2008). Last but not least, concrete rewards do not seem to drive children's helping. Specifically, in a study of 18-month-olds, children who were offered a toy as a reward for helping were not more likely to help than children who helped without being given a reward (Warneken et al., 2007). As a matter of fact, concrete rewards can even have a negative effect on children's helping. After adapting the paradigm by Lepper and colleagues on the "overjustification effect" (Lepper, Greene, & Nisbett, 1973), we found that children who received rewards for helping were less likely to help in future situations than those who had not received a reward, indicating that children's helping is intrinsically motivated and external rewards can undermine this tendency (Warneken & Tomasello, 2008).

Taken together, these results provide evidence for an early emergence of basic altruistic tendencies. Toddlers use their social cognitive capacities to help others in need. Experimental manipulations rule out certain situational factors such as rewards or parental encouragement. Moreover, the fact that these helping behaviors emerge so early in life renders certain hypotheses about socialization practices as the driving factor rather implausible. For example, we can rule out the claim that children are initially oblivious to the needs of others and help only when promised concrete rewards (e.g., Cialdini, Kenrick, & Baumann, 1982) or that humans develop spontaneous helping behaviors only after a long reward history until ultimately helping becomes self-rewarding around adolescence (e.g., Bar-Tal, 1982). It is similarly implausible to assume that these young children have already adopted an explicit moral value system that guides their behavior. Moreover, there is no indication that these young children are adept at reputation management, an ability that does not seem to emerge before school age (Banerjee, 2002). It is of course possible that parental reinforcement had shaped these behaviors. However, there are several problems with an approach that relies on external reinforcement alone. First, natural observations with children show that parents do not appear to systematically reward altruistic behaviors with material rewards, but most of the time they just acknowledge the helpful act (Grusec, 1991). Second, even if rewards occurred, infants 14 to 18 months of age had little opportunity to be reinforced for helping. Third, studies with older children show that the inducement of altruistic behaviors through concrete reinforcements does not transfer to other types of situations or interactions with other people—when the incentive disappears, so does the behavior (Moore & Eisenberg, 1984). The reported studies, in contrast, demonstrate that children also help an unfamiliar adult in novel situations for which they could not possibly have been rewarded in the past. Fourth, as described earlier, external rewards can have negative effects on helping in an experimental situation. This is corroborated by a longitudinal observational study in which the amount of parental reinforcement of compliant altruistic behavior was *negatively* correlated with behaviors toward a peer 2 years later (Eisenberg, Wolchik, Goldberg, & Engel, 1992). Given these data, it seems rather implausible to assume that young children are initially totally self-focused and oblivious to the needs of others, with socialization practices completely reprogramming children's motivations.

Nevertheless, it is still possible that there are certain socialization practices early in life that have not been captured in previous studies. Perhaps children are particularly adept social learners when it comes to helping behaviors, or perhaps adults are particularly motivated to raise altruistic offspring. For example, children may learn to help because they imitate other people's helping behaviors. Unfortunately, no studies with infants and toddlers directly address this topic. However, indirect evidence comes from a very different source: studies of chimpanzees. If socialization practices such as teaching helpful behavior or internalizing social norms are a necessary prerequisite for the emergence of the kinds of altruistic behaviors we see in young children, we would not expect to find them in chimpanzees. Although chimpanzees show flexible social-cognitive skills (Tomasello et al., 2005) and may transmit some cultural information about some domains of life such as tool use (Whiten, McGuigan, Marshall-Pescini, & Hopper, 2009), there is currently no indication that chimpanzees transmit cultural norms about appropriate social behavior or actively reward their offspring for social behaviors toward others. Thus, studies with chimpanzees can inform us whether these types of socialization factors are actually necessary for helping behaviors to emerge. Not only that, comparative studies of humans and chimpanzees enable us to time-travel into our evolutionary past, differentiating between those aspects that might have characterized the common ancestor of humans and nonhuman apes 5 to 7 million years ago from those behaviors that evolved only in the human lineage.

HELPING IN CHIMPANZEES

It is currently a matter of debate to what extent chimpanzees display altruistic behaviors similar to those of humans. On the one hand, there are recent experiments demonstrating that chimpanzees do not take the opportunity to act on behalf of another individual. In particular, chimpanzees do not reliably deliver food to a conspecific by pulling a board within reach of them (Jensen et al., 2006) and do not choose a mutualistic over a selfish outcome in a forced-choice situation (Silk et al. 2005; see Chapter 6.6, this volume). On the other hand, our studies of instrumental helping provide evidence that chimpanzees might in fact have altruistic motivations. These different results raise interesting questions about the proximate mechanisms that are involved in altruistic behavior and highlight important differences and similarities in humans and chimpanzees.

The first piece of experimental evidence suggesting that chimpanzees might be altruistic in some contexts came from a study on instrumental helping in human-reared chimpanzees. When we tested them in the same tasks as the 18-month-old toddlers described earlier, we found that chimpanzees would also help their caregiver when she was reaching for an object (Warneken & Tomasello, 2006). They did this without being offered a reward and did not pick up the objects in matched control conditions in which there was no indication by the caregiver that she needed help. Moreover, this phenomenon is not restricted to human-raised chimpanzees who interact with their human surrogate mother; a second study with semi-free-ranging chimpanzees indicated that they would help a human stranger with whom they had no prior interaction when he was reaching for objects (Warneken et al., 2007). Perhaps most surprisingly, as with children, the apes were equally likely to help when the human was offering a reward (here, a piece of food) as when he did not offer a reward. This indicates that the chimpanzees were motivated to help the experimenter with his unachieved goal, and not by the possibility of retrieving a material reward for themselves.

To test whether chimpanzees would also help their conspecifics, we created an experimental situation in which one chimpanzee (the recipient) was faced with the problem that a door leading to a room with a piece of food was fixed with a chain that she could not unlock (Warneken et al., 2007).

But if another chimpanzee (the actor) released this chain from an adjacent room, the recipient would be able to enter. Results showed that chimpanzees often released the chain (and significantly more often than in various controls). This shows that subjects were attentive to the recipient's goal, intervening on the recipient's behalf when she was unsuccessfully trying to open the door. Taken together, this line of experiments indicates that chimpanzees also have the cognitive and motivational prerequisites to perform acts of instrumental helping.

These experiments provide an interesting contrast to other experimental paradigms in which chimpanzees did not actively deliver food rewards to conspecifics, raising questions about the types of altruistic behavior that humans and our closest relatives engage in. Specifically, we hypothesized that perhaps chimpanzees are so competitive over food that they are reluctant to actively provide food to others, even if they are unable to obtain it for themselves. Alternatively, the active problem-solving activity that is inherent in the instrumental helping situation might make the recipient's unfulfilled goal and the need for intervention more salient than the sharing contexts in which the recipients are not engaged in a task and remain mainly passive. To measure the importance of both factors, we manipulated them experimentally within a single experimental paradigm (Melis et al., 2010). Here, the actor could release a bag with a reward, which would slide down a chute to the recipient in another room. To test the food hypothesis, we manipulated whether the bag contained food or a token. To test the activity hypothesis, we also manipulated whether the recipient could actively try to pull at a rope attached to the bag or had no such opportunity. Results showed that chimpanzees were equally likely to help with food rewards or tokens: helping was not diminished when food was involved. Importantly, actors helped more often when the recipient was actively trying to access the reward by pulling the rope or communicated with the actor than when the recipient remained passive (see Yamamoto, Humle, & Tanaka, 2009, for a similar finding). Thus, an important factor predicting helping in chimpanzees appears to be the activity of the recipient signaling the need for help.

Taken together, these studies show that not unlike human infants, chimpanzees instrumentally help others—at least when the problem is made salient. It is important to note, however,

that despite this similarity, altruistic behaviors in chimpanzees appear to be much more restricted than what we see in humans. This is particularly true when it comes to food sharing. Chimpanzees rarely share food that they could keep for themselves, and food transfers occur mainly in instances of "tolerated theft," in which one individual allows another individual to take food after being harassed rather than handing it over voluntarily (Gilby, 2006) over voluntarily (Gilby, 2006)." However, in situations with other demands, such as a concrete instrumental problem, chimpanzees appear to be willing to lend a hand. Thus, to compare species, it seems important to assess a variety of behaviors. This will enable us to better understand the proximate factors that enable and constrain altruistic behaviors in humans and our closest relatives.

CONCLUSION

Young children engage in helping behaviors and so do chimpanzees. These findings indicate that the basic social cognitive and motivational processes have deep roots in ontogeny and phylogeny. In particular, these results challenge the idea that human altruistic behaviors are due to socialization practices in the form of parental instruction or the internalization of norms alone. There is no question that socialization practices can profoundly influence children's basic altruistic tendencies (for better or worse). However, it seems that these practices build upon processes that we share with our closest evolutionary relatives, rather than completely reshape our biological endowment.

Moreover, recent findings from comparative and developmental psychology indicate that altruistic behavior should not be viewed as a unitary trait. There are different ways that humans can engage in altruistic behavior, and these varieties may be supported by distinct psychological mechanisms. Moreover, different varieties of altruism may differ in how they are manifested across species, such as in terms of food provision and instrumental helping in chimpanzees. Thus, investigating the circumstances under which humans and other animals do and do not act on behalf of others will provide further insight into the similarities and differences in a behavior that is a cornerstone of human social life.

ACKNOWLEDGMENTS

Thanks to Alexandra Rosati for helpful comments on an earlier draft.

REFERENCES

Banerjee, R. (2002). Children's understanding of self-presentational behavior: Links with mental-state reasoning and the attribution of embarrassment. *Merrill-Palmer Quarterly, 48*, 378–404.

Bar-Tal, D. (1982). Sequential development of helping behavior: A cognitive-learning approach. *Developmental Review, 2*, 101–124.

Buttelmann, D., Carpenter, M., & Tomasello, M. (2009). Eighteen-month-old infants show false belief understanding in an active helping paradigm. *Cognition, 112*, 337–342.

Cialdini, R. B., Kenrick, D. T., & Baumann, D. J. (1982). Effects of mood on prosocial behavior in children and adults. In N. Eisenberg (Ed.), *The development of prosocial behavior* (pp. 339–359). San Diego, CA: Academic Press.

Eisenberg, N., Wolchik, S., Goldberg, L., & Engel, I. (1992). Parental values, reinforcement, and young children's prosocial behavior. *Journal of Genetic Psychology, 153*, 19–36.

Gilby, I. C. (2006). Meat sharing among the Gombe chimpanzees: Harassment and reciprocal exchange. *Animal Behavior, 71*, 953–963.

Grusec, J. (1991). Socializing concern for others in the home. *Developmental Psychology, 27*, 338–342.

Jensen, K., Hare, B., Call, J., & Tomasello, M. (2006). What's in it for me? Self-regard precludes altruism and spite in chimpanzees. *Proceedings of the Royal Society B, 273*, 1013–1021.

Lepper, M. R., Greene, D., & Nisbett, R. E. (1973). Undermining children's intrinsic interest with extrinsic reward: A test of the "overjustification" hypothesis. *Journal of Personality and Social Psychology, 28*, 129–137.

Melis, A. P., Warneken, F., Jensen, K., Schneider, A-C., Call, J., & Tomasello, M. (2010). Chimpanzees help conspecifics obtain food and non-food items. *Proceedings of the Royal Society B*. doi:10.1098/rspb.2010.1735

Moore, B., & Eisenberg, N. (1984). The development of altruism. *Annals of Child Development, 1*, 107–174.

Silk, J., Brosnan, S., Vonk, J., Henrich, J., Povinelli, D., Richardson, A. S.,…Schapiro, S. J. (2005). Chimpanzees are indifferent to the welfare of unrelated group members. *Nature, 437*, 1357–1359.

Svetlova, M., Nichols, S. R., & Brownell, C. A. (2010). Toddlers' prosocial behavior: From instrumental to empathic to altruistic helping. *Child Development, 81*, 1814–1827.

Tomasello, M., Carpenter, M., Call, J., Behne, T., & Moll, H. (2005). Understanding and sharing intentions: The ontogeny and phylogeny of cultural cognition. *Behavioral & Brain Sciences, 28*(5), 675–691.

Warneken, F., Hare, B., Melis, A. P., Hanus, D., & Tomasello, M. (2007). Spontaneous altruism by chimpanzees and young children. *PLoS Biology, 5*, 1414–1420.

Warneken, F., & Tomasello, M. (2006). Altruistic helping in human infants and young chimpanzees. *Science, 311*, 1301–1303.

Warneken, F., & Tomasello, M. (2007). Helping and cooperation at 14 months of age. *Infancy, 11*, 271–294.

Warneken, F., & Tomasello, M. (2008). Extrinsic rewards undermine altruistic tendencies in 20-month-olds. *Developmental Psychology, 44*, 1785–1788.

Warneken, F., & Tomasello, M. (2009). Varieties of altruism in children and chimpanzees. *Trends in Cognitive Sciences, 13*, 397–482.

Warneken, F., & Tomasello, M. (2012). Parental presence and encouragement do not influence helping in young children. *Infancy (Early View)*, 1–24.

Whiten, A., McGuigan, N., Marshall-Pescini, S., & Hopper, L. M. (2009) Emulation, imitation, over-imitation and the scope of culture for child and chimpanzee. *Philosophical Transactions of the Royal Society B, 364*, 2417–242.

Yamamoto, S., Humle, T., & Tanaka, M. (2009). Chimpanzees help each other upon request. *PLoS One 4*(10), e7416.

INDEX